Economics of the Labour Market

Economics of the Labour Market

Unemployment and the Costs of Unemployment

P. N. (Raja) Junankar
Honorary Professor, Industrial Relations Research Centre, UNSW Australia,
Emeritus Professor, Western Sydney University
and
Research Fellow, IZA, Bonn, Germany

palgrave
macmillan

ECONOMICS OF THE LABOUR MARKET: UNEMPLOYMENT AND THE COSTS OF UNEMPLOYMENT

First published 2016 by
PALGRAVE MACMILLAN

Palgrave Macmillan in the UK is an imprint of Macmillan Publishers Limited, registered in England, company number 785998, of Houndmills, Basingstoke, Hampshire RG21 6XS.

Palgrave Macmillan in the US is a division of Nature America, Inc., One New York Plaza, Suite 4500
New York, NY 10004–1562.

Palgrave Macmillan is the global academic imprint of the above companies and has companies and representatives throughout the world.

Hardback ISBN: 978–1–137–55518–2
E-PUB ISBN: 978–1–137–55520–5
ISBN 978-1-137-55518-2 ISBN 978-1-137-55919-9 (eBook)
DOI 10.1007/978-1-137-55919-9

Distribution in the UK, Europe and the rest of the world is by Palgrave Macmillan®, a division of Macmillan Publishers Limited, registered in England, company number 785998, of Houndmills, Basingstoke, Hampshire RG21 6XS.

Library of Congress Cataloging-in-Publication Data
Names: Junankar, P. N., author.
Title: Economics of the labour market : unemployment and the costs of unemployment / P. N. (Raja) Junankar.
Description: Houndmills, Basingstoke, Hampshire ; New York, NY : Palgrave Macmillan, 2015. | Includes index.
Identifiers: LCCN 2015033261 | ISBN 978-1-137-55518-2 (hardback)
Subjects: LCSH: Labor market. | Unemployment.
Classification: LCC HD5706 .J86 2015 | DDC 331.12—dc23
LC record available at http://lccn.loc.gov/2015033261

A catalogue record for this book is available from the Library of Congress.

A catalogue record for this book is available from the British Library.

Typeset by MPS Limited, Chennai, India.

To

My wife Susie Junankar,

my daughter

Kamini and

my son

Simon

Contents

List of Figures and Tables

Figures

Tables

Foreword

For many decades now, Raja Junankar's writings have been renowned for their concentration on vital social issues arising from the malfunctioning of economies, careful gathering of data, sensible, down-to-earth econometric analysis of it and the provision of humane practical policies with which to tackle the social ills revealed. It is excellent and fitting that the essays of this fine economist have now been gathered together in a number of volumes.

The present volume is concerned with his many contributions to the economics of the labour market, emphasising the causes and costs of unemployment in both developed and developing economies. His case studies include Britain, continental Europe and Australia, with an especially important essay on unemployment among Australia's indigenous communities.

The author has included a valuable introduction that discusses the characteristics of various competing theories of why unemployment occurs and what can be done about it. Junankar emphasises especially the role of insufficient aggregate demand as a primary cause of involuntary unemployment. He also writes sensibly about technological and structural unemployment. Especially helpful is the contrast he brings out between the nature of unemployment in developed economies as compared to that in developing economies.

All said, this is a volume that contains astute analysis of fundamental principles and processes, to which he has brought a compassionate stance to complement his dispassionate analyses and criticisms.

Professor Emeritus G. C. Harcourt
School of Economics, UNSW Business School

Preface and Acknowledgements

My interest in Labour Economics was first aroused by a set of lectures at the University of Essex by Professor Frank Brechling in the early 1970s. While I was a lecturer at the University of Essex I had several colleagues who provided me with an excellent environment for learning. I had the pleasure of having Professor Tony Atkinson as a colleague and mentor. Subsequently, I worked at the University of Warwick in the Institute for Employment Research where my work on Labour Economics continued. On joining the Australian National University I worked with Professor Bob Gregory, Professor Bruce Chapman and Dr Cezary Kapuscinski on various aspects of Australian labour markets. Although I have not published jointly with Bob Gregory, he has been an important mentor to me. Since I joined UNSW Australia I have had the pleasure of working with Professor G.C. Harcourt and Associate Professor Peter Kriesler who have given me wonderful support. I am grateful to all the above-mentioned people and to many other colleagues of mine who have helped me in my intellectual journey. This book is a selected collection of my published papers over many years that investigate the labour market in Britain, Europe, Indonesia, and Australia.

1
Introduction

P. N. (Raja) Junankar

The world economies have gone through one of the worst depressions since the Great Depression of 1929. It appears that some of the OECD countries are now slowly recovering from the crisis, although many European countries have very high unemployment rates and their Gross Domestic Product (GDP) has still not reached the pre-crisis levels. As Atkinson (2008) argues:

> Government budgets are under stress, but citizens are going to expect that, if funds can be found to rescue banks, then governments can fund unemployment benefits and employment subsidies. **If governments can take on the role of lender of last resort, then we should be willing to see government as the employer of last resort** (emphasis in original).

In a recent paper, Larry Summers (2015) has argued that countries are now going through a process of "secular stagnation," that is unemployment levels are likely to remain at high levels. Over the past few years there has been a debate about the role of technological change in influencing employment and unemployment. On the employment side, technological change has led to a shift in demand away from unskilled to skilled labour. Technological change has also led to replacing labour by capital, and hence displacing workers. But at the same time increasing incomes have increased the demand for all goods and services and hence there has not been a trend increase in unemployment. However, a recent worry has been that while technological change has been taking place and incomes have been rising, income inequality has been increasing and as a result aggregate consumption may not increase sufficiently to prevent unemployment from increasing. In a modern economy, there is continual change with new firms being set up and old firms closing down. Jobs are created and jobs are destroyed simultaneously in the process, see Davis, Haltiwanger and Schuh (1996). The net impact on the economy and the labour market then depends on the relative magnitudes of these two opposing (dialectical?) forces. In an upswing more firms are expanding and being set up, while in a downturn more firms are declining and closing down. Capitalist economies go through a cyclical process that Keynes argues are due to fluctuations in the "animal spirits" of firms investing in real capital goods.

This book studies the labour market of developed and developing countries. It then studies the causes and consequences of unemployment in these countries. It is a collection of selected published papers in various journals.

One of the features of this collection of papers, chapters now, is that it emphasises the social nature of the labour market. In the labour market, workers do not sell themselves (slavery is illegal in most countries) but they sell their labour power (labour services, or the flow of services offered from the stock of employment). The quality of the labour services they provide depends on both the worker and the employer: if workers are treated well, they would go out of their way to help the employer. If they are treated badly, workers may simply provide limited services to avoid being sacked. The labour market is (or labour markets are) not like the market for fresh tomatoes in a farmers' market. At the end of the day in a farmers' market, tomatoes are sold off at very low prices otherwise they will just get spoilt. In a labour market, even if a firm finds out that it has too many workers it just cannot throw them out into a garbage bin. The workers are not going to sell their labour services at knock-down prices! To coin a phrase: a labour market is different from markets for other commodities because **workers think**. If an employer tried to cut their wages to keep their costs down, workers would either work less efficiently or just leave the employer. If the workers are unionised they would go on strike. Tomatoes do not go on strike if their price is lowered! Labour markets are different from other markets. In particular they are not like auction markets that clear instantaneously. They are influenced by "custom and practice," (Okun, 1981). When an employer is hiring a worker, s/he has to think about how the worker would perform over a period of time into the future, while the worker offered a job has to consider how his/her income and conditions of work would play out over a period of time. They are both making an investment in a "job".

What is a labour market?

Distinctive features of labour as a commodity:

(a) Except for a slave society we can only buy and sell labour *services*. As a result the skills of a worker cannot be separately sold. If an employer trains a worker who subsequently leaves the firm, the worker takes away with her the skills she acquired in her employment.

(b) The quality of the labour services provided depends not only on the innate ability of the workers but also on their attitudes to work, to their fellow workers and to their employers (bosses).

(c) The motivation of workers is very important in the production process. This motivation may be influenced not only by monetary incentives like better pay, but also by "social" factors.
(d) Most employment contracts last for a fairly long time and hence we do not have frequent repeat purchases of the "commodity". However, there has been an increasing trend towards part-time work and the casualisation of labour.
(e) There is asymmetric information in the labour market: the employee has a better idea of his/her abilities while the employer simply has some information about formal qualifications and work experience. The employer may use some worker characteristics (e.g. gender, colour, dress, etc.) to provide a "signal" about the worker's productivity.
(f) There is an unequal power relationship in the labour market: the employer is in a much stronger bargaining position, see quotation from Marx in Section (iv) Radical and Marxist.
(g) Decisions to supply labour may be influenced by the family (e.g. child care availability) and other social factors; it may not depend simply on wages.
(h) The labour market is a social institution, see Solow (1990).

Different labour markets

There is not one but several labour markets differentiated by:

(i) Regions,
(ii) Skills,
(iii) Occupations,
(iv) Industries,
(v) Gender, and
(vi) Race, etc.

It has been argued that there are segmented labour markets: there is a primary labour market and a secondary labour market. The primary labour market consists of workers who have proper contracts, good pay and conditions, while the secondary labour market consists of workers on part-time, temporary or casual work contracts on poor pay and conditions of work.

Institutional constraints

Unlike markets for other commodities there are several institutional and legal constraints which affect the working of labour markets:

(i) Trade unions,
(ii) Wage bargaining procedures,
(iii) Minimum wage legislation,
(iv) Employment protection legislation,

(v) Equal rights legislation, and
(vi) Custom and practice.

What are the questions?

Employment

(i) Why do employers prefer to hire workers who already hold a job somewhere else? Or why is it easier to find a job when you already have a job? Generally, when employers are faced with two applicants for one job, they would prefer the person with experience, and the fact that s/he is employed is evidence of good employability characteristics. An unemployed job seeker may be treated as someone with problems of holding a job.

(ii) Why do employers prefer to hire part-time workers rather than full-time workers? Employers may prefer part-time workers as they can adjust the working hours flexibly and they may not have to pay for leave, etc.

(iii) Why do employers tend to promote people within the firm rather than hire outsiders? Many employers work on the basis of promoting internally as it is likely to give workers an incentive to be more productive (internal labour markets). A promotion is like a reward for good behaviour.

(iv) Do employers discriminate against women, migrants, blacks, etc.? There is a large literature on discrimination in the labour market against particular groups. According to Becker (1957) employers may have a taste for discrimination which leads them to hire particular groups even if it leads to higher costs. Another explanation is called "statistical discrimination": if employers believe that a "minority/ethnic" group is less productive (either through past experience or through some contacts) they would assume that all members of that group are less productive.

(v) In a downturn which workers are fired (sacked) first? Why? When an economy slows down in a recession, firms cut down the hours of part-time workers, and fire temporary and part-time workers first. Experienced workers may be kept on in case of an upturn in demand; furthermore, permanent workers cannot be sacked, for legal or institutional reasons without paying them redundancy payments – hence it is more costly to get rid of them.

(vi) In a recession why do firms not fire more workers and then rehire them in an upswing? There is an interesting literature on the concept of reciprocity in the labour market. If firms treat workers well then workers will be more productive for the employers. In a downturn, if employers fire workers then when the economy picks up they may not be able to hire the better (more productive) workers as they were not treated well.

Unemployment

Before beginning a discussion about unemployment, it is important to note that different countries from the OECD have faced different conditions since the global crisis. Most of the OECD countries had unemployment rates increase significantly, with Germany managing to run its economy with the unemployment rate falling due to work sharing. However, some countries like Spain had unemployment rise to dramatic levels (over 25%), see Figure 1.1.

(i) Why does unemployment exist? Is it accidental or necessary? Some unemployment in capitalist societies is inevitable. There are always going to be some people who are between jobs (transitional unemployment) looking for new work. But more importantly, the economy goes through a business cycle with periods of declining aggregate demand for goods and services which leads to increasing unemployment. When the economy picks up, demand for labour increases and employment increases and unemployment decreases. It has also been argued that to

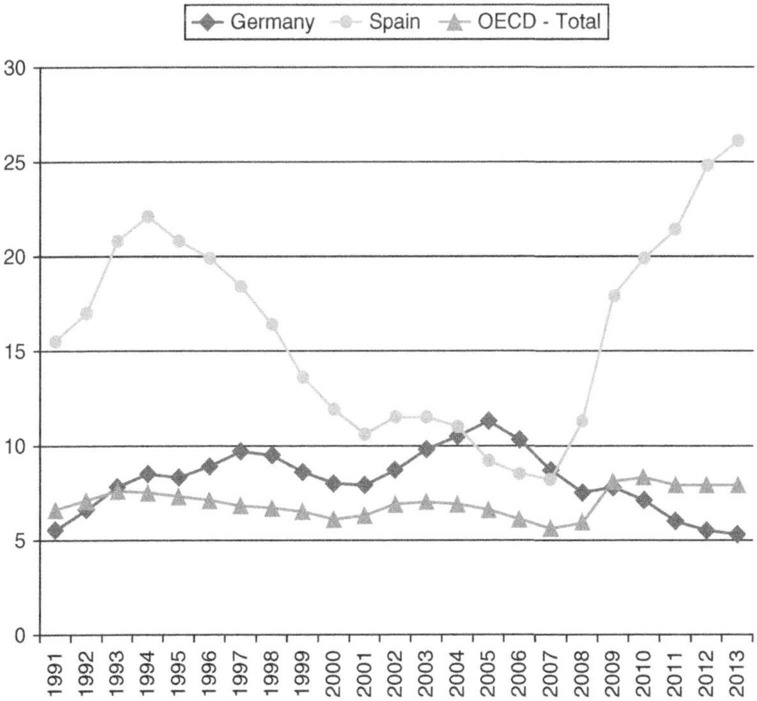

Figure 1.1 Unemployment rates in the OECD (%)
Source: OECD.Stat.

contain inflation, there is a certain amount of unemployment necessary. Neoclassical economists talk about a "non-accelerating inflation rate of unemployment" (NAIRU). Marx and Kalecki had argued that in a capitalist system unemployment helps to control wages and prices and keeps the workers' "pretensions in check". It also makes the sack an effective (credible) threat.

(ii) Is unemployment voluntary or involuntary? Over decades there has been a debate in the economics literature on whether unemployment is voluntary or involuntary. Keynes in his *General Theory* argued convincingly that unemployment is involuntary. In the post-war period neoclassical (and New Classical) economists have been arguing that unemployment is voluntary and influenced by the existence of unemployment benefits or high (minimum) wages. A group of neoclassical economist argue that the unemployed are simply "searching" for a suitable job and if unemployment benefits are available and generous they will continue to search for a higher paid job. Keynesian economists have long argued that unemployment is involuntary and due to a lack of aggregate demand.

(iii) Why are there fluctuations in unemployment? Keynesian economists argue that fluctuations in unemployment are caused by fluctuations in aggregate demand. Neoclassical and New Classical economists argue that these fluctuations are either random or due to sudden changes in the preferences of people for "leisure."

(iv) Does immigration cause unemployment? There is overwhelming evidence that immigration does not cause unemployment in the recipient country. Immigration leads to an increase in the supply of workers but at the same time it leads to an increase in aggregate demand.

(v) Why is the unemployment rate among youths and migrants higher than for other Australians? Why do unskilled workers have higher rates of unemployment? Why do less educated people have higher rates of unemployment? Youths and migrants enter the labour market with little knowledge of the availability of jobs. Young people have less experience in the workforce, and migrants' experience from the home country may not be recognised by employers. Young people who leave school early have less educational qualifications and hence are assumed to be lower productivity workers and hence less likely to be employed. The literature on human capital suggests that increasing education and skills increases the workers' productivity and hence they are more profitable for the employers. During a recession, when there are a large number of workers seeking employment, employers can be more choosy and hire those workers who have better qualifications and skills, hence leaving the less educated and less skilled unemployed.

(vi) Why do some people have repeat spells of unemployment? Why do some of the unemployed have long durations of unemployment?

As mentioned earlier, those people with less skills and education are more likely to be unemployed. In addition, employers treat unemployment as a signal of some poor work qualities and hence do not employ unemployed workers. In addition, the experience of unemployment makes the person lose skills and motivation, which makes it less likely that they find work.

(vii) What are the costs and benefits of unemployment? Some economists argue that an economy must be run with a certain amount of unemployment to control inflation. However, unemployment imposes significant costs on society, on individuals and on families. The existence of large pools of unemployed people signifies the loss of production that they could have produced if they were employed, in other words, there is a significant loss of GDP. In addition, unemployment leads to increases in poor physical and mental health, family disputes, social problems and crime.

Different approaches to unemployment

Neoclassical and New Classical economists

Although there are some differences of emphasis, neoclassical economists argue that all unemployment is voluntary and due to high wages (either because of unions or due to government-imposed minimum wages), or due to workers voluntarily choosing to remain unemployed because they expect to get a higher wage offer by searching longer or they are making an "intertemporal substitution" of leisure between now and later. This intertemporal substitution is made possible by "generous" unemployment benefits. However, unemployment benefits provide insurance against involuntary unemployment. In fact, unemployment benefits may make the worker find a job that is more suitable and hence be more productive. Neoclassical economists explain unemployment in terms of misinformation in the labour market that leads some unemployed people not to accept wage offers in the (sometimes mistaken) belief that a better wage offer is just around the corner. Search theories of unemployment provide some new insights into the functioning of labour market, see for example, Diamond (2011). New Classical economists argue that unemployment is simply due to random technological shocks to the economy or that workers have misperceptions about wage offers and voluntarily reject them. In particular, they argue that the government should let the market determine outcomes and should not intervene in the economy.

Keynesian and Post-Keynesian economists

For both Keynesian and Post-Keynesian economists, unemployment is involuntary and caused by a lack of adequate aggregate demand for goods and services. Frictional and seasonal unemployment, of course, is likely to be voluntary. They argue that wages do *not* adjust rapidly (rigid) to clear the market (that is to remove unemployment). Even if wages were perfectly flexible, it would not clear the labour market and lead to full employment, as falling wages leads to a fall in aggregate demand and hence leads to a downward spiral. In particular, they argue that the government should increase aggregate demand mainly *via* fiscal policies (increased government expenditures and decreased taxation) to increase GDP and hence unemployment decreases. As opposed to the view that minimum wages leads to unemployment, Keynesian and Post-Keynesians would argue that the minimum wages leads to a higher level of aggregate demand and hence *lower* unemployment rates.

Neo-Keynesian economists

Neo-Keynesian economists argue that unemployment does not automatically fall due to wage adjustments. For a variety of reasons it is argued that the labour market is not an auction market and wages are "rigid." Wages are not flexible (downwards) because many workers are on annual contracts, or because firms pay efficiency wages (wages higher than a market wage to get increased efficiency/productivity) or because increased turnover imposes costs on the firm. It was argued that higher than market clearing wages are set by employers either to get a more skilled labour force (adverse selection models), or to provide the workers with an incentive to be more productive.

Radical and Marxist

For Marx and radical economists, unemployment is a necessary consequence of a capitalist economy. Unemployment (or the Industrial Reserve Army, IRA) helps to keep workers under "control" (Marx (1867, 1977); Kalecki (1943), Shapiro and Stiglitz (1984)). Hence, a capitalist economy requires a level of unemployment. Marx and Schumpeter argued that technological and structural changes were inherent in a capitalist economy, and due to the volatility of investment unemployment would also be cyclical.

In some recent work, using experimental economics methods, various authors have discussed the role of "fairness" and "reciprocity" in much of human behaviour that influences decisions on effort, wages, etc. Much of this recent work throws doubt on the self-regulating features of a labour market: employers do not cut wages in times of unemployment, wages are set above market-clearing rates to get higher productivity, workers are willing to accept lower wages but employers do not hire these workers, etc.

Marx argues that on the surface competition prevails, but when the worker enters the factory the relationship between the worker and employer (boss) changes:

> "We now know how the value paid by the purchaser to the possessor of this peculiar commodity, labour-power, is determined. The use-value

which the former gets in exchange, manifests itself only in the actual utilisation, in the consumption of the labour-power. The money-owner buys everything necessary for this purpose, such as raw material, in the market, and pays for it at its full value. The consumption of labour-power is at one and the same time the production of commodities and of surplus value. The consumption of labour-power is completed, as in the case of every other commodity, outside the limits of the market or of the sphere of circulation. Accompanied by Mr. Moneybags and by the possessor of labour-power, we therefore take leave for a time of this noisy sphere, where everything takes place on the surface and in view of all men, and follow them both into the hidden abode of production, on whose threshold there stares us in the face 'No admittance except on business.' Here we shall see, not only how capital produces, but how capital is produced. We shall at last force the secret of profit making.

This sphere that we are deserting, within whose boundaries the sale and purchase of labour-power goes on, is in fact a very Eden of the innate rights of man. There alone rule Freedom, Equality, Property and Bentham. Freedom, because both buyer and seller of a commodity, say of labour-power, are constrained only by their own free will. They contract as free agents, and the agreement they come to, is but the form in which they give legal expression to their common will. Equality, because each enters into relation with the other, as with a simple owner of commodities, and they exchange equivalent for equivalent. Property, because each disposes only of what is his own. And Bentham, because each looks only to himself. The only force that brings them together and puts them in relation with each other, is the selfishness, the gain and the private interests of each. Each looks to himself only, and no one troubles himself about the rest, and just because they do so, do they all, in accordance with the pre-established harmony of things, or under the auspices of an all-shrewd providence, work together to their mutual advantage, for the common weal and in the interest of all.

On leaving this sphere of simple circulation or of exchange of commodities, which furnishes the 'Free-trader Vulgaris' with his views and ideas, and with the standard by which he judges a society based on capital and wages, we think we can perceive a change in the physiognomy of our *dramatis personae*. He, who before was the money-owner, now strides in front as capitalist; the possessor of labour-power follows as his labourer. The one with an air of importance, smirking, intent on business; the other, timid and holding back, like one who is bringing his own hide to market and has nothing to expect but – a hiding." (Marx, Karl, *Capital,* Volume 1, Chapter 6, p. 121, from Marx-Engels Archive)

Unemployment is a serious and continuing problem faced by capitalist economies. Unemployment is analogous to a malign cancer attacking the body politic. It spreads throughout the world and its treatment appears only to provide temporary remission from its consequences. Sometimes the treatments offered are worse than the disease! Unfortunately, unemployment is very selective in finding its victims. Usually, they are the poor, the disadvantaged, the less educated, the less skilled, migrants, blacks, and the young. Just like a diagnosis of cancer for a patient can mean many months (years) of suffering, so it is for the unemployed. Again, like people who suffer from cancer, they may get better for some time until cancer comes back again, perhaps more virulently. For the unemployed, it is more likely that they would suffer repeated spells of unemployment.

The book consists of an Introduction and five parts:

Overview of the Book

The Labour Market

This part provides brief surveys of the "labour economics," the "demand for labour," the "supply of labour" and the "labour force participation rate." It then discusses the concept of employment and unemployment in developed and developing countries. Finally, it discusses the concept of human capital in the context of indigenous workers in Australia. In particular, it argues that providing better education for indigenous people would have a high social rate of return.

Youth Labour Markets

In this part, youth labour markets in Britain, Australia and Indonesia are analysed using econometric/statistical methods. The chapters emphasise that youth labour markets have several distinctive properties. First, there is a high turnover in the labour market with large numbers of young people joining the labour market at the end of schooling/education. Furthermore, since a large proportion of young people work in casual and temporary jobs they are more likely to lose their jobs. Since, they are less experienced they tend to be at the end of a hiring queue. The chapters show that the youth labour market is particularly sensitive to changes in the business cycle, with big increases in their unemployment rate during recessions.

In Chapter 3.1, the essay discusses the nature of youth unemployment in Britain and shows that given that young people have very long durations of unemployment it is unlikely to be voluntary. In particular, it notes that many of the young who are unemployed are not accessing unemployment benefits hence they could not be unemployed voluntarily. It argues that this problem needs to be tackled by increasing government expenditures.

Chapter 3.2 suggests that the youth labour market is a "secondary" labour market with a very high turnover. It begins with a critical examination of a government publication that claims to show that youth unemployment in Britain was due to high wages. It then tests this thesis in a "switching regression" disequilibrium econometric model (a relatively new technique at that time), that is, one where the data determines whether there is an excess demand or excess supply in the labour market. The econometric results show that youth employment is determined by aggregate demand and not by relative wages.

Chapter 3.3 turns to an analysis of Australian youth labour markets. It begins with a critique of a neoclassical competitive labour market to explain the behaviour of the youth labour market. It points out that a large proportion of workplaces do not hire any young people even though youth wages are less than adult wages. It then goes on to estimate employment functions for youths and show that in most cases the estimated wage elasticity is either incorrectly signed or insignificant.

Chapter 3.4 uses data from an Australian longitudinal study to study the dynamics of unemployment. It shows that there is "occurrence dependence", that is, if a young person has one unemployment spell there is a very high probability that s/he will have a repeat spell of unemployment. It shows that these young people who have repeat spells of unemployment account for most of the unemployment experience.

Chapter 3.5 studies the impact of the recent Global Financial Crisis (GFC) on the Australian youth labour market. It demonstrates that the GFC had a significant impact on the youth labour market with unemployment and long-term unemployment for youths rising to levels not seen since the crisis of the early 1990s, even though Australia did not go into a recession (as usually defined). It shows that the labour market for teenagers is more volatile than that for the 20–24-year-old groups. Again, looking at relative wages and unemployment benefits there is no evidence to support the neoclassical explanations. The fall in aggregate demand after the GFC is the main reason for the rapid rise in youth unemployment and long-term unemployment.

Chapter 3.6 studies the problem of youth unemployment in Indonesia, a developing country. In particular it questions the hypothesis that youth unemployment is a "luxury" that only the rich can afford since there is no access to unemployment benefits. It discusses the puzzle that although the Indonesian economy was booming and adult unemployment rates were relatively low, youth unemployment rates were high. It discusses the role of informal labour markets in developing countries. The findings suggest that although youth unemployment is very low among the poorest class it is significantly high among the rest of the social classes. Policies to tackle youth unemployment include more work-based training schemes.

Unemployment

Chapter 4.1 argues that structural changes in the economy (from the industrial sector to the services sector) were one of the major causes of the growth of unemployment in Britain. The level and composition of aggregate demand, not the increase in unemployment benefits is the primary cause of the growth of unemployment.

Chapter 4.2 is one of the earliest essays in Britain to emphasise the importance of studying unemployment flows, rather than the unemployment stock. It emphasises the dynamics of unemployment in terms of the changing inflows into the unemployment stock and the outflows from unemployment. It argues that changes in aggregate demand, tastes and technology lead to changes in the distribution of firms that are growing and declining. It estimates models for the inflows into unemployment and outflows from unemployment. Interestingly, an increase in the inflows leads to an increase in outflows. Structural change variables are statistically significant in both the inflows and outflows equations. An increase in unemployment benefits increases the outflows from unemployment suggesting that higher unemployment benefits increase aggregate demand and hence increase outflows. Wage cost increases lead to an increase of inflows into unemployment and a decrease of outflows suggesting a movement along a labour demand curve. The evidence supports the hypothesis that increases in aggregate demand decrease inflows and increase outflows from unemployment.

Chapter 4.3 studies the manner in which wage-setting institutions affect unemployment in Australia. In an important experiment in Australia the then Hawke Labor government introduced an agreement in 1983 (the Accord) between the unions and government (the employers were meant to be part of this agreement but withdrew) which was an effective "incomes policy". Under this agreement, the unions would agree to money-wage restraint in return for a "social wage" where the government would provide various welfare benefits, lower taxes for low income earners, increased pensions, etc. The chapter shows that the Accord was successful in controlling wage and price inflation and helped to increase aggregate demand and hence led to lower unemployment and long-term unemployment rates. This Accord held for several years, although modified from time to time and ended with the return of a conservative (Coalition) government of John Howard.

Chapter 4.4 provides an overview of the economic problems faced by Aboriginal (indigenous) people in Australia. Although the essay was written a long time ago, unfortunately, conditions of indigenous people in Australia have not improved significantly. To use Hobbes' terms, life for indigenous people is "nasty, brutish, and short". Aboriginal people have low employment rates, high unemployment rates, and are employed as casual and temporary workers, with low earnings. They have a very high rate of imprisonment, poor health and shorter life spans. For many years there was a labour market programme called the Community Development Employment Projects (CDEP) (set up in 1976–77) under which unemployed people give up their rights to social security payments and these payments were made to the community which then created part-time employment in traditional activities, for example producing artworks, traditional wooden products, etc. for sale. This scheme was ended in 2007. The scheme was controversial as most of the participants in CDEP were completely reliant on that scheme and did not usually move into regular employment. However, in remote areas where employment prospects are negligible, it gave participants a useful role in society.

Chapter 4.5 critically discusses various explanations of unemployment in Australia. It argues that structural and technological changes in the economy are an important factor in explaining the growth of unemployment. Although there has been a trend increase in the proportion of students staying on at school until the age of 18, and a trend increase in the number of students completing undergraduate degrees there has been an increase in unemployment rates. In other words, simply increasing educational levels does not help to solve the unemployment problem. Policies are required to increase the level of aggregate demand in an economy. The chapter argues that labour market deregulation does not help to lower unemployment rates.

Chapter 4.6 evaluates the hypothesis that the lowering of real wages would help to decrease the unemployment rate. It shows that in a capitalist economy profit-maximising firms set wage rates at levels higher than so-called equilibrium rates to encourage higher productivity by workers. Hence firms would not cut wages to increase employment. Research by Truman Bewley (1999) showed that in America during a recession firms were not willing to cut wages to increase employment as it would affect their relationship with their workers that may lower productivity. Governments do not have any controls to cut wages and hence it is not a sensible policy prescription. Even if it were possible, it would not increase employment.

Chapter 4.7 argues, following Kalecki (1943), that it is in the interests of the capitalists to have a certain amount of unemployment to help to control the wage demands of workers and to make them more compliant to the demands of their bosses. In a highly cited paper Shapiro and Stiglitz (1984) also argue that unemployment is a "worker discipline device," although they appear unaware of Marx or the classic Kalecki (1943) paper. The paper discusses alternative theories of unemployment and emphasises the significant costs of unemployment.

Long-Term Unemployment

Chapter 5.1 discusses the issue of long-term unemployment in Australia. It argues that as unemployment increases the long-term unemployed get pushed further and further to the back of a hiring queue. The less skilled and older workers tend to be at the back of employers hiring queues. Furthermore, the longer a person is unemployed the more s/he gets disillusioned and loses motivation to search for a job. They also lose their skills (skill atrophy) and this makes them less employable. A simple model is set up to explain the proportion of long-term unemployed in the total unemployed stock as a function of the level of unemployment rates (current and lagged). These estimates were then used to forecast what would happen to long-term unemployment in the future if the unemployment rate followed some alternative paths. The results suggested that the prospects for long-term unemployed were desperate and any policy measures introduced were unlikely to help in the short run. Hence, to avoid high levels of long-term unemployment it is crucial to keep the unemployment rates low. Even if there is a temporary rise in the unemployment rate it has a continuing impact on long-term unemployment.

Chapter 5.2 evaluates the success of Australian labour market programmes introduced by the Keating government in 1994 under the title of "Working Nation." The programmes were targeted at the unemployed who had been unemployed for longer than 18 months. Comparing the performance of the Australian economy over the two recessions (1980s and 1990s) the chapter shows that the Working Nation programmes helped to control long-term unemployment. Furthermore, estimating employment functions the chapter shows that the Working Nation programmes helped to increase employment more than would have happened without these programmes.

Costs of Unemployment

Chapter 6.1 provides estimates for the costs of unemployment in the European Community. After a brief discussion about the costs of unemployment to individuals, families, social groups, government and to society, it suggests ways of providing some quantitative estimates of the loss of GDP. The chapter uses two alternative scenarios: labelled "High" if we use the average unemployment levels of 1968–73 or "Low" if we use the average unemployment levels of the period 1974–79. For example, the estimate for Germany in 1983 was 13.38 % for the "Low" scenario and 20.63% for the "High" scenario. That is GDP would have been 13% and 20% larger in 1983 if unemployment had been reduced to previous levels. For the United Kingdom for the same time, the estimates of 13% and 17% of GDP were lost due to high unemployment. Of course, if we were to provide estimates for the present time when the OECD countries have gone through a global crisis the estimates would be frighteningly high. For countries like Spain and Greece where unemployment levels in January 2015 were 23% and 25% respectively the loss of GDP would be dramatically high. It argues that policies to control inflation, and nowadays, the government debt are imposing huge costs to society.

Chapter 6.2 provides a detailed analysis of the costs of unemployment in Australia using alternative methods. The GDP loss to Australian society was between 6% and 9%. It also assesses the costs to unemployed individuals who are losing their income and simply receiving very low levels of unemployment benefits. The chapter also provides some estimates of the costs to society in terms of an increase in divorces and increased crime caused by high levels of unemployment. Overall, it emphasises that the costs to society of high levels of unemployment are very significant and hence governments should introduce policies to lower unemployment. Simply focusing on lowering inflation (or in the recent period since the Global Crisis) focusing on lower government budget deficits and government debt imposes huge costs on individuals, families, on government and on society as a whole.

Chapter 6.3 begins with a discussion of the importance of employment to the individual, not only in terms of providing an income, but also in providing a set of social relationships that provides a structure and meaning to life. The loss of a job has significant impact on the psychological well-being of an individual and may cause physical and mental illness. Employers may reduce safety standards in the workplace and increase pressure on workers to be more productive that may lead to more workplace accidents. In opposition to this a higher level of unemployment decreases work-related accidents and health costs of workplace pollution. Reduced traffic to and from work is also likely to reduce road accidents. It then provides an econometric study to show that mortality rates in England and Wales increases with unemployment rates. The econometric evidence supports the work done by epidemiologists and demographers that show that increased unemployment increases morbidity and mortality rates.

Now the reader should read the following chapters to study various aspects of the labour market and unemployment.

Bibliography

Aaronson, D., B. Mazumder and S. Schechter (2010). "What Is Behind the Rise in Long-term Unemployment," Federal Reserve Bank of Chicago, *Economic Perspectives*, 2Q, 2010.

Agell, J. (1999). "On the Benefits from Rigid Labour Markets: Norms, Market Failures, and Social Insurance," *Economic Journal*, 109, F143–64.

Akerlof, G. A. (1982). "Labor Market Contracts as Partial Gift-Exchange," *Quarterly Journal of Economics*, 97, 543–69.

Akerlof, G. A. and J. L. Yellen (eds) (1986). *Efficiency Wage Models of the Labor Market*, Cambridge: Cambridge University Press.

Allegretto, S. and D. Lynch (2010). "The Composition of the Unemployed and Long-term Unemployed in Tough Labour Markets," *Monthly Labour Review*, October, 3–18.

Atkinson, A. B. (2008). "Unequal Growth, Unequal Recession," *OECD Observer* No. 270/271, December 2008–January 2009.

Baker, M. (1992). "Unemployment Duration: Compositional Effects and Cyclical Variability," *American Economic Review*, 82, 313–21.

Ball, L. (2009). "Hysteresis in Unemployment: Old and New Evidence," NBER WP 14818.

Becker, G. (1957). *The Economics of Discrimination*, Chicago: Chicago University Press.

Bernanke, B. S. (2011). Statement by Ben S. Bernanke, Chairman, Board of Governors of the Federal Reserve System before the Committee on Financial Services, US House of Representatives, 13 July 2011.

Bewley, T. F. (1999). *Why Wages Don't Fall during a Recession*, Cambridge and London: Harvard University Press.

Blanchard, O. (2003). *Macroeconomics*, Third Edition, New Jersey; Prentice Hall, Chapter 6.

Blanchard, O. and J. Wolfers (2000). "The Role of Shocks and Institutions in the Rise of European Unemployment: The Aggregate Evidence," *Economic Journal* (Conference Papers) 110, C1–C33.
Blanchard, O. and L. Summers (1986). "Hysteresis and the European Unemployment Problem," in S. Fischer (ed.), *NBER Macroeconomics Annual 1986.*
Blanchard, O. and P. Diamond (1989). "The Beveridge Curve," *Brookings Papers on Economic Activity*, 1, 1–60.
Boone, J., A. Sadrieh and J. C. van Ours (2004). "Experiments on Unemployment Benefit Sanctions and Job Search Behavior," IZA Discussion Paper No. 1000.
Brown, M., A. Falk and E. Fehr (2004). "Relational Contracts and the Nature of Market Interactions," *Econometrica*, 72, 747–80.
Bureau of Labour Statistics (2012). "The Recession of 2007–2009," US Bureau of Labour Statistics (www.bls.gov/spotlight)
Calmfors, L. and J. Driffill (1988). "Bargaining Structure, Corporatism, and Macroeconomic Performance," *Economic Policy*, 6, April 1988, 14–61.
Card, D., R. Chetty and A. Weber (2007). "'The Spike at Benefit Exhaustion' Leaving the Unemployment System or Starting a New Job?" *American Economic Review*, 97, 113–18.
Chapman, B. J., P. N. Junankar and C. A. Kapuscinski (1992). "Projections of Long-term Unemployment," *Australian Bulletin of Labour*, 18, September 1992, 195–207.
Daly, M. C., B. Hobijn, A. Sahin and R. G. Valletta (2012). "A Search and Matching Approach to Labour Markets: Did the Natural Rate of Unemployment Rise?" *Journal of Economic Perspectives*, 26, 3–26.
Dao, M. and P. Loungani (2010). "The Human Cost of Recessions: Assessing it, Reducing it," IMF Staff Position Note, SPN/10/17, 11 November 2010.
Davis, S. J. and J. A. Kahn (2008). "Interpreting the Great Moderation: Changes in the Volatility of Economic Activity at the Macro and Micro Levels," *Journal of Economic Perspectives*, 22, 155–80.
Davis, S. J. and T. M. von Wachter (2011). "Recessions and the Cost of Job Loss," *Brookings Papers on Economic Activity*, Fall 2011, 1–72.
Davis, S. J., J. C. Haltiwanger and S. Schuh (1996). *Job Creation and Job Destruction*, Cambridge, MA: MIT Press.
Diamond, P. (2011). "Unemployment, Vacancies, and Wages," *American Economic Review*, 101, 1045–72.
Eckstein, Z. and G. J. van den Berg (2003). "Empirical Labor Search: A Survey," IZA Discussion Paper No. 929.
Eichorst, W., V. Escudero, P. Marx and S. Tobin (2010). "The Impact of the Crisis on Employment and the Role of the Labour Market Institutions," ILO, Geneva.
Elsby, M. W. L., A. Hobijn and A. Ahin (2010). "The Labour Market in the Great Recession: Comments and Discussion," *Brookings Papers on Economic Activity*, Spring, 1–69.
Farber, H. S. (2012). "Unemployment in the Great Recession: Did the Housing Market Crisis Prevent the Unemployed from Moving to Take Jobs," paper presented to the AEA Meetings, Chicago, 2011.
Farber, H. S. and R. G. Valetta (2013). "Do Extended Unemployment Benefits Extend Unemployment Spells?" IZA Discussion Paper 7347.
Fehr, E. and A. Falk (1999). "Wage Rigidity in a Competitive Incomplete Contract Market," *Journal of Political Economy*, 107, 106–34.
Fehr, E. and S. Gachter (2000). "Fairness and Retaliation: The Economics of Reciprocity," *Journal of Economic Perspectives*, 14, 159–81.

Gamberoni, E., E. Von Uexkull, and S. Weber (2010). "The Roles of Openness and Labour Market Institutions for Employment Dynamics during Economic Crises," World Bank Economic Premise, No. 29 (forthcoming as an ILO Working Paper, 2011).

Guichard, S. and E. Rusticelli (2010). "Assessing the Impact of the Financial Crisis on Structural Unemployment in OECD Countries," OECD Economics Department Working Paper No. 767.

Hall, R. E. (2011). "The Long Slump," *American Economic Review*, 101, 431–69.

Heckman, J. J., R. J. Lalonde and J. A. Smith (1999). "The Economics and Econometrics of Active Labor Market Programs," in *Handbook of Labor Economics*, vol. 3A, ed. Orley Ashenfelter and David Card, Amsterdam: Elsevier.

Hoon, H. T. and E. S. Phelps (1992). "Macroeconomic Shocks in a Dynamised Model of the Natural Rate of Unemployment," *American Economic Review*, 82, 889–900.

Hoynes, H., D. L. Miller and J. Schaller (2012). "Who Suffers during Recessions?" *Journal of Economic Perspectives*, 26, 27–48.

International Monetary Fund (2010). "Unemployment Dynamics during Recessions and Recoveries: Okun's Law and Beyond," Chapter 3, *World Economic Outlook*, April, 69–107.

Jackman, R. and R. Layard (1991). "Does Long-term Unemployment Reduce a Person's Chance of a Job: A Time-Series Test," *Economica*, 58, 93–106.

Johnson, G. E. and P. R. G. Layard (1986). "The Natural Rate of Unemployment: Explanations and Policy," in *Handbook of Labor Economics*, ed. Orley Ashenfelter and R. Layard, Amsterdam: Elsevier.

Junankar, P. N. (1986). *Costs of Unemployment: Main Report*. Luxembourg: Office for the Official Publications of the European Communities, 1986 (pp. vi + 111).

Junankar, P. N. (1987). *Social Costs of Unemployment: Annex to Costs of Unemployment*. Luxembourg: Office for the Official Publications of the European Communities, 1987 (p. 34).

Junankar, P. N. (1988). *Very-Long-Term Unemployment* (ed.) Luxembourg: Office for the Official Publications of the European Communities, 1988 (p. 142).

Junankar, P. N. (2000a). "Are Wage Cuts the Answer? Theory and Evidence," in *The Unemployment Crisis in Australia: Which Way Out?*, ed. Stephen Bell, Cambridge: Cambridge University Press.

Junankar, P. N. (2000b). *Economics of Unemployment: Causes, Consequences and Policies*, (ed.), 4 vols, International Library of Critical Writings, Cheltenham: Edward Elgar Publishing Limited.

Junankar, P. N. (2011). "The Global Economic Crisis: Long Term Unemployment in the OECD." IZA Discussion Paper No. 6057, Bonn, Germany.

Junankar, P. N. and C. A. Kapuscinski (1991). "The Incidence of Long Term Unemployment in Australia," *Australian Bulletin of Labour*, 17, 325–52.

Junankar, P. N. and C. A. Kapuscinski (1992). *The Costs of Unemployment in Australia*, Economic Planning Advisory Council, Background Paper No. 24, Canberra, AGPS, 1993 (p. 63).

Junankar, P. N. and J. B. Madsen (2004). "Unemployment in the OECD: Models and Mysteries," IZA Discussion Paper No. 1168.

Kalecki, M. (1943). "Political Aspects of Full Employment," *Political Quarterly*, 14, 322–31.

Kochan, T. A. (2013). "The American Jobs Crisis and Its Implications for the Future of Employment Policy: A Call for a New Jobs Compact," *Industrial and Labour Relations Review*, 66, 291–315.

Krueger, A. B. (2008). Hearing on "Unemployment in a Volatile Economy: How to Secure Families and Build Opportunity," Prepared Statement by Alan B. Krueger, 6 March 2008, Dirksen Senate Office Building.

Krueger, A. B. and A. Mueller (2012). "The Lot of the Unemployed: A Time Use Perspective," *Journal of the European Economic Association*, 10, 765–94.

Krugman, P. R. and R. Z. Lawrence (1994). "Trade, Jobs and Wages," *Scientific American*, 270, 22–27.

Layard, P. R. G. and S. J. Nickell (1986). "Unemployment in Britain," *Economica*, 53, S121–70.

Layard, R., S. Nickell and R. Jackman (1991). *Unemployment: Macroeconomic Performance and the Labour Market*, Oxford: Oxford University Press.

Lindbeck, A. (1993). *Unemployment and Macroeconomics*, London: MIT Press.

Lindbeck, A. and D. Snower (1988). "Cooperation, Harassment and Involuntary Unemployment," *American Economic Review*, March 1988, 71, 896–908.

Lippman, S. A. and J. J. McCall (1976a). "The Economics of Job Search: A Survey: Part I," *Economic Inquiry*, 14, 155–89.

Lippman, S. A. and J. J. McCall (1976b). "The Economics of Job Search: A Survey: Part II," *Economic Inquiry*, 14, 347–68.

Ljungqvist, L. and T. J. Sargent (1998). "The European Unemployment Dilemma," *Journal of Political Economy*, 106, 514–50.

Lucas, R. E., Jr and L. A. Rapping (1969). "Real Wages, Employment, and Inflation," *Journal of Political Economy*, 77, Sept./Oct. 1969, 721–54.

Machin, S. and A. Manning (1999). "The Causes and Consequences of Long-term Unemployment in Europe," in *Handbook of Labor Economics*, vol. 3, ed. O. Ashenfelter and D. Card, Amsterdam: Elsevier.

Mark, K. (1977). *Capital*, vols I, II, III, London: Lawrence and Wishart (first published volume I, 1867, volume II, 1885, volume III, 1894).

Matthews, R. C. O. (1968). "Why Has Britain Had Full Employment Since the War?", *Economic Journal*, 78, 555–69.

Mortensen, D. T. (1970). "Job Search, the Duration of Unemployment, and the Phillips Curve," *American-Economic-Review*, 60, Dec. 1970, 847–62.

Mortensen, D. T. (1986). "Job Search and Labor Market Analysis," in *Handbook of Labor Economics*, vol. 2, ed. O. C. Ashenfelter and R. Layard, Amsterdam: Elsevier.

Mortensen, D. T. (2011). "Markets with Search Friction and the DMP Model," *American Economic Review*, 101, 1073–91.

Mortensen, D. T. and C. A. Pissarides (1999). "New Developments in Models of Search in the Labour Market," in *Handbook of Labour Economics*, vol. 3, ed. O. C. Ashenfelter and D. Card, Amsterdam: Elsevier.

Nickell, S. (1990). "Unemployment: A Survey," *Economic Journal*, 100, 391–439.

Nickell, S. and R. Layard (1999). "Labor Market Institutions and Economic Performance," in *Handbook of Labor Economics*, vol. 3, ed. O. Ashenfelter and D. Card, Amsterdam: Elsevier.

Nickell, S., L. Nunziata and W. Ochel (2005). "Unemployment in the OECD Since the 1960s. What Do We Know?" *Economic Journal*, 115, 1–27.

OECD (2002). "The Ins and Outs of Long-term Unemployment," Chapter 4, *OECD Employment Outlook* 2002.

OECD (2009). "The Jobs Crisis: What Are the Implications for Employment and Social Policy," Chapter 1, *OECD Employment Outlook* 2009.

OECD (2010a). "Moving Beyond the Jobs Crisis," *OECD Employment Outlook* 2010, 15–102.

OECD (2010b). "Labour Markets and the Crisis," OECD Economics Department Working Paper No. 756.

Okun, A. (1981). *Prices and Quantities: A Macroeconomic Analysis*, Oxford: Basil Blackwell.

Petrongolo, B. and C. A. Pissarides (2001). "Looking into the Black Box: A Survey of the Matching Function," *Journal of Economic Literature*, 39, 390–431.

Phelps, E. S. (1970). *Microeconomic Foundations of Employment & Inflation Theory*, New York: W.W. Norton & Co. Inc.

Pissarides, C. A. (2011). "Equilibrium in the Labor Market with Search Frictions," *American Economic Review*, 101, 1092–105.

Rabin, M. (1993). "Incorporating Fairness into Game Theory and Economics," *American Economic Review*, 83, 1281–302.

Rinne, U. and K. Zimmermann (2012). "Another Economic Miracle? The German Labor Market and the Great Recession," *IZA Journal of Labor Policy*, 1, 1–21.

Rothstein, J. (2011). "Unemployment Insurance and Job Search in the Great Recession," *Brookings Papers on Economic Activity* (Fall), 143–96.

Rowthorn, R. E. (1977). "Conflict, Inflation and Money," *Cambridge Journal of Economics*, 1, Sept. 1977, 215–39.

Saunders, P. and R. Taylor (2002). *The Price of Prosperity: The Economic and Social Costs of Unemployment*, Sydney: UNSW Press.

Schotter, A. and Y. M. Braunstein (1981). "Economic Search: An Experimental Study," *Economic Inquiry*, 19, 1–25.

Shapiro, C. and J. E. Stiglitz (1984). "Equilibrium Unemployment as a Worker Discipline Device," *American Economic Review*, 74, June 1984, 433–44.

Shimer, R. (2012). "Reassessing the Ins and Outs of Unemployment," *Review of Economic Dynamics*, 15, 127–48.

Solow, R. M. (1986). "Unemployment: Getting the Questions Right," *Economica*, 53, Supplement 1986, S23–34.

Solow, R. M. (1990). *The Labour Market as a Social Institution*, Oxford: Blackwell.

Stockhammer, E. and E. Klar (2011). "Capital Accumulation, Labour Market Institutions and Unemployment in the Medium Run," *Cambridge Journal of Economics*, 35, 437–57.

Summers, L. H. (2015). "US Economic Prospects: Secular Stagnation, Hysteresis, and the Zero Lower Bound," *Business Economics*, 49, 65–73.

Valetta, R. and K. Kuang (2010). "Extended Unemployment and UI Benefits," FRBSF Economic Letter, 19 April 2010.

Yellen, J. L. (1984). "Efficiency Wage Models of Unemployment," *American Economic Review*, 74, May 1984, 200–05.

2
The Labour Market

2.1
Labor Economics

P. N. Junankar

The field of labor economics is involved with the study of the labor market, including the determinants of employment, unemployment, and wages. The labor market developed as societies moved from feudal to capitalist processes. The development of capitalism in turn led to powerful capitalist owners and an industrial workforce that was concentrated in factories. Conditions of work became, by present Western standards, dirty, demanding, and dangerous. As a result, workers organized unions and began to demand better pay and working conditions, and they set up political organizations like the Labour Party in the United Kingdom. Over the years, organized labor managed to achieve many of their goals, as legislation was introduced in many countries to provide minimum wages, poverty relief, unemployment benefits, and pensions, and to ensure safe working conditions.

The labor market consists of employers, workers, and a government that provides an institutional and legal framework. The distinctive features of labor as a commodity are: (1) except for a slave society, people can only buy and sell labor services; (2) the quality of the labor services provided depends not only on the innate ability of the workers but also on their attitudes to work, to their fellow workers, and to their employers; (3) most employment contracts last for a fairly long time, so there are not frequent repeat purchases of this "commodity"; (4) there is asymmetric information in the labor market about the "quality" of labor services; and, (5) there is an unequal power relationship in the labor market.

Labor markets are different from other markets. As Arthur Okun points out in *Prices and Quantities* (1981), they are not auction markets that clear instantaneously, but are influenced by "custom and practice." For example, firing is usually based on last in, first out, and seniority is often given special

---

Reprinted from 'Labor Economics' by P. N. Junankar in *International Encyclopedia of the Social Sciences*, 2nd edition, 9 vols, edited by William A. Darity Jr. Detroit: Macmillan Reference USA, 2008. With kind permission from Macmillan Publishers Ltd.

privileges. There are many interrelated labor markets, differentiated by geography, occupation, industry, and often by gender and race. Analyses of segmented labor markets (primary and secondary markets) provide an interesting window into the role of "power" in labor markets, as demonstrated in the work of Peter Doeringer and Michael Piore (1971). Robert Solow, meanwhile, has emphasized the idea that the labor market is a social institution, and that it is therefore important to consider issues of equity and fairness in labor markets (1990). The labor market is different from other markets because the commodity being traded (labor) is capable of reasoned thought. Hence, the way employers treat workers, and the way other workers treat each other, influences their behavior and productivity, as well as wages.

Labor economics was once an interdisciplinary (institutionalist) study that included historical analysis, industrial relations, sociology, and political science. In the early literature, Adam Smith, David Ricardo, and Karl Marx employed versions of the labor theory of value, which states that the determinant of the value of a commodity is the amount of labor embodied in it. Marx pointed to the "exploitation" of labor, believing that workers produced "surplus value." Subsequently, at some point in the post-World War II era, labor economics became a narrow economics subdiscipline in terms of methodology that used neoclassical economic theory (assumptions of maximizing behavior in atomistic, mainly, competitive markets) to analyze various aspects of the labor market, including aspects of employment, unemployment, wages, gender and race discrimination, and immigration. It expanded its boundaries in terms of subject matter, exploring areas of demography, crime, health, marriage, and social relationships ("economics imperialism") under the guidance of the Nobel Prize-winning economist Gary Becker.

Econometric methods have been used on time-series, cross-section, and panel or longitudinal data to study labor economics and the evaluation of government policies on the labor market. Thus, under the influence of another Nobel Prize-winning economist, George Akerlof, modern labor economics has moved full circle—it now studies labor markets in an interdisciplinary framework (although with formal economic models) that includes concepts of psychology, anthropology, industrial relations, and management theory. Modern labor economics has developed new econometric methods to analyze social safety policies by using controlled experiments, "matching" techniques, and panel estimation techniques with fixed and random effects. Since the mid-1990s, labor economics has embraced "experimental economics" methods devised by innovative economists such as Ernst Fehr and Simon Gächter (2000). In these studies, the concepts of fairness, reciprocity, and equity in the labor market are investigated.

The Great Depression of the 1930s led to studies of unemployment, including long-term unemployment, the impact of unemployment on society, and human degradation caused by unemployment. Much work was done to explain the massive rise of unemployment in terms of "rigid wages" (classical economics), and of inadequate aggregate demand (Keynesian economics). The big increase in unemployment following the "oil shocks" of the 1970s led to theories of "stagflation." Subsequently, explanations of unemployment pointed to imperfectly functioning markets, with regulated labor market institutions being blamed. Theories then moved on to using concepts of search in a labor market with imperfect information, as described by Edmund Phelps (1970) and Dale Mortenson and Christopher Pissarides (1999). In these models workers are looking for a job when they receive wage offers which follow a normal distribution; some are good and some are bad. They have to decide whether to accept the offer or reject it. If they reject the offer, they are unable to return to it if the subsequent offers are worse.

The rise of rational expectations led to the concept of the "natural rate of unemployment" (Friedman 1968), and to a Keynesian variant, the non-accelerating inflation rate of unemployment (NAIRU), which was supposed to be constant and immutable. However, econometric work has found this concept to be ill-defined and poorly estimated. More important, it was found that there is "hysteresis" in the behavior of unemployment and in the so-called natural rate. The current rate of unemployment depends on the past evolution of the unemployment rate. Hence the "natural rate" is not a constant to which the unemployment rate will gravitate.

Much has been made about the role of "monopolistic" unions in raising wages above market-clearing wages and causing unemployment. Several studies have compared the differences between the wages of union and nonunion members. In an important book published in 1984, Richard Freeman and James Medoff argued that unions have a positive impact on the functioning of labor markets.

The post-1960s literature on labor economics moved from macroeconomic analyses of labor markets and industry-level studies to the study of microeconomics (on a firm and individual/household level) of the demand and supply of labor. The development of the human capital approach to analyzing the investments of rational maximizing individuals in education and skills, as outlined by Gary Becker in *Human Capital* (1964), led to a better understanding of labor supply. Given that investment in human capital is irreversible, work done in the 1990s treated the acquisition of skills as an "investment option" under uncertainty.

The growth of computer usage, and the subsequent development of large data sets, has led to an explosion of econometric analyses. Most of the research to explain wage rates (or earnings) has used earnings functions. Thus, the logarithm of wages (earnings) was explained by human capital, work experience, and various other control variables. Although most studies have found human capital variables to be significant, the explanatory power of these equations is very low. Yet the role of human capital in explaining economic growth has had important policy implications. Minimum wage policies have been analyzed to see if they have helped the poor and led to a fall in employment. David Card and Alan Kreuger's 1995 critical analysis of the data for the United States suggested that minimum wages had little impact on unemployment. This conclusion led to a huge controversy that has continued into the early twenty-first century. The re-introduction of minimum wages in the United Kingdom in 1998 was found by Alan Manning (using monopsonistic models in 2003) to have had no significant impact on employment.

There have been significant advances in the study of the determinants of labor supply and demand using modern econometric techniques and panel data. In studies of labor supply, individuals are assumed to maximize lifetime utility, subject to given budget and time constraints, where they choose an optimal amount of education, work, and leisure. Tax and welfare policies are studied in this framework and have important implications for the policy analysis of negative income taxes and social security benefits. Labor demand is studied for firms that maximize present values of profits by choosing optimal amounts of labor. Labor is treated by firms as a "quasi-fixed" input, according to Walter Oi (1962), and it is analogous to investing in physical capital goods. Advanced studies suggest that firms choose wages to maximize the efficiency of labor (Akerlof and Yellen 1986), or else choose an appropriate sequence of wages to maximize present values (Lazear 1995).

Labor economics has made significant theoretical and empirical strides in understanding the workings of labor markets. Econometric analyses of various tax, welfare, and active labor-market policies have helped to develop new policies for improving the functioning of the labor market and helping the unemployed and the poorer segments of society. However, there is still much work to be done to truly understand the nature of unemployment and poverty.

Bibliography

Akerlof, George A. 1982. Labor Market Contracts as Partial Gift-Exchange. *Quarterly Journal of Economics* 97: 543–569.

Akerlof, George A., and Janet L. Yellen, eds. 1986. *Efficiency Wage Models of the Labor Market*, Cambridge, U.K.: Cambridge University Press.

Ashenfelter, Orley C., and David Card, eds. 1999. *Handbook of Labor Economics*. Vols. 3A, 3B, and 3C. Amsterdam: North Holland.

Ashenfelter, Orley C., and Kevin F. Hallock, eds. 1995. *Labor Economics*. 4 vols. International Library of Critical Writings. Cheltenham, U.K.: Edward Elgar.

Ashenfelter, Orley C., and Richard Layard, eds. 1986. *Handbook of Labor Economics*. Vols. 1 and 2. Amsterdam: North Holland.

Becker, Gary. 1964. *Human Capital*. New York: Columbia University Press.

Becker, Gary. 1976. *The Economic Approach to Human Behavior*. Chicago: University of Chicago Press.

Card, David, and Alan B. Krueger. 1995. *Myth and Measurement: The New Economics of the Minimum Wage*. Princeton, NJ: Princeton University Press.

Doeringer, Peter B., and Michael J. Piore. 1971. *Internal Labor Markets and Manpower Analysis*. Lexington, MA: Heath Lexington Books.

Fehr, Ernst, and Simon Gächter. 2000. Fairness and Retaliation: The Economics of Reciprocity. *Journal of Economic Perspectives* 14 (3): 159–181.

Freeman, Richard, and James L. Medoff. 1984. *What Do Unions Do?* New York: Basic Books.

Friedman, Milton. 1968. The Role of Monetary Policy. *American Economic Review* 58 (1): 1–17.

Junankar, P. N., ed. 2000. *Economics of Unemployment: Causes, Consequences, and Policies*. 4 vols. International Library of Critical Writings. Cheltenham, U.K.: Edward Elgar.

Lazear, Edward P. 1995. *Personnel Economics*. Cambridge, MA: MIT Press.

Manning, Alan. 2003. *Monopsony in Motion: Imperfect Competition in Labor Markets*. Princeton, NJ: Princeton University Press.

Mortensen, Dale T., and Christopher A. Pissarides. 1999. New Developments in Models of Search in the Labor Market. In *Handbook of Labor Economics*. Vol. 3, eds. Orley C. Ashenfelter and David Card. Amsterdam: North Holland.

Okun, Arthur. 1981. *Prices and Quantities: A Macroeconomic Analysis*. Oxford: Basil Blackwell.

Oi, Walter J. 1962. Labor as a Quasi-Fixed Factor. *Journal of Political Economy* 70 (6): 538–555.

Phelps, Edmund S. 1970. *Microeconomic Foundations of Employment and Inflation Theory*. New York: Norton.

Solow, Robert M. 1990. *The Labor Market as a Social Institution*. Oxford: Blackwell.

2.2
Labor Demand

P. N. Junankar

The "demand for labor" is usually understood by economists to mean the demand for labor services by a firm, an industry, or the economy at a given real wage. In a capitalist economy, labor becomes a commodity that is bought and sold on the market just like any other commodity, such as bread or butter. Labor is a unique commodity, however, and when an employer buys labor, he or she obtains a worker's "labor power" which is the amount of services that the employer gets from the worker. These services depend on the power the employer has over the worker. If there is high unemployment, for example, the worker is in a weak position and greater labor services can be extracted from him or her. The amount of labor services that the employer obtains (not only in terms of hours of work, but in terms of the efficiency of those services) also depends on the nature of the employment contract, the real wage paid to the worker, the conditions of employment, and the attitude of the employer to the worker (and vice versa).

Labor services consist of three components: the number of workers (employees), the average hours worked per worker, and the efficiency per hour of the worker. There are several institutional and legal constraints on employers in most developed countries. For example, there may be laws against discrimination, equal pay legislation, minimum wages (henceforth, the term *wages* refer to real wages), occupational health and safety requirements, hiring and firing restrictions, and penalty rates for overtime.

The demand for labor is a derived demand: Firms wish to hire workers to produce goods and services that they sell in order to earn profits. Alfred Marshall, in his *Principles of Economics* (1930) suggested that labor demand becomes more responsive to wage changes if the substitution possibilities between labor and capital increase. In other words, the easier it is to

---

Reprinted from 'Labor Demand' by P. N. Junankar in *International Encyclopedia of the Social Sciences*, 2nd edition. 9 vols, edited by William A. Darity Jr. Detroit: Macmillan Reference USA, 2008. With kind permission from Macmillan Publishers Ltd.

substitute capital for labor, the greater the share of wages in total costs, and the more responsive the other factors of production are to their prices.

Much of the formal economics literature is based on simple models of firm behavior in a perfectly competitive economy (for a closed economy, that is, without any international trade), assuming that labor is a homogeneous commodity. In a prototype model, a firm is assumed to maximize profits (or minimize costs) subject to a so-called "well-behaved" production function that depends on homogeneous labor and capital. By simple mathematical manipulation, it is easy to show that the firm's demand for labor is a negatively sloped marginal revenue product (MRP) curve, and that employment is determined by equating the marginal revenue product of labor with the wage rate. In such models, it is usually assumed that labor and capital are substitutable (usually in a Cobb-Douglas production function). There are some difficulties, however, in moving from a firm labor-demand function to an industry or aggregate labor-demand function because of the possible interactions between firms, the heterogeneity of labor, and other factors.

In most of these models, it is assumed that the technology of production is given and unchanging. Alternatively, technological change is simply an exogenous variable that falls like manna from heaven on all existing inputs. Labor services are often assumed to be such that hours of work and employees are perfectly substitutable.

The impact of technological change on the labor market and on labor mobility is very significant, but it often has contradictory effects. Technological change is usually defined as being either a change in the product or a change in the process of production. Technological change that leads to the introduction of new products will lead to either new firms being set up or old firms expanding into a new product line, which would lead to increased employment through job creation and job destruction. Job destruction leads to the closing down of firms producing some products that are replaced by new firms producing new products. However, demand for a new product may lessen demand for competing products, leading to a reduction in labor demand elsewhere in the economy. Similarly, a technological change in the production process may lead to the substitution of capital for unskilled labor, and hence to a decrease in labor demand. It may also lead to an increase in the demand for skilled labor, however, due to a complementarity of capital with skilled labor.

In more advanced models, labor is treated as a "quasi-fixed" input, like a capital good (see Oi 1962; Nickell 1986). In other words, there are significant fixed costs associated with changing employment, due to hiring and firing costs. Usually, it is assumed that these costs of adjustment are quadratic (implying increasing marginal costs of adjustment), so that if there is an increase in the demand for goods the impact on the demand for labor is spread out over a few periods. In the short run, the demand for labor adjusts slowly in response to any external shock. Given that there are costs of adjustment, the firm would find it easier to either adjust the hours of work of existing workers or hire casual part-time workers. It is cheaper, however, to hire and fire casual part-time workers. European countries that have a more regulated labor market, with larger hiring and firing costs, have been found to have a slower adjustment process to shocks. However, the evidence on this is very controversial and needs further research (see Blanchard 2006).

There has been a large amount of econometric work to estimate the impact of a change in real wage rates (corrected for inflation) on labor demand holding the level of production constant using large datasets. Most of these studies have found that elasticity (the percentage change in labor demand in response to a 1 percent change in the real wage rate) lies between –0.15 and –0.75, with "a best guess" of –0.30. However, studies of the impact of minimum wages on employment suggest that there is no significant impact (see Card and Krueger 1995). David Neumark and William Wascher have found otherwise, however, perhaps because it is mainly unskilled labor, while usual studies of labor demand are for skilled and unskilled labor taken as a whole. The scale elasticity (i.e., the impact of increased output) is almost unity: a 1 percent increase in the level of production (output) leads to a 1 percent increase in labor demand.

Firms demand labor services from employees who provide honest, committed, and productive work at wage rates that the employer determines (either unilaterally or as a bargain between the employer and employee). Ideally, employers would like to employ workers who take a positive long-term interest in their work and make useful suggestions to improve the production process. In general, firms have flexibility in the wage (and other conditions of work, including perquisites) they offer to their employees. There are also theories of deferred payment, tournaments to provide a stimulus to get wage increases, and "efficiency wages." It has been shown that employers can get higher productivity from their workers, and hence make higher profits, if they pay a higher real wage. This idea was first put forward in a classic paper by Harvey Leibenstein (1957), who argued that in a developing country, paying higher wages led to workers getting better nutrition and providing better productivity.

This essential link between wages and productivity, or "efficiency wages," was extended in a series of papers: In 1984, Carl Shapiro and Joseph Stiglitz put forward the view that higher wages decreased shirking by employees; Steven Salop argued in 1979 that higher wages lowered worker turnover, increased productivity, and increased profits; and Andrew Weiss (in 1980) and George Akerlof (in 1982) both showed that if employers paid higher wages as a partial gift, workers would reciprocate by providing greater effort. Thus, there is no unique negative relationship between the real wage and employment, because an employer who pays a wage in excess of the "market wage" gets greater productivity. Lowering the wage does not increase employment.

Experimental economics, particularly the work of Ernst Fehr and Simon Gächter, has shown the importance of considerations of "reciprocity" (e.g., fairness, equity, and other issues) in the employment relationship.

In a globalized world, the demand for labor becomes more confused as various activities are "outsourced." In other words, the firm can produce a larger quantity of output by either hiring more labor, buying more capital goods, improving its technology, or simply by outsourcing a particular activity. Call centers in less developed countries are good examples of this. Hence, the link between the output of a firm and its demand for labor is no longer constrained by a given production function.

There has been a large amount of econometric analyses of the demand for labor, suggesting, in general, a negative link between wages and employment. There are important policy implications that can flow from the research about minimum wages, but the results are contradictory and controversial (see Card and Krueger 1995; Neumark and Wascher 1992). Similarly, the efficiency wage literature also throws some doubt on a simple negative relation between wages and employment. The literature on hiring and firing costs has been used to suggest that a deregulated labor market would lead to higher employment, but this is still being debated.

Bibliography

Akerlof, George A. 1982. Labor Contracts as Partial Gift Exchange. *Quarterly Journal of Economics* 97 (4): 543–569.

Akerlof, George A., and Janet L. Yellen, eds. 1986. *Efficiency Wage Models of the Labor Market.* Cambridge, U.K.: Cambridge University Press.

Blanchard, Olivier. 2006. European Unemployment: The Evolution of Facts and Ideas. *Economic Policy* 21 (45): 5–59.

Card, David, and Alan B. Krueger. 1995. *Myth and Measurement: The New Economics of the Minimum Wage.* Princeton, NJ: Princeton University Press.

Fehr, Ernst, and Simon Gächter. 2000. Fairness and Retaliation: The Economics of Reciprocity. *Journal of Economic Perspectives* 14 (3): 159–181.

Griliches, Zvi 1969. Capital-Skill Complementarity. *Review of Economics and Statistics* 51 (4): 465–468.

Hamermesh, Daniel S. 1993. *Labor Demand.* Princeton, NJ: Princeton University Press.

Junankar, P. N. 1982. *Marx's Economics.* Oxford: Philip Allan.

Lazear, Edward P. 1995. *Personnel Economics.* Cambridge, MA: MIT Press.

Leibenstein, Harvey. 1957. The Theory of Underemployment in Backward Economies. *Journal of Political Economy* 65 (2): 91–103.

Marshall, Alfred. 1930. *Principles of Economics.* 8th ed. London: Macmillan.

Marx, Karl 1867. *Capital.* Vol. 1. London: Lawrence and Wishart, 1977.

Neumark, David, and William Wascher. 1992. Employment Effects of Minimum and Subminimum Wages. *Industrial and Labor Relations Review* 46 (1): 55–81.

Nickell, Stephen. 1986. Dynamic Models of Labor Demand. In *Handbook of Labor Economics,* Vol.1, ed. Orley C. Ashenfelter, and Richard Layard. Amsterdam: North Holland.

Oi, Walter J. 1962. Labor as a Quasi-Fixed Factor. *Journal of Political Economy* 70 (6): 538–555.

Salop, Steven. 1979. A Model of the Natural Rate of Unemployment. *American Economic Review* 69 (1): 117–125.

Shapiro, Carl, and Joseph Stiglitz. 1984. Equilibrium Unemployment as a Worker Discipline Device. *American Economic Review* 74 (3): 433–444.

Solow, Robert. 1990. *The Labor Market as a Social Institution.* Oxford, U.K.: Blackwell.

Weiss, Andrew. 1980. Job Queues and Layoffs in Labor Markets with Flexible Wages. *Journal of Political Economy* 88 (3): 526–538.

2.3 Labor Supply

P. N. Junankar

For economists, "labor supply" usually means the hours of work, usually per week, offered for pay or profit. This definition therefore excludes unpaid household work and voluntary work. Usually, the question of labor-force participation (the question of whether a person is working or looking for work) is treated separately. Research on both the theoretical and applied labor supply exploded in the 1980s and 1990s, with the work ranging from models of individual behavior in a static one-period model to dynamic multi-period models for a household. Simple theoretical models that gave a backward-bending supply curve (where labor supply first increased and then decreased with wage rates, for which little evidence exists) have given way to empirical labor-supply curves that are usually (but not always) positively sloped with respect to the wage rate. Beginning in the late twentieth century, much of the focus of research has been on labor supply as a whole, not on particular firms, industries, or occupations.

The concept of "labor supply" is defined for economies with a well-developed labor market; that is, a market where wage labor is employed. The concept of labor supply in less developed countries (LDCs) is less clearly defined, because culture, history, and institutions affect labor supply. In some LDCs, women are not involved in the formal labor market, and the labor activities that women perform may be limited by tradition, either for religious or cultural reasons. Because precapitalist conditions exist in LDCs, labor in these nations is often tied to a particular feudal lord, and the worker does not have the freedom to move from one employer to another, or from one location to another.

In LDCs, as the economy develops, labor moves from the agricultural sector to the industrial sector. W. Arthur Lewis, in his seminal 1954 paper

---

Reprinted from 'Labor Supply' by P. N. Junankar in *International Encyclopedia of the Social Sciences*, 2nd edition. 9 vols, edited by William A. Darity Jr. Detroit: Macmillan Reference USA, 2008. With kind permission from Macmillan Publishers Ltd.

"Economic Development with Unlimited Supplies of Labour," put forward a dual-economy model in which the surplus agricultural labor (defined as labor with a zero marginal product) moved to the industrial (modern) sector, providing a nearly infinite supply of labor at a constant wage. This provided a boost to economic development because the industrial sector could expand with a "surplus" (i.e., a profit) being created with cheap labor. The rapid growth of the Chinese economy in the first decade of the twenty-first century provides an example of how surplus labor from agriculture can provide a boost to economic growth.

In general, there are important differences in labor supply for males and females. Biology, history, and society have led to women spending more time in housework, child rearing, and various other domestic duties. For various reasons, including discrimination, society appears to have accepted a gender segregation of roles in the labor market. For example, women work in the textile industry while men work in mining, and women work as primary school teachers while men work as lawyers. Fortunately, many of these stereotypes are breaking down slowly, at least in most Western countries.

The labor supply in a particular economy can increase through population growth (natural increase), immigration, an increase in people employed or looking for work, and through workers offering longer hours of work in each period. Although the labor supply of different educational or skill levels is considered in many models, the issue of the efficiency of labor services (i.e., how hard and diligently a person works) is usually ignored.

In most models of labor supply, the determination of the hours of work is derived from an assumption of utility-maximizing individuals who face given wage rates and prices and a time constraint. In all these models, it is assumed that there is a disutility from work—that is, it is assumed that people do not like working. There is a good deal of evidence, however, from psychologists, sociologists, and industrial relations experts that work provides an individual with a set of contacts, imposes a time structure on the waking day, provides social status and identity, and enforces activity (see Jahoda 1982). Further, an unemployed person often suffers from a level of despair that may lead to mental illness.

Standard neoclassical models are set up to analyze competitive capitalist economies with a well-developed wage-labor market. The utility function, which is unchanging over the life cycle, depends on leisure and consumption goods. An increase in the wage rate leads to a substitution effect (leisure becomes expensive) and an income effect (a person can purchase more leisure and goods). If leisure is a normal good, then these two effects work in opposite directions. The net effect of a wage rate change is therefore ambiguous. The introduction of income taxes and social security payments make the analysis more complex, since the budget constraint becomes nonlinear.

In a novel extension to the concept of labor supply, George Becker argued in a 1965 paper that individuals choose "commodities" that are produced by combining consumer goods with the individual's time. Hence, a consumer good that is purchased, such as meat, also needs time (e.g., cooking time, washing-up time) to form the "commodity" called dinner. The time used in cooking thus has an "opportunity cost." Alternatively, the "dinner" can be purchased in a restaurant with less time spent in obtaining it. The choice of cooking at home or eating out depends on the opportunity costs of time. For a professional person, the opportunity costs of cooking a meal are generally too high. This approach is especially useful in analyzing nonmarket work done (mainly) by women.

In an early model, labor supply was dependent on current wages and (expected) future wages, such that people would offer to work less in the current period if future wages were expected to be higher. Robert Lucas and Leonard Rapping deal with the intertemporal substitution of labor in "Real Wages, Employment, and Inflation" (1969). In advanced models, labor supply is dependent on the planned time path of consumption goods and leisure, along with a choice of saving and wealth accumulation over an entire lifetime. A critical assumption in these dynamic models is of a utility function that is not affected by habits or learning (intertemporal separability over time), as this could make the wage rates depend on individual's behavior (see Card 1994). There are significant differences in the labor supply of males and females due to cultural and institutional factors. Typically, the female labor supply is significantly affected by the number of preschool children in the family.

Expanded models of labor supply allow for joint household decision making, with bargaining between husband and wife (see Vermeulen 2002). The aggregate supply of hours depends on the number of people who are willing to work (given wage offers and their reservation wage) and the hours offered per person. Individuals are assumed to work out a "reservation wage," meaning a wage below which they are not willing to work because the opportunity cost of leisure is too high. This reservation wage is obviously influenced by an individual's age, education, experience, family commitments, social security benefits, and wealth status. Changes in the minimum wage are likely to lead to a change in the distribution of reservation wages, because the idea of "fair wages" will also change (see Falk, Fehr, and Zehnder 2005). Changes in reservation wages can also affect the aggregate supply of labor.

It is generally assumed that the individual can work as many hours at a given wage as she or he desires (either within a firm, choosing different offers from different firms, or with multiple jobs). It is also usually assumed that there are no institutional constraints (e.g., a specified work week for a full-time person), and that the nonavailability of work (i.e., involuntary unemployment) is not a factor. Most estimates of labor supply are based on people who are working. This creates a selection bias, because it excludes those who want to work but cannot find work or have refused the wage offered to them. However, an individual can influence his or her wage through an appropriate investment in human capital, such as acquiring new skills or additional education. In some labor markets (especially for highly skilled labor) an individual may be able to bargain for a package of wages, hours, and other perquisites.

Some empirical regularities have been seen in OECD (Organisation for Economic Co-operation and Development) countries in the post-war period. These include an increase in the number of women working, a decrease in the number of older males working, a fall in the average number of hours worked, and educated people working longer hours. Most of the research on this subject has focused on an econometric estimation of labor supply for males, females, and households. Econometric estimation has moved progressively from time-series data to cross-section data to panel data. Most estimates of labor supply find a small positive link between wages and hours worked—known as "elasticity," the percentage increase in labor supply as a result of a one percent change in the wage rate—although there is a large element of "unexplained" variance. A major interest has been the extent to which welfare benefits and changes in tax rates affect the labor supply. Policy changes in these and other areas could affect people's decision whether or not to seek work. Again, because most labor-supply models are based on data on working people, the possibility of selection bias must be considered.

Labor supply is also important from a policy perspective. How people respond to changes in tax rates, social security payments, and other institutional features like minimum wages are all relevant. Much of the evidence is based on simple models of single-person (or "unitary") households, and is thus subject to debate. The evidence on many of these issues is very controversial, especially the impact of minimum wage on employment. And as Richard Blundell and Thomas Macurdy point out, there is little evidence to support the view that welfare programs have a disincentive effect on the labor supply.

Even though there have been significant advances in the theoretical modeling of labor supply, and in econometric estimation techniques, there are still large gaps in our understanding of the impact of policy changes on labor supply. Models need to be extended to households in which people decide simultaneously whether to work and how many hours to work over a longer period, including their saving behavior, and with some allowance made for the existence of demand-constrained choices. The existence of persistent unemployment in most OECD economies suggests that a basic underlying assumption of labor supply models is unrealistic, namely that workers can choose whether to work and how many hours to work.

Bibliography

Becker, George. 1965. A Theory of the Allocation of Time. *Economic Journal* 75 (299): 493–517.

Blau, Francine D., and Marianne A. Ferber. 1992. *The Economics of Women, Men, and Work*. 2nd ed. Englewood Cliffs, NJ: Prentice-Hall.

Blundell, Richard, and Thomas Macurdy. 1999. Labor Supply: A Review of Alternative Approaches. In *Handbook of Labor Economics*, Vol. 3A, eds. Orley C. Ashenfelter and David Card. Amsterdam: North Holland.

Card, David. 1994. Intertemporal Labor Supply: An Assessment. In *Advances in Econometrics*, ed. Christopher Sims. Cambridge, U.K.: Cambridge University Press.

Card, David, and Alan B. Krueger. 1995. *Myth and Measurement: The New Economics of the Minimum Wage*. Princeton, NJ: Princeton University Press.

Chang, Yongsung, and Sun-Bin Kim. 2006. From Individual to Aggregate Labor Supply: A Quantitative Analysis Based on a Heterogeneous Agent Macroeconomy. *International Economic Review* 47 (1): 1–27.

Falk, Armin, Ernst Fehr, and Christian Zehnder. 2005. The Behavioral Effects of Minimum Wages. IZA Discussion Paper No. 1625. Bonn, Germany: Institute for the Study of Labor.

Jahoda, Marie. 1982. *Employment and Unemployment: A Social-Psychological Analysis*. Cambridge, U.K.: Cambridge University Press.

Killingsworth, Mark R. 1983. *Labor Supply*. Cambridge, UK: Cambridge University Press.

Killingsworth, Mark R., and James J. Heckman. 1986. Female Labor Supply: A Survey. In *Handbook of Labor Economics*, Vol. 1, eds. Orley C. Ashenfelter and Richard Layard. Amsterdam: North Holland.

Lazear, Edward P. 1995. *Personnel Economics*. Cambridge, MA: MIT Press.

Lewis, W. Arthur 1954. Economic Development with Unlimited Supplies of Labour. *Manchester School of Economic and Social Studies* 22: 139–192.

Lucas, Robert E., Jr., and Leonard A. Rapping. 1969. Real Wages, Employment, and Inflation. *Journal of Political Economy* 77 (5): 721–754.

Mortensen, Dale T., and Christopher A. Pissarides. 1999. New Developments in Models of Search in the Labor Market. In *Handbook of Labor Economics*, Vol. 3, eds. Orley C. Ashenfelter and David Card. Amsterdam: North Holland.

Neumark, David, and William Wascher. 1992. Employment Effects of Minimum and Subminimum Wages. *Industrial and Labor Relations Review* 46 (1): 55–81.

Pencavel, John 1986. Labor Supply of Men. In *Handbook of Labor Economics*, Vol. 1, eds. Orley C. Ashenfelter and Richard Layard. 1986. Amsterdam: North Holland.

Senesky, Sarah. 2005. Testing the Intertemporal Labor Supply Model: Are Jobs Important? *Labour Economics* 12 (6): 749–772.

Vermeulen, Frederic. 2002. Collective Household Models: Principles and Main Results. *Journal of Economic Surveys*. 16 (4): 533–564.

2.4
Labor Force Participation

P. N. Junankar

The labor force participation rate is defined as the proportion of a population that is either employed for pay or profit (for one hour or more in the reference week or fortnight) or looking for paid work over some period of time. By definition, people who are carrying out unpaid work in the home or voluntary work are not counted as employed.

The concepts of employment and unemployment are more easily defined for a developed capitalist economy that has a market for wage labor. In less developed countries (LDCs), where wage labor is not a predominant form of employment, the concept of unemployment becomes "fuzzy": The line between employment in the informal sector (e.g., selling cigarettes on street corners) and unemployment is not clearly defined (see Turnham 1993). Similarly, the concept of "looking for work" becomes vague when social security benefits are not available and when labor markets are not developed. Often, when the unemployed are unable to find work for any length of time they give up looking for work and hence are not in the labor force (they are the so-called "discouraged workers"). In societies that provide welfare benefits to people with disabilities, people often move between the unemployed and disabled categories, and hence the participation rate as measured is unclear. Because the concept of unemployment is problematic in some countries, economists often compare employment-population ratios instead of participation rates.

Social customs, culture, and institutions (including the legal framework) play a large part in the participation of women and younger people in the labor market. In LDCs where there is no compulsory schooling, children are part of the labor force. In certain cultures where religion plays an important role, females do not engage in paid work and hence are not part of the labor force.

Reprinted from 'Labor Force Participation' by P. N. Junankar in *International Encyclopedia of the Social Sciences*, 2nd edition. 9 vols, edited by William A. Darity Jr. Detroit: Macmillan Reference USA, 2008. With kind permission from Macmillan Publishers Ltd.

It is common to distinguish between the participation rate of males and females, and more detailed studies look at differences in the participation rates of several subgroups, such as married females and single females, whites and blacks, young and old, migrants and natives. In general, female labor force participation rates have been rising and male participation rates have been falling in most countries of the Organization for Economic Cooperation and Development (OECD), except for Japan, where male participation rates have risen. Male participation rates for older workers have been rising since the mid-1990s, possibly because of better employment conditions and better superannuation provisions for retirement after sixty-five years of age, or due to (in the United States) provision of health care for employed workers. Note, however, that the participation rate of both males and females has fallen in the United States since 2000, and whether this is a trend fall or a cyclical fall is a contentious issue (see Aaronson et al. 2006 and Juhn and Potter 2006). Participation rates tend to first rise with age and then fall as people get older. Participation rates of more educated people are usually higher than those of less educated people.

During World War II many women from the combatant countries worked in the war industries, and after the end of the war continued in the labor force. The increase in female participation rate is sometimes explained by the change in the structure of the economy from a dominant manufacturing sector to a dominant services sector that demands (allegedly) "feminine" skills such as computer keyboard skills. The increased level of education of females has also led to increased female participation, especially in white-collar jobs, often in part-time employment. The changing social mores that came with the women's liberation movement and the increased access to and ease of contraception via the Pill, which provided greater control over and timing of childbearing, lowered fertility rates and increased female participation rates. Increased real wages of women, as well as the introduction of equal pay legislation in many OECD countries, increased female participation rates. The development of household appliances (e.g., washing machines, microwave ovens, and so on) that lower time spent in household work for females have also had a positive impact on female participation rates (see Blau and Ferber 1992).

Male participation rates have declined with a fall in employment in the manufacturing sector, especially for older males who were made redundant and were unable to find work in the newer industries. However, in most OECD countries expanding economies (and perhaps the tightening of access to welfare benefits) appear to have increased participation rates for all males (including older males) since about 2000.

It is important to note that the labor force participation rate depends on both demand and supply factors: For example, a higher proportion of women are working if the demand for the skills that women offer is high. Generally, participation rates are procyclical: They rise during booms and fall in recessions. If for some reason employers discriminate against women in one country, their participation rate is lower than in a society where such discrimination does not exist. Similarly, women's participation rate is higher when they place a lower value on their time spent at home, and so are willing to supply more labor.

Economic analysis of labor force participation begins with neoclassical models of utility maximization subject to a budget constraint: Individuals are assumed to be maximizing their individual welfare (dependent on consumption and leisure or nonmarket time) subject to a given wage rate and some nonlabor income (either from social security or from family sources). (Usually the models are based on individual maximization, rather than family decision-making.) This typically provides an individual with a "reservation wage" that depends on the value of leisure (or nonmarket time). A "reservation wage" is defined as that wage below which the individual prefers not to work. Individuals have different reservation wages depending on their preferences for leisure, their access to nonlabor incomes, and their educational background. Female labor force participation is more difficult to analyze due to their roles as household managers, childbearers and caretakers, and paid market work. Even though social mores have changed over the past few decades, women continue to do the same amount of unpaid household work.

Models that allow for family decision-making (where the husband and wife choose whether to work or not, and decide who produces "household goods," e.g., child care at home, meals at home, etc.) are more complex and difficult to estimate econometrically. Some models treat these as "bargaining models" in a game theoretic context. In general, the probability of a wife working is positively related to her husband working (Pencavel 1998). This may, of course, also be explained in terms of "assortative mating,"—that is, highly educated and well paid males tend to marry highly educated and well paid females.

In a life-cycle context, males invest in education in their youth, then work and acquire pension or superannuation benefits, and retire in older age. Females invest in education (more so since World War II), work for some time, have children and leave the labor force, return to the labor force when the children are of school-leaving age, and then work until retirement. This stylized life-cycle behavior is easily explained by simple models of utility maximization. Participation rates of young people decreased with the increased participation in education in the postwar period. Retirement decisions were based on availability of pension or social security funds, accumulation of wealth over the life cycle, and health and family considerations.

There is an important interaction between the tax and welfare systems and participation rates, which makes the budget constraint nonlinear and sometimes nonconvex: Simple models of maximization of utility become complex and difficult to estimate. It is often argued that welfare benefits tend to lower participation rates, especially of women, as their nonlabor income is higher and hence their valuation of nonmarket time is higher. Child care support for families generally increases participation rates for married females.

To summarize, the research on labor force participation has expanded dramatically over the last decade, especially studies of the impact of tax and welfare policy changes. There is little hard evidence to support the popular view that welfare and social security provide disincentives to work. Most of the empirical evidence is based on simple static (one-period) individualistic models that do not allow for family decision-making. Work on household decision-making is still in its early stages, and further research is needed that allows for life-cycle decisions that include household saving jointly with labor-supply decisions and family formation and dissolution. Most empirical studies of labor-force participation find that noneconomic considerations play an important role in explaining behavior.

Bibliography

Aaronson, Stephanie, Bruce Fallick, Andrew Figura, et al. 2006. The Recent Decline in the Labor Force Participation Rate and Its Implications for Potential Labor Supply. *Brookings Papers on Economic Activity* 1: 69–134.

Blau, Francine, and Marianne A. Ferber. 1992. *The Economics of Women, Men, and Work*. 2nd ed. Englewood Cliffs, NJ: Prentice Hall.

Blundell, Richard, and Thomas Macurdy. 1999. Labor Supply: A Review of Alternative Approaches. In *Handbook of Labor Economics*, vol. 3A, ed. Orley C. Ashenfelter and David Card, 1559–1695. Amsterdam: North-Holland.

Card, David. 1994. Intertemporal Labor Supply: An Assessment. In *Advances in Econometrics*, ed. Christopher Sims, 49–78. Cambridge, U.K.: Cambridge University Press.

Hotchkiss, Julie L. 2006. Changes in Behavioral and Characteristic Determination of Female Labor Force Participation, 1975–2005. *Economic Review* 91 (2): 1–20.

Juhn, Chinhui, and Simon Potter. 2006. Changes in Labor Force Participation in the United States. *Journal of Economic Perspectives* 20 (3): 27–46.

Killingsworth, Mark R. 1983. *Labor Supply*. Cambridge, U.K.: Cambridge University Press.

Killingsworth, Mark R., and James J. Heckman. 1986. Female Labor Supply: A Survey. In *Handbook of Labor Economics*, vol. 1, ed. Orley C. Ashenfelter and Richard Layard, 105–204. Amsterdam: North-Holland.

Pencavel, John. 1986. Labor Supply of Men. In *Handbook of Labor Economics*, vol. 1, ed. Orley C. Ashenfelter and Richard Layard, 3–102. Amsterdam: North-Holland.

Pencavel, John. 1998. The Market Work Behavior and Wages of Women. *Journal of Human Resources* 33: 771–804.

Senesky, Sarah. 2005. Testing the Intertemporal Labor Supply Model: Are Jobs Important? *Labour Economics* 12: 749–772.

Turnham, David. 1993. *Employment and Development: A New Review of Evidence*. Paris: Organization for Economic Cooperation and Development.

2.5
Employment and Unemployment

P. N. Junankar

The concepts of employment and unemployment are most easily defined for a developed capitalist economy that has a market for wage labour. Employment is defined as working for at least one hour a week for some payment, either for a wage or for profit, or commission, or without pay in a family business. However, this definition usually excludes people (mainly women) who provide unpaid household services. Unemployment is defined in terms of not being employed while being available and looking for work. In less developed countries, where wage labour is not a predominant form of employment, the concept of unemployment becomes 'fuzzy': the line between employment in the informal sector (selling cigarettes on the street corners) and unemployment is not clearly defined (Turnham 1993). In most economies people may not 'look for work' when there are no obvious vacancies available and drop out of the labour force (i.e. the participation rate varies). Since the concept of unemployment may not be well defined labour economists sometimes use the concept of employment–population ratios (or the not-employed to population ratio).

In OECD countries, the postwar decades have seen a growth of the service sector and a relative decline of the industrial and agricultural sectors. At the same time, there has been a growth in part-time female employment and a decline in full-time male employment. Further, there has been an increase in white-collar employment and a decline in blue-collar employment. Wage inequality has also increased. After a short period of full employment in the 1950s and 1960s, most of the OECD economies have faced increasing unemployment and long-term unemployment (the latter defined, at present, as continuous durations of unemployment of 12 months or more). This has led to economists (e.g. Matthews 1968) asking whether this period was unusual

---

Reprinted from 'Employment and Unemployment' by P. N. Junankar in *The Social Science Encyclopedia*, 3rd edition, edited by Adam Kuper and Jessica Kuper, London: Routledge, pp. 294–297, 2004. With kind permission from Routledge.

and whether the norm for developed capitalist economies is of periods of high unemployment. The only OECD countries that appear to have avoided the problems of high unemployment have been Japan, and to a lesser extent the USA. However, the USA appears to have lowered its unemployment rate at the expense of increasing the 'working poor' and creating an underclass, and by a growth of informal sector activities like hustling on the streets.

In conventional economics, employment is determined by demand for labour and supply of labour. Demand for labour is determined in the same way as the demand for non-human inputs (e.g. raw materials, or capital): by firms maximizing profits. Labour supply is determined by individuals maximizing utility and making a choice between leisure and work (where work is considered to be a necessary evil). In this paradigm wages clear the labour market and unemployment is purely voluntary. In Keynesian and post-Keynesian theories wages do not adjust instantaneously to clear the labour market and involuntary unemployment eventuates. Employment is determined by labour demand: the excess of labour supply at the market wages is called unemployment.

Full employment is defined as a state where the demand for labour equals the supply, at existing wage rates. More recently, the concept of the NAIRU has been proposed: this is the non-accelerating inflation rate of unemployment (Johnson and Layard 1986). This level of unemployment, sometimes called the 'natural' rate of unemployment, is often thought of as the full employment level. Many economists argue that the labour market operates in such a way as to make the present level of unemployment depend on the previous history of the time path of unemployment: the idea of *hysteresis* in the labour market that leads to unemployment rates increasing with time in a 'ratchet' fashion. The reasons for hysteresis are thought to be the lower probability of the long-term unemployed finding work because of decreased search by them due to a loss of self esteem; because of skill atrophy; and because employers use unemployment as a signal of poor qualities. In addition, in the macroeconomic sphere the long-term unemployed have no impact on wage bargaining and the NAIRU increases. In contrast to this view, new classical economists argue that employment and unemployment follow a random path; exogenous shocks simply perturb the 'natural' rate. For the few countries for which we have data spanning a long period (say over 50 years) there is no obvious trend in the unemployment rate (see Layard et al. 1991).

Unemployment is usually separated into the following components: seasonal, frictional (due to temporary mismatch between workers and vacancies), cyclical (due to aggregate demand changes) and structural (due to long-term changes in the economic structure, including technological change). Sometimes hidden unemployment (people who leave the labour force in times of recession) is distinguished from open unemployment. Underemployment is the situation where workers who are placed on short-time working, or who can only find part-time work, would prefer full-time work.

The major explanations of unemployment (and fluctuations in unemployment) are as follows: aggregate demand, technological and structural change, wage rigidity, information problems, and aggregate supply (see Junankar 2000). Some economists have postulated that unemployment in OECD countries has been caused by the growth of low-wage Newly Industrialized Countries (Korea, Singapore, Thailand, etc.), which are taking away markets from the richer high-wage economies (see Krugman and Lawrence 1994; and Economist 1994).

Keynesians explain unemployment in terms of a shortfall in the aggregate demand for goods and services, together with a labour market where wages do not adjust instantaneously. Marx and Schumpeter argued that technological and structural change were inherent in a capitalist economy, and due to the volatility of investment, unemployment would also be cyclical. In an interesting development of such ideas, Davis et al. (1996) discussed job creation and job destruction that took place simultaneously due to changing technology, demand, etc. Marx also argued that the industrial reserve army (unemployment) would act as a brake on wage growth as well as controlling the 'pretensions of the workers'. Neoclassical economists explain unemployment in terms of misinformation in the labour market that leads some unemployed people not to accept wage offers in the (sometimes mistaken) belief that a better wage offer is just around the corner. This is made possible by the availability of unemployment benefits. In some versions this is simply an optimizing strategy where the unemployed are carrying out an intertemporal substitution of leisure. In some recent versions, firms are supposed to create jobs and put up vacancies, and unemployed workers are searching in a market with imperfect information. 'Matching functions' are set up that are productive matches between unemployed workers searching for jobs and firms posting vacancies looking for appropriate employees (Petrongolo and Pissarides 2001). In other versions, unemployment is due to random supply shocks. However, it is not explained why these 'random' shocks hit a number of countries simultaneously.

Most theories of unemployment focus on reasons for wages not adjusting downwards in textbook fashion in the face of excess supply (unemployment). Neo-classical theories tend to emphasize the 'rigidities' introduced by unions, unemployment benefits and minimum wage legislation. An alternative explanation, the 'insider–outsider' hypothesis, has wage bargaining conducted between employers and unions such that they only concern themselves with the employed labour force (the insiders), while the unemployed (the outsiders) are ignored (Lindbeck 1993).

In the 1980s and 1990s, theories of employment and unemployment focused on emphasizing the distinctive properties of the labour market and the role of wages in providing incentives to offer more or higher-quality (more productive) labour services (Solow 1990). It was argued that higher than market clearing wages are set by employers either to get a more skilled labour force (adverse selection models), or to provide the workers with an incentive to be more productive. These efficiency wage models suggest that where wages are set higher than necessary, workers who do not perform adequately would be fired (the 'shirking' model). The threat of unemployment, or of having to find a poorly paid job, gives workers an incentive to be productive. In another version, higher wages decrease turnover. Consequently, employers have a more stable (and so more productive) work-force (see Akerlof and Yellen 1986). Akerlof has also suggested that social custom plays a part, and that a partial gift-exchange takes place: workers get paid a wage higher than necessary and workers provide more (better) labour services than they are required to.

In some recent work, using experimental economics methods, various authors have discussed the role of 'fairness' and 'reciprocity' in much of human behaviour that influences decisions on effort, wages, etc. Many economists have argued that the labour market is distinctive, since social considerations influence the way that a labour market operates (Akerlof and Yellen 1986; Fehr and Gachter 2000; Junankar 2000; Solow 1990). Much of this recent work throws doubt on the self-regulating features of a labour market: employers do not cut wages in times of unemployment, wages are set above market clearing rates to get higher productivity, workers are willing to accept lower wages but employers do not hire these workers, etc. (Agell 1999).

Unemployment imposes severe costs on the economy in terms of lost GDP (both now and in the future), costs to the government in terms of lost revenues, loss of earnings for the unemployed individuals and families, and a loss in terms of physical and mental illness, social disruption and crime in society (Junankar 1986).

Many OECD governments have given up their commitment to full employment, either on the basis that they believe that the free market would eventually solve the problem, or that the danger of inflationary forces is too great to introduce explicit policies for full employment. Recent pronouncements tended to stress the advantages, or supposed necessity, of more flexible labour markets (i.e. increased downwards flexibility of wages, fewer constraints on employers in hiring and firing practices, weakening of the powers of the unions, etc.). The major policy interventions have been in introducing labour market training programmes, the use of private-sector agencies to provide labour market assistance, improving the efficiency of labour market exchanges, and deregulation of the labour markets.

References

J. Agell (1999) 'On the benefits from rigid labour markets: Norms, market failures, and social insurance', *Economic Journal* 109 (453): F143–64.

G.A. Akerlof and J.L. Yellen (eds) (1986) *Efficiency Wage Models of the Labor Market*, Cambridge, UK.
S.J. Davis, J.C. Haltiwanger and S. Schuh (1996) *Job Creation and Job Destruction*, Cambridge, MA.
Economist (1994) 'The global economy: A survey', 1 October, 233 (7,883): Survey 1–42.
E. Fehr and S. Gachter (2000) 'Fairness and retaliation: The economics of reciprocity', *Journal of Economic Perspectives* 14 (3): 159–81.
G.E. Johnson and P.G. Layard (1986) 'The natural rate of unemployment: Explanations and policy', in O. Ashenfelter and R. Layard (eds) *Handbook of Labor Economics*, Amsterdam.
P.N. Junankar (1986) *Costs of Unemployment: Main Report*, Luxembourg.
P.N. Junankar (ed.) (2000) *Economics of Unemployment: Causes, Consequences and Policies*, 4 vols, Cheltenham.
P.R. Krugman and R.Z. Lawrence (1994)' Trade, jobs and wages', *Scientific American* 270 (4): 22–7.
R. Layard, S. Nickell and R. Jackman (1991) *Unemployment: Macroeconomic Performance and the Labour Market*, Oxford.
A. Lindbeck (1993) *Unemployment and Macroeconomics*, London.
R.O. Matthews (1968) 'Why has Britain had full employment since the war?' *Economic Journal* 78: 555–69.
B. Petrongolo and C.A. Pissarides (2001) 'Looking into the black box: A survey of the matching function', *Journal of Economic Literature* 39 (2): 390–431.
R. Solow (1990) *The Labour Market as a Social Institution*, Oxford.
D. Turnham (1993) *Employment and Development: A Review of the Evidence*, Paris.

2.6

Estimating the Social Rate of Return to Education for Indigenous Australians

P. N. Junankar and J. Liu

The present paper compares estimates of the social rate of return to education for Indigenous Australians with those for non-Indigenous Australians. The social rate of return measures the net benefits to society of educating its citizens. If education is treated as an investment by society in its people, then Australian society will be made better off by an increase in educational investment as long as the social rate of return is higher than that for other public investments. This paper provides a discussion of the concept of the social rate of return to education and some estimates for Indigenous Australians.

Higher levels of education, in general, lead to an increased probability of finding employment and higher levels of income in employment. Hence, an increased level of education for an Indigenous person would be of advantage in economic terms; the private rate of return to education is likely to be quite high. In addition, we argue that increasing education has important social benefits (so-called 'externalities') for Indigenous people, and society in general: improved education would lead to better nutrition, to better living conditions, to better access to health services, and hence to a longer and healthier life. This means that productivity would be higher for Indigenous people and they would have higher incomes over a longer period of time. In addition, we argue that improved levels of education have the capacity to contribute to a decrease in the numbers of Indigenous people who are imprisoned, and thus lead to a direct reduction in the costs of imprisonment. Thus, increased education increases the earnings span, decreases prison costs and hence increases the social rate of return. We find that the social rate of return for education is generally higher for Indigenous Australians than for non-Indigenous Australians. This suggests, from a public policy perspective, that government should allocate increased funding for the education of Indigenous people since this

---

Reprinted from 'Estimating the Social Rate of Return to Education for Indigenous Australians' by P. N. Junankar and J. Liu in *Education Economics*, 11 (2), August 2003, 169–190. With kind permission from Taylor and Francis.

social rate of return is greater than the Department of Finance recommended cut-off rates for government investment projects.

Introduction

The aim of the present paper is to compare estimates of the social rate of return to education for Indigenous Australians with those for non-Indigenous Australians.[1] The social rate of return measures the net benefits to society of educating its citizens. If education is treated as an investment by society in its people, then Australian society should be better off by increasing educational investment as long as the social rate of return is higher than that for other public investments.[2] Although there are numerous studies of the private rate of return to education (i.e., the return accruing to individuals) for several countries and for different time periods, there are very few studies of the social rate of return. The distinctive contribution of this paper is to provide a discussion of the concept of the social rate of return to education and to provide some estimates for Indigenous Australians.

Indigenous Australians suffer severe disadvantages in society. They have, on average, significantly lower incomes, lower employment, lower participation rates, and higher unemployment rates than non-indigenous Australians (see Junankar & Kapuscinski, 1991). They have lower levels of education, and are more likely to have left school before the school leaving age of 15 (see Appendix Table 2.6.A1). Indigenous Australians have poor housing, and significantly worse health outcomes, lower life expectancy and higher mortality rates than non-Indigenous Australians. They are more likely to be arrested and imprisoned than other Australians. In many ways, their position in society is similar to the American Indians (Indigenous Americans) (see Gregory & Daly, 1997).

The present paper extends the private rate of return estimation to consider social costs and benefits.[3] Most people consider that education plays a very important role in society. Education is considered to lead to a more fulfilling life, and the ability to participate in all aspects of a modern society. In the language of John Herron, a former Coalition Minister for Aboriginal and Torres Strait Islander Affairs, improved education for Indigenous people is the key to 'empowering' them (Herron, 1996). Higher levels of education, in general, lead to an increased probability of finding employment and obtaining higher levels of income. Hence, other things being equal, an increased level of education for an Indigenous person would be of advantage to that person, and the private rate of return to education is likely to be quite high. In addition, we argue that increasing one's level of education has important social benefits (so-called 'externalities') for Indigenous people, and society in general: improved education has the capacity to lead to better nutrition, better living conditions, access to health services, and hence a longer and healthier life (increased life expectancy). This means that productivity would be higher for Indigenous people and they would have higher incomes over a longer period of time. This also implies that education leads to increased economic growth (see the endogenous growth literature; for example, Romer, 1994). In addition, we argue that improved levels of education have the capacity to contribute to a decrease in the numbers of Indigenous people who are imprisoned, and thus lead to a direct reduction in the costs of imprisonment. Thus, increased education increases the earnings span, decreases prison costs, and hence increases the social rate of return.

We use data from the 1991 Census of Population and Housing to estimate the likely earnings of a person with differing levels of education and work experience at different ages. We then use these estimates to project into the future the additional earnings he/she would expect to earn if he/she had spent some additional time in education. We then estimate extra social benefits and social costs involved to calculate a rate of return to the investment in education. This is analogous to working out a rate of profit on investing in (say) a new factory. Not surprisingly this is a controversial area, and we highlight the limitations of our analysis in Appendix 2.6.A2.

Investing in People

Although it is common for us to think about spending more time studying so that we may get a better and more highly paid job, Becker (1964) formalized the idea as investment in human capital. He argued that we can consider the decision to spend a longer time in educational institutions as a form of investment that was similar to investing in (say) a factory or a new cafe. In the same way, Becker suggested that if we consider the additional income from staying on for a little longer in school or college and compared it with the costs of education, we could work out the rate of profit (or the rate of return).[4] The costs of education for a person are not only the extra costs of tuition fees, books, and other direct costs of staying on in additional education, but also the forgone income that the person will not be earning while studying. These forgone earnings can be a very significant cost for, say, a 3-year degree, if this rate of return exceeds the market rate of interest he/she invests in his/her education. The precise method for carrying out these calculations is discussed in Appendix 2.6.A1.

Investing in People: A Social Perspective[5]

Human capital theory, with all its qualifications, is sometimes extended to estimate a social rate of return to education. Most studies simply use the pre-tax earnings in these calculations (instead of post-tax earnings as in the private rate of return estimates) and include not only the private costs of education, but also the full costs of education for the government sector (see Psachoropoulos, 1969, 1981; Johnes, 1993). Since the costs of education are in the early part of the lifecycle and are much larger for society than for the individual (since in most countries the government subsidizes education), the social rate of return is usually much lower than the private rate of return.

Information on taxes enables the distinction to be made between the social and private benefits of education. For example, if the before-tax earnings of a university graduate employed in the competitive sector of the economy is W per year, one can reasonably assume that this approximates the value society places on a graduate. However, if the graduate has to pay t% in taxes, then the benefit the individual realises is only $W(1-t)$. The logic of using gross earnings in a social rate of return calculation is that, although taxes are paid out of the individual's pocket, gross earnings reflect the addition to society's production, and hence welfare. Gross earnings are a better reflection of the contribution the individual makes to the productivity of society.

However, since the social rate of return measured using this method is lower than the private rate, it is argued by some that the government should decrease its investment in education. In general, if we are estimating the social rate of return we must allow for all social costs (including the forgone earnings of students) and social benefits, and then compare the social rate of return with the opportunity cost of investing in education. If alternative government projects provide a lower social rate of return, there is an argument to expand education.[6]

The private returns aspect considers the relation between the costs incurred by private individuals in obtaining education and the benefits they, as individuals, derive from this education. The social rate of return includes the impact that one person's education can have on the welfare of others – for example, a reduction in delinquency and an improvement in standards of social responsibility (Johnes, 1993). The increased earnings from education generate not only private benefits, but also social benefits in the form of public goods paid for by these increased earnings, and savings in public welfare costs (McMahon, 1998, 1999). The external benefits of education are those benefits to society that are above and beyond the private benefits realized by the individual decision-maker (i.e., the student and the family). External benefits to others that may be postulated include, for example, the satisfaction of living in a society with functioning democratic institutions and their related freedoms, lower crime rates, more books, more newspapers, and more literature.

If we are to define the social rate of return to education properly, we need to know the addition to society's welfare of an additional unit of education for (say) one person. If we use an individualistic welfare function (society's welfare is simply the sum of individual welfare), then if an individual gets additional income due to more education it would increase social welfare, and hence increase the social rate of return. If, however, this additional income is simply compensated by someone else getting a lower income, then society's welfare would be unchanged unless there is some explicit weighting given to income distribution. Another social welfare function, proposed by Rawls (1971), argues that society's welfare depends on the welfare of the least well-off member of society. Since Indigenous people are by far the worst-off members of society, anything that improves their welfare improves society's welfare in the Rawlsian sense.[7]

In addition to the increased individual income, society may benefit from the additional education by increasing the benefit to other people in society. Thus, it is often argued that a more educated society can introduce new technology more easily. These 'externalities' are difficult to quantify. However, there is a large literature on the macro-economic productivity benefits of education that suggests there are significant externalities (see Denison, 1962; World Bank, 1993; Romer, 1994). Ideally, we should also include in social benefits the 'consumption benefits' of education, which are also difficult to quantify.

There are basically three types of benefits that belong to the social domain. They include:

(i) the additional income stream that the individual obtains from additional education. This should be included as a social benefit as long as education is actually increasing the productivity of the person. This means that if education is simply a signalling device or is used as credentialism, then some of the income stream is not a social benefit. In our estimates later we assume that increased education increases the productivity of the worker, and hence is a social benefit as well. Tax payments associated with the educational benefit (i.e., income taxes paid out of one's lifetime income stream) should be included in social benefit;

(ii) 'external' benefits, which are those benefits that are due to the educational investment but that the individual cannot capture. An example of the external benefits of education is the ability of the government to rely on individual filing of income tax returns, which would be impossible to achieve without general literacy (Cohn & Geske, 1990). Another externality would be the impact of increased education on the health of the community, and hence an increase in life expectancy. An important externality for Indigenous people may be that increased education decreases the probability of being imprisoned, hence decreasing costs for society of the prison system; and

(iii) indirect and intangible benefits to education would include the increases in productivity and incomes of workers other than those who receive education, whether through the diffusion of skills or the reorganization of work procedures; education promotes technical change (and thus, ultimately, productivity and output growth) in various ways, ranging from the undertaking of research and development to the spread of knowledge through literacy; education increases allocative efficiency, by increasing the flexibility and mobility of the labour force, in response to changes in the demand for labour; and education brings about many other gains of a social as well as economic character, including increased social cohesion, stability and democratic values.

The social costs are the real issue involved in education. If we assume market prices reflect equilibrium social opportunity costs,[8] then we should include the additional costs of education, the forgone income of an individual, and any other social costs. In our analysis, we allow education to increase the life expectancy of Indigenous people, hence increasing the social benefits as they have a longer period over which they are earning an income. Another way we attempt to allow for externalities in our analysis is by allowing education to lower the probability of Indigenous people being imprisoned. We argue that, since a significant proportion of Indigenous people are imprisoned (especially younger males), if society increases the education of Indigenous people then there will be fewer people who go to prison (there is a clear negative association between education levels and probability of being imprisoned).[9] If we now estimate the social costs as being lower due to the increased education levels, then we would find that the social rate of return would be higher. We do not make any allowance for the fact that if there is a decrease in the levels of criminal activity due to increased education, there would also be increased benefits to the potential victims of crime, and to society in general. Hence, any estimate we provide for the social rate of return would be a lower bound to the 'true' social rate of return. Table 2.6.1 summarizes some of the potential costs and benefits.[10]

Table 2.6.1 Private and social costs and benefits

Benefits	Costs
Private	Private
While in school	Direct
Part-time after tax earnings	Tuition and incidental schooling costs
While in the labour force	Indirect
After tax earnings	Forgone after tax earnings
Social	**Social**
While in school	Direct
Part-time before tax earnings	Total schooling costs
While in the labour force	Indirect
Before tax earnings for a longer period of time	Forgone earnings before tax
Externalities	**Externalities**
Better democracy	Lower prison costs
Increased technological change	

Source: Adapted from Psacharopoulos (1969).

The Data and Methods

The data used for the present study are derived from the 1991 Census. As there are significant differences between the earnings of native-born Australians and overseas-born Australians, we have focused simply on comparisons of Indigenous people with other native-born Australians. Regression equations have been estimated and used to calculate the internal rate of return to an additional year of schooling and to the completion of a post-schooling qualification for males and females aged 15–64 years in full-time and part-time employment (summary statistics on the variables used and these results are presented in Appendix Table 2.6.A2). The results for other Australians have been derived from the 1% public-use sample of the census, and those for Indigenous Australians from the full Aboriginal sub-file of the 1991 census. The 1% public-use sample of the population census includes a very small number of Indigenous adults, which would not provide sufficient degrees of freedom for econometric estimation of earnings functions. The Australian Bureau of Statistics ran the regression equations on the full sub-file of Indigenous Australians.

The private benefits of education are the additional earnings of the higher level of education compared with the previous level of education, and are based on the predicted earnings for both groups. We have allowed for these earnings to increase over time according to the mean wage growth between the two census dates of 1986 and 1991 for each educational level and age left school. This is in addition to the higher wages according to the cross-sectional data. In effect, we are assuming that individuals, in formulating expectations about future earnings, not only look at the earnings of people now with different levels of education at different ages, but also assume that the increases in earnings over the past (due to increased productivity and growth in the economy) will continue into the future. Obviously, this assumes a certain amount of 'rationality', but no more than involved in carrying out large-scale present-value calculations.

The private costs of investing in education are additional incidental school-related costs incurred by individuals, such as direct costs of tuition fees and books, Higher Education Contribution Scheme (HECS) charges for those at university,[11] and forgone incomes net of income tax. These forgone earnings are a significant cost in the earlier part of the lifecycle, and hence have a large impact on the calculated private rate of returns. In calculating these private rates of return, we also allow for the fact that students from low-income households are eligible for AUSTUDY and ABSTUDY[12] (Daly & Liu Jin, 1997). Since the earnings are estimated from cross-sectional data, we have allowed for increases in wages over time due to general productivity growth in the economy. These growth rates are estimated over 1986–1991 for each educational level and assumed to apply to Indigenous and non-Indigenous Australians.[13] In addition, we have also allowed the probability of employment to be affected by the increased education, hence increasing the expected future incomes because of improved levels of education.

We have treated the social benefits as including the private benefits of additional incomes (but taken as gross earnings, rather than net earnings) assuming that there is no difference between market wages and shadow wages (equilibrium wages from a societal point of view). We argue that increased education not only increases the income stream at each date in the future, but also extends the life of Indigenous people, and hence their working life. This externality of increased working life expectancy could be applied in estimating social rates of return.[14] The average life expectancy for male and female Indigenous persons was assumed to be 44 and 46, years respectively,[15] and for other Australians a working life terminating at 64 years. 'Life expectancy for Aboriginal males was estimated to be 16 to 18 years shorter than for non-Aboriginal males during 1990–92; the gap was slightly wider for Aboriginal females' (Bhatia & Anderson, 1995, p. 12). The differences of rates of return between working a life expectancy of 44 years (female) or 46 years (male) and an increasing working life expectancy to 64 years for Indigenous Australians are only marginal because of the process of discounting lifetime earnings after the peak earning capacity.[16] Since the results did not differ significantly, the results presented in the current paper assume that increased education leaves the working life of indigenous people unchanged.

For the social costs of education, we have allowed for the total resource costs to society. Besides opportunity costs incurred by individuals – namely, income forgone during school attendance – there are additional incidental school-related costs incurred by individuals for private rates of return such as direct costs of tuition fees and books, and HECS charges for those at university. In addition, we include government costs for education per person (at all levels of government) for those in post-compulsory secondary education, which includes school costs incurred by society (i.e., teachers' salaries, supplies, interest and depreciation on capital, and society's costs, which are normally defrayed though taxation). Income support to individuals under AUSTUDY and ABSTUDY are considered as transfer payments rather than as part of social cost to education. The only element that would be relevant would be the real resource costs involved in administering such allowances. As we have inadequate information about these administrative costs (and in any case they are likely to be small), we have ignored them in our estimates.

Another issue that we explicitly assumed as an externality is that education lowers crime and hence decreases the numbers of people imprisoned, which decreases the prison costs for society.[17] Appendix Table 2.6.B1 shows that 3.4% of Indigenous males are in prison compared with 0.18% of other male Australians. Appendix Table 2.6.B2 provides information on the distribution of the percentage of prisoners by age group. This shows that the highest percentage of prisoners for males are at age 20–24 years and for females at 25–29 years, but for both males and females most of them are concentrated in the age range 20–40 years. Appendix Table 2.6.B3 provides information by labour market status, and shows that most prisoners are likely to be unemployed or of unknown labour market status. Appendix Table 2.6.B4 shows that people with lower levels of education are more likely to be arrested. We estimate the social rates of return allowing for this dimension by assuming that Indigenous Australians have the same employment probability and the same percentage of prisoners as other Australians, so that average lifetime earnings are adjusted accordingly. This is obviously a fairly strong assumption and hence the results are likely to bias the rates of return upwards.

To summarize, we estimate the social rates of return by using gross earnings, allowing for total expenditures on education by the individual and by society; and for indigenous people we allow education to extend the working life (which in fact does not make a significant difference to the estimated rates of return), and allow education to decrease the probability of being imprisoned, and hence lower social costs by decreasing the costs of imprisonment. We exclude any financial assistance payments for students on AUSTUDY and ABSTUDY as these are pure transfer payments and not a real resource cost to society.

Results and Interpretation

In this section we provide estimates of the private and social rates of return to additional years of education. The private rate of return is likely to influence the decision of individuals to continue their education if they choose to maximize their lifetime incomes. It is probably true that a significant proportion of Indigenous people do not make this choice, especially if they live a traditional lifestyle in remote regions. However, the social rate of return builds on this private rate of return by including various social costs and benefits discussed earlier. For a government, it is important to know what would be the additional benefit to society of increasing expenditure on additional education for (say) Indigenous people. As discussed earlier, if the social rate of return to additional expenditure on education is large and greater than some alternative public investment, then the government should expand education.

The results and interpretation reported in this section estimate the internal private and social rates of return to education based on predicted income from estimates based on earning functions regressions (using annual earnings; see Appendix Tables 2.6.A3 and 2.6.A4) with appropriate adjustments for additional costs and benefits. Results are reported for both males and females, Indigenous and other Australians.

Table 2.6.2 presents comparisons of the private rate of return to education for Indigenous and other Australian males and females with adjustments

Table 2.6.2 Private rate of return to education with AUSTUDY or ABSTUDY aged 15–64 years, 1991 (assuming proportional income support, adjusting for mean wage growth rates and employment probabilities)

Aboriginality, age and sex	ALS 15/16 (%)	ALS 15/17 (%)	ALS 15/18 (%)	Age 17[1] Cert. (%)	Age 17[2] Dip. (%)	Age 18–20[3] Degree (%)	Age 18–21[4] Degree (%)
Females							
(a) Other, 64 years	18.3	14.7	9.9	3.4	12.6	12.4	13.4
(b) Indigenous, 44 years	11.5	15.7	11.8	14.9	26.4	19.2	20.6
(c) Indigenous same as other*	12.6	15.0	9.7	8.3	22.9	16.7	17.6
Males							
(d) Other, 64 years	23.2	16.9	12.3	13.6	16.7	19.6	19.7
(e) Indigenous, 46 years	10.7	14.4	12.4	27.6	28.5	21.8	23.3
(f) Indigenous same as other*	10.7	12.6	9.8	26.7	25.2	20.9	20.8

Notes:
(a) Other Australian females with working life terminating at 64 years with own employment probability adjustment.
(b) Indigenous females with working life terminating at 44 years with own employment probability adjustment.
(c) Indigenous females same as Other Australian females in terms of employment probabilities.
(d) Other Australian males with working life terminating at 64 years with own employment probability adjustment.
(e) Indigenous males with working life terminating at 46 years with own employment probability adjustment.
(f) Indigenous males same as Other Australian males in terms of employment probabilities.
* Rows (c) and (f) are virtually unchanged if we allow for Indigenous workers to work until 64 years of age like other Australians.
[1] Assuming a certificate (Cert.) involves 2 years of full-time study.
[2] Assuming a diploma (Dip.) involves 2 years of full-time study.
[3] Assuming a degree (Age 18–20/Degree) involves 3 years of full-time study.
[4] Assuming a degree (Age 18–21/Degree) involves 4 years of full-time study. Age 18–21/Degree is under assumption that the income growth rate equals the average growth rate over the period 1986–1991. It is also assumed that we have full employment.

for the proportion of students receiving AUSTUDY or ABSTUDY (also see Appendix Table 2.6.A5). Seventeen per cent paid HECS in advance with 15% discount in 1991, and 83% of students paid HECS after graduation above a certain income level. ABSTUDY or AUSTUDY payment is calculated as an average of the payment for maximum 'living at home', maximum 'living away' and maximum 'independent'.

Table 2.6.3 presents comparisons of the social rate of return to education for Indigenous and other Australian males and females. All these results are adjusted for mean wage growth[18] rates and different employment probabilities and externalities. The mean wage growth rates are for the period 1986–1991 by degree and age left school for males and females respectively (see Appendix Table 2.6.A4). The first half of the tables relates to the rate of return to continuing secondary education, and the second part of these tables relates to post-secondary qualifications. The social cost (i.e., per-capita expenditure in 1991 for education) is highest for higher education ($6797),[19] then $3329 for schooling and $1920 for Technical and Further Education (TAFE) college (Australian Bureau of Statistics, 1991). Table 2.6.4 provides information on the differences between the social rate of return and private rate of return by gender.

The private rate of return in Table 2.6.2 provides calculated rates for other Australians in row (a) assuming that the incomes are expected incomes using the predicted earnings for people with the appropriate levels of education and weighted by the probabilities of employment for each age and education category. It is assumed that other Australians work until they reach the age of 65 years. In each cell, the income component is the (mathematical) expected value of additional earnings for the level of education (compared with the previous level of education). In other words, we take the additional earnings times the probability of employment plus the unemployment benefit times the probability of unemployment. Row (b) provides calculated rates of return for Indigenous people with a life expectancy of 44 years for females[20] and with the employment probabilities of that group. To provide some 'sensitivity' results, we provide information in row (c) that provides similar information, assuming a scenario that Indigenous females have similar employment probabilities to Other Australians. Rows (d), (e), and (f) give similar calculations for males who are assumed to work until the age of 64 years for other Australians and 46 years for indigenous Australians. Sensitivity analyses for private rates of return (such as assuming a student with or without ABSTUDY or AUSTUDY) are attached in Appendix Tables 2.6.C1 and 2.6.C2.

Indigenous people with low levels of education have lower private rates of return to education than non-Indigenous Australians, suggesting that for this group there may be significant difficulties in finding employment, and they may have lower wage rates if they do find employment. This may be due to discrimination. It is interesting to see, however, that Indigenous people with higher levels of education have higher employment probabilities than other Australians. This suggests that, since only a small minority of Indigenous people have higher levels of education, they are in a favourable position in the labour market. If everyone from this group had a higher level of education, we might have to adjust the employment probabilities towards that of non-Indigenous Australians to get a better idea of how the

Table 2.6.3 Social rate of return to education, aged 15–64 years, 1991 (adjusting for mean wage growth rates, employment and crime probabilities)

Aboriginality, age and sex	ALS 15/16 (%)	ALS 15/17 (%)	ALS 15/18 (%)	Age 17[1] Cert. (%)	Age 17[2] Dip. (%)	Age 18–20[3] Degree (%)	Age 18–21[4] Degree (%)
Females							
(a) Other, 64 years	15.5	11.7	7.4	2.3	11.0	8.9	10.9
(b) Indigenous, 44 years*	9.1	9.7	6.7	12.0	19.2	15.3	17.5
(c) Indigenous same as other	11.2	11.2	6.8	6.3	16.3	13.5	15.0
(d) Indigenous with crime cost	9.3	9.8	6.8	12.2	19.3	15.5	17.6
Males							
(e) Other, 64 years	20.4	14.8	10.9	13.4	14.8	18.1	18.9
(f) Indigenous, 46 years*	8.9	9.5	8.2	22.6	21.3	19.0	20.8
(g) Indigenous same as other	9.7	9.6	7.5	22.0	18.9	18.2	18.8
(h) Indigenous with crime cost	9.2	9.7	8.4	22.8	21.6	19.1	21.0

Notes:

(a) Other Australian females with working life terminating at 64 years with own employment probability adjustment.

(b) Indigenous females with working life terminating at 46 years with own employment probability adjustment.

(c) Indigenous females same as Other Australian females in terms of employment probabilities.

(d) Indigenous females same as (b) but with additional adjustment by crime cost.

(e) Other Australian males with working life terminating at 64 years with own employment probability adjustment.

(f) Indigenous males with working life terminating at 46 years with own employment probability adjustment.

(g) Indigenous males same as Other Australian males in terms of employment probabilities.

(h) Indigenous males same as (f) but with additional adjustment by crime cost.

* Rows (b) and (f) are virtually unchanged if we allow for Indigenous workers to work until 64 years of age like other Australians.

[1] Assuming a certificate (Cert.) involves 2 years of full-time study.

[2] Assuming a diploma (Dip.) involves 2 years of full-time study.

[3] Assuming a degree (Age 18–20/Degree) involves 3 years of full-time study.

[4] Assuming a degree (Age 18–21/Degree) involves 4 years of full-time study. Age 18–21/Degree is under assumption that the income growth rate equals the average growth rate over the period 1986–1991. It is also assumed that we have full employment.

Table 2.6.4 Differences between social and private rates of return to education, aged 15–64 years, 1991 (assuming full income support, adjusting for mean wage growth rates, employment and crime probabilities, and proportional student receiving AUSTUDY or ABSTUDY)

Aboriginality, age and sex	ALS 15/16 (%)	ALS 15/17 (%)	ALS 15/18 (%)	Age 17[1] Cert. (%)	Age 17[2] Dip. (%)	Age 18–20[3] Degree (%)	Age 18–21[4] Degree (%)
Females							
(a) Other, 64 years	–2.9	–3.0	–2.5	–1.1	–1.6	–3.5	–2.5
(b) Indigenous, 44 years	–2.4	–6.0	–5.1	–2.9	–7.2	–3.9	–3.1
(c) Indigenous same as other	–1.4	–3.8	–2.9	–2.0	–6.6	–3.2	–2.6
(d) Indigenous with crime cost	–2.3	–5.9	–5.0	–2.7	–7.1	–3.7	–2.9
Males							
(e) Other, 64 years	–2.8	–2.1	–1.4	–0.2	–1.9	–1.5	–0.8
(f) Indigenous, 46 years	–1.8	–4.9	–4.1	–5.0	–7.2	–2.8	–2.5
(g) Indigenous same as other	–1.0	–2.9	–2.3	–4.7	–6.3	–2.7	–2.0
(h) Indigenous with crime cost	–1.4	–4.7	–4.0	–4.8	–6.9	–2.6	–2.3

Notes:
(a) The difference between social and private rate of return for other Australian females.
(b) The difference between social and private rate of return for Indigenous females.
(c) The difference between social and private rate of return with same employment probability for Indigenous females.
(d) The difference between social (with additional crime cost) and private rate of return for Indigenous females.
(e) The difference between social and private rate of return for other Australian males.
(f) The difference between social and private rate of return for Indigenous males.
(g) The difference between social and private rate of return with same employment probability for Indigenous males.
(h) The difference between social (with additional crime cost) and private rate of return for Indigenous males.
[1] Assuming a certificate (Cert.) involves 2 years of full-time study.
[2] Assuming a diploma (Dip.) involves 2 years of full-time study.
[3] Assuming a degree (Age 18–20/Deg.) involves 3 years of full-time study.
[4] Assuming a degree (Age 18–21/Deg.) involves 4 years of full-time study.

rate of return would appear. At present, highly educated Indigenous people may have relatively high employment probabilities compared with non-Indigenous Australians due to some kind of scarcity value. However, we have not made such corrections.

Let us focus on the private rate of return for males, who have a higher probability of a continuous working life, and hence these estimates are probably more reasonable for males than for females. When we compare the private rate of return for different levels of education for a particular group, we see that for non-Indigenous Australians they seem to follow a U-shape with high rates for low levels of education, falling for intermediate levels and then rising for degrees. For Indigenous people, there appears to be an inverted U-shape: low rates for low levels of education, rising steeply for intermediate levels, and then falling slightly for degree levels. This significantly different pattern needs further exploration. It may be a reflection of greater inequality of earnings amongst Indigenous people compared with non-Indigenous Australians.

Table 2.6.3 provides our estimates of the social rate of return to education for Indigenous and non-Indigenous Australians. As mentioned earlier, these estimates use gross earnings, and include all social expenditures on education, and allow for an individual's forgone earnings. Rows (c) and (g) make an adjustment to the calculated rates of return by assuming that the employment probabilities are the same as for non-Indigenous Australians and implicitly assuming that the probabilities of being imprisoned are the same for Indigenous and non-Indigenous Australians. In addition, for Indigenous people we have included prison costs (see Appendix Table 2.6.B1), using the probabilities of being in prison; see rows (d) and (h) of Table 2.6.3 (assumed to be the same in 1991 as in 1994, and assuming that the probabilities of being in prison are the same as being arrested; see Appendix Tables 2.6.B2, 2.6.B3 and 2.6.B4). This is an attempt to allow for the costs to society of imprisoning someone by taking the cost of incarceration and multiplying it by the differences in probabilities of being imprisoned for indigenous and other Australians. This inclusion obviously raises the social rate of return for Indigenous people, *ceteris paribus*, since there is reduced expenditure on prisons due to improved education.[21]

Table 2.6.4 summarizes the differences between social and private rates of return for males and females. This shows clearly that the social rate of return is lower than the comparable private rate of return. It is interesting to note that the private rate of return for a degree is extremely high (for both Indigenous and non-Indigenous people) compared with any alternative investment that the individual could make. The private rate for staying on in school until age 18 years is also fairly high. It is also interesting to note that if Indigenous people with education have the same employment probability as non-Indigenous people, then the private rate of return is less than if their own employment probabilities are used. This is because few

Indigenous people achieve such levels of education and then have higher employment probabilities than for non-Indigenous people. If we allow education to decrease the probability of being imprisoned, then the social rate of return is higher (compare row (b) with row (d) for females, and row (f) with row (h) for males, in Table 2.6.4).

Although we do not present tables where we allow for Indigenous people with more education to have an increased life expectancy to equal that of non-Indigenous Australians, we found that it made very little difference to the rate of return. This is because the earnings of Indigenous people had already peaked by the age of 46 years (for males) and 44 years (for females), and the extra years of declining earnings when discounted made very little difference.[22]

Conclusion

In the present paper we have provided estimates of private and social rates of return to education for Indigenous and non-Indigenous Australians under different assumptions. In our analysis we discussed the social benefits of education for Indigenous people. In particular, we argued that increasing the levels of education would improve the health of Indigenous people, and hence increase their life expectancy. This increased life expectancy would increase the number of years that Indigenous people would be working productively, and hence increase the benefits to society. Another important social benefit, we argued, was that improved education led to a lower probability of being arrested, and hence imprisoned. Following on from this, we argued that a lowering of imprisonment would increase the working life of Indigenous people and hence increase society's well-being. In addition, a lower rate of crime would decrease society's expenditure on policing and prisons, and hence lead to a social improvement.

Using a fairly common methodology for calculating the private benefits of education, we extended this method to quantify some of the social costs and benefits, and were able to get estimates of the private and social rates of return to education. Our results show that the rate of return (both private and social) to education is fairly high. In particular, we pointed out the curious result that, as education levels increased, the rate of return followed a U-shape for non-Indigenous Australians but an inverted U-shape for Indigenous Australians. This result needs further exploration to provide an explanation. Our results also show that the social rate of return is in general lower than the private rate of return, primarily because social expenditure on education exceeds private expenditure (education is subsidized by the state). In our estimates of the social rate of return, we argued that we should allow for all social costs and benefits, and we made a tentative beginning by allowing education to lower the probability of going to prison and hence lowering social costs. We also allowed for education to improve health by allowing life expectancy to increase. Our results show that making these allowances increases the social rate of return marginally.

In all cases we find that the social rates of return are very high and clearly exceed the Department of Finance's recommended cut-off rate of 8% per annum (in real terms) for public projects. This analysis suggests that the government should increase its funding of education for Indigenous people.

Acknowledgements

The research for this paper was performed when Jin Liu was at the Centre for Aboriginal Economic Policy Research (CAEPR), Australian National University, and the authors thank CAEPR for their support. An earlier version of this paper was presented to a seminar at CAEPR and the authors thank the participants for helpful comments. We are also very grateful for extensive and helpful comments from Bruce Chapman, Anne Daly and Boyd Hunter. We are grateful for comments from an anonymous referee that helped to improve the paper.

Notes

1. The paper is an extension of a previous paper by Daly and Jin (1997), which provided estimates of the private rates of return to education for Indigenous and non-Indigenous Australians.
2. In Australia, the Department of Finance requires all public investments to achieve a real rate of return in excess of 8% per annum.
3. The paper is located firmly in the human capital context (Becker, 1964; Blaug, 1970; Mincer, 1974; Psacharopoulos, 1981, 1985), and is subject to the same limitations as most of the studies in this genre.
4. There are distinctions between the marginal and average rates of return, as well as between *ex ante* and *ex post* rates of return.
5. For an extensive and thoughtful discussion of the externalities involved in education, see McMahon (1998, 1999).
6. Strictly speaking this is true if the 'marginal' social rate of return is high. However, all estimates of rates of return are the 'average' rates.
7. The Rawlsian Social Welfare Function is based on the idea of the 'veil of ignorance': if we do not know where in the income distribution we may happen to fall, we may wish society to help the worst-off person. This is based on the assumption that everyone has an equal probability of being in someone else's place in the income distribution, and hence to avoid being badly off we try to help the least well off in case one happens to fall into that trap. Clearly, it is difficult for a non-Indigenous person to fall into an Indigenous society; that is, a non-indigenous person is unlikely to believe that he/she would fall into a remote Aboriginal community.
8. To the extent this assumption is invalid we would need use shadow prices. However, that is a huge task that we do not even attempt.
9. In some preliminary research (using data on Indigenous people) we have carried out, there is a significant relationship between the level of education and the

probability of being arrested, controlling for various factors including age and income. We assume that there is a fairly stable relationship between the probability of being arrested and being imprisoned.

10. It is of course possible that the increased labour supply of Indigenous labour may lead to a fall in wages, and hence in taxes collected by the government. However, this is likely to be a very small effect.
11. HECS is a method of charging fees for higher education, but is payable only when the student begins earning and the earnings exceed a critical amount. In effect, the student is provided an income-contingent loan by the government that is collected via the income tax system. See Chapman (1997).
12. AUSTUDY and ABSTUDY are financial assistance payments made to students in secondary and tertiary educational courses, which are means tested. ABSTUDY payments are only made to indigenous students and are not means tested as rigorously as AUSTUDY.
13. It is assumed that these growth rates are the same for both groups for each education level. Since these apply to both private and social rates of return, they do not affect the relativities.
14. It is, of course, true that if Indigenous people live longer that there may be increased expenditures on health. However, in most other cases for non-Indigenous people we think of a longer life as a benefit.
15. This is the life expectancy at birth, not at the relevant age of (say) 16 years, which is likely to be larger. However, we do not have any estimates for life expectancy at different ages and are therefore unable to make any allowance for these differences.
16. The peak estimated earnings for Indigenous males are at 44 years, compared with 'Other Australians' males whose peak earnings are at 42 years. The peak estimated earnings for Indigenous females are at 41 years compared with 'Other Australian' females at 42 years.
17. As mentioned earlier, our preliminary results (using NATSIS data) show such a relationship.
18. We obtained a similar set of results if we ignored any growth of wages over time, in addition to those implied by cross-sectional estimates. These results are available from the authors on request.
19. Note that these costs include an element that covers research in higher education. It is difficult to allocate what proportion of this should be excluded.
20. Note that other, Australians are assumed to work continuously until the age of 64 years. This is a shaky assumption for males and is certainly untrue for females. However, incomes towards the end of the working life have a very small effect on the rates of return as they are heavily discounted.
21. Note that these rows cannot be compared with similar rows in Table 2.6.2. Ideally, we should provide a row that shows the social rates of return when we include the costs of prison and then allow education to decrease these prison costs. Implicitly, we are assuming that an individual is imprisoned for 1 year if arrested.
22. When we have discount rates of over 20%, earnings 20 or so years in the future are almost zero in present value terms. Simple experiments where we increased the terminal earnings by over a 100-fold made little difference to the rates of return.
23. The Australian Longitudinal Survey (ALS) is a small sample of young people aged 16–25, and the Australian Youth Survey has only young people aged 16–19. Neither study has a significant number of Aboriginal people in it.

References

Altman, J. C. & Daly, A. E. (1992) The CDEP scheme: a census-based analysis of the labour market status of participants in 1986, *CAEPR Discussion Paper No. 36* (Canberra, Centre for Aboriginal Economic Policy Research, The Australian National University).

Ashenfelter, O. & Krueger, A. (1994) Estimates of the economic return to schooling from a new sample of twins, *American Economic Review,* **84**, pp. 1157–1173.

Ashworth, J. (1997) A waste of time? Private rates of return to higher education in the 1990s, *Higher Education Quarterly,* **51**, pp. 164–188.

Australian Bureau of Statistics (1991) *Year Book Australia* (Canberra, ABS).

Australian Bureau of Statistics (1995) *National Aboriginal and Torres Strait Islander Survey 1994: Detailed Findings,* (Canberra, ABS).

Becker, G. S. (1964) *Human Capital: A Theoretical and Empirical. Analysis with Special Reference to Education,* 1st Edn (New York, National Bureau of Economic Research).

Bhatia, K. & Anderson, P. (1995) An overview of Aboriginal and Torres Strait Islander health: present status and future trends, *Information Paper* (Canberra, Aboriginal and Torres Strait Islander Health Unit, Australian Institute of Health and Welfare).

Blaug, M. (1970) *The Economics of Education* (Harmondsworth, Penguin).

Bowles, S. & Gintis, H. (1975) The problem with human capital theory: a Marxian critique, *American Economic Review,* **65**, pp. 74–82.

Chapman, B. (1997) Conceptual issues and the Australian experience with income contingent charges for higher education, *Economic Journal,* **107**, pp. 738–751.

Cohn, E. & Geske, T. G. (1990) *The Economics of Education,* 3rd Edn. (Oxford, Pergamon Press).

Daly, A. E. & Liu Jin (1997) Estimating the private rate of return to education for Indigenous Australians, *Australian Economic Papers,* **0**, pp. 100–112.

Denison, E. F. (1962) *Sources of Economic Growth in the US* (New York, Committee for Economic Development).

Gregory, R. G. & Daly, A. E. (1997) Welfare and economic progress of indigenous men of Australia and the US 1980–1990, *Economic Record,* **73**, pp. 101–119.

Groot, W. (1994) Differences in rates of return by type of education, *Education Economics,* **2**, pp. 209–214.

Herron, J. (1996) Joe and Dame Enid Lyons Memorial Lecture, unpublished speech presented at The Australian National University, Canberra.

Johnes, G. (1993) *The Economics of Education* (Hong Kong, Macmillan Press).

Junankar, P. N. & Kapuscinski, C. A. (1991) Aboriginal employment and unemployment: an overview, *Economic Papers,* **10**, pp. 30–43.

McMahon, W. W. (1998) Conceptual framework for the analysis of the social benefits of lifelong learning, *Education Economics,* **6**, pp. 309–346.

McMahon, W. W. (1999) *Education and Development: Measuring the Social Benefits* (Oxford, Oxford University Press).

Miller, P., Mulvey, C. & Martin, N. (1995) What do twins studies reveal about the economic returns to education? A comparison of Australian and US findings, *American Economic Review,* **85**, pp. 586–599.

Mincer, J. (1974) *Schooling, Experience and Earnings* (New York, National Bureau of Economic Research).

Psacharopoulos, G. (1969) *The Rate of Return on Investment in Education at The Regional Level: Estimates for the State of Hawaii,* (Honolulu, Economic Research Centre).

Psacharopoulos, G. (1981) Returns to education: an updated international comparison, *Comparative Education*, **17**, pp. 321–341.
Psacharopoulos, G. (1985) Returns to education: a further international update and implications, *Journal of Human Resources*, **20**, pp. 583–604.
Rawls, J. (1971) *A Theory of Justice*, (Cambridge, MA, Harvard University Press).
Romer, P. M. (1994) The origins of endogenous growth, *Journal of Economic Perspectives*, **8**, pp. 3–22.
Spence, M. A. (1973) Job market signalling, *Quarterly Journal of Economics*, **87**, pp. 355–375.
Walker, J. (1991) *Australian Prisoners: Results of the National Prison Census*, (Canberra, Australian Institute of Criminology).
Weale, M. (1993) A critical evaluation of rate of return analysis, *Economic Journal*, **103**, pp. 729–737.
Willis, R. J. (1986) Wage determinants: a survey of human capital earnings functions in: O. Ashenfelter and R. Layard (Eds) *Handbook of Labor Economics, vol. 1* (Amsterdam, North Holland).
World Bank (1993) *The East Asian Miracle*, (Washington, DC, Oxford University Press).

Appendix 2.6.A1: Estimating the Rate of Return

The empirical procedure for estimating the rate of return on education is as follows: Earnings functions are estimated with the log of earnings as the dependent variable and with independent variables that include years of schooling (or educational dummy variables), work experience (usually proxied as age minus age left school), and controlling for some demographic characteristics like marital status, number of children, and so on. Usually these equations are estimated on cross-sectional data. It is then postulated that the expected future earnings would follow the same path as the pre-existing cross-sectional estimates. This extrapolation is obviously based on some strong assumptions, including steady-state equilibrium conditions with no growth in earnings, and no changes in wage differentials due to changing demand or supply conditions. If we used longitudinal data it would be an improvement: however, there are very few studies based on longitudinal data and, since these data do not exist in Australia,[23] we have to rely on cross-sectional estimates. Ideally, we need to know the expected future lifetime income stream of each individual, which is of course not feasible. In our analysis we have assumed that individuals extrapolate from the immediate past. We assume that the mean wage growth for each education level and age left school for the period between 1986 and 1991 continues into the future. Hence, the individuals are assumed to have expectations that they would receive the earnings of a person who has the higher level of education at that time if they decided to invest in education, but in addition they would receive the mean wage growth increases that someone with that level of education has received in the past.

These predicted earnings are then used to calculate the rate of return as that discount rate, which makes the present value of the resulting net benefit stream (the difference between the benefits and costs) equal to zero:

$$\Sigma B_{ij}/(1 + r)^i - \Sigma C_{ij}/(1 + r)^i = \mathrm{P}_j = 0 \qquad (1)$$

where B_{ij} is the additional earnings at each age i associated with additional education j, C_{ij} = are the costs of education at age i associated with additional education

j, and P_j is the present value of additional education j. The rate of return to education is defined as that rate of discount that equates the sum of the discounted value of benefits to the sum of the discounted value of costs of education. An alternative method of computing the rate of return to education is to regress the natural logarithm of earnings on schooling (Mincer, 1974; Willis, 1986). The resulting coefficient of schooling is interpreted as the rate of return.

Appendix 2.6.A2: The Limitations of the Estimated Rate of Return

There are several limitations related to this estimation.

(i) We are comparing the rate of return for a very small group of Indigenous people with post-secondary and higher levels of education with a much larger group of non-Indigenous Australians. If the levels of education of Indigenous people were up to the levels of that of non-Indigenous Australians, then the wage differentials might change (in a general equilibrium sense). Hence, we may be over-estimating the rate of return to education for a general increase in education levels, although they would be appropriate to an individual increasing her/his level of education.

(ii) We have assumed that wage growth between the 1986 and 1991 Censuses will be continued. We also assumed that this wage growth is identical for Indigenous and non-Indigenous Australians. Since we have used cross-sectional estimates to get our predicted earnings, we are implicitly assuming that existing wage differentials will continue into the indefinite future. In other words, any changes in behaviour that would increase the supply of (say) people with degrees does not affect the equilibrium wage.

(iii) We make all the usual human capital theory assumptions, including that individuals choose the investment plan that maximizes the present value of earnings over the lifecycle. This assumption is particularly problematic for Indigenous people. Given the cultural and historical background of Indigenous people, it is unlikely that they would be following such an optimizing approach.

(iv) For Indigenous people, the earnings that we have used would not include non-market earnings such as from hunting and fishing, which would bias our estimates. In our estimates of earnings functions we have used total income as the dependent variable, which includes the income from Community Development Employment Projects (CDEP) scheme employment for Indigenous people. This may lead to a bias since some participants in the CDEP scheme appear to have been classified not only as 'unemployed', but also 'not in the labour force' in the census (Altman & Daly, 1992). We have not included those people who are 'not in labour force' in our sample.

(v) The social rate of return is estimated by using observed market earnings assuming that wages are equal to the value of the marginal product of labour (labour markets are perfect). If we did not make this assumption we would have to estimate shadow wages. In a centralized wage bargaining system like we have in Australia, it is not clear to what extent the centralized wage bargains simply rubber-stamp competitive market wages or to what extent they introduce distortions. This is another area that needs further exploration.

(vi) We have made no corrections for the possibility that there is selection bias (i.e., the more educated are of higher ability). We have assumed that the higher earnings of the more educated simply reflect a return on that education.

Appendix Table 2.6.A1 Age on leaving school for indigenous and other Australians aged 15 years and over, 1976–1991[a]

	1976 (%)	1981 (%)	1986 (%)	1991 (%)	Change in share 1976–1991 (%)
Indigenous persons					
Younger than 15 years	28.4	25.9	22.6	19.7	-30.6
15–16 years	48.8	51.0	55.7	54.3	11.3
17+ years	8.6	10.7	13.7	20.6	139.5
Did not attend school	14.3	12.5	7.9	5.4	-62.2
Total	100.0	100.0	100.0	100.0	
Other Australians					
Younger than 15 years	31.0	26.9	22.8	17.2	-44.5
15–16 years	47.5	48.1	47.8	45.8	-3.6
17+ years	20.4	24.2	28.6	36.0	76.5
Did not attend school	1.0	0.8	0.8	1.0	0.0
Total	100.0	100.0	100.0	100.0	
Ratio of Indigenous/other Australians					
Younger than 15 years	0.9	1.0	1.0	1.2	
15–16 years	1.0	1.1	1.2	1.2	
17+ years	0.4	0.4	0.5	0.6	
Did not attend school	14.3	15.6	9.9	5.4	

Source: Daly and Liu (1995).

[a] Information on the school-leaving age of the Aboriginal adult population was not presented in 1971. Data are available, however, for the highest level of schooling for the whole Aboriginal population, including both adults and children. Among those not currently attending school at the time of the 1971 Census, 26.3% had never attended school. The data presented in Table 2.6.1 for later years do not include those still attending school.

Appendix Table 2.6.A2 Descriptive statistics of variables for Indigenous Australians (full sample 1991 Census, aged 15–64 years) and for native-born non-Indigenous Australians (1% sample 1991 Census, aged 15–64 years)

Variable	Mean	Standard deviation	Minimum	Maximum	Valid *N*
Indigenous Australians					
Sex	1.51	0.50	1	2	153113
AGE	31.47	12.52	15.00	64.00	153113
QLL	3.87	0.46	1.00	4.00	134238
ALS	2.63	1.26	1.00	6.00	123841
Males	1.00	0.00	1	1	74330
AGE	31.25	12.47	15.00	64.00	74330
QLL	3.86	0.44	1.00	4.00	65167
ALS	2.58	1.28	1.00	6.00	59770
Females	2.00	0.00	2	2	78783
AGE	31.68	12.57	15.00	64.00	78783
QLL	3.88	0.47	1.00	4.00	69071
ALS	2.68	1.25	1.00	6.00	64071
Non-Indigenous Australians					
Total					
AGE	35.35	13.80	15.00	64.00	77728
QLL	3.49	0.93	1.00	4.00	77728
ALS	4.07	1.32	1.00	7.00	69567
MST	1.73	0.63	1.00	3.00	77728
CDP	1.95	0.98	0.00	8.00	37825
LANG	0.00	0.04	0.00	1.00	77485
Males					
AGE	35.17	13.79	15.00	64.00	38745
QLL	3.43	0.92	1.00	4.00	38745
ALS	4.10	1.36	1.00	7.00	34614
MST	1.67	0.62	1.00	3.00	38745
CDP	1.95	0.98	0.00	8.00	17762
LANG	0.00	0.04	0.00	1.00	38603
Females					
AGE	35.53	13.81	15.00	64.00	38983
QLL	3.55	0.93	1.00	4.00	38983
ALS	4.05	1.29	1.00	7.00	34953
MST	1.79	0.64	1.00	3.00	38983
CDP	1.95	0.97	0.00	8.00	20063
LANG	0.00	0.04	0.00	1.00	38882

Appendix Table 2.6.A3 Earnings function for Indigenous and non-Indigenous Australians by gender, 1991

Variables[a]	**Indigenous**		**Others**	
	Males	**Females**	**Males**	**Females**
Constant	7.8101	7.4795	7.3264	6.7494
	(224.4)*	(157.8)*	(184.5)*	(131.7)*
Age	0.0889	0.0983	0.1188	0.1243
	(43.4)*	(34.1)*	(52.7)*	(40.9)*
Age squared	–0.0010	–0.0012	–0.0014	–0.0015
	(–37.6)*	(–29.2)*	(–49.1)*	(–37.8)*
Age on leaving school[b]				
No schooling	–0.3834	–0.2671	–0.2720	–0.3452
	(–15.4)*	(–6.6)*	(–3.0)*	(–2.16)**
≤ 14 years	–0.0606	–0.0425	–0.0412	–0.0335
	(–5.4)*	(–2.6)*	(–2.7)*	(–1.4)
16 years	0.0519	0.1333	0.1432	0.2176
	(5.3)*	(10.7)*	(13.0)*	(15.1)*
17 years	0.1208	0.2414	0.1858	0.2864
	(10.1)*	(16.7)*	(15.7)*	(18.9)*
18 years	0.1591	0.2388	0.1964	0.2693
	(9.7)*	(12.0)*	(13.8)*	(14.0)*
19 years	–0.0303	0.0920	0.1363	0.2641
	(–1.3)	(3.3)*	(–6.7)*	(9.6)*
Qualifications[b]				
Certificate	0.3495	0.2278	0.1702	0.1546
	(33.7)*	(13.3)*	(18.5)*	(9.1)*
Diploma	0.4178	0.4147	0.2997	0.2952
	(15.4)*	(20.4)*	(16.7)*	(16.7)*
University degree	0.5759	0.5772	0.5226	0.4393
	(19.4)*	(20.3)*	(38.1)*	(25.2)*
Marital status				
Married	0.1398	–0.1414	0.1628	–0.1524
	(14.9)*	(–11.8)*	(13.4)*	(–9.8)*
Other	0.0974	0.0537	0.1056	0.1239
	(6.6)*	(3.2)*	(5.9)*	(5.8)*
Dependent children	0.0089	0.0242	0.0167	0.0568
	(8.0)*	(17.6)*	(13.9)*	(37.9)*
Language	–0.4528	–0.3188	0.0978	–0.1070
	(–19.0)*	(–9.5)*	(0.8)	(0.8)
R^2	0.23	0.19	0.30	0.26

Source: 1991 Census.
[a] '*t*' statistics in parentheses.
[b] Joint *F*-test significant at 1% level (one-side or two-side tests as appropriate).
* Significant at 1% level, **Significant at 5% level.

Appendix Table 2.6.A4 Mean wage and growth rate from 1986–1991 for all Australians, by sex, section-of-state, qualification level and age left school, 1986 and 1991 Census

Qualification levels	1986 males	1991 males	Growth rate	1986 females	1991 females	Growth rate
Total areas						
Degree	32417	45702	1.41	19719	26707	1.35
Diploma	28761	35347	1.23	15440	20747	1.34
Certificate	20140	26307	1.31	11340	15091	1.33
Non-qualification	14387	18954	1.32	7781	11910	1.53
Average	17719	23758	1.34	9266	14040	1.52
Age left school total areas						
Als 15	17307	23074	1.33	8217	12658	1.54
Als 16	18135	24177	1.33	9891	14425	1.46
Als 17	21384	28704	1.34	12613	17466	1.38
Als 18	21890	29155	1.33	12829	17550	1.37
Als 19	23461	30950	1.32	13571	19481	1.44
Average	19186	25994	1.35	10142	15238	1.50

Source: 1986 and 1991 Census.
Note: Other areas include other urban and rural areas.
(1) Assuming that wage rate for Indigenous is same as for others by the level of qualification and by section-of-state.
(2) Average wage growth rate is assumed no discrimination for Indigenous and marginal productivity equal to wage rate.
(3) Wage growth rate will be calculated from 1986 rather than 1981 and 1991 censuses. There are two reasons why the 1981 Census cannot be used for this purpose: the limited sample for Indigenous Australians (about 1500 cases), and no geographic areas divided wage rate for other Australians.

Appendix Table 2.6.A5 Percentage of recipients of AUSTUDY or ABSTUDY by sex, age 15–22 years, 1991

	Indigenous ABSTUDY		Other AUSTUDY	
	Males	Females	Males	Females
16 years	56.2	65.0	32.5	35.8
17 years	44.9	52.3	22.9	27.5
18 years	20.2	24.0	15.5	20.3
19 years	14.0	18.5	10.6	14.3
20 years	12.2	15.0	7.2	9.0
21 years	9.6	13.9	5.1	5.5
22 years	9.2	11.8	3.7	3.6

Source: Department of Employment, Education, Training and Youth Affairs.

Appendix Table 2.6.B1 Number and percentage of prisoners, by sex and Aboriginality, 1991

	Number	%	per 100000	Number percentage
Indigenous				
Male	2045	(94.4)	3403	3.40
Female	121	(5.6)	188	0.19
Sub-total	2166	(100)	1739	1.74
Other				
Male	11716	(95.1)	183	0.18
Female	607	(4.9)	9	0.01
Sub-total	12323	(100)	95	0.10
Total				
Male	13761	(95.0)	221	0.22
Female	728	(5.0)	11	0.01
Sub-total	14489	(100)	115	0.12

Source: Walker (1991, pp. 22, 23).
Notes:
(1) The additional crime costs for Indigenous males and female compared with other Australians are $1466 and $81, which is calculated by $45 537 cost per prisoner in 1991 times the difference percentage 3.22 (male) and 0.18 (female) of prisoners between Indigenous (male or female) and other Australians (male or female).
(2) The proportional deduction of social benefit from being in prison by level of education is applied, which causes increased rate of return. The increased rate of return after adjusting for crime cost is because of widening the stream of lifetime earnings. The widening increased stream of lifetime, earning is because of higher probability of being in prison (bigger loss of social benefit). Left school at 15 years and at non-qualification among the age groups are both comparative benchmarks for the increased stream of lifetime earnings.

Appendix Table 2.6.B2 Percentage of prisoners by sex and age, all Australians, 1991

Age group	Male	Female	Total
17 years	0.4	0.3	0.4
18 years	2.5	1.9	2.4
19 years	4.1	3.4	4.1
20–24 years	26.4	20.2	26.1
25–29 years	21.7	29.0	22.0
30–34 years	17.1	21.7	17.3
35–39 years	11.7	10.2	11.6
40–44 years	7.0	7.4	7.0
45–49 years	4.3	3.0	4.3
50–54 years	2.6	1.9	2.6
55–59 years	1.2	0.3	1.2
60–64 years	0.7	0.5	0.7
65 years and over	0.4	0.1	0.4
All years	100.0	100.0	100.0

Source: Walker (1991, p. 18).
Persons younger than 17 years go to juvenile centre.

Appendix Table 2.6.B3 Number and percentage of prisoners, by sex and known employment status, all Australians, 1991

Numbers	Male	Female	Total
Employment status			
Employed	2100	64	2164
Unemployed	3927	152	4079
Home duties	1013	69	1082
Student	27	14	41
Other	197	29	226
Unknown	7029	400	7429
Total	14293	728	15021
Percentage employment status			
Employed	14.7	8.8	14.4
Unemployed	27.5	20.9	27.2
Home duties	7.1	9.5	7.2
Student	0.2	1.9	0.3
Other	1.4	4.0	1.5
Unknown	49.2	54.9	49.5
Total	100.0	100.0	100.0

Source: Walker (1991, p. 32).

Appendix Table 2.6.B4 Percentage of Indigenous Australians arrested by police in the past 5 years by age and education, NATSIS 1994

Years	Als 15	Als 16	Als 17	Als 18	Degree	Diploma	Certificate	Non-qualified
Males								
15–19	7.7	4.6	3.5	0.9	0.0	0.0	1.5	0.7
20–24	10.6	9.0	11.4	11.0	0.0	0.0	8.5	13.4
25–29	9.7	9.0	8.1	6.4	0.0	2.3	8.9	7.4
30–34	5.9	8.0	3.0	4.9	12.1	10.7	7.7	6.0
35–39	5.8	2.5	2.2	2.6	0.0	2.1	4.3	5.6
40–44	2.6	2.0	1.2	0.4	0.0	5.0	3.1	0.6
45–49	1.7	0.3	0.3	0.5	0.0	0.0	0.9	0.0
50–54	0.4	0.3	0.1	0.0	0.0	2.7	0.2	0.3
55–59	0.1	0.0	0.0	0.2	0.0	0.0	0.1	0.0
60–64	0.1	0.1	0.0	0.0	0.0	0.0	0.0	0.0
Total	44.5	35.8	30.0	26.9	12.1	22.8	35.2	34.0
Females								
15–19	1.6	0.9	0.8	0.7	0.0	0.0	0.7	0.2
20–24	4.4	2.2	4.1	5.2	0.0	2.1	1.7	5.5
25–29	2.8	2.3	1.4	1.8	0.0	1.2	2.3	0.8
30–34	3.0	1.9	1.2	1.3	1.0	0.5	2.1	3.5
35–39	1.8	1.0	0.9	0.6	1.1	0.7	1.3	2.1
40–44	0.6	0.7	0.2	0.4	0.0	0.0	0.3	0.5
45–49	0.0	0.3	0.1	0.0	1.3	0.0	0.0	0.0
50–54	0.1	0.1	0.0	0.2	4.7	0.0	0.1	0.0
55–59	0.0	0.0	0.0	0.0	0.0	0.0	0.0	0.0
60–64	0.0	0.0	0.0	0.0	0.0	0.0	0.0	0.0
Total	14.3	9.4	8.7	10.1	8.2	4.5	8.6	12.5

Source: Australian Bureau of Statistics (1995).

Appendix Table 2.6.C1 Private rate of return to education without AUSTUDY or ABSTUDY aged 15–64 years (assuming full income support, adjusting for mean wage growth rates and employment probabilities), 1991

Aboriginality, age and sex	AIs 15/16 (%)	AIs 15/17 (%)	AIs 15/18 (%)	Age 17[a] Cert· (%)	Age 17[b] Dip· (%)	Age 18–20[c] Degree (%)	Age 18–21[d] Degree (%)
Females							
(a) Other, 64 years	18.3	13.5	8.8	2.7	11.3	11.6	12.8
(b) Indigenous, 44 years	11.5	11.8	8.5	11.3	21.0	17.5	19.0
(c) Indigenous same as other	12.6	12.4	7.6	5.7	18.0	15.2	16.3
Males							
(d) Other, 64 years	23.2	16.0	11.5	12.4	15.5	19.0	19.1
(e) Indigenous, 46 years	10.7	11.1	9.5	21.6	23.1	20.2	21.7
(f) Indigenous same as other	10.7	10.4	8.0	21.0	20.4	19.3	19.4

Notes:
(a) Other Australian females 64 years for working life expectancy with own employment probability adjustment.
(b) Indigenous females 44 years for working life expectancy with own employment probability adjustment.
(c) Indigenous females same as other Australian females in terms of employment probabilities.
(d) Other Australian males 64 years for working life expectancy with own employment probability adjustment.
(e) Indigenous males 44 years for working life expectancy with own employment probability adjustment.
(f) Indigenous males same as other Australians males in terms of employment probabilities.

Appendix Table 2.6.C2 Private rate of return to education without AUSTUDY or ABSTUDY aged 15–64 years (assuming full income support, adjusting for mean wage growth rates and employment probabilities), 1991

Aboriginality, age and sex	AIs 15/16 (%)	AIs 15/17 (%)	AIs 15/18 (%)	Age 17[a] Cert· (%)	Age 17[b] Dip· (%)	Age 18–20[c] Degree (%)	Age 18–21[d] Degree (%)
Females							
(a) Other, 64 years	18.3	19.1	15.4	7.4	20.7	20.2	20.7
(b) Indigenous, 44 years	11.5	21.7	22.8	30.7	48.1	31.9	32.0
(c) Indigenous same as other	12.6	18.4	15.0	17.2	39.3	26.9	27.1
Males							
(d) Other, 64 years	23.2	20.8	16.8	21.9	25.0	27.8	27.4
(c) Indigenous, 46 years	10.7	18.9	20.5	51.2	46.7	32.4	34.6
(f) Indigenous same as other	10.7	15.3	14.2	46.4	40.2	31.4	30.6

Notes:
[a] Assuming a certificate (Cert.) involves 2 years of full-time study.
[b] Assuming a diploma (Dip.) involves 2 years of full-time study.
[c] Assuming a degree (Age 18–20/Deg.) involves 3 years of full-time study.
[d] Assuming a degree (Age 18–21/Deg.) involves 4 years of full-time study. Age 18–21/Deg. is under assumption of the same proportion of additional year income increased and full employment probability. The rate of return for Age 18–21/Deg. will be less than that for Age 18–20/Deg. if no assumption of full employment probability.

3
Youth Labour Markets

3.1
The British Youth Labour Market in Crisis

P.N. Junankar

The paper argues that the British youth labour market is in a crisis with employment falling, unemployment and long-term unemployment rising rapidly. In section one the paper reviews the evidence and, in particular, looks at alternative measures of unemployment duration. Section two discusses various explanations for the growth of youth unemployment and dismisses the view that it is due to the increase in relative wages of young people. It is argued that the youth labour market has several distinctive features that make it more sensitive to cyclical fluctuations. Section three takes a brief look at various policies to alleviate the problem. Section four concludes the paper stressing that a reflation of the economy is necessary to make a significant impact on youth unemployment.

The youth labour market[1] in Britain is in a state of crisis with a dramatic increase in unemployment. Each year about three-quarters of a million children reach school-leaving age (in England and Wales) and decide whether to stay on at school or whether to enter the labour market. In 1983 about 44% stayed on in school (or higher education) and about 56% entered the labour market. Of those entering the labour market only 38% found employment, 48% joined various government training schemes (Youth Training Schemes) and 14% were unemployed. Over the past few years there has been a dramatic collapse in the youth labour market with an increasing proportion of young people unemployed and a decreasing proportion finding employment. In spite of being an avowedly *laissez-faire* government, there has been massive intervention in this labour market by the Conservative government with the introduction of the Youth Training Scheme (YTS, a successor to the Youth Opportunities Programme, YOP), Young Workers Scheme (YWS), and recently the removal of the minimum wages legislative cover for people under 21 years of age.

Reprinted from 3.1 'The British Youth Labour Market in Crisis' by P. N. Junankar in *International Review of Applied Economics*, 1 (1), 1987, 48–71. With kind permission from Taylor and Francis.

Various explanations have been provided for the collapse of the youth labour market. Firstly, the impact of the recession (perhaps as part of the international recession) has led to a decline in the demand for labour services, and hence a fall in the hiring of school leavers and young people. Secondly, as a result of the so-called post-industrial (or deindustrialized) society, there has been a shift in employment from full-time employment in manufacturing to part-time employment in the service sector. Thirdly, as a result of a demographic 'bulge', there has been an increase in labour supply of young people. Fourthly, (as argued by Conservative politicans and neoclassical economists) the explanation lies in an increase in relative wages of young people, minimum wage legislation, the 'pernicious' influence of trade unions, and allegedly 'generous' social security benefits.

Before we turn to an evaluation of these hypotheses, it is worth noting certain peculiar (distinctive) characteristics of the labour market for young people. Most young people who enter the labour market are normally unskilled and enter non-professional occupations and non-career grade jobs. They often enter 'dead-end' jobs which require little in the form of skills, little training is provided 'on the job', and a very small percentage of them are unionized. A high proportion of them enter part-time, poorly paid jobs. In an uncertain environment employers should *prefer* to hire young people as they are paid less, they are non-unionized, are likely to quit voluntarily, and they are easy to fire, unlike older workers who are protected by employment protection legislation. Ignoring any training (general or specific) that young people may get on the job, employers could follow a policy of replacing one batch of young workers by another batch, so that they need never pay adult wage rates. (This policy is described graphically in Greenwood (1933).) However, young workers are less skilled, less experienced, less mature, viewed as being less reliable and trustworthy. Employers may prefer to have a 'balanced' age composition for their workforce to allow for training, taking on responsibility, to avoid having discontinuous natural wastage, etc.

A feature of this labour market that is commonly pointed out is that there is a very high turnover. Every year a new cohort of school-leavers join this labour market, and of course through the ageing process a cohort leaves the youth labour market. Some of the school-leavers decide to stay on in higher education, some find employment, some join the YTS, some are unemployed, and some are not in the labour force. Of the employed labour force a large number of people quit or are fired. Some of these people become unemployed while a substantial number temporarily withdraw from the labour force. At the same time, some of the unemployed are hired, some decide to enter (or reenter) higher education, while some withdraw from the labour force. This high turnover is reflected in the higher rates of inflows into, and outflows from, the unemployment stock. For example, for males in April-July 1985 the likelihood of becoming unemployed was 17.6 per cent for the under 18s and 3.9 per cent for the 30–34 year olds. The likelihood of ceasing to be unemployed was 57.8 per cent for the under 18s and 33.0 per cent for the 30–34 year olds (*Employment Gazette,* October 1985, Table 2.21). In general, the young provide a convenient reserve army of labour to be hired and fired according to the level of economic activity. Because they are young they are the first to be fired under agreed industrial relations practice: last-in-first-out (LIFO). Employment protection legislation reinforces this. This paper, in section one, discusses the evidence on the crisis of the youth labour market; section two reviews some of the explanations; section three reviews some of the policies to combat the problem; section four concludes the paper.

I Growth of youth unemployment

Almost all data sources show that the youth labour market is in crisis with a decline in employment, an increase in unemployment, and in recent years an enormous growth in YTS. An especially worrying feature has been the rapid growth of long-term unemployment. For example, for males 10.3 per cent of the unemployed 17 year olds had been unemployed for over a year, 3.7 per cent of the unemployed 18 year olds had been unemployed for over two years, and 3.1 per cent of the unemployed 19 year olds had been unemployed for over three years! In other words, there are school leavers in the labour market who have *never* experienced employment (*Employment Gazette,* June 1986, Table 2–6, p. 527).

One of the main problems in describing and studying the labour market for young people in Britain (or the UK) is that the time series data are seriously inadequate. Until 1972 there was an annual time series on employment by age obtained from the National Insurance card count. However, with the abolition of NI cards this vital source of data was destroyed. There are some data available on a biennial (now annual) basis, from the Labour Force Surveys (LFS) which began in 1973, although for various reasons the first reasonable estimates are available for 1975. From 1972 another source of data on employment is the (annual) General Household Survey (GHS). However, this is a relatively small sample survey and the numbers of young people in the sample are fairly small and may not be very reliable indicators. There is also an annual survey of school leavers. The data on the numbers of young people unemployed are, by comparison, good. However the percentage *rates* of youth unemployment are difficult to obtain because the employment data by age are poor. Moreover various legislative changes make comparisons over time difficult. In particular, the raising of the school leaving age in 1972, various changes in regulation affecting *when* a school leaver can register as unemployed, and in recent years various schemes like YOP and YTS make comparisons over time hazardous. A key problem with this data series is that it understates the true level of youth unemployment as it includes only those young people who *register,* and after 1982 only those in receipt of benefits. There is much evidence from surveys that many young people do not register as unemployed, see for example

Roberts *et al.* (1981) and Lynch (1984). Estimates of unregistered unemployment in some cities are of the order of about 40 per cent of the truly unemployed (i.e. only 60 per cent register as unemployed). This non-registration is greater for ethnic minorities and females. In other words, the distinction between unemployed and not in the labour force is 'fuzzy' and hence the real problem is greater than the measured unemployment rate. In addition, many young people may move from unemployment into not in the labour force and hence unemployment durations may be an underestimate. The problem of repeat spells of unemployment also leads to the same bias.

The data on earnings of young people are also very limited. Until 1979 there used to be an annual October Earnings Enquiry carried out by the Department of Employment which provided information on earnings of males under 21, and 21 and over and for females under 18, and 18 and over. The survey is of establishments in the United Kingdom with more than 10 employees and covers manual workers in manufacturing, mining and quarrying (except coal mining), construction, gas, electricity and water, transport and communications (except railways and sea transport), certain miscellaneous services and public administration. To the extent that the young work in small establishments, non-manual occupations, and the services sector (in particular) these earnings data are misleading. In general these data are less representative of females and as the industrial sector has declined, the data are becoming less and less representative of young male employees. Since 1970 an alternative source of data is the New Earnings Survey (NES). This survey is carried out in April of individual employees in Great Britain in all occupations, establishments and industries. In 1974/75 the sampling frame changed to include only employees in the PAYE system thereby excluding low income (and hence many young) people. This is likely to lead to an over-estimate of their true earnings. However, the NES data provide a finer age breakdown than the October Earnings Enquiry.

In our discussion below we shall use alternative data sources to complement our picture of the labour market for young people. For the purposes of bur discussion we define the young to be those people under 25 years. Table 3.1.1 illustrates some aspects of the changes in the labour market for those reaching school leaving age in England and Wales. In the space of five years (1978 to 1983) employment falls from 53 per cent to 21 per cent (a fall of 60 per cent). From 1979 to 1980 unemployment (or not in the labour force) increases by over two hundred per cent! If we include those in YTS as being in the unemployed (or not in the labour force) category – which is how they are treated in official statistics – there is an increase of 400 per cent between 1978 and 1983! It is clear that the bottom has dropped out of this particular labour market over the space of five years. Estimates for 1984 and J985 suggest a continuation of this trend.

Using the GHS data for Great Britain (Figures 3.1.1 and 3.1.2), we can see a fall in employment of young males and females (except the 18–24

Table 3.1.1 First employment of young people (England and Wales) (Of those reaching school-leaving age)

	Percentages			
	1978[1]	1979[2]	1980[3]	1983[4]
(a) Employed (by end Dec)	53	45	33	21
(b) Staying on at school (or entered full-time higher education or training)	40	50	50	44
(c) Unemployed (or not in labour force)	7	5	17	8
(d) Entering YTS				27

Sources:
[1] DE *Gazette*, Dec. 1980 (pp. 1201–1203).
[2] DE *Gazette*, March 1982 (pp. 117–120).
[3] DE *Gazette*, May 1984 (pp. 230–234).
[4] DE *Gazette*, Oct. 1984 (pp. 445–448).

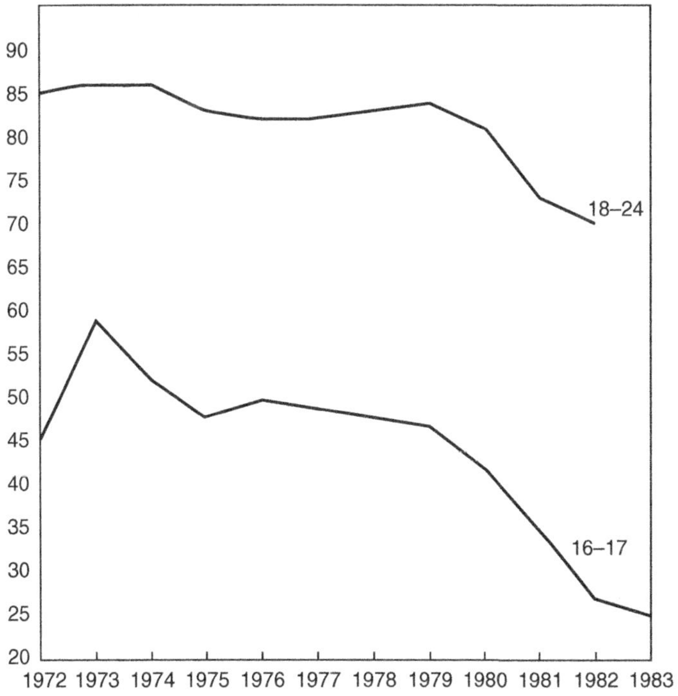

Figure 3.1.1 Youth employment: males (percentages)
Note: Percentage of population ol age group (i) that is in employment.
Source: GHS.

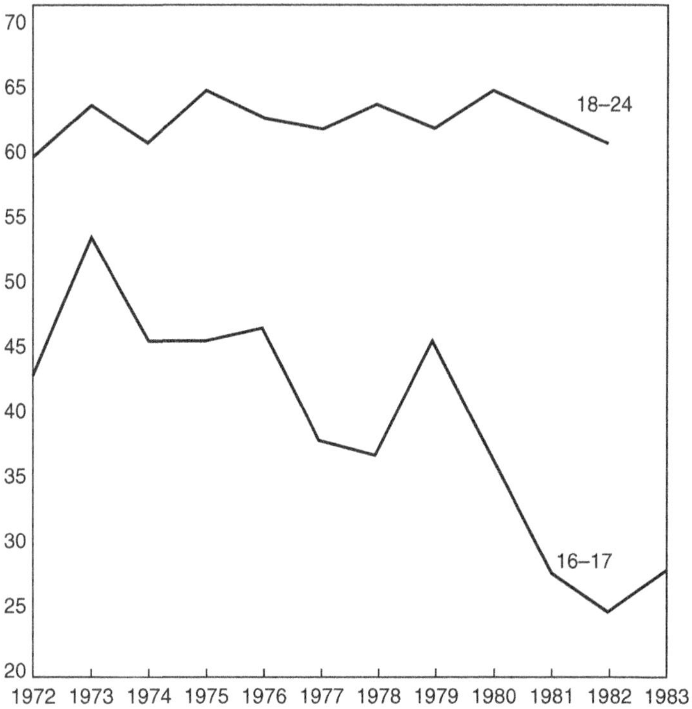

Figure 3.1.2 Youth employment: females (percentages)
Note: See note to Figure 3.1.3.
Source: GHS.

females) from 1973 onwards. The relatively good showing of the 18–24 females reflects in part the growth of the services sector which has expanded by hiring part-time workers. A similar picture emerges if we look at youth unemployment (Figures 3.1.3 and 3.1.4) which has risen since 1973 with a fall for 16–17 year old males between 1982–83.[2] This latter 'blip' is presumably due to the big expansion in YTS/YOP. The increasing unemployment of 18–24 females (and more-or-less stable employment) reflects the increasing participation rate of that group.

The Department of Employment (DE) data for the United Kingdom on unemployment (Figures 3.1.5 and 3.1.6) show similar trends to the GHS although the age categories are different. The break (and lower levels after) in the fourth quarter of 1982 reflects the change in the data series from registered unemployed to *claimant* unemployed. Strictly speaking, the data before and after 1982 are not comparable. However, the diagrams make clear

Figure 3.1.3 Youth unemployment: males (percentages)
Note: Percentage of population ol age group (i) that is in employment.
Source: GHS.

that the change-over gives a different (and perhaps misleading) view of the labour market.

Figures 3.1.7 and 3.1.8 based on DE data are the best indication of the scale of the problem; long-term unemployment (duration greater than 52 weeks) has been growing throughout the period. The proportion of the young who have been unemployed for more than a year has increased to over thirty per cent for males and over twenty per cent for females. This provides an especially worrying feature of the labour market for young people. It is hard to believe that these people are voluntarily unemployed, refusing wage offers because their reservation wage is too high! Let us take a closer look at the duration of unemployment by looking at information on median durations of uncompleted and completed spells of unemployment, based on data from the Department of Employment.

Figure 3.1.4 Youth unemployment: females (percentages)
Note: See note to Figure 3.1.3.
Source: GHS.

As mentioned earlier, there are large flows into and out of the unemployment stock of young people. According to the so-called 'new view' of unemployment (see Feldstein, 1973; Hall, 1972), the large turnover (with short duration spells) implies that unemployment is not a problem: the labour market is functioning efficiently. There are several alternative concepts used to measure the duration of unemployment (see Main (1981) and references cited therein). When we look at the unemployment *stock* and the duration distribution of that stock it provides information about *uncompleted* (interrupted) spells of unemployment: many of those people will continue to be unemployed in the future. Since October 1982 we have information on *completed* spells of unemployment, and we can look at the distribution of these completed spells. Although most completed spells are relatively short, most of the *weeks* of unemployment are due to long spells of unemployment. For example, assume that over a period of a year there were 52 different individuals with completed spells of one week each (spread evenly) and

Figure 3.1.5 Youth unemployment: males (thousands)
Source: DE Gazette.

one individual with a completed spell of 52 weeks. The average completed duration of unemployment spells would be less than two weeks. However, half of the total weeks of unemployment would be accounted for by one spell of one year. To allow for this we could use a concept called an experience weighted average duration (analogous to, in demographic terminology, the average age at death of the *current* population) which is *approximately* twice the average of the uncompleted spells of the currently unemployed (see Main, 1981). In our example, at any point in time the average spell length of the currently unemployed would be 26.5 weeks. Assuming a stable register, where inflows equal outflows, we can calculate the expected duration of all spells as the ratio of unemployment stock to inflows (or outflows). As we have increasing unemployment we can obtain an approximation by dividing the stock by the average of inflows and outflows.

Tables 3.1.2a, 3.1.2b and 3.1.2c illustrate the growing problem facing the young. If we look at the median duration of all completed spells (column 3 in each table) we may infer that there is a high turnover in an 'active'

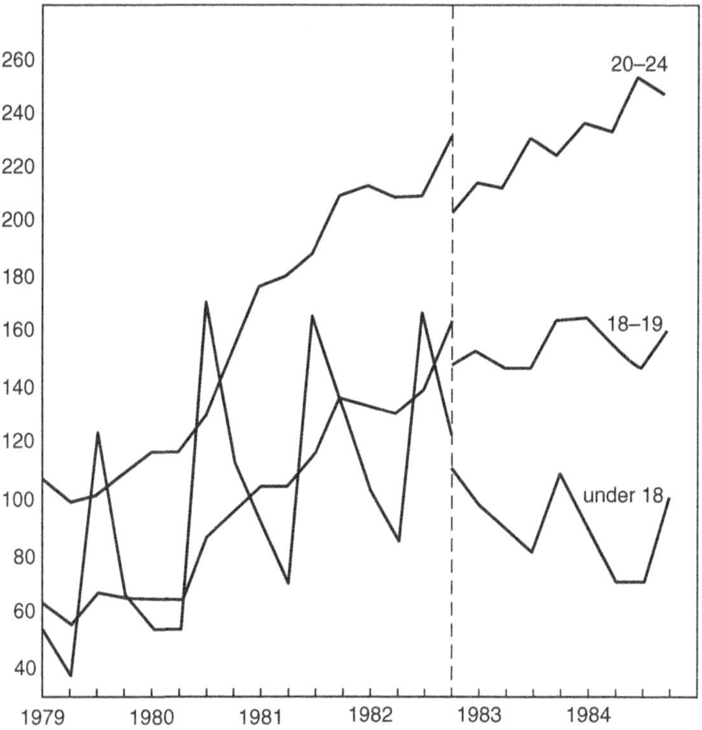

Figure 3.1.6 Youth unemployment: females (thousands)
Source: DE Gazette.

labour market: there are a large number of young people who have very short spells of unemployment. The series also display a very high degree of seasonal influences (because of the bunching of school leavers). The average (arithmetic mean) duration of all completed spells for the under 18s was 8.2 weeks, for the 18–19s it was 25.6 weeks and for the 20–24 year olds it was 15.0 weeks in 1984. A very different picture emerges if we look at the average of the median durations of uncompleted spells (column 1): the corresponding averages are 14.4 weeks, 29.4 weeks and 34.3 weeks in 1984 respectively. An even more alarming picture emerges if we look at the experience weighted average durations (column 2): 28.9 weeks, 58.7 weeks, and 68.7 weeks in 1984 respectively. Finally, if we look at the proportion of weeks of unemployment accounted for by the long-term unemployed (with durations greater than 52 weeks) the percentages are 14.6, 48.6 and 58.1 respectively. In other words, long-term unemployment is a serious problem for the eighteen and over age groups. Although we do

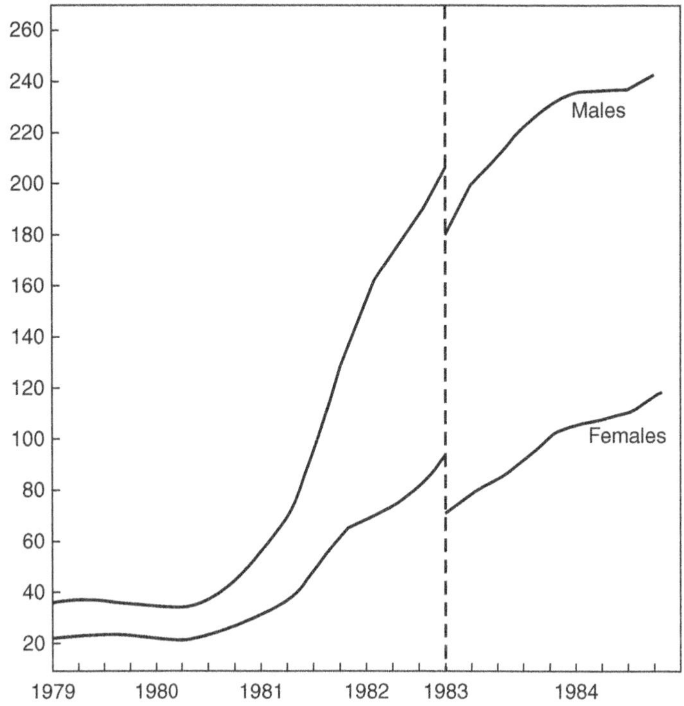

Figure 3.1.7 Long-term youth unemployment (thousands)
Note: Persons less than 25 years, unemployed for more than 52 weeks.
Source: DE Gazette.

not have a longer time series, unemployment durations (however measured) lengthened from 1983 to 1985. As noted earlier, these estimates of duration are biased downwards, because of the fuzzy distinction between unemployment and not in the labour force, as well as due to repeat spells of unemployment.

It is interesting to note that the duration distribution of particular age groups is *truncated due to the ageing process.* A sixteen year old who has been unemployed for more than two years no longer falls in the category of someone 18 and under. Similarly, a seventeen year old cannot be unemployed for more than a year and remain in the 18 and under category. Hence, the estimates of median duration are *biased downwards.* To conclude this section, we see that all the available labour market indicators show that the young are facing a serious problem. In particular, we find that long-term unemployment is a growing problem.

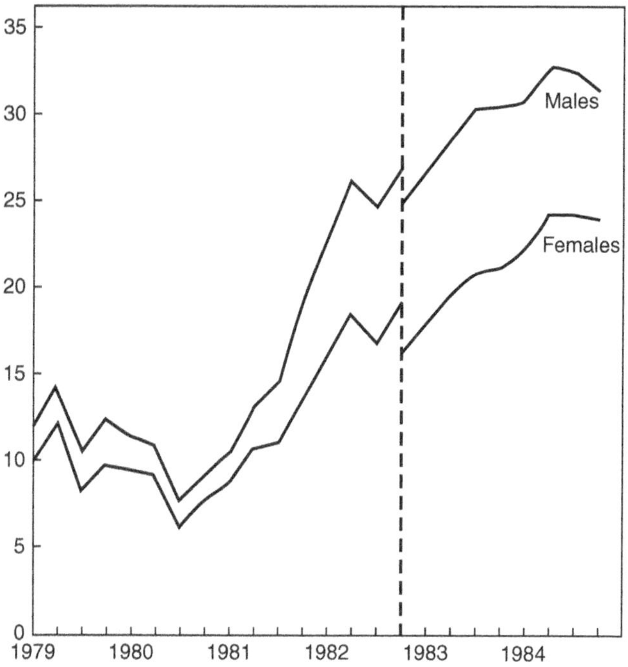

Figure 3.1.8 Long-term youth unemployment (percentages)

Note: Persons less than 25 years, unemployed for more than 52 weeks as a proportion of all persons less than 25 years.

Source: DE Gazette.

II Some explanations

Explanations of the crisis in the youth labour market range from blaming the young for being lazy and dishonest to treating it as a reflection of the international crisis. As mentioned earlier, the youth labour market has some special characteristics which make it more difficult to analyse. In addition to all the problems raised earlier, in recent years government intervention on a massive scale makes it very difficult to model this labour market. Two alternative approaches have been followed. Firstly, the use of time series data to estimate models of supply and demand. In this case various assumptions can be made: (a) market clearing with flexible (real) wage rates, (b) non-market clearing with *a priori* sample selection, and (c) non-market clearing with disequilibrium estimation methods. Secondly, the use of cross-sectional (or occasionally longitudinal/panel) data to explain the probability of a young person being employed (unemployed) in terms of a vector of individual characteristics, and occasionally some market characteristics.

Table 3.1.2a Duration of unemployment. Males under 18 (including school leavers)

Great Britain	**(1)**	**(2)**	**(3)**	**(4)**	**(5)**
	Median duration of uncompleted spells	**Median duration of completed spells of currently unemployed**	**Median duration of all completed spells**	**Expected duration of completed spells**	**Percentage of unemployment accounted for by those with more than 52 weeks of unemployment**
1982 October	5.9	11.8	3.3	2.5	11.3
1983 January	14.9	29.8	10.6	4.6	10.8
April	12.4	24.8	9.5	3.7	10.9
July	16.8	33.6	8.9	5.0	10.9
October	7.0	14.0	3.2	2.6	12.8
1984 January	17.2	34.4	11.1	5.6	13.9
April	20.3	40.6	10.4	5.9	14.9
July	13.4	26.8	7.8	5.7	14.7
October	6.8	13.6	3.5	3.6	14.9
1985 January	16.9	33.8	11.7	6.2	13.1

Notes: Col (1) = Median of unemployment stocks.
Col (2) = Col 1 × 2.
Col (3) = Median of completed spells of outflows.
Col (4) = Unemployment stock ÷ (inflows + outflows)/2.
Col (5) = Weeks of unemployment of those with completed durations of more than 52 weeks ÷ total weeks of unemployment (mid points of duration categories were used and for the final class a maximum of 3.5 years was assumed).

Source: Department of Employment.

Table 3.1.2b Duration of unemployment. Males 18–19 (including school leavers)

Great Britain	(1)	(2)	(3)	(4)	(5)
	Median duration of uncompleted spells	Median duration of completed spells of currently unemployed	Median duration of all completed spells	Expected duration of completed spells	Percentage of unemployment accounted for by those with more than 52 weeks of unemployment
1982 October	22.6	45.2	8.7	4.8	37.8
1983 January	24.9	49.8	14.8	9.8	38 6
April	30.7	61.4	18.5	8.2	40.4
July	32.0	64.0	19.9	6.6	45.8
October	25.0	50.0	8.6	4.4	49.6
1984 January	25.5	51.0	14.7	9.6	45.2
April	33.0	66.0	18.8	9.2	45.9
July	34.4	68.8	21.1	7.5	49.6
October	24.5	49.0	7.7	5.2	53.5
1985 January	24.5	49.0	14.3	9.3	48.3

Notes: Col (1) = Median of unemployment stocks.
Col (2) = Col 1 × 2
Col (3) = Median of completed spells of outflows.
Col (4) = Unemployment stock ÷ (inflows + outflows)/2.
Col (5) = Weeksof unemployment of those with completed durations of more than 52 weeks ÷ total weeks of unemployment (mid points of duration categories were used and for the final class a maximum of 3.5 years was assumed).

Source: Department of Employment.

Table 3.1.2c Duration of unemployment. Males 20–24 (including school leavers)

Great Britain	(1)	(2)	(3)	(4)	(5)
	Median duration of uncompleted spells	Median duration of completed spells of currently unemployed	Median duration of all completed spells	Expected duration of completed spells	Percentage of unemployment accounted for by those with more than 52 weeks of unemployment
1982 October	28.3	49.6	12.1	5.4	47.6
1983 January	30.0	60.0	13.8	9.4	49.6
April	35.1	70.2	18.0	7.9	51.0
July	34.9	69.8	18.0	5.7	55.5
October	33.8	67.6	12.9	5.3	59.5
1984 January	32.7	65.4	13.1	9.2	55.7
April	36.4	72.8	16.9	9.2	56.5
July	35.0	70.0	17.6	6.9	59.0
October	33.2	66.4	12.3	6.8	61.1
1985 January	32.2	64.4	13.7	4.8	55.2

Notes: Col (1) = Median of unemployment stocks.
Col (2) = Col 1 × 2.
Col (3) = Median of completed spells of outflows.
Col (4) = Unemployment stock ÷ (inflows + outflows)/2.
Col (5) = Weeks of unemployment of those with completed durations of more than 52 weeks ÷ total weeks of unemployment (mid points of duration categories were used and for the final class a maximum of 3.5 years was assumed).

Source: Department of Employment.

In recent years, a third method has been to study labour market flows from one state to another and to analyse the duration of unemployment. The changes in the youth labour market over the past few decades are usually explained in terms of changes in the demand for, and supply of young people. In some models it is *assumed* that (real) wages are sufficiently flexible to clear the market so that the only unemployment that exists is involuntary. If for various reasons the output market does not clear (and there is inadequate aggregate demand) then it leads to involuntary unemployment even if the real wage were perfectly flexible. (For a detailed analysis, see Junankar and Neale, 1986.)

If the output market is a non-Walrasian market (that is output prices are not perfectly flexible and trade takes place at disequilibrium prices) producers are rationed in how much they can sell and hence they reduce their labour demand. During the past few years there has been a severe recession with industrial output just beginning to overtake the level in 1979. During this recession many firms have gone to the wall and fired their workers, the firms that survived have decreased their employment levels by firing workers and hiring fewer new workers. The public sector has also been squeezed and has made people redundant and hired fewer new workers. The young are particularly sensitive to such changes: as firms fire workers the young are the first to lose their jobs. The young have fewer skills and less experience (specific or general) and workers with lower productivity are the first to be fired. The last-in-first-out policy as well as employment protection legislation reinforces this. With a decrease in hiring, the young are again affected since they are just entering the labour market, or because of their higher mobility reentering the labour market. There is much evidence to support the view that youth unemployment has risen due to the recession, see Junankar and Neale (1986).

Another explanation of the growth of unemployed young people is that there are structural changes taking place in the economy away from 'youth-intensive' industries. Although there is some evidence for this view, it is a relatively controversial issue, see Raffe (1984). During the past few years there has been a spectacular decline in the manufacturing sector and hence a decline in hiring by that sector. In particular, young people (in the past) would have joined the manufacturing industries as apprentices and these apprenticeships have also declined. The decline in the manufacturing sector has been accompanied by a growth in the service sector. Much of the expansion of employment in the service sector has been of part-time female (married) workers. Again the young who are looking for full-time jobs have suffered.

A possible explanation for the growth in unemployment (but now for the fall in employment) may be that due to demographic reasons there has been an increase in numbers of young people in the past few years. However, data published in the *Employment Gazette* (August 1985, p. 323) shows that the bulge of school leavers peaked in 1982/83. In addition there has been-a marked increase in the participation rate of females. It appears that the labour market has been unable to absorb the increased supply. (The raising of school leaving age in 1972 led to a sudden fall in labour supply which was reflected in a fall in unemployment.) However, this cannot explain the *fall* in employment.

A currently popular explanation of the problems of the youth labour market is in terms of employers not hiring young people because of increased wages of young people relative to adults. However, a casual glance at the data (from the NES) on relative labour costs of the young (Figure 3.1.9) shows that since the mid-seventies they have been *declining* and yet employment has been falling (unemployment rising). Figure 3.1.10 shows that the real earnings of the young have been declining over the past few years.[3] In Table 3.1.3 and Figures 3.1.11 and 3.1.12 we have calculated and plotted

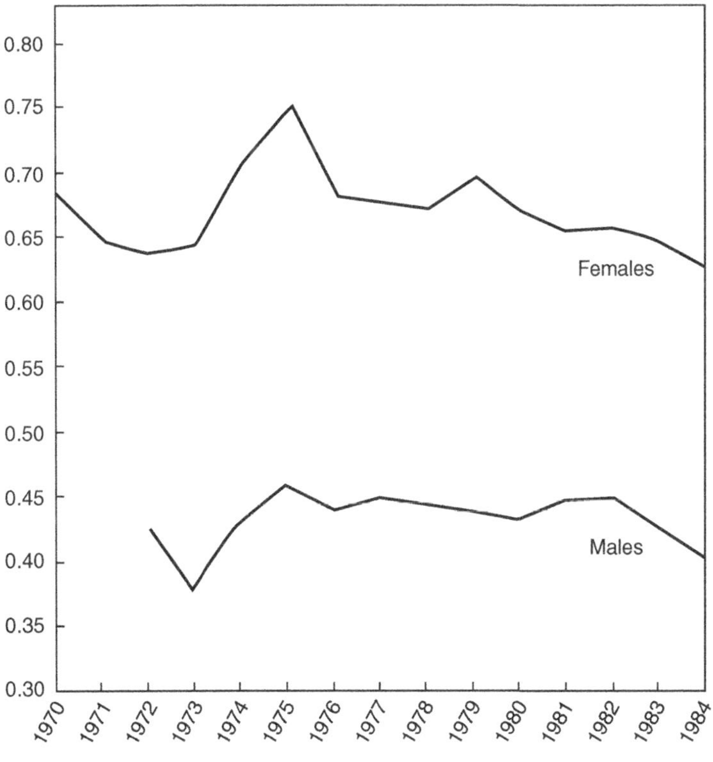

Figure 3.1.9 Relative labour costs
Notes: 1) Males under 18 to 21 and over.
2) Females under 18 to 18 and over.

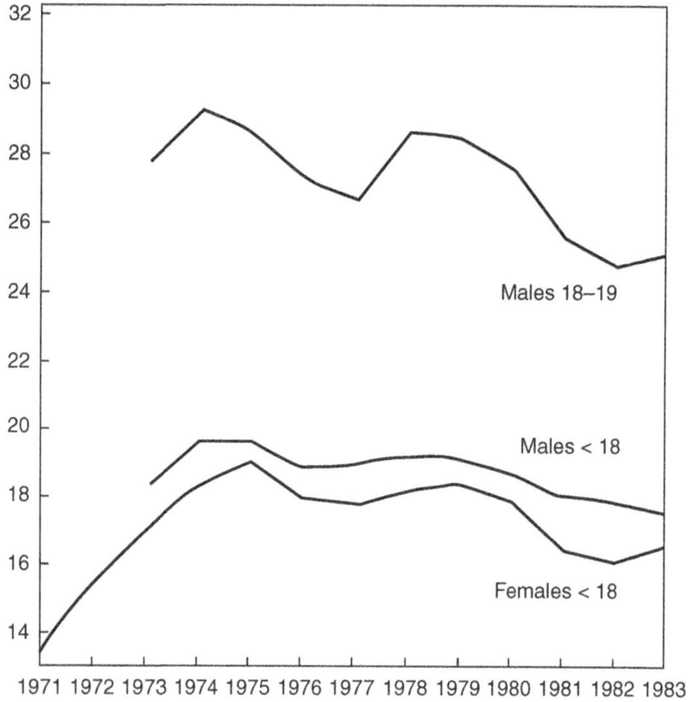

Figure 3.1.10 Real earnings
Note: Real earnings = NES Earnings – (Tax + National Insurance) ÷ Retail Price Index.
Source: NES.

the wage-age profiles for males/females (manual/non-manual) for 1974 and 1984. It is clear that in all cases (except for non-manual males) the relative earnings of the young have declined. It has also been argued by monetarists that unions have led to increase unemployment of the young by raising their relative wages. As we saw above there is little evidence for increased relative wages. In addition, union membership has declined in the past few years and, in any case, the young are. relatively under unionized (partly because they are in industries/occupations with low unionization). A final monetarist argument is that generous social security benefits explain increased unemployment. However, again in recent years, the *real* benefits have fallen very slightly for young people, see Figure 3.1.13. (Due to recent changes in legislation school-leavers cannot claim benefits for the summer and have to wait until September.) As mentioned earlier, the long durations of unemployment are also inconsistent with the view that the young are voluntarily unemployed.

In some cross-sectional studies of this labour market (Lynch, 1984; Main, 1981), it has been found that the poorly educated, unskilled, those with

Table 3.1.3 Wage age profiles

	Full-time manual employees				Full-time non -manual employees			
	Males		Females		Males		Females	
	Males 1974 *Earnings (i)* ÷ Earnings	Males 1984 *Earnings (i)* ÷ Earnings	Females 1974 *Earnings (i)* ÷ Earnings	Females 1984 *Earnings (i)* ÷ Earnings	Males 1974 *Earnings (i)* ÷ Earnings	Males 1984 *Earnings (i)* ÷ Earnings	Females 1974 *Earnings (i)* ÷ Earnings	Females 1984 *Earnings (i)* ÷ Earnings
Age (i)	All	All	All	All	All	All	All	All
Under 18	0.4439	0.4219	0.7284	0.6423	0.3130	0.3130	0.5507	0.4799
18–20	0.7327	0.6908	0.9569	0.8760	0.4656	0.4680	0.7355	0.6828
21–24	0.9714	0.8974	1.0345	0.9869	0.6794	0.6492	0.9529	0.8735
25–29	1.0668	1.0067	1.0603	1.0818	0.9084	0.8566	1.0906	1.0707
30–39	1.1074	1.0986	1.0129	1.0545	1.1011	1.0698	1.1341	1.1438
40–49	1.0788	1.0999	1.0302	1.0589	1.1756	1.1686	1.1123	1.1142
50–59	1.0119	1.0255	1.0259	1.0251	1.1240	1.1061	1.1667	1.1019
60–64	0.9189	0.9591	0.9397	0.9477	0.9885	0.9593		1.0781
65 & over	0.7542							

Notes: 1) Earnings are 'average gross weekly earnings' for each age group (i).
2) Earnings for group (i) are normalized by the overall average gross earnings.
Source: New Earnings Surveys.

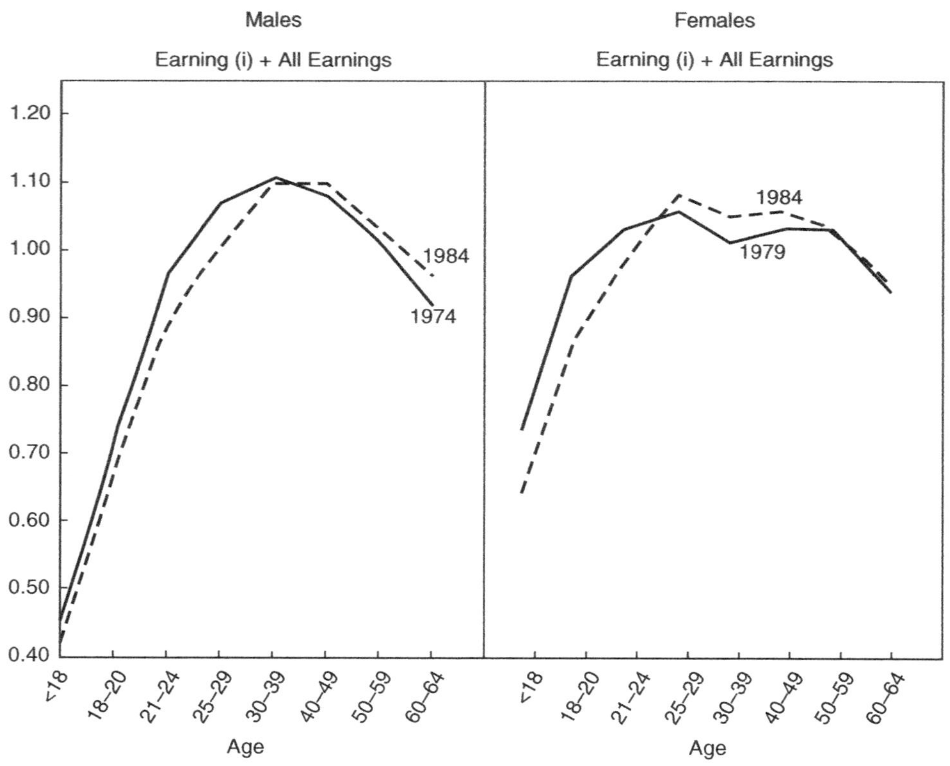

Figure 3.1.11 Full-time manual employees earnings

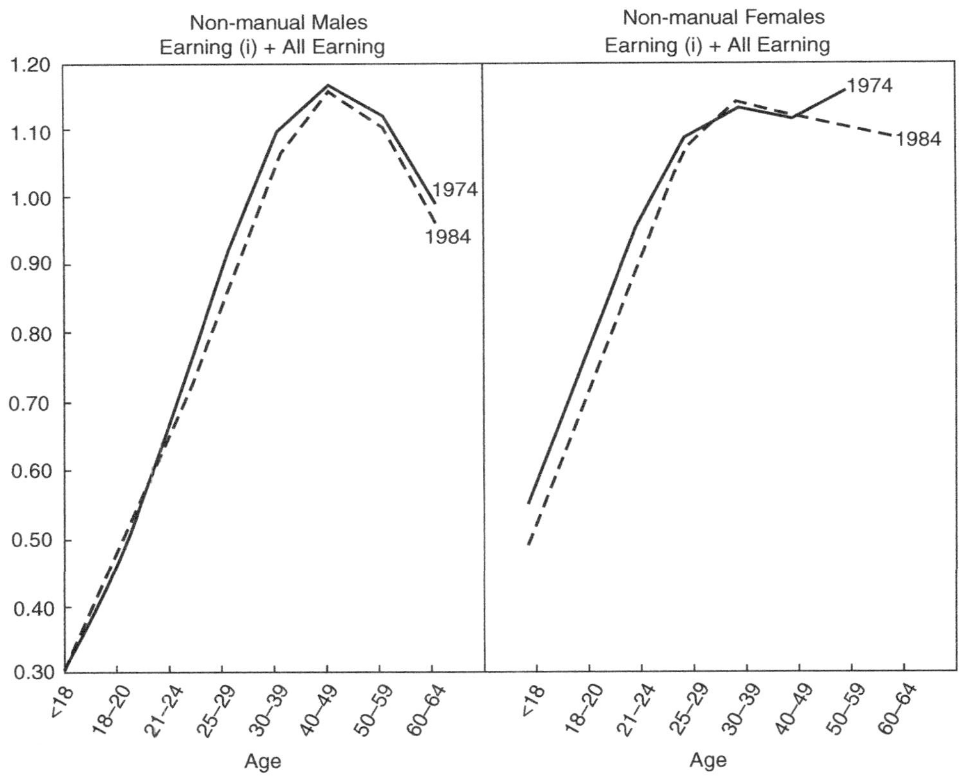

Figure 3.1.12 Non-manual employees earnings

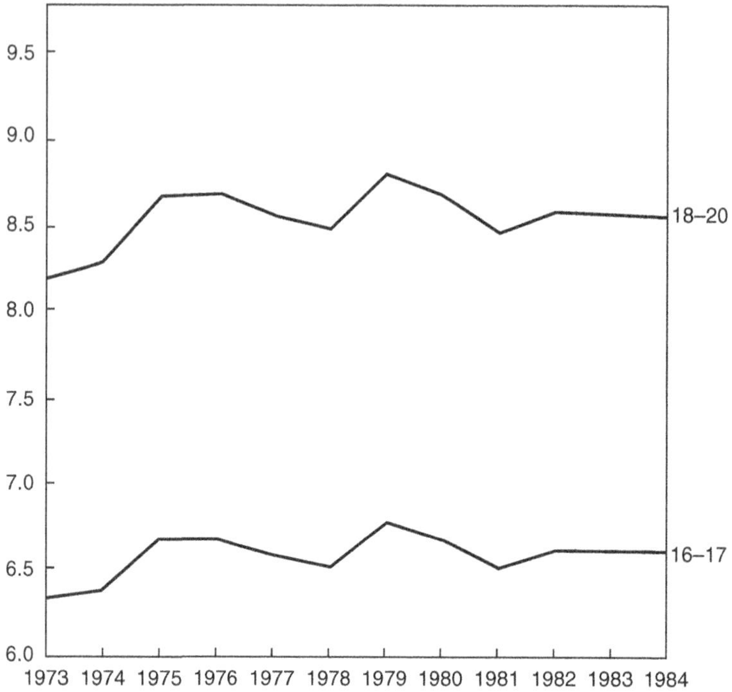

Figure 3.1.13 Real supplementary benefits
Note: Ordinary Rate Supplementary Benefits ÷ Retail Price Index.
Source: Social Security Statistics, 1984.

poor parental background, and ethnic minorities are more likely to be unemployed. For example, according to the Labour Force Survey in 1981 the unemployment rates for the under 25s were 19, 38 and 25 per cent for White, West Indian and Asians respectively. Lynch (1984) also finds that the longer a young person has been unemployed the less likely (s)he is to find a job (so called 'state-dependence'). These cross-sectional studies also find a large number of the unemployed young are not registered as unemployed. This suggests that many of them are not 'rational (maximizing) economic agents' but due to various social and institutional reasons prefer not to be stigmatized as the 'unemployed'. Note that even of the registered unemployed (until 1982) many young people are not receiving *any* benefits (unemployment or supplementary). The proportion of unemployed boys and girls less than 18 years old receiving any benefits increased from approximately 40 per cent in 1968 to 75 per cent in 1974. Of unemployed young people less than 20, the proportion increased from 80 per cent in 1975 to almost 90 per cent in 1983. This increased take up may reflect the increased duration of unemployment as well as a change in social climate. Thus, although there is evidence of increasing take up of benefits, it is still not universal.

III Policies

There are four major methods of affecting the labour market:

1. increase aggregate demand,
2. decrease labour costs of young people,
3. increase the skills of the young either through formal higher education or through training and apprenticeship schemes,
4. affect the incentives of the young towards work/leisure.

As argued earlier, the most important way of improving the employment prospects of young people is by increasing aggregate demand. As the economy expands, firms would hire more young people and fires (dismissals) would go down. Given that there is usually a period before changes in aggregate demand affect employment, the results of policy changes may take over a year before any significant change in employment/unemployment takes place. Neoclassical economists (especially) argue that the *relative* labour costs of the young must be reduced (by the abolition.of minimum wages, by weakening trade unions, or by lowering National Insurance charges) to increase employment. As mentioned earlier, even though the under 18s have been getting cheaper, the level of employment (unemployment) has been falling (rising). At present the government is trying to put downward pressure on wage rates via the Young Workers Scheme (which subsidizes firms if they pay less than the 'going rate').[4] Similarly it is hoped that the low YTS allowance would put pressure on wage rates. A decrease of (or exemption from) National Insurance charges for young employees should make young people more 'competitive'. Recent budget changes have lowered the employers' National Insurance charges for lower paid workers. In addition, the government has just excluded young people under twenty-one from the Wages Councils, in an attempt to stimulate employment of the young. However, most estimates of the relative labour cost elasticities are fairly small.

The major plank of the government's policy towards young people has been the introduction of the Youth Training Scheme (YTS). The object of this is, in theory, to lower the training costs for the firm (employer) and to increase the 'human capital' of young people. However, if there is a lack of demand, *all* that may happen is that firms substitute YTS people for employees (or trainee employees). At the end of the YTS, firms can use the YTS as a 'screening device' and hence lower their hiring and firing costs. Again, given a shortage of demand, only the 'better' YTS people would find jobs: the total number of jobs may not change but YTS simply *selects* who is successful in finding a job. There is accumulating anecdotal evidence to suggest that some (many?) employers are simply taking on YTS people as cheap labour and taking on a new set at the end of the so-called traineeship. However, there is no 'hard' evidence on the success rates of YTS people. A much quoted figure by the government is that 60 per cent of the YTS people found jobs or went into further education. However, this figure has been criticized by many people and organizations, in particular, Youth Aid.

Unfortunately, there has been no proper study of the effectiveness of YTS comparing it with a (matched) control group. There is certainly anecdotal evidence that some YTS schemes are good and do provide training while others are purely disguised cheap labour. A further assessment of this must await the results of the Manpower Services Commission follow-up surveys of the YTS people.

Neoclassical economists, believe that young people are refusing job offers because social security payments are too generous. They suggest that these benefits should be decreased or withdrawn completely. As mentioned earlier, many young people do not register as unemployed (or claim benefits) which suggests that even if the argument is true for some young people, the impact on employment is likely to be very small. It was mentioned earlier that the lengthy periods of unemployment do not suggest people are refusing job offers.

IV Conclusions

In this paper we argued that the labour market for young people is in a crisis: employment has been falling, unemployment rising, and long-term unemployment growing rapidly. We argued that this was due to the recession with the youth labour market being more sensitive than the adult labour market. In particular, we stressed the distinctive features of the youth labour market which have led to increase unemployment. One of the most worrying aspects of this problem is the growth of long-term unemployment, with some school leavers never finding work. Although the government has introduced various policies to alleviate this problem (e.g. YOP, YTS) only a reflation of the economy is likely to lead to a significant improvement. Beveridge (1944) said, '[f]failure to find any use for adaptable youth is one of the worst blots on the record of the periods between the wars' (p. 72). It is a sad reflection on society that forty years later the situation is much worse!

Acknowledgements

I am grateful to Ruth Hermitage for research assistance. Comments from Pat Dutton and Peter Elias helped to improve the paper. I am responsible for prejudices and errors. An abridged version of this paper was published in *Social Europe,* Supplement on Youth Pay and Employers' Recruitment Practices for Young People in the Community, 1986.

Notes

1. For purposes of this paper young people are defined as those between 16 and 25 years of age. We shall look at some subsets of this age-band later in this paper.
2. The apparent improvement in 1973 was due to the raising of the school leaving age (ROSLA) in 1972. This decreased the supply of young people onto the labour market.
3. A detailed econometric analysis is presented in Junankar and Neale (1986).
4. Evidence presented in Rajan (1986) suggests a very small impact on employment. For a more recent evaluation see Bushell (1986).

References

Beveridge, Sir William 1944: *Full employment in a free society.* London: Allen and Unwin.

Bushell, R. 1986: Evaluation of the Young Workers Scheme. *Employment Gazette,* May 1986, pp. 145–152.

Clarke, K.B. and Summers, L.H. 1982: The dynamics of youth unemployment. In *The Youth Labor Market Problem,* Chicago: University of Chicago Press.

Feldstein, M. 1973: Lowering the permanent rate of unemployment. A study prepared for the use of the Joint Economic Committee, Congress of the United States. Washington: US Government Printing Office.

Greenwood, W. 1933: *Love on the dole.* London: Jonathan Cape.

Hall, R.E. 1972: Turnover in the labor force. *Brookings Papers on Economic Activity* Vol. 3, pp. 709–764.

House of Lords 1982: *Report from the Select Committee of the House of Lords on Unemployment Vol. I – Report.* London: HMSO.

Junankar, P.N. 1984: Youth unemployment and youth crime: a preliminary analysis. Australian National University, Centre for Economic Policy Research, Discussion paper No. 106.

Junankar, P.N. and Neale, A.J. 1986: Relative wages and the youth labour market. In *Junankar, P.N., editor, From school to unemployment? The labour market for young people,* London: Macmillan.

Lynch, L. 1984: State dependence in youth unemployment: a lost generation. Centre for Labour Economics, London School of Economics, Discussion paper No. 184.

Main, G.M. 1981: The length of employment and unemployment in Great Britain. *Scottish Journal of Political Economy* 28, 146–64.

Malinvaud, E. 1977: *The theory of unemployment reconsidered.* Oxford: Basil Black well.

OECD: The nature of youth adult unemployment differentials. OECD *Employment Outlook,* September 1983, pp. 73–80.

Raffe, D. 1984: Change and continuity in the. youth labour market: a critical review of structural explanations of youth unemployment. Paper presented to the British Sociological Association Conference on Work, Employment and Unemployment, Bradford, April 1984.

Rajan, A. 1986: The Young Workers Scheme: a preliminary assessment. In Junankar, P.N., editor, *From school to unemployment? The labour market for young people,* London: Macmillan.

Roberts, K., Duggan, J. and Noble, M. 1981: *Unregistered youth unemployment and outreach careers work.* Department of Employment Research Paper No. 31 (November, 1981).

3.2
Relative Wages and the Youth Labour Market

P. N. Junankar and A. J. Neale

3.2.1 Introduction

The dramatic rise of youth unemployment in recent years in most OECD countries has led to the introduction of various policies targetted at youths. Although there are competing explanations of this phenomenon (as of aggregate unemployment), the British government (in particular) has been seduced by the explanation that the growth in youth unemployment is due to a rise in the relative wages of youths. The Prime Minister stated in Parliament (Hansard 27 July 1981, Cols 835–6) '[b]ecause the wages of young people are often too high in relation to those of experienced adults, employers cannot afford to take them on'. The Department of Employment produced a research paper (Wells, 1983) allegedly providing econometric evidence for this view. *The Times* gave this favourable publicity, and entitled an article 'Pay Cuts Would Create Jobs for Young People' (20 December 1983). In this chapter we review some of the evidence on the relationship between relative wages and youth (unemployment in Great Britain and then estimate a disequilibrium model of the youth labour market.

The rapid growth of youth unemployment has been viewed with concern by the young, by their parents, by economists and by politicians. Unemployment in the early years of a potential working life may have permanent 'scarring' effects, and affect the future prospects of employment and/or the future earnings profiles.[2] In addition, there is concern that youth unemployment may have harmful social consequences in terms of violence and crime.[3] This has led to massive government intervention (by an allegedly *laissez-faire* government) in this market by the introduction of various schemes like the

Reprinted from 'Relative Wages and the Youth Labour Market' by P. N. Junankar and A. J. Neale in *From School to Unemployment? Labour Market for Young People* edited by P. N. Junankar, Macmillan, 1987, pp. 79–107. With kind permission from Palgrave Macmillan Ltd.

Youth Opportunities Programme (YOP), Youth Training Scheme (YTS), Young Workers' Scheme (YWS), etc.[4] It is worth noting that young people on these schemes are not treated as being unemployed (or employed). It is, therefore, a (politically) convenient method of lowering the monthly count of the unemployed: it is a method of 'massaging the unemployment figures'.

Most explanations of the rise in youth unemployment stress the peculiarities of this particular sub-group of the labour market. If employers believed that youth and adult labour was homogeneous, youth labour would be hired in preference to adult (since youth wages are lower). For several reasons, employers have a demand for youth labour as distinct from adult labour: typically because young people are inexperienced and need training. Similarly, youth labour supply is clearly different from adult labour supply. Employers could substitute adult for youth labour on the demand side, while youths supplying labour have an option of supplying labour, remaining in education, or not participating in the labour market at all. It has been argued that the youth labour market is a 'secondary' labour market:[5] workers are hired on short-term contracts with low wages and poor working conditions, promotion prospects are limited, there is a large pool of new employees available, etc. Changes in aggregate demand lead firms to use this secondary labour market as a buffer: it is easier to hire and fire in this labour market. Given the higher turnover of young people, employers can also rely on natural wastage to tide them over difficult times.

An alternative view of the labour market (which has some common elements with the 'secondary' or 'dual' labour market hypothesis) explains the growth of youth unemployment in terms of the recession (a fall in aggregate demand), with employers preferring experienced adult workers and firing on the basis of last-in-first-out (LIFO) inexperienced youths. The existence of employment protection legislation also makes it more expensive to fire older workers (employees with longer service). However, LIFO is an agreed industrial relations procedure which predates employment protection legislation. Another explanation is in terms of structural change in the economy, leading to a fall in production in youth-intensive industries. A factor emphasised by neoclassical economists is that a rise in the relative wages of youths leads to a decrease in demand (and an increase in supply) for them, hence increasing unemployment. Allied to this is an argument (based on a *competitive* model) that the imposition (or raising) of minimum wages has led to a decrease in demand for youths. From the supply side, the increase in youth unemployment is explained by a demographic bulge in this age group, by youths preferring to live on (allegedly generous) social security benefits, or by youths preferring to hustle in the informal economy rather than accept 'legitimate' but poorly-paid work. Finally, for various reasons youths have higher turnover and quit rate, so that in a slack market they would have higher unemployment rates. In their earlier years in the labour market they spend time 'sampling' jobs and searching for better paid (or more satisfying) jobs. It is worth noting that youths are a large proportion of the total flow of people who are looking for work, although they are a relatively small proportion of the stock of employment.

The remainder of this chapter is structured as follows: section 3.2.2 discusses alternative methods of modelling youth (un)employment and reviews the evidence from British time-series studies. Section 3.2.3 evaluates Wells (1983). Section 3.2.4 provides some results using a disequilibrium estimation method, and Section 3.2.5 concludes the paper. To anticipate our conclusions, we find that the youth labour market is best described by a disequilibrium model, that the growth of youth unemployment is primarily due to the recession, and that the effects of relative wages are relatively small.

3.2.2 Econometric modelling and evidence

In this section we review the alternative methods of modelling the youth labour market using British time-series data. Before we turn to the econometric modelling, let us briefly look at the data sources. The data on employment by age are readily available (on an annual basis for June-July) until 1972 and were obtained from the National Insurance (NI) card count. However, after the abolition of NI cards this vital source of data was destroyed. After 1972 data can be obtained from the biennial (now annual) Labour Force Surveys (LFS) which began in 1973 (although for various reasons the first 'reasonable' estimates are available in 1975). Data on employment by age are also available (on an annual basis) from the General Household Survey from 1971. However, as this is a relatively small sample the numbers of young people in it are very small and may not be very good indicators of youth employment overall. In other words, we do not have a reliable annual time-series of employment of young people. The data on youth unemployment are (relatively speaking) good. They are available on a quarterly and annual basis, although various legislative changes make comparisons over time difficult. In particular, the ending of National Service (conscription) in 1959, the raising of the school leaving age (ROSLA) in1972, various changes in regulations about how soon after leaving school the young could register as unemployed, and in recent years various government schemes like the YOP and YTS make comparisons over time hazardous. A key problem with this data series is that it understates the true level of youth unemployment, as it includes only those young people who *register,* and after 1982 only those in receipt of benefits.[6] There is much evidence from surveys that many young people do not register as unemployed (see, for example, Roberts *et al.,* 1981 and Lynch, 1985). Although the data on the *numbers* unemployed are readily available, the data on percentage *rates* of unemployment are based on *estimates* of employment by age.

The data on youth earnings–a key variable (especially) for neoclassical economists – are fairly limited. The main source until 1979 for these data were the (annual) October Earnings Enquiry carried out by the Department of Employment. These provide information on earnings for males under 21, and 21 and over, and for females under 18, and 18 and over. The October Earnings Enquiry is a survey of establishments in the UK with more than 10 employees and covers *manual* workers in manufacturing, mining and quarrying (except coal mining), construction, gas, electricity and water, transport and communication (except railways and sea transport), certain miscellaneous services and public administration. To the extent that the young work in small establishments, non-manual occupations, and the services sector (in particular) these earnings data are misleading. In general, these data are unrepresentative for young females and as the industrial sector has declined, the data are becoming less and less representative of young male employees as well. Since 1970 (on an annual basis) a rich source of earnings data are the New Earnings Survey (NES). This survey is carried out in April of *individual employees* in *Great Britain* in all occupations/establishments/industries. In 1974–5 the sampling frame changed to include only employees in the PAYE system, thereby excluding low-income (and hence often young) people. However the advantage of the NES data is that it has a more comprehensive coverage, as well as giving a finer breakdown of earnings (for example, under 18s for males and females as well as under 21s for males, etc.). However, the time series is relatively short.

To summarise, the different data series have different coverage (geographical, industrial, age, etc.), are collected at different months in the year, and are not available on a *consistent* basis for the whole post-war period. It is important to keep in mind this problem of data limitation when we review some of the conflicting evidence.

Let us now turn to the formal (econometric) modelling of the youth labour market and a review of British time-series evidence. There are three different approaches:

1. Unemployment functions
2. Employment functions
3. Labour demand and supply functions:
   (i) Equilibrium
   (ii) Disequilibrium.

For the purposes of this chapter we shall concentrate our attention on one research study which 'typifies' each approach.

Unemployment Functions

A common approach is to estimate youth unemployment *stock* (either as *numbers* unemployed or as an unemployment *rate)* as a function of variables which are selected on a more or less *ad hoc* basis. Any variable which affects youth labour demand or supply is introduced in the unemployment function: it is a quasi-reduced form.[7] Examples of this approach are Collier (1978), Makeham (1980), Layard (1982), Lynch and Richardson (1982) and OECD (1980). This approach can be formalised as follows.[8]

$$L^D = L^D(Z_1) \tag{3.2.1}$$

$$L^S = L^S(Z_2) \tag{3.2.2}$$

$$U = L^S - L^D = L^S(Z_2) - L^D(Z_1) \tag{3.2.3}$$

$$U = f(Z_1, Z_2) \tag{3.2.4}$$

where:
L^D and L^S are labour demand and supply, U is unemployment and Z_1 and Z_2 are vectors of (allegedly) exogenous variables (a common element in Z_1 and Z_2 may be wage rates).

In this approach it is assumed that there is always an excess labour supply and that Z_1 and Z_2 are exogenous variables. Implicitly it is assumed that wage rates are exogenous and do not adjust (at least in that period) to clear the labour market – i.e., they are predetermined. In addition, it is implicitly assumed that the 'min' condition applies – that is, employment equals the minimum of L^D, L^S which by assumption is always L^D. (Note that if equations (3.2.1) and (3.2.2) were in logs, equations (3.2.3) and (3.2.4) could be treated as unemployment *rates*.)

Equation (3.2.4) is usually estimated in linear or log-linear form after adding a white noise random error term.

If the demand and supply functions are derived from an optimisation process then the components of the vectors Z_1 and Z_2 are determined by the precise specification of the maximand and the constraints. For example, if the demand function is derived from a cost-minimising model (subject to an exogenous output level, and input prices) then Z_1 would contain the output level and relative input prices. In a profit-maximising model of a competitive firm output is endogenous and would be *excluded* from Z_1. If the supply function was derived from utility maximisation subject to exogenous wage rates and unemployment benefits, then the supply function would contain these variables. However, as most of the work using unemployment functions does not set out a formal model the variables included in equation (3.2.4) are purely *ad hoc*. In most cases the unemployment function is estimated with some index of aggregate demand (often the male unemployment rate or vacancies), a relative (youths to adults) earnings or labour cost variable, a potential population variable (as an index of labour supply), and assorted variables like replacement ratios (benefit–income ratios), dummies to capture legislative or other changes, etc. Note that if we derive equation (3.2.4) from the underlying demand and supply equations we should have unemployment depend on relative labour costs (from the demand side) *and* the *level* of youth wages (from the supply side).

A general finding of this genre of studies is that aggregate demand is an important determinant of youth unemployment – see Makeham (1980), Layard (1982), Lynch and Richardson (1982), OECD (1980), Wells (1983). In contrast, the relative wages (or earnings, or labour costs including national insurance) variable has a very mixed outcome. Makeham (1980)[9] using annual data (1959–76) and the OECD (1980) using annual data (1959–79) find no significant effect of relative wage costs. However, Layard (1982) using annual data (1959–76), Wells (1983) (using annual data 1969–81 for males and 1971–81 for females) and Lynch and Richardson (1982) using annual data (1950–78) find significant (or almost significant) effects of relative wage costs.

Let us take the Lynch and Richardson (1982) research as 'typifying' this approach. They estimate an equation for the *proportion* of the *numbers* of young male (female) unemployed to the *numbers* of total unemployed males (females). The young are defined as 'aged less than 20 years' (p. 371). (It is worth noting that others have often estimated equations with the dependent variable as the *level* of the young unemployed.) The independent variables they tried out in their equations were an index of 'general business conditions' (which they proxied by the male unemployment rate and by total vacancies),[10] employment costs of young workers relative to adults (implicitly ignoring other input costs), a measure of supply of young workers, an index of demand conditions in 'youth intensive' industries, a replacement ratio, and a dummy. The equations were estimated in log-linear form using a Cochrane–Orcutt estimation method for males and females using the January (July) annual time series from 1950–78. The results for the January equations are reported, although they state that similar results were obtained for the July data. It is curious that the data were not pooled (that is, biannual data) as most variables (except the relative employment costs) are available on (even) a quarterly basis. The main findings are that for males the aggregate demand *indices* are statistically significant, but that the replacement ratio and the supply of young workers variables are *not* significant. The employment cost variable (lagged one period) is not significant ($t = 0.74$) when using the male unemployment rate as an index of aggregate demand. However, when vacancies are used instead of the male unemployment rate, the relative employment cost variable increases in significance ($t = 1.98$), but is still poorly determined. For females the results are similar except that relative employment costs are significant (whichever aggregate demand index is used), as are aggregate demand, labour supply, and the youth-intensive industry index. Overall these results are 'better', but there is evidence of structural instability in 1979–80 (unlike for males) which they explain in terms of changes in NI legislation which increased registration of females. However, they neglect the possible impact of special employment measures.

The main conclusions to be derived from these studies are that the estimated equations are very sensitive to the exact dates of the sample data and to the inclusion (or exclusion) of variables. However, in all studies aggregate demand is a significant variable while relative wages (costs) are significant only in some studies. Overall, these results are a useful step in formulating a rigorous model of the youth labour market but the results should be treated with caution.

Employment Functions

Following in the footsteps of Brechling (1965), employment is postulated to adjust slowly towards an equilibrium stock due to increasing marginal costs of adjustment. The equilibrium employment stock is usually derived from a cost-minimising model and hence depends on output and relative input prices.[11] In this model labour is treated as a quasi-fixed input with convex costs of adjusting labour stock. Note that in a certain world if we did not have *increasing* marginal costs of adjustment we would have a 'bang bang' solution: firms would adjust instantaneously. With uncertainty firms may respond slowly to exogenous changes in demand to 'wait and see' if the changes are 'permanent'.

Hutchinson, Barr and Drobny (1984) follow this approach in their investigation of the male youth labour market. They explicitly assume (p. 188) that there is disequilibrium (excess labour supply) in this market (in their estimation period, 1952–72), with employers always on their demand functions. Assuming cost-minimising firms, optimal employment stock is determined by the exogenous output level and the wage costs of male youths relative to other groups, and a quadratic time trend to proxy (exogenous) capital stock growth. They write

$$L_y^* = g(Q, t, t^2, W_y/W_1, W_y/W_2, \ldots, W_y/W_n) \qquad (3.2.5)$$

where:
L_y^* is the demand for male youths, Q is output, t, t^2 a quadratic time trend and W_y/W_i are the wages of male youths relative to male adults, female adults, etc.

A partial adjustment equation where actual employment L_y adjusts slowly is postulated:

$$L_y(t) - L_y(t-1) = a(L_y^*(t) - L_y(t-1)) \qquad (3.2.6)$$

The model (substituting equation (3.2.5) in equation (3.2.6)) is estimated in log-linear form on annual data (1952–72). The authors follow recent econometric methodology to find an appropriate dynamic specification. The results (using autoregressive least squares) are robust (for that period) and suggests that youth labour is a *substitute* for female labour. They find that the relative labour cost elasticities are significant and relatively large. The output elasticity is greater then (but not significantly different from) unity, which supports the view that youths suffer proportionately more in cyclical downturns.

Unlike much of the work on young people, the Hutchinson *et al.* research is a careful piece of systematic and rigorous econometric modelling. However, not too much weight should be put on these results for four reasons:

1. The data are from an early period prior to changes in the age of majority (which happened towards the end of their sample), the introduction of various government policies aimed at the youth labour market, etc. The results may, therefore, be misleading for the present time.
2. At least part of the sample period is widely believed to be a period of excess demand in the labour market. As such, they may be observing points on a supply function (assuming a 'min' condition) – so that, for example, the finding of complementarity with adult males may be misleading. On the other hand, if this was a period of equilibrium they may have estimated a 'mongrel' relationship.
3. Strictly speaking, equation (3.2.5) is one of a system of equations with similar equations for young females, adult males, and adult females. Similarly, equation (3.2.6) should be specified with a matrix of adjustment coefficients so that the adjustment of *one* input depends on deviations from optimal levels of *all* inputs (*à la* Nadiri and Rosen, 1969).
4. As other input prices are excluded the estimated parameters may be biased. However, most other research in this field also ignores other input prices.

Labour Demand and Supply Equations

An obvious way to model the youth labour market is to set up demand and supply functions and to estimate the model by appropriate methods. In this framework we can either assume market clearing or not. In a market clearing model, if the identification conditions are satisfied, we can obtain the parameters of the structural equations. Some authors simply specify a demand equation assuming away problems of identification and treat wages as exogenous. This is analogous to the employment functions approach, except that it assumes complete adjustment within the unit period. For most non-market clearing models it is usually assumed that the quantities transacted are determined by the short side of the market: the so-called 'min' condition. These models can be estimated by either:

1. Assuming *a priori* which period is a demand- (supply)-constrained regime (see, for example, Merrilees and Wilson, 1979 and Wells, 1983).

or

2. Maximum likelihood estimation methods and letting the data determine the switching point(s) (see, for example, Rice, 1986 and section 3.2.4 below). The advantage of this method is that we use *all* the data to estimate the supply and demand functions, and that we can allow for more than one switch in regimes.

In an interesting study, Layard (1982) estimates a demand system (derived from a translog cost function) using data for manual workers in the British manufacturing sector (biannual 1949–69). Assuming that wages are exogenous and that the demand function is identified he estimates a system of equations for four inputs (boys, girls, adult males, adult females) using Zellner's (1962) SURE methods imposing symmetry restrictions.[12] Layard finds significant and negative own-price elasticities (girls do not have a significant coefficient) and finds that there is a high degree of substitutability between the different kinds of labour. In parentheses, it is worth noting that only half of the wage terms are significant at usual levels. These results should be treated with caution for four reasons:

1. The data are for manufacturing only. The evidence suggests that a large proportion of youths (especially females) work in the services sector. The data are very old and the manufacturing sector has declined substantially since 1969.
2. Although the use of duality theory is valid under the assumption of exogenous wages and cost-minimising behaviour, there is no guarantee that the stochastic equations are dual. There is some evidence of misspecification in the low Durbin–Watson statistics reported. Note also that he does not allow for any dynamics but assumes instantaneous adjustment.
3. If – as we shall argue – there was a disequilibrium in the labour market, it is invalid to estimate a labour demand system over his sample period. Many people would argue that the period 1949–69 was one of excess demand, and hence the observations may be coming from a supply function. Even in an equilibrium framework, the demand function may not be identified.
4. The estimated elasticities may be sensitive to the use of alternative cost shares. Many of the elasticities have relatively large standard errors. With a high proportion of females working in the services sector, these elasticities cannot be extrapolated to the whole economy.

Overall, although this is an interesting application of duality theory to the labour market, it ignores the supply side of the market and the results should therefore be handled carefully.

We now turn to recent attempts which treat the youth labour market as being in disequilibrium. An important study using this approach was by Merrilees and Wilson (1979), using annual data from 1952 to 1978.

The authors use *a priori* information to separate the sample into excess demand (supply-constrained) and excess supply (demand-constrained) regimes. In their study they evaluate the evidence on unemployment and vacancies and reports from the Youth Employment Service to determine that the period 1952–69 was a period of excess demand for males and the period after that one of excess supply. For females they consider the period 1952–71 as one of excess demand and the period 1972–8 as one of excess supply. They also use (Chow) stability tests to confirm their 'professional judgement'.[13] They find that an equilibrium model performs poorly compared to a disequilibrium model: the supply equation is identified for the earlier period and the demand equation for the latter period. Further, they find that real wages do not adjust to clear the market. Overall, the study is an important first step in estimating a disequilibrium model. Their results suggest an important role for aggregate demand, a significant relative wage coefficient, and a positive effect on employment of government policies.[14] As we shall argue in the next section, OLS estimation of this model with *a priori* sample separation leads to truncated error terms and hence inconsistent parameter estimates.

In a recent study Rice (1986) estimates a disequilibrium model using annual data for 1953–79.[15] Using the Maddala-Nelson (1974) approach she finds that for teenage males the period until 1972 was one of excess demand and after 1972 one of excess supply. For teenage females she finds the period until 1963 one of excess demand, excess supply until 1966, excess demand until 1970 and excess supply thereafter – in other words, multiple switches. She finds that-although relative wages are significant in explaining the rise in unemployment-the aggregate demand effects are quantitatively more important for males. This study is a significant contribution to the literature and is impressive in the way that she carried out a sequence of hypothesis tests. Unfortunately, her data set ends just before the sudden increase in unemployment.[16]

3.2.3 A critique of wells (1983)

In this section we evaluate Wells (1983) using his model as a vehicle for investigating various aspects of the youth labour market. We begin this section by an outline and evaluation of Wells's theoretical model and a summary of his conclusions, followed by a battery of tests of dynamic specification, error specification, stability tests, and tests of robustness.

The Model

Following in the footsteps of Merrilees and Wilson (1979) (henceforth M–W) Wells sets up in Chapter 7 a log-linear disequilibrium model. Wells uses several different aspects of the labour market to justify the view that relative wages are exogenously determined. However, he does not attempt to formulate an econometric model to justify these conclusions. His model is specified as follows:

$$\ell n L_i^S = a_0 + a_1 \ell n(PPOP)_i + a_2 \ell n(WAGE)_i + \varepsilon_1 \quad (3.2.7)$$

$$\ell n L_i^D = b_0 + b_1 \ell n(UX_M) + b_2 \ell n(RLC)_i + \varepsilon_2 \quad (3.2.8)$$

$$\ell n L_i = \min(\ell n L_i^S, \ell n L_i^D) \quad (3.2.9)$$

where:

L_i^S is labour supply of the *i*th group
L_i^D is labour demand of the *i*th group
$PPOP_i$ is the population of the relevant age group less the number in full-time education, *less* the number in the armed forces (including National Service)
UX_M is the male unemployment rate excluding school leavers
$WAGE_i$ is the real average weekly earnings *less* tax and national insurance of full-time manual workers of the relevant group (strictly speaking, a supply function should use a *wage rate* and not earnings)
RLC_i are the relative labour costs (gross earnings *plus* the employers' national insurance contribution) of youths (males under 21, females under 18) relative to adults.

This specification (estimated in first differences of logs) and the sample separation (1969 for male, 1971 for females) is taken directly from M–W.[17] In general he also includes a lagged relative labour cost term. The model is presumably based on usual neoclassical maximising theory. To justify an aggregate demand (cyclical) variable in the labour demand function we need to assume cost-minimising firms. This implies that the appropriate variable should be an index of production (for example, GDP or industrial output): the unemployment rate is a 'lazy indicator' of cyclical movements. Although the study emanates from the Department of Employment, there is no attempt to model the impact of various Special Employment Measures (SEM), There are, however, numerous references to SEMs to explain poor or conflicting results. *A priori* we would expect the SEMs to affect the demand for youths, perhaps by altering the elasticity with respect to *RLC* (since the SEMs are implicit subsidies to employers).

The labour supply function is specified in such a manner (in the definition of *PPOP*) that individuals have no choice to stay on in education or to join the armed forces.[18] There is also no attempt to study the impact of social security benefits on labour supply, and so the estimated wage elasticity may be biased.

One final comment on the specification: the model is estimated separately for males and females, for under 18 year olds, 18–19 years olds, and under 20 year olds. This assumes a heterogeneity of labour with employers demanding each kind of labour. Presumably the demand for 18 19 year olds will be derived from the *previous* employment of under 18 year olds, since they would have acquired relevant skills and experience. The unemployed 18–19 year olds would not be competing in the same market. It is worth stressing that the labour market is *not* an auction market where the entire labour supply is thrown on the market in each period: there are several existing contracts (implicit or explicit). This suggests that aggregation over the different age groups is a hypothesis to be tested. In particular we would expect the results of the under 18 year olds to be affected by the SEMs. This suggests that Wells's model needs to be respecified differently for different age groups.

The Data and Wells's Results

Wells uses annual data from1953 to1981and estimates supply functions for 1953–69 (for males) and 1953–71 (for females) and demand functions for 1969–81 (males) and 1971–81 (females). In other words, his regressions are run on 17 and 13 observations for males and 19 and 11 for females which means there are very few degrees of freedom and the usual caveats for small samples apply. Perhaps more importantly, the data for the crucial dependent variables (employment by age groups) are obtained from the NI card count up to 1972 and after that by extrapolation (for 1973 and 1974) and interpolation (as an arithmetic mean) between the biennial Labour Force Surveys. In other words, *for the latter period approximately half the observations for the dependent variables were crudely interpolated data.* Similarly, a key (for Wells) right hand side variable-the wage or relative cost variable – was obtained from the October Enquiry until 1979 and *the data for 1980 and 1981 were estimates obtained from the New Earnings Survey.*[19] This was obtained by regressing the October Earnings data on the New Earnings Survey (NES) data from 1971–9. Again, this makes the estimates for the latter period shaky: no sensitivity analysis was carried out. The data are for mainly the industrial sector and exclude many services and hence are (in particular) inappropriate for females. (It is also worth noting that the employment data are mid-year estimates while the wages (costs) data are for October. We have centred these data and report our results later.)

Let us now summarise Wells s findings:

1. The disequilibrium approach (with *a priori* sample separation) is superior to the equilibrium approach
2. The results for the under 18 year olds allegedly support his model, while the results for 18–19 year olds and under 20 year olds are recognised to be inadequate
3. Labour supply is positively related to wages (earnings) and *PPOP*
4. Labour demand is negatively related to relative labour costs and to the unemployment rate which is an index of aggregate demand (the cyclical

factor); however, the cyclical variable is not significant for females[20] – it is this result which has given much joy to *The Times* editorial writer (20 December 1983) and to the Thatcher government.

Before we provide a detailed critique it is worth noting that the only 'reasonable' results he obtains are for males under 18 years old. However, the wage variable is a relative wage *of under 21* to the 21 and over group. In general his Durbin–Watson statistics are in the indeterminate range which may suggest a misspecified model. Although Wells often treats the incidence of a structural break as supporting a (disequilibrium) switch point, it is worth stressing that this too could also reflect a misspecified model.

A Critique

Although we are sympathetic to the view that we should treat the youth labour market in terms of a disequilibrium model, we find that Wells's work is inadequate on several grounds. First, although he provides a plethora of results, he does not carry out any specification tests to compare alternative models. In particular, although he estimates numerous models (especially in Chapter 9) there are no tests provided which would show the superiority of one model over the others.[21] Second, there are no tests of dynamic specification of the model. On p. 71 he argues that some alternative lag structures were tried and 'if the explanatory power of the equation collapses with a different lag structure, it may cast suspicion on the results'. Again, this is an unusual approach. Third, there are no tests of the error specification implied by the first differencing of the equations. Finally, OLS estimation leads to inconsistent results when the sample is separated (because of truncated error distributions).

In our work we first replicated Wells's results, and then carried out various hypotheses tests:

1. Dynamic and error specification
2. Stability tests
3. Tests of robustness.

Dynamic and error specification

Wells estimates his model in terms of first differences of logarithms without any justification. To test his specification we carried out the following tests on the data for the sub-periods. Let:

$$y_t = \alpha_0' + \sum \alpha_i' X_{it} + u_t \tag{3.2.10}$$

and

$$u_t = \rho u_{t-1} + \varepsilon_t \tag{3.2.11}$$

where the *ys* and *Xs* are logged variables except one *X* variable which is a time trend. First differencing (3.2.10) gives:

$$\Delta y_t = a_0 + \Sigma a_i \Delta X_{it} + \varepsilon_t \tag{3.2.12}$$

which is the form of equation estimated by Wells. We could test the error specification by estimating equation (3.2.10) by autoregressive least squares and test the hypothesis $\rho = 1$. Another test of error specification is to use a Lagrange Multiplier (LM) test for residual autocorrelation in equation (3.2.12). We find that Wells's equations do fairly well on an LM test except for the female labour supply equations for the under 18s and the 18 19 year old groups. However, when we estimate equation (3.2.10) and test for $\rho = 1$ we find that we reject the hypotheses *in all cases* for males but accept the hypothesis for half the cases for females (case = age/demand/supply).[22]

A summary of these results is presented in Table 3.2.1.

A further test was to rewrite equation (3.2.12) as:

$$y_t = a_0 + \lambda y_{t-1} + \sum a_i X_{it} + \sum \beta_i X_{it-1} + \varepsilon_t \tag{3.2.13}$$

and test the restrictions: $\lambda = 1$ and $a_i = -\beta_i$ for all i. A likelihood ratio test rejected the restrictions for all the supply equations (the earlier period) except for the under 18s. For the demand equations (the latter period) the restrictions were rejected only for the females under 18 (see Table 3.2.1).

Table 3.2.1 Test results

	Hypothesis	$\rho = 1$	U_t not auto-correlated	$\lambda = 1, \alpha_i = -\beta_i$	Parameter stability*
Males					
Demand	<18	Reject	Accept	Accept	Accept
equations	18–19	Reject	Accept	Accept	Accept
1969–81	<20	Reject	Accept	Accept	Accept
Supply	<18	Reject	Accept	Accept	Accept
equations	18–19	Reject	Accept	Reject	Accept
1953–69	<20	Reject	Accept	Reject	Accept
Females					
Demand	<18	Accept	Accept	Reject	Reject 1972
equations	18–19	Reject	Accept	Accept	Accept
1971–81	<20	Reject	Accept	Accept	Accept
Supply	<18	Accept	Reject	Accept	Accept
equations	18–19	Reject	Reject	Reject	Reject 1965
1953–71	<20	Accept	Accept	Reject	Reject 1969
Rejection frequency (%)		75	17	42	25

Notes: All tested at 95% level.

*Equations estimated over the *whole* period, by Recursive least squares.

Overall these results provide only partial support for the dynamic specification adopted by Wells.

Stability tests

As mentioned earlier, tests of the parameter stability provide us with information about the robustness of the model and may also indicate switches in regimes. We used Brown, Durbin and Evans's (1975) recursive residuals Cusum Square test for this purpose.[23] Interestingly, this method suggests a significant break *only for females.* The significant breaks are for under 18 year old females at 1972 (demand equation), 18–19 year old females (supply equation) at 1965, and under 20 year old females (supply equation) at 1969. The absence of any obvious 'switch' point (especially for males) suggests that Wells's model may be inadequate to detect disequilibrium behaviour. This issue is discussed further in section 3.2.4 below.

Tests of robustness

In this sub-section we estimated Wells's model with an alternative definition of the cyclical variable and with alternative wage (cost) variables. We argued earlier that – if the labour demand function is derived from cost-minimising behaviour – an appropriate aggregate demand (cyclical) variable is an index of GDP (excluding North Sea Oil) and not the unemployment rate.

The results with the difference of the log unemployment being replaced by the difference of the log of GDP (*less* oil, *MLH 104*) in Wells's demand equations – led to some changes. The significance of the relative labour cost terms (*RLC*, RLC_{t-1}) increased for males but decreased for females (see Table 3.2.2). In addition, the absolute value of the output elasticity increased with this specification, although still not significant. See Appendix Table 3.2.A1 for Wells's results with the unemployment rate.

In an earlier section we commented on the fact that while the employment data were for June, the wages (costs) data were for October. For consistency, we used a weighted average of the wages variable:

$$\bar{W}_t = 0.75W_t + 0.25W_{t-1}$$

Introducing this weighted average wages term in the labour supply equations leads to a decrease in the coefficients and an increase in its significance.[24] We then estimated the demand equations with a GDP index and with weighted relative labour costs. As before, the GDP index was not significant for any group but the weighted labour cost terms were significant only for males under 18.

As a further test of the sensitivity of Wells's results we estimated his labour demand equations with a relative labour cost variable for the under 18s to the 21 and over group for males (females) to correspond with the dependent variable (employment of under 18s). This relative labour cost

Table 3.2.2 Wells's demand equations: tests for robustness

	Constant	Relative labour costs	Relative labour costs (t–1)	GDP	R^2	DW
Males 1969–81						
<18	–0.008	–3.993	1.682	0.359	0.73	2.52
	(0.58)	(4.54)	(1.99)	(0.81)		
18–19	–0.032	–0.870	1.808	0.882	0.25	2.17
	(1.55)	(0.63)	(1.35)	(1.26)		
<20	–0.022	–2.264	1.823	0.628	0.44	1.65
	(1.68)	(2.62)	(2.20)	(1.45)		
Females 1971–81						
<18	–0.060	–0.781	–0.938	0.562	0.36	0.69
	(2.35)	(0.93)	(1.56)	(0.43)		
18–19	–0.007	–0.118	0.004	0.303	0.02	1.41
	(0.40)	(0.23)	(0.01)	(0.38)		
<20	–0.031	–0.472	–0.414	0.430	0.27	0.54
	(2.04)	(0.93)	(1.15)	(0.55)		

Notes:
1. All variables are first differences of logs.
2. Absolute *t*-statistics in parentheses.

Overall, Wells's model is poorly specified and his results are not robust. They should, therefore, not be used for any policy purposes.

variable was constructed from NES data (which we believe is more representative for the young) and then following Wells's procedure to obtain estimates for the pre-1970 (in some cases pre-1974) data.[25] It is interesting to note that these data series are very different for males but very similar for females (see Figures 3.2.1 & 3.2.2).[26] For Wells, the male relative labour cost series is upward trended (more or less) throughout the period, which picks up the *declining* trend in employment since the 1960s. Using the NES data we have a declining trend for males until the early 1970s, rising due to the raising of school leaving age and then declining again (except for a minor blip in 1979).

The results with our NES-based series (Table 3.2.3) suggest that Wells's model breaks down completely for males with *no* significant parameters, poor R^2s and very low *DW*s. The female equations, although slightly better, suffer from problems of serial correlation.

3.2.4 A disequilibrium model of the youth labour market

In this section we outline a disequilibrium model of the youth labour market taking account of some of the criticisms we made of earlier work. We estimate this model by maximum likelihood methods using the density

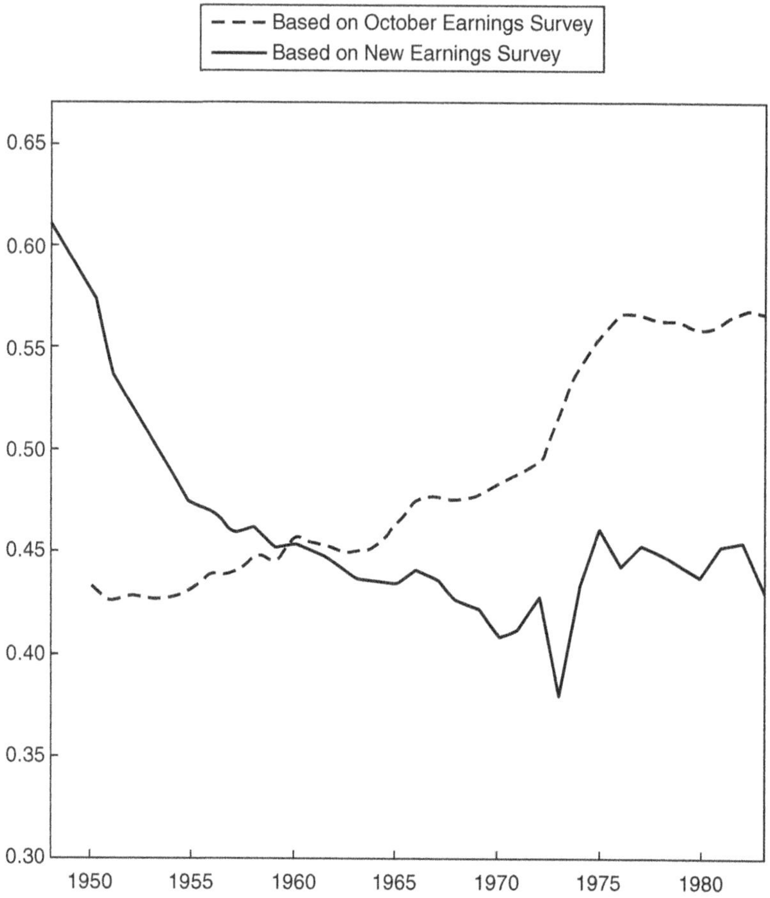

Figure 3.2.1 Relative labour costs: males

functions provided by Maddala and Nelson (1974, Model 1). Before we turn to our model and estimates we list our four objections to the *a priori* sample separation assumed by M–W and Wells (1983).

1. Their method is extreme in classifying regimes with probability 1
2. They assume a single switch point
3. It removes from the field of empirical study what is perhaps the most interesting phenomenon in this area, namely the timing and extent of disequilibrium
4. When used in combination with OLS, even if the assumed sample separation is correct, it will give rise to inconsistent estimates.

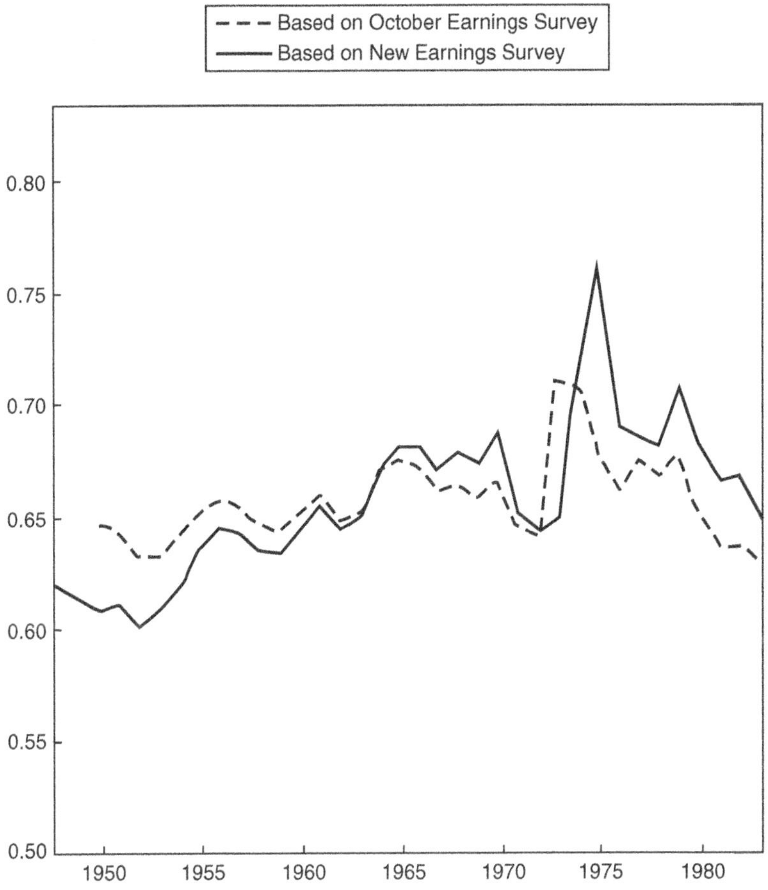

Figure 3.2.2 Relative labour costs: females

As M–W and Wells estimated their models in first differences of logs it would not make sense to estimate their model with a min condition. We are therefore unable to provide a set of comparable disequilibrium estimates.

We propose the following model:

$$L_t^D = L^D(\bar{Q}_t, WRLC_t, SMD, t, L_{t-1}) + \varepsilon_1 \quad (3.2.14)$$

$$L_t^S = L^S(Pop_t, W_t, SB_t, NSD, t, UR_t) + \varepsilon_2 \quad (3.2.15)$$

$$\mathrm{L} = \min(\mathrm{L}^D, L^s) \quad (3.2.16)$$

Table 3.2.3 Alternative models of employment: A reworking of Wells's Tables 13 and 14 (dependent variables: employment (females) under 18)

	Estimating Period	C	NES RLC	NES RLC(t–1)	CYC	R^2	DW
Males under 18	(1)	–0.0222	–0.4308	–0.5300	–0.0388	0.1264	0.6154
		(1.10)	(0.48)	(0.54)	(0.76)		
	(2)	–0.0396	0.0384	–0.0487	0.0332	0.0245	0.8080
		(1.81)	(0.09)	(0.12)	(0.32)		
	(3)	–0.0200	0.0231	–0.1012	–0.0249	0.0234	0.7225
		(1.69)	(0.08)	(0.35)	(0.54)		
Females under 18	(4)	0.0035	–0.0319	–1.3304	–0.0728	0.2692	0.6617
		(0.25)	(0.04)	(1.73)	(1.19)		
	(5)	–0.0557	–0.8236	–0.4324	0.0119	0.4254	0.6345
		(2.24)	(1.90)	(0.97)	(0.12)		
	(6)	–0.0150	–0.7632	–0.3315	–0.0692	0.2186	0.6253
		(1.26)	(2.19)	(1.01)	(1.46)		
Males under 18	(1)	–0.0434	–0.2661	–0.8858	0.0085	0.1316	0.4892
		(1.63)	(0.29)	(1.01)	(0.81)		
	(2)	–0.0334	0.0340	–0.0047	–0.0029	0.0229	0.8388
		(1.58)	(0.07)	(0.01)	(0.29)		
	(3)	–0.0244	0.0015	–0.1484	0.0013	0.0143	0.7021
		(1.74)	(0.00)	(0.53)	(0.19)		
Females under 18	(4)	–0.0079	0.6613	–0.9991	0.0008	0.2001	0.5462
		(0.28)	(1.02)	(1.18)	(0.07)		
	(5)	–0.0509	–0.8743	–0.5034	–0.0054	0.4563	0.7445
		(2.34)	(2.15)	(1.18)	(0.64)		
	(6)	–0.0283	–0.5756	0.3279	0.0047	0.1726	0.5167
		(1.92)	(1.74)	(0.94)	(0.79)		

Notes:
All variables are first differences of logs.
NES RLC is a relative labour cost variable derived from NES data (see Appendix). *CYC* is the male unemployment rate.
All equations were estimated by OLS.
Estimating periods are: (1) 1953–69; (2) 1969–81; (3) 1953–81; (4) 1953–71; (5) 1971–81; (6) 1953–81.
Parentheses contain absolute value of *t*-statistics.

where:

$\bar{Q}_t = \sum_{i=t}^{40} \left(\frac{e_i}{E} q_i \right)$ = an employment weighted output index

e_i = employment in the ith industry
q_i = output of the ith industry
L = aggregate employment
$WRLC$ = weighted relative labour cost
SMD = a zero–one special measures dummy
t = time trend
L_{t-1} = lagged employment
Pop = population of males (females) under 18
W_t = earnings
SB = supplementary benefits
NSD = a zero–one National Service dummy (for males only)[27]
UR_t = adult unemployment rate.

The labour demand function is derived from a cost-minimising model with partial adjustment. $\bar{Q}_t$ is an index of aggregate production which takes account of changing industrial structure. A time trend is included to proxy for the growth of capital stock and changes in technology. The labour supply function allows for supplementary benefits to affect the decisions of the young and a time trend allows for changing preferences. The male unemployment rate is included to allow for any 'discouraged worker' effect.

The model was estimated (in log-linear form) by maximum likelihood methods on annual data 1953–81, and the results are presented in Table 3.2.4; the notes to Table 3.2.4 give details of the optimisation method. Using Kiefer's (1980) classification technique we find that there was excess supply for males for the period 1960–81 and for females for the periods 1956–63 and 1974–81. The labour demand function has plausible signs and magnitudes for most of the estimated parameters. The aggregate demand variable is significant but has a fairly small (large) elasticity for males (females). The relative labour cost variable has a small and insignificant (large and significant) coefficient for males (females). The SEM dummy turns out to be *positive* and significant.[28] The supply function also has plausible signs and magnitudes in most cases. There is evidence of a discouraged worker effect and the sign on supplementary benefits is 'perverse'.[29] Overall, these results are fairly encouraging. To reiterate, we find aggregate demand a significant variable in determining employment and relative labour costs are not well defined for males. It is interesting to note that the switch point(s) are very different from those that were chosen *a priori* by M–W and Wells. These results are very encouraging, and we feel that further work should investigate such models.

Table 3.2.4 A disequilibrium model: Maximum likelihood estimates

	Males <18	Females < 18
Demand		
CONSTANT	0.47(0.41)	–17.41 (0.49)
$\ell n\bar{Q}_t$	0.19(0.06)	2.16(0.06)
$\ell nWRLC_t$	–0.23 (0.13)	–3.92(0.02)
SMD	0.14(0.02)	0.11 (0.01)
t	–0.02(0.002)	–0.05(0.002)
ℓnE_{t-1}	0.71 (0.04)	0.87 (0.006)
σ_D^2	0.0009 (0.0002)	0.0001 (0.00002)
Supply		
CONSTANT	–2.64(0.04)	–2.56(0.30)
$InPOP_t$	1.43 (0.004)	1.17 (0.02)
$InWAGE_t$	0.29 (0.006)	0.65 (0.06)
$InSUPBEN_t$	0.33 (0.02)	0.04 (0.04)
NSD	–0.001 (0.0008)	
t	0.01 (0.0002)	–0.003(0.002)
InUR_t	–0.15(0.0006)	–0.15(0.004)
σ_S^2	0.00001 (0.000002)	0.001 (0.0002)
R_D^2	0.93	0.94
R_S^2	0.90	0.93
R_{min}^2	0.99	0.99
log likelihood	86.50	75.80
Periods of excess supply		
	M 1960–1981	
	F 1956–1963, 1974–1981	

Notes:
Asymptotic standard errors in parentheses
Optimisation was carried out by quasi-Newton methods using NAg routine EO4LBF on a Burroughs 6800 machine, using an analytical Jacobian and Hessian. The Hessian was also used to derive asymptotic standard errors of the parameters. Despite 'flattish' likelihood functions, the converged estimates are virtually invariant to the parameter starting values chosen, although from certain points the algorithm would crash first and, of course, the number of iterations involved could vary considerably.

3.2.5 Conclusions

In this chapter we have reviewed some of the literature on relative wages and the youth labour market. Our major finding is that the youth labour market is best described as being in disequilibrium, with some periods of excess demand and some of excess supply. We argued that much of the earlier work which assumed an equilibrium to estimate demand or employment functions should be treated with caution. We paid particular attention to Wells's work and found that his model is poorly specified, theoretically and econometrically. In particular, we find that cyclical or aggregate demand variables are important in explaining the growth of unemployment. The impact of relative wages on youth employment is often not significant (in some models) and even when significant is quantitatively small. In our chapter we have pointed out several problems with the data, especially key variables like employment and relative wages. We would like to stress that the limited number of observations in an annual time series model when we use *a priori* sample separation makes the results very sensitive to the particular specification of the model. We argue that a way forward is to investigate the youth labour market using disequilibrium estimation techniques. Future work should also pay particular attention to SEMs.

Notes

1. The first draft of this chapter was written while the authors were at the Institute for Employment Research, University of Warwick. We are grateful to Ruth Hermitage for competent research assistance. We thank Bill Wells for providing his data set and details of sources can be found in Wells (1983) and in section 4.3 above. This chapter was first presented as a paper at the 'Young Persons' Labour Market Conference' held at the IER, University of Warwick. We thank our ex-colleagues at the IER and Conference participants for helpful comments. We would like to thank Bill Wells for comments on our paper although we did not agree with all of them. Remaining errors are our own responsibility.
2. See Lynch (1985)'
3. See Junankar (1984).
4. Of those not remaining in full-time education in 1983, 48 per cent entered the YTS: (*Employment Gazette*. October 1984–446).
5. See Doeringer and Piorc (1971).
6. To the extent that the young are involved in the underground economy this bias is, in part, mitigated.
7. See, for example, Maki and Spindler (1975) and criticisms of that approach in Junankar (1981).
8. However, this is not the way it is usually presented. In general, authors simply estimate equation (4.4) without any justification.
9. In some unpublished work Makeham (1981) reported a significant relative wage effect.
10. Note that a formal model suggests they should use aggregate *output* and not the unemployment rate or vacancies.
11. For a survey of this literature see Hazledine (1981).
12. Layard does not specify whether he tested the imposition of this restriction. As this model is estimated for the whole manufacturing sector, due to aggregation problems we suspect the restriction would be rejected by the data. Hart (1984) elaborates on this point.
13. Note that instability of parameters may reflect a misspecified model in a more general sense than simply a switch in regimes.
14. They estimated their model in first differences of logs and they stated that the implied restrictions 'were generally accepted at the 5 per cent level' (p. 34).

15. Our work on similar lines was carried out before we came across Rice (1986). There are some differences but we shall not deal with them in this paper.
16. This was because the October Earnings Enquiry ended in 1979, Since then, earnings data by age arc from the New Earnings Survey which is not a comparable data set. Wells has spliced the two series.
17. There are some minor differences which are of little significance. In chapters 9 and 10, Wells estimates several variants of the demand equation for the latter period. Wells estimates a large number of equations (approximately 100) with slightly different definitions of the dependent variables and alternative sets of independent variables. Given a very small data set, the tests of significance are pretty meaningless under these circumstances.
18. Note there was conscription (National Service; for males until 1959.
19. Note that the wage (cost) variables are for males (females) less than 21 (18) years and 21 (18) years and over. Although the dependent variables are more finely defined (e.g., males less than 18 years old) the right hand side variables have wage (costs) for less than 21 year olds as a proportion of persons 21 years and over,
20. In Chapter 9 he also estimates unemployment functions, where he finds the cyclical variable is very significant.
    In Chapter 9, Wells estimates alternative versions of the labour demand equation and generally finds that the female equation performs poorly. However, in almost all these *ad hoc* employment demand functions the cyclical variable is insignificant. It is possible that the relative labour cost variable (based on *earnings,* not wage rates) is picking up some cyclical effects.
21. At one stage (p. 71) he argues that in order to concentrate on substitutability or complementarity of different age and sex groups 'the cyclical term was dropped from the equations'. This is an untisual way of doing applied econometrics!
22. Details of these tests arc available on request.
23. Note that Garbade (1977) finds that this test has low power and a tendency to produce type II errors under the null hypothesis of stability. However, when we attempted to examine parameter stability via the Kalman filter route the estimates *never* converged; again indicative of poor specification.
24. Results available on request.
25. The precise method is described in the Appendix, p. 104.
26. This is probably because for males the NES data allows us to look at the under 18s, while Wells's data is for under 21s. For females the age separation (under to over 18s) is the same for both series.
27. Although conscription affected only the 18–21 age group, it may have indirect effects on the labour supply of the under 18s because of changing preferences to staying on at school as higher education would be interrupted.
28. This needs further investigation.
29. Similar 'perverse' results were found in Junankar and Price (1984). Note that an increase in supplementary benefit would (according to economic theory) reduce the actual labour supply. It may, however, lead to an increase in the 'apparent' labour supply as individuals 'pretend' to be in the labour market.

References

Brechling, F. P. R. (1965) "The Relationship Between Output and Employment in British Manufacturing Industries", *The Review of Economic Studies* 32 (3), 187–216.

Brown, R. L., J. Durbin, and J. M. Evans (1975) "Techniques for Testing the Constancy of Regression Relationships over Time", *Journal of the Royal Statistical Society. Series B (methodological)* 37 (2), 149–92.

Collier, P "Crisis in Youth Unemployment?" Manpower Research Group, research paper 33, 1978, Coventry: University of Warwick.

Doeringer, Peter B. and Michael J. Piore (1971) *Internal labor markets and manpower analysis*. Lexington, Mass: Heath.

Garbade, Kenneth (1977) "Two Methods for Examining the Stability of Regression Coefficients", *Journal of the American Statistical Association,* 72 (357), 54–63.

Hart, PE (1984) "Youth Unemployment and Relative Wages in the UK: A Survey of Recent Econometric Evidence", National Institute of Economic and Social Research, DP 70.

Hazledine, T (1981) "Employment Functions and the Demand for Labour in the Short-run", in Zmira Hornstein, Joseph Grice and Alfred Webb (eds.) *The Economics of the Labour Market* (London, HMSO)

Hutchinson, G., N. A. Barr and A. Drobny (1984) "The employment of young males in a segmented labour market: the case of Great Britain", *Applied Economics,* 16 (2), 187–204,

Junankar, P.N & S. Price (1984) "The Dynamics of Unemployment: Structural Change and Unemployment Flows" *Economic Journal,* Vol. 94, March 1984 (pp. 158–165).

Kiefer, Nicholas M. (1980) "A Note on Regime Classification in Disequilibrium Models", *The Review of Economic Studies* 47 (3). [Oxford University Press, Review of Economic Studies, Ltd.]: 637–39. http://www.jstor.org/stable/2297314.

Layard, Richard (1982) "Unemployment in Britain and the United States Compared" in The *Youth Labor Market Problem: Its Nature, Causes, and Consequences,* Richard B. Freeman and David A. Wise, eds., University of Chicago Press, Chicago.

Lynch, L. M. and Richardson, R. (1982), Unemployment of Young Workers in Britain, *British Journal of Industrial Relations,* 20, 362–372.

Maddala, G. S., and Forrest D. Nelson (1974) "Maximum Likelihood Methods for Models of Markets in Disequilibrium", *Econometrica,* 42 (6), 1013–30.

Makeham, P. (1980) "Youth Unemployment: An Examination of the Evidence on Youth Unemployment Using National Statistics, Department of Employment Research Paper 10, London, HMSO.

Makeham, P. (1981) "Youth Unemployment: Further Analysis", Department of Employment Technical Note, London, HMSO.

Maki, D. and Z.A. Spindler (1975) "The effect of unemployment compensation on the rate of unemployment in Great Britain", *Oxford Economic Papers,* vol. 27, no. 3.

Merrilees, W.J. and R.A. Wilson (1979) "Disequilibrium in the Labour Market for Young People in Great Britain", Manpower Research Group, Discussion Paper 10, Coventry: University of Warwick.

Nadiri, M.I and S. Rosen (1969) "Interrelated Factor Demand Functions", *American Economic Review,* 59 (4), 457–71.

OECD (1980) *Youth Unemployment: The Causes and Consequences,* Paris: OECD.

Rice, Patricia G. (1986) "Juvenile Unemployment, Relative Wages and Social Security in Great Britain", *The Economic Journal,* 96 (382), 352–74.

Wells, W. (1983) *The Relative Pay and Employment of Young People,* Department of Employment research paper 42, London: HMSO.

Zellner, A. (1962) "An efficient method of estimating seemingly unrelated regressions and tests for aggregation bias", *Journal of the American Statistical Association.* 57, 348–68.

Appendix relative labour costs

The New Earnings Survey (NES) based data on relative labour costs (*NES RLC*) used in the text were derived in the following way.

A. The NES manual earnings were regressed on the October Earnings Enquiry (*OEE*) data and a raising of school leaving age (*ROSLA*) dummy. The results obtained are presented below:

1. **Males**
   (a) Under 18

$$NES = 0.674 + 0.748\ OES(<21) - 1.921\ ROSLA$$
$$(0.47)\quad (22.89)\qquad\qquad (-2.46)$$
$$R^2 = 0.998 \qquad DW = 2.19$$

(Estimated on annual data, 1973–81)

   (b) 21 and over

$$NES = -2.210 + 1.002\ OES(\geqslant 21) - 1.798\ ROSLA$$
$$(-1.96)\quad (56.39)\qquad\qquad (-1.87)$$
$$R^2 = 0.998 \qquad DW = 2.19$$

(Estimated on annual data, 1970–81)

2. **Females**
   (a) Under 18

$$NES = -0.439 + 1.017\ OES(<18) - 2.225\ ROSLA$$
$$(-0.76)\quad (47.22)\qquad\qquad (-4.59)$$
$$R^2 = 0.998 \qquad DW = 1.49$$

(Estimated on annual data, 1971–81)

   (b) 18 and over

$$NES = -0.240 + 0.971\ OES(\geqslant 18) - 1.491\ ROSLA$$
$$(-0.31)\quad (47.61)\qquad\qquad (-1.99)$$
$$R^2 = 0.997 \qquad DW = 2.03$$

(Estimated on annual data, 1970–81)

B. The above estimated regressions were used to predict values for earnings from 1948 until *NES* data were published.

C. Labour costs were then obtained by adding the employer's NI contribution to the earnings data (part published and part 'predicted').

D. Relative labour costs were then derived as the ratio of labour costs of the under 18s to the 21 and over for males. For females it is a ratio of under 18s to 18 and over.

E. Note that since the age category for females is the same as in Wells the alternative series are similar. However, for males our NES-based series is a ratio of under 18s to 21 and over, while for Wells it is under 21s to 21 and over. In this case the series diverge quite markedly. In the OLS demand equations (Table 3.2.3) for the latter period (1969–81 for males, 1971–81 for females) predicted values are used for four observations for males and only one observation for females.

Table 3.2.A1 A selection of results from Wells (1983)

Demand equations

Table	11	13	15	12	14	16
Eq. no.	*D4*	*D4*	*D4*	*D4*	*D4*	*D4*
Period	1969–81	1969–81	1969–81	1971–81	1971–81	1971–81
Age	Teenage	<18	18–19	Teenage	<18	18–19
Sex	Male	Male	Male	Female	Female	Female
Constant	–0.01	0.00	–0.02	–0.00	–0.02	0.01
	(0.6)	(0.3)	(0.7)	(0.4)	(0.9)	(0.5)
RLC	–2.30	–4.31	–0.69	–1.44	–2.27	–0.67
	(2.5)	(5.1)	(0.5)	(2.9)	(2.5)	(1.0)
RLC_{t-1}	1.49	1.91	1.60	–0.81	–1.52	–0.23
	(1.8)	(2.4)	(1.1)	(2.9)	(3.0)	(0.7)
CYC	–0.06	–0.07	–0.06	–0.22	–0.34	–0.13
	(1.2)	(1.5)	(0.8)	(2.7)	(2.3)	(1.3)
R^2	0.22	0.70	0.00	0.47	0.45	0.00
DW	2.17	2.82	2.49	1.21	0.90	1.87

Supply equations

Table	11	13	15	12	14	16
Eq. No.	*S2*	*S2*	*S2*	*S2*	*S2*	*S2*
Period	1953–69	1953–69	1953–69	1953–71	1953–71	1953–71
Age	Teenage	<18	18–19	Teenage	<18	18–19
Sex	Male	Male	Male	Female	Female	Female
Constant	–0.01	–0.01	–0.02	–0.01	–0.00	–0.00
	(2.0)	(2.2)	(1.3)	(1.2)	(0.9)	(0.6)
PPOP	1.04	0.86	0.97	1.10	0.94	1.05
	(8.9)	(9.3)	(8.1)	(9.8)	(9.6)	(8.9)
WAGE	0.45	0.54	0.31	0.35	0.44	1.16
	(2.6)	(3.7)	(1.0)	(3.0)	(3.5)	(0.9)
R^2	0.85	0.86	0.81	0.85	0.84	0.81
DW	2.00	1.67	2.28	1.30	1.14	1.81

3.3
The Youth Labour Market: Anecdotes, Fables and Evidence

P.N. (Raja) Junankar, Matthew Waite and Grant Belchamber

1 Introduction

The aim of this chapter is to discuss some of the issues involved in assessing the evidence presented in empirical studies of the youth labour market (YLM). The main theme of this chapter is to emphasise the fragile nature of most of the evidence on YLMs. There have been numerous studies carried out in the USA and UK, and relatively few in Australia, which purport to show that youth unemployment is caused by the relatively high wages of youths relative to adults. However, most of these studies are based on poorly specified models, inadequate data, and inappropriate econometric techniques. Some of the evidence is based on anecdotes, some on text-book elementary competitive economy models (the fables of the title), and some eclectic models that attempt to take account of the very peculiar nature of the youth labour market. Section 2 discusses some general aspects of the youth labour market. Section 3 of the chapter discusses the different methods employed by economists to determine various aspects of the YLMs. Section 4 evaluates some of the existing research on the role of wages in influencing youth employment. Section 5 provides a critique of the Productivity Commission Report authored by Daly *et al.* (1998). Section 6 sets up a simple model of youth employment and provides estimates using data disaggregated by age, gender, and by industry. A critical question in the empirical evidence is to do with the elasticity of demand for youths with respect to wage rates. To give a preview of the main results, we find that in most cases the relative wage elasticity is statistically insignificant. Section 7 concludes the chapter with suggestions for future research.

Reprinted from 'The Youth Labour Market: Anecdotes, Fables and Evidence' by P. N. (Raja) Junankar, Matthew Waite and Grant Belchamber in *Employment and Labour Relations Review*, supplement to volume 11, 2000, 159–186. With kind permission from SAGE Publications.

2 Background

Firstly, it should be noted that there are very large inflows each year into the YLM, there are large flows between different labour market states, and the ageing process naturally leads to large outflows from the market. For various social, cultural, and institutional reasons there is a sequential decision process, if you leave school early then a few doors are closed to you in the future, e.g. tertiary education, white collar jobs, etc. Finally, it should be noted that the YLM (or for that matter any labour market) is not an auction market where the labour flows are auctioned at each period. Most people once they find work stay there for some time even if an alternative wage is higher, while employers do not fire employees when relative wages change. Changes in the economic environment simply lead to changes in wastage rates, in hiring rates, etc. In other words, it is *the flows* that may respond to economic changes; the stocks of employees do not change significantly, see Junankar and Neale (1987). Figure 3.3.1 provides a simple flow chart that shows the different "choices" (some voluntary, some involuntary) available at key ages. In fact reality is even more complicated than the flow chart since many people in school/higher education are also part-time workers (employment status and educational status are not mutually exclusive).

Employers may prefer young people because they are paid a lower wage, are less likely to be unionised, and are less likely to complain. When times are good employers hire the young, but when things worsen the young are not hired, and are the first to be fired on a last-in-first-out basis, see the papers in Junankar and Neale (1987). The young are also likely to be more mobile and leave voluntarily and suit the employers who do not need skilled labour. The young are also willing to take on repetitive and boring tasks as long as it is only part-time work and which they do not see as leading to a long-term career. Most of the young are hired in retail trades as salespersons and general hands. These occupations and industries are cyclically sensitive and hence there are big changes in employment and unemployment (see ABS Cat. 6203).

Underlying the neoclassical paradigm is the view that price signals play a paramount role in resource allocation, while an alternative paradigm (e.g. the segmented labour market paradigm) suggests that there are many sociocultural influences that play an important role. Recently, see Marceau (1989) there has been a move towards thinking of the industrial and employment structure as being influenced by the rapid advance of new technology, in particular the growth of the microprocessor revolution. Thus the rapid growth of part-time employment is explained, not by the lower costs of hiring part-time labour, but because of the change in technology relatively unskilled workers can be employed in small well defined tasks, the just-in-time-technology requires an adaptable and flexible labour force. It has been argued, see Marceau (1989, 1990), this has also led to a change in industrial

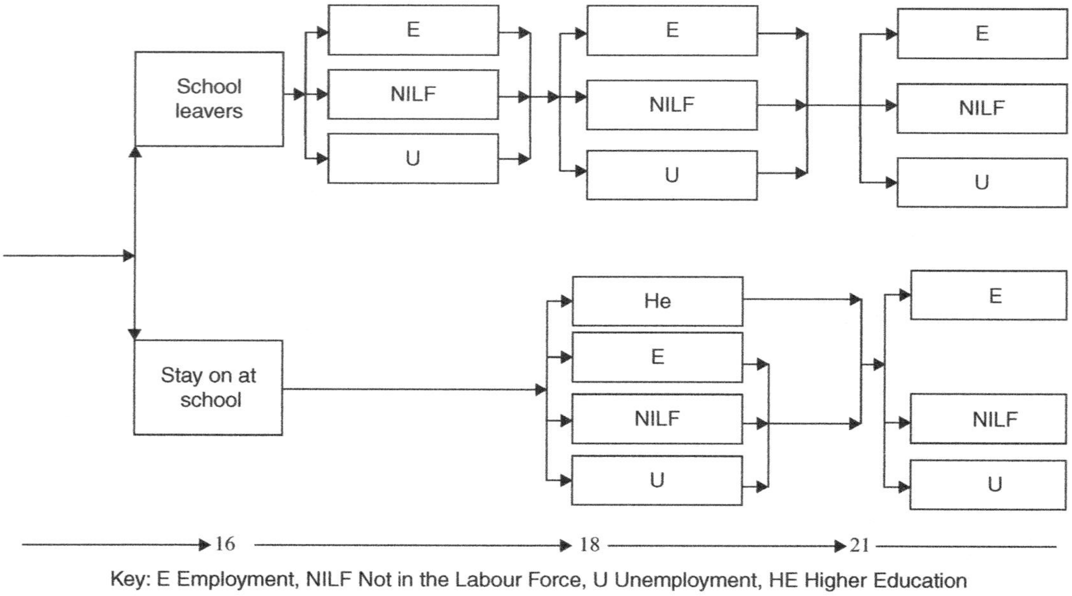

Figure 3.3.1 "Choices" at Critical Ages for Youths

structure such that the large corporate firm has many small dependent firms that provide the intermediate inputs. These small firms rely heavily on part-time labour. Also, in the service sector it is impossible to keep inventories, hence firms simply hire casual and part-time labour when the demand for their output is high. Secondary school students provide a pliant part-time labour force.

An analysis of youth labour markets (YLMs) may focus on the determinants of the different labour market states (employment, full-time or part-time, unemployment, not-in-the-labour force, education) or the *transitions* between different states (or gross flows between different states), or the wage rates of the young relative to adults. These studies could focus on determining the demand for, or supply of, different varieties of employment, training, education etc. either on an individual level or an aggregate level. The youth labour market is a fascinating market because of certain peculiar characteristics: there are large inflows each year into the labour market, there are large flows between different labour states, and the ageing process naturally leads to large outflows from the market. For various institutional reasons there is a sequential decision process: if you do not stay on at school at 15 then you cannot (usually) go into many forms of tertiary education, or into professional occupations like law or accountancy. If you leave school at 15 then you are likely to enter a secondary labour market with low wages, greater probabilities of being unemployed, and a flatter age-earning profile. Past government policies attempted to increase "retention rates" (i.e. of the 15 plus at schools) and there have been fairly large increases in students staying on in school.

Because of low wages and high turnover of youths (and low unionisation rates) firms might be expected to prefer hiring young workers. However, firms may prefer more responsible and better trained (older) workers. Some of the larger firms may go in for recruiting young workers to have a balanced age composition of their workforce. Why is it then, that the youth unemployment (employment) rates are more cyclically sensitive? Firstly, during a recession the first thing a firm does is to stop new recruitment that hits the young disproportionately. Secondly, this is exacerbated by the application of the last-in-first-out practice.

3 Models of the Youth Labour Market

The conventional analysis of YLMs begins with a neoclassical competitive labour market. The labour supply, education and training decisions are made by rational maximising individuals who look at the market wage rates, the expected wage rates after education/training, and the alternatives in terms of unemployment benefits. Labour demand is determined by looking at marginal productivity and relative (youth/adult) wage rates. Unemployment is explained either as a rational (voluntary) search strategy or as a result of

Government introduced minimum wage legislation, union imposed restrictions on wage rates etc. This suggests a set of economic variables that should be included in either a time-series or cross-sectional model.

An alternative framework contains elements of imperfectly competitive cost minimising firms working in non-Walrasian output rationed markets, segmented labour markets, and efficiency wages in the primary sector. Changes in aggregate demand accompanied by the changes in industrial structure (from large scale production in smoke-stack industries to small scale production in micro-chip firms, and to service industries) has shifted demand from full-time workers to part-time (and often married women) workers. Some of the youths join the primary sector where employers pay "high" efficiency wages (either to prevent shirking or to ensure peak efficiency levels are achieved for expensive capital equipment, or to decrease turnover). Insiders in the primary sector keep wages high and hence exclude new entrants into the labour market – the outsiders (youths). Because of efficiency wages, employers discriminate against youths because they *expect* them to have a high turnover, or expect them to shirk more, or to have a lower wage-productivity relation. In the secondary market, market clearing wages would be below "minimum wages" or below the social security benefits. Hence, there is unemployment.

This alternative framework would suggest that an analysis of YLMs should look at the characteristics of the output market of the firms, the wage-policies of firms, segmentation of labour markets, etc. Clearly, one important aspect would be the nature of the contract for casual part-time workers who would have few of the long-term benefits of full-time workers in the primary sector. It would also look at flows into the primary sector. It would look at flows between states (employment/unemployment/not-in-the-labour force) for different groups of workers in different types of firms. This would require a large amount of linked data on workers and firms.

The econometric work on YLMs using mainly time series data has consisted of:

(i) Unemployment functions
(ii) Employment functions
(iii) Labour supply functions
(iv) Participation rate functions (in the labour market, or in education)
(v) Labour demand and supply functions, either assuming equilibrium or allowing for disequilibrium. In the latter case the models are estimated by either separating the data, using *a priori* methods, into periods of excess demand or excess supply or by using a switching regression technique.

Econometric analysis of cross-section data, see Daly et al. (1998) estimates employment demand functions using data from the AWIRS 95 with the workplace as the unit of observation. The model assumes cost minimisation by firms subject to a production function.

Further details are provided below in Section 5.

Analysis of individual level data, or of panel data raises many interesting questions that are not relevant to this study. These studies usually estimate the probability of being unemployed (or employed or being at school) or the probability of transition from one state to another. Most of these studies then link these probabilities to the individual's characteristics and occasionally the local labour market tightness. These studies need to look at the characteristics of the firm, as well as the general state of the firm in relation to the output market.

Most of the time series models are based on single equations assuming competitive markets with equilibrium being *assumed* and identification of the demand or supply equation being assumed explicitly or implicitly. In many of these models it is assumed that the wage rate is exogenous, which is in contradiction to the maintained hypothesis of competitive markets! To reiterate the point, if we have competitive markets then the wage rate is an endogenous variable and we cannot manipulate it to increase youth employment or decrease unemployment. Strictly speaking we need to set up a model with a supply and demand equation, and assuming identifiability we can get separate estimates for each equation. However, once we allow for non-market clearing the situation is a little murky. Some of the papers simply assume excess supply (or excess demand) and assume a minimum condition for the market (i.e. the short side clearing condition). But this is a simplification with little justification in competitive theory. An alternative procedure is to use maximum likelihood estimation methods to estimate a switching regression model; i.e. let the data decide when we are in an excess demand or excess supply regime. See for example Rice (1986), Junankar and Neale (1987).

The actual estimates of wage elasticities we get are quite sensitive to the actual model specification, as well as to the data period over which the model is estimated. Often times it has a negative sign, although we suspect most people do not try to publish papers (or are not accepted for publication) if they find a positively sloped demand curve![2] Junankar and Neale (1987) provide a critical analysis of most of the British studies and those criticisms will not be listed here.

One of the main shortcomings of most of these papers is that they tend to concentrate on full-time employment (and unemployment) but do not go into estimating a system of equations where individuals are assumed to choose full-time or part-time employment, full-time or part-time education, or full-time or part-time training or apprenticeships. The logic of the neoclassical model dictates that these decisions are interdependent and hence a complete system of equations should be estimated with restrictions within and across equations. Especially since there has been such a significant growth in part-time employment of youths, especially of students, earlier estimates are likely to be seriously biased.

As mentioned earlier, most of the estimated equations have used inadequate data. In Australian studies most have focused on full-time employment, on using average weekly earnings, which may ignore changes in the composition of occupation or industry, see Section 5 below. Most seem to have ignored any influence of incomes policies, minimum wage policies, and labour market programs.

4 A Review of Some Earlier Research

In an important and influential report, BLMR (1983) *Youth Wages, Employment and the Labour Force* estimated employment demand functions for male and female youths. The report assumes competitive markets to estimate employment functions for female and male youths in terms of relative wages of youths to adults, of female adults to male adults, and total female and male employment. The model is based on cost minimising subject to a common production function over 17 different industries and over 6 years, (sliding along an isqquant for alternative relative wage rates). The model is estimated using Zellner's SURE method allowing for within and across equation constraints (although tests of the restrictions are not provided). The results provide negative and significant own price elasticities and positive cross elasticities. To focus on the own price elasticities, they find an elasticity of –1.8 for male youths and –4.58 for female youths, which is excessively large (the results are summarised in Table 3.3.2 in Daly et al., 1998).

Although the estimation is done with state of the art technology at that time, there appears to be a problem with assuming competitive markets and cost minimising employment demand functions. Strictly speaking with profit maximising behaviour we should have the real input prices (i.e. deflated by output price) and there should be no output (or aggregate employment) on the right hand side. We suspect a simple profit maximising model does not work unless we have output on the right hand side. A second problem with this estimation is the assumption of the same production function for all industries, but with different relative prices. In a competitive model there should be no difference in relative prices unless there are quality differences in the inputs. But then the estimation is not valid by aggregating labour into youths and adults. We think the negative elasticities are derived from the data more by differences in production functions across industries and by the quality differences in the types of labour employed in different industries. Note that the time dummies are insignificant implying all the variation is across industries. Also note the complete absence of dynamics in the estimation. For example in many of the service industries the labour employed is mainly unskilled. It seems what the estimates are saying is that some industries that employ relatively fewer youths have to pay higher wages for better quality of labour. The distribution of employment across industries is really determined by differences in technology. Given the award wage structure was such that relativities were more or less constant for several years we cannot conclude from these results that employment of youths can be increased by lowering relative wages. If we were to attempt to improve on this estimation it may be better to extend the data set and allow for fixed industry effects in the estimation.

To summarise, there are several qualifications that need to be made, and many are in the BLMR Report, before we can accept these estimates. However, most estimates from most studies suggest a negative relationship, so it might be argued that perhaps there is something in the sign even if the magnitude is suspect.

In a recent study of the impact of minimum wages on employment, the OECD Employment Outlook 1998 estimated cross country (pooled over time) regressions for a sample of OECD countries which had minimum wage legislation (curiously excluding Australia). They found that:

> Firstly, the results suggest that a rise in the minimum wage have a negative effect on teenage employment. Secondly, negative employment effects for young adults are generally close to or insignificantly different from zero. Thirdly, for prime-age adults, the most plausible specifications suggest that minimum wages have no impact on their employment outcomes. (OECD, Employment Outlook 1998:47-48)

However, they are cautious in their conclusion and emphasise the "fragility of the results in Table 3.2.5", (OECD 1998: 47). They add:

> At the same time, it is important to note that these estimated effects are relatively insignificant in terms of explaining the large decline that has occurred in the teenage employment-population ratio in some countries. (OECD, Employment Outlook 1998:48)

The employment elasticities are significant for the 15–19 year old groups but are relatively small, of the order of about minus 0.4. These are relatively small and for a group of young people for whom there has been a large increase in education. In other words, they have not allowed for young people choosing to stay on in education and simply assumed that the differences in employment over time and country are due to the employers cost minimising demand functions. The OECD *Employment Outlook* (1998: 70) indicates that differences and changes in school retention rates are likely to affect the estimates and this is a matter for further research. In fact it is likely the result is due to estimating a hybrid demand and supply equation.

The recent Productivity Commission report, Daly et al. (1998) provides a thorough investigation of the youth labour market and provides a review of the international literature. In the formal modeling they assume a cost minimisation process using the cost function approach pioneered by McFadden (1978). Due to econometric software constraints they use only youth labour (not disaggregated by gender) and adult male and adult female labour in the production process. Assuming weak separability they ignore the role of capital although they include a so-called "environmental variable": educational attainment. From this cost function approach it is easy to derive input demand functions by simply differentiating the cost function (which is the minimised costs as a function of input prices and other variables). This gives share equations (share of labour costs for labour of type i in total labour costs) in terms of relative wages and output (and environmental variables). Assuming an additive error term, imposing homogeneity and symmetry, and allowing for the implicit restriction (shares add to one) they estimate two share equations, (equations 9a or 9b: 51).

The data used were based on AWIRS 95 but the sample was restricted to workplaces where youths (15-20 year olds) were more likely to be employed: retail trade, accommodation, construction and manufacturing. A subset of this sample was also used where youths were used intensively. The data used were hours of employment, average weekly earnings, output was proxied by total hours worked in the workplace, and a "virtual education index" (presumably to proxy for compositional differences in the labour force). Since many workplaces did not employ any youths a "virtual wage" was estimated using a hedonic price index method. The authors use a bivariate tobit estimation procedure to allow for censored data: approximately 75 percent of workplaces do not employ any youth.

The Daly et al. study features an econometric exercise using cross-sectional data from AWIRS '95, yielding "best estimates [which] suggest that a 1 per cent increase in youth wages would lead to a decrease in youth employment of between 2 and 5 percent in industries employing a relatively high proportion of youth" [p. xiii].

5 Critique of Daly et al. (1998)

The data

The Daly et al. paper was intended and prepared as a "technical exercise to help inform the forthcoming review of junior rates of pay by the Australian Industrial Relations Commission" [AIRC], (p. iii).

The AIRC review of junior rates is concerned with *minimum rates of pay*, however Daly's elasticity estimates are based on an *average earnings* data set covering three groups – youth, adult males, and adult females.

Daly et al. assert:

> "... even among teenagers, who are often most affected by minimum wages, the proportion being paid the minimum wage is relatively small.

> Minimum wage studies do not say anything about what would happen if the wages of the remaining teenagers were changed relative to employees in other demographic groups."
> "Studies that can examine this question look at substitution between particular types of labour. The estimated responsiveness of youth employment to youth wages in these studies is considerably higher than the estimates from the minimum wage studies. The weight of evidence suggests a relatively large (much more than proportionate) decline in youth employment in response to an increase in the youth wage." [pp. xii, xiii]

Daly et al. do not discuss the relationship between changes in minimum wages for juniors and consequent changes in youth average earnings. The study does not attempt to quantify the 'spillover' effect to which it points in justification for its focus on youth average earnings. It does not assist to answer to question: "By how much will youth average earnings rise, for [any specified] increase in junior award rates of pay?"

We return to this issue below. However one point must immediately be acknowledged as a matter of logic. If *average* wages elasticities are 'considerably higher' than *minimum* wage elasticities for the same demographic group and the same minimum wage change, then the employment consequences of any increase in the minimum wage must be higher amongst workers not directly affected (i.e. those being paid more than minimum wage) than amongst those receiving wages at or in the neighbourhood of the minimum!

A further problem associated with use of average earnings data in lieu of minimum wage rates in the estimation of elasticities, is that average earnings may (and do in fact) vary over time or differ across sectors independently of any change in wage rates. Tables 3.3.1 and 3.3.2 demonstrate the importance of this effect.

In Table 3.3.1, the true price variable is held constant; we use retail rates as at June 1996 in this example. The employment data are those used for our own elasticity estimation (see below), and are described in the Appendix. The age-profile employment shares for 1986/87 and 1996/97 show a fall in the relative shares of the younger age groups and a rise for the older age groups, which together comprise "youth employment" in the Daly et al. study. This change in the age profile *within* junior employment causes "junior wages" as measured by junior average earnings, to rise significantly over the decade in the absence of any change in the price of labour.

A similar effect occurs in cross-section data, as Table 3.3.2 shows. Here, the age profile of junior employment in 1995 differs significantly between retail and manufacturing and accommodation, generating profound differences in "junior wages" as measured by youth average earnings.

Table 3.3.2 sets out a comparison of "junior earnings" calculated using award rates against the Daly et al. estimates of youth average earnings. It also shows benchmark award rates in each sector as at June 1995. An

Table 3.3.1 Compositional Change in Age: Employment Profile within Youth Employment

Age (year)		15	16	17	18	19	20	'Juniors'
Retail rates	($/wk)	163.10	203.90	244.70	285.50	326.20	367.00	
June 1996	($/hr)	4.29	5.37	6.44	7.51	8.58	9.66	
Hours worked								
Employment Shares								
All Employees	1986/87	6.3%	13.4%	18.5%	20.9%	21.3%	19.7%	100.0%
	1995/96	6.2%	11.1%	15.2%	21.5%	23.1%	23.0%	100.0%
Full-time	1986/87	2.6%	8.7%	16.3%	22.2%	25.3%	24.9%	100.0%
	1995/96	1.6%	5.3%	12.2%	22.2%	27.7%	31.0%	100.0%
Part-time	1986/87	16.5%	21.6%	19.1%	16.9%	13.4%	12.5%	100.0%
	1995/96	11.1%	17.2%	17.4%	19.7%	18.1%	16.5%	100.0%

'Youth Wages' as indicated by 'average youth earnings' assuming constant retail award rates

		All Employees ($/wk)	Full-Time ($/wk)	Part-Time ($/hr)
	1986/87	284.15	299.10	6.72
	1995/96	290.80	310.75	7.15
Percentage change		2.3%	3.9%	6.3%

immediate implication of this comparison is that the 'bite' of minimum wage regulation is much more pronounced in retail than in the manufacturing or accommodation sectors. The Daly et al. hourly youth earnings figure for retail is around 6% higher than the level indicated by retail award rates ($7.75 compared to award rates of $7.28); however for manufacturing the Daly et al. youth hourly earnings figure is more than 40% higher than benchmark award rates would suggest ($9.42 compared to award rates of $6.56). In accommodation the divergence is around 15% ($9.30 compared to award rates of $8.04).

If the orders of magnitude attaching to the age profile differences shown here are truly reflective of youth employment in the Australian labour market, then the Daly et al. elasticity is simply a statistical artifact quite inadequate for any assessment of the responsiveness of youth employment to changes in youth wages. The sectoral differences in youth average earnings are evidently *endogenous*, probably a function of firm choice of production technologies, and jointly determined with youth employment.

A further issue concerns the rather ad hoc restriction of the sample intended to overcome the high degree of censoring in the returns on youth employment – fully three quarters of firms in the AWIRS data set employ no youths. Since such a large percentage of the workplaces surveyed do not

Table 3.3.2 Compositional Difference in Age: Employment Profile within Youth Employment

Age (year)	15	16	17	18	19	20	'Juniors'
Award rates June 1995 ($/hr)							
Retail	4.21	5.26	6.31	7.37	8.42	9.47	
Manufacturing	3.06	3.93	4.80	5.67	6.85	8.11	
Accom etc	4.93	5.92	6.49	7.42	8.35	9.28	
1995/96 hours worked employment shares							
Retail	8.0%	13.4%	16.6%	22.0%	20.7%	19.2%	100.0%
Manufacturing	2.3%	4.8%	10.7%	20.5%	29.9%	31.7%	100.0%
Accom etc	3.1%	6.5%	10.1%	18.6%	27.7%	34.0%	100.0%
1995/96 'Youth Wages' implied by retail award wage rates*							'Junior wages' ($/hr)
Retail	0.34	0.71	1.05	1.62	1.74	1.82	7.28
Manufacturing	0.10	0.25	0.68	1.51	2.51	3.00	8.06
Accom etc	0.13	0.34	0.64	1.37	2.33	3.22	8.03
1995/96 'Youth Wages' implied by own award wage rates**							
Retail	0.34	0.71	1.05	1.62	1.74	1.82	7.28
Manufacturing	0.07	0.19	0.52	1.16	2.05	2.57	6.56
Accom etc	0.15	0.38	0.65	1.38	2.32	3.16	8.04
Productivity Commission estimate – average youth hourly wage***							
Retail							7.75
Manufacturing							9.42
Accom etc							9.30

Notes: * These are calculated using employment shares times the *retail* award rates for each age category

** These rates are the sum of wage rates for each year group divided by employment in each group

$$\sum\left(\frac{Minwage15}{Employment15}+\frac{Minwage16}{Employment16}+....+\frac{Minwage20}{Employment20}\right)$$

*** These rates taken from Table B.3 in Daly et al page 83.

employ young workers, it seems important to address the question "why not".[3] Simply allowing for censored data in an econometric analysis does not really explain why workplaces are not willing to hire youths who are relatively cheaper: firms should foe sliding along their isoquants to minimise costs and employ positive amounts of all varieties of labour.

Beyond these concerns focusing on the data used by Daly et al., we have great reservations about the econometrics reported.

Critique of Econometric Results

(i) One of the major shortcomings of this research paper is the measurement bias as a result of using average weekly earnings. Since employers (workplaces) could hire youths at the minimum wage, an interesting *economic* issue is why do they pay more than the minimum wage? Why are there differences across workplaces? If AWE are different from minimum wages is it because of efficiency wage considerations? Are AWE different across workplaces because of different firm (workplace) characteristics which also affect the firms' employment of youths? If so AWE is not an exogenous variable and it leads to estimation bias. For example in the manufacturing sector the AWE is much higher than the minimum wages, but in the retail sector the AWE are barely above minimum wages. In other words, minimum wages seem to "bite" in the retail sector but not the manufacturing sector. Another problem with using AWE on the right hand side is that the left hand side includes employment (which is used to derive the AWE variable, which may introduce spurious correlation).

(ii) Since a large proportion of workplaces do not hire youths the researchers use a "virtual wage" which is estimated using workplace characteristics. (The adjusted R^2 for the wage equations range from 0.07 to 0.17, in other words not a very good fit.) If wages in a workplace are a function of workplace characteristics then they recognise that wages are *endogenous*. If they use a virtual wage for a subset of the data they are introducing bias in their estimates. They should at least do some sensitivity analysis to see how their results vary if they estimate virtual wages for the *whole* sample, and allow for two standard error bands on virtual wages for this sensitivity analysis.

(iii) The use of a virtual wage however leaves unanswered the question, why do workplaces not hire youths? According to usual neoclassical theory for a convex compact production set firms would always employ a non-zero quantity of all inputs unless the input prices were infinitely high. It seems that a survey question should be added in future: "why do you not hire youths?"

(iv) Using cross section analysis to draw implications for changing minimum wages is fraught with problems. All they are estimating is the impact of wage *differences* on employment *differences*, not the impact of wage *changes* on employment *changes*.

(v) By imposing a common production structure on all workplaces in the sample they are potentially introducing aggregation biases in their estimates. This is recognised when they estimate industry regressions towards the end of Chapter 4.

(vi) Use of total hours instead of output (which is the appropriate variable with cost minimising) may lead to unknown bias in the estimates.

(vii) The PC study did attempt a time-series analysis using pooled data, but the results are not reported (purportedly) because of "unreliable estimates" attributed to multicollinearity in the data.

(viii) The youth own wage elasticity estimates are several times larger in the full sample than in the sub-samples focussing on industries where youths are employed intensively or in large numbers, yet the latter estimates are "roughly the same as the highest estimates obtained in overseas studies" (p. 57).

(ix) A major criticism of the results presented in Daly et al. is that they reject the homogeneity and symmetry restrictions of economic theory. As a result their estimates are invalid. They have assumed weak separability (p. 46) but then argue that the rejection of the restrictions may be due to the imposition of weak separability. In other words, their results are invalid: the theoretical restrictions are completely rejected and hence the estimated elasticities are meaningless.

It is immediately apparent that the question must be asked: "What *is* the PC elasticity and what does it measure?" The study does not assist the AIRC review of minimum wages, because the relationship between minimum and average wages for youth is left unspecified; moreover it is implicitly assumed to be the same across sectors in contradiction to the apparent evidence. In any event, the PC study does not produce real elasticity estimates relating the responsiveness of quantities to changes in prices.

Several other peculiarities attach to the PC study, including its curious result that finds adult women (and men) are *complements* not substitutes for youth in employment. That is, employment of adult women falls consequent on any rise in youth wages, according to the latest PC results; this is in contradiction with the 1983 BLMR results and with common sense.

The conclusions of the Report provide an interesting contradiction:

> "While the teenage wage has not changed much relative to the adult wage over time, teenage employment has declined relative to adult employment. For teenage full-time workers, wage costs and employment have both fallen relative to adults. For teenage part-time workers, wage costs and employment have both increased relative to adults. Neither trend is consistent with a strong degree of substitution between teenage and adult workers. Indeed, the trends suggest the opposite."
>
> "It is remarkable that these casual observations made by examining industry and economy-wide data over time, are born (sic) out by more formal econometric analysis of an entirely different dataset (sic)."
>
> "The analysis using AWIRS 95 dataset finds a significant and negative relationship between youth employment and youth wages." (Daly et al. 1998:67)

The first paragraph quoted above says there is *no* relationship between youth employment and youth wages and the latter two paragraphs claim

AWIRS 95 estimates support time series evidence even though they claim to have found a *negative elasticity* for youth wages! What are they trying to argue? How can the cross section results support the time series results, unless they do not believe the significance of the cross section results because of rejection of symmetry and homogeneity!

6 Modelling minimum wages and youth employment

In this section we set up a simple model to study the effects of minimum wages on youth employment. We assume that firms are cost minimising subject to a given level of output. This gives an equilibrium relationship between employment and relative wages and the level of output.[4] Assuming this equilibrium relationship is log linear we then allow for employment to adjust slowly towards its equilibrium value. This model is estimated for the following sectors: retail trade and manufacturing industries. The employment data are average hours times number of persons. The employment data covers all occupational groups except those deliberately excluded (1) Managers, (2) Professionals, (3) Para-professionals, and (4) Tradespersons and related workers. In other words the groups included are (5) Clerks, (6) Sales workers, (7) Plant and machine operators and drivers, and (8) Labourers. This includes the groups most likely to be affected by minimum wages and hence should provide the largest elasticity for the impact of minimum wages. In other words, we are stacking the cards against the probability of finding a zero elasticity. The data used in our estimation are discussed in detail in an Appendix (available on request from the authors) which also discusses the institutional aspects of minimum wage fixing in Australia. What is important to note is that we have used *minimum wage* data for youths (by gender) and disaggregated by individual year of age, part-time and full-time, and by industry: this means that we estimate 38 equations for each case. The adult wages used are the adult minimum wage or Average Weekly Earnings. All wages data are deflated by the CPI to obtain real minimum wages and real AWE. When we use relative wages we use the ratio of the youth minimum wage to the adult average weekly earnings (as the junior minimum wages are a fixed percentage of the adult minimum wages) in the appropriate industry. However, for manufacturing we used both: the relative wage of youths to adult minimum wage, and to AWE. The output data are obtained from the ABS for the appropriate industry. All data are seasonally unadjusted quarterly data from 1987(1) to 1997 (2).

Figures 3.3.2 and 3.3.3 provide a guide to the subsequent econometric work: they show the hours of employment for full-time workers alongside their relative wages for the different years of age. In manufacturing industry employment is declining gently and at the same time relative wages are also declining, which is contrary to simple neoclassical economics. In the retail trade we see employment is either declining gently or more or less constant

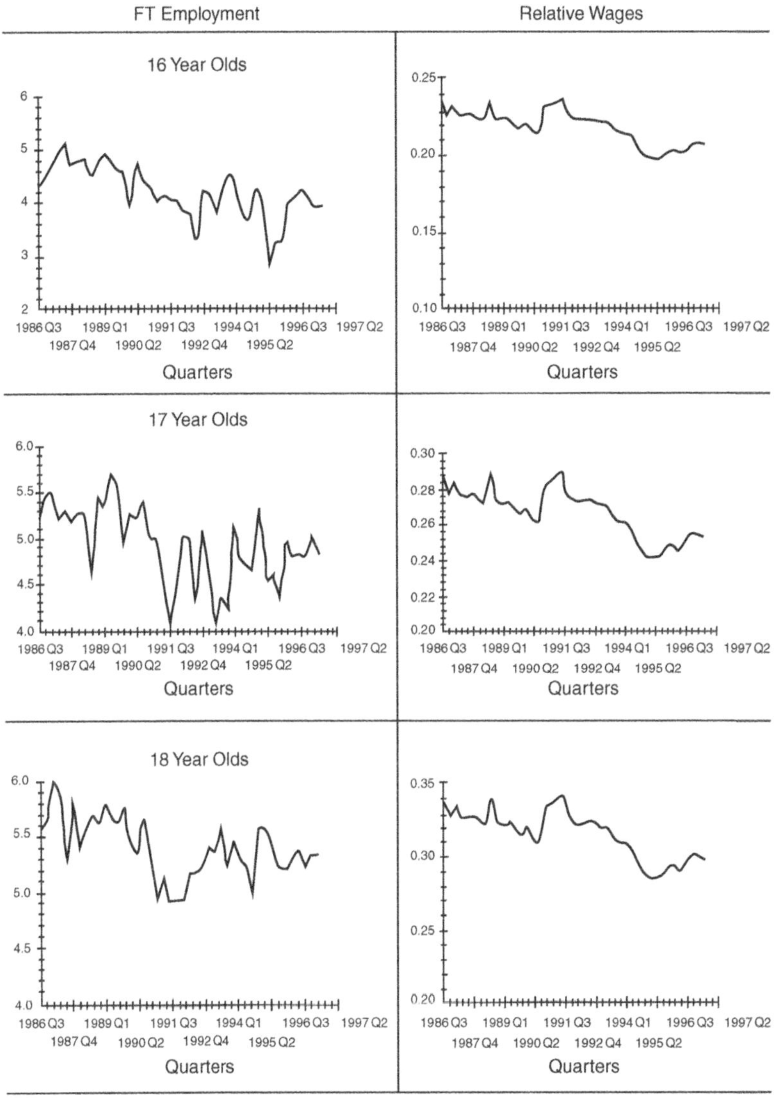

Figure 3.3.2 Manufacturing, 3rd Quarter 1986 to 2nd Quarter 1997
Notes: Employment = Average hours worked * No. of persons employed
Wages = Ratio of youth minimum wages to adult Average Weekly Earnings for the industry.

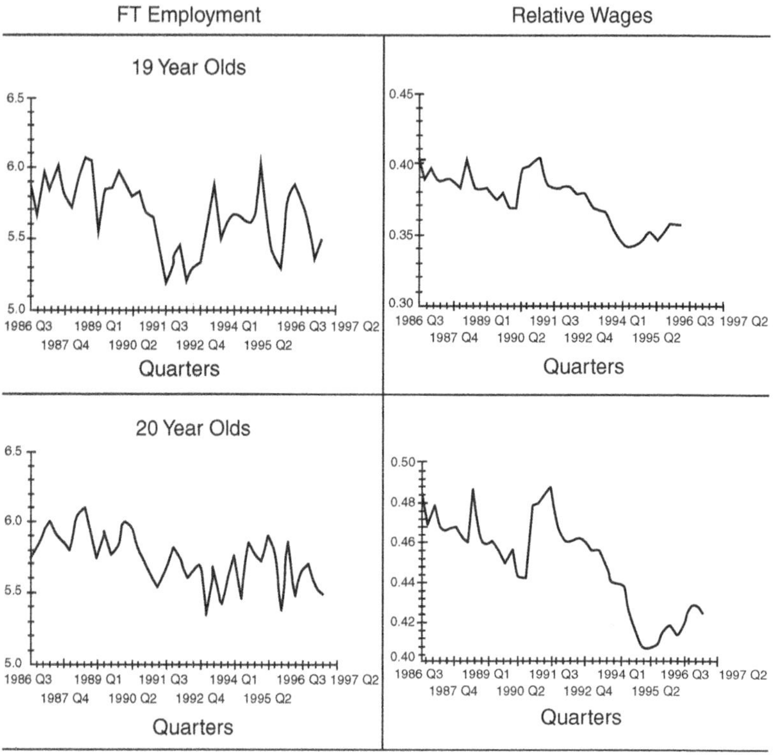

Figure 3.3.2 Continued

over time while relative wages first decline and then rise sharply. Again this graphical evidence does not give unambiguous support to finding a negative relationship between employment and relative wages.

The estimated models are given below:

Estimation of the model in log linear form with youth and adult wages entered separately:

$$hours_t = \alpha + \beta_1 hours_{t-1} + \beta_2 Youthwage + \beta_3 AdultAWE + \beta_4 output_{t-1} + \varepsilon$$

We then tested the restriction that $\beta_2 = -\beta_3$ and if the restriction was not rejected we estimated the model in log linear form with *relative* wages:

$$hours_t = \alpha + \beta_1 hours_{t-1} + \beta_2 Relwage_{t-1} + \beta_3 output_{t-1} + \varepsilon$$

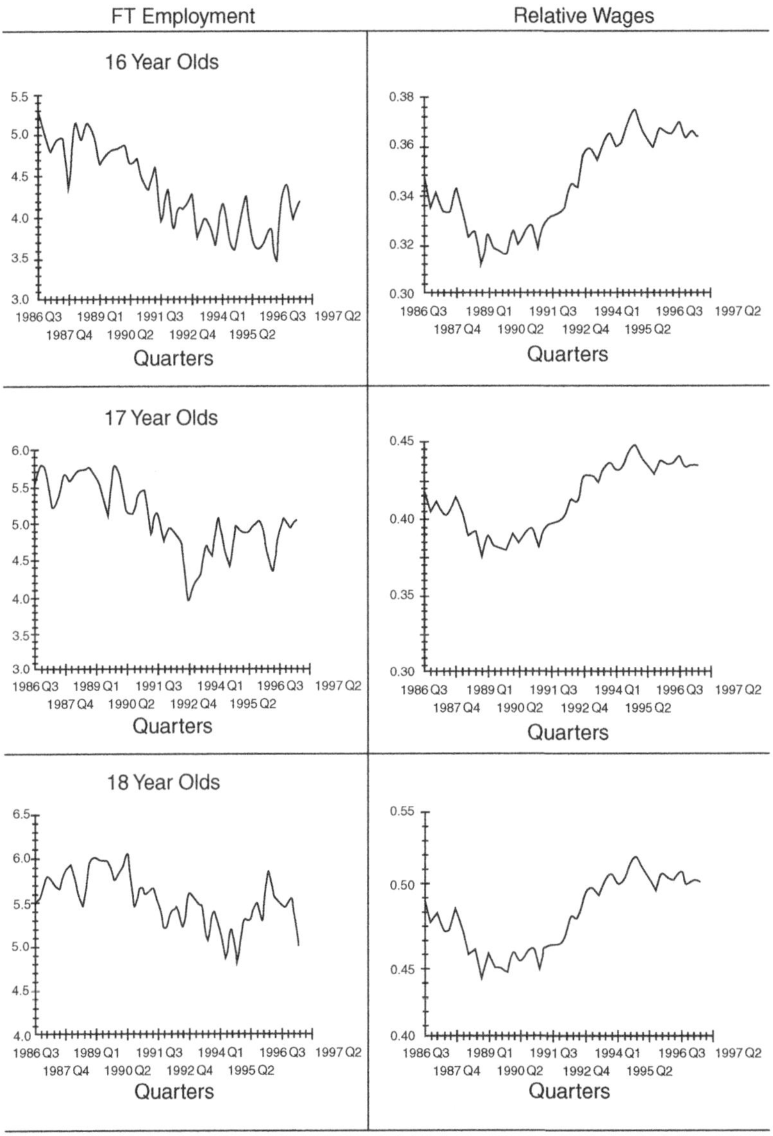

Figure 3.3.3 Retail Trade, 3rd Quarter 1986 to 2nd Quarter 1997

Notes: Employment = Average hours worked * No. of persons employed

Wages = Ratio of youth minimum wages to adult Average Weekly Earnings for the industry.

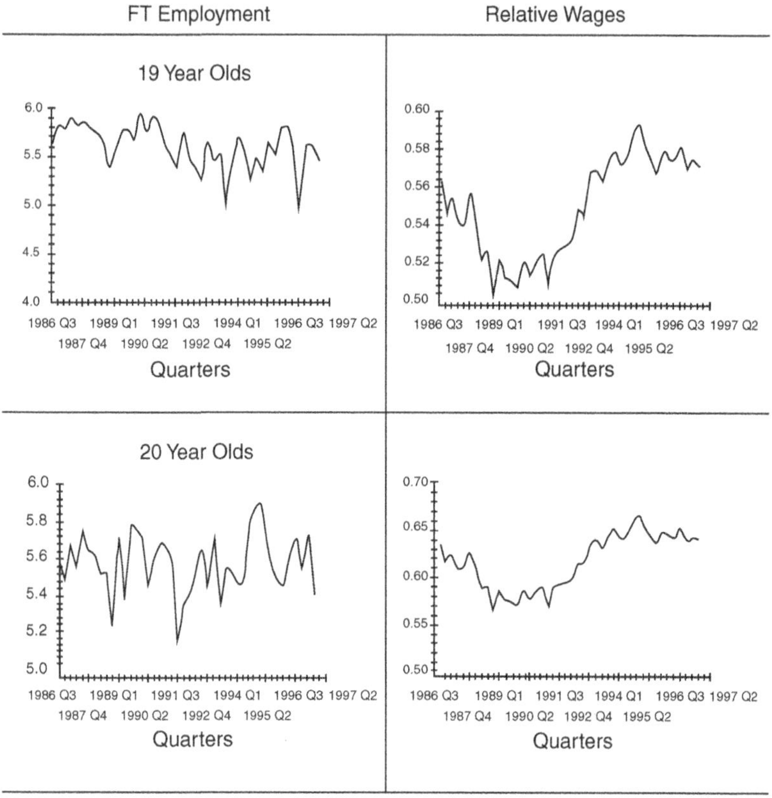

Figure 3.3.3 Continued

Finally, to allow for problems of unit roots and cointegration we estimate an error correction model following the approach in Debelle and Vickery (1998) where all variables are in logs and first difference of logs:

$$\Delta hours_t = \alpha + \beta_1[hours_{t-1} + \beta_2 Relwage_{t-1} + \beta_3 output_{t-1}] + \gamma_1 \Delta hours_{t-1} + \gamma_2 \Delta Relwage_{t-1} + \gamma_3 \Delta output_{t-1} + \varepsilon$$

The dependent variable is the average number of hours worked times the number of employees, the youthwage is the minimum wage for the appropriate youth age group, the Relwage is the appropriate minimum wage for the age group divided by the Average Weekly Earnings for adults. All variables are logged and differences are differences of logs. (In the case of manufacturing we also present results with the relative wage as a ratio of youth to adult minimum wages since there is a fairly high variance of this variable.)

Before we carried out the estimation we tested for unit roots for all the variables and then estimated the ECM and tested for unit roots of the residuals of that equation. As the sample is fairly small and the power of the tests of integration and cointegration is relatively low, we provide estimates of the equation in level forms and in the error correction model form. The error correction model is estimated after we found that most of the variables were I(1) (a few were I(0)). The estimation was carried out by ordinary least squares, as the right hand side variables were all predetermined variables.

In the first stage of our analysis we estimated simple log linear equations where we estimated the wages freely (i.e. we estimated them with youth wages and adult wages separately, equation 1 above). A summary of these results is presented in Table 3.3.3. (Detailed results are available on request from the authors.) It is interesting that in most cases the youth minimum wage is either the wrong sign (i.e. positive) or not significant: in only four out of 38 cases do we find negative and significant coefficients. For males the youth minimum wage is always incorrectly signed or insignificant. For females the results suggest that in retail trade there is a negative elasticity of full-time 16–18 year olds and for part-time 16 year olds. However, the apparently large elasticities are beyond any reasonable expectation and hence should be treated with caution. It is possible that these peculiar results are due to collinearity between youth and adult minimum wages. Alternatively, they may simply reflect the increased participation rate of females over the period in the labour market.

We tested to see if we could estimate these significant cases using a relative wage and we rejected the implicit restrictions on the parameters (that the parameters on the wage terms were equal and opposite in sign) except for 18 year old full-time females. Again this may be due to the fact that there is a close relationship between youth and adult minimum wages.

When we estimated the same equation with youth minimum wages and adult AWE (separately) the results came out strongly with negative minimum wage elasticities for full-time males and females only in the retail trades for

Table 3.3.3 Levels equation for total hours employed using Youth Minimum Wages and Adult Minimum wages separately

Industry	FT/PT	M/F	Age	Min Wage	t-stat.
Retail	FT	F	16	–23.1	–2.68
	FT	F	17	–19.0	–2.99
	FT	F	18	–10.2	–2.02
	PT	F	16	–4.06	–2.02

Note: We estimated 38 equations and all other results are non significant.

Table 3.3.4 Levels equation for total hours employed using Youth Minimum Wages and Adult AWE separately

Industry	FT/PT	M/F	Age	Min Wage	t-stat.
Retail	FT	M	16	–8.41	–4.37
	FT	M	17	–7.48	–3.75
	FT	M	18	–5.05	–3.26
	FT	F	17	–2.97	–2.01
	FT	F	18	–2.56	–2.17
	FT	F	19	–2.44	–2.65
Manuf.	PT	M	18	–3.25	–2.03

Note: We estimated 38 equations and all other results are non-significant.

the younger age groups. *(Note that since we had data only on full-time AWE we estimated equations for part-time workers using youth minimum wages and full-time adult AWE separately. This is important; both our data and that reported by Daly et al show strong growth in part-time employment in retail over the period, while full-time employment falls sharply.)* The elasticities ranged from –2 to –8, which are still on the high side. These results are presented in Table 3.3.4.

We tested to see if we could estimate these significant cases using a relative wage and we rejected the implicit restrictions on the parameters (that the parameters on the wage terms were equal and opposite in sign) for 16, 17, and 18 year old full-time males.

In the next stage we estimated the equations with relative wages using youth minimum wages relative to adult minimum wages.

All coefficients are either incorrectly signed and/or insignificant. For female part-time 18 and 19 year olds the sign is wrong and is significant.

We then estimated the same equation with youth minimum wages relative to adult AWE. In this case we found that except for male 16 and 18 year olds and female 19 year olds in retail trade all the other elasticities were insignificant or incorrectly signed, see Table 3.3.6.

Finally we estimated an error correction model following on the De-belle and Vickery (1998) paper. These results are presented in Tables 3.3.7 and 3.3.8. Table 3.3.7 includes equations using youth minimum wages relative to adult minimum wages for the manufacturing sector. These results show that both the short and long run relative wage elasticities are insignificant or incorrectly signed except for 18 year old part-time males in manufacturing where the long run relative wage elasticity is negative and significant (–9.4).

Table 3.3.8 presents results using youth minimum wages relative to adult AWE for retail and manufacturing sectors. These ECM results again come out with all wage elasticities as insignificant or incorrectly signed except for full-time 18 year old males in manufacturing with a short run elasticity of –3.1 and female full-time 19 year old workers in retail trade with a long run elasticity of –2.05.

Table 3.3.5 Levels with relative wage (youth min/adult min), manufacturing

Industry	FT/PT	M/F	Age	Rel. Wage	t-stat.
Manuf.	FT	M	17	–3.85	–1.34
	FT	M	18	–2.94	–1.42
Manuf.	PT	M	16	11.7	1.89
	PT	M	18	–6.90	–1.47
Manuf.	PT	F	18	14.89	3.11
	PT	F	19	12.9	2.73
	PT	F	20	3.73	1.70

Note: We estimated 38 equations and all other results are non significant.

Table 3.3.6 Levels equation for total hours employed using relative wages (Youth Minimum Wages/Adult AWE)

Industry	FT/PT	M/F	Age	Rel Wage	t-value
Retail	FT	M	16	–4.03	–2.68
	FT	M	18	–2.59	–2.3
	FT	F	19	–1.6	–2.19

Note: We estimated 38 equations and all other results are non significant.

Table 3.3.7 ECM using Relative Wage (Youth Minimum Wage/Adult Minimum Wage)

Industry	FT/PT	M/F	Age	Relwage L-R Elasticity	Significant	Relwage S-R Elasticity	Significant
Manuf.	FT	M	16	9	No	–0.6	No
	FT	M	17	6.2	No	0.2	No
	FT	M	18	–0.8	No	0.2	No
	FT	M	19	2	No	0.1	No
	FT	M	20	1.8	No	–0.2	No
	PT	M	16	–0.7	No	–2.9	No
	PT	M	17	–3.7	No	–1.4	No
	PT	M	18	–9.4	Yes	4.42	No
	PT	M	19	–0.4	No	0.1	No
	PT	M	20	3.8	No	–0.4	No
	PT	F	16	–6.9	No	1.1	No
	PT	F	17	4.8	No	–1.3	No
	PT	F	18	–0.7	No	–1.8	No
	PT	F	19	–1.2	No	–4.4	No

Table 3.3.8 ECM using Relative Wage (Youth Minimum Wage/Adult AWE)

Industry	FT/PT	M/F	Age	Rel Wage L-R Elasticity	t-value	Rel Wage S-R Elasticity	t-value
Manuf.	FT	M	18			−3.1	−2.17
Retail	FT	F	19	−2.05	−2.58		

Note: We estimated 38 equations and all other results are non significant.

To summarise, in each case we estimated 38 equations and only in a very few cases were wage elasticities negative and significant.

7 Conclusions

There are several estimates of wage elasticities floating about, most of the published ones being negative or zero. However, most of the estimation is based on inadequate data, and inappropriate estimation techniques.

In the exercise in this chapter we have gone hunting for youth wage elasticities in a large Australian minimum wage and employment data set which weighs against the finding of zero elasticities. The smaller (manufacturing only) analysis uniquely allows an elasticity estimate using minimum rates for juniors and for adults. This avoids compositional problems inherent in the use of AWE as a measure of wages in such exercises. The estimated elasticities are almost always incorrectly signed or statistically insignificant.

The larger analysis has elasticities for youth minimum wages relative to total full-time average earnings. Compositional effects will generally affect the latter variable for reasons similar to those demonstrated here to be present in measured youth AWE with implications for spurious correlation, and this fact conditions our results. The estimated elasticities are again almost always incorrectly signed or statistically insignificant.

We report that we have still not found the elusive Australian elasticities, and we don't think anyone else has beaten us to it. Our hunt is not yet over. The data set will support further investigation, and we will keep looking – at the data for the Accommodation etc sector, allowing for changes to shop trading hours over the period, estimating equations 4, 6, and 8 using part-time employment, allowing for education participation, and estimating a system of equations. We are continuing our hunt for the Thylacine[5]!

In our view the simple neoclassical model needs extensive redevelopment to take account of a whole range of features mentioned earlier, or else labour market economists will increasingly be looking to begin afresh with a new paradigm.

Notes

1. We would like to thank Lisa Cameron, University of Melbourne, for providing us with incisive and helpful comments. We also thank Cezary Kapuscinski for

helpful discussions on the subject. All errors are our own. An earlier version of this paper was presented to the Joint Workshop on "Do youth wages matter?" at the Centre for Economic Policy Research, ANU and Productivity Commission, 23rd November 1998.

2. Card and Krueger (1995) refer to this as publication bias. This point was raised by Junankar in his comment on a paper by Phil Lewis to a DEET/CEPR Conference in 1990.
3. Wooden (1998) discusses this issue and argues that teenagers are employed predominantly in small firms because skilled labour is less important for small firms, see p. 41.
4. Ideally we should estimate a system of equations for employment of youths and adults as well as an equation to explain participation in education for youths. The time period is very short, however, as the retention rate data are available only on an annual basis. Unfortunately, time constraints prevent this for the present and we hope to estimate a complete model in the near future.
5. According to the Oxford Concise Dictionary: "thylacine, n. Zebra wolf, a Tasmanian carnivorous marsupial. [F. f. Gk. Thulakos pouch, -INE]"

References

Australian Bureau of Statistics (various) *Labour Force, Australia,* Cat.No. 6203.0.

Bureau of Labour Market Research (1983) *Youth Wages, Employment and the Labour Force,* AGPS, Canberra.

Card D. and Krueger A.B. (1995) *Myth and Measurement: The New Economics of the Minimum Wage,* Princeton University Press, New Jersey.

Daly A., Nguyen-Hong D., Eldridge D., Gabbitas O. and McCalman P. (1998) *Youth Wages and Employment,* Productivity Commission Staff Research Paper, AusInfo, Canberra, October.

Debelle G. and Vickery J. (1998) 'The Macroeconomics of Unemployment', in G. Debelle and J. Borland (eds.), *Unemployment and the Australian Labour Market,* Reserve Bank of Australia, Sydney.

Junankar P.N. and Neale A. (1987) 'Relative Wages and the Youth Labour Market' in Junankar. P.N. (ed.) *From School to Unemployment? The Labour Market for Young People,* Macmillan, London.

Marceau J. (1990) 'Neither Fish nor Fowl: Theorising Emerging Organisational Forms in a Small Open Economy (Australia)' Paper for the World Congress of the International Sociological Association, July 9–13, (mimeo, ANU).

Marceau J. et al. (1989) 'Giants and Dwarves: Changing Technologies and Productive Interlinkages in Australian Manufacturing Industry', Paper for the Third International APROS Colloquium, ANU, 13–15 December.

McFadden D. (1978) 'Estimation techniques for the elasticity of substitution and other production parameters', in M. Fuss and D. McFadden (eds.) *Production Economics: A Dual Approach to Theory and Applications,* Volumes 1 and 2, North-Holland, Amsterdam.

OECD (1994) *The OECD Jobs Study,* Parts 1 and 2, OECD, Paris.

OECD (1998) *Employment Outlook,* OECD, Paris.

Rice P.G. (1986) 'Juvenile Unemployment, Relative Wages and Social Security in Great Britain', *Economic Journal,* 96, 352–374.

Wooden M. (1998) 'The labour market for young Australians', in Australia's Youth: Reality and Risk, Dusseldorp Skills Forum, Sydney

3.4

The Dynamics of Youth Unemployment: An Analysis of Recurrent Unemployment

P.N. Junankar and Margaret Wood

1 Introduction

In this paper we focus on recurrent unemployment using the Australian Longitudinal Surveys. Earlier studies on recurrent unemployment include Heckman and Borjas (1980), OECD (1985), Hui (1986a,b), Corcoran and Hill (1985), Stern (1986), Trivedi and Alexander (1986, 1989), and Adena (1989). The aim of this paper is to determine whether there are some people who are more likely to face recurrent spells (defined as those people who have more than one spell in a calendar year) and whether they are more likely to have had prior spells of unemployment, i.e. whether there is occurrence dependence, or scarring. We study whether people who come from poor socio-economic and poor educational backgrounds enter into secondary labour markets with low wages and insecure employment and hence face recurrent unemployment or spells in the not-in-the-labour-force (NILF) category. Our results show that there is clearly a problem of recurrent unemployment faced by a sub-set of the youth labour market and that there some is evidence for occurrence dependence. Those people who have recurrent spells account for a large proportion of the total weeks of unemployment experience, as well as facing a cumulatively large number of weeks of unemployment. Section 2 briefly outlines some theories; Section 3 describes the data we have used from the Australian Longitudinal Surveys, the methods used, and some results; and Section 4 concludes the paper.

Reprinted from 'The Dynamics of Unemployment: An Analysis of Recurrent Unemployment' by P. N. Junankar and Margaret Wood in *Youth in the Eighties: Papers from the Australian Longitudinal Surveys* edited by R.G. Gregory and T. Karmel, Canberra: Department of Employment, Education and Training & Centre for Economic Policy Research, ANU, Canberra, 1992, pp. 282–304. With kind permission from Australian National University.

2 Some Explanations

Let us consider the various ways in which individuals may have *recurrent spells* of unemployment, that is more than one spell of unemployment in (say) one year. If we consider the labour market in terms of flows then the recurrent spells may originate from individuals losing their jobs frequently either due to voluntary separations (quits or termination of short term contracts) or involuntary ones (redundancy or being fired for poor performance). But in either case, unless a person receives acceptable job offers soon after becoming unemployed they cannot have *recurrent spells* of unemployment. The one exception is when a person leaves the unemployment state simply to leave the labour force temporarily and then re-enters the labour force by joining the unemployed pool. For many young people, it has been argued, there is a fuzzy boundary between unemployment and NILF states. Hence, in our econometric work we consider the case of recurrent spells of unemployment as well as recurrent spells of unemployment or not-in-the-labour-force. It is clear that if an individual has a long spell of unemployment, then s/he cannot have too many repeat spells of unemployment in a (calendar) year, or more formally the probability of recurrent spells is not independent of the duration of spells. Some people (those in the so-called 'fast lane') may hold a series of jobs in a short spell of time, but they would not have any unemployment spells in between the different jobs. Section 3 provides some evidence on this issue. To summarise, to have recurrent spells of unemployment an individual must have a high probability of losing a job (either voluntarily or involuntarily) as well as a high probability of receiving acceptable job offers. One way of presenting this schematically is given below:[1]

To have a high probability of obtaining a job a person must have a high probability of receiving (good) job offers and a high probability of accepting the offers (or, in other words, must have a low reservation wage).

The probability of job loss depends either on the employee (voluntary separations), on the nature of the employment contract, or on involuntary separations—the probability of being fired by the employer.

Some workers may have very weak attachment to a job, employer, or geographic location and may voluntarily quit to look for different employment.

Table 3.4.1 A Taxonomy of Recurrent Spells

Probability of Job Loss:	**Probability of Obtaining a Job:**	
	Low	**High**
Low	Few long spells	Few short spells
High	Repeat long spells	Repeat short spells

This decision may be affected by the availability and magnitude of unemployment benefits.[2] They may quit because they do not like the nature of the work, or the employer (or their supervisor), or they may wish to try their luck in a different part of the country. Some young people may sample a sequence of jobs in an attempt to choose an optimal career while others may change jobs frequently to increase their incomes. Workers in the secondary sector in dead end jobs, no career structure, with little or no firm specific training are more likely to quit. Some workers have, due to personal reasons (e.g. poor health), a very unstable employment record.

In many cases the job loss is simply due to the ending of a short term contract, for example, the workers in seasonal industries/occupations (such as agriculture, tourism, hotels, restaurants, building trades, ice cream sales persons, etc.) are hired only for short periods.

Involuntary job separations could be due to: (a) the firm becoming bankrupt and all employees losing their jobs; or (b) redundancy, that is the job comes to an end because of financial stringency or due to technological change; or (c) due to the worker being fired for inefficiency, incompetence, or corrupt behaviour. The latter requires an employer to have good monitoring practices or a workforce that does not like shirkers. Redundancies obviously depend on the buoyancy of the product market in general and the success of the firm in particular. In buoyant markets a worker may simply have to shift from one line of work to another even if his/her particular work has been superseded by new technology. Early school leavers, unskilled workers with little training, and in non-unionised jobs are more likely to be laid off, or made redundant, or dismissed.

The probability of obtaining a job depends on the joint probability of receiving an offer and the probability of accepting the offer. The probability of receiving an offer would depend on the state of the labour market and on the personal characteristics of the worker searching for work. A person with better education, skills and experience would be more likely to receive an offer. If the employer uses unemployment as a negative signal of a worker's productivity, then (*ceteris paribus*) the probability of an offer would be lower. Similarly, the probability of receiving an offer would depend on the search intensity of the worker, and the duration of unemployment may decrease the search intensity.

The probability of accepting the offer depends on the individual's reservation wage which in turn is determined by the distribution of wage offers and the costs of search, hence it may be affected by unemployment benefit. Young people are often posited to sample jobs in their early career in order to find their optimal career, and this would explain recurrent spells of unemployment. In other words, age or experience should explain recurrent spells of unemployment.

Another reason for having recurrent unemployment spells is that people may leave unemployment due to sickness, or they join a labour market program, or because they get discouraged and leave the labour force. Subsequently they may rejoin the unemployment stock and appear to have had multiple spells of unemployment even though they have not held a job in the intervening period. This means that they do not fit in the earlier conceptualisation of people losing and gaining jobs. People who are in this category would have, it has been argued, similar characteristics to those who go through multiple jobs. A proper treatment of this issue would require us to look at the probabilities of transition from one labour market state to another. Some indirect evidence on this issue is provided later in the paper when we look at the number of unemployment spells cross tabulated against the number of jobs held.

According to the segmented labour market hypothesis, workers in the bottom segment have a higher probability of job loss and a higher probability of obtaining a (short-term) job because they have low expectations, a low reservation wage, and work in occupations with short term contracts.[3] However, this is also consistent with human capital theory where people with less training would be the most likely to be dismissed, as well as having a lower probability of employment. *The main difference is that the segmented labour market hypothesis would suggest recurrent spells of unemployment while the human capital hypothesis would suggest long spells of unemployment.*

This analysis suggests a set of economic variables that should be included in reduced form cross-sectional, or longitudinal models, namely, local unemployment rates, age (or experience), migrant or Australian born, state of health, previous occupation, urban or rural, educational and training variables, unemployment benefits, union member or not, etc.. An important aspect of such studies is to look for scarring effects, that is does the experience of unemployment increase the probability of remaining unemployed. Thismay be due to decreasing search intensity as the person becomes despondent, or because the prospective employer regards a previous spell of unemployment as a negative signal, and treats the searcher as having some unmeasured poor characteristics including depreciated human capital: there must be something wrong with an unemployed person! In the context of studying *recurrent* unemployment we shall look for occurrence dependence, that is, whether previous spells of unemployment affect the probability of facing recurrent spells of unemployment.

In summary, the probability of recurrent spells of unemployment depends on a high probability of job loss and on a high probability of obtaining another job. Both probabilities depend on the nature of the employer and the employee.

3 Data, Methods and Results[4]

The data we have used are extracted from the Australian Longitudinal Surveys. In this study we have used the Area Sample (a stratified multi-stage random sample) of 4515 male respondents between the ages of 16 and 25 in 1985 who were then followed through until 1988 by which time sample attrition led to a sample of 3026. *For our econometric analysis we have looked at those* ***males in 1988*** *for whom data existed on* ***all*** *the relevant variables. In other words, the sample excludes those males in 1988 who had 'missing values' for the regressors. This left us with a sample of 2255 males that we used in our econometric analysis.* Thus sample attrition over time plus the deletion of observations due to missing values may have led to some unknown biases in our results.[5]

Data description

Before we carry out formal econometric analysis let us look at some some descriptive statistics for the sample of male respondents who were in each wave of the survey over the period 1985–88. Table 3.4.2 provides information,for each year, on the percentage of the sample who were unemployed, in long term unemployment (defined as being unemployed continuously for over a year), or who faced recurrent spells of unemployment or unemployment or NILF. Recurrent spells are defined here as more than one spell of unemployment or NILF experienced by a person in one year. The sample we used is a sub-set of the original sample of 4515 males: as a result of attrition the sample size decreases and due to incomplete information on relevant variables some observations had to be deleted from the sample.[6]

The percentage of unemployment in the sample decreases with time as does the long term unemployment (LTU), although the fall is much greater in the reduced sample of 2255 males. The number of males facing recurrent spells increases suddenly between 1985 and 1986 and then declines, again the decline is more rapid in the smaller sample. It is interesting to note that this picture is the same whether we look only at unemployment spells or whether we include NILF spells. *It appears that the problem of sample attrition and missing values is biased towards those males who are unemployed and have recurrent spells of unemployment: the percentages are consistently higher for the larger samples.*[7] Thus our econometric results should be interpreted with some caution.

Table 3.4.2 Unemployment, Long Term Unemployment, and Recurrent Spells (Sample of survivors with complete data)

	1985	1986	1987	1988
Percentage Unemployed in Sample	9.8	7.4	7.1	4.0
Percentage LTU in Sample	2.6	2.5	2.1	0.9
Percentage of sample with recurrent spells of unemployment	2.9	10.1	8.9	5.2
Percentage of sample with recurrent spells of unemployment or NILF	5.6	15.7	12.0	7.8
Sample Size	2255	2255	2255	2255

Source: ALS Calendar Dataset.

A feature of this sample (whether the larger or smaller sub-sets) is that for some reason there is a sudden increase in recurrent spells between 1985 and 1986 followed by a gradual decline. It is curious that this occurs at a time when the percentage unemployed in the sample falls over the entire period (as is true of youth unemployment rates in the whole population). This is another issue that needs further investigation.

In order to exploit the longitudinal nature of the sample, we look at the number (and percentage) of the sample in 1985 who continued in the same state. That is, those people who had zero (one, and more than one spells) in 1985 who continued to have zero (one, and more than one) spells in 1986, 1987, and 1988. These data are presented in Tables 3.4.3, 3.4.4, and 3.4.5.

Table 3.4.3(a) Unemployment Spells = 0

	1985	**1986**	**1987**	**1988**
1985	1715	1334	1169	1076
	(100.0)	(77.8)	(68.2)	(62.7)
1986		1524	1318	1199
		(100.0)	(86.5)	(78.7)
1987			1654	1483
			(100.0)	(89.7)

Table 3.4.3(b) Unemployment and Not-in-the-labour-force Spells = 0

	1985	**1986**	**1987**	**1988**
1985	1238	946	822	727
	(100.0)	(76.4)	(66.4)	(58.7)
1986		1257	1066	931
		(100.0)	(84. 8)	(74.1)
1987			1470	1248
			(100.0)	(84.9)

Table 3.4.4(a) Unemployment Spells = 1

	1985	**1986**	**1987**	**1988**
1985	475	196	62	22
	(100.0)	(41.3)	(13.1)	(4.6)
1986		503	164	51
		(100.0)	(32.6)	(10.1)
1987			400	118
			(100.0)	(29.5)

Table 3.4.4(b) Unemployment and Not-in-the-labour-force Spells = 1

	1985	1986	1987	1988
1985	738	223	67	20
	(100.0)	(30.2)	(9.1)	(2.7)
1986		461	116	37
		(100.0)	(25.2)	(8.0)
1987			374	97
			(100.0)	(25.9)

Table 3.4.5(a) Unemployment Spells > 1

	1985	1986	1987	1988
1985	65	17	4	0
	(100.0)	(26.2)	(6.2)	
1986		228	68	14
		(100.0)	(29.8)	(6.1)
1987			201	39
			(100.0)	(19.4)

Table 3.4.5(b) Unemployment and Not-in-the-labour-force Spells > 1

	1985	1986	1987	1988
1985	279	131	53	15
	(100.0)	(46.9)	(19.0)	(5.4)
1986		537	212	69
		(100.0)	(39.5)	(12.8)
1987			411	126
			(100.0)	(30.6)

These tables show the persistence of spells from one year to another. If we look at Tables 3.4.4 and 3.4.5 we see that a fairly high percentage of the sample seem to have repeat spells of unemployment (or unemployment and NILF spells). For example, of the 65 who had more than one spell of unemployment in 1985, 26 per cent had more than one spell in 1986 and 6 per cent in 1987. Of the 201 who had more than one unemployment spell in 1987, 19 per cent had more than one spell in 1988. Similarly, about 30 per cent of those who had recurrent spells of unemployment or NILF had a repeat experience in the subsequent year. At the other end of the spectrum, a huge majority (between 58 to 90 per cent) of those who had zero spells usually continued to have zero spells. In particular, 63 per cent of the sample had no spells of unemployment throughout the period, or, in other words,

37 per cent of the sample had at least one spell of unemployment over the period. This suggests that there is a concentration of unemployment experience among some groups. Further evidence presented below supports this finding.

Results from our sample are similar to those of Clark and Summers (1979) who found that most people (males in our sample) have short spells. *However, they account for a very small proportion of the total weeks of unemployment.* For example over the period 1985–88, 20.1 per cent of the males (who had at least one spell of unemployment) had spells of less than 4 weeks but accounted for only 1.2 per cent of the total weeks of unemployment and 42.2 per cent who had spells longer than 26 weeks accounted for 84.9 per cent of the total weeks of unemployment. Figure 3.4.1 shows how the longer durations account for a large percentage of the total weeks of unemployment experience. The data reveal an increase in inequality from 1985 to 1986, and then remained constant for the next two years.

We now look at the number and duration of spells experienced by the unemployed over the period 1985–88, see Tables 3.4.6 and 3.4.7. Table 3.4.6 shows that although 40.6 per cent of those who experienced unemployment had short spells (less than 13 weeks) they accounted for only 6.0 per cent of the total weeks of unemployment experienced. At the other end of the spectrum, 3 per cent with very long spells (greater than 157 weeks) accounted for almost 15 per cent of the total weeks of unemployment. In other words, although a majority of the unemployed had fairly short spells (less than 26 weeks) they account for only 15 per cent of the total weeks of unemployment.

Table 3.4.6 Total Weeks of Unemployment, 1985–88

Spell Length	Number	Percent	Weeks	% of all Weeks
1–4 weeks	308	20.1	655	1.18
5–13 weeks	314	20.5	2643	4.76
1–26 weeks	264	17.2	5092	9.16
27–39 weeks	165	10.8	5380	9.68
40–52 weeks	125	8.2	5747	10.34
53–65 weeks	77	5.0	4482	8.06
66–78 weeks	70	4.6	4997	8.99
79–91 weeks	37	2.4	3156	5.68
92–104 weeks	32	2.1	3137	5.64
105–117 weeks	37	2.4	4132	7.43
118–130 weeks	18	1.2	2233	4.02
131–143 weeks	20	1.3	2728	4.91
144–156 weeks	21	1.4	3161	5.69
157+ weeks	46	3.0	8035	14.46
All	1534	100.0	55578	100.0

Table 3.4.7 Unemployment Spells, 1985–88

Unemp. Spells	Males No.	Males %	No. of Spells	% of all Spells	Total Weeks	Mean Weeks/ Person	% of all Weeks
1	653	42.6	653	19.18	12547	19.21	22.58
2	387	25.2	774	22.73	15057	38.95	27.12
3	240	15.6	720	21.15	11353	47.30	20.43
4	124	8.1	496	14.57	7635	61.57	13.47
5	77	5.0	385	11.31	5076	65.92	9.13
6	23	1.5	138	4.05	1951	84.83	3.51
7	16	1.0	112	3.29	719	44.94	1.29
8	6	0.4	48	1.41	487	81.17	0.88
9	6	0.4	54	1.59	590	98.33	1.06
10	1	0.1	10	0.29	31	31.00	0.06
15	1	0.1	15	0.44	114	114.00	0.21
All	1534	100.0	3405	100.0	55578	36.23	100.0

Source: ALS Calendar Dataset (for Tables 3.4.6 and 3.4.7).

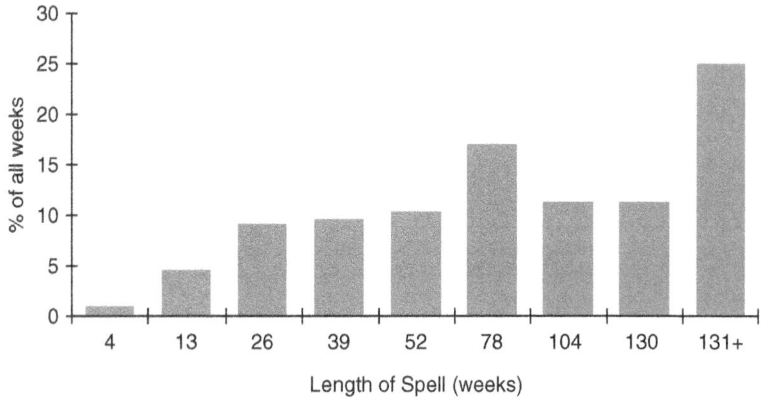

Figure 3.4.1 Duration of completed spells, 1985–88

Table 3.4.7 shows that over the period 1985–88 although 42.6 per cent of the sample (who experienced unemployment) had only one spell, they accounted for a small percentage (19.18 per cent) of the total number of spells of unemployment and accounted for a small percentage (22.58 per cent) of the total weeks of unemployment. Or put another way, over three quarters of the total weeks of unemployment were accounted for

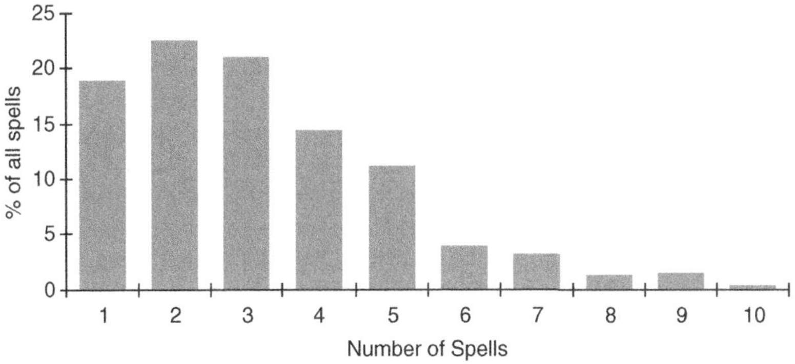

Figure 3.4.2 Completed spells of unemployment, 1985–88

Table 3.4.8 Duration of Unemployment Spells, 1985–88

Unemp.Spells	Males	1st Spell	2nd Spell	3rd Spell	4th Spell	5th spell	6th Spell
				(MeanWeeks)			
1 spell	653	19.21	0	0	0	0	0
2 spells	387	20.87	18.09	0	0	0	0
3 spells	240	17.08	15.22	15.00	0	0	0
4 spells	124	18.90	15.00	14.37	13.30	0	0
5 spells	77	16.38	12.23	13.97	10.84	12.49	0
6 spells	53	17.85	10.34	8.38	10.47	10.30	7.70

Source: ALS Calendar Dataset.

by males who had more than one spell of unemployment. Figure 3.4.2 illustrates the point. In general we find that the more the spells of unemployment, the longer the average duration of weeks of unemployment faced by the individual. For example the average duration per person increases from 19.21 weeks for those who face only one spell to 84.83 weeks for those who experienced six spells. The problem is probably worse as we are ignoring many people whose unemployment spell ends not in a job but simply in NILF. Evidence presented in Kryger (1990) suggests that the longer the duration of a spell the less likely is an exit into a job and the more likely the exit is into NILF. (See Kryger 1990, Table 25.)

This suggests that the recurrent spells are not a rational search strategy (job shopping) being practised by optimising workers. They appear much more likely to be an involuntary response to the market.

Table 3.4.8 provides interesting information on the average duration of a spell for those people who have recurrent spells. In general, for those with multiple spells of unemployment the duration of *each subsequent spell* gets gradually smaller. For example if we look at the period 1985–88, those males who have *only* one spell have a mean duration of 19.21 weeks. For those who have *four* spells the mean durations are 18.9 weeks for the first spell, 15.00 weeks for the second, 14.37 weeks for the third, and 13.30 weeks for the fourth and final spell.

Another interesting aspect of the problem of recurrent unemployment is revealed by looking at a cross tabulation, see Table 3.4.9 of the number of unemployment spells by the number of jobs held over the period 1985–88. We find that 21 per cent of our sample held more than five jobs, and a massive 35 per cent held more than four jobs. This table also reveals that frequent job changers have very few spells of unemployment, and that almost 28 per cent of those who held four jobs, 25 per cent of those who held five jobs, and 20 per cent who held 6 or more jobs *had zero spells of unemployment.* If frequent job changers went through an intermediate labour market state of unemployment, then we should find that the elements of the principal diagonal in Table 3.4.9 should dominate the off-diagonal elements. However, a casual glance at the table reveals that (generally) the off-diagonal elements dominate the principal diagonal. In other words, those people who have several spells of unemployment are not job shopping and voluntarily 'taking' unemployment as a rational search strategy: almost 50 per cent of the multiple job holders (four or more jobs) had no more than one spell of unemployment.

Tables 3.4.10 and 3.4.11 provide summary statistics on some of the variables used in our analysis. The results are presented by the number of unemployment spells in 1988.

It is interesting to note that for all those who have had at least one spell of unemployment, the mean number of unemployment spells increased over time. For example, looking down a column for those with two or more spells in 1988 the mean number of spells increased from 0.47 in 1985 to 1.3 in 1987. Again, looking along the rows of unemployment spells in previous years, we see that the mean number of spells in (say) 1987 increases with the number of spells in 1988. Similarly, mean unemployment increased over time for each spell group, for example for those with two or more spells in 1988 the mean went up from 0.20 in 1985 to 0.46 in 1987. Turning to occupation, the greater the number of spells the less likely they are to be professionals and more likely to be manual workers. We now turn to some more formal analysis.

Results

In this study we use maximum likelihood estimation of multinomial logit equations to analyse the probability of having zero, one, or recurrent spells (two or more spells) of unemployment and not in the labour force in 1988. As mentioned earlier there is reason to believe that for youths, unemployment and not in the labour force are very similar labour market states.

Table 3.4.9 Unemployment Spells by Jobs Held, 1985–88

Unemployment Spells	Number of Jobs:							
	0	1	2	3	4	5	6	Total
0 spells: (a)	17	556	304	201	108	59	75	1320
(b)	0.60	19.48	10.65	7.04	3.78	2.07	2.63	46.25
(c)	1.29	42.12	23.03	15.23	8.18	4.47	5.68	
(d)	38.64	75.24	49.43	42.86	28.35	25.54	20.00	
1 spell:	22	128	181	108	97	54	63	653
	0.77	4.48	6.34	3.78	3.40	1.89	2.21	22.88
	3.37	19.60	27.72	16.54	14.85	8.27	9.65	
	50.00	17.32	29.43	23.03	25.46	23.38	16.80	
2 spells:	3	44	94	84	81	36	45	387
	0.11	1.54	3.29	2.94	2.84	1.26	1.58	13.56
	0.78	11.37	24.29	21.71	20.93	9.30	11.63	
	6.82	5.95	15.28	17.91	21.26	15.58	12.00	
3 spells:	2	8	31	51	49	44	55	240
	0.07	0.28	1.09	1.79	1.72	1.54	1.93	8.41
	0.83	3.33	12.92	21.25	20.42	18.33	22.92	
	4.55	1.08	5.04	10.87	12.86	19.05	14.67	
4 spells:	0	3	3	21	35	19	43	124
	0.00	0.11	0.11	0.74	1.23	0.67	1.51	4.34
	0.00	2.42	2.42	16.94	28.23	15.23	34.68	
	0.00	0.41	0.49	4.48	9.19	8.23	11.47	
5 spells:	0	0	2	4	8	16	47	77
	0.00	0.00	0.07	0.14	0.28	0.56	1.65	2.50
	0.00	0.00	2.60	5.19	10.39	20.78	61.04	
	0.00	0.00	0.33	0.85	2.10	6.93	12.53	
6+ spells:	0	0	0	0	3	3	47	53
	0.00	0.00	0.00	0.00	0.11	0.11	4.65	1.86
	0.00	0.00	0.00	0.00	5.66	5.66	88.68	
	0.00	0.00	0.00	0.00	0.79	1.30	12.53	
Total	44	739	615	469	381	231	375	2854
	1.54	25.89	21.55	16.43	13.35	8.09	13.14	100.0

Note: For each of the spell blocks 1 – 6+
Row (a) = Frquency; Row (b) = Percent of total;
Row (c) = Percent of row total; Row (d) = Percent of column total
Source: ALS Calendar Dataset.

Table 3.4.10 Summary statistics, unemployment spells

YSPELLS	0 spells N = 1788	1 spells N = 349	>1 spells N = 118	All N = 2255
NSWACT	0.4044	0.4413	0.3814	0.4089
VIC	0.2321	0.1633	0.1780	0.2186
QLD	0.1560	0.1404	0.1525	0.1534
SANT	0.1051	0.1089	0.1271	0.1069
WA	0.0727	0.0974	0.1356	0.0798
TAS	0.0296	0.0487	0.0254	0.0324
YMARRIED	0.2863	0.1748	0.2542	0.2674
VHEALTH	0.0095	0.0143	0.0339	0.0115
WHEALTH	0.0056	0.0200	0.0593	0.0106
XHEALTH	0.0006	0.0315	0.0678	0.0089
YCAPCITY	0.5487	0.6246	0.5169	0.5588
YOTHCITY	0.2338	0.2178	0.2288	0.2310
YTOWN	0.1572	0.1347	0.2034	0.1561
YRURA L	0.0604	0.0229	0.0508	0.0541
LOOK82	0.0291	0.0372	0.1186	0.0350
LOOK83	0.0503	0.0974	0.1102	0.0607
LOOK84	0.0610	0.1519	0.1441	0.0794
PROF	0.2824	0.1719	0.0932	0.2554
CLERCAL	0.1057	0.1261	0.1356	0.1104
MANUAL	0.0861	0.1891	0.2627	0.1113
SALESER	0.1342	0.1633	0.1525	0.1397
TRADE	0.2679	0.2120	0.2203	0.2568
MANUF	0.2125	0.1862	0.2119	0.2084
CONSTR	0.1186	0.1289	0.1186	0.1202
TRADIND	0.2075	0.1948	0.2373	0.2071
FINADM	0.1560	0.1289	0.0678	0.1472
SERIND	0.0660	0.1375	0.1186	0.0798
YRS4	0.0140	0.4069	1.0000	0.1264
VUN	0.0777	0.1633	0.2034	0.0976
WUN	0.0447	0.1948	0.1610	0.0741
XUN	0.0056	0.2779	0.4576	0.0714
XHHSIZE	3.4111	3.5903	3.7203	3.4550
AUSNZ	0.8714	0.8768	0.79661	0.8683
WHITE	0.9592	0.9312	0.9661	0.9552
ENGLISH	0.9217	0.9226	0.9152	0.9215
AUSQUAL	0.2640	0.1404	0.1356	0.2381
VSCHL10	0.2013	0.2751	0.3136	0.2186
VSCHL12	0.3389	0.3267	0.3220	0.3361
YUNION	0.4284	0.2493	0.2034	0.3889
XINDCURR	367.68	207.36	198.64	334.03
UNEMPSP	0.2405	0.3926	0.4746	0.2763
WUNEMPSP	0.3552	0.7393	1.0254	0.4497
XUNEMPSP	0.2220	0.9112	1.2627	0.3832
MIGRANT	0.1286	0.1232	0.2034	0.1317
VLNGSTAY	1.5962	1.5301	2.4407	1.6302
YLTU	0.0000	0.0430	0.0424	0.0089
TOTSP	0.8177	2.0430	2.7627	1.1091
TOTUN	8.8384	28.60	32.407	13.129
YAGE	23.32	22.42	22.60	23.14

Table 3.4.11 Summary statistics, not-in-the-labour force spells

YSPNILF	0 spells N = 1583	1 spells N = 387	>1 spells N = 285	All N = 2255
NSWACT	0.3961	0.4419	0.4351	0.4089
VIC	0.2281	0.2041	0.1860	0.2186
QLD	0.1604	0.1292	0.1474	0.1534
SANT	0.1093	0.1034	0.0982	0.1069
WA	0.0745	0.0853	0.1017	0.0798
TAS	0.0316	0.0362	0.0316	0.0324
YMARRIED	0.3032	0.1938	0.1684	0.2674
VHEALTH	0.0082	0.0181	0.0210	0.0115
WHEALTH	0.0044	0.0129	0.0421	0.0106
XHEALTH	0.0006	0.0258	0.0316	0.0089
YCAPCITY	0.5370	0.6176	0.6000	0.5588
YOTHCITY	0.2382	0.2145	0.2140	0.2310
YTOWN	0.1630	0.1292	0.1544	0.1561
YRURAL	0.0619	0.0388	0.0316	0.0541
LOOK82	0.0284	0.0388	0.0667	0.0350
LOOK83	0.0505	0.0749	0.0982	0.0607
LOOK84	0.0619	0.1163	0.1263	0.0794
PROF	0.2817	0.2067	0.1754	0.2554
CLERCAL	0.1131	0.0982	0.1123	0.1104
MANUAL	0.0796	0.1628	0.2175	0.1113
SALESER	0.1200	0.1860	0.1860	0.1397
TRADE	0.2817	0.2067	0.1860	0.2568
MANUF	0.2198	0.1835	0.1789	0.2084
CONSTR	0.1181	0.1318	0.1158	0.1202
TRADIND	0.2028	0.2067	0.2316	0.2071
FINADM	0.1630	0.1137	0.1053	0.1472
SERIND	0.0575	0.1266	0.1403	0.0798
YRS4	0.0000	0.0000	1.0000	0.1264
VUN	0.0739	0.1447	0.1649	0.0976
WUN	0.0373	0.1447	0.1825	0.0741
XUN	0.0031	0.2067	0.2667	0.0714
XHHSIZE	3.4037	3.5711	3.5825	3.4550
AUSNZ	0.8800	0.8398	0.8421	0.8683
WHITE	0.9627	0.9302	0.9474	0.9552
ENGLISH	0.9255	0.8992	0.9298	0.9215
AUSQUAL	0.2704	0.1886	0.1263	0.2381
VSCHL10	0.2085	0.2300	0.2596	0.2186
VSCHL12	0.3354	0.3282	0.3509	0.3361
YUNION	0.4523	0.2662	0.2035	0.3889
XINDCURR	378.69	258.00	189.16	334.03
UNEMPSP	0.2293	0.3773	0.4000	0.2763
WUNEMPSP	0.3342	0.6615	0.8035	0.4497
XUNEMPSP	0.2028	0.7338	0.9088	0.3832
MIGRANT	0.1200	0.1602	0.1579	0.1317
VLNGSTAY	1.4902	1.9948	1.9123	1.6302
YLTU	0.0000	0.0362	0.0210	0.0089
TOTSP	0.7663	1.7726	2.1123	1.1091
TOTUN	8.0120	24.837	25.656	13.129
YAGE	23.39	22.74	22.32	23.14

The models we estimate are of the form

$$P_j = \exp(x\beta)/\Delta \ (j=1,2,.., m-1)$$

and

$$P_m = 1/\Delta$$

$$\Delta = 1 + \Sigma \exp (x\beta)$$

where P is the appropriate probability and x is a vector of regressors and β is an appropriately defined vector of parameters.

Our main hypotheses are: (a) whether we can discern a secondary labour market, and (b) whether there is evidence of scarring or occurrence dependence. In this paper we estimate reduced form equations which cannot really distinguish between the segmented labour market hypothesis and an amended neoclassical model which allows for scarring. However, as mentioned earlier, the segmented labour market hypothesis provides an explanation for recurrent spells while the human capital/neoclassical model is more an explanation for long term unemployment.

In our estimation we have used a set of variables which describe the characteristics of the individual (e.g. age, education, marital status, union membership, etc.); labour market history variables (e.g. previous unemployment spells); occupation and industry of last previous employment, etc..

List of Variables

LHS Variables:

Spells of Unemployment in 1988.

Spells of Unemployment or Not-in the-Labour-Force in 1988.

RHS Variables:

Most of the variables have been recoded to one-zero variables. A variable name beginning with V,W,X,Y stands for the date of that variable and is for 1985, 1986, 1987, 1988 respectively.

LOOK 84(83,82)	Looking for work in 1984(83,82) = 1, 0 otherwise
UN	1 if Unemployed in the reference period, 0 otherwise
LTU	1 if unemployment duration greater than 1 year, 0 otherwise
UNEMPSP	Number of unemployment spells in one year
YMUR	Male Unemployment Rate in 1988 in State of residence in 1985
AGE	In years
MARRIED	1 if married or de facto, 0 otherwise
SCHL10	SCHL10 = 1 if 10 or less years of school, 0 otherwise
SCHL12	SCHL12 = 1 if 11 or 12 years of school, 0 otherwise
EXP	Years of experience
MIGRANT	1 if born overseas, 0 otherwise.

TOWN	Other city location = 1, 0 otherwise.
RURAL	Rural location = 1, 0 otherwise.
UNION	Union member = 1, 0 otherwise.
WHITE	Race, English or European = 1, 0 otherwise.
HEALTH	Health problems looking for work = 1, 0 otherwise.
INDCURR	Derived Current Income ($)
YFIRED	1 if fired from the last job held, 0 otherwise.
MANUAL	1 if in manual occupations, 0 otherwise.

In some preliminary work we considered a simple binary logit model allowing for those who had two or more spells (recurrent spells) as against those who had either zero or one spell, or one spell only. In this framework we tried several variables describing the individuals characteristics, including type of school, region of origin of migrant, English language ability, previous industry and father's occupation, but most were not significant.[8]

Tables 3.4.12 and 3.4.13 provide results of multinomial logit estimation for spells of unemployment and for spells of unemployment and NILF respectively. Because of the fewer numbers of males who had two or more spells we decided to allow for three alternatives: males who had zero spells (the reference group), those who had one spell, and those who had two or more spells.

Table 3.4.12 shows that the probability of having one spell of unemployment (compared to zero spells) is less if the male is married, lives in a town or rural area (compared to the reference group, those living in cities) in Victoria, is a union member, or had a high income in the previous year. He would have a greater probability of facing a spell of unemployment if he had been fired from the last job he held, the greater the spells of unemployment in the previous year, and had been unemployed at the interview date in the previous year. Manual workers and those who left school early were more likely to have one spell, although the variables have low t-values.

The probability of having recurrent spells of unemployment was less for union members and those who had a high income in the previous year. The probability was greater if they lived in Western Australia, had been fired from the previous job held, the greater the number of previous spells, and if they had been unemployed in the previous year at interview date, and if they were migrants. Curiously, the experience variable is not significant nor was age (used in previous runs), and education variables had low t-values. Manual workers, and those who had a spell of long term unemployment in the first year of the sample were more likely to have unemployment spells but with low t-values.

Table 3.4.13 for unemployment and NILF spells tells (essentially) the same story with generally stronger t-statistics. In effect the results support the view that there is occurrence dependence, that those with low incomes and who are not union members are more likely to face recurrent spells. The main difference is that manual workers are more likely to have more than one spell

Table 3.4.12 Multinomial logit, unemployment spells

Variable	Coefficient	Std. Error	T-ratio
		Outcome = YSPELLS = 1	
ONE	–0.9436	0.3741	-2.522
VIC	–0.3853	0.1972	-1.954
QLD	–0.3448	0.2130	-1.619
SANT	–0.1998	0.2497	-0.800
WA	0.3418	0.2515	1.359
TAS	0.4267	0.3854	1.107
YMARRIED	–0.2865	0.1941	-1.476
YFIRED	1.1351	0.1884	6.026
YTOWN	–0.4374	0.2148	-2.036
YRURAL	-1.2676	0.4189	-3.026
LOOK82	–0.2184	0.4126	–0.529
WUNEMPSP	0.0910	0.0944	0.963
XUNEMPSP	0.6009	0.0960	6.261
YUNION	–0.5177	0.1569	-3.299
XINDCURR	–0.0029	0.0005	-5.907
WHITE	–0.3043	0.3154	–0.965
MIGRANT	–0.2597	0.2259	-1.150
YEXP	0.0031	0.0271	0.116
XUN	2.7246	0.3656	7.451
VLTU	0.5613	0.3611	1.554
VSCHL10	0.2707	0.1871	1.447
VSCHL12	0.1991	0.1635	1.218
YHEALTH	18.4658	1407.3300	0.013
MANUAL	0.2651	0.2101	1.262
		Outcome = YSPELLS = 2	
ONE	–4.2491	0.7031	–6.043
VIC	–0.1029	0.380	–0.324
QLD	–0.1473	0.3379	–0.436
SANT	–0.0376	0.3884	–0.097
WA	0.7454	0.3667	2.032
TAS	–0.5484	0.7179	–0.764
YMARRIED	0.0213	0.2906	0.073
YFIRED	0.9510	0.2839	3.350
YTOWN	0.0456	0.3087	0.148
YRURAL	–0.3555	0.5368	–0.662
LOOK82	0.6830	0.4736	1.442
WUNEMPSP	0.3313	0.1285	2.579
XUNEMPSP	0.6904	0.1307	5.284
YUNION	–0.8853	0.2743	-3.227
XINDCURR	–0.0015	0.0008	-1.808
WHITE	0.7607	0.6065	1.254
MIGRANT	0.5295	0.3084	1.717
YEXP	–0.0195	0.0426	–0.458
XUN	3.5723	0.4229	8.4446
VLTU	0.7112	0.4801	1.481
VSCHL10	0.2847	0.2930	0.972
VSCHL12	0.2906	0.2664	1.091
YHEALTH	18.6893	1407.3300	0.013
MANUAL	0.4070	0.2955	1.377

Table 3.4.13 Multinomial logit, not-in-the-labour force spells

Variable	Coefficient	Std. Error	T-ratio
	Outcome = YSPNILF = 1		
ONE	–0.6522	0.3437	–1.898
VIC	–0.1686	0.1687	–1.000
QLD	–0.4843	0.1981	–2.444
SANT	–0.3576	0.2276	–1.571
WA	0.0740	0.2396	0.309
TAS	–0.0836	0.3844	–0.217
YMARRIED	–0.4028	0.1687	–2.388
YFIRED	1.0689	0.1838	5.815
YTOWN	–0.4298	0.1949	–2.205
YRURAL	–0.6765	0.3135	–2.157
LOOK82	–0.0268	0.3715	–0.072
WUNEMPSP	0.1341	0.0892	1.502
XUNEMPSP	0.4819	0.0947	5.090
YUNION	–0.6466	0.1396	–4.632
XINDCURR	–0.0014	0.0004	–3.637
WHITE	–0.3701	0.2875	–1.287
MIGRANT	0.2558	0.1910	1.339
YEXP	–0.0003	0.0242	0.012
XUN	3.2353	0.4861	6.656
VLTU	0.4898	0.3701	1.323
VSCHL10	–0.1464	0.1744	–0.839
VSCHL12	0.0040	0.1454	0.027
YHEALTH	17.0282	1474.0900	0.012
MANUAL	0.3588	0.2013	1.782
		Outcome = YSPNILF = 2	
ONE	–0.9346	0.4154	–2.250
VIC	–0.2703	0.2049	–1.320
QLD	–0.38`8	0.2264	–1.687
SANT	–0.5105	0.2764	–1.847
WA	0.2507	0.2748	0.912
TAS	–0.1743	0.4617	–0.377
YMARRIED	–0.4477	0.2159	–2.073
YFIRED	0.9958	0.2149	4.633
YTOWN	–0.2439	0.2215	–1.101
YRURAL	–1.1550	0.4109	–2.811
LOOK82	0.5890	0.3782	1.557
WUNEMPSP	0.2328	0.0982	2.370
XUNEMPSP	0.5388	0.1043	5.167
YUNION	–0.9017	0.1777	–5.073
XINDCURR	–0.0041	0.0006	–7.261
WHITE	0.0745	0.3581	0.208
MIGRANT	0.3310	0.2235	1.481
YEXP	–0.0137	0.0294	–0.466
XUN	2.9195	0.4941	5.909
VLTU	0.3875	0.3934	0.985
VSCHL10	0.0691	0.2071	0.334
VSCHL12	0.3288	0.1746	1.883
YHEALTH	18.5184	1474.0900	0.013
MANUAL	0.5716	0.2165	2.641

of unemployment or NILF, and those who had 11 or 12 years of schooling were more likely to have recurrent spells. This provides some support to the view of a secondary labour market where the same people face recurrent spells of unemployment, those who are migrants, who are non-union members, and had low paid work in the past, and those who had previous experience of unemployment. Of course these results could be rationalised in terms of a neoclassical story: those who are low paid are those with few skills and limited education, have a weak attachment to the labour market, are low quality workers and hence are more likely to be fired and less likely to be hired. However, it does not explain why they would have *recurrent spells of unemployment.* In either case these people get trapped in a lower segment of the labour market. The main finding of interest in this study is the impact previous unemployment and previous spells of unemployment play in reinforcing the problems of this group of males.

The surprising part of this analysis was the mixed performance of education variables. This may be because previous unemployment experience was proxying for the education levels. Similarly, the insignificance of age and experience was unexpected. We would expect the younger males to go through a job shopping period, but perhaps because the sample is fairly restricted over the age variable (19–28 years) it may not show up. We were also surprised at the low significance of occupation dummies and insignificance of industry dummies. Again, this may be because of the previous unemployment experience proxying for them. Finally, we did not find a significant effect for the unemployment rate in the state of residence. This may have been because we only had the state of origin of the respondent in 1985. Ideally we would like to use the unemployment rate in the local labour market, but these data are not available to us.

4 Conclusions

Our study of recurrent unemployment suggests that recurrent unemployment is an important problem which has not received sufficient attention in the past. We found that people who had recurrent spells over the period 1985–88 cumulated several months of unemployment experience, even though, on average, each spell may only have been about 13 to 20 weeks long. We found, for example, that those people who had six spells had an average total duration of 85 weeks. We also found that the percentage share of unemployment experience of short spells, and of those people with single spells, was very small. Long spells and people with multiple spells accounted for a very large percentage of the total weeks of unemployment experience. We found evidence for spell repetition, and for spell lengths to decline for people with recurrent spells.

Our evidence from estimation of multinomial logit equations suggests that there is occurrence dependence (scarring), and that males who had been fired from their last job, are migrants, non-union members, had low paid work in the past seem to face recurrent spells. This provides some support for a segmented labour market interpretation of the labour market. However, it is also consistent with some versions of a model that is based on human capital theory, but we cannot discriminate between the models.

The ALS data set provides a unique information base for the study of the Australian youth labour market. We hope that subsequent work will be able to throw some light on the transitions between different labour market states. Policy makers are especially concerned about the high rates of youth unemployment and we need to find ways of preventing the recurring spells of unemployment which lead some people to accumulate very long periods of time in unemployment or not in the labour force. We believe our study provides some insights into this relatively under-researched area.

Notes

The authors are grateful to the Centre for Economic Policy Research, Australian National University and the Department of Employment, Education and Training for financial support. We thank Yong Ping Li for excellent research assistance. Comments from Tony Atkinson, Bruce Chapman, John Creedy, Peter Dolton, Bob Gregory and Dan Hamermesh are gratefully acknowledged.

1. I am grateful to John Creedy for suggesting this framework.
2. This assumes that on-the-job search is less efficient than off-the-job search. However, there is very little evidence to support this view.
3. See Atkinson (1990) for an analysis of an interesting theoretical model.
4. Earlier studies of youth labour markets include Miller and Volker (1987), Junankar (1987), and Lynch (1989).
5. In subsequent work we hope to look at females in the sample.
6. Missing values of UNEMPSP were set equal to zero, and hence are likely to underestimate the problem.
7. Tables showing this bias are available from the authors on request.
8. Due to the restrictions of the LIMDEP version on the mainframe computer, we could only allow for a limited number of variables in the multinomial logit equations.

References

Adena, M.A. (1989) 'Associations Between Frequency and Duration of Unemployment and Later Unemployment Status in Young Australians', Canberra: INSTAT.

Atkinson, A.B. (1990) 'Institutional Features of Unemployment Insurance and the Working of the Labour Market', Welfare State Discussion Paper WSP/50, STICERD, London School of Economics.

Clark, K.B and L.H. Summers (1979) 'Labour Market Dynamics and Unemployment: A Reconsideration', *Brookings Papers on Economic Activity*, 1, 13–60.

Corcoran, M. and M.S. Hill (1985) 'Reoccurrence of Unemployment Among Young Adult Men', *Journal of Human Resources*, 20, 165–183.

Heckman, J.J and G.J. Borjas (1980) 'Does Unemployment Cause Future Unemployment?', *Economica*, 47, August, 247–284.

Hui, W-T (1986) 'Modelling Multiple Spells of Unemployment', Working Papers in Economics and Econometrics No. 135, Australian National University.

Hui, W-T. (1986) 'State Dependence and Youth Unemployment in Australia: A Survival Analysis', Working Papers in Economics and Econometrics No. 138, Australian National University.

Junankar, P.N. (ed.) (1987) *From School to Unemployment? The Labour Market for Young People*, London: Macmillan.

Kryger, T. (1990) *The Australian Longitudinal Survey: 1985 to 1988: Dynamics of the Youth Labour Market*, Canberra: AGPS.

Lynch, L.M. (1989) 'The Youth Labour Market in the Eighties: Determinants of Re-Employment Probabilities for Young Men and Women', *Review of Economics and Statistics*, LXXI, February, 37–45.

Miller, P. and P. Volker (1987) 'The Youth Labour Market in Australia: A Survey of Issues and Evidence, Discussion Paper No. 171, Centre for Economic Policy Research, Australian National University.

OECD (1985) *Employment Outloo 1985*, Paris.

Parsons, D.O. (1977) 'Models of Labor Market Turnover: A Theoretical and Empirical Survey', in R. Ehrenberg (ed) *Research in Labor Economics*, Greenwich, Conn.: JAI Press, 185–219.

Pedersen, P.J. and N. Westergard-Nielsen (1987) 'Multiple Spells of Unemployment-The Danish Experience', in P.J. Pedersen and R. Lund (eds) *Unemployment: Theory, Policy and Structure*, Berlin, Walter de Gruyter.

Stern, J. (1986) 'Repeat Unemployment Spells: The Effect of Unemployment Benefits on Unemployment Entry', in R. Blundell and I. Walker (eds) *Unemployment Search and Labour Supply*, Cambridge: Cambridge University Press.

Trivedi, P. and J.N. Alexander (1986) 'Re-employment Probability and Multiple Unemployment Spells: A Semi-Parametric Approach', Working Papers in Economics and Econometrics No. 139, Australian National University..

Trivedi, P.K. and J.N. Alexander (1989) 'Re-employment Probability and Multiple Unemployment Spells: A Partial Likelihood Approach', *Journal of Business and Economic Statistics*, 7, 395–401.

Trivedi, P.K. and G.M. Baker (1983) 'Unemployment in Australia: Duration and Recurrent Spells', *Economic Record*, 59, 132–148.

3.5
The Impact of the Global Financial Crisis on Youth Unemployment

PN (Raja) Junankar

Australia was one of the few OECD countries to emerge from the Global Financial Crisis (GFC) without facing a recession, usually defined as negative GDP growth for two consecutive quarters. However, the (overall) unemployment rate did increase following the GFC and has still not returned to pre–GFC levels. Unemployment rates for young people went up much more dramatically and remain high. This article investigates the impact of the GFC on youth unemployment and long-term unemployment. To anticipate our results, we find that the youth unemployment rates increased significantly owing to a fall in aggregate demand, although youth wages had been falling relative to adult wages. These findings do not support the commonly heard claim that youth wages are pricing young people out of the market.

Introduction

Australia was one of the few Organisation for Economic Co-operation and Development (OECD) member countries to emerge from the Global Financial Crisis (GFC) without facing a recession, usually defined as negative growth in gross domestic product (GDP) for two consecutive quarters. However, the (overall) unemployment rate did increase following the 2008–2009 onset of the GFC and has still not returned to the pre-GFC levels. Youth unemployment rates went up much more dramatically than average rates across the workforce and remain high. Chris Kent, Assistant Governor of the Reserve Bank of Australia, stated to a House of Representatives Standing Committee on Economics that youth unemployment 'is certainly a significant concern' (Commonwealth of Australia, 2015: 15). This article investigates the impact of the GFC on youth unemployment and long-term unemployment. In particular, we study whether

Reprinted from 'The Impact of the Global Financial Crisis on Youth Unemployment' by P. N. (Raja) Junankar in *Economic and Labour Relations Review*, 26 (2), 2015, 1–27. With kind permission from SAGE Publications.

youth unemployment rates increased due to an increase in youth wages relative to adult wages. To anticipate our results, we find that the youth unemployment rates increased significantly although youth wages had been falling relative to adult wages. These findings do not support the commonly heard claim that youth wages are pricing young people out of the market.

Changes announced in the May 2014 Coalition Government Budget (but still not legislated by February 2015) meant that anyone below 30 years of age would not have access to unemployment benefits for 6 months and after that would be required to engage in compulsory work for the dole. The prospects facing a large and growing number of young people are therefore grim. Recent research (Clark et al., 2014; Mavromaras et al., 2013; Stewart, 2007) suggests a long-term scarring effect of taking on a job that is below the skill level of the person who does so: the probability of subsequently getting a good job (i.e. one that is appropriate for that person's skills and education levels) is decreased significantly. The Coalition Government in 2014 proposed that anyone under the age of 30 years must accept any job at all as a condition of receiving unemployment benefits.[1] This is a policy likely to cause serious problems for the young. The OECD (2013) in its Action Plan for Youth argues that 'Even if public resources are constrained, especially where fiscal consolidation is required, it is important to guarantee that youth, including those with little or no work experience, have access to unemployment and social assistance' (p. 7).

In the context of the Coalition Government's policy approach to young people's employment, this article examines the dimensions of the Australian youth labour market and changes to it in the wake of the GFC. The section 'Literature review' provides a literature review of the debate over the determinants of youth unemployment, including the relationship between minimum wages and unemployment levels. The section 'The Australian youth labour market' provides a statistical overview of the nature and dynamics of the youth labour market since 1997, including a regression analysis showing that unemployment trends in the adult labour market are amplified in the youth labour market, which is concentrated into narrow casualised segments, vulnerable to downturns. The section 'The youth labour market after the GFC' identifies the scarring effects on young people of post-GFC unemployment and its failure to return to pre-GFC levels. In a discussion of the causes of youth unemployment in the section 'What explains the rise in youth unemployment?' it is shown that claimed links to the levels of either youth wages or unemployment benefits are not supported by the evidence. The article concludes with some concrete proposals for reducing youth unemployment and by arguing the potentially very harmful effects of policy proposals announced in 2014.

Literature review

There is a large research literature on youth labour markets in the OECD in general, and there are a smaller number of papers about the Australian experience. Many of the European OECD countries have faced a massive increase in youth unemployment and long-term unemployment (Junankar, 2011). A common feature of this literature is the social impact of youth unemployment. When young people are unemployed, they may face various problems including heightened levels of social alienation and depression and an increase in the use of non-prescribed drugs, petty crime and suicide rates (Eurofound, 2014).

In the economics literature, there has been a continuing debate about the impact of minimum wages on (youth) unemployment, with the traditional view assuming competitive labour markets where it is argued that minimum wages lead to unemployment (Junankar, 1987). This view has been very popular with Conservative politicians and with the business sector. However, in recent years, a growing number of economists have argued that in imperfect markets, minimum wages do not lead to increased unemployment (Booth, 2014; Card and Krueger, 1995; Manning, 2003, 2010). They argue that the labour market is not perfectly competitive but that employers have market power in wage setting (monopsony). There is asymmetric information in the labour market, workers have heterogeneous preferences and so on, all of which make the labour market behave differently from a competitive market. Manning (2003, 2010) has shown that in such markets employment can increase with an increase in wage rates.

The controversy on the impact of minimum wages on unemployment was kindled by the work of Card and Krueger (1994, 1995) which was followed by several critiques by (among others) Neumark and Wascher (2007). The international evidence is mixed with recent studies by Dube et al. (2010) for the United States showing that there is no evidence for the 'disemployment' effects of minimum wages. Dube (2011) in a book review of Neumark and Wascher (2008) argues that the evidence provided for such effects is selective and that '[D]ynamic specifications show that the measured disemployment in the state panel models tend to occur before (and sometimes many years before) the minimum wage increases' (p. 763).

In 1999, Britain introduced a national minimum wage (NMW). The impact of this NMW has been studied by several economists. David Metcalf (2008), for example, shows that the NMW did increase wages, but there is no evidence to show that it led to a fall in employment. He argues that a minimum wage rise could increase labour supply and the increased wages (via efficiency wages) could increase productivity.

There is now much evidence that minimum wages do not lead to increased unemployment. In an open letter on 14 January 2014, 600 US Economists wrote to the US Congress:

> In recent years there have been important developments in the academic literature on the effect of increases in the minimum wage on employment, with the weight of evidence now showing that increases in the minimum wage have had little or no negative effect on the employment

> of minimum-wage workers, even during times of weakness in the labor market. Research suggests that a minimum-wage increase could have a small stimulative effect on the economy as low-wage workers spend their additional earnings, raising demand and job growth, and providing some help on the jobs front. (Economic Policy Institute, 2014)

Another branch of traditional economics argues that generous unemployment benefits lead to increased unemployment. The underlying economic theory is based on a model of unemployed workers searching for a job with imperfect information (Mortensen and Pissarides, 1999). The unemployed searching for employment receive various job offers, but depending on the wage offered they may accept or reject that offer. If they have substantial unemployment benefits, they have a higher 'reservation wage' and reject low wage offers, remaining unemployed. Nickell and Layard (1999) have argued that unemployment benefits are one of the reasons for high unemployment. They also argue that various labour market institutions like unions, centralised wage bargaining and so on also lead to higher unemployment. These results have been criticised by various people including Howell (2005, 2011), and Howell et al. (2007). Heckman (2007) also argues that the orthodox results are 'fragile' and unable to support the conclusions that labour market institutions are the main cause of high unemployment.

Curiously, there is very little recent literature on Australian youth labour markets. There were a few survey papers several years ago (Lewis and Mclean, 1998; Miller and Volker, 1987), a few papers using longitudinal data (Junankar and Wood, 1992; Marks et al., 2003), panel studies by Leigh (2003), Watson (2004) and some time-series estimates of employment (Daly et al.,1998; Junankar et al., 2000). In a paper using Australian time-series data, Junankar et al. (2000) estimated employment functions for youth in different industries using time-series data and found no evidence to support the view that minimum wages decrease employment rates. Leigh (2003), in a study using difference in difference methodology, compared one State (Western Australia) that had increased minimum wages with other States. He found a negative impact of minimum wages on employment. This article was heavily criticised by Watson (2004) and Junankar (2004). One important issue that is sometimes ignored in cross-sectional studies is that if minimum wages are increased, this leads to an increase in total incomes of that group; hence, there would be Keynesian aggregate demand effects that can help to increase employment overall.

Sewell (2013) carried out a time-series analysis (quarterly data from 1997 (Q1) to 2012 Q(1)) of the Australian youth labour market. He estimated a model using Ordinary Least Squares where the youth unemployment rate is a function of lagged changes in the growth rate of GDP (as a proxy for aggregate demand), lagged real minimum wage, a replacement rate (RR) and an indicator variable to allow for non-linearities in the impact of positive and negative changes in growth. He found that the impact of the real minimum wage was statistically insignificant for male youth but significant for females. The RR was statistically insignificant, but he noted that he used the adult wage rate (as he did not have data on youth wage rates), which means that we need to be wary in accepting these results. He also found that increases in aggregate demand lead to falls in the youth unemployment rate. An interesting finding was that when GDP growth is negative, it has a greater effect on youth unemployment than when it is positive.

There is some evidence for scarring (reduced long-term life chances) and occurrence dependence (an event of unemployment increases the probability of a repeat spell). A relatively recent paper by Doiron and Gorgens (2008) found evidence for state dependence, using the Household and Income Labour Dynamics (HILDA) longitudinal data. Another recent paper by Hérault et al. (2012) estimated a multinomial logit model for the youth labour market using cohort data from the Longitudinal Surveys of Australian Youth and Youth in Transition Surveys and found that growth and unemployment have different effects on different components of the youth labour market (analysed by education, whether working part-time or full-time, and gender). An increase in the overall unemployment rate increases the risk of youth unemployment.

Overall, the various studies of the youth labour market suggest that there is considerable doubt about the impact of minimum wages on youth unemployment. However, most studies find that increases in aggregate demand lead to a fall in youth unemployment.

The Australian youth labour market[2]

The youth labour market in Australia is a complex market: young people have a choice of leaving school at age 16 or 17 (the compulsory schooling ages) or of continuing until age 18 (and completing Year 12). If they leave school early, they may look for work or a traineeship. If they continue until age 18, they may look for work or continue in tertiary education (either at a TAFE or at University). As the number of unskilled jobs seems to have been on a declining trend over the past few decades, most young people who leave school early find it difficult to get a job. As a result, they may decide to re-enter the education sector. If they continue into tertiary education, they may leave education at 20 (say with a TAFE qualification) or a university degree at 21 or 22. It is important to note that since government policies were introduced in July 2009, young people aged under 19 years have to be in full-time education (at least 25 hours a week); otherwise, they do not have access to the youth allowance (unemployment benefits), and hence are unlikely to respond to an Australian Bureau of Statistics (ABS) Survey as being unemployed. Even 20- to 24-year-olds without a Year 12 or equivalent would have access to subsidised education or training place. Again, this may affect this group from being listed as unemployed.[3]

Many young people who are studying at TAFE or University work part-time as well. There are even a significant number of young people who are full-time students and who work full-time! There are large flows between different states: from employment to unemployment or education, from unemployment to education or employment and from education to employment or unemployment.

Since there is a surge of young people entering the labour market at the end of a school year or university year, the sudden increase in supply means that it is difficult to find a job quickly and unemployment rises. If some young people are unable to find work for some time, they may move from unemployment to the education sector or to not-in-the-labour force (NILF) status, and the labour force participation rate and unemployment rate fall as a result. In a recession, as firms stop hiring, the young are hit as they are just entering the labour market. In addition, during a recession, firms tend to fire the young because they work on a last-in-first-out basis. As many young people may be in casual or short-term employment, during a recession their contracts are not renewed. Another important feature of the youth labour market is that young people are typically employed in cyclically sensitive areas like Manufacturing and Construction (for males) and Retail trade and Accommodation and food services (especially for females) (see Table 3.5.1). During the GFC, these industries were hit significantly and youth unemployment increased substantially.[4] A study by the OECD (2014) shows that

> in terms of employment changes by age the initial decline in the OECD employment rate (persons aged 15 and over) up to the end of 2009 was largely driven by job losses among prime-age workers and youth, reflecting the relative dominance of prime-age workers in the population and the disproportionate impact of the crisis on jobs held by youth. (p. 26)

Furthermore, the OECD states, 'The worst off are youth and low skilled workers. Young and unskilled workers face the highest unemployment rates. Hence, they cumulate the poorest performance in terms of job quantity with the worst outcomes with respect to job quality' (p. 120).

As a result, young people are likely to face higher rates of unemployment compared to adults, as Figure 3.5.1 indicates. In particular, the 15- to 19-year-old group has much higher unemployment rates than the 20- to 24-year-old group, which in turn has higher rates than adults (25- to 64-year-olds). As young people see the labour market getting tighter, they may respond by delaying entering it and continuing their education (a phenomenon I call 'encouraged students'). Similarly, when people have been unemployed for a long period, they may give up searching for employment ('discouraged workers').

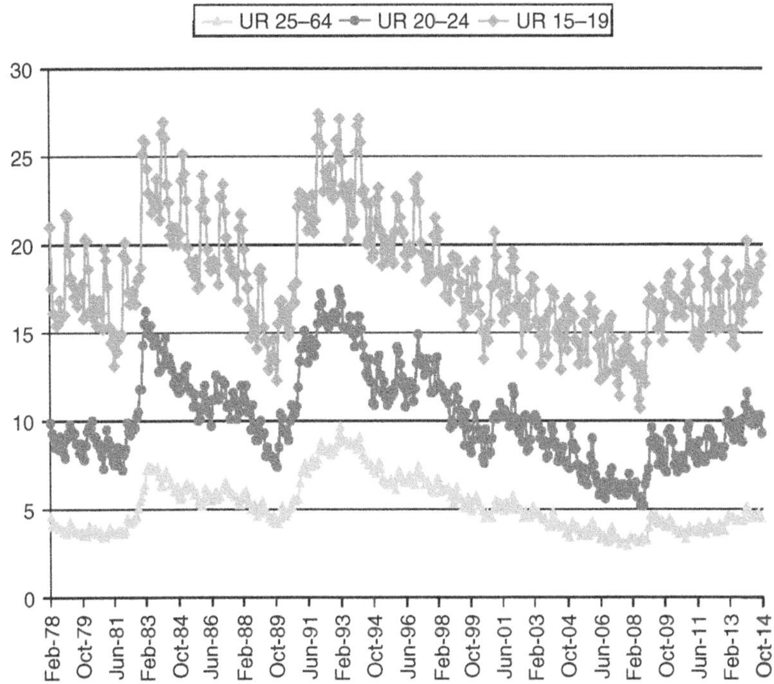

Figure 3.5.1 Unemployment rates, people aged 15–24, 20–24 and 25–64 years. Australia, 1978–2014

UR 15–19: unemployment rate, 15- to 19-year-olds; UR 20–24: unemployment rate, 20- to 24-year-olds;

UR 25–64: unemployment rate, 25- to 64-year-olds.

Source: ABS (2014e). GM1, Labour force status and gross changes (flows) by sex, state, age (LM8srd).

A simple ordinary least squares regression of the Australian youth unemployment rate (15–24 age group) on the adult unemployment rate (25–64 age group), using monthly seasonally adjusted data from November 1997 to November 2013, gives the following

$$YUR = 4.64 + 1.67UR \quad (1)$$
$$(18.35) \; (28.61)$$

$$R^2 = 0.81$$

In words, for every 1 percentage point increase in the adult unemployment rate, the youth unemployment rate increases by 1.67 percentage points.

There appears to have been a change in this relationship after the GFC (using a dummy variable equal to zero from November 1997 to December 2007, and one thereafter)[5]

$$\text{YUR} = \underset{(14.87)}{4.25} + \underset{(27.93)}{1.75\text{UR}} + \underset{(2.76)}{0.30\text{GFC}} \quad (2)$$

$$R^2 = 0.82$$

This suggests that for every 1 percentage point increase in the adult unemployment rate, the youth unemployment rate increased by 1.75 percentage points and after the GFC by 2.05 percentage points. In each case, the variables are statistically significant at the 1% level.[6]

A similar equation was estimated in terms of an annual change in unemployment rates (to remove any trend)

$$\Delta\text{YUR} = \underset{(0.68)}{0.04} + \underset{(17.43)}{1.89\Delta\text{Adult UR}} \quad (3)$$

$$R^2 = 0.63$$

This result in turn suggests that an increase of 1 percentage point in the adult unemployment rate led to a 1.89 percentage point increase in the youth unemployment rate. Note that changes in access to unemployment benefits, especially since July 2009, may have led to lower youth unemployment rates, *ceteris paribus*. No attempt has been made to test this relationship for structural stability.

As Tables 3.5.1 and 3.5.2 show, youth employment is concentrated in a few industries (shown in bold face type); 15- to 19-year-old males are mainly in full-time employment in the Construction, Manufacturing and Retail trade and in part-time employment in the Retail trade and Accommodation and food services. Full-time employment of 20- to 24-year-old males is concentrated in the Construction, Manufacturing and Retail trade, and 25- to 34-year-old males are mainly in full-time employment in Manufacturing while their part-time employment is concentrated in the Retail trade and Accommodation and food services. However, there is much greater concentration of males aged under 25 years in a few industries, compared with the older age group of 25- to 34-year-olds (a group that could be considered as substitutes for younger people);15- to 19-year-old females in full-time employment are concentrated in Health care and social assistance, the Retail trade and Accommodation and food services, while part-time female employment is heavily concentrated in Accommodation and food services and the Retail trade; 20- to 24-year-old females in full-time employment are concentrated in Health care and social assistance, the Retail trade, and Professional, scientific and technical services. Part-time employment for this age group is mainly in the Retail trade, Accommodation and food services, and Health care and social assistance.

Thus, whereas 25- to 34-year-old males working full-time are concentrated in the Construction industry, those working part-time are concentrated

Table 3.5.1 Shares of employment by age and industry (%), males, Australia, May Quarter 2014

Males – young and aged 25–34 years	MEFT, 15–19 (%)	MEPT, 15–19 (%)	MEFT, 20–24 (%)	MEPT, 20–24 (%)	MEFT, 25–34 (%)	MEPT. 25–34 (%)
Agriculture, forestry and fishing	4.59	2.08	3.27	0.42	2.34	3.13
Mining	0.63	0.15	4.57	0.26	4.57	0.00
Manufacturing	**11.43**	2.38	**10.29**	**4.08**	10.83	7.92
Electricity, gas, water and waste services	2.52	0.10	1.05	0.26	1.90	1.00
Construction	**34.29**	2.67	**25.52**	6.84	16.93	8.33
Wholesale trade	2.70	1.14	2.80	0.68	3.92	1.89
Retail trade	**12.06**	**35.89**	**10.29**	**26.28**	7.86	13.89
Accommodation and food services	5.76	**35.25**	6.69	**21.37**	4.50	12.59
Transport, postal and warehousing	4.41	1.98	5.24	5.49	6.02	6.21
Information media and communications	3.06	0.69	2.17	1.57	2.36	1.12
Financial and insurance services		0.20	1.52	0.89	4.17	0.71
Rental, hiring and real estate services	0.18	1.04	1.05	2.77	1.98	0.35
Professional, scientific and technical services	2.34	2.52	4.89	2.66	10.34	5.02
Administrative and support services	0.63	2.48	2.10	3.61	2.17	7.39
Public administration and safety	2.61		3.60	2.35	5.44	3.01
Education and training	0.72	1.83	1.12	5.12	3.64	7.27
Health care and social assistance	0.72	2.52	2.90	7.37	5.15	11.29
Arts and recreation services	1.17	5.69	2.05	5.49	1.30	3.37
Other services	**10.17**	1.39	8.89	2.51	4.58	5.50
Total (×1000)	111.1	202	400.5	191.4	1322.70	169.20

MEFT: share of males employed full-time in industry x; MEPT: share of males employed part-time in industry x.

Source: ABS (2014f). Employed persons (ST E12) by industry (Australian New Zealand Standard Industrial Classification (ANZSIC) division), sex, state and territory, age and actual hours worked, August 1991 onwards.

Table 3.5.2 Shares of employment by age and industry (%), females, Australia, May Quarter 2014.

Females – young and aged 25–34 years	**FEFT, 15–19 (%)**	**FEPT, 15–19 (%)**	**FEFT, 20–24 (%)**	**FEPT, 20–24 (%)**	**FEFT, 25–34 (%)**	**FEPT, 25–34 (%)**
Agriculture, forestry and fishing	0.71	0.52	1.08	0.25	0.41	0.85
Mining			0.97	0.11	1.49	0.18
Manufacturing	7.30	4.19	3.95	2.64	4.08	4.12
Electricity, gas, water and waste services	0.89		0.68	0.32	1.10	0.40
Construction	1.07	0.26	1.69	1.00	1.99	2.51
Wholesale trade	0.53	0.33	2.55	0.64	2.89	1.81
Retail trade	**17.26**	**36.00**	**12.03**	**30.31**	9.42	14.76
Accommodation and food services	**15.66**	**38.86**	8.04	**21.43**	5.71	11.07
Transport, postal and warehousing	3.20	0.96	3.59	1.57	2.10	1.41
Information media and communications	2.14	1.15	1.26	2.46	2.48	0.60
Financial and insurance services	3.74	0.30	5.10	1.07	7.07	2.99
Rental, hiring and real estate services	3.91	1.45	5.46	1.82	2.95	2.11
Professional, scientific and technical services	5.16	0.85	**10.99**	3.21	12.11	6.50
Administrative and support services	1.42	0.89	2.37	2.82	3.54	6.20
Public administration and safety	2.67	0.04	6.93	1.43	7.89	4.52
Education and training	3.02	3.23	5.82	8.06	10.77	11.02
Health care and social assistance	**17.44**	4.60	**19.46**	**12.70**	18.55	22.12
Arts and recreation services	0.89	3.34	1.22	3.74	1.55	2.11
Other services	**12.99**	3.04	6.82	4.42	3.92	4.72
Total (×1000)	56.2	269.7	278.5	280.4	810.90	398.30

FEFT: share of females employed full-time in industry x; FEPT: share of females employed part-time in industry x.

Source: ABS (2014f). Employed persons (ST E12) by industry (Australian New Zealand Standard Industrial Classification (ANZSIC) division), sex, state and territory, age and actual hours worked, August 1991 onwards.

in similar industries to females: Accommodation and food services and the Retail trade. However, it is clear that there are significant differences between the different age groups with a greater concentration in a fewer industries for the young.

Although youth are usually defined as young people between the ages of 15 and 24 years, the labour market for the 15–19 age group is very different from that of the 20–24 age group. Young people aged 15–24 years are more likely to be working part-time or in casual jobs. Note that casual employment is defined as workers without leave entitlements.[7] As Figures 3.5.2 and 3.5.3 show, for young males and females (15–19), a large majority are part-time workers, but even for the 20–24 age group, a significant proportion are working in part-time jobs. In addition, there has been a significant increase in part-time working for young males as well as females over the past decades. As we can see from Figures 3.5.4 and 3.5.5, part-time workers are more likely to be casual workers and hence subject to a greater threat of losing their jobs. Even a large proportion of young full-time workers are in casual employment and would most likely be the first to lose their jobs in a recession.

The youth labour market after the GFC

After the GFC (post 2008), Australia fared much better than most OECD countries, and its youth unemployment rates for 15- to 24-year-olds were almost the lowest, with only Japan and Germany having lower rates (Table 3.5.3;

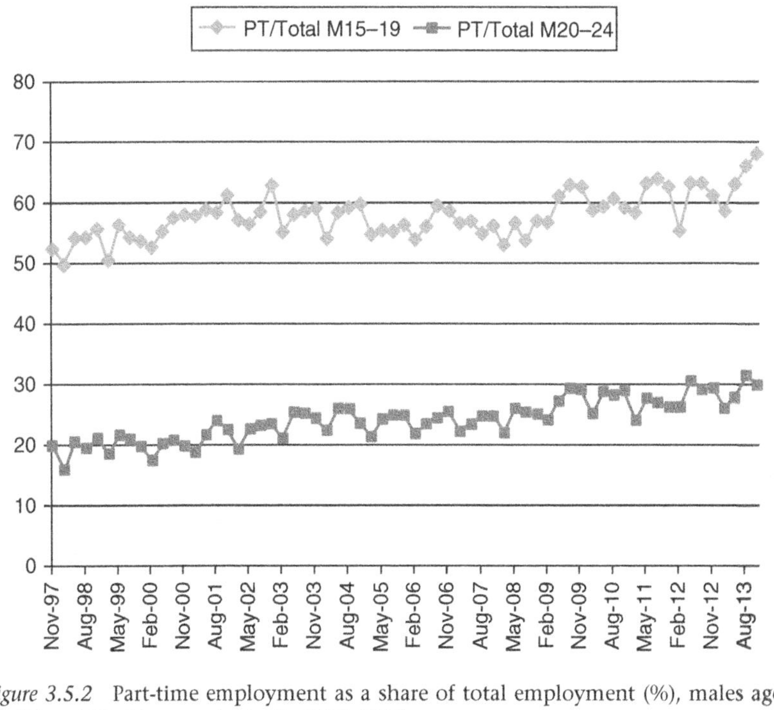

Figure 3.5.2 Part-time employment as a share of total employment (%), males aged 15–19 and 20–24 years, Australia 1997–2013
Source: ABS (2014e).

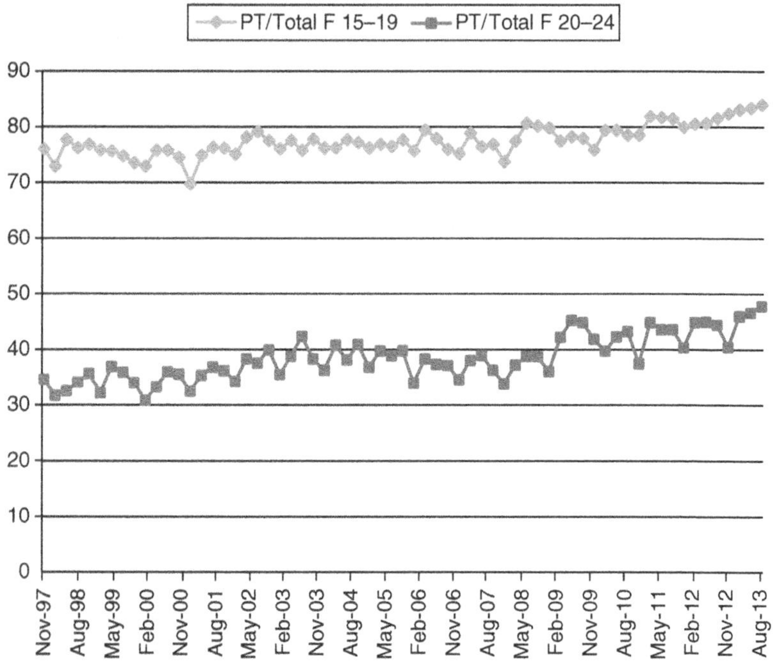

Figure 3.5.3 Part-time employment as a share of total employment (%), females aged 15–19 and 20–24 years, Australia, 1997–2013
Source: ABS (2014e).

highest and lowest values shown in bold type). Even New Zealand, which is sometimes listed as a country that has done well since the GFC, had higher unemployment rates. Greece and Spain have had increasingly high youth unemployment rates, while Germany was one of the few countries where youth unemployment rates continued to fall over this period.

The GFC led to significant falls in GDP for most of the OECD countries, but Australia managed to grow throughout this period. Many economists (but not the National Bureau of Economic Research, New York) define a recession as a situation in which a country faces two consecutive quarters of negative GDP growth.[8] In terms of that definition, Australia avoided a recession. However, although Australian GDP fell only in one quarter during the GFC, unemployment rates (especially for youth) increased and had not returned to pre-GFC levels even by August 2013 (Table 3.5.4). A broader definition of a recession that includes employment/unemployment would consider that Australia suffered a recession in the aftermath of the GFC. The youth labour market was hit badly by the GFC, and unemployment and long-term unemployment increased substantially for both males and

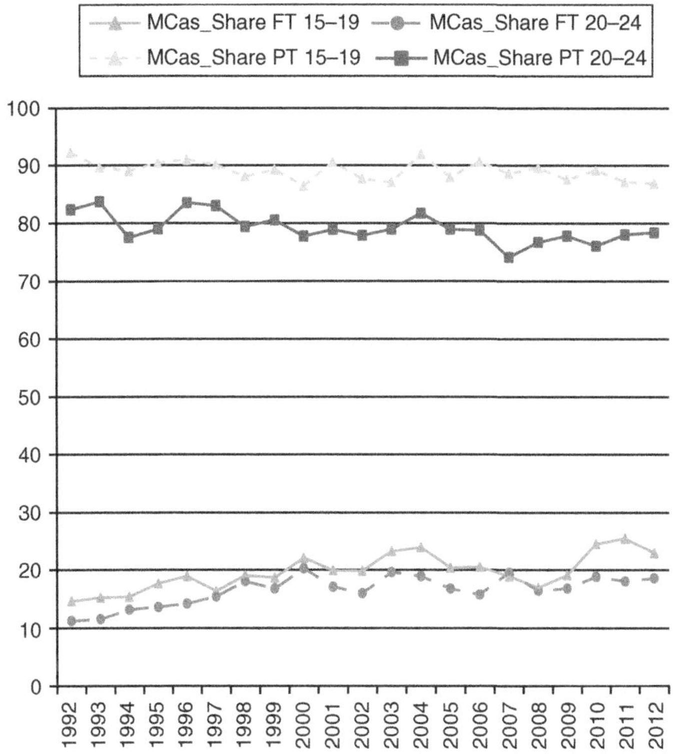

Figure 3.5.4 Casual employment as a share of full-time and part-time employment (%), males aged 15–19 and 20–24 years, Australia, 1992–2012
Source: ABS (2014a).

Table 3.5.3 Unemployment rates (%), young people aged 15–24 years, OECD.

	2008	2009	2010	2011	2012	2013	% Increase
Australia	8.8	11.5	11.6	11.4	11.7	12.2	38.5
Canada	11.6	15.2	14.8	14.2	14.3	13.7	18.0
France	18.6	23.2	22.9	22.1	23.9	23.9	28.7
Germany	10.4	11.0	9.7	8.5	8.1	7.9	–23.7
Greece	22.1	25.8	32.9	44.4	55.3	**58.3**	164.1
Ireland	12.4	25.5	28.3	29.9	33.0	29.6	137.9
Italy	21.3	25.4	27.9	29.1	35.3	40.0	88.2
Japan	7.2	9.1	9.2	8.0	7.9	**6.9**	–4.9
New Zealand	11.4	16.6	17.1	17.3	17.7	15.8	38.9
Spain	24.5	37.7	41.5	46.2	52.9	55.5	126.9
Sweden	20.2	24.9	24.8	22.8	23.7	23.6	16.8
United Kingdom	14.1	19.0	19.3	20.0	21.0	20.9	48.1
United States	12.8	17.6	18.4	17.3	16.2	15.5	21.0
OECD	12.7	16.7	16.7	16.2	16.3	16.2	27.0

Source: Organisation for Economic Co-operation and Development (OECD, 2015).

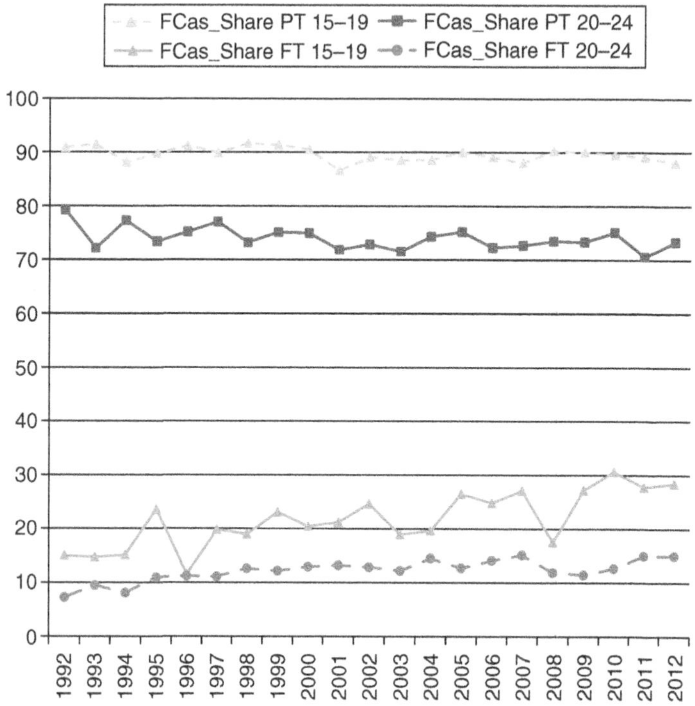

Figure 3.5.5 Casual employment as a share of full-time and part-time employment (%), females aged 15–19 and 20–24 years, Australia, 1992–2012

Source: ABS (2014a).

females. However, since Australian GDP did not fall substantially, unemployment rates did not reach the very high levels that Australian youth had faced during the previous recessions of the early 1980s and the early 1990s (Figure 3.5.6). Similarly, youth underemployment rates (the unemployed plus those young people who would like to work longer hours) and youth underutilisation rates (the unemployed, plus the underemployed, plus the marginally attached to the labour force) increased and reached very high levels (Figures 3.5.7 and 3.5.8).

These figures suggest that the problem for young people is more serious than can be discerned simply looking at the unemployment rates. As a recession hits, the youth employment-to-population ratio falls (Figure 3.5.9). This occurs both because unemployment rises and because the labour force participation rate falls (Figure 3.5.10). Note that the female labour force participation rates had been growing consistently in previous decades and then fell, while the male labour force participation rates had been slowly falling and then fell sharply with the GFC. As a result of these

Table 3.5.4 Increases in youth unemployment in Australia, post-GFC (%)

	Unemployment rate (%)			
	Males aged 15–19 years	**Males aged 20–24 years**	**Females aged 15–19 years**	**Females aged 20–24 years**
August 2008	10.2	5.6	9.9	4.9
August 2013	16.4	9.8	13.6	8.6
% Increase since GFC (August 2008 to August 2013)	61.1	77.0	36.3	72.8

GFC: Global Financial Crisis.
Source: ABS (2014e).

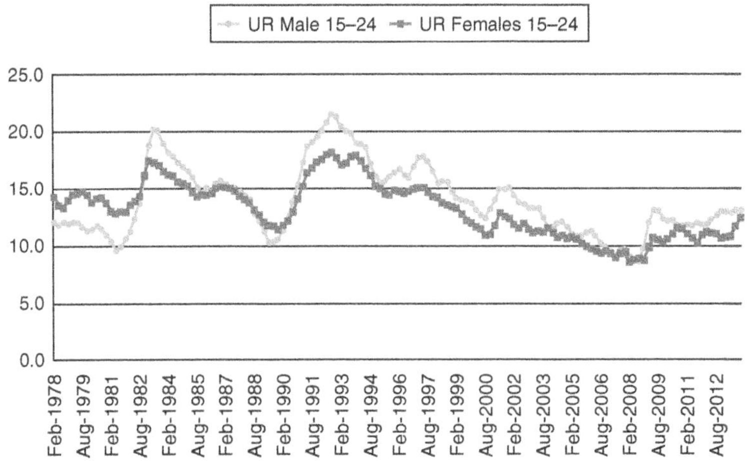

Figure 3.5.6 Unemployment rates (%), males and females aged 15–24 years, Australia, 1978–2012
Source: ABS (2013b) –. Labour force status by sex – persons aged 15–24 years – trend, seasonally adjusted and original.

changes in the participation rate, youth unemployment rate increases are underestimated.

As the GFC developed, although we did not have a technical recession, unemployment rates increased significantly for males, females and young people of both genders. For the reasons discussed earlier, young people face significant increases in unemployment in recessions.

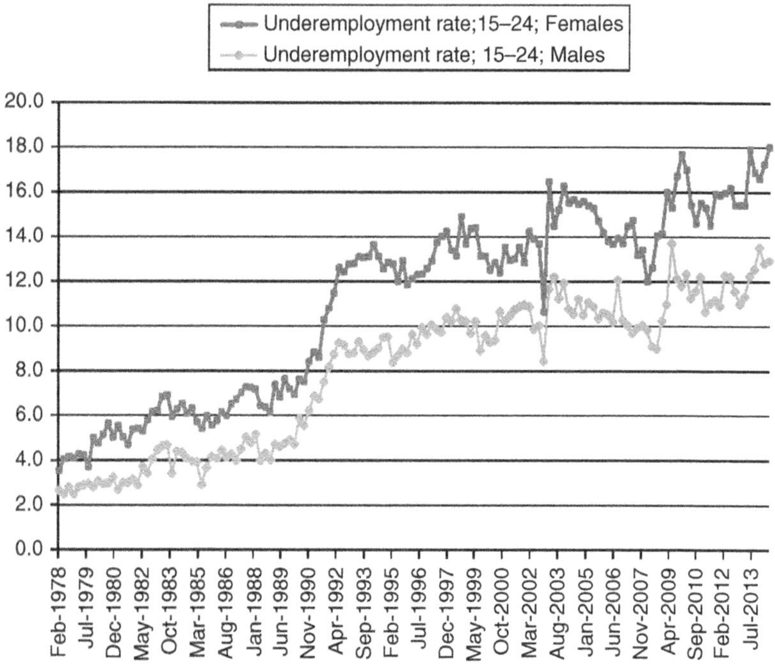

Figure 3.5.7 Underemployment rates (%), males and females aged 15–24 years, Australia, 1978–2013

Source: ABS (2014d) – Table 22. Labour underutilisation by age and sex – trend, seasonally adjusted and original.

When the GFC hit Australia, unemployment rates for adults and young people rose and so did the rates of long-term unemployment.[9] The percentage of the young unemployed who were unemployed for 12 months or more (i.e. the incidence of long-term unemployment) increased significantly (percentage of long-term unemployment (PLTU)). *Again, this long-term unemployment has not returned to pre-GFC days* (Figure 3.5.11). It is worth noting that since some of the unemployed may give up looking for work and move into the education sector, they are not recorded as long-term unemployed, which means that long-term unemployment rates are underestimated. Similarly, as young people age, they may move out of the age group (say 15–19) that is being considered (a person who is just 18 years old cannot be included in the measure of youth unemployed for more than a year). For a 20-year-old young person, to be unemployed for *1 year* is to have lost 5% of one's life to date in unemployment; to be unemployed for *2 years* is to have lost 10% of one's life in unemployment! Added to that is the problem of scarring: one spell of unemployment is likely to lead to repeat spells (Junankar and Wood,

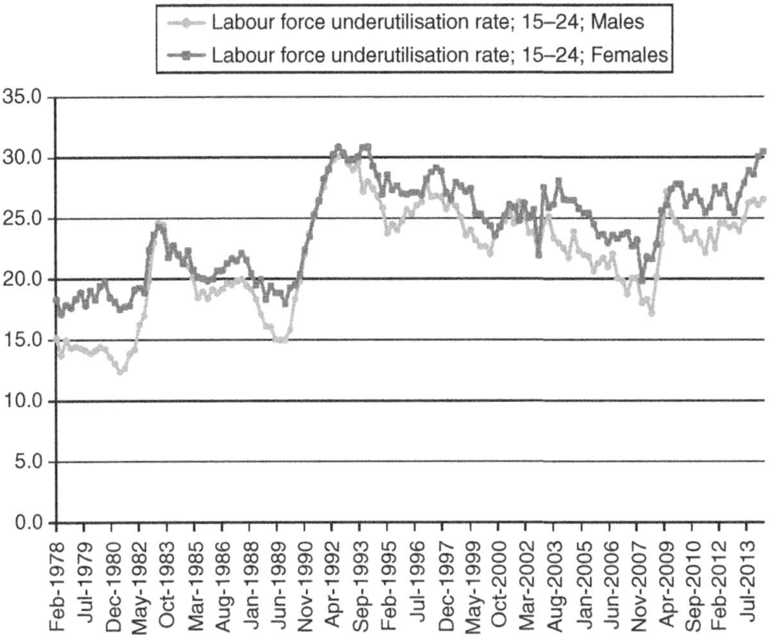

Figure 3.5.8 Labour underutilisation rates (%), males and females aged 15–24 years, Australia, 1978–2013

Source: ABS (2014d) – Table 22. Labour underutilisation by age and sex – trend, seasonally adjusted and original.

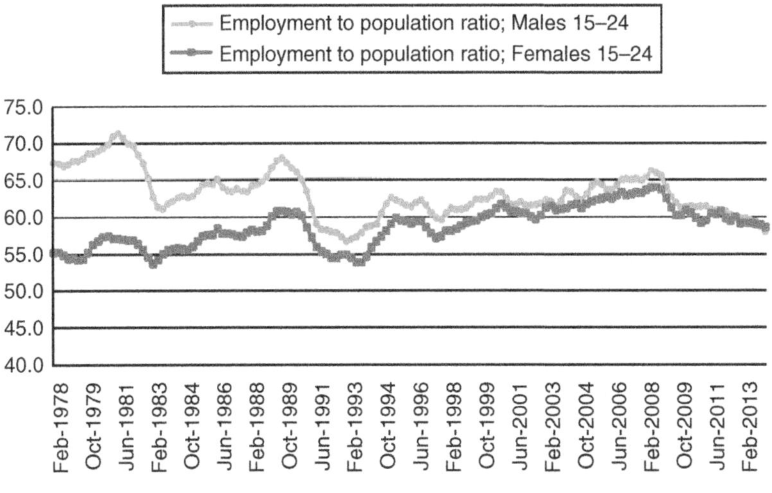

Figure 3.5.9 Youth employment-population ratios, Australia, 1978–2013

Source: ABS (2013b) – Table 17. Labour force status by sex – persons aged 15–24 years – trend, seasonally adjusted and original.

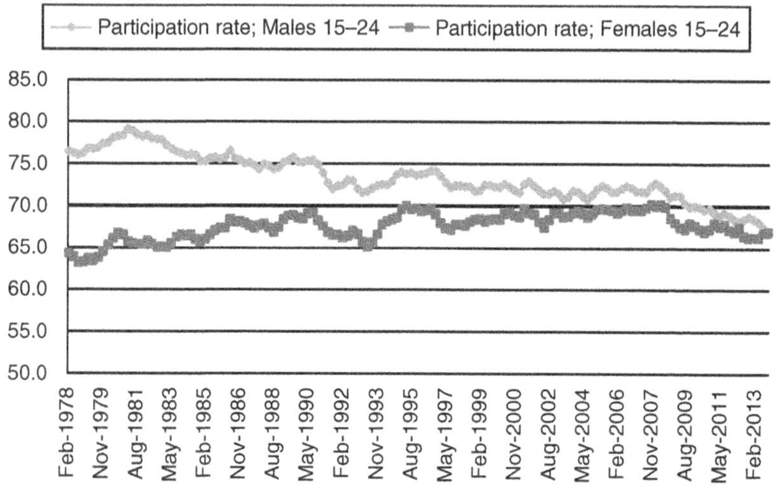

Figure 3.5.10 Labour force participation rates (%), males and females aged 15–24 years, Australia, 1978–2013

Source: ABS (2013b) – Table 17. Labour force status by sex – persons aged 15–24 years – trend, seasonally adjusted and original.

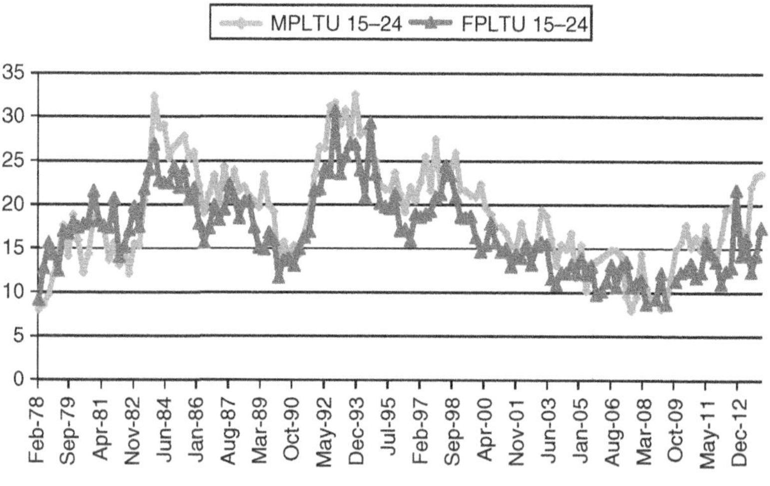

Figure 3.5.11 Incidence of male and female youth long-term unemployment (%), Australia, 1978–2012

MPLTU 15–24: male percentage of long-term unemployment, 15- to 24-year-olds; FPLTU 15–24: female percentage of long-term unemployment, 15- to 24-year-olds.

Source: ABS (2014e). ST UM1 unemployed persons by state and territory, age, sex and duration of unemployment since last full-time job, February 1978 onwards.

1992) and to lower life-time earnings (Clark et al., 2014). Is it surprising that the long-term unemployed suffer from alienation, psychological problems and depression?

What explains the rise in youth unemployment?

What explains the rise in youth unemployment and long-term unemployment? Although Australian GDP growth during the GFC (2008–2010) was negative for only one quarter (but negative for two consecutive quarters in terms of the GDP index), the rate of growth of GDP slowed down after 2008 (Figure 3.5.12). Firms became cautious about hiring new workers, and since a large proportion of young people are first time entrants into the (full-time) labour market, they find it difficult to find work. Firms faced with a global crisis not only cut back on hiring new workers but also cut back on renewing contracts of casual and part-time workers, and these workers now joined the unemployment queue.

Most economists would agree that if the economy goes into a recession or if the growth rate of GDP slows down, this will lead to an increase in the overall unemployment rate. An Okun's Law relationship was estimated for Australia on quarterly data, 1978 Q1 to 2013 Q4 (four-quarter change in the unemployment rate regressed on the growth rate), and it was found that the Okun coefficient was –0.40, suggesting that a 1 percentage point fall in the growth rate led to a 0.40 percentage point increase in the unemployment rate. At the same time, youth unemployment rates tended to increase more than proportionately (by 1.67 percentage points, as estimated in Equation (1)). We can see that as Australian growth rates slowed down, youth unemployment rates went up significantly. According to our estimates, the annual growth rate would have to be at 3.1% to keep the overall unemployment rate constant

$$\begin{aligned} \Delta UR &= 1.29 - 0.40\ \text{GrowthRate} \\ &\quad (11.1)\ (-12.9) \qquad (4) \\ R^2 &= 0.5 \end{aligned}$$

Many economists and employers' organisations argue that the growth of youth unemployment is either due to the high rate of the minimum wage they have to pay or because the unemployment-benefit system is 'over-generous'. There are always strident calls from the employer organisations that Australian minimum wages are too high compared with those in our competitive countries.

To evaluate these claims, we will study, for Australia between 1990 and 2012, the movement of youth wages relative to those of adults. We will also examine the behaviour of the minimum wage relative to Average Weekly Earnings (AWE) and the movement of the RR (ratio of unemployment benefits to AWE) for the period 1998–2012.

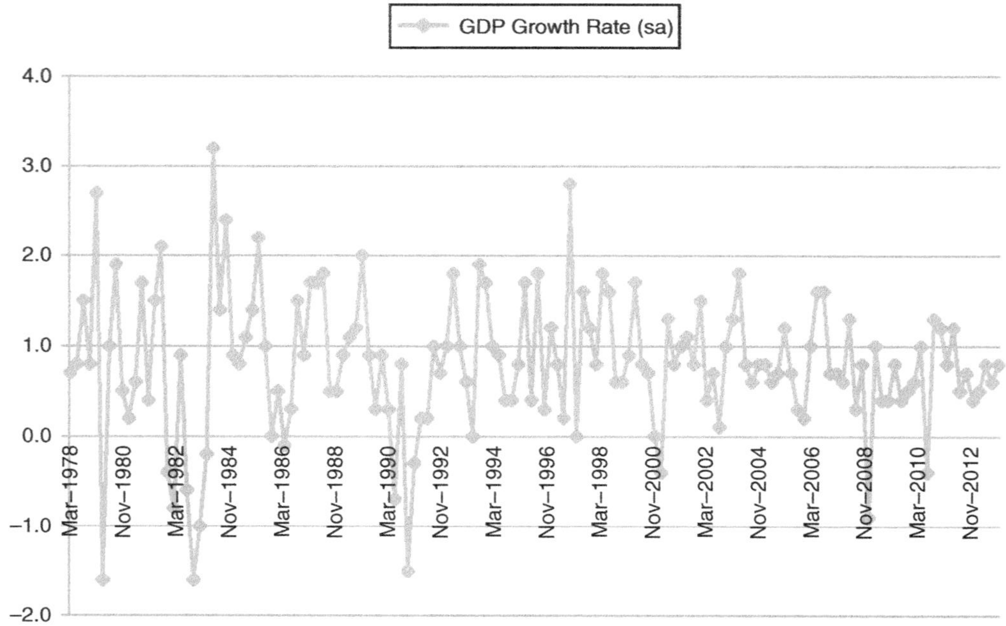

Figure 3.5.12 GDP growth rate (% seasonally adjusted) Australia, 1978–2012
Source: ABS (2014b) – Table 1. Key National Accounts aggregates.

Figures 3.5.13 to 3.5.16 clearly show that youth wages relative to adult wages declined in 2008–2009 and had been on a declining trend since the 1990s. This is true for both males and females. This suggests that the increase in youth unemployment rates was not due to youth wages being 'too high', if we assume that youth labour productivity had not fallen relative to adult labour productivity. Such a decline is unlikely, given that the average educational levels of youth have been increasing over the past few decades with higher retention rates in high schools and increased participation in the higher education sector.

Another argument that is often raised is that the minimum wage overall is 'too high', and hence, employers are cutting back on employing young people. In Figures 3.5.17 and 3.5.18, we see that although the minimum wage was almost constant (increasing very slowly from 1998), unemployment rates for male and female youths had been falling continuously until the GFC. It is only after the GFC that unemployment rates increased while minimum wages increased slightly. This suggests that the view that youth unemployment rates increase with minimum wages is not supported by the data.

We then study the possibility that unemployment benefits were too high compared to AWE, reducing the incentive of young people to accept jobs.[10] In general, according to search theory, if the RR (the ratio of unemployment

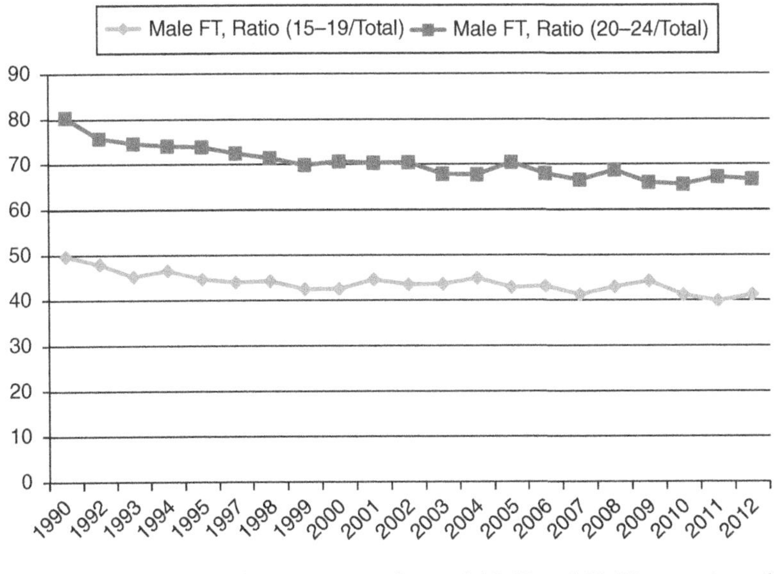

Figure 3.5.13 Full-time earnings ratios, males aged 15–19 and 20–24 years, Australia, 1990–2012

Source: ABS (2013a) – Table 4. Employees in main job, mean weekly earnings in main job, by full-time or part-time status in main job, by age group (years), by sex, 1990–2012.

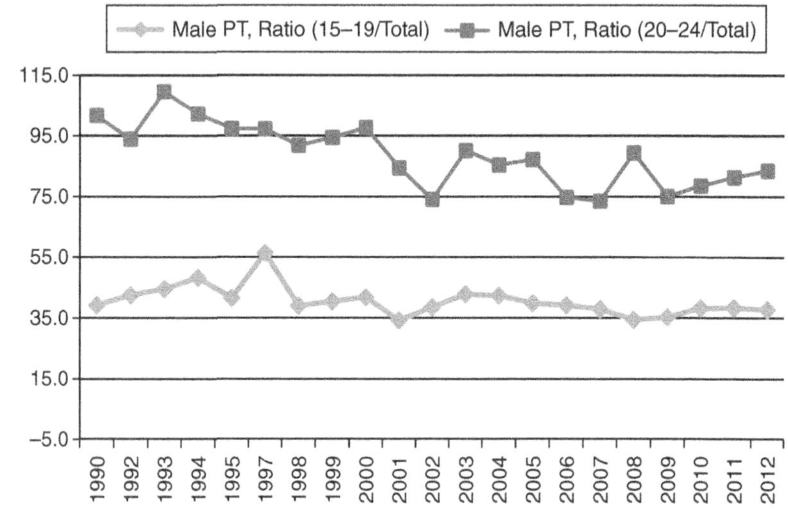

Figure 3.5.14 Part-time earnings ratios, males aged 15–19 and 20–24 years, Australia, 1990–2012

Source: ABS (2013a) – Table 4. Employees in main job, mean weekly earnings in main job, by full-time or part-time status in main job, by age group (years), by sex, 1990–2012.

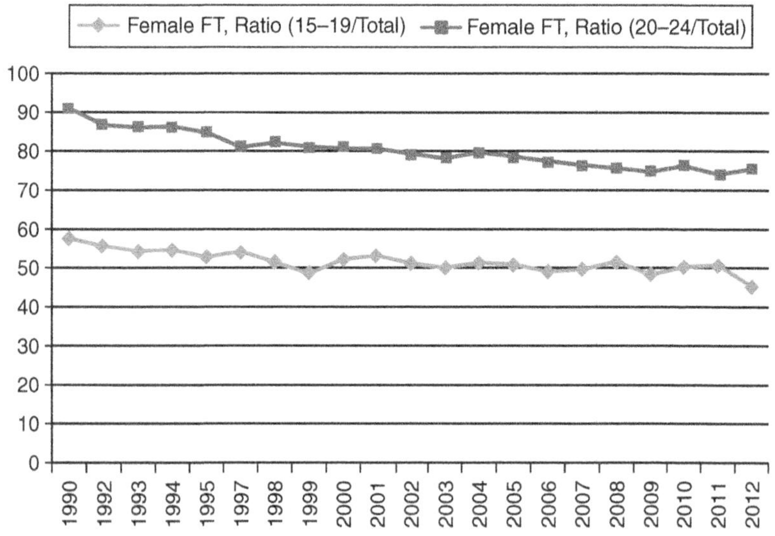

Figure 3.5.15 Full-time earnings ratios, females aged 15–19 and 20–24 years, Australia, 1990–2012

Source: ABS (2013a) – Table 4. Employees in main job, mean weekly earnings in main job, by full-time or part-time status in main job, by age group (years), by sex, 1990–2012.

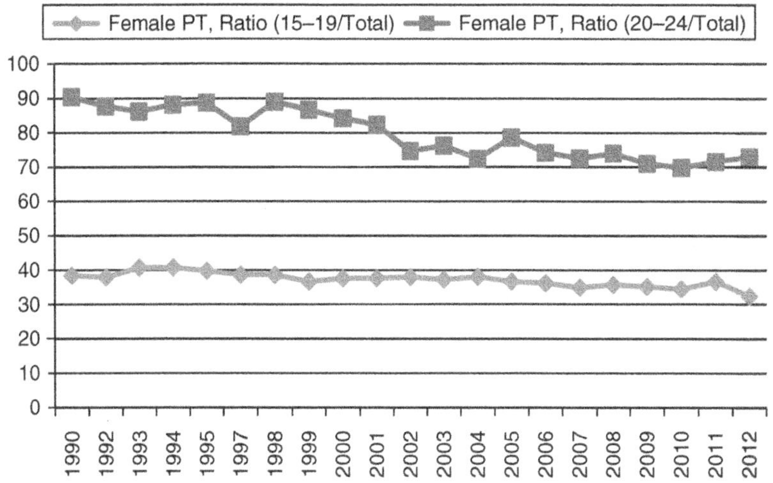

Figure 3.5.16 Part-time earnings ratios, females aged 15–19 and 20–24 years, Australia, 1990–2012

Source: ABS (2013a) – Table 4. Employees in main job, mean weekly earnings in main job, by full-time or part-time status in main job, by age group (years), by sex, 1990–2012.

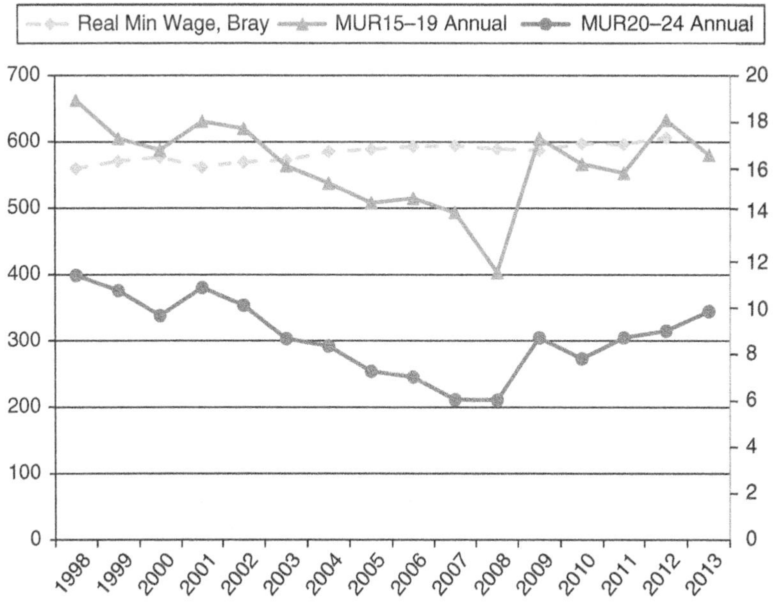

Figure 3.5.17 Male youth unemployment rates (%) and the real minimum wage (AUD), Australia, 1998–2013

MUR: male unemployment rate.

The real minimum wage data (AUD) are from Bray (2013) and are on the left-hand scale, while unemployment rates (%) are represented on the right-hand scale.

Source: ABS (2014e). GM1 – Labour force status and gross changes (flows) by sex, state, age; and Bray (2013).

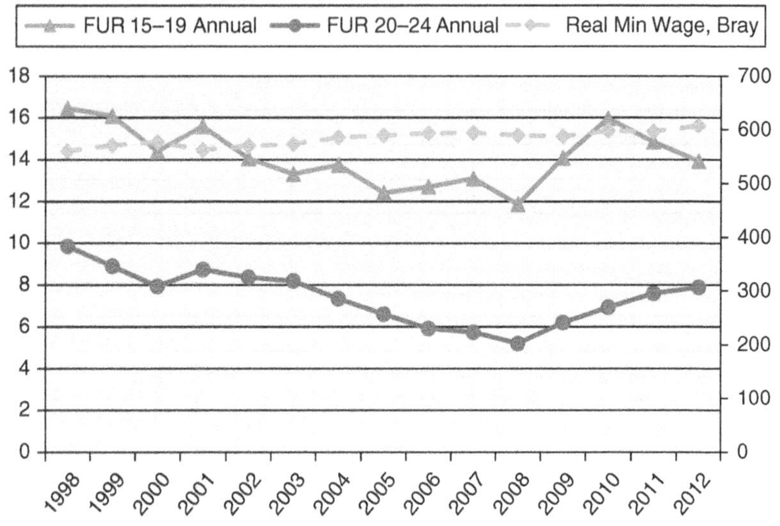

Figure 3.5.18 Female youth unemployment rates and the real minimum wage, Australia, 1998–2012

FUR: female unemployment rate.

The real minimum wage data (AUD) are from Bray (2013) and are on the right-hand scale, while unemployment rates (%) are represented on the left-hand scale.

Source: ABS (2014e). GM1 – Labour force status and gross changes (flows) by sex, state, age; and Bray (2013).

benefits to *expected* wage rates) increases, unemployed job searchers would become more 'choosy' and reject job offers; as a result, unemployment goes up when RR increases. Analogously, if the RR falls, unemployment will fall.[11] As Australia had been growing rapidly for several years (without a serious recession), unemployment rates had been falling and real wages increasing. However, in a recession, we would find that the *expected* wage would fall, and if unemployment benefits are constant,[12] the RR would rise! *Note that the expected wage falls for two reasons*. First, wage rates are likely to fall in a recession. Second, the probability of gaining a job offer falls, hence the expected wage declines (taking the wage as the price of an employee). In other words, the RR is *endogenous*.[13]

The RR is defined as the real unemployment benefits as a proportion of the real minimum wage for our figures (diagrams), assuming that young people are mainly working at minimum wages and hence expect to receive minimum wages. We have not corrected for a fall in the probability of a wage offer. (A similar picture emerges if we define the RR to AWE of youths.) In Figure 3.5.19, we see that the RR fell and unemployment rates were falling with the growing economy. However, as discussed above, the causation is from unemployment to RRs, not the other way round. Since the GFC, the

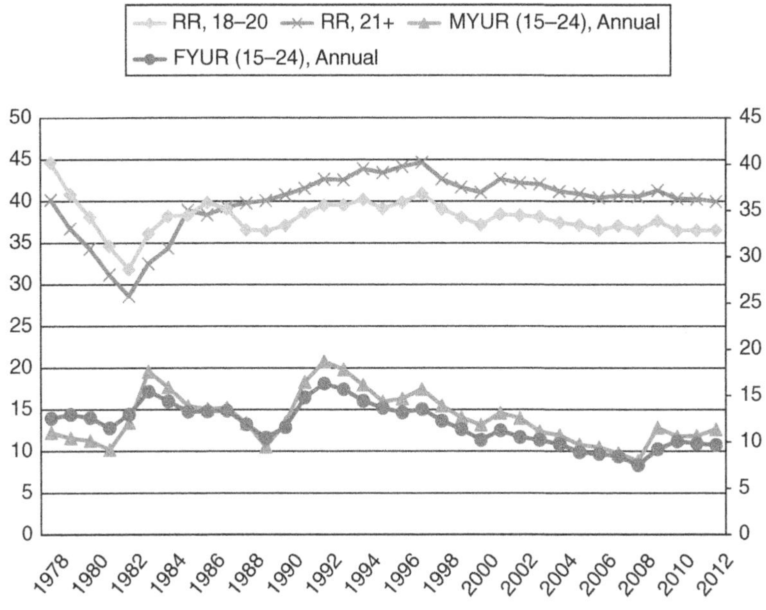

Figure 3.5.19 Youth unemployment rates and replacement rates, Australia 1978–2012
MUR: male unemployment rate; FUR: female unemployment rate
Left-hand side (LHS) axis: replacement rates; right-hand side (RHS) axis: unemployment rates.
Source: ABS (2013b) – Table 17. Labour force status by sex – persons aged 15–24 years – trend, seasonally adjusted and original; and Bray (2013).

RR has continued to fall but unemployment rates have been rising. There is no obvious relationship.[14]

Conclusion

This article has studied the Australian youth labour market and its response to thc Global Financial Crisis. It has established that the youth labour market is significantly different from the adult labour market. Youth unemployment rates increase more rapidly during a recession because many young people work in cyclically sensitive sectors and in part-time casual employment. As a result, when a recession hits, employers stop hiring new entrants (the young) and begin to fire young people who are in vulnerable employment. It was shown that high youth unemployment could not be explained by high youth wages, by the minimum wage or by so-called generous unemployment benefits.

To reduce youth unemployment rates, it is important to create increased growth, particularly in the industries that are the main employers of young people, namely, Construction, Manufacturing, Retail trade, Accommodation and food services, and Health care and social assistance.[15] Since Manufacturing has been on a declining trend for decades, the main way to help young people would be a stimulus to (say) tourism that would help Retail trade and Accommodation and food services. In recent years, there has been an increase in temporary visas for migrants (e.g. backpackers and the so-called 457 visas) who compete with youth for jobs in restaurants, accommodation and so on. With an ageing population, there needs to be an increase in Health services, and this would increase the employment of young people as (say) nurses. For long-term unemployed youth, it would help to provide a job guarantee, where the work included training in useful skills and activities. To summarise, if the growth rate of the economy was stimulated, this would decrease youth unemployment rates. In the context of a growing economy, young people would need greater access to apprenticeships and to on-the-job training schemes.[16]

Policies announced in 2014 by the Abbott government precluding young people (now defined by this government as anyone aged 30 years or less) from receiving unemployment benefits for the first 6 months of unemployment and requiring work for the dole in the succeeding 6 months would, in effect, exclude the young from the welfare system. There is clear evidence that work for the dole does not help the unemployed to find jobs and more importantly that it has a negative effect on the participants in the scheme (Borland and Tseng, 2011). How young people are expected to survive without any social security benefits is left to one's imagination. If they do not come from families with sufficient resources (and/or they are living independently), they face homelessness and either dependence on charitable organisations or resort to petty crime. Is that the kind of society we would like to live in?

Acknowledgements

This paper was written while I held an Honorary Professorship at the Industrial Relations Research Centre, UNSW Australia. I am grateful to Michael Quinlan Peter Kriesler, Anne Junor, John Lodewijks (all from UNSW), Jeff Borland (Melbourne) and Matt Cowgill (ACTU) for comments that have helped to improve the article. An early version of this article was presented to an Academy of Social Sciences in Australia seminar organised by Michael Bittman (UNE) at the University of Sydney. I would also like to thank an anonymous referee for helpful comments. I am, of course, responsible for remaining errors.

Funding

Under this project (*Family Fortunes and the Global Financial Crisis – The consequences of an economic downturn for work, families and children*), a small grant from the Academy of the Social Sciences in Australia (ASSA) helped to undertake this research.

Notes

1. Note that the Organisation for Economic Co-operation and Development (OECD, 2013) argues, 'Even if public resources are constrained, especially in countries where fiscal consolidation is required, it is important to guarantee that youth, including those with little or no work experience, have access to unemployment and social assistance systems' (p. 7).
2. See Sewell (2013) for an extended literature review and econometric analysis. O'Brien (2006) provides a study of the impact of Work Choices legislation on the youth labour market.
3. See Australian Government (n.d.) Fact Sheet, http://deta.qld.gov.au/resources/pdf/compact-fs-young.pdf and Cuervo et al. (2013).
4. Marcus and Gavrilovic (2010) provide evidence that youth 'occupy a marginalised position in the labour market ... young people form the backbone of vulnerable industries such as manufacturing, construction and services' (p. 10). International Labour Organisation (ILO, 2010) states, 'Youth unemployment rates have proven more sensitive to economic shocks than adult rates' (p. 5).
5. In an earlier version of this paper I had used the overall unemployment rate from the Australian Bureau of Statistics (ABS), 2014c.
6. This is a purely descriptive statement, and not a causal statement. Note that since we are using monthly data (from Australian Bureau of Statistics (ABS, 2014e) ABS 6291.0.55.001 – Labour Force, Australia, Detailed – Electronic Delivery, GM1 – Labour Force Status and Gross Changes (flows) by Sex, State, Age), the series is very noisy.
7. Flatau et al. (2008) provide further details about young people aged 15–20 years for an earlier period.
8. The National Bureau of Economic Research's (NBER, n.d.) definition is as follows:

   The Committee does not have a fixed definition of economic activity. It examines and compares the behavior of various measures of broad activity: real GDP measured on the product and income sides, economy-wide employment, and real income. The Committee also may consider indicators that do not cover the entire economy, such as real sales and the Federal Reserve's index of industrial production (IP).

9. These data are for duration of unemployment since the last full-time job. Data for a shorter period are available for durations since the last job. There are similarities although duration since last full-time job is likely to be longer than since the last job.
10. In an interesting paper, Morris and Wilson (2014) show that young people have great difficulties in living when they receive unemployment benefits.
11. In a recent publication, the Federal Reserve Board (2014) comment that in a survey they recently conducted, 'Respondents identified personal networks as a primary source in their job search'. In other words, their search was not undirected and was influenced by wage offers.
12. In fact, real unemployment benefits had remained more or less constant for a decade or more.
13. What would Kahneman (2011) say about this so-called rational choice? Do young people really go through this 'system 2' thinking?

14. Ideally, we need to have a complete econometric model to test for this relationship, allowing for the endogeneity of the replacement rate (RR). However, the time-series data on the youth labour market are not sufficiently rich for a rigorous examination. There have been numerous changes made to the rates of benefits paid and more importantly to the conditions under which these benefits were accessible. In an Honours thesis, Sewell (2013) showed (with limited data) that there was no significant relationship between youth unemployment and the RR.
15. Note that OECD (2013) in its Action Plan to tackle the current youth unemployment crisis recommends that the first priority is to 'Tackle weak aggregate demand and boost job creation' (p. 3).
16. To discuss the policies to help lower unemployment rates would require another paper. See Appendix for the OECD Action Plan for Youth, June 2013. In the OECD and ILO (2014) paper on 'Promoting better labour market outcomes for youth', it argues that job training is important and that is unlikely to be provided in temporary jobs. Furthermore, 'many low-skilled youths get locked into such jobs or leave the labour market altogether' (p. 7).

References

Australian Bureau of Statistics (ABS) (2013a) *Employee earnings, benefits and trade union membership – mean weekly earnings*. Cat. no. 63100TS0002. Canberra, ACT, Australia: Commonwealth of Australia. Available at: http://www.abs.gov.au/AUSSTATS/abs@.nsf/DetailsPage/6310.0August%202013 (accessed 10 March 2015).

Australian Bureau of Statistics (ABS) (2013b) *Labour force Australia*. December. Cat. no. 6202.0. Canberra, ACT, Australia; Commonwealth of Australia. Available at: http://www.abs.gov.au/AUSSTATS/abs@.nsf/DetailsPage/6202.0Dec%202013?OpenDocument (accessed 10 March 2015).

Australian Bureau of Statistics (ABS) (2014a) *Australian labour market statistics*. July. Cat. no. 6105.0. Canberra, ACT, Australia: Commonwealth of Australia. Available at: http://www.abs.gov.au/ausstats/abs@.nsf/mf/6105.0 (accessed 10 March 2015).

Australian Bureau of Statistics (ABS) (2014b) *Australian National Accounts: National income, expenditure and product*. June. Cat. no. 5206.0. Canberra, ACT, Australia: Commonwealth of Australia. Available at: http://www.abs.gov.au/AUSSTATS/abs@.nsf/DetailsPage/5206.0Jun%202014 (accessed 10 March 2015).

Australian Bureau of Statistics (ABS) (2014c) *Labour force Australia*. November, Table 02. Labour force status by sex – seasonally adjusted. Cat. no. 6202.0. Canberra, ACT, Australia: Commonwealth of Australia. Available at: http://www.abs.gov.au/AUSSTATS/abs@.nsf/DetailsPage/6202.0Nov%202014?OpenDocument (accessed 10 March 2015).

Australian Bureau of Statistics (ABS) (2014d) *Labour force Australia*. November. Cat. no. 6202.0. Canberra, ACT, Australia: Commonwealth of Australia. Available at: http://www.abs.gov.au/AUSSTATS/abs@.nsf/DetailsPage/6202.0Nov%202014?OpenDocument (accessed 10 March 2015).

Australian Bureau of Statistics (ABS) (2014e) *Labour force Australia, detailed – electronic delivery*. Cat. No. 6291.0.55.001. Canberra, ACT, Australia: Commonwealth of Australia. Available at: http://www.abs.gov.au/AUSSTATS/abs@.nsf/DetailsPage/6291.0.55.001Nov%20 2014?OpenDocument (accessed 10 March 2015).

Australian Bureau of Statistics (ABS) (2014f) *Labour force Australia, detailed, quarterly*. November. Cat. No. 6291.0.55.003. Canberra, ACT, Australia: Commonwealth of Australia. Available at: http://www.abs.gov.au/ausstats/abs@.nsf/mf/6291.0.55.003 (accessed 10 March 2015).

Australian Government (n.d.) Fact sheet. Learning or earning: new education and training requirements for 15–24 year olds. Available at: http://deta.qld.gov.au/resources/pdf/compact-fs-young.pdf (accessed 16 Febaruary2015).

Booth A (2014) *Wage Determination and imperfect competition.* IZA discussion paper no. 8034, March 2014. Bonn: IZA.

Borland J and Tseng Y-P (2011) Does 'work for the dole' work? An Australian perspective on work experience programmes. *Applied Economics* 43(28): 4353–4368.

Bray JR (2013) *Reflections on the evolution of the minimum wage in Australia: options for the future.* Paper, HC Coombs Policy Forum, May. Canberra, ACT, Australia: *Crawford School of Public Policy, Australian National University.*

Card D and Krueger A (1994) Minimum wages and unemployment: a case study of the fast-food industry in New Jersey and Pennsylvania. *American Economic Review* 84(4): 772–793.

Card D and Krueger A (1995) *Myth and Measurement: The New Economics of the Minimum Wage.* Princeton, NJ: Princeton University Press.

Clark B, Joubert C and Maurel A (2014) *The career prospects of overeducated Americans.* NBER working paper w20167, May. Cambridge, MA: National Bureau of Economic Research. Available at: http://www.nber.org/papers/w20167 (accessed 10 February 2015).

Commonwealth of Australia (2015) *House of Representatives, Standing Committee on Economics.* Reserve Bank of Australia annual report 2014. Hurstville, NSW, Australia.

Cuervo H, Crofts J and Wyn J (2013) *Generational insights into new labour market landscapes for youth.* Research report 42. Melbourne, VIC, Australia: Youth Research Centre, Melbourne Graduate School of Education, University of Melbourne.

Daly A, Nguyen-Hong D, Eldridge D, et al. (1998) *Youth Wages and Employment* (Productivity Commission Staff Research Paper). Canberra, ACT, Australia: AusInfo.

Doiron D and Gorgens T (2008) State dependence in youth labor market experiences, and the evaluation of policy interventions. *Journal of Econometrics* 145(1): 81–97.

Dube A (2011) Book Review: David Neumark and William L. Wascher, *Minimum Wages,* Cambridge, MA and London, MIT Press, 2008. *Journal of Economic Literature* 49(3): 762–766.

Dube A, Lester TW and Reich M (2010) Minimum wage effects across state boundaries: estimates using contiguous counties. *Review of Economics and Statistics* 92(4): 945–964.

Economic Policy Institute (2014) Over 600 economists sign letter in support of $10.10 minimum wage. Available at: http://www.epi.org/minimum-wage-statement/ (accessed 5 March 2015).

Eurofound (2014) *Social Situation of Young People in Europe.* Luxembourg: Publications Office of the European Union.

Federal Reserve Board (FRB) (2014) *In the Shadow of the Great Recession: Experiences and Perspectives of Young Workers.* Washington, DC: Board of Governors of the Federal Reserve System. Available at: http://www.federalreserve.gov/econresdata/2013-experiences-and-per-spectives-of-young-workers-201411.pdf

Flatau P, Dockery M and Stromback T (2008) *The economic and social circumstances of Australian young people aged 15–20 years.* Australian Fair Pay Commission, Research report no. 1/108. Canberra, ACT, Australia: Commonwealth of Australia.

Heckman JJ (2007) Comments on 'Are protective labor market institutions at the root of unemployment? A critical review of the evidence' by David Howell, Dean Baker, Andrew Glyn and John Schmitt. *Capitalism and Society* 2(1): 1–4.

Hérault N, Kostenko W, Marks G, et al. (2012) The effects of macroeconomic conditions on the education and employment outcomes of youth. *Australian Journal of Labour Economics* 15(1): 17–36.

Howell DR (ed.) (2005) *Fighting Unemployment: The Limits of Free Market Orthodoxy*. Oxford: Oxford University Press.

Howell DR (2011) Institutions, aggregate demand and cross-country employment performance: alternative theoretical perspectives and the evidence. In: Hein E and Stockhammer E (eds) *A Modern Guide to Keynesian Macroeconomics and Economic Policies*. Cheltenham: Elgar, pp. 165–190.

Howell DR, Baker D, Glyn A, et al. (2007) Are protective labor market institutions at the root of unemployment? A critical review of the evidence. *Capitalism and Society* 2(1): 1–73.

International Labour Organisation (ILO) (2010) *Global employment trends for youth* (Special issue on The Impact of the Global Economic Crisis on Youth). August. Geneva: ILO.

Junankar PN (ed.) (1987) *From School to Unemployment? The Labour Market for Young People*. London: Macmillan.

Junankar PN (2004) Employment effects of minimum wages: evidence from a quasi-experiment, by Andrew Leigh: a preliminary critique. In: *ACTU (Australian Council of Trade Unions) Minimum Wages Case. Tag Number 7 in Composite Exhibit*. Melbourne, VIC, Australia: Australian Industrial Relations Commission Safety Net Review.

Junankar PN (2011) *The global economic crisis: long term unemployment in the OECD*. IZA Discussion Paper No. 6057, Bonn: IZA.

Junankar PN and Wood M (1992) The dynamics of unemployment: an analysis of recurrent unemployment. In: Gregory RG and Karmel T (eds) *Youth in the Eighties: Papers from the Australian Longitudinal Surveys*. Canberra, ACT, Australia: Department of Employment, Education and Training and Centre for Economic Policy Research, ANU, pp. 282–304.

Junankar PN, Waite M and Belchamber G (2000) The youth labour market: anecdotes, fables and evidence. *Economic and Labour Relations Review* 11(Suppl.): 159–186.

Kahneman D (2011) *Thinking Fast and Slow*. New York: Farrar, Straus and Giroux.

Leigh A (2003) Employment effects of minimum wages: evidence from a quasi-experiment. *Australian Economic Review* 36(4): 361–373.

Lewis P and Mclean B (1998) The youth labour market in Australia: a survey. *Australian Journal of Labour Economics* 2(2): 158–172.

Manning A (2003) *Monopsony in Motion: Imperfect Competition in Labor Markets*. Princeton, NJ: Princeton University Press.

Manning A (2010) Imperfect competition in the labor market. In: Ashenfelter OC and Card D (eds) *Handbook of Labor Economics*, vol. 4B. Burlington, NJ: Elsevier Science, pp. 973–1041.

Marcus R with Gavrilovic M (2010) *The Impacts of the Economic Crisis on Youth: Review of the Evidence*. London: Overseas Development Institute.

Marks GN, Hillman K and Beavis A (2003) *Dynamics of the Australian Youth Labour Market: The 1975 Cohort, 1996–2000*. Melbourne, VIC, Australia: Australian Council for Educational Research.

Mavromaras K, Sloane P and Zhang W (2013) *The scarring effects of unemployment, low pay and skills under-utilisation in Australia compared*. IZA discussion paper no. 7440. Bonn: IZA.

Metcalf D (2008) Why has the British national minimum wage had little or no impact on employment? *Journal of Industrial Relations* 50(3): 489–512.

Miller P and Volker P (1987) The youth labour market in Australia. *Economic Record* 63(3): 203–219.

Morris A and Wilson S (2014) Struggling on the Newstart unemployment benefit in Australia: the experience of a neoliberal form of employment assistance. *Economic and Labour Relations Review* 25(2): 202–221.

Mortensen DT and Pissarides CA (1999) New developments in models of search in the labor market. In: Ashenfelter OC and Card D (eds) *Handbook of Labor Economics*, vol. 3. Amsterdam: Elsevier, pp. 2567–2627.

National Bureau of Economic Research (NBER) (n.d.) The NBER's Business Cycle Dating Committee. Available at: http://www.nber.org/cycles/recessions.html (accessed 16 February 2015)

Neumark D and Wascher W (2007) *Minimum wages and unemployment*. IZA Discussion Paper Series No. 2570.

Bonn: IZA. Neumark D and Wascher W (2008) *Minimum Wages*. Cambridge, MA and London: MIT Press.

Nickell S and Layard R (1999) Labor market institutions and economic performance. In: Ashenfelter OC and Card D (eds) *Handbook of Labor Economics*, vol. 3. Amsterdam: Elsevier, pp. 3029–3084.

O'Brien M (2006) *The youth labour market in Australia – implications from Work Choices legislation*. Department of Economics, Working paper 06–08. Wollongong, NSW, Australia: University of Wollongong.

Organisation for Economic Cooperation and Development (OECD) (2013) *The OECD Action Plan for Youth-Giving Youth a Better Start in the Labour Market*. Paris: OECD. Available at: http://www.oecd.org/employment/Action-plan-youth.pdf (accessed 12 February 2015).

Organisation for Economic Cooperation and Development (OECD) (2014) *Employment Outlook*. Paris: OECD.

Organisation for Economic Cooperation and Development (OECD) (2015) *LFS by sex and age – composition*. OECD.StatExtracts. Available at: http://stats.oecd.org/Index.aspx?DatasetCode=STLABOUR (accessed 12 March 2015).

Organisation for Economic Cooperation and Development (OECD) and International Labour Organisation (ILO) (2014) Promoting better labour market outcomes for youths, Report on youth employment and apprenticeships prepared for the G20 Labour and Employment Ministerial Meeting, Melbourne, Australia, 10–11 September 2014.

Overseas Development Institute (ODI) (2010) *The Impacts of the Economic Crisis n Youth: Review of the Evidence*. London: ODI.

Sewell C (2013) *An analysis of youth labour markets*. Bachelor of Commerce, Honours Thesis. Sydney, NSW, Australia: The University of New South Wales.

Stewart M (2007) The inter-related dynamics of unemployment and low wage employment. *Journal of Applied Econometrics* 22(3): 511–531.

Watson I (2004) Minimum wages and employment: comment. *Australian Economic Review* 37(2): 166–172.

3.6
Choosy Youth or Unwanted Youth? A Survey of Unemployment

Chris Manning and P.N. Junankar

This paper examines structure and change in unemployment in Indonesia from the 1970s through to 1996 The analysis focuses on high unemployment rates among urban youth, set in the context of similar problems experienced in other developing countries It also deals with some of the conceptual and measurement issues It is concluded that high youth unemployment is partly a queuing phenomenon among middle class families, related to processes of job search and wage structure. But rates of under-utilisation are also high among children of poorer households in the working age population Over time, the paper finds considerable stability in the structure of unemployment, with some tendency for overall rates to increase Some rises in unemployment were experienced by youth with either low educational status or tertiary qualifications, and by women Explanations include increased minimum wages and a slowdown in manufacturing activity, although changing definitions have also played a part

Introduction

Even prior to the economic crisis in 1997–98, official national unemployment had risen sharply in Indonesia in 1994–96, and urban rates had increased to almost double digit figures for the first time. These increases raised concerns about the rate of job creation, and especially about the social and political effects of high youth unemployment. Why should youth joblessness rise in a period of economic boom? To what extent does this reflect changes in the structure of unemployment? What are the social and economic implications of the problem, and what remedies should be used? This paper seeks to answer some of these questions by examining the structure of unemployment in the mid 1990s and changes in joblessness over the past two decades.

Reprinted from 'Choosy Youth or Unwanted Youth? A Survey of Unemployment' by Chris Manning and P. N. Junankar in *Bulletin of Indonesian Economic Studies*, 34 (1), April, 1998, 55–93. With kind permission from Taylor and Francis.

Before the crisis, which may well see the doubling of unemployment rates by early 1998, the subject of unemployment was not high on the economic policy agenda Under-employment, low wages and low productivity were viewed as much more pressing labour market problems. It has often been argued that the poor cannot afford to be unemployed in the early stages of development. Joblessness is merely a symptom of extensive search for better jobs (a 'luxury') among better-off households, as in earlier periods in other LDCs (Turnham 1971; Berry 1975, Berry and Sabot 1978)

An alternative viewpoint, seemingly consistent with recent trends in Indonesia, stresses unemployment as a genuine structural problem related to insufficient labour demand or excess labour supply. It imposes hardship especially on poorer households, partly because of 'informal' recruiting policies that tend to favour the better-off. In a recent review of the LDC evidence, Turnham (1993, pp. 54–6), an earlier sceptic, now questions the dismissal of unemployment as a trivial problem. He points to high rates especially in urban areas, even by developed country standards, as a challenge to the 'luxury unemployment' hypothesis.[1] There is also evidence that as countries become more industrialised and urbanised, older workers from less affluent families increasingly dominate unemployment queues (Rodgers 1989).

Indonesia provides fertile ground for examining these competing views of the unemployment problem. Rapid economic growth might suggest that unemployment should have fallen, as it did in several other East Asian countries during the 1960s and 1970s (Kuo 1983; Kim 1986; Galenson 1992). The persistence of high unemployment under such conditions could be seen as support for the 'luxury' hypothesis. However, several other developments may work in the opposite direction the relatively slow growth in manufacturing employment and a sharp increase in the supply of educated manpower, as has occurred in some other LDCs (World Bank 1995a)[2]

The paper first examines the structure of unemployment, and discusses alternative approaches to measuring unemployment and under-employment. We then focus on unemployment rates across socio-economic classes, applying some tests to the 'luxury unemployment' hypothesis. An examination of changes in unemployment over time gives special attention to recent trends in joblessness among urban youth.

The discussion is based largely on analysis of National Labour Force Survey (Sakernas) data undertaken in Indonesia since 1976.[3] We focus on analysis of the published data for 1996 and of data tapes from the 1992 survey. Sakernas is the richest (though by no means an exhaustive) source on labour market issues in Indonesia, but it collects data on very few individual characteristics and no data on household socio-economic status. Thus we are precluded from conducting a more comprehensive analysis of how several key variables interrelate with unemployment.[4]

The structure of unemployment

Unemployment in Indonesia presents something of a puzzle. Aggregate rates in 1996 (4% nationally) were quite low compared with those in most developed or even developing countries. Yet urban rates were much higher (8%), and well above those in rural areas (3%). Youth and educated unemployment was very high: rates hovered around 15–30% in 1996. They were higher among females than among males, although not significantly higher among students from academic schools than among those in more costly vocational schools (figures 3.6.1 and 3.6.2). Among the younger, more educated cohorts, most of them first job seekers, unemployment in 1996 was closer to 20–30% for upper secondary and tertiary graduates of both sexes in urban Indonesia (figures 3.6.3 and 3.6.4).

These rates of educated and youth unemployment are high by international standards, and similar to those recorded in industrial countries grappling with major problems of youth unemployment. Among young people in their late teens and early twenties Indonesia's rate of joblessness was surpassed only in Sri Lanka among 10 Asian countries for which data are reported by Turnham (1993, p. 80) for the mid to late 1980s. Over half of all the unemployed in 1996 were upper secondary graduates (from both academic and vocational streams) m their early twenties, and tertiary graduates in their late twenties.

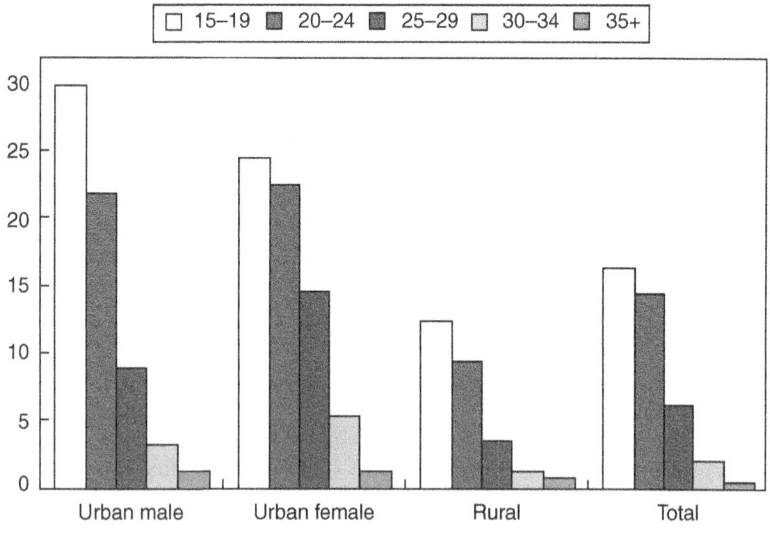

Figure 3.6.1 Unemployment Rates by Age, Indonesia,1996 (%)
Source: BPS, Sakernas (National Labour Force Survey), 1996.

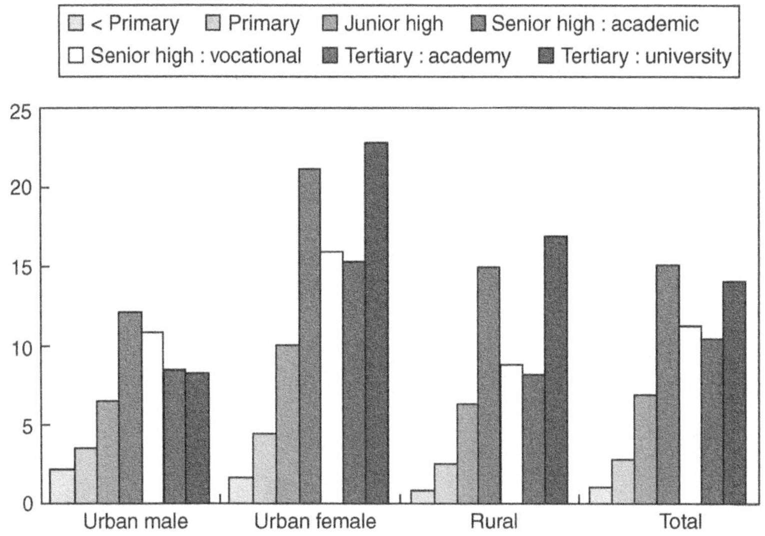

Figure 3.6.2 Unemployment Rates by Education, Indonesia, 1996 (%)
Source: As for figure 3.6.1.

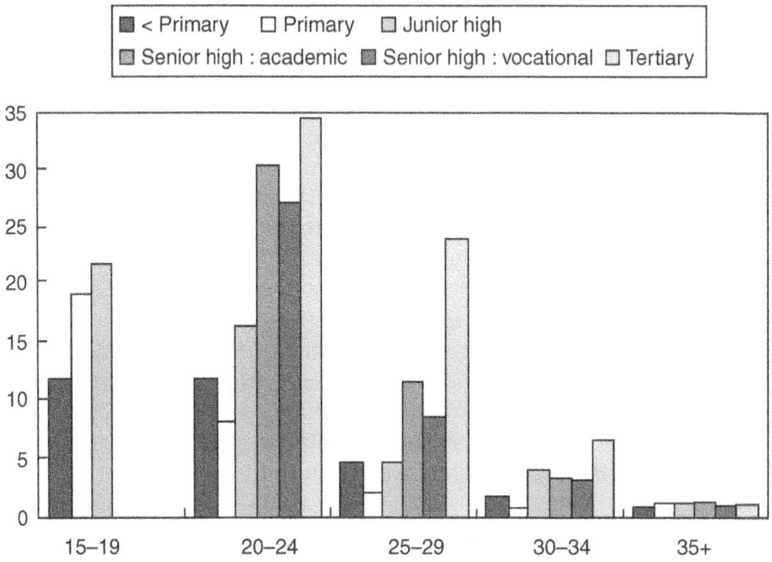

Figure 3.6.3 Unemployment by Age and Education, Urban Males, Indonesia, 1996 (%)
Source: As for figure 3.6.1.

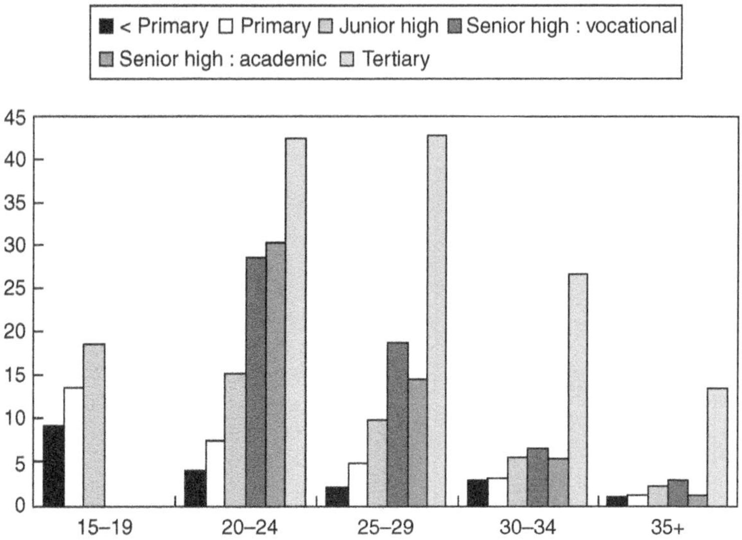

Figure 3.6.4 Unemployment by Age and Education, Urban Females, Indonesia, 1996 (%)
Source: As for figure 3.6.1.

Thus low aggregate unemployment relative to other countries was due partly to low levels of joblessness among older people in particular, the extraordinarily low rates of recorded unemployment among people aged 35 or above. The ratio of youth unemployment to rates among older cohorts was very high in Indonesia compared with the sample of countries surveyed by Turnham.[5] The low unemployment rates among this group imply that the ratio of younger and more educated unemployed to all prime age unemployed (ages 15–49), whether educated or not, is around 20:1. It is not surprising that total unemployment rates were so low, given the very low unemployment rates among older persons that emerge in all national surveys since the 1970s. This picture has not changed much since the 1970s, notwithstanding the apparent increases in 1994–96.

Part of the explanation for such low rates of joblessness in the older population is the predominance of non-wage employment among older, less educated persons in rural areas. Few of these people can afford to be out of work. Another factor may be the institutional rigidity that discourages people from moving between employers both in the government sector and in the modern private sector, which began to take an increasing share of educated workers in the 1990s (Manning 1998). Thus the data suggest either that older educated persons move very quickly between jobs or that once people get into modern sector jobs, they tend to stay there.[6]

Finally, some mention should be made of variations in unemployment across provinces. Despite Indonesia's size and regional diversity, the relative uniformity in joblessness across provinces is quite remarkable. Almost all provinces consistently recorded total rates within a band of 3–5% and urban rates within a band of 7–10% in 1996 (table 3.6.1). To the extent that there were interprovincial variations, joblessness was generally lower on Java, and also in other parts of 'inner' Indonesia, such as Lampung, Bali and West Nusa Tenggara (Manning and Junankar 1994, table 4.4).

Outside Java, two patterns of development were associated with high urban unemployment: rapid, resource based economic growth, and interregional differences in the supply of educated persons relative to employment opportunities.[7] Higher than average unemployment rates were also discernible in several relatively isolated and poor eastern Indonesian provinces, such as East Nusa Tenggara and East Timor. The pattern of unemployment by gender, age and education was rather similar across provinces. Where unemployment was high outside Java, joblessness among females and youth was also high (these data are contained in an appendix available from the authors).[8]

In sum, three distinct features of Indonesian unemployment stood out in the mid 1990s, and, for the most part, in national surveys conducted since the 1970s: high levels of joblessness among educated youth, extremely low rates recorded in rural areas and among older people, and relatively uniform rates across provinces.

These patterns seem to support the view that unemployment is not a very useful labour market indicator, particularly in rural areas, where under-employment (measured by hours worked) may be a more useful measure. Moreover, the high incidence of unemployment among the young and educated compared with older and less educated workers seems to provide evidence that joblessness is a 'luxury' in Indonesia. At face value, the data suggest that most unemployed educated youth remain out of work because they can afford to be selective in job search, but that most find jobs when they marry and set up independent households.

Before dealing with these propositions, we need first to examine how 'unemployment' and 'under-employment' are defined in Indonesia. A careful look at the data suggests that total unemployment may not be quite as low relative to under-employment as is commonly assumed. Furthermore, as several authors have shown, under-utilisation of youth is heavily understated in the official data, especially if one takes into account the duration of unemployment.

Measuring unemployment and surplus labour

Uncertainty about the level of unemployment, and its significance, derives partly from problems of conceptualisation and measurement. The estimation of rates of unemployment and under-employment is a tricky business in LDCs, where a high proportion of the workforce consists of non-wage workers, many of them females and children. Rates can vary substantially depending on the time period chosen to assess labour force attachment (the reference period) and on the precise definition (and perception) of work.

Table 3.6.1 Urban Unemployment in Selected Provinces in Indonesia, 1987–96

	Rate (%)			Ratio (Indonesia = 10)			% of Unemployed	
	1987	1992	1996	1987	1992	1996	1987	1996
Java-Bali								
Jakarta	10.2	6.4	9.4	1.5	1.1	1.1	22.4	14.4
West Java	7.9	6.3	9.1	1.1	1.1	1.1	21.2	24.3
Other Java-Bali	5.8	4.6	6.2	0.8	0.8	0.7	34.1	27.0
Sumatra								
North Sumatra	5.2	6.1	10.6	0.8	1.1	1.3	4.0	7.7
South Sumatra	6.6	7.6	7.9	0.9	1.3	1.0	2.9	2.6
Other Sumatra	6.3	7.2	9.3	0.9	1.3	1.1	5.1	8.5
Sulawesi	6.3	7.1	12.2	0.9	1.2	1.5	3.7	7.2
Kalimantan	6.5	5.6	8.5	0.9	1.0	1.0	3.8	4.7
Eastern Indonesia	6.6	6.2	9.4	1.0	1.1	1.1	2.8	3.6
Indonesia	7.0	5.8	8.3	1.0	1.0	1.0	100	100

Source: BPS, Sakernas, 1987, 1992, 1996.

Among those working less than normal hours, an individual's employment status hinges on whether those who *choose* to work less than normal hours (part-time workers) are categorised as under-employed, in addition to those *involuntarily denied access* to the amount of work they seek.

A comparison of different measures of unemployment and under-employment illustrates these points in the case of Indonesia. We first distinguish between (*open*) unemployment, *voluntary* under-employment and *involuntary* under-employment, and present estimates of the incidence of each in table 3.6.2, based on the 1992 National Labour Force Survey.[9] We then calculate unemployment rates based on the *wage earning* workforce rather than the total workforce.

Unemployment and Under-employment

The following definitions are used (Manning and Junankar 1994, appendix 1):

- *'Labour force'* refers to all persons employed or looking for work in the reference week,
- *'Unemployed'* refers to persons working less than one hour per week, looking for work and available for work during the reference week,
- *'Involuntary under-employed'* refers to persons working less than a stipulated minimum hours of work a week and looking for or available for work (two cut-off points are chosen: less than 25 hours and less than 35 hours);

Table 3.6.2 Unemployment and Under-employment by Gender, Urban and Rural Areas, Indonesia, 1992

	Urban		Rural		Total
	Male	Female	Male	Female	
Number ('000)					
Unemployed	771	533	494	388	2,186
Under-Employed:					
Involuntary[a]	676	534	4,152	3,138	8,500
Voluntary[b]	1,375	1,678	8,193	10,614	21,859
Total labour force ('000)	14,462	8,093	34,970	23,179	80,704
Rate (column %)					
Unemployed	5.3	6.6	1.4	1.6	2.7
Under-employed:					
Involuntary[a]	4.7	6.6	11.9	13.5	10.5
Voluntary[b]	9.5	20.7	23.4	45.8	27.1
Distribution (row %)					
Unemployed	35	24	23	18	100
Under-employed.					
Involuntary[a]	8	6	49	37	100
Voluntary[b]	6	8	37	49	100
Total labour force (%)	18	10	43	29	100

[a]Working < 35 hours and looking or available for work.
[b] Working < 35 hours and not looking/available for work.
Source: BPS, Sakernas, 1992, computer tape.

- *'Voluntary under-employed'* refers to those persons working less than the stipulated number of hours, and *not* looking for or available for work

The table suggests that crude rates of both unemployment *and involuntary under-employment* were quite low. Involuntary under-employment (covering those working less than 35 hours a week) accounted for 11% of the total labour force. In all, just on 14% of the labour force could be categorised as under-utilised (not having a job or working less than normal hours and looking for work, or alternatively 'willing' to extend their hours of work or seek a new job).[10] This total level of under-utilisation is far below most estimates of 'surplus labour' in Indonesia. It is only slightly over one-third of the Ministry of Manpower's estimate of the rate of 'global unemployment', which covers both unemployment and under-employment, and was estimated to affect slightly under 40% of the workforce in the early 1990s. The main difference is that the voluntary under-employed or part-time workers—27% of the total workforce in 1992 (table 3.6.2)—are excluded in the above measure but included m the Ministry of Manpower's estimate.

Who Are the Jobseekers? The Role of Wage Employment

We next assume, on the basis of research in other LDCs, that most persons who report that they are looking for work are likely to be searching for wage jobs. We then attempt to take account of the bias introduced by the small share of wage employment in non-agricultural work in Indonesia, by making an alternative estimate of unemployment rates based on the number of job seekers calculated as a percentage of all *wage employees* (as the denominator). When this measure is used, the rate of unemployment jumps to three times the official rate: 8.7% overall in 1992, and over 10% in urban areas.[11] Unemployment is only slightly lower than involuntary underemployment under this definition.[12] This procedure biases the picture of unemployment in one sense, one should be concerned with what proportion of the *total working age population* is actively searching for work. However, it does provide a more useful basis for comparison with figures from more industrialised countries, and gives an alternative estimate of the importance of unemployment relative to under-employment as an economic and social problem.

Hidden Unemployment: Participation and Employment Rates

Under-utilisation of labour occurs not only as a result of open unemployment and under-employment, but also because people are outside the labour force, either as discouraged workers or for other reasons. Thus, labour market specialists have tended increasingly to focus on the structure of *employment rates*—which measure the employed as percentage of the working age population—as a useful summary measure of total labour utilisation and participation (Gregory 1991). Employment rates reflect variations m both unemployment and participation rates, which may offset one another. They also capture the extent of 'hidden' or 'disguised' unemployment affecting persons who are outside the labour market.[13]

'Surplus labour' among young people in Indonesia is clearly a much bigger problem if one focuses on participation and employment rates, rather than on open unemployment rates alone. Employment rates have been quite low.[14] In 1992 and 1994, they were about 50% among the male workforce aged 15–29, and closer to one-third for young females in this age group. The male rates appear low compared with those in countries with similar levels of school enrolment.[15]

Low employment rates among young males in particular were related to three factors relatively high unemployment rates; high levels of schooling participation; and a significant share of persons (officially classified as 'other') who were not employed and not at school or involved in housework as a principal activity. For example, around one half of all young males were employed, a further one-third in school, 8% unemployed and 9% classified as 'other' in 1992. The latter group, in particular, have received considerable attention in the analysis of the labour force in Indonesia.[16]

One might refer to young people who were not employed and not engaged actively in job search, but were *available for work*, as the 'hidden' unemployed. In urban Indonesia in 1992, approximately two-thirds of young males and half of young females who were outside the workforce and not engaged in housework or in school (classified as 'other') reported that they were available for work.[17] If this group of 'hidden' unemployed is added to the 'open' unemployed, then overall rates rise from 13–14% to 21–22% among all youth, and to over 30% for upper secondary and tertiary graduates.

The percentages are much higher if we include people at school and performing housework who reported that they were also available for work. The proportion of young persons who might be considered as hidden unemployed then rises to 27% for young males and to as high as 37% for females.[18] The latter figure is clearly an upper limit. It would include many who chose to be outside the workforce but were perhaps prepared to enter it if the right kind of job presented itself. But 20–30% of youth cohorts involuntarily without work is a high proportion by any standards.

Why were so many young people recorded as not working and available for work, yet not involved in job search activities? Several possibilities can be suggested. Some people were probably genuinely discouraged workers. However, we can surmise that a considerable proportion were indeed hopeful of obtaining modern sector jobs but saw Little point in partaking in formal processes of job search. Classifying as jobseekers only those engaged in active job search in the past week is clearly too restrictive. Further, the official data suggest that almost one-quarter even of the officially defined unemployed reported they used only job search methods that were outside formal channels. Among young, urban people in 1994, nearly half used these 'other' methods of job search in combination with more formal methods. Contacts made through family and friends (*koneksi*) play a key role in most job search, especially for higher wage jobs, where informal payment of often substantial fees to middlemen or company recruiting officers is a common practice.

What activities did the non-working youth undertake? Aside from full-time schooling, many are engaged in short, privately run training courses: English language, computing and other basic courses for aspiring white collar workers are widespread in urban Indonesia (Cremer 1990; World Bank 1995b). In addition, many were probably earning some income assisting in family businesses, self-employed (for example, as self-appointed traffic directors and intermediaries in a range of other services) or engaged in petty crime.[19] For many, the distinction between work and non-work does not accord with official definitions: 'a job' is perceived largely as formal sector wage and white-collar employment, particularly by those who aspire to such jobs.

The Long-Term Unemployed. The extent of long-term unemployment provides further evidence of the severity of joblessness among youth.[20] Durations of recorded unemployment have typically been quite long among young people in Indonesia in 1992 they averaged 10 months for male and female first job seekers, and slightly less for those who had worked before (table 3.6.3).[21] One-third of both young male and young female first job seekers reported looking for work for 12 months or more, and a relatively high percentage (12%) reported searching for two years or more.[22] Young secondary school leavers, in particular, endure long periods out of work. While mean durations in 1992 were just under one year among first job seekers, they were 7–8 months among previously employed youth (table 3.6.3), and 4–5 months for people aged 30 and above. Among the latter, the transition between jobs appears to be short for most workers, in the absence of unemployment benefits and social insurance, or sufficient family support.[23]

Tracer studies among tertiary graduates support these findings (Strudwick 1991; Redecon 1994). A sizeable fraction of all graduates found work in the first six months after completing university. However, durations of unemployment were typically 1–2 years among 20–30% of graduates from some faculties, and from state and private universities. The Redecon study showed that the transition from school to work was shorter among graduates from technical faculties and from the more prestigious universities. More females suffered long-term unemployment, although the difference with males was substantially reduced once account was taken of the particular university and field of study.

As rates of unemployment by age imply, young unemployed are eventually absorbed into the labour force as they reach their mid twenties for senior high graduates and thirties for tertiary graduates. This fall-off in unemployment rates with age has been a feature of the Indonesian labour market for some time.[24] And rates of return to education were high—at least m the 1970s and 1980s—even for those who spent a long time in job search activities (Clark 1983; McMahon and Boediono 1991).

Is unemployment a luxury among the better-off?

This brings us back to the issue of 'luxury' unemployment is it true that the better-off can afford to be unemployed, whereas poorer job seekers are unable to wait for better jobs because of lack of financial support? Support for the luxury hypothesis came from earlier studies in Third World settings where higher unemployment among the rich—often proxied in empirical studies by those with more educated dependants—was characterised as 'wait unemplovment' (Udall and Sinclair 1982). In contrast, other evidence shows that the poor frequently suffer quite high rates of unemployment (Visaria 198 L; Rodgers 1989).

Earlier studies of Indonesian employment also stressed this 'luxury' aspect of unemployment. For example, Arndt and Sundrum (1980, p. 65), in a discussion of unemployment data in Indonesia, state blandly that

> Open unemployment is heavily concentrated among the young and better-educated in urban areas often waiting for better jobs than those

Table 3.6.3 Duration of Unemployment among Young First job Seekers and the Previously Employed (Ages 15–29), by Level of Schooling, Indonesia, 1992

Gender and Education	First job Seekers					Previously Employed				
	Mean Duration (months)	N('000)	Percentage Searching			Mean Duration (months)	N('000)	Percentage Searching		
			< 6 months	12 months +	24 months +			< 6 months	12 months +	24 months +
Male										
≤ Primary	8	(61)	53	27	9	5	(38)	75	12	6
Junior high	9	(76)	42	30	10	7	(37)	62	26	5
Senior high	10	(329)	38	37	13	9	(82)	47	29	10
Tertiary	9	(43)	48	32	11	7	(7)	46	24	7
All levels	10	(509)	42	34	12	7	164	57	24	7
Female										
≤ Primary	9	(36)	43	35	14	6	(19)	62	17	15
Junior high	9	(52)	47	28	7	12	(10)	55	32	13
Senior high	11	(322)	37	36	16	9	(43)	51	24	9
Tertiary	7	(44)	51	24	3	7	(7)	38	26	0
All levels	10	(454)	40	34	13	8	(79)	52	23	7

Source: As for table 3.6.2.

> readily available, and supported by their relatively well-off families. ... Open unemployment is thus a political rather than an economic problem for governments.

To test the 'luxury unemployment' hypothesis, we examined unemployment rates among dependants (most of them aged less than 30) according to the social-economic status of the household head.[25] Some data appear to confirm the hypothesis. For example, both among all household members and among members aged 15–29, unemployment rates tended to be much lower for job-seekers whose household head was primary educated or below (Manning and Junankar 1994, table 5.3). The finding was. especially marked for males.[26]

However, most other evidence from Indonesia in the early 1990s did not support the luxury hypothesis. First, there was little difference in unemployment rates for dependants in households whose head was lower secondary, upper secondary or tertiary educated. For all male urban dependants, these rates were close to 21%, and for young persons they ranged from 24 to 28%.

Second, if we standardise for the education of job seekers themselves, the difference in unemployment rates among lower and higher socio-economic status households narrows. This is shown in table 3.6.4 for young dependants who were upper secondary educated, by far the largest group among the unemployed. The table shows quite small differences in unemployment of dependants in the lowest socio-economic status households (especially as categorised by education of the head) compared with those in higher status groups.[27] This is especially so if the 'other' group discussed above (those outside the workforce and with no recorded activity) is included among the unemployed. Unemployment rates of 20–30% among children of lower socio-economic status households suggest that many faced considerable difficulty in getting jobs.[28]

Third, following our earlier discussion, it is also useful to represent the unemployed as a share of the working age population, given the apparently large numbers of young people outside the workforce who might be considered as 'hidden' unemployed. According to this measure, the share of the unemployed peaked among households where the head had completed lower secondary education. Equally telling, it was substantially *lower* among households where the head was upper secondary or tertiary educated (table 3.6.4).[29]

In one sense, this latter ratio is a more meaningful representation of the relationship between socio-economic status and labour force attachment than are unemployment rates. This is highlighted by the differences in employment and school participation rates among various socio-economic classes shown in the last two columns of table 3.6.4. Young secondary educated dependants from the lower status groups were much more likely to be in the workforce and less likely to continue their schooling to tertiary levels—presumably owing mainly to economic pressures. Half of this lower status group were employed and a further 15–20% unemployed, whereas

Table 3.6.4 Unemployment and Employment Rates of Senior High School Educated Urban Youth (Ages 15–29), by Education and Income of Household Head, Indonesia, 1992

Education and Income of Head	**Measures of Unemployment**				**Employment Rate[c]**	**School Participation Rate[d]**
	% of Labour Force[a]		**% of Working Age Population[a]**			
	Unemployed	**Unemployed + Other[b]**	**Unemployed**	**Unemployed + Other[b]**		
Schooling of head						
≤ Primary	25	37	18	32	54	13
Junior high	31	43	19	33	43	23
Senior high	28	41	14	24	35	40
Tertiary	36	48	10	17	18	65
Income of head (Rp '000)[e]						
<Rp50	19	37	13	26	54	11
50 – <100	31	40	24	35	54	19
100 – < 200	29	41	19	32	46	25
200 +	32	44	14	23	29	42
All persons	27	40	16	29	44	27

[a]Percentage of labour force and population who are urban, senior high school educated and aged 15–29.
[b](U | O)/(I + O), where U = unemployed, L = labour force, O = other (outside labour force).
[c](Employed – working age population)*100.
[d](Number whose main activity is school – population aged 15–29)*100.
[e] Because there are no data on incomes of the self-employed, this part of the table only presents data on unemployed members of households whose head is a wage earner.
Source: As for table 2.

only around 10–15% were enrolled in tertiary institutions. In contrast, around half of the population of secondary educated persons in the highest socio-economic classes were enrolled in tertiary institutions, only 20% were employed, and 10% had joined the unemployment queues.

Thus in terms of activities of the working age population, rather than just the labour force, there is quite a clear contrast between lower status and better-off households. High school educated people in the lower status group were much more likely than their better-off counterparts to enter the workforce after graduating, and quite a high proportion of the entire cohort found themselves unemployed. Many more of those from better-off households could afford to go on to tertiary education, and a relatively small proportion were unemployed, even though quite a high percentage of those who opted to work experienced difficulty in getting the jobs they desired.

A final piece of evidence that questions the 'luxury' hypothesis is that quite long *durations* of unemployment were recorded for individuals from low status households. In households whose head had completed only primary schooling or less, almost 30% of the unemployed, whether male or female, were long-term unemployed. Durations of unemployment were similar to those experienced by higher status households.

These findings are generally supported by logit analysis undertaken by Manning and Junankar (1994, ch. 6). This study used data from the National Labour Force Surveys for 1992 and focused on urban youth, defined as those aged 15–29 years. It investigated the relationship between the likelihood of someone being unemployed and a set of individual and household characteristics, including household socio-economic status and the individual's age, education, gender and region of residence. The results suggested that the probability of being unemployed was lower for the very poor, but higher for all other groups. The hypothesis that it is the rich (who can afford it) who are most likely to be unemployed in Indonesia was thus rejected, although we found evidence to support the contention that the very poor are least likely to remain long, if at all, in unemployment queues.

In general, therefore, the data for Indonesia in the early 1990s lead us to reject the 'luxury unemployment' hypothesis. It is a reminder that many young, educated people from less privileged socio-economic backgrounds are likely to find it as hard as, if not harder than, those from better-off families to break into the modern sector job market. They may also have as much difficulty in getting employment in the informal sector.

These findings have added significance given that secondary level education itself is no longer the luxury in Indonesia that it was in the early years of the New Order. By the early 1990s, gross enrolment rates at secondary level were approximately 50% nationally and over two-thirds in urban areas Although few of the poorest households could support their children through to upper secondary school, many relatively low-income households were *now able to do so*, albert at substantial cost. Long durations of unemployment endured by children in these families were probably associated with considerable hardship, especially if the jobs to which they aspired remained out of reach

Changes in unemployment

Three patterns are apparent in unemployment trends evidenced by official data in Indonesia. First, the national rate appeared to rise in 1994 after a long period of stability. Second, prior to this, there was a remarkable period of stability in national rates and even in the structure of unemployment, despite fluctuations in macroeconomic fortunes and changing labour supply conditions. Third, changes that did take place affected mainly less educated youth, tertiary educated people and women. Each of these developments is discussed in turn

Recent Trends

Official national unemployment remained very low by developed and developing country standards from 1971 to 1993 (2–4%), before rising to 7% in 1995 and falling back to 4% again in 1996.[30] Although the data for 1995 are problematic,[31] quite large rises in recorded rates are evident in 1994 and 1996, compared with earlier years (figure 3.6.5).

Does this represent a significant change in labour market conditions in the mid 1990s? The answer is a categorical 'no', with some minor qualifications. There was no dramatic change in overall labour supply or demand conditions to suggest that the labour market was suffering undue strain at this time. Labour supply growth rates had begun to slow in the 1990s, especially on Java, as the delayed effects of fertility decline began to slow the expansion of the working age population.[12] More pointedly, among young people (aged 15–29) growth in labour supply halved to only a little above 1% in the period 1990–95, largely owing to an absolute fall in the number of young people who entered the labour force with no schooling or an incomplete primary education.

On the labour demand side, the economy continued to grow strongly in the 1990s, although there is some indication that labour demand trends were not as favourable to employment as in the latter half of the 1980s. Trends in employment and wages suggest a tightening labour market in the 1990s. There was an absolute decline in agricultural employment for the first time—one indicator of a 'turning point' in the unskilled labour market, as the balance shifts away from general conditions of labour surplus. Second, real wages increased in a range of Sectors—agriculture, manufacturing and services—from around 1990, after a period of stagnation in the previous decade (Manning and Jayasuriya 1996).

Why then did unemployment rates appear to rise in in these years, despite the tightening labour market. The main explanation for this apparent

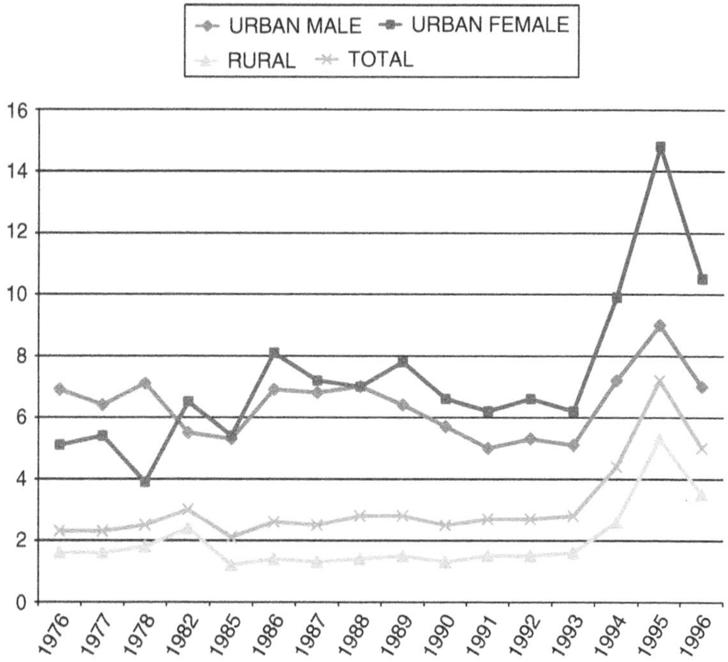

Figure 3.6.5 Trends in Unemployment in Indonesia, 1976–96[a] *(%)*

[a] There are no data for 1979–81 and 1983–84, because no Sakernas surveys were conducted in these years, except for an incomplete survey in 1979. Census data for 1980 are not used, for reasons of comparability.

Source: BPS, Sakernas, 1976–78, 1986–94, Susenas, 1982, Supas, 1995.

contradiction is definitional rather than real. It relates to the substantial lengthening of the reference period for job search activities from one week in all surveys and censuses prior to 1993 to one year from 1994 onwards. The former definition was unduly restrictive, whereas the one-year reference period is uncommonly long. Most countries define unemployment as job search activity conducted over a one-month or three-month period. The change to the longer reference period is probably more in tune with labour market realities in Indonesia. It is unfortunate, however, that such a dramatic change to the definition precludes comparisons of recent developments with earlier recorded unemployment rates.

Two other factors might help explain sustained high rates of educated youth unemployment. Some of the gains in job opportunities associated with a tighter labour market may have been offset by signals from the rise in the real minimum wage, which accelerated in 1994 and 1995 (Manning and Jayasuriya 1996). Young job seekers were probably encouraged to join queues for jobs in the larger establishments, which were under greater pressure to implement minimum wage policy. Rural workers were also likely to respond to potential gains in earnings offered by the minimum wage. Harris–Todaro rural–urban migration movements in response to expected wages may well have begun to play a more important role in Indonesia than previously. Such processes have probably contributed to more rapid increases in unemployment in some regions outside Java, given that the majority of low-income rural workers are now concentrated in the Outer Island provinces.

This trend could be expected to affect particularly those less educated young people seeking jobs at new minimum *wage rates m* the rapidly growing formal sector. Indeed a rise in the unemployment rate of the less educated relative to overall rates was one notable change in the structure of unemployment shown in the 1995 intercensal survey (but not in the National Labour Force Surveys). This was in contrast to a decline in this ratio in the previous two decades. It is precisely this group of less educated workers that one might expect to have been lured by job prospects in rapidly growing labour-intensive manufacturing industries and hence to have experienced low levels of joblessness in the 1980s. They may have found their way into unemployment queues as minimum wages began to bite in the mid 1990s.

A second development in the job market may also be relevant to rates of unemployment among the less educated. Manufacturing employment growth slowed in the 1990s, following a spurt associated with deregulation in the latter half of previous decade (Manning 1998). Employment growth in manufacturing was below that in other major sectors in the early 1990s (table 3.6.5).[33] Even if one accepts the higher Sakernas estimates, the employment elasticity of manufacturing was only around 0.5 (given output growth of around 12% per annum), and generally no better than that of other non-agricultural sectors. Part of the explanation may be the

Table 3.6.5 Growth in Employment by Major Sector, Indonesia, 1971–95[a] (% p.a.)

Sector	Census		Census/Supas	Sakernas
	1971–80	1980–90	1990–95	1989/90–1993/94[b]
Agriculture	1.2	21	–0.6	–18
Manufacturing	4.7	5.6	41	6.7
Trade	49	4.6	53	4.7
Transport	4.9	58	5.4	8.4
Services	6.3	2.7	4.9	4.3
All sectors[c]	3.0	3.2	2.2	1.9

[a] Data adjusted for uneven coverage of Irian and East Timor, 1971 and 1980.
[b] Two-year average.
[c] Includes mining, banking and finance, public utilities, construction.
Sources: BPS, Population Census, 1971, 1980, 1990; Supas, 1995; Sakernas, 1994.

shift in the composition of output and investment away from the more labour-intensive industries (textiles, clothing and footwear in particular) towards industries such as chemicals and non-metallic minerals (Manning and Jayasuriya 1996). Other evidence confirms this trend, namely the shift in foreign investment approvals in favour of paper and chemicals in the two years 1994–95 compared with 1989–90 when the deregulation reform program was at its height.[34]

Longer-Term Trends: Stability

National Trends In this paper we do not examine in detail cyclical trends in unemployment. But a close look at the data in figure 3.6.5 suggests that macroeconomic circumstances seem to be weakly, if at all, related to aggregate or youth unemployment (at least prior to the 1997–98 crisis). Thus rates of aggregate and youth unemployment did not rise during slower economic growth in 1982 and 1986 (although urban rates did increase slightly in the latter year). Nor did they fall when the economy picked up from 1987–88 following deregulation and the non-oil export boom.[35] Similarly, while youth unemployment seems to have risen in 1986, it did not fall again until 1990 (a year in which economic growth was little different from the previous three years), and then remained relatively stable.

In general, the dominant pattern was one of stability in overall, urban and educated youth unemployment rates over time. The trends in total urban and rural unemployment rates shown in figure 3.6.5 were also reflected m relative stability in rates among young educated people and older people during the 1970s, 1980s and into the 1990s (table 3.6.6).[36]

This stability in the incidence of unemployment over time is shown in figures 3.6.6–3.6.7 for selected years from 1976 among key population subgroups. Thus, for example, the rate of joblessness changed little from 1976 among people aged 20–24 and 25–29, the largest groups of unemployed, at most levels of schooling.[37]

There has also been considerable stability m the regional structure of urban unemployment over time, although unemployment rates increased more rapidly in several of the Outer Island regions than on Java after 1987 (table 3.6.1)[38] From the mid 1970s, unemployment rates were consistently above the national average in the provinces where manufacturing employment grew rapidly. Jakarta and West Java, and to a lesser extent North Sumatra). They were also high m the resource rich provinces of Aceh, Riau and Irian Jaya, and in the more isolated eastern Indonesian provinces where education has historically been quite advanced. Conversely, almost all the 'inner Indonesia' provinces in which unemployment was low in 1977/78 recorded low unemployment rates 14 years later in 1991/92.

Urban Youth Similarly, under-utilisation of urban youth—especially the high proportion of 'others' outside the labour force—has been a feature of the labour market in Indonesia since the 1970s. For example, among urban

Table 3.6.6 Unemployment Rates and Distribution of Unemployed by Age and Schooling, Urban Areas, Indonesia, 1976–96

	Unemployment Rate (%)					% of Total Unemployed		
	1976	1982	1986	1992	1996	1976	1992	1996
Age group								
15–19	20.4	16.8	14.3	22.0	27.1	36	20	25
20–24	17.1	18.0	19.4	23.1	22.1	42	50	41
25–29	5.7	5.4	7.7	10.5	11.0	12	20	21
30+	1.0	1.1	0.9	1.6	1.7	10	10	13
						100	100	100
Level of completed schooling[a]								
< Primary	3.7	2.7	1.2	1.4	1.9	24	4	3
Primary	6.8	4.9	2,4	3.6	3.2	30	12	13
Junior high	8.7	6.6	5.3	7.7	7.6	19	15	15
Senior high								
Academic	11.2	12.9	14.2	17.9	14.9	14	41	37
Vocational	11.1	11.2	9.2	12.5	12.7	11	19	21
Tertiary[b]	4.0	5.6	9.7	12.5	12.3	2	9	11
						100	100	100
Overall rates[c]	6.3	5.8	5.8	8.2	8.3			
N ('000)[c]						467	1,159	2,511

[a] Population aged 15 and above.
[b] Three years completed tertiary education (BA level) and above.
[c] Total workforce aged 10 and above.
Sources: BPS, Sakernas, 1976, 1986, 1992 and 1996; Susenas (National Socio-Economic Survey), 1982.

males aged 20–24, the labour force participation rate was only 65% in 1992, declining slightly from 73% in 1977 owing to growth in school enrolments. A quite high proportion (6–10%) of young persons enumerated as 'other' and outside the workforce has also been recorded consistently since the early National Labour Force Surveys in 1976–77 (Cremer 1990).

From one perspective, we might have expected the already high youth unemployment rates to have risen in Indonesia since the 1970s. There was an extraordinary expansion in the supply of educated manpower, with secondary and tertiary graduate numbers increasing by over 10% per annum since the 1970s. That youth unemployment did not increase has been a considerable achievement. Nevertheless, urban rates have remained high among educated youth, and the unemployment queues have become increasingly dominated by the more educated. The rapid expansion of the economy has not been able to make inroads on what had already emerged as a key labour market problem early in the Soeharto period.

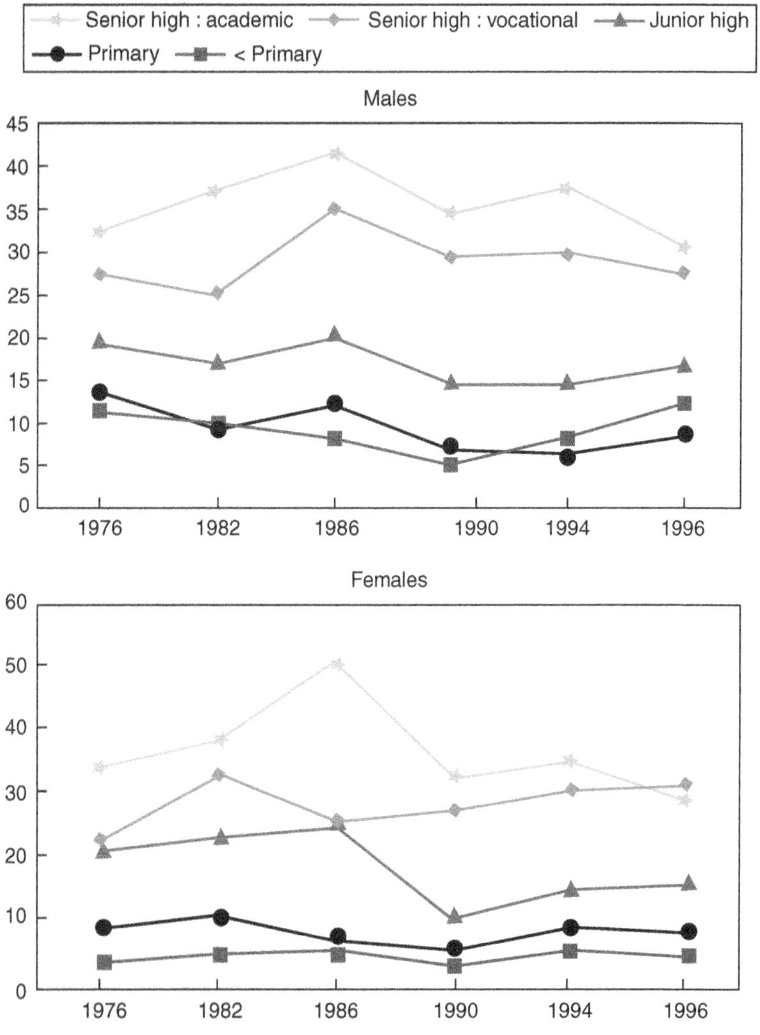

Figure 3.6.6 Trends in Unemployment by Education among Males and Females Aged 20–24, Urban Indonesian, 1976–96 (%)
Source: BPS, Sakernas, 1976, 1986, 1990, 1994 and 1996.

Longer-Term Trends: Change

Despite this dominant pattern of stability, there were some visible changes in the structure of unemployment through to the mid 1990s.[39] Changes in the rate of joblessness among less educated people, the tertiary educated and females are shown in figures 3.6.6–3.6.7, and in an appendix available from the authors

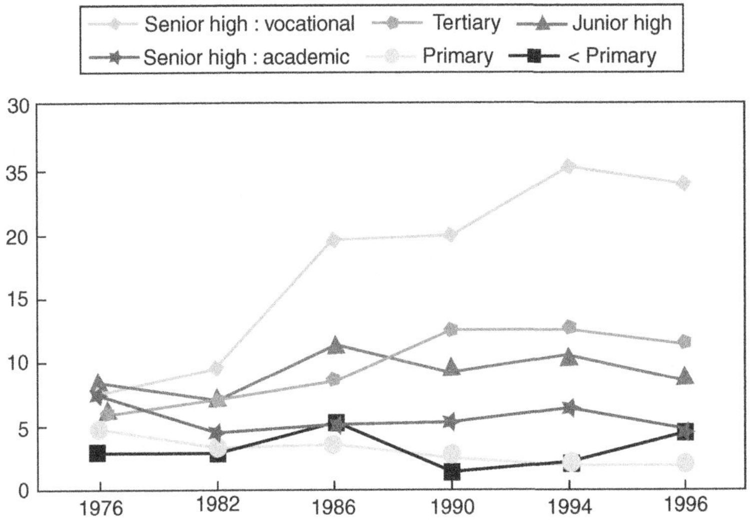

Figure 3.6.7 Trends in unemployment by education among males aged 25–29, urban Indonesia, 1976–94 (%)
Source: As for figure 3.6.6.

Less Educated Youth Aggregate unemployment rates did not rise, partly because higher unemployment among the increasing number of more educated was offset by falling rates among younger persons who left school earlier. In the mid 1970s, unemployment rates were quite similar (20–30%) among young upper secondary graduates and young male job seekers aged 15–19 who had only completed lower secondary education or less. Subsequently, unemployment nearly halved among the group of less educated, younger job seekers. As the number graduating from senior high school rose quickly—their share of all unemployed increasing from around 20% in 1976 to over 40% in 1996—less educated persons appear to have left the better-paid modern sector job queues

The data suggest a clear pattern of 'bumping up' of educational requirements for modern sector jobs, This tendency is related to 'credentialism' (reliance on credentials rather than other criteria in selecting staff)—a pattern that has been common in other developing countries.[40] Whereas primary and lower secondary graduates could realistically aspire to modern sector jobs in the 1970s, and were prepared to queue for them, this had changed by the 1990s. Public sector jobs were virtually closed to primary graduates from the late 1970s and to lower secondary graduates from the mid 1980s, and it is likely that this was also true of many modern private sector jobs, even for relatively unskilled workers

The growth of job opportunities in export-oriented manufacturing probably contributed to lower unemployment among the less educated. While young primary and lower secondary graduates have been 'bumped out' of modern sector jobs, many appear to have found employment in the new industries. The low age and educational status of many workers in the clothing and footwear industries exemplifies this (White *et al* 1992)

Tertiary Educated Youth. In contrast to the relatively stable rates among young senior high graduates, unemployment rose markedly for tertiary graduates in the 1980s and into the 1990s. Both their unemployment rates and their share of all unemployed doubled from 4% to around 10%. This included a tripling of rates recorded for males, and a smaller increase among females, since the mid 1970s. For both sexes the rates for those aged 25–29 years were 20–25% in 1992 and closer to 30% in 1996

These increases in unemployment rates at tertiary levels of schooling were accompanied by quite long durations of job search—on average approximately nine months in the early 1990s. From the standpoints of both under-utilisation of skilled manpower and social returns to investment in education, they represent a worrying trend. Given the experience of countries like Malaysia in earlier periods (Mazumdar 1981), high levels of unemployment among the tertiary educated seem likely to remain an important feature of the Indonesian labour market in the 1990s.

Thus, high graduate salaries, linked to an acute shortage of certain categories of highly skilled manpower, clearly did not apply to all tertiary educated persons (although high tertiary unemployment was no doubt partly a response to such inducements). An increasing excess supply of graduates with qualifications not highly valued in the market place—the still heavy emphasis on law, social sciences and the humanities rather than pure and applied sciences—also helps explain rising unemployment among tertiary educated people. Studies have found that huge differences between institutions in the quality of higher education also impact significantly on durations of unemployment (Keyfitz 1989; Hough and Wiranta 1994; Redecon 1994).

Unemployment by Sex. The share of females among all unemployed (more than 45% in 1996) and total female unemployments rate rose relative to those of males.[41] In the latter half of the 1970s, male unemployment rates were 20–30% higher than female rates, but by the 1990s the situation was reversed.

Contrary to popular views, the high unemployment rates among females do not represent significant disadvantage compared with males from the same age–education cohorts. Thus, for example, educated youth unemployment rates were generally not higher among females than among males.[42] The greater incidence of overall female unemployment relative to males is mainly the result of a higher proportion of younger, educated females than males entering the labour market in recent years[43]

One qualification needs to be added, however. Upper secondary and especially tertiary educated women in slightly older cohorts appear to have faced greater problems than men in gaining employment. Thus in 1992 and

1994 unemployment rates among senior high graduates in their late twenties and early thirties were considerably higher for women than for men, as they were among tertiary educated women aged m their thirties.[44] Less than 30% of unemployed women aged 25–34 reported previous work experience in 1992, These data suggest that a sizeable number of educated women who do not get into the upper segment of the labour market quickly seem to face discrimination in competition with younger women, or men, of the same age and educational status[45]

In part, the reversal in unemployment rates between the sexes is the result of declining rates among less educated males. In the 1970s, primary and lower secondary males recorded much higher unemployment rates than females. Increased supply of less educated females in work is reflected in rising participation rates and employment rates among those not at school. Nevertheless, although unskilled and semi-skilled females have been preferred in labour-intensive industries such as footwear and garments, this does not appear to have been at the expense of growth in job opportunities among less educated males. The expansion of employment in other industries such as chemicals, metals and machinery, construction, and service activities such as repair shops has been sufficient to absorb considerable numbers of less educated males (Manning 1998).

To sum up, we have stressed the stability of unemployment levels and structure over time, especially among the largest group of unemployed—the young senior high graduates—and among all older persons. The main changes among less educated youth and tertiary educated males and females were related to changing labour market conditions' unemployment was not entirely unresponsive to economic and demographic circumstances. But unemployment among senior high school graduates seems to have had little to do with economic conditions, although the socio-economic composition of this group has changed. Finally, we have suggested that the apparent recent increases in aggregate unemployment are probably related to the minimum wage policy and the slowdown in manufacturing employment growth in the 1990s, although they have much to do with changing survey definitions.

Conclusions

The findings of our research suggest that unemployment rates have been very high among youth in Indonesia for some time, even before the economic crisis hit in 1997. In part, we concur with those who argue that high unemployment reflects selective job search behaviour among better educated youth in a segmented labour market. But unlike several commentators we do not dismiss the issue as trivial, drawing attention to the social costs of youth unemployment, and the representation of poorer households among the urban unemployed. The 'choice' to have unemployed youth in their ranks is exercised not only by better-off families but also by lower-income households—although we found it was less likely to be exercised by individuals from the poorest families

The social (public) cost of unemployment—the waste of human resources—is considerable even if private rewards may still justify long periods of search for employment in the modern sector. Very recent trends linked to a new definition of joblessness aside, a stable incidence of unemployment in urban areas was associated with a tripling of the total number of unemployed, and a more than sevenfold increase in the number of unemployed upper secondary graduates, from 1977 to 1996. The scale of the problem cannot be ignored as youth unemployment spreads across cities and towns in Indonesia. The fiery nature of social disturbances m 1996 and early 1997, even prior to the crisis, seems to be related in part to unmet expectations among urban youth, fanned by specific conflicts. This was set against a backdrop of dissatisfaction over political freedoms and income distribution.

We have drawn attention to a qualitative change in the unemployment problem over time Arndt and Sundrum (1980) were right in stressing 15 years ago that unemployment was probably mainly the preserve of the small number of middle class families with access to secondary and tertiary education. Children in these households could at that time realistically aspire to and queue for at least a stable government job on graduation. The market for educated labour has changed dramatically since then. As access to education has spread, many in the lower middle class have struggled to provide their children with a chance to enter modern sector jobs. They appear to have found such avenues often barred to them because of discriminatory recruiting procedures and the high cost of gaining entry.

Differences between Indonesia's experience and that of several other rapidly growing countries in East Asia (where unemployment fell as labour markets tightened) are probably due to specific institutional circumstances inflexible modern sector employment contracts and relatively high modern sector wages. Both are associated with the early dominant role of the government in providing employment for educated manpower. Also of importance have been mining, state-owned and foreign enterprises in industrial development, and the protection of some modern sector activities for long periods These factors have encouraged greater labour market rigidity than in countries with more atomised labour markets and competitive institutions, such as Taiwan, Hong Kong or even perhaps Thailand (Galenson 1992, Sussangkarn 1987), Rigidities include long durations of 'informal' job search through personal contacts (*koneksi*) in pursuit of modern sector jobs, and low rates of turnover once people get into desired jobs.

These conclusions challenge the notion that there can be a 'quick fix' to the problem of joblessness in Indonesia. In recent years, the cause of the problem has been identified as a lack of skills that can be readily used by the private sector. The Ministries of Education and Manpower have recommended increased vocational content m secondary education. They have set up arrangements for greater involvement of the private sector in 'twinning' programs, in which students are given practical work experience as part of their formal education.

However, unemployment rates and durations of unemployment do not support the conclusion that a substantially more vocationalised secondary education system would necessarily serve Indonesia better. We have seen that unemployment rates were slightly but not significantly lower among vocational school graduates than among academic stream graduates in the same age cohorts. At tertiary levels, the area of specialisation (applied and pure sciences versus social sciences) and the quality of institutions seems to have been more significant than the general readiness of graduates for work. Provided they did the right courses in better institutions, tertiary graduates faced relatively little difficulty in getting jobs.

What then are the policy implications of our findings? First, assuming the economy returns to an even keel in the medium term, greater competition in commodity and capital markets is likely to contribute to a better functioning labour market, insofar as high unemployment is related to a differentiated earnings structure. Second, efforts to improve transparency in systems of recruitment, especially in the public sector, can be expected to give greater job access, especially to those outside the main cities. Third, providing more equal access for poorer individuals to a high quality education through loan and scholarship programs could improve income distribution and reduce the social costs of unemployment, bearing in mind the significant number of less advantaged unemployed among upper secondary leavers. Fourth, greater efforts to give on-the-job experience to students during their final years of education could reduce durations of job search, provided practical training schemes are strongly supported (and at least partly funded) by employers in the major growth industries. However, experiments with state funded training programs should be evaluated on a small-scale basis for their cost effectiveness before the programs proceed further.

As a final caveat, we are largely in the dark about several issues such as the role of credentialism, discrimination in the labour labour market and the extent of labour market attachment of unemployed and discouraged workers. This arises in part from the paucity of available data. The major source of information, the National Labour Force Survey (Sakernas), has been conducted quarterly or annually (with some gaps) since the mid 1970s. While these surveys have filled an important gap in Indonesia's data base on labour market issues, Sakernas in 1996 collected even less information than it did in the late 1970s, despite the growing complexity of the economy and differentiation of the workforce. Several key questions—such as the connection of unemployment to migration and household socio-economic status—cannot be answered adequately without more information.[46]

Notes

Parts of this paper are based on analysis for an earlier study by Manning and Junankar (1994) undertaken for the Ministry of Manpower. Much of the data presented in that report have been updated and further analysed The authors particularly thank staff members of the Demographic Institute, University of Indonesia, of the Population Studies Centre at Gadjah Mada University, of Satya Wacana University and of the Economics Faculty, Andalas University, for comments at seminars given at these institutions in 1994 We also greatly appreciate the helpful comments of three anonymous referees

1. Myrdal (1968, vol. 2, p 1,231) popularised the term 'luxury unemployment'; he focused on disguised unemployment, dismissing unemployment as a 'bourgeois' problem experienced mainly by better-off households.
2. High rates of urban unemployment have been associated especially with large urban–rural wage differentials and migration to urban areas (Todaro 1976)
3. The data were collected annually in 1976, and quarterly from 1977 to 1992 (excluding 1981–85 when no Sakernas surveys were conducted), the survey reverted to an annual basis in 1993. The decision to switch back to annual data collection was due to the relative absence of seasonal fluctuations found in the more expensive quarterly surveys. The sample size has fluctuated between 60,000 and 80,000 households each year, with greater weight being given to urban and to relatively sparsely populated regions
4. The key variables on which there are no data are relationship to the household head, marital and migration status, and household income and expenditure. In the paper's conclusion we suggest briefly how this situation might be rectified.
5. The ratios reported by Turnham (1993, table 2.3, p. 80) are of those aged 15–24 and ages 25 and above in urban areas. The ratio in urban Indonesia was slightly over 101 compared with the next highest ratio of approximately 6.1 in India and ratios of closer to 3–4:1 in most of the other Asian countries included in the table
6. A further possible explanation is that frictional, seasonal or temporary unemployment among less educated older persons (who tend to be concentrated in self-employed and family work) is probably rarely recorded in the official unemployment figures.
7. Some provinces (East Kalimantan, Irian Jaya, Aceh, and to a lesser extent Riau) have experienced resource booms—and busts—and attracted interregional migrants from poorer regions, hopeful of obtaining high wage jobs. In several other outer island provinces, schooling has traditionally been more widespread (North Sumatra, North Sulawesi and Maluku) and educated unemployment is a more pressing problem
8. Female unemployment rates were also substantially above those for males in Jakarta and West Java, two regions where females were heavily concentrated in manufacturing employment.
9. The same general orders of magnitude are found in unemployment measures obtained from the national censuses (1980 and 1990) and other National Labour Force Surveys conducted during the 1980s and early 1990s (Manning and Junankar 1994)
10. The definition of 'under-employment' makes no distinction between looking for more work in the same job and looking for another job
11. In this measure, unemployment rates are calculated as follows' (U/[W+U])*100, where U represents the number of unemployed and W the number of wage workers.

12. If involuntary under-employment is calculated in terms of full-time equivalents, the rate of under-employment falls, to only 3.9%, ranging from a law 1.5% for urban males to 5.6% for rural females (Manning and Junankar 1994, ch 3).
13. Even if rates of unemployment are higher than normal (i.e the percentage of those looking for work is high relative to the labour force), rates of employment also tend to be above average if labour force participation rates are high. Conversely, although unemployment rates may be low, low participation rates will contribute to low employment rates and overall labour utilisation. Increases in unemployment rates may be associated with increases in labour force participation and hence in employment rates. This has been the case in many industrialised countries in the past decade
14. The problem of under-utilisation of young urban males, in particular, was noted by Lluch and Mazumdar (19S5) in their examination of the 1977 Sakernas data
15. The ratio of participation rates for males aged 20–24 to total urban was much lower in Indonesia than in Malaysia, Sri Lanka, Pakistan and Thailand around 1990, with only the Philippines recording the same ratio as Indonesia (Manning and Junankar 1994). The data for other Asian countries are from national labour force surveys reported in the ILO Yearbook of Labour Statistics (1993).
16. The problem was first identified by Jones (1974) in his examination of labour force trends in the 1971 Population Census, and is a pattern revealed in both the National Population Censuses and the National Labour Force Surveys (see also Lluch and Mazumdar 1985; Rucker 1985, and Cremer 1990).
17. Those aged 20–24 and young persons with upper secondary schooling not only recorded the highest rates of unemployment and inactivity, but also constituted a high proportion of the inactive who were available for more work.
18. Caution must be used, of course, in assuming that those *available* for work but outside the work force can be considered unemployed in the same sense that those looking for work are defined as such. For example, those whose principal activity is school (and to a lesser extent housework) may be available only for part-time work
19. Labour force surveys in the late 1970s found that although most unemployed people depended mainly on their families for support, 10–15% (closer to 20% among males) were engaged in occasional jobs
20. In contrast to the considerable literature about the problems of the long-term unemployed in industrialised countries (Junankar 1988; OECD 1993), relatively little has been written on this group in LDCs, and in Indonesia in particular.
21. The data refer to durations of uninterrupted spells of unemployment at the time of the survey Median durations of unemployment among young people were shorter, around six months, in urban areas in the early 1990s (Dhanani 1994, table 2 2 13).
22. See also Clark (1983) for data on the late 1970s.
23. This aspect of the unemployment problem has been more severe in Indonesia than was found to be the case in several earlier studies of other Asian countries. Durations of more than one year's unemployment were recorded by a significant proportion of the workforce only in Malaysia among several Asian countries (the Philippines, Thailand, Sri Lanka and India) for which data were available around 1970 (Mazumdar 1981, p. 281)
24. For example, there is sharp decline in unemployment rates among upper secondary graduates aged 25–29 in 1982, 1986 and 1992 compared with those aged 20–24 in 1976, 19S2 and 1986 respectively (Manning and Junankar 1994).

25. Ideally one would want to link unemployment to the socio-economic status of the unemployed, but there were no general indicators of household socioeconomic status apart from the attributes of the household head included in the National Labour Force Surveys
26. For example, among young males from households where the head was only primary educated or less, unemployment rates were around 15% compared with 24–28% where the head was more educated (Manning and Junankar 1994). The rate of unemployment was quite similar (6%) among young females in households where the head was primary educated or less, and in those whose head was tertiary educated
27. The group of households classified by the wage of the household head is, of course, a biased sample, since it does not include self-employed household heads—although this group was unlikely to be more highly represented among the poor (Huppi and Ravallion 1991). The findings for households classified by head's wage were, however, generally consistent with those for all households (classified by head's educational status)
28. Almost half of unemployed individuals with secondary schooling came from the lowest socio-economic status groups—those in which the head had only primary schooling or a low wage income. Nevertheless, it is true that unemployment rates were still slightly lower (around 10% below the rate for all secondary educated) in cases where the head had only a primary education or less, or earned a low wage income, they were also slightly higher than the overall mean (10–30%) if the head had a tertiary education or had a relatively high income
29. In the population represented by table 4 (upper secondary educated urban youth aged 15–29), the share of those classified as 'other' (those outside the work force and reporting no other activity) was also higher among dependants of the less educated. If this group and the unemployed are taken together, their ratio to the population is similarly much higher among those whose household head had lower secondary schooling or below.
30. The 1971 figures are based on the Series C subsample results, which are more consistent with those of other surveys than the much higher rates recorded in the full sample Series D publication
31. The 1995 intercensal (Supas) rates of unemployment were much higher for all provinces and age–education categories than those shown by the Sakernas Survey in any preceding year, or in 1996. As in 1994 and 1996, a different definition of unemployment was adopted (see below), hence the data cannot be compared directly with those from earlier years. Nevertheless, the results are puzzling, given that economic performance was generally impressive in 1995 and there were no obvious supply-side shocks
32. On Java labour force growth fell from a peak of 3% per annum in the 1980s to 2.6% in the 1990s. Outer Island labour force growth remained high, however (estimated at close to 4% on an annual basis 1990–95), and is only likely to decline in the early part of the next century (Manning 1998)
33. In general, one can place greater faith in the Census–Supas comparisons for longer-term trends, given quite large year-to-year fluctuations in the Sakernas data on employment structure. However, even according to Sakernas, manufacturing employment growth was only slightly higher than all non-agricultural jobs expansion (including the construction, mining and banking/finance sectors not shown in table 3.6.5)
34. These two industries accounted for over half of all investment approvals in 1994/95, while foreign direct investment (FDI) approvals in TCF industries fell

from 12%. five years earlier to just over 1% of FDI approvals in 1994/95. Thus one would expect a reversal in the shift towards more jobs in the TCF industries that occurred in the period 1986–93 (Manning 1998)

35. Unfortunately, there is a gap in the data for several years in the early 1980s (1981, 1983–84) which precludes a more careful look at the response of the labour market to slower economic growth in this period
36. Dhanani (1994) provides details of trends over time for specific age and education subgroups between 1977 and 1993.
37. Two exceptions were a sharp rise in recorded unemployment rates among 20–24 year old senior secondary graduates in academic streams in 1986, a year of economic hardship when oil prices plummeted, and for male tertiary graduates aged 25–29, who experienced a sustained increase in unemployment rates from 1982 (see below). The data for females aged 25–29 are not shown in the graphs, but trends in these rates showed a pattern similar to those for males in all schooling groups.
38. See Manning and Junankar (1994, figure 4.10) for longer-term trends. The increases were most marked in Sumatra and Sulawest, while Jakarta unemployment rates fel relative to the national average (Jakarta had recorded one of the highest rates of unemployment in urban Indonesia in the 1970s and 1980s)
39. Unfortunately comparisons of the structure can only be made for data up to 1993, owing the change in definition mentioned above. Most of the data presented in this section are for the period up to 1992, although we draw attention to some apparent trends based on the 1994 National Labour Force Survey data
40. See especially Sabot's (1977) study of labour market adjustment in urban Tanzania for an interesting discussion of the 'bumping up' of educational requirements for jobs
41. These changes were due mainly to rapid increases in labour force participation rates, especially among younger educated women (who were more likely to be unemployed), and smaller falls (relative to males) in already low unemployment rates among less educated women
42. In other words, there was relatively little difference in age standardised unemployment rates among educated and less educated men and women. For example if unemployment rates among females at academic senior high and at tertiary levels are standardised using the male age distributions, unemployment rates fall from 21 and 16% to 13 and 8% respectively, both these latter rates are only slightly higher than those for males (12 and 7% respectively)
43. Thus while a minority of the educated male work force were aged in their twenties (around 40% the of upper secondary and tertiary educated) in 1992, the majority of female upper secondary (around 60%) and tertiary graduates (50%) were in this age category
44. For example, upper secondary educated (academic stream) males aged 25–29 experienced unemployment rate of 13% compared with 18% among females in 1994, male rates were 7% and female rates 13% among the tertiary educated aged 30–34
45. This does not mean, of course, that women of these ages are necessarily discriminated against because of gender, but rather that a break in labour market experience puts them at a disadvantage. However, there is considerable evidence that married females and those with children are discriminated against in recruitment for modern sector jobs, especially in banking and business
46. This would not require a radical departure from the successful format that Sakernas has followed over the years. The main changes needed include (i) the introduction of new questions covering occupation, socio-economic status of households and key socio-demographic characteristics of individuals (marital

status, relationship to the head of household and migration status in particular); and (ii) more careful definition of several unemployment measures (especially the reference period for job search, the nature of search activities and the concept of availability for work)

References

Arndt, H W, and R M. Sundrum (1980), 'Employment, Unemployment and Under-Employment', *Bulletin of Indonesian Economic Studies* 16 (3), pp. 61–82.

Berry, Albert (1975), 'Unemployment as a Social Problem in Columbia. Myth and Reality', *Economic Development and Cultural Change* 23 (2), pp 276–91.

Berry, Albert, and Richard Sabot (1978), 'Labour Market Performance in Developing Countries', *World Development* 6 (11/12), pp 1, 199–1, 242.

Breman. J.C (1980), *The Informal Sector in Research Theory and Practice,* Comparative Asian Studies Program, Erasmus University, Rotterdam.

Clark, David H (1983), *How Secondary School Graduates Perform in the Labor Market A Study of Indonesia,* World Bank Staff Working Paper no 615, Washington DC.

Cremer, G (1990). 'Who Are Those Misclassified as Others' A Note on the Indonesian Labour Force Statistics', *Bulletin of Indonesian Economic Studies* 26 (1), pp 69–91.

Dhanani, S (1994), Unemployment and Underemployment in Indonesia in the 1980s, Unpublished paper, Jakarta.

Galenson, Walter (1992), *Labor and Economic Growth in Five Asian Countries South Korea, Malaysia, Taiwan, Thailand and the Philippines,* Praeger, New York.

Gregory, RG (1991), 'Jobs and Gender A Lego Approach to the Australian Market', in Kenneth W Clements Robert C Gregory and Takashi Takayama (eds), *International Economic Postgraduate Research Conference Volume,* Supplement to *The Economic Record,* Economic Research Centre, Department of Economics, University of Western Australia, Perth, pp 20–40.

Hough, James, and Sukarna Wiranta (1994), 'Labour Market and Higher Education Graduate Employment in Indonesia', *Masyarakat Indonesia* 21 (1), pp 33–52.

Huppi, Monika, and Martin Ravallion (1991), 'The Sectoral Structure of Poverty during an Adjustment Period. Evidence for Indonesia in the Mid 1980s', *World Development* 19 (12), pp 1.653–1,678.

Jones, Gavin W (1974), What Do We Know about the Labour Force in Indonesia?', *Majalah Demografi Indonesia* 1 (2), pp 7–36.

Junankar, P N (1988), *Very Long Term Unemployment,* Commission of the European Communities, Luxembourg.

Keyfitz, Nathan (19S9), Putting Trained Labour Power to Work The Dilemma of Education and Employment', *Bulletin of Indonesian Economic Studies* 25 (3), pp 35–56

Kim, Jang Ho (1936), *Wages, Employment and Income Distribution in South Korea: 1160–83,* ARTEP-ILO, New Delhi.

Kuo, Shirley (1983), *The Taiwan Economy in Transition,* Westview Press, Colorado.

Lluch, C. and D Mazumdar (1985), *Wages and Employment in Indonesia,* World Bank, Washington DC.

McMahon, Walter, and Boediono (1991), *Education and the Economy,* Education Policy and Planning Project, Department of Education and Culture, Jakarta.

Manning, C (1998), *Indonesian Labour in Transition. An East Asian Success Story?* Cambridge University Press, Cambridge.

Manning, C., and PN Junankar (1994), *Unemployment in Indonesia A Focus on Urban Youth,* Report prepared for the Ministry of Manpower, Republic of Indonesia, ANUTECH Pty Ltd, Canberra.

Manning, C., and S. Jayasuriya (1496), 'Survey of Recent Developments', *Bulletin of Indonesian Economic Studies* 35 (2), pp. 3–45.

Mazumdar, Dipak (1981). *The Urban Labour Market and Income Distribution A Study of Malaysia,* Oxford University Press, New York.

Myrdal, G (1968), *Asian Drama,* Penguin Books, Harmondsworth.

OECD (1993), *Employment Outlook,* OECD. Paris.

Redecon (1994), *Studi Pelacakan Lulusan Perguruan Tinggi di Indonesia,* Department of Education and Culture, Jakarta.

Rodgers, Gerry (1989) (ed), *Urban Poverty and the Labour Market Access to jobs and Incomes in Asian and Latin American Cities,* ILO, Geneva.

Rucker, Robert L. (1985), *A Preliminary View of Indonesia's Employment Problem and Some Options for Solving It,* United States Agency for International Development, Jakarta.

Sabot, Richard H (1977), 'The Meaning and Measurement of Urban Surplus Labour,' *Oxford Economic Papers* 29 (3), pp 389–411.

Strudwick, J., and A Cresswell (1994), *Secondary Education Outcomes in Indonesia,* USAID, Jakarta.

Sussangkarn, Chalongphob (1987), 'Labour Markets', in Peter Warr (ed.). *The Thai Economy in Transition,* Cambridge University Press, Cambridge, pp. 355–400.

Todaro, Michael P. (1976), *Internal Migration in Developing Countries,* ILO, Geneva.

Turnham, David (1971), *The Employment Problem in Less Developed Countries: A Review of the Evidence,* Development Centre, OECD, Paris.

_____ (1993), *Employment and Development A New Review of Evidence,* Development Centre, OECD, Paris.

Udall, A T, and S Sinclair (1982), 'The "Luxury Unemployment" Hypothesis A Review of the Recent Evidence', *World Development* 10, pp 49–62.

Visaria, P, (1981), 'Poverty and Unemployment in India An Analysis of Recent Evidence', *World Development* 9 (3), pp 277–300.

White, Benjamin, *et al* (1992), Workshops and Factories: Dynamics of Production, Organisation and Employment in West Java's Rural Footwear Industries, Paper presented at the 9th Biennial Conference of the Asian Studies Association of Australia, 6–9 July 1992.

World Bank (1995a), *World Development Report Workers in an Integrating World,* Oxford University Press, Washington DC.

_____ (1995b), *Training and the Labor Market in Indonesia Policies for Productivity Gains and Employment Growth,* World Bank, Washington DC.

4
Unemployment

4.1
An Econometric Analysis of Unemployment in Great Britain, 1952–75

P. N. Junankar

1 Introduction

In this paper we shall argue that the main causes of high unemployment m Britain since the mid-sixties, are the level and composition of aggregate demand. We shall argue that structural changes in the economy that have led to a change in the composition of output (from the industrial sector to the services sector) are an important explanation of the high levels of unemployment. Further, we shall argue that the increased unemployment benefits since 1966 do not have a significant effect on the level of unemployment. Our econometric results suggest that although we can highlight the main determinants of unemployment, the relationship is inherently unstable suggesting the need for a more completely specified model of the labour market.

In a controversial paper Maki and Spindler (1975) argue that a large part of the increase in post-1966 unemployment can be explained by increased unemployment benefits. Sawyer (1979) disputes their findings on both theoretical and empirical grounds. Specifically he questions their measure of the replacement ratio (benefit-income ratio) as a very small proportion of the unemployed were actually in receipt of an Earnings Related Supplement (ERS). In this paper we shall show that the replacement ratio used by Maki and Spindler (henceforth M–S) is a mis-specification and that the rise in unemployment can be explained by structural changes in the economy.

2

In this section we present some econometric results for unemployment in Great Britain using annual data, 1952–75.[1] We begin by taking the M-S

Reprinted from 'An Econometric Analysis of Unemployment in Great Britain, 1952–75' by P. N. Junankar in *Oxford Economic Papers*, 33 (3), November 1981, 387–400. With kind permission from Oxford University Press.

equation and test the specifications of the benefit-income *ratio* and we test the equation for structural stability. Their estimating equation is:

$$\ln U_t = \beta_0 + \beta_1 \ln R_t + \beta_2 \ln D_t + \beta_3 \ln D_{t-1} + \beta_4 S_t + e_t \qquad (1)$$

where U_t is the unemployment rate, R_t is the replacement ratio (benefit-income ratio), D_t and D_{t-1} are indexes of aggregate demand, S_t is a labour supply measure and e_t is an error term assumed to satisfy classical least squares properties. (This equation is identical to Spindler-Maki (1979) equation (1) except that we have taken logarithms of the replacement ratio.) The argument is that as the replacement ratio rises more people prefer to "buy" leisure and either to leave employment or remain unemployed for longer periods. M–S impose the implicit constraint that it is only the *ratio* of benefits to income that is relevant. We propose to test this constraint. The demand variables are to represent shifts in the labour demand curve due to changes in effective aggregate demand. They are measured as a ratio of actual GDP to trend GDP. The S_t variable is to allow for shifts in the labour supply curve due to demographic changes and changes in labour supply in *efficiency* units by using a productivity index.[2] Rewriting equation (1) by separating the benefit-income ratio we get:

$$\ln U_t = \beta_0 + \beta_1 \ln (B/P) + b_1 \ln (Y/P) + \beta_2 \ln D_t + \beta_3 \ln D_{t-1} + \beta_4 S_t + e_t \qquad (2)$$

(Note that $R = (B/P)/(Y/P)$ where B are benefits, Y is net income, and P is the price level.)

We now estimate equation (2) by Ordinary Least Squares and then by Restricted Least Squares to test the restriction that the parameter on Real Benefits and Real Income are equal and opposite in sign. As there is some evidence (see Bowers, Cheshire and Weedon (1970, 1972), Gujarati (1972), and Sawyer (1979)) to suggest that the labour market seems to have had structural changes occur in 1965–66, and some evidence to suggest a break in 1970 (see later) we estimated the equation for the different sub-samples and then carried out tests of structural stability (Chow tests).

We test the hypothesis:

H_{01}: $\beta_1 = -b_1$ (1952–65)
H_{02}: $\beta_1 = -b_1$ (1952–66)
H_{03}: $\beta_1 = -b_1$ (1952–70)
H_{04}: $\beta_1 = -b_1$ (1952–75)
H_{05}: $\beta(1952–65) = \beta(1952–75)$
H_{06}: $\beta(1952–66) = \beta(1952–75)$
H_{07}: $\beta(1952–70) = \beta(1952–75)$

Looking at the OLS results first (see Table 4.1.1) we note that LRBEN (the log of *real* benefits) is not significant for any of the sub-periods and is even negative for the period 1952–66), but is significant (and positive) for the whole period. We reject the hypotheses of equality (and opposite in sign) of coefficients for all the sub-periods (H_{01}, H_{02}, H_{03}) but cannot reject the hypothesis for the whole period (H_{04}). However, when we test for structural stability, we cannot reject H_{05}, H_{06} but we reject H_{07}: the parameter vector β is not stable over the period 1952–70 and 1952–75. Thus we must be cautious of the results for the entire period. It appears that the replacement ratio turns out to be significant because in some sense the income variable is "doing all the work". When we separate out the variable into its component parts the benefits variable "collapses".[3]

To carry out formal tests of "money illusion" we rewrite equation (2) as

$$\ln U_t = \beta_0 + \beta_1 \ln B + b_1 \ln Y + \gamma_1 \ln P + \beta_2 \ln D_t + \beta_3 \ln D_{t-1} + \beta_4 S_t + e_t \qquad (3)$$

We now test the hypotheses:

$$H_{01}\colon \beta_1 = -b_1$$

$$H_{02}\colon \gamma_1 = 0$$

$$H_{03}\colon \beta_1 = -b_1 \text{ and } \gamma_1 = 0$$

Table 4.1.2 presents results of these tests of hypotheses, without giving the detailed results.[4] What we find is that for all the sub-periods the *joint* hypothesis (H_{03}) is rejected. Moreover, it is not rejected for the entire period. But, tests of structural stability (Chow tests) reject stability of the β vector over the sub-periods. For each sample we find that the OLS estimate of the benefits variable is insignificant. Once again we are led to the conclusion that the benefits variable is not significant and that there is structural instability of the parameter vector. However, in all versions we find that aggregate demand is an important explanatory variable.

In an attempt to pin-point the instability of the M-S regression equation we carried out further tests of structural stability. Following Brown, Durbin and Evans (1975) (henceforth BDE) we analysed the residual sums of squares from recursive regressions and moving regressions. A computer program (TIMVAR) which carries out this analysis also provides a graphical output of the parameter estimates. Also provided is a plot of the "Cusum Squares" which should follow a diagonal from the bottom left hand corner to the top right hand corner under the null hypothesis of structural stability. We applied this method to the M–S regression with the replacement ratio as defined by them, and then separated into its real components. As the output from this computer program is voluminous we summarise the results and illustrate with a sample of them.

In both cases we find that the plot of the Cusum Squares diverges from the diagonal, especially around 1966–67. (See Figure 4.1.1 and 4.1.3.) Using

Table 4.1.1 Unemployment in Great Britain. 1952–75 (Dependent Variable is LURATE)

Eq.	*Estimation method*	*Sample*	*Constant*	($\ln B/P$) LRBEN	($\ln Y/P$) LRINC	($\ln D_t$) LCAPAC	($\ln D_{t-1}$) LAGCAP	(S_t) ILSET	$\bar{R}^2$	*F*	*DW*	*F value for restrictions*
(1)	OLS	52–65	–7.072	0.072	–3.040	–9.986	–6.073	0.0003	0.91	26.6	1.86	
			(–2.194)	(0.160)	(–2.954)	(–5.740)	(–4.254)	(2.846)				
(2)	ROLS	52–65	0.413	0.757	–0.757	–8.529	–6.582	0.00006				$F(1,8)$ =
			(0.643)	(1.794)	(–1.794)	(–4.277)	(–3.803)	(1.728)				5.54*
(3)	OLS	52–66	–8.588	–0.355	–3.040	–10.860	–6.030	0.0003	0.89	24.9	1.67	
			(–2.801)	(–1.199)	(–2.871)	(–6.644)	(–4.107)	(3.522)				
(4)	ROLS	52–66	–0.308	0.215	–0.215	–9.624	–6.632	0.0008				$F(1,9)$ =
			(–0.628)	(0.800)	(–0.800)	(–4.784)	(–3.567)	(2.673)				7.41*
(5)	OLS	52–70	–7.587	0.008	–3.172	–9.967	–6.669	0.0003	0.92	40.1	2.08	
			(–3.194)	(0.031)	(–3.875)	(–6.000)	(–4.327)	(4.197)				
(6)	ROLS	52–70	0.333	0.579	–0.579	–9.081	–6.975	0.00009				$F(1,13)$ =
			(0.068)	(2.453)	(–2.453)	(–4.273)	(–3.496)	(2.524)				10.55†
(7)	OLS	52–75	–2.188	0.639	–1.774	–8.196	–7.652	0.0001	0.94	56.7	1.70	
			(–0.913)	(2.725)	(–1.924)	(–6.169)	(–4.396)	(1.958)				
(8)	ROLS	52–75	0.411	0.786	–0.786	–8.404	–7.633	0.00006				$F(1,18)$ =
			(1.181)	(4.064)	(–4.064)	(–6.357)	(–4.363)	(2.874)				1.20

1. *The Restrictions are rejected at 5%.
2. †The Restrictions are rejected at 1%.
3. A Chow test rejects at the 5% level stability of the parameters for 1952–70 and 1952–75, but does not reject stability for either of the other sub-periods.
4. Parentheses contain *t*-values.

Table 4.1.2 Unemployment in Great Britain, 1952–75

Eq.	*Sample*	H_{01}	H_{02}	H_{03}
(1)	52–65	$F(1,7) = 1.56$	$F(1,7) = 2.21$	$F(2,7) = 9.26^*$
(2)	52–66	$F(1,8) = 2.01$	$F(1,8) = 2.19$	$F(2,8) = 13.94^\dagger$
(3)	52–70	$F(1,12) = 7.61^*$	$F(1,12) = 0.03$	$F(2,12) = 8.04^\dagger$
(4)	52–75	$F(1,17) = 2.99$	$F(1,17) = 0.82$	$F(2,17) = 2.43$

LURATE = $\beta_0 + \beta_1$ LBENERS + b_1 LINC + γ_1LPRICE + β_2LCAPAC + β_3LAGCAP + β_4ILSET
1. *Reject at 5%.
2. †Reject at 1%.
3. Chow Tests rejected structural stability for equations (1) and (4); (2) and (4); and (3) and (4).

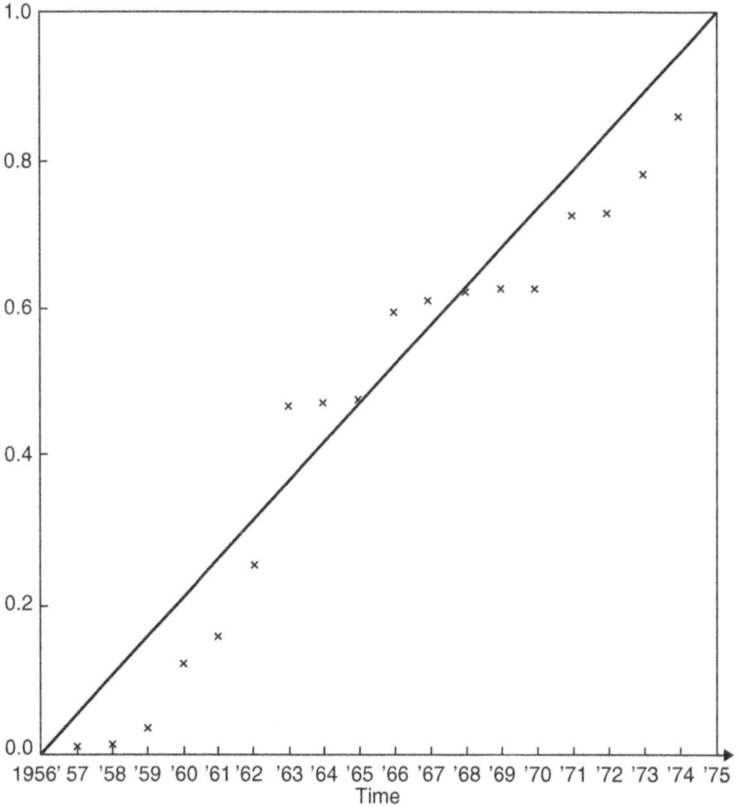

Figure 4.1.1 Forward recursive regression: Cusum squared residuals normalised (LURATE C BENCN LCAPAC LAGCAP ILSET)

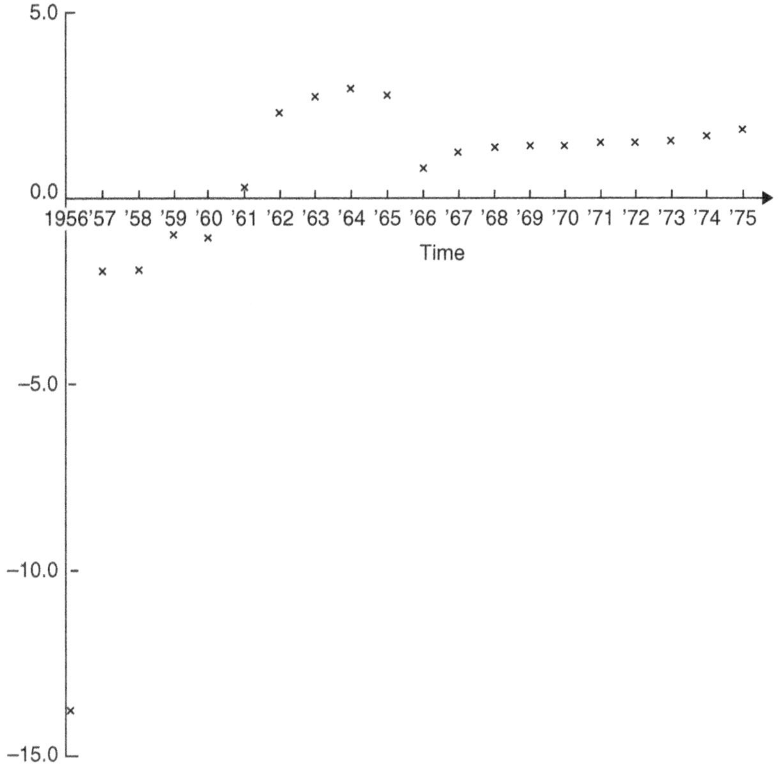

Figure 4.1.2 Forward recursive regression: Coefficient on BENCN

the Cusum Squares test on forward recursive regressions we cannot reject the null hypothesis of structural stability. However for backward recursive regressions we reject the null hypothesis of structural stability. What is especially interesting is to look at the parameter estimates on the benefit-income ratio (BENCN) (Figure 4.1.2) which starts as a negative quantity, then becomes positive, and appears to stabilise after 1966. When we look at the coefficient on the log of real benefits (LRBEN) (Figure 4.1.4) we see that it also changes sign and that it is very volatile. Thus this analysis confirms our earlier findings of instability of the M-S equation, especially the instability of the parameter on the benefits variable. Changing the functional form by taking logs of the benefit-income variable or the supply variable (ILSET) did not help to remove this instability. We therefore conclude this section by arguing that the relation between unemployment benefits and the unemployment rate is not supported by the data. Any policy prescriptions based

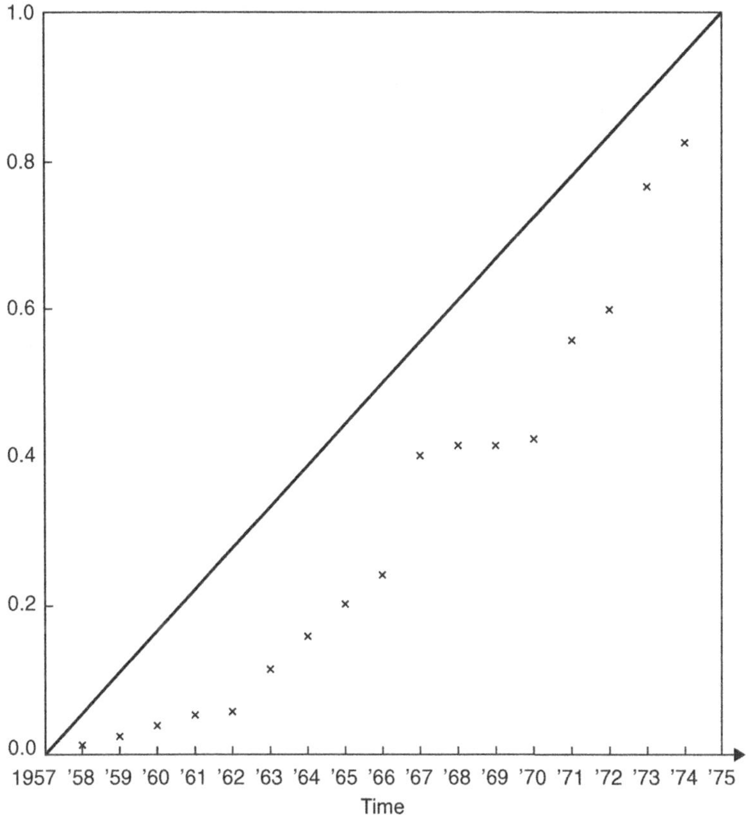

Figure 4.1.3 Forward recursive regression: Cusum squared residuals normalised (LURATE C LRINC LRBEN LCAPAC LAGCAP ILSET)

on such an unstable relation are purely fallacious. Even M–S agree that their parameter estimate on the replacement ratio is unbelievably large given the number of people receiving unemployment benefits (especially ERS).[5]

3

Up to this point we had used the M–S framework for explaining unemployment using data provided by them. We now postulate (unlike M–S) that the changing structure of the British economy has led to increasing unemployment. Three aspects need to be emphasised: firstly, there has been a decline in the industrial sector relative to the service sector; secondly, there has been technological change (and in recent years we have seen the beginnings of

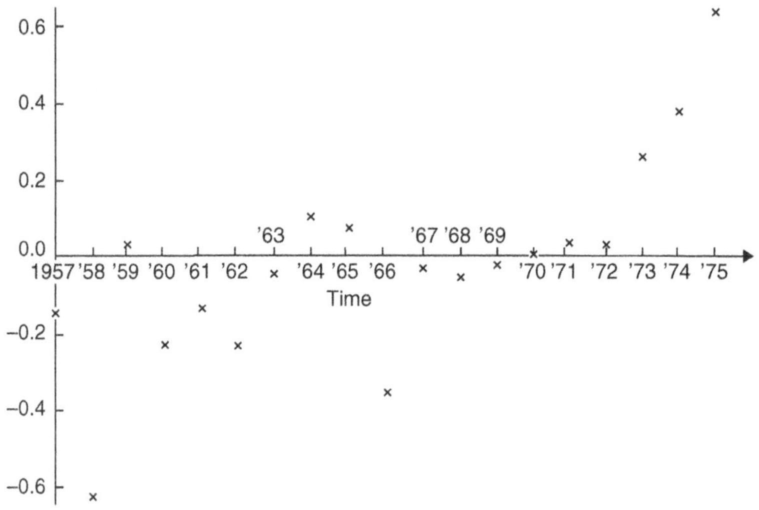

Figure 4.1.4 Forward recursive regression: coefficient on LRBEN

the 'micro-processor' revolution); and thirdly, there have been social and demographic change that have led to increasing female participation in the labour force.

Several economists have remarked on the large changes that have taken place in the British economy since mid-sixties. Bacon and Eltis (1976) in an influential book have highlighted the relative decline of the "market sector" and the falling share of the industrial sector. The theme has also been taken up in Blackaby (1979) which discusses the de-industrialisation of the British Economy. Thatcher (1979) has a careful analysis of that changing structure of the labour market where he stresses the increasing supply of females to the labour market and the decreasing demand for labour by the industrial sector.[6] Technological change combined with a relative decline in the industrial sector has led to a decrease in employment in that sector. Since most of them were males they would register as unemployed and hence increase unemployment. The increase in employment in the services sector has been mainly by employing *female* labour, especially part-time female labour. Because of an increase in the participation rate this increase in unemployment did not show up as a decrease in unemployment. Hence overall unemployment increased. To operationalise these ideas, we used as an explanatory variable the log of the ratio of industrial output to the output of the services sector (for an exact definition of this variable, LMIX, see Appendix 1). In addition we used as an index of technological change the log of output per employed person (LOPE) instead of the composite ILSET variable used by M-S. These results are presented in Table 4.1.3.

Table 4.1.3 Unemployment in Great Britain, 1952–75 (Dependent Variable is LURATE)

Eq.	*Sample*	*Constant*	LBENERS	LINC	LCAPAC	LAGCAP	LMLX	LOPE	$\bar{R}^2$	*DW*
(1)	1952–65	-58.267	-0.559	-0.753	-10.525	-2.484	-5.861	5.607	0.96	2.71
		(-5.703)	(-1.535)	(-0.919)	(-3.256)	(-1.643)	(-4.106)	(2.812)		
(2)	1952–70	-47.090	-0.276	-2.631	-14.952	-1.834	-3.055	7.932	0.95	1.68
		(-4.622)	(-1.260)	(-4.734)	(-6.297)	(-1.195)	(-2.383)	(5.561)		
(3)	1952–75	-48.919	-0.158	-1.807	-13.195	-1.890	-4.104	6.389	0.97	1.88
		(-5.682)	(-0.781)	(-8.149)	(-8.096)	(-1.321)	(-4.516)	(6.409)		

1. A Chow test Rejects (at 1%) the stability of the parameters over either period.
2. Parentheses contain *t*-values.

The results provide some support to our hypothesis. The aggregate demand variables (LCAPAC and LAGCAP) always have a correct sign and the current aggregate demand variable is always significant. This suggests that an increase in aggregate demand would lower unemployment. The composition of output variable (LMIX) is always negative and significant for all the periods. This supports our hypothesis that a decrease in the industrial sector output relative to the services sector has increased unemployment. The technological change variable (log of output per employed person, LOPE) is also always positive and significant. The nominal benefits variable has an incorrect sign but is always insignificant. The nominal income variable is negative and significant for 1952–70 and 1952–75. Thus these results support our hypothesis that aggregate demand, the *composition* of output, and technological change are important determinants of unemployment.[7]

4 Further complications

In the paper so far we have followed the Spindler-Maki approach fairly closely and even used their data for most of the econometric work. In this section we turn to look at some problems involved in using some of these variables. First, we turn to the unemployment variable.

The unemployment rate in Britain is a measure of those people who *register* as unemployed. Any changes that take place in the *proportion* of unemployed registering would lead to a changed relationship between unemployment and the explanatory variables. In Britain it is estimated that about 20% of the unemployed do not register: they are the hidden unemployed.[8] Another problem with using the unemployment rate is that it is a *stock* measure (or rather an average of a monthly stock figure divided by the stock of labour force): there are large flows in and out of the unemployment register *between* two unemployment counts. Besides this problem, what happens to the unemployment rate depends on what determines the inflows and outflows. It is possible for an explanatory variable to affect both the inflows and the outflows such that the net inflows are zero (and hence the unemployment stock may be unchanged). A proper analysis should therefore look at these flows. Some preliminary work done by the author supports our earlier findings that the replacement ratio does not affect these flows.

When we look at the replacement ratio more closely we find that the variable used in our econometric work may not be a good measure. The variable we used was the benefits which a married man with two children was *eligible* for. When we look at the data carefully, as Atkinson and Flemming (1978) emphasize, we find that over half of the unemployed did not receive *any* unemployment benefits. Of the men receiving unemployment benefits a large proportion had no dependents. The big increase in the replacement ratio in 1966 (which coincided with an increase in unemployment) was due to the introduction of the earnings related supplement. But a very small proportion were receiving this supplement. Thus the idea of using a replacement ratio for a 'typical' unemployed person is a vacuous one. (Atkinson and Flemming comment on the recent *fall* in the replacement ratio being associated with a *rise* in unemployment throwing doubt on a simple relation between benefits and unemployment.) Sawyer (1979) criticises M-S for the use of the benefits variable on similar grounds.

Nickell (1979) and Lancaster (1979) using cross-section data find a small but significant effect of the replacement ratio on the probability of leaving the unemployment stock, and hence on duration. These results are in contrast to our findings that for the sub-periods the real benefits are not significant and when we tested for money illusion nominal benefits were never significant (when price was included separately as a variable). Only for the period 1952–75 do we find real benefits as significant, but the equation is structurally unstable. One possible way of reconciling the conflict between cross-section and time series data is to argue that the higher unemployment benefits simply select who is unemployed, without affecting the total.[9] The Nickell and Lancaster papers assume workers searching in a labour market with imperfect information but facing a *given* wage distribution *which is unaffected by the changes in the benefits and consequent changes in the behaviour of suppliers of labour.* To illustrate with an example: assume there are 100 vacancies and 1000 heterogeneous "searchers". As benefits are increased let all the searchers increase their "desire for leisure". As employers find that they cannot fill the 100 vacancies they may do one of two things—(a) raise wages, or, more likely (b) lower their "standards". Ignoring (a), 100 searchers will be taken on: those that were least affected by the increase in benefits. Hence an increase in benefits has left unemployment unaffected: it has simply *selected* a different group who get employed. Nickell (1979) seems to be worried about the aggregation problem, "our estimates ... arise from averaging over two types of individuals ... If this is so, when benefits are increased, the latter will tend to postpone job acceptance and the extra vacancies made available may be taken up by those who remain unaffected, thereby *shortening* their expected durations and reducing the impact of the change on aggregate unemployment." (p. 46) However, he does not allow the employers to change their behaviour. Cross-section results cannot be generalised to a time series context without making some explicit supplementary hypotheses.

We have argued that we need to specify a model of the labour market which looks at the flows in and out of unemployment. Unfortunately, some data are available only from 1967 but they do not distinguish whether the inflows are from the labour force or from outside the labour force. Similarly, they do not distinguish the outflows into categories who have joined the employed labour force and those who have left the labour force. An interesting paper for the U.S. by Clark and Summers (1979) discusses the large movements from outside the labour force into employment/unemployment, and from employment to out of the labour force. These movements do not get picked up by simply looking at the unemployed stock. There is a need for a better data base for labour market flows in Britain.

Conclusions

Our econometric work suggests that the increase in unemployment benefits did not cause the increase in unemployment in Britain since the mid-sixties. Specifically, we find the parameter estimates on the replacement ratio, or on benefits is either insignificant or very unstable. Hence we cannot derive any policy conclusions about whether to raise or lower benefits. More importantly, unemployment *is* a problem: the unemployed are not voluntarily searching for a (non-existent!) better job. We should try to reduce the unusually high levels of unemployment by appropriate fiscal and monetary policies. Our results suggest that the level and composition of aggregate demand is an important explanation of increasing unemployment.

Unlike many other areas, we can clearly say more work needs to be done in this area, especially in modelling and estimating labour market flows.

Notes

I should like to thank Ms. Rachel Britton and Mr. V. Rapanos for computing assistance. Professor Gordon Fisher gave much of his time discussing some of the econometric problems discussed in the paper, and also brought to my notice the Brown, Durbin and Evans (1975) paper, for which I am very grateful. The paper was completed at Queen's University while on leave from the University of Essex. Earlier versions of this paper were presented at McMaster University, University of British Columbia, and Simon Fraser University and the comments received have helped to improve this paper. None of the above is responsible for remaining errors or the prejudices expressed.

1. The data were kindly provided by Professor Z. A. Spindler. The appendix describes the data and definitions of variables used.
2. See M–S (1975, 1979) for details.

3. Similar results were obtained when we used *nominal* benefits and *nominal* income. Sawyer (1979) also finds the M-S equation unstable, see p. 141.
4. These are available on request from the author.
5. "We confess that we do not have any concrete suggestions on how to reliably estimate the size of that replacement ratio effect". Spindler and Maki (1979) p. 19. They are convinced however, that the replacement ratio "does matter". See Sawyer (1979) and Nickell (1979) for criticisms of M–S's estimates.
6. See the DE report (1976) prepared by a Committee under the Chairmanship of Mr. A. R. Thatcher.
7. Note however that a Chow test still rejects structural stability. Also note that the Durbin-Watson statistics are higher than for the M–S specification, although they are still in the indeterminate range for equations 2 and 3.
8. See DE Gazette (Dec. 1976) and Atkinson and Hemming (1978).
9. See Thatcher (1979) p. 37.

References

ATKINSON, A. B. and FLEMMING, J. S. "Unemployment, Social Security, and Incentives", *Midland Bank Review,* Autumn, 1978.

BACON, R. and Eltis, W. *Britain's Economic Problem,* London: Macmillan, 1976.

BARRO, R. and GROSSMAN, H. "A General Disequilibrium Model of Income and Employment", *American Economic Review,* March 1971.

BOWERS, J. K., CHESHIRE, P. C. and WEBB, A. E. "The Change in the Relationship Between Unemployment and Earnings Increases", *National Institute Economic Review,* No. 54, November 1970.

BOWERS, J. K. *et al.,* "Some Aspects of Unemployment and the Labour Market, 1966–71", *National Institute Economic Review,* No. 62, November 1972.

BROWN, R. L., DURBIN J. and EVANS, J. M. "Techniques for Testing the Constancy of Regression Relationships over Time", *Journal of the Royal Statistical Society* (Series B), 1975.

CLARK, K. B. and SUMMERS, L. H. "Labour Force Transitions and Unemployment", *Brookings Papers on Economic Activity* 1979. No. 1.

CUBBIN, J. S. and FOLEY, K. "The Extent of Benefit Induced Unemployment in Great Britain: Some New Evidence", *Oxford Economic Papers,* March 1977.

Department of Employment, "Working Party on the Change Relationship Between Unemployment and Vacancies: Final Report of the Working Party", Mimeo, 1976.

_____, "Unemployment and Notified Vacancies—Flow Statistics, D.E. *Gazette,* September 1976.

_____, "The Unregistered Unemployed in Great Britain", D.E. *Gazette,* December 1976.

_____, "Statistics on Long-term Unemployed", D.E. *Gazette,* June 1978.

FIELD, F. (Ed.), *The Conscript* Army: A Study *of Britain's Unemployed,* London: Routledge & Kegan Paul, 1977.

GUJARATI, D., "The Behaviour of Unemployment and Unfilled Vacancies: Great Britain, 1958–71", *Economic Journal,* Vol. 82, March 1972.

HOROWITZ, S. A., "A Model of Unemployment Insurance and the Work Test", *Industrial and Labor Relations Review,* Vol. 30, No. 4, July 1977.

LANCASTER, T., "Econometric Methods for the Duration of Unemployment", *Econometrica,* Vol. 47, No. 4, July 1979.

MAKI, D. and SPINDLER, Z. A., "The Effect of Unemployment Compensation on the Rate of Unemployment in Great Britain", *Oxford Economic Papers,* Vol. 27, No. 3, 1975.

Marsden, D. and Duff, E., *Workless*, Harmondsworth: Penguin, 1975.
Mortensen, D., "Unemployment Insurance and Job Search Decisions", *Industrial and Labor Relations Review*, Vol. 30, No. 4, July 1977.
Nickell, S., "The Effect of Unemployment and Related Benefits on the Duration of Unemployment", *Economic Journal*, March 1979.
Sawyer, M., "Effects of Unemployment Compensation on the Rate of Unemployment in Great Britain: A Comment" *Oxford Economic Papers*, 1979.
Solow, R. M., "What to do (Macroeconomically) when OPEC comes", Mimeo 1978? undated.
Spindler, Z. A. and Maki, D., "More on the Effects of Unemployment Compensation on the Rate of Unemployment in Great Britain", *Oxford Economic Papers*, 1979.

Appendix

For purposes of comparability, most of the data used are taken from Spindler-Maki (1979). We reproduce below their description of data sources:

Data Sources:

U Rate: Calculated as *average of quarterly unemployment* counts for calendar year as per cent of civilian labour force similarly averaged. Data for 1952–1968 from Department of Employment and Productivity, *British Labour Statistics, Historical Abstract: 1886–1968*. p. 223; 1969–1972 from *Labour Statistics Yearbook*, 1973, p. 120; 1973–1975 from Department of Employment, *Gazette*, Dec. 1976, p. 1372. All figures refer to Total male and females, Great Britain. Prior to June 1971 figures estimated on national insurance card count basis, subsequently on census of employment basis.

GDP Index: Gross Domestic Product at constant factor cost, from Central Statistical Office, *Annual Abstract of Statistics*, various issues. Part of the original series was reported on a 1948 base, part on a 1958 base, part on a 1963 base, and 1965–1975 on a 1970 base. We converted everything to a 1970 base using the average adjustment factor derived from the 4 or 5 year overlaps available.

Ben/Inc: Standard rate of sickness or unemployment benefit plus ERS divided by net income after deducting tax and NI contributions, for a married couple with two children, from Department of Health and Social Security, *Social Security Statistics*, various issues. *Data refer to Oct. 1 of each year, and were converted to annual basis by making* $(\text{Ben/Inc})_t = 0.25(\text{Ben/Inc})_{\text{Oct 1},t} + 0.75(\text{Ben/Inc})_{\text{Oct 1},t-1}$.

O/PE: Index of output per head—all production industries. Data for 1952–1968 from Department of Employment and Productivity, *British Labour Statistics, Historical Abstract, 1886–1968;* for 1962–1970 from Central Statistical Office, *Monthly Digest of Statistics*, June 1971, p. 46; and for 1969–1976 from *Monthly Digest of Statistics*, June 1977, p. 55. Data for 1969–1975 available to 1970 base, for 1952–1970 to 1963 base. We converted 1971–1975 to a 1963 base using the average adjustment factor derived from the 1969–70 overlap.

LFI: Constructed by converting civilian labour force as discussed above under *U Rate* to an index number, 1963 = 100.

In addition to the above data we used

Price:	An index of the General Index of Retail Prices (All Items), 1970 = 100. Source *Economic Trends: Annual Supplement*, 1977. (C.S.O.) (page 96).
Industrial production:	Index of Industrial Production, 1970=100. Source: as above (page 70).
Trades:	Index of Distributive Trades, 1970=100. Source: as above (page 70).
Services:	Index of Other Services, 1970=100. Source: as above (page 70).

List of variables used

1. LURATE = Log (U Rate)
2. BENCN = Ben/Inc (see above)
3. LBENCN = Log (BENCN)
4. BRSY = $(\text{Benefits})_t/(\text{Net Income})_t$
5. LBRSY = Log (BRSY)
6. LBENERS = Log $(\text{Benefits})_t$
7. LINC = Log (Net Income)
8. LRBEN = Log $(\text{Benefits/Price})_t$
9. LRINC = Log (Net Income/Price)
10. LCAPAC = Log (GDP/Trend GDP) (The Trend GDP was estimated by fitting Log GDP = $\alpha + \beta$ TIME.)
11. LAGCAP = $(\text{LCAPAC})_{t-1}$
12. ILSET = (0/PE)(LFI)
13. LOPE = Log (O/PE)
14. LMIX = Log {(Industrial Production)/(104 · TRADES+ 343 · SERVICES)} where 104 and 343 are the weights in the GDP.
15. LPRICE = Log (PRICE)

4.2

The Dynamics of Unemployment: Structural Change and Unemployment Flows

P.N. Junankar and Simon Price

In this paper we attempt to explain the inflows onto and the outflows from the unemployment stock. In spite of great interest in explaining unemployment, very little work has been done using time series data on flows.[1] *It is useful to think of the labour market as being in a perpetual state of flux with people moving from job to job, from jobs to unemployment and from unemployment to jobs. An analysis of flows allows us to study the dynamics of the labour market and provides us with useful insights which may be clouded by studying unemployment stocks. Our model explaining the flows is based on cost-minimising firms and individuals searching for jobs.*[2] *We postulate an economy consisting of two types of firms: expanding firms that hire and declining firms that fire. Changes in aggregate demand, tastes and technology lead to changes in the distribution of firms and hence to the flows. Section I considers the empirical specification and discusses the results for Great Britain for the period 1967 (III) to 1980(II). To anticipate our results we find that inadequate aggregate demand is a crucial determinant of the growth of unemployment in Britain.*

I Empirical specification and results

Inflows and Outflows at date t can be decomposed into:

$$I_t \equiv \text{Inflows} = \text{Fires} + \text{Quits} + \text{New and Re-entrants}$$

$$O_t \equiv \text{Outflows} = \text{Hires} + \text{Discouraged workers} + \text{Retirements.}$$

The stock of unemployment U_t is given by

$$U_t = U_{t-1} + (I_t - O_t) \tag{1}$$

Reprinted from 'The Dynamics of Unemployment: Structural Change and Unemployment Flows' by P. N. Junankar and Simon Price in *Economic Journal*, 94, March 1984, 158–165 and updated to reflect the change reported in the erratum from *Economic Journal* 94 (376), 1060. With kind permission from The Royal Economic Society.

where unemployment is defined at the *end* of the period and I_t and O_t are the flows *during* that period. As data on separate components of the flows are unavailable, we had to estimate equations for aggregate flows. We estimated our model using quarterly (seasonally unadjusted) data for Great Britain from 1967(III) to 1980(II). The methods of estimation used were Instrumental Variables (IV) and Seemingly Unrelated Regressions Estimation (SURE). We report our empirical work under two heads: (*a*) Methodology and (*b*) Results.

(a) Methodology

We used as our dependent variables the logarithms of total inflows and total outflows.[3] Nickell (1982) normalised his flow variables by the relevant current stocks, although we would argue the relevant normalisation is by the stock at the beginning of each period (U_{t-1}). In the absence of a steady state, normalisation may provide biased estimates of true exit or entry probabilities. It also excludes the possibility of the level of unemployment itself affecting the probability of exit. We therefore estimated equations of the general form

$$\ln I_t = \alpha_1 \ln E_{t-1} + \sum_2^n \alpha_i \ln X_{it} + \varepsilon_{1t} \tag{2}$$

and

$$\ln O_t = \beta_1 \ln U_{t-1} + \sum_2^m \beta_i \ln Z_{it} + \varepsilon_{2t} \tag{3}$$

where X_i and Z_i are explanatory variables and E_t is the stock of employed workers. We tested the hypothesis that $a_1 = \beta_1 = 1$, i.e. tested Nickell's specification. This has an additional econometric advantage as ln (O_t/U_{t-1}) is strongly trended while In O_t is more nearly a stationary series. We followed a common methodology in beginning with fairly general specifications and testing zero restrictions and other restrictions to see whether the variables should be entered in log-differences or as proportions.[4]

In terms of our model we have broadly six categories of independent variables:

(*i*) *Structural Change Variables:* We proxied structural change in the economy by the ratio of industrial to service employment. An increase in this may increase both inflows and outflows as the industrial sector is relatively more vulnerable to cyclical variations than the services sector, which includes government. As proportionally more, men are employed in industry, this will also increase *registered* flows. Bankruptcies were also used as an index of structural change which leads to increased inflows.

(*ii*) *Aggregate Demand Variables:* We assumed that aggregate demand for output could be proxied by a capacity utilisation measure (deviations from a log-linear trend of GDP) while the level of vacancies is the appropriate supply side demand variable. There are inherent ambiguities in the theory as to what signs to expect from these variables: while fires will fall, quits may rise in response to increases in demand. We expect outflows to increase (although there is ambiguity here too, as the unemployed may search longer if the perceived probability of finding a job increases).

(*iii*) *Price Variables*: To distinguish demand and supply effects we used the real wage cost per unit of output to capture the behaviour of firms and real benefits (including earnings related supplements, ERS) and real earnings introduced as separate variables to pick up supply responses. We expect increases in wage costs to reduce outflows and increase inflows, while benefits are expected to encourage inflows and reduce outflows.

(*iv*) *Demographic and Compositional Variables:* We were unable to find a significant relationship for the proportion of youth or older workers in the labour force. We expected an increase in the proportion of the unemployed who have experienced long durations to reduce outflows, as workers lower reservation wages or as employers take long duration as a signal of undesirable characteristics. An important compositional effect on outflows is via the level of past and current inflows. Increase in inflows increase the proportion of the unemployed who have high exit probabilities, while, on the demand side, firms will be hiring to replace workers.

(*v*) *Dynamic Adjustment Variables:* We used lagged dependent variables as well as the level of inventories (stocks) and average hours. Given constant long run equilibrium values for the two latter variables, we expect inventories (hours) to fall (rise) initially in response to an increase in demand but, for the long run effect to be zero. Thus outflows should be negatively (positively) related to changes in inventories (hours) and the reverse to hold for inflows.

(*vi*) *Dummy Variables:* As we used seasonally unadjusted data, we included seasonal dummies. In addition we included dummies for extraordinary events like the three-day week, the crisis leading up to the 1976 IMF loan and for observations that had to be interpolated due to civil service industrial disputes in 1974 and 1976. Finally, to allow for the effects of employment legislation, we introduced a variable measuring the number of unfair dismissals cases heard which is zero up to 1972(II).[5]

(*b*) *Results*

In estimating the inflows and outflows equations we assumed that the errors satisfied the usual properties. Although we present results estimated by instrumental variable techniques, we also allowed for covariance of errors across equations and then used Zellner's SURE method. The SURE results were very similar and are not reported. On the whole, the parameter signs are not inconsistent with our model and the parameter magnitudes are 'reasonable'. Having selected out final equation, we tested for structural stability by bisecting the sample at 1973(IV) and doing a Chow test. We also used a post-sample parameter stability test[6] with three observations after our sample period.

In Table 4.2.1 we present our IV estimates of the inflows equation.[7] Overall the equation is well determined with no evidence of serial correlation but some evidence of structural instability. Our structural change variables are very significant: changes in the relative importance of sectors lead to increased inflows. Similarly, bankruptcies (which pick up a discontinuity in declining firms) come out very significantly even with aggregate demand included in the equation. Our aggregate demand measure (capacity utilisation) comes out significantly: the greater the capacity utilisation, the lower the inflows. The real wage costs variable comes out very strongly with the expected sign. The higher the wage costs, the lower the employment and hence the greater the fires (inflows). Although our model suggests that this variable should be in differences, the data reject this and we find the level is the appropriate specification. We may be estimating the effect of a deviation from a constant equilibrium value of wage costs. There is some evidence for the benefit-earnings ('replacement') ratio influencing quits and increasing

Table 4.2.1 Instrumental Variables Estimates of the Inflows Equation Dependent Variable: $\ln(\text{inflows})_t$

Variable	**Coefficient**	**Absolute t-statistic**
$\ln(\text{inflows})_{t-1}$	0.401	5.94
ln (deviation from trend GDP)$_t$	–0.067	2.25
ln (real wages and salaries per unit of output)$_{t-3}$	1.296	8.63
Δ_1 ln (employment in production/ employment in services)$_{t-3}$	1.572	2.43
ln (bankruptcies)$_t$	0.180	4.05
Δ_1 ln (hours)$_t$*	–0.729	1.70
ln (real benefits)$_{t-1}$ – ln (real earnings)$_{t-2}$	0.315	2.76
Δ_1 ln (stocks/GDP)$_{t-1}$	1.034	4.58
Δ_1 ln (stocks/GDP)$_{t-2}$	0.690	5.26
no. of unfair dismissal cases$_t$	–0.069	2.40
Constant	3.663	8.32
seasonal: Q2	–0.126	4.38
interpolated observation dummy (1974(IV))	0.135	3.70
interpolated observation dummy (1976(IV))	0.117	2.94

* indicates variable was instrumented
$\bar{R}^2 = 0.92$
Q(8) = 7.265 (Box-Pierce)
Z(4) = 3.094 (Lagrange Multiplier)
Structural change 1973(IV)/1974(I): F(14, 24) = 2.13
P(3) = 17.587 (Parameter Stability).

inflows[8]. We entered benefits and earnings separately and ended up with a ratio with earnings lagged behind benefits. The dynamic adjustment variables (inventories and hours) also affect inflows significantly. Government legislation regarding unfair dismissals has apparently decreased the number of fires by firms. Overall, our equation performs well and unlike Nickell (1982) we do not have to introduce (inexplicable) time trends. Although the results are not reported here, if lagged employment is added to the equation, its coefficient is not significantly different from zero, although it is so badly determined it is also not significantly different from unity. Using the normalised dependent variable yields very similar results.

Let us now turn to our estimates of the outflows equation in Table 4.2.2. Overall these results support our model although they are not as good as the inflows equation. An important feature of this equation is that because of

Table 4.2.2 Instrumental Variables Estimates of the Outflows Equation Dependent variable: ln(outflows)$_t$

Variable	Coefficient	Absolute t-statistic
ln (inflows)$_t$*	0.374	5.54
ln (inflows)$_{t-2}$	0.113	1.76
ln (outflows)$_{t-1}$	0.281	3.86
ln (unemployment stock)$_{t-1}$	0.033	1.87
Δ_1 ln (real wages and salaries per unit of output)$_t$*	–0.571	1.99
Δ_1 ln (real wages and salaries per unit of output)$_{t-1}$	–0.444	1.85
ln (deviations from trend GDP)$_{t-3}$	0.092	3.66
Δ_1 ln (employment in production/ employment in services)$_t$	1.856	3.67
Δ_1 ln (vacancies)$_{t-1}$	0.149	2.90
ln (proportion of unemployed with duration $\geqslant$ six months)$_{t-1}$	–0.227	4.65
Δ_1 ln (real weighted benefits)$_{t-1}$	0.703	5.92
ln (real weighted benefits)$_{t-3}$	0.456	5.16
Three day week dummy	–0.120	3.61
1975 crisis dummy	–0.183	6.04
Interpolated observation dummy (1976 (IV))	0.093	2.72
Constant	2.914	6.14
seasonal: Q1	0.090	5.66
seasonal: Q2	0.127	9.17
seasonal: Q3	0.040	2.54

* indicates variable was instrumented
$\bar{R}^2 = 0.95$
Q(8) = 6.460 (Box Pierce)
Z(4) = 7.082 (Lagrange Multiplier)
Structural change 1973(IV)/1974(I): F(19,14) = 1.29
P(3) = 0·686 (Parameter Stability)

compositional effects, an increase in *inflows* increases outflows. Our results suggest that a 10% increase in inflows leads to a 3.7% increase in outflows *in the same quarter.* The structural change variable comes out very significantly as does the aggregate demand (capacity utilisation) variable. An increase in vacancies increases the probability of a job offer and increases outflows. The wage cost variables are significant at the 10% level and suggest that increases in wage costs decrease outflows (again a labour demand relation). Real benefits and earnings were entered separately but inclusion of the earnings variable was rejected by the data. The benefits variable is a weighted average of flat rate real benefits and real benefits plus ERS where the weights represent the proportion in the unemployment stock receiving each type of benefit. Surprisingly, the coefficients turn out positive and very significant, which may be explained by the Mortensen (1977) 'entitlement' effect. It may also be due to aggregate demand increasing via increased benefits. Except for lagged outflows, the dynamic adjustment variables are insignificant, implying that there may be a large asymmetry in the adjustment process. None of the demographic variables was significant although the duration variable is significant. There was no evidence for a structural break at 1973(IV). The very small coefficient on the lagged unemployment term throws doubt upon a probabilistic interpretation: a regression using the normalised dependent variable yields a coefficient on the lagged unemployment term of –0.71 (S.E. = 0.08). In other words, we reject the hypothesis that outflows should be normalised by the lagged unemployment stock.

We began this paper by arguing that a proper analysis of unemployment requires a study of the determinants of inflows and outflows. To study how successful we have been we used our estimated inflow and outflow equations to forecast unemployment stocks using equation (1). The dynamic predictions track the data very well in a period of sharply increasing unemployment (see Figure 4.2.1). We feel satisfied that a study of flows provides us with a good understanding of the behaviour of the unemployment stock. This procedure enables us to assess the causes of the recent dramatic rise in unemployment. Between 1979(I) and 1981(I) (three quarters outside our sample) our measure of unemployment rose from 1,269,000 to 2,285,000 while the predicted rise was to 2,176,000. Using simulation methods Table 4.2.3 reveals that demand deficiency was the most important determinant of unemployment in that period, although the steep rise in labour costs per unit of output after 1979 also played an important part.[9]

II Conclusions

In this paper we have argued that a study of the determinants of inflows and outflows provides us with a better understanding of the growth of unemployment in Britain. Our model of inflows and outflows is based on cost minimising firms and search behaviour by individuals where there are

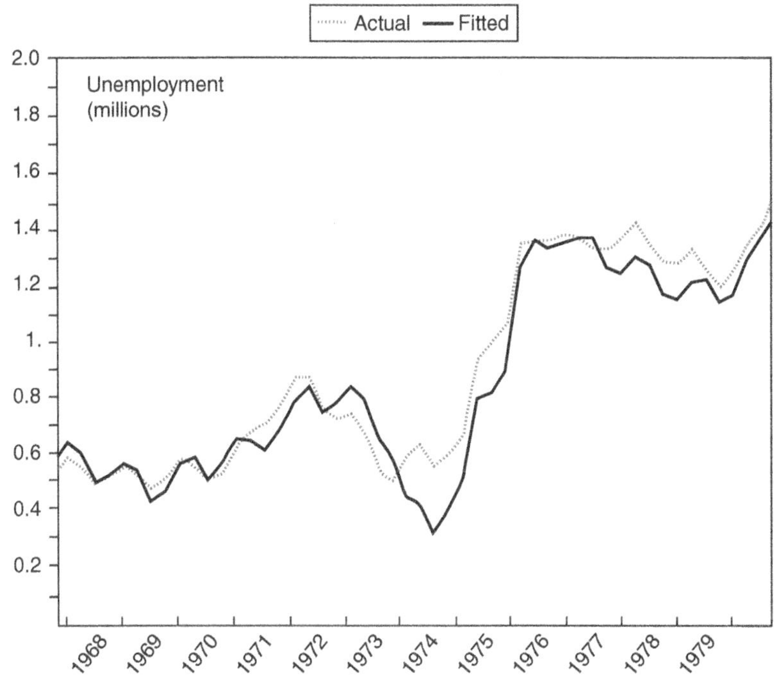

Figure 4.2.1 Actual and fitted unemployment stocks, 1967 (III) to 1980 (II)

Table 4.2.3 Estimated Contributions to the Rise in Unemployment 1979(I) to 1981(I)

All factors	Demand Deficiency	Structural Change	Benefits	Labour Costs	Unfair dismissal Legislation
855	573	61	–71	274	37

Thousands.

two sets of firms: one that is hiring and another that is firing workers. We argued that the distribution of firms across these two sets varies with structural change and aggregate demand. We estimated our inflow and outflow equations for Great Britain using quarterly data from 1967(III) to 1980(II) and find that our estimated equations perform quite well in terms of usual statistical criteria. Our main finding is that the growth of unemployment has been caused by a lack of aggregate demand. We found that changes in the composition of the unemployment stock affected the dynamics of the outflows. We used these estimated inflow and outflow equations to forecast unemployment stocks. Our within sample predictions of unemployment tracked the actual unemployment series fairly well.

Notes

We are grateful to the SSRC for financial support for our project under Grant HR 7274/1. We would like to thank our colleagues on the project, Mono Chatterji and Tim Hatton for helpful advice and comments. We are grateful to participants at the AUTE/RES Conference who commented on our paper and to an anonymous referee for helpful comments. A more detailed version of this paper is available on request from the authors. We would also like to thank Sheila Ogden for her tireless and accurate typing. We, of course, are guilty of any sins of omission and/or commission.

1. With the notable exception of Nickell (1982). However, our approach differs from the equilibrium approach employed by Nickell.
2. Here we merely restate existing theory with a few minor amendments. This theory provides a guide to the econometric model. See Mortensen(1970), Nickell (1982), Wickens(1978) and Nadiri and Rosen (1973).
3. We used the total flows, male and female. Nickell (1982) used only male flows. Our data excludes 'self-service' flows unlike Nickell.
4. With a fairly limited number of observations and several independent variables, we had to follow a pragmatic procedure: we could not allow large lags on each variable at the same time.
5. See Nickell (1982).
6. See Davidson *et al.* (1978)
7. Instruments were generated by regressing the relevant variables on a common set of exogenous and pre-determined variables.
8. The benefits include the earnings related supplement and refer to a 'typical' married man with two children. Nickell (1982) does not find a significant coefficient on the replacement ratio in the inflows equation.
9. Our estimates of 'equilibrium unemployment' were implausible perhaps due to a poor estimate of β_1 due to collinearity.

References

Davidson, J. E. H., Hendry, D. F., Srba, F. and Yeo, S. (1978), 'Econometric modelling of the aggregate time-series relationship between consumers' expenditure and income in the United Kingdom', ECONOMIC JOURNAL, vol. 88, pp. 661–92.

Mortensen, D. T. (1970), 'A theory of wage and employment dynamics' in E. Phelps (ed.) *Micro-economic Foundations of Employment and Inflation Theory,* New York: Norton.

_____(1977), 'Unemployment insurance and job search decisions', *Industrial and Labor Relations Review,* vol. 30, pp. 505–17.

Nadiri, M. I. and Rosen, S. (1973), 'A disequilibrium model of demand for factors of production', *N.B.E.R.,* New York: Columbia University Press.

Nickell, S. (1982), 'The determinants of equilibrium unemployment in Britain', ECONOMIC JOURNAL, vol. 22, pp. 555–75.

Wickens, M. R. (1978), 'An econometric model of labour turnover in U.K. manufacturing industries 1956–73', *Review of Economic Studies,* vol. 45, pp. 469–77.

4.3

Perspectives on Australian Unemployment: The Impact of Wage Setting Institutions in the 1980s

Bruce J. Chapman, Steve Dowrick and P.N. Junankar

1 Introduction

The 1980s stand out in Australian post-World War II economic history as the decade of high unemployment. Unemployment rates have risen over the last forty years, averaging less than 2 per cent in the 1950s and 1960s, 3.7 per cent in the 1970s and 7.3 per cent over the 1980s. The consistent ratchetting up of unemployment rates since the early 1970s has only been reversed to any substantial extent in the period since 1983 (see Figure 4.3.1).[1] The causes and implications of this recent experience constitute the subject of this paper.

Less than full utilisation of the available labour force implies output loss, both in the short-run, when producing inside the production possibility frontier, and in the long run due to losses of human capital through skill atrophy and negative impacts on the rate of accumulation of physical capital[2]. Moreover, unemployment is usually associated with movements to less equal income distributions and opportunities. These costs are probably particularly acute when individuals experience prolonged spells of involuntary joblessness. Unemployment in general and long term unemployment in particular are issues of fundamental policy relevance.

The causes, nature and consequences of unemployment constitute a vast topic. We have chosen to focus on some of the issues raised by recent international comparisons of wage and employment outcomes across a range of OECD economies. These studies have led several authors to conclude that centralisation of wage setting decisions can lead to lower sustainable levels of unemployment, or at least a quicker move back to low unemployment

Reprinted from 'Perspectives on Australian Unemployment: The Impact of Wage setting Institutions in the 1980s' by Bruce J. Chapman, Steve Dowrick, and P. N. Junankar in *Australian Economic Policy: Conference Proceedings* edited by F. H. Gruen, Centre for Economic Policy Research, Australian National University, Canberra, 1991, pp. 21–57.

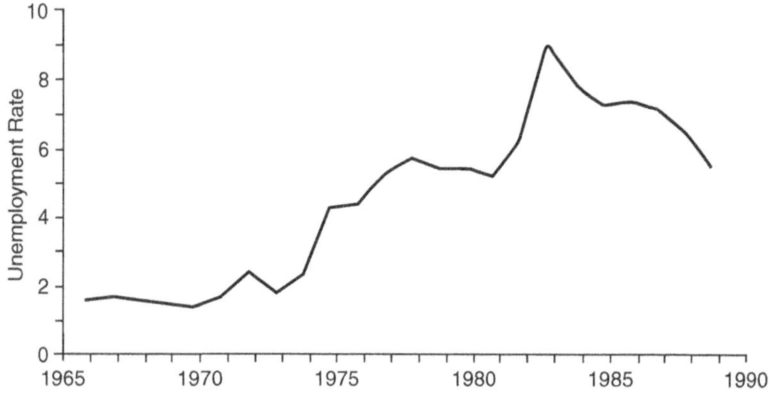

Figure 4.3.1 The Aggregate Australian Unemployment Rate, 1966–89
Note: All data for this and subsequent Figures and Tables refer to August of each year and come from ABS 6203.0 (unless otherwise specified).

after adverse shocks. The possible implication of this for Australian policy is clear given that the Federal government, with the Australian Council of Trade Unions (ACTU), instituted the prices and incomes Accord in May 1983. The Accord can be interpreted reasonably as an attempt to move wage-setting practices towards so-called 'corporatism'. We seek to explore the consequences, if any, this has had for aggregate short-run labour market outcomes.

The important questions addressed in this paper may be summarised by the possible causal chain illustration of Figure 4.3.2. Our line of inquiry is to examine whether the initiation of the Accord changed wage setting attitudes and arrangements, leading to lower wage settlements and increased employment. This in turn may have induced changes in both labour supply and (measured) unemployment with concomitant implications for long term unemployment. Understanding the theoretical bases of and empirical evidence for each of these links constitutes the major challenge of our analysis.

To set the scene Section 2 offers descriptive material on some important aspects of the Australian record of wage and labour force behaviour over the last twenty five years or so. Section 3 examines theory and evidence on the hypothesised link between wage setting institutions and wage outcomes. In Section 4 we discuss ways in which institutionally-induced variations in wage outcomes may feed through to employment, and report estimates of the magnitude of these effects in the Australian economy. Section 5 investigates the links between wage-employment outcomes and the growth of the labour force, from which we can deduce the consequences for unemployment. We proceed in Section 6 to examine the relationship between levels of (and changes in) the unemployment stock and its composition in terms of duration.

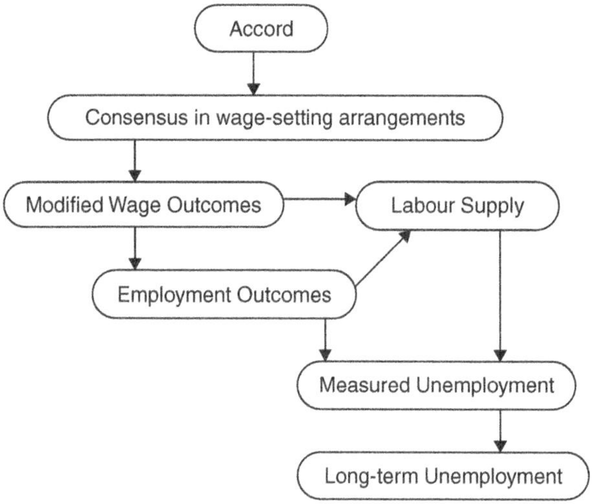

Figure 4.3.2 The Accord and unemployment

The broad conclusion of our analysis is that centralisation of wage setting has contributed significantly to reductions in both short term and long term unemployment. In the concluding section we summarise these findings and discuss some qualifications and implications.

2 The Australian Labour Market 1966–89

A brier illustrated discussion or some of the salient features or the Australian labour market over the past quarter century or so is set out below. The ensuing discussion combines full- and part-time jobs, although it is clear that there are significant issues in this area (Gregory, 1989). In aggregate, for both sexes total employment growth was strong up to about 1974/75, and similarly has been robust since 1983. The important periods of job growth stagnation were in 1975/76 and 1982/83, a point highlighted in Figure 4.3.3 which allows important insights into the relationships between the labour force, employment and unemployment.

The data of Figure 4.3.3 show the relationship between the measured labour force and employment, the vertical distance between them representing the number of (measured) unemployed. Several points emerge from the figure. One is that the labour force follows a clear and consistent upward trend[3], but with observable decreases during and after periods of job growth stagnation. This latter characteristic of labour force change is explained by participation rate responses to unemployment, and is evidence for the widely-held view that hidden unemployment increases in recessions.

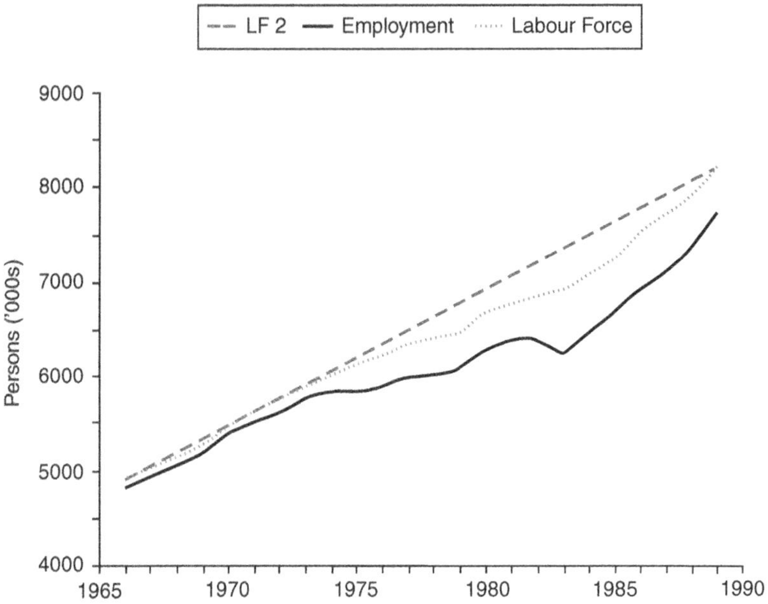

Figure 4.3.3 Australian Labour Force and Employment, 1966–89

Clearly, participation rate variations dampen fluctuations in measured unemployment.

An extremely simple, but revealing, illustration of the possible extent of hidden unemployment is shown by the dashed line in Figure 4.3.3 (LF 2) which is simply the straight line connecting the observed labour force in 1966 with the observed labour force in 1989. These start and end years are times of relatively high employment (as reflected in employment/population ratios). Assuming that the level of hidden unemployment was the same in 1966 as in 1988 (approximately zero), and that the measured labour force plus hidden unemployment has grown at a constant amount of approximately 150,000 per year, then the dashed line would represent the hypothetical 'true' labour force. It follows that the vertical distance between the dashed line and the observed labour force can be regarded as a measure (admittedly an extremely crude one) of the extent of possible hidden unemployment.

In a following section we estimate fluctuations in this gap econometrically and find that the results correspond roughly to those illustrated. This reinforces our view that when job growth slows, as in the mid and late 1970s, or goes into reverse as in the early 1980s, the extent of unmeasured unemployment increases considerably. It seems to be the case that the measured unemployment figures of the mid 1980s are an important understatement of the magnitude of the unemployment.

The phenomenon of unrecorded unemployment and the strong trend growth in the labour force help explain the apparent asymmetry associated with increases and decreases in measured unemployment. Years of zero or negative job growth result in substantial increases in unemployment which (on the basis of past experience) take a considerable period to unwind, even when subsequent job creation is very rapid. This point is important enough to be illustrated differently as it is now in Table 4.3.1.

The two very large annual increases in unemployment, from 2.4 to 4.6 per cent in 1975, and from 6.7 to 9.9 per cent in 1983, are explainable mostly by stagnation in job creation. Periods of very rapid employment growth, on the other hand, appear to have had relatively minor impacts on the unemployment rate. Over the period August 1983 to August 89, when employment growth averaged around 3.6 per cent per annum – a not unprecedented, but certainly a most unusually strong experience in the post World War II

Table 4.3.1 Australian Labour Force, Job Growth and Unemployment, 1966–89

Year	Labour Force Growth (%pa)	Job Growth (%pa)	Unemployment Rate (%)
1967	2.39	2.21	1.7
1968	2.33	2.49	1.6
1969	2.43	2.51	1.5
1970	4.03	4.11	1.4
1971	2.45	2.22	1.7
1972	2.60	1.70	2.5
1973	2.35	3.08	1.8
1974	1.82	1.25	2.4
1975	2.07	–0.24	4.6
1976	1.16	0.98	4.7
1977	2.65	1.64	5.7
1978	0.77	0.17	6.2
1979	0.81	1.23	5.9
1980	3.41	3.32	5.9
1981	1.47	1.80	5.6
1982	0.99	–0.23	6.7
1983	1.27	–2.16	9.9
1984	2.01	3.54	8.6
1985	2.12	2.85	7.9
1986	3.67	3.61	8.0
1987	2.59	2.72	7.8
1988	2.83	3.96	7.1
1989	3.85	4.89	5.9
Average	2.26	2.07	5.00
Coefficient of variation	0.378	1.302	1.420

Note: All data are taken from August of each year.

period – the unemployment rate fell on average by only 0.66 percentage points per year. This is in part because employment expansion 'unwinds' the substantial increase in unmeasured unemployment induced by the previous recession.[4] Clearly, even very short periods of job growth stagnation have important medium-term unemployment consequences.

2.1 Nominal wage inflation and real wage levels

The paths of nominal wage inflation and real wage levels for the period 1967 to 1989 are illustrated in Figures 4.3.4 and 4.3.5. The data show that annual wage inflation, which tends to be at least 5 per cent, was at an extraordinary level in 1974–75 – over 30 per cent -and was at a very high level of about 18 per cent in 1981–82. These two unusual experiences were soon followed by large increases in unemployment. Of relevance here are the changes in real wage levels (pre- and post-tax), illustrated in Figure 4.3.5.

From the these figures it would appear that significant jumps in wage inflation have been accompanied by higher real wage levels, this being true most obviously for 1974. Interestingly, however, the late 1960s and early 1970s were periods of sustained growth in real wages, but without any clear implications for increases in joblessness, a point that is not true for

Figure 4.3.4 Australian Wage Inflation, 1967–89

Average hourly earnings of full-time adults in all sectors October 1972–89, private sector only 1966–7.

Source: ABS Cat. No. 6304.0.

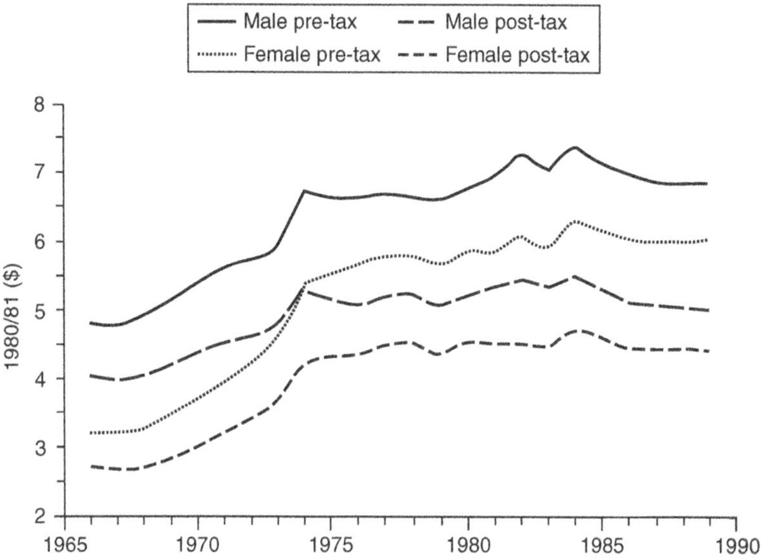

Figure 4.3.5 Australian Real Hourly Earnings, 1966–89
Source and definition as for Figure 4.3.4; Nominal earnings deflated by CPI; average ratio of PAYE to earnings from NIF.

1975–76 and 1982–83. (The links between wages and employment creation are examined further in Section 4). It should also be noted that there has been a fall in real wages since 1984. Possible explanations are explored in Section 3.

2.2 Long term unemployment

Our final area of interest is long term unemployment (LTU), which is defined as continuous unemployment for twelve months or more. Figure 4.3.6 illustrates the absolute numbers involved for the period in which data are available.[5] LTU rose dramatically in 1983–84 before beginning a gentle decline. The absolute number of male LTU increased from 34.2 thousand (15.4 per cent of male unemployment) in August 1978 to a peak of 154.1 thousand (35.4 per cent) in February 1984, falling to 73.0 thousand (28 per cent) in Augustl989. Female LTU increased from 27.6 thousand (15.8 per cent of female unemployment) in August 1978 to a peak of 76.9 thousand (25.4 per cent) in February 1984, and then falling to 35.3 thousand (16.9 per cent) in August 1989. Further useful information on this phenomenon is shown in Figures 4.3.7 and 4.3.8. It is apparently the case that the proportion of the unemployed who are LTU increased substantially a short while after the large jump in the unemployment rate in 1982–83. Both the absolute number and the proportion of LTU seem to increase considerably as unemployment rises,

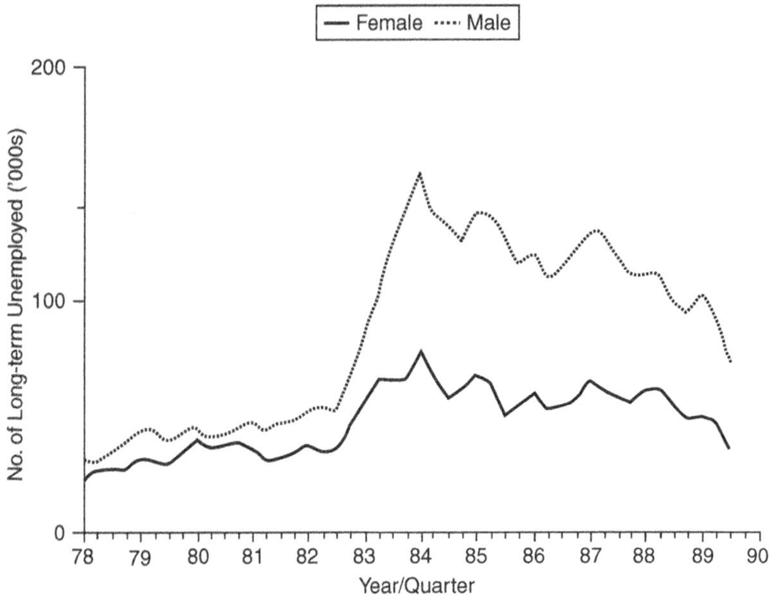

Figure 4.3.6 Australian Long Term Unemployment, 1978–89

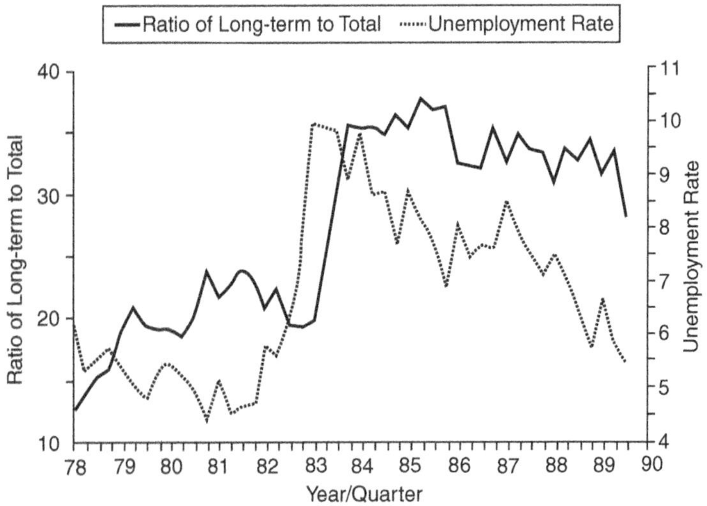

Figure 4.3.7 Australian Male Proportions of the Unemployed Who Were LTU, 1978–89

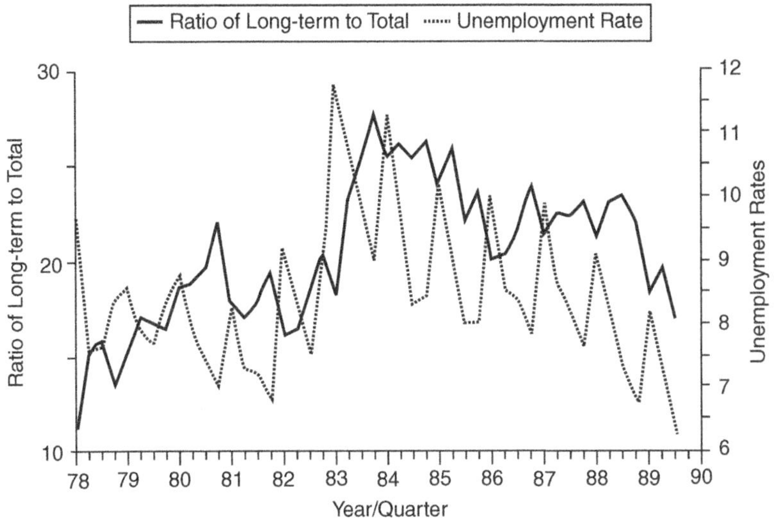

Figure 4.3.8 Australian Female Proportions of the Unemployed Who Were LTU, 1978–89

falling relatively slowly with the subsequent unemployment rate decreases. These relationships are examined econometrically in Section 6.

Another aspect of LTU is the mean (or median) duration of the current stock of unemployment. In data presented in the Appendix the mean (median) duration of males rose from 25 (14) weeks in 1978 to a peak of 58 (30) weeks in 1985, falling to 55 (18) weeks in 1989. For females, the mean (median) rose from 27 (13) weeks in 1978 to a peak of 40 (21) weeks in 1984, falling to 32 (12) weeks in 1989. Apparently the means (median) rise rapidly (with a lag), but fall rather slowly with decreasing unemployment rates.

Data on LTU as reported by the Department of Social Security (DSS) show some discrepancies in relation to the ABS data. From this source disaggregations of LTU by age show that in 1989 older males (over 55 years) who were LTU constituted 17.8 per cent of all male LTU. However, of those older males who were unemployed a large proportion (48.9 per cent) were in LTU. The phenomenon of LTU amongst older males is understated to the extent that many took early retirement, since the participation rate of this group has fallen significantly over the past few years. Older females (over 55 years) who were LTU constituted only 4.2 per cent of all female LTU. However, in 1989 of older females who were unemployed a large proportion (31.9 per cent) were in LTU.

Disaggregation also reveals that migrants, especially non-English speaking migrants (NESM), are over represented in the LTU. As an example, the mean (median) duration for NESM in 1987 was 70 (33) weeks while for Australian born males it was 54 (26) weeks. Other investigations show that Aborigines have a higher duration of unemployment compared to the rest (Committee of Review of Aboriginal Employment and Training Programs, 1987).

3 Wage Setting Institutions and Wage Outcomes

3.1 A theory of wage-setting institutions and outcomes

Recent contributions to analysis of wage and employment determination suggest that the role of labour market arrangements can be crucial (Freeman, 1987; Newell and Symons, 1987 (henceforth N-S); Calmfors and Driffill, 1988, (henceforth C-D)). The general finding is that economies characterised by high levels of 'insider power'[6] – usually understood to be a consequence of significant union strength – tend to deliver the highest levels of real wages and/or the highest rates of growth of nominal wages, leading to the least propitious employment outcomes, unless this insider power is marshalled towards a concern for the outsiders (the unemployed, or prospective unemployed).

The key argument underlying the C-D analysis is that centralisation of wage setting gives the wage setters a degree of market power which can be exploited to raise wages. However, such wage increases have effects on other groups. One union's wage rise leads to another union facing price rises; and aggregate wage rises may lead to higher unemployment. When wage setting is decentralised, the individual wage setters are largely insulated from these flow-on effects; but with increasing centralisation, taken to imply consensus between bargaining units on the value of wage restraint, the wage setters 'internalise the externalities', realising that they themselves can be hurt by the price and employment consequences of their decisions.

N-S argue that a centralised bargaining structure will encourage unions to take account of the unemployed, because of 'an increase in communal harmony' and/or because of the consequence of 'lower taxes for unemployment relief. C-D also recognise fiscal externalities as a possible motive for centralised unions to restrain their wage-setting power, but they concentrate their analysis on the price externalities. In their perspective unions have an incentive to coordinate their wage bargaining in order to avoid a competitive process of bidding up nominal wages. Uncoordinated wage bargaining may lead to inflation but not necessarily to any increase in aggregate real wages.

Whereas these authors assume that it is labour which exploits market power in wage setting, Dowrick (1987; 1989) argues that both real wage levels and wage inflation are the outcome of bargaining between unions and employers who have a degree of monopoly power in the labour and product markets respectively. Wage rises won by a union feed through to prices only to the extent that the employer has oligopolistic price setting power. At the same time, firms' product market power creates monopoly rents which encourage unions to push for higher wages. In this analysis, real wage outcomes and the rates of wage and price inflation are influenced by the degree of coordination and market power not only of labour but also of capital. If this point is accepted, the C-D analysis of centralisation of union power can be interpreted in the more general context of the centralisation of wage-and price-setting by both unions and employers.

Arguably both the C–D analysis and Dowrick's extension of it are better suited to institutional settings characterised by firm and industry-based unions than they are for systems dominated by craft or occupation unions, such as in Australia. The greater the extent of these types of unionism the less likely it is for unions to be concerned with firm- or industry-specific price rises, and the less obvious are the links between wage rises, product market power, and price increases. This does not deny the usefulness of the C-D and Dowrick perspectives in the Australian context since some unions may dominate particular industries, and others are close to establishment-based, at least in terms of their wage-price outcome potential. But the point implies that some caution is required in transferring uncritically modelling perspectives across different systems.

C–D argue that there is a hump-shaped relationship between wages and the degree of centralisation of the wage setting process (in contrast to N–S who postulate a linear relationship). At one extreme, competitive wage setting by many small independent firms and groups of workers is likely to result in relatively low wage outcomes. Partial centralisation of wage setting may give the groups market power, which enables them to raise wages and prices without concern for the consequences for other groups, including the unemployed. Further centralisation, however, may lead to 'large and all-encompassing trade unions [who] naturally recognise their market power and take into account both the inflationary and unemployment consequences of wage increases' (C–D, p. 14). As a result, the wage outcome under full centralisation is argued to be lower than that which occurs under partial centralisation.

The jargon of this literature refers to such a process of centralisation of wage setting as 'corporatism', defined by Panitch (1980) as:

> ...the integration of trade unions in economic policy making in exchange for their incorporation of capitalist growth criteria in union wage policy and their administration of wage restraint to their members.

and by N-S as:

> ...wage setting by central organisation, commanding the obedience of individual workers and employers to achieve a higher level of employment.

Austria and Sweden are typically given as examples of corporatist economies.

As noted, but worth stressing, the C–D framework does not suggest that corporatism is the only labour market arrangement that delivers relatively favourable employment outcomes, because of the presumed hump-shaped relationship referred to above. At the other end of the spectrum are economies with weak insider power, those with relatively decentralised labour markets, such as the US and Japan. The C–D analysis suggests that such environments similarly deliver relatively high wage flexibility in response to economic shocks, essentially because the employed have comparatively little influence over factor shares.

The above implies that lower real wages, and by assumption higher employment outcomes, accrue to countries at either end of the spectrum. Systems with high union coverage but without centralised wage setting tend to have poorer labour market results in this view. The examples given of such countries include typically the UK, West Germany and Belgium.

While the C–D model focuses on real wage levels as a measure of labour market flexibility, their analysis is readily extended to structural relationships concerned with nominal wage inflation, and thus the position of the non-accelerating inflation rate of unemployment (NAIRU).[7] For instance, Dowrick (1989) suggests that incorporation of union-employer bargaining models into the macro-economic framework of Layard and Nickell (1986) implies a direct correspondence between inflationary pressure and micro-level conflict over the distribution of economic surplus. This is a fundamental issue for the analysis following.

3.2 Testing the move towards corporatism in Australia

Practically all of the empirical work related to the above modelling considers the issue cross-sectionally through a comparison of the performance of different countries (Bruno and Sachs, 1985; N–S; C–D). Such approaches necessitate the quantification of how corporatist or decentralised an economy is. Typically less than twenty countries are included, which must cast important doubt on the validity of the results obtained. Since commentators disagree on their rankings of corporatism it is difficult to accept that the data can give consistent and easily interpreted results.

Interestingly, Australia has usually been placed in the middle group of countries. This observation suggests that the Australian NAIRU positioning should have been poor, at least for the periods concerned (up to 1985). Generally this is found in the cross-national studies.

A point of considerable interest for the current analysis is that the Australian experience over the 1980s offers an opportunity to test part of the corporatist perspective on time-series rather than cross-sectional data.[8] The formal statement of the intention of the parties to the prices and incomes Accord signed in May 1983, and subsequent pronouncements by both government and union leaders, suggest that it represents a significant change in the wage-setting framework, implying a move towards corporatism as defined above.

Of course, there can be a substantial gap between statements of intent and reality. Thus it is important to establish whether or not the Accord did actually initiate a significant change in labour market institutions and behaviour. The analysis of Chapman and Gruen (1990), building on earlier work by Beggs and Chapman (1987a, 1987b, 1987c), uses measured industrial disputation as an indicator of consensus. They find a statistically significant and substantial reduction in strike activity (around 70 per cent) since the second quarter of 1983. The extent of this structural break in strikes is evident not only in relation to previous Australian experience but also in comparison with the general downward trend in OECD working days lost from strikes over the same period. We take this evidence to indicate that the Accord did indeed suggest a significant change in the Australian industrial relations environment.[9]

3.3 The implications of corporatism for wage outcomes in Australia

Given this indication that the move towards corporatism in Australia has involved more than mere rhetoric, a significant policy question concerns the impact, if any, this change has had on wage outcomes. Certainly, casual inspection of the wage inflation and real wage data illustrated in Figures 4.3.4 and 4.3.5 suggests that the five year decline since 1984 represents a change in wage behaviour. But to rely on aggregative data such as these to draw conclusions is imprudent because of the many factors (presumably) influencing wage outcomes that differed between the periods. Most notably, the Accord was signed in the calendar year with the highest recorded unemployment for nearly fifty years. Obviously, econometric work is needed.

In an attempt to determine whether or not the Accord has been associated with structural changes in wage equations, Chapman and Gruen (1990) invited five practitioners of Australian macroeconomic quarterly wage models to subject their equations to similar methodological approaches. These were designed to illuminate what changes, if any, there have been in wage inflation or real wage levels since the second quarter of 1983. While analysis and details are left to Chapman and Gruen, the following brief description of the models is useful.

Three of the five equations are concerned with changes in nominal wages. They are from the Australian Treasury's NIF 88 model (Simes, 1988; Simes and Richardson, 1987), Martin Watts and Bill Mitchell (Watts and Mitchell, 1989) and Chris Murphy's macroeconomic forecasting model (Murphy, 1989). While they differ in terms of theoretical framework, each includes various representations of both a short-run Phillips curve and price expectations, and measures of the influence of the positioning of the NAIRU.

Two real wage level equations were used, from Phil Lewis (Lewis and Kirby, 1987; Lewis and Kirby, 1988) and Ian Russell, who drew on a model first developed by Pissarides (1987). These are quite different modelling approaches, the Lewis equation being a reduced form representation of labour supply and demand forces, including as independent variables the level of output, real unemployment benefits and a series of incomes policy dummies. The Russell model is derived from a perspective of bargaining between small firms and small unions, with labour productivity, tax leakages and inflation expectations, among others, as regressors.

Each of the five equations was used to test the existence or otherwise of incomes policy effects on wages in two separate, but related, ways. The first was to estimate the equations from the beginning of the data periods – usually the late 1960s – to 1983(1), and to use the estimated coefficients to predict the dependent variable over the Accord period, assumed to be from 1983 (2) to the end of the available data. Predictions of the dependent variable using the actual values of the independent variables were then compared to actual wage outcomes, a technique usually known as the simulation approach

In all five wage equations projections of the dependent variable lay above actual experience for the great majority of quarterly observations (70 per cent for the lowest, 100 per cent for the highest, with the average being 87 per cent). This is suggestive evidence that wage outcomes were lower in the Accord period than expected on the basis of pre-Accord econometric experience.

The second method used in all models was the estimation of the equations over the entire sample including an intercept-dummy variable for the post-1983(2) period. This approach has the advantage of providing an easily interpretable coefficient and a test of significance, its main limitation being that it constrains regressor coefficients to be identical across regimes. As well, the Accord dummy coefficient illustrates the average effect only since it is constrained not to vary through time.

With these caveats in mind it is interesting to note that of the three wage inflation equations, the latter two revealed significant falls after 1983(2) with NIF 88 showing an insignificantly negative effect. Taking the point estimates of the coefficients literally, two of the equations implied a decrease of around three to four percentage points in wage growth per year (2.97 from NIF 88 and 3.30 to 4.32 from Murphy, depending on specification), the other suggesting a much larger (dynamic) decrease of around fourteen percentage points per annum at the middle of the period. The real wage level equations of both Lewis and Russell both implied average decreases of about 10 per cent over the 1983–89 period, although Russell's Accord effect was not significantly different from zero. The results are reported more fully in the Appendix.

These findings allow us to make an overall summary judgement of the effect of the Accord on structural wage relationships. This is that the evidence is consistent with the proposition that wage outcomes decreased after 1983(2). To motivate ensuing analysis, the order of magnitude for wage inflation is estimated to be three percentage points per annum (that is, given the same value of the right hand side variables, without the Accord wage inflation per annum would have been, for example, 11 per cent per year instead of 8 per cent). Importantly, we believe this estimate to be a lower bound, a conservative assessment, given that it is approximately the same as that implied by about the lowest Accord dummy variable coefficient (although in this case the effect was not statistically different from zero at the 5 per cent level). If we had chosen the largest wage inflation effect the estimated impact would have been around three times higher.

For the real wage effect of the Accord we have taken the point estimates revealed from the coefficients of each equation. This is that, *ceteris paribus,* the average real wage level was 10 per cent lower over 1983(2) - 1989(1) than was expected on the basis of both the regressor values and pre-Accord econometric experience. Again, it is circumspect to acknowledge that in one of the two equations the effect is not statistically significantly different from zero at the 5 per cent level.

A major caveat to the above judgements is that it is possible that the experience of wage inflations followed by recessions in 1974/75 and 1982/83 may have changed worker's attitudes to wage rises and concomitantly their bargaining behaviour, both in Australia and internationally. The greater is the empirical relevance of this observation the more questionable is the judgement that we have identified incomes policy outcomes only. But we are reassured by the fact that comparisons of the growth of real wages and real unit labour costs between the 1978–83 and 1984–88 periods show greater decreases in Australia than the average for the seven largest OECD countries (Chapman and Gruen, 1990). This is additional evidence that Australian wage relationships changed after the signing of the Accord.

4 Wage Restraint and Employment

4.1 Theoretical issues

The question of the relative importance of wage changes and wage levels for unemployment outcomes has received much attention in this country (see Reserve Bank of Australia, 1979). Over the decade following the marked rise in joblessness in 1974/75 the existence and relevance of the so-called 'real wage overhang' (RWO) dominated the unemployment debate and, indeed, apparently influenced significantly government policy approaches to the issue.

While it is our judgement that neither the empirical evidence[10] nor the RWO conceptual framework[11] are such as to encourage confident acceptance of its underlying message, from the available empirical evidence it is hard to deny that wages matter for employment. The continuing points of contention are the causal mechanisms involved, the size of the elasticity of labour demand with respect to both wage inflation and the real wage, and the role of aggregate demand as an independent determinant of employment.

It is sufficient for our purposes to note that today most commentators give weight to the role of wage outcomes on employment, but we acknowledge readily that the issues are complex and many of the linkages are indirect. A useful distinction for such a discussion differentiates between the implications for job creation of nominal wage inflation and real wage levels.

Potentially, nominal wage inflation can affect employment via its impact on price inflation. It is not controversial to suggest that higher price inflation affects employment, through several possible channels: a decrease in certainty for business leading to lower investment, because of the likely positive association of the variance in relative prices and the level of price inflation; and through an encouragement of moves by government towards more restrictive monetary and fiscal policy in an attempt to influence both inflation expectations and nominal wage growth.

Of course, when nominal wage inflation exceeds price inflation real wages increase and real unit labour costs tend to increase or decrease more slowly, which may imply higher unemployment. A popular perspective is that relative factor price changes move the economy around an aggregate production frontier, since real wage increases result in a substitution of capital for labour. More compelling is the possibility that real wage increases imply decreases in the profit share, concomitantly investment, and thus employment (Higgins, 1979).

From macroeconomic theory, most of these potential relationships point to the same thing. If nominal wage inflation decreases, *ceteris paribus,* this suggests that the NAIRU has shifted to the left, implying a more propitious inflation/unemployment scenario. This is taken to be a major goal of corporatism.

Clearly the relationships between wage changes and levels and their employment implications are complex in theory and we have chosen not to explore them further. Moreover, we offer no new evidence on the empirical dimensions to these issues, nor do we judge the efforts reported so far on the magnitudes involved. Analysis of these issues is unnecessary for our purposes so long as the wage-employment elasticities estimated from other models are plausible, since it is these we use for predictions concerning the role of the Accord in generating employment through wage restraint.

4.2 Corporatism and employment creation in Australia: An empirical exercise

Our judgement that the Accord decreased wage inflation by three percentage points per annum on average, and real wages by ten per cent over 1983–89, can be used in an attempt to cast light on the following counterfactual question: without the wage restraint associated with the move to corporatism in 1983, what would Australian employment outcomes have been in the ensuing six years?

The first method used was to simulate in a macroeconomic model the effects of a permanent decrease in wage inflation at the rate of three percentage points per annum. The model used was that of Chris Murphy (see

Murphy, 1989) which is, approximately, a one hundred equation system characterised by rational expectations in financial markets and with no long run tradeoff between inflation and unemployment. The employment effects arise because wage inflation decreases result in equivalent cuts in real wage levels as a result of short-run price stickiness, with the economy settling on a lower NAIRU.

The second method used in the wage inflation experiment entailed employing Challen's (1984) estimate of the Australian money wage – employment elasticity. His judgement was made on the basis of analysis conducted on five macro-econometric models, NEVILE, NIF-10, RBII, IMP and ORANI. The conclusion he comes to is that 'a 10 per cent money-wage cut will produce an increase in employment of more than 3 per cent after two years or a little more ' (Challen, 1984, p. 39). We interpret this to imply that the employment effects are long lasting, and assume for simplicity both that the estimate is linear and that the effects of 10 per cent money wage cut are equivalent to a decrease in nominal wage inflation of 10 percentage points.

Real wage effects on employment have been estimated using the elasticities from Agrawal (1988) and Lewis and Kirby (1988), the latter authors having undertaken an exercise very similar to the one reported here. Respectively the elasticities are –1.0 and –0.8.

The Murphy experiment and the Challen, Agrawal and Lewis and Kirby elasticity estimates revealed employment effects from a three percentage point per annum decrease in wage inflation or a ten per cent cut in real wages as illustrated in Table 4.3.2.

It is important to be clear as to the meaning of the data of Table 4.3.2. The Murphy experiment suggests that the Accord reduced the equilibrium NAIRU from 6.37 per cent to 4.16 per cent, with the estimated 3.7 per cent employment growth over the period implying about 290,000 additional jobs. The data associated with Challen result simply from imposing a 3 per cent lower money wage level per year than would otherwise have been attained. Since his experiments revealed that a 10 per cent cut in wages was associated with a 3 per cent increase in employment, we assume a 3 per cent cut in wage levels implies a 0.9 per cent annual growth in employment, or around 420,000 extra jobs for 1983–89. The real wage effects estimated from Agrawal and from Lewis and Kirby of a 10 per cent reduction have

Table 4.3.2 Estimated Employment Effects from The Accord's Wage Restraint

	Nominal Wage Inflation		Real Wage Levels	
	Murphy	**Challen**	**Agrawal**	**Lewis and Kirby**
Job growth % 1983–89	3.7	5.4	10.0	8.0
Additional jobs by 1989	289,000	423,000	782,000	626,000

been translated into Accord employment consequences by multiplying their elasticities by 0.1, which implies total job creation of about 780,000 and 630,000 respectively. Lewis and Kirby (1988) did their own estimates of the effect of the Accord on employment with the same result we report for them here.

It is important also to understand what the data of Table 4.3.2 do *not* mean. The only alleged impact of the Accord identified here arises from the assumed structural change in the wage inflation and real wage processes. It is possible that the Accord had other, indirect, effects on employment, one plausible avenue being through increased business confidence and investment as a consequence of diminished strike activity. On the other hand, some commentators assert that increased centralisation in wage-setting processes decreases flexibility at the firm level (Moore, 1989), which might suggest that there are adverse long run consequences. The point is that we have produced estimates here only of the direct short-term employment consequences of the Accord.

Our overall judgement is that the Accord, through its effects on the structure of wage relationships, resulted in (at least) 4 per cent employment in 1983–89, over and above what would have eventuated had there been no changes in institutional arrangements. This amounts to around 310,000 jobs for the period. We believe this judgement to be conservative, given that an averaging across the wage-employment models suggest a figure in excess of 500,000 jobs.

5 Australian Corporatism, Labour Force Growth and Unemployment.

5.1 Theoretical issues

The change in unemployment which has occurred over the period of the Accord is definitionally equal to the growth of the labour force minus the change in employment. We have already examined the extent to which employment growth can be attributed to the change in the wage setting framework, but in order to explain the impact on measured unemployment it is necessary to analyse the response of labour supply. In particular, we investigate below the extent to which the exceptionally fast labour force growth of the past six years has resulted from the employment and wage changes which we have identified with the Accord.

There are four main components of the growth of the labour force to be examined:

(i) *demographic trends:* recent labour force growth has been fuelled by Australia's relatively high rate of immigration and population growth (in comparison with other advanced industrialised countries) and also by the effects of the 'baby boomers' reaching prime working age;

(ii) *real wages:* real wages have fallen over the past six years. This could either contribute to an increase in the labour force (an income effect as families seek to maintain household incomes by sending more members to work) or to a decrease (substitution towards leisure);

(iii) *cyclical effects:* job opportunities have opened up in the recovery from the cyclical trough of 1983, so people may have been encouraged to spend time looking for work and thus be recorded as members of the officially defined labour force (reversing the 'discouraged worker' effect), or they may have dropped out of the labour force as other members of the household found work (an income effect);

(iv) *sociological and other factors:* which lead to a systematic, but unexplained, trend in participation rates.

5.2 Evidence on the determinants of labour supply

Previous research on changes over time in Australian labour supply[12] has suggested that cyclical effects are strong, that time trends are clearly evident, that age and gender differences are significant, and that real wage effects are not very important. The Appendix summarises the results of our OLS regressions explaining participation rates for each of ten age-gender groups over the period 1966–89 in terms of time trends, job opportunities, and real wages.

The results suggest that participation rates are pro-cyclical after the late 1970s for all groups except prime-age males and older women. We infer that the discouraged worker effect – people who drop out of the official unemployment statistics when employment opportunities are scarce, but rejoin when more jobs become available – is particularly strong for women and for the young and old. The aggregate effect is that for every 100 extra jobs, about forty people join the labour force[13] and unemployment drops by sixty. (This is also the order of magnitude implied for hidden unemployment from Figure 4.3.3).

On the other hand the real wage effects are mixed: for men they are statistically insignificant for the period since the late 1970s, except for those aged under 20 years whose participation responds positively to real wage rises. The own-wage effect for women under the age of 55 is generally positive – implying that leisure-work substitution does occur – but it is apparently offset by a negative income effect of the male wage on adult participation. These are important research findings since they help explain both why aggregate participation equations show no real wage effects (Murphy, 1988), and why our total real wage absolute elasticity is small – less than 0.25 at the sample means.

The relationships suggest that the changes in employment and in real wages which have been attributed to the Accord have in turn had impacts on labour supply. Estimates of these labour force effects are presented in Table 4.3.3. Actual earnings, employment and labour force data are given

Table 4.3.3 The Labour Force Aged 15–64: Actual and Simulated

	1983	1989	Alternative scenarios for 1989:		
			a	b	c
Average real adult male hourly earnings*	$7.05	$6.82	$6.82	$6.82	$7.52
Employment/population ratio (%)	61.2	68.4	68.4	65.7	65.7
	Actual		Predicted		
Female participation rate %	51.7	60.4	60.6	59.1	58.5
Male Participation rate %	83.5	84.7	84.3	83.5	83.8
Persons participation rate %	68.0	72.7	72.6	71.5	71.4
Female % of labour force	37.6	40.9	41.1	40.7	40.4
Unemployment rate %	10.0	5.9	5.8	8.1	8.0

(Predictions are based on the age and gender specific estimates of participation rates as reported in the Appendix).
Note: * 1980/81 $.

for 1983 and for 1989 in the first two columns. The third column, labelled scenario a, presents the labour force figures, which are *predicted* for 1989 by the participation model summarised in the Appendix, using actual employment and wages. These notional figures can be compared with those derived from scenario b where *employment is assumed to be 4 per cent lower.* Scenario c adds in the predicted effects of real wages being 10 per cent higher. The wage and employment outcomes of scenario c are those which we estimate would have occurred in the absence of the Accord. (Comparison with scenarios a and b enables us to distinguish labour supply responses induced by the wage effects of the Accord from the responses induced by the employment effects).

The results should be interpreted as follows. If real wages had been 10 per cent higher and employment 4 per cent lower in 1989 than was the case, aggregate labour supply is estimated to have been 1.7 per cent lower. (Comparison of scenarios b and c indicates that almost all of the estimated change in the size of the labour force is due to the discouraged worker effect; the main consequence of a real wage rise is to substitute male for female participation.) In consequence, the 4 per cent rise in employment which we have attributed to the Accord translates into a 2.2 percentage point fall in the measured rate of unemployment.

We have used this labour supply model, in association with the population projections presented in ABS (1988), to examine the implications for unemployment in the medium term. Underlying demographic trends imply that while the working age population is expected to grow at 1.5 per cent per annum, the prime-age group 25–55 will grow at 2.2 per cent. – a 'baby-boom' effect. Given the high participation rates of prime age males and females, and also the strong trend growth of participation amongst prime age women, the underlying growth rate of the labour force up to 1996 is calculated to be 2.3 per cent.

These labour force projections suggest that continued strong employment growth (of at least 2.3 per cent per annum) is required over the medium term if the unemployment rate is not to rise. This point can be illustrated by considering the implications should annual job growth be as low as 1.5 per cent (which is the Australian average for job growth over the period 1966 to 1983 and would be regarded as very high growth in other advanced industrialised countries). In this case, our labour supply model predicts that the measured unemployment rate would rise to 9.3 per cent by 1996.[14]

It is interesting to note that estimation of disaggregated labour supply equations confirms the observation made in Section 2 that labour force participation is highly pro-cyclical, particularly for women. This evidence supports the view that there is substantial hidden unemployment in recessions.

Disaggregating by sex the effects of the employment growth on participation, we are able to deduce that the increase in employment has brought an extra 107,000 women and an extra 24,000 men into the labour force.

6 Long Term Unemployment

The change identified in unemployment as a result of the Accord leads to the question of what, if any, have been the implications for LTU. Thus in this section we explore the proposition that the proportion of unemployment that is LTU, and consequently the absolute numbers of LTU, have been affected by these changes.

While most work in this area has concentrated on cross-section and individual panel data sets, recent studies by OECD (1983), Trivedi and Hui (1987), Budd, Levine and Smith (1988a, 1988b) and Jackman and Layard (1988) report equations estimated for LTU (either absolute numbers or as a proportion of total unemployment), the general conclusion supporting the view that the higher the unemployment rate the higher the (proportion of) LTU.[15]

6.1 Theoretical issues

It is useful to think of the labour market as continually changing with inflows into, and outflows from, the unemployment stock. That is,

$$U_t = U_{t-1} + I_t - O_t$$

where Ut is the end of period t unemployment level, and I_t and O_t are respectively into inflows and outflows from employment over the period t. The inflows consist of quits (voluntary separations), fires and layoffs (involuntary separations), and new entrants (or reentrants) to the labour force. The outflows consist of people who either find jobs, become discouraged and leave the labour force, fall ill, retire, or enter labour market programs.

There is some evidence to suggest that the experience of LTU affects the probability of escape from unemployment.[16] This arises for two possible reasons. One is because either the individuals lose part of their skills (skill atrophy), become discouraged and search less intensively, or that employers use LTU as a signal of 'less marketable characteristics' possessed by the unemployed person. In either case so called state-dependence (or duration dependence) arises. The second reason for the LTU as a group to have a lower escape probability is due to the possibility that employers select those job seekers with the more marketable characteristics (with high escape probabilities) leaving behind those with less marketable characteristics, a phenomenon known as 'heterogeneity'. In a time series analysis, an increase in the proportion of LTU can increase as a result of either or both state dependence and heterogeneity.

The proportion of LTU can also increase if the probability of reemployment falls for *all* of the unemployed; this might occur during a recession when less vacancies arise and more people compete for each vacancy.

The approach reported below is the estimation of a reduced form equation attempting to explain the proportion of LTU by lagged unemployment rates. It does not attempt to distinguish between the different causal mechanisms outlined above.

6.2 Some econometric estimates

It is postulated that the proportion of unemployment which is LTU (PLTU) depends on a lagged distribution of unemployment rates. That is, we tested:

$$A(L)\ PLTU = B(L)\ UR + e$$

where A(L) and B(L) are polynomials in the lag operator L, UR is the unemployment rate, and e is assumed to be a white noise error term.

Separate equations were estimated for males and females using ABS quarterly data from 1978(1) to 1988(4), allowing for up to 8 lags on UR and 4 lags on the dependent variable, PLTU. A time trend was included to capture any changes in social or institutional features, and various zero restrictions in the lagged variables were tested. The variables are measured as percentages. Using the 'general-to-specific' methodology, the best equations are presented below (with t-statistics in brackets):

Males

$$\underset{}{MPLTU} = \underset{(0.729)}{1.382} + \underset{(0.653)}{0.492}MUR(-4) + \underset{(1.632)}{1.359}MUR(-5) - \underset{(-1.723)}{1.406}MUR(-6)$$

$$+ \underset{(2.355)}{1.501}MUR(-7) + \underset{(5.287)}{1.004}MPLTU(-1) - \underset{(-3.053)}{0.596}MPLTU(-2)$$

$$- \underset{(-0.823)}{0.144}MPLTU(-4) + \underset{(2.274)}{0.159}T + \text{Seasonal Dummies}$$

$R^2 = 0.943$; DW = 2.078;
LM (Serial Correlation) Chi-Sq(4) = 5.37
Mean Lag = 6.6 quarters
Long Run Coefficient = 2.6

Females (1979Q1 – 1988Q4)

$$FPLTU = \underset{(2.650)}{-4.918} + \underset{(5.481)}{1.356}FUR(-1) + \underset{(10.047)}{0.639}FPLTU(-1)$$

+ Seasonal Dummies
$R^2 = 0.867$; DW = 2.223
LM (Serial Correlation) Chi Sq(4) = 4.502
Mean Lag = 2.8 quarters
Long Run Coefficient = 3.8

The estimations reported have satisfactory econometric properties[17], and suggest the following. For males, while there is a long and complicated lag distribution, the essence of the relationship uncovered is that a one percentage point decrease in the male unemployment rate is associated with a long run fall of 2.6 percentage points in the proportion of the male unemployed who are LTU, with 50 per cent of this effect occurring within seven quarters. For females, a one percentage point decrease in the female unemployment rate is associated with a reduction of the proportion of the female unemployed who are LTU by about 3.8 percentage points, half of this effect being reached after only three quarters.

These estimates imply that, if the Accord reduced (measured) unemployment by around 2.2 percentage points, the associated fall in the (aggregate) proportion of unemployment which is LTU is around 7 percentage points, from a predicted (non-Accord) world in 1989 of 30 per cent to the observed 23 per cent. In absolute numbers this represents a fall in 1989 LTU from a predicted 194,000, to the observed level of 108,000,[18] a difference of the order of 85,000 persons.

This exercise warrants two caveats. Firstly, the econometric estimates do not control for other factors that might affect LTU which may have changed over the period. Most obviously, no variables have been included to account for variations in job mismatches from structural changes, or the real value of unemployment benefits which may have affected work-leisure choices. Secondly, the significant time trend in the male estimation can be interpreted as a misspecification, or it could be picking up some part of the influence of omitted variables. Thus the statistical analysis is both approximate and useful only as a forecasting exercise.

We have applied our estimates of the long run relationship[19] between the unemployment rate and the LTU ratio to the labour force projections for 1996 discussed in Section 5. Should the unemployment rate stay at its current level of 5.9 per cent, we predict 134,000 people in LTU by 1996. Under our 'slow' employment growth scenario, however, unemployment reaches 9.3 per cent and the predicted number of people in LTU rises to 299,000. Present trends in the labour market suggest that this is a conservative estimate. These predictions serve as an indication of the costs of adopting a wage-fixing system, or macro-economic policies, which might slow employment creation. Arrangements which decrease annual employment creation from 2.3 to 1.5 per cent will more than double the number of people in measured LTU by 1996.

7 Summary and Implications

While the 1980s have been characterised by the highest recorded unemployment rates since the 1930s and the largest number of persons ever in this category in Australia, the last six years have witnessed a sustained fall in joblessness. In previous work unemployment has been analysed in macroeconomic frameworks best characterised as distinguishing between the roles of supply factors – such as the influence of unemployment benefits and the labour/leisure choice – and demand conditions – such as the state of private investment or the government's macroeconomic stance. Our point of departure has been to focus on the implications for Australian unemployment of an apparent change in institutional wage-setting arrangements.

The study can be interpreted in a conventional contemporary macrotheory framework as an analysis of the effects of changes in the structure of wage-bargaining on both the NAIRU and on disequilibrium unemployment. Our goal has been to determine what this has meant for employment, unemployment and LTU. This is one of the few time-series tests of the implications of a move to corporatism.

We have taken as our starting point the evidence adduced elsewhere that the prices and incomes Accord has delivered both lower wage inflation and lower real wages than would have occurred if institutional arrangements for wage setting had not been altered. This evidence fits both with theories of centralised wage setting and also with the cross-sectional international evidence. Our estimate of the implications of these wage effects for aggregate labour market outcomes are summarised in Table 4.3.4, which compares the situation in 1983 with both actual outcomes in 1989 and our estimate of the data from a counter-factual with no institutional change in wage setting arrangements.

As an example to explain the data of Table 4.3.4, the implication is that the number of unemployed persons in 1983 of about 960,000 fell to 492,000

Table 4.3.4 1983 and 1989 Labour Maiket Outcomes: Actual and Estimated Given No Accord (August Levels)

Variable	1983 Actual	1989 Actual	1989 Estimated
Average Real Adult Hourly Earnings (1980–81)	7.05	6.82	7.52
Employment ('000s)	6241.1	7800.0	7488.0
Male Labour Force ('000s)	4333.3	4883.0	4859.0
Female Labour Force ('000s)	2594.6	3409.3	3302.3
Total Labour Force ('000s)	6927.9	8292.3	8161.3
Unemployment ('000s)	686.8	492.3	641.1
Unemployment Rate (%)	10.0	5.9	8.1
Long-Term Unemployment ('000s)	189,000	108,000	194,000
Long Term Unemployment (Proportion of Unemployment, %)	27	23	30

in 1989. But in the absence of the structural break in wage relationships attributed by us to the Accord, unemployment in August 1989 would have been of the order of 640,000.

We have also predicted that unless wage fixing institutions in combination with macro-economic policy are able to deliver annual average employment growth of over 2 per cent over the medium term, unemployment and LTU will rise again. This point is of particular relevance to the current debates both over the future of the Accord and also over the desirability or otherwise of short-term dampening of domestic demand.

Estimating the impact of the Accord has required us to make judgements on a number of contentious issues, particularly with regard to wage behaviour and subsequent employment responses. Our approach has been to test these relationships over a variety of elasticity estimates and econometric models. The models on which the evidence is based have all been tested previously in the public domain and represent a wide cross-section of the best practice in current Australian macroeconomic research. While the estimated magnitudes (and the degree of statistical precision) of the wage and employment responses differ across models, they all point in the same direction. We have been deliberately conservative in our choice of working estimates, so the figures quoted above for the effects of the Accord are more likely to be underestimates than overestimates.[20] But it is pertinent to note that the recent growth in unemployment with continued wage restraint underlines the fact that other factors (besides real wages) influence unemployment.

The evidence does not in itself constitute an overwhelming case in favour of the Australian corporatist experiment. There are three important qualifications. First, from theory, similar wage and employment outcomes might also have been achieved by a *reduction* in the degree of centralisation and market power of the wage-setting institutions, although the British experience of a decade of this alternative policy suggests that the benefits to employment of such an approach may take many years to come through. Given our findings the list of interesting research topics would include a comparative analysis of Australian – UK experience, since the policy approaches to labour market institutions have been completely different.

Secondly, our analysis offers no insights into the role of wage-setting practices for micro-efficiency, or other possible areas of reform. *A priori* it is not obvious that work-place efficiency is impaired or encouraged by moves to corporatism: the Accord experience seems to have been both that restrictive work practices have decreased and that labour productivity growth has so far been relatively low.

Perhaps most importantly our analysis offers nothing on distributional issues. The following points are relevant. One, while increased employment probably leads to a more equal distribution of income within the potential labour force, it is possible that inequality has widened between employees and the self-employed (including professionals) since the latter may have been able to escape the restraints of Accord. Two, is the question of factor shares. Newell and Symons (1987) suggest that 'corporatism... will operate in favour of capital, in favour of the otherwise unemployed and, to some extent, against the interests of the employed'. This prediction seems to have been borne out in the Australian case since the share of GDP going to capital has increased substantially over 1983–89. This probably implies widening inequality in the distribution of wealth (Stilwell, 1986). And three, there is the complex issue of the distribution of income between and within households. While real wages have fallen, household incomes have *on average* increased (Treasury, 1989). What is unclear is to what extent those receiving the additional jobs have been able to compensate in the household for the real income losses of those in employment.

These distributional issues are potentially very important for the future prospects of the Accord since one of the factors which probably has so far prevented its collapse either through wage breakouts or through a change of political direction is a widespread belief that it has promoted social justice. Further research is needed into the occupational, gender and household distributions of the gains and losses from the Accord.

A final methodological point is that the extent of the effects ajudged to have arisen from the move to corporatism are sufficiently large as to imply that a reorientation of unemployment research to the issue of distributional arrangements between and within labour and capital would be highly useful. That is, conventional macro-economic demand and supply models need to be supplemented with analyses of wage setting institutions.

Notes

We acknowledge gratefully the excellent research assistance provided by Karen Byng, Cezary Kapuscinski, Gloriavic Salveron and Tracy Tiong, and also the typing assistance provided by Eileen Berry. We received helpful advice from Chris Murphy, Bob Gregory, Fred Gruen and George Fane. Vince FitzGerald and Bill Mitchell provided useful and stimulating commentary as discussants of the papers, as did other Conference participants. P.N. Junankar gratefully acknowledges financial assistance from the ANU Faculties Research Fund.

1. Since the beginning of 1990 there has been a reversal of this declining trend in unemployment and we would expect the number of long term unemployed to increase.
2. Formal welfare analysis implies a welfare loss as long as unemployment is involuntary, ie, if the unemployed would choose to work if employment were available at or below the current wage. Unemployment also implies welfare loss if there are externalities involved in the search process with voluntary unemployment (see Diamond, 1981, and Mortensen, 1986). See Junankar (1986, 1987) for discussion of the costs of unemployment.
3. Trend labour force growth is due mainly to population increase (stemming in roughly equal parts from natural increase and immigration) supplemented by increasing female participation.
4. The comparative impact of the role of employment and labour force growth on unemployment outcomes is implied by the sizes of the coefficients of variation of the variables, shown in the table.
5. The relative strengths and weaknesses of the different data series for LTU are considered in Junankar and Kapuscinski (1990). The ABS data are used here. For a detailed discussion of LTU also see Junankar and Kapuscinski (1991).
6. See Gregory (1982).
7. For analysis of the NAIRU in the Australian context, see Mitchell (1987).
8. For comparable analyses sec Lewis and Kirby (1988), and Kenyon (1990).
9. The Chapman and Gruen conclusion is not unqualified, for two notable reasons. One is that other forms of disputation (e.g. bans) may have increased over the period (Sheen, 1990); the other is that the apparent increase in industrial harmony could have been as a consequence of the seeming increased willingness of employers to resort to legal means to break strikes (Moore, 1989).
10. See Covick (1984) and Bonnell (1984) for discussion of statistical difficulties in interpreting RWO data.
11. See Gregory and Duncan (1979) and INDECS (1981).
12. See BLMR (1985), Cox (1986), Murphy (1989), and Agrawal (1988).
13. Agrawal (1988) reports a response of between 38% and 42%. The Murphy (1989) estimate is similar.
14. The considerable increase in unemployment in 1990–91 has two obvious implications: one, the measured unemployment rate is already approaching this level because of the recent stagnation in job creation; and two, given that real wages have not increased, it is clear that aggregate demand has profound independent effects on unemployment.
15. See Junankar (1988).
16. In a time-series context it is useful to think of the inflows as 'births' and the outflows as 'deaths' so that certain results from demographic theory may be used (see, for example, Keyfitz, 1977). In this theory a stable population is one where

for a given birth rate (rate of inflows) and given age specific mortality distribution (a given duration specific escape probability distribution) the age composition of the population (the duration of the unemployment stock) remains constant over time. A special case of a stable population is a stationary population with births equal to deaths (inflows equal to outflows and a constant age (duration) distribution). Demographic theory suggests that in the steady state (stable population) an increase in the birth rate, given a mortality distribution, leads to a 'younger' population, or in our context to a decrease in the proportion of LTU. However, in a stationary state the proportion of LTU is independent of the birth rate (inflows). If there is a sudden increase in inflows as occurred with the recession in 1982–83 (with an unchanged outflow distribution) then the proportion of LTU first falls and then eventually rises. Assuming another stationary state is reached, the proportion of LTU should return to its previous level, unless the escape probability distribution shifts downwards. This might occur because of changes to those experiencing LTU.

17. That is, there are no identified problems with functional form, heteroscedasticity or serial correlation (up to eight quarters). When coefficient restrictions were not rejected at the 5 per cent level of significance they were re-estimated and are reported above.
18. Or, more exactly, to the 1989 *predicted* number of LTU of 111,000.
19. We have not included the time trend for males in these projections.
20. As noted, it is clearly the case that our estimates are small compared to those reported in Lewis and Kirby (1988).

References

Australian Bureau of Statistics (1988), *Projections of the Populations of Australia, States and Territories 1987 to 2031,* Cat. No. 3222.0, Canberra.

Agrawal N. (1988), 'The Effects of Structural Change on Employment, Unemployment and Labour Force Participation', General Paper No. G-88, IMPACT Research Centre, Melbourne.

Beggs J.J. and B.J. Chapman (1987a) 'An Empirical Analysis of Australian Strike Activity', *The Economic Record,* 63, 46–60.

Beggs J.J. and B.J. Chapman (1987b) 'Declining Strike Activity in Australia, 1983–85: An International Phenomenon', *The Economic Record,* 63, 330–339.

Beggs J.J. and B.J. Chapman (1987c) 'Australian Strike Activity in International Context: 1964–85', *Journal of Industrial Relations,* 49, 149–161.

Bureau of Labour Market Research (1985), "Who's In The Labour Force', Research Report No. 7, Canberra.

Bonnell S (1984), 'The "Real Wage Overhang" and the Wage Share of Output', in B.J. Chapman *et al* (eds) *Australian Labour Economics: Readings,* 3rd edn., Macmillan, Melbourne.

Bruno M. and J. Sachs (1985) *The Economics of Worldwide Stagflation,* Oxford, Basil Blackwell.

Budd A., P. Levine and P. Smith (1988a) 'Real Wage Adjustment and Long-term Unemployment', in R. Cross (ed). *Unemployment, Hysteresis and the Natural Rate Hypothesis,* Oxford, Blackwell.

Budd A., P. Levine and P. Smith (1988b) 'Unemployment, Vacancies and the Long-term Unemployed', *Economic Journal,* 98, 1071–1091.

Calmfors Lars and John Driffill (1988), 'Centralisation of Wage Bargaining', *Economic Policy,* 6, April, 14–61.

Cass B. (1988), 'Income Support for the Unemployed in Australia: Towards a More Active System', *Social Security Review Issues Paper No. 4,* Canberra, AGPS.

Challen D. (1984), *The Wages-Employment Relationship in Australian Macroeconomic Models,* Bureau of Labour Market Research, Canberra, AGPS.

Chapman B J and F. Gruen (1990), 'An Analysis of the Australian Consensual Incomes Policy: The Prices and Income Accord'. Discussion Paper No. 221, Centre for Economic Policy Research, Australian National University.

Committee of Review of Aboriginal Employment and Training Programs (M. Miller, Chairman) (1985) *Report,* Canberra, AGPS.

Covick O. (1984), 'Productivity-Geared Wages Policy, Labour's Share of Gross Product, and the "Real Wage Overhang"', in B.J.Chapman *et al* (eds), *Australian Labour Economics: Readings,* 3rd edition, Macmillan, Melbourne.

Cox J.P. (1986), 'Economic Growth and Income Support Policies in Australia, *Economic Record,* 62(178): 268–285.

Diamond P. (1981), 'Mobility Costs, Frictional Unemployment and Efficiency', *Journal of Political Economy,* 89: 789–812.

Dowrick S. (1987), 'Union-oligopoly Bargaining: Micro- and Macro-economic Implications', Working Papers in Economics and Econometrics No. 145, Australian National University, Canberra.

Dowrick S. (1989) 'Union-oligopoly Bargaining, *Economic Journal,* 99 (398), 1123–1142.

Economic Planning Advisory Council (EPAC) (1989) 'Productivity in Australia: Results of Recent Studies', Council Paper No. 39, AGPS, Canberra.

Freeman R. (1987) 'International Comparisons of Macroeconomic Performance', paper presented to the ACT Branch of the Australian Economic Society, Canberra.

Gregory R.G. and R.C. Duncan (1979) 'The Labour Market in the 1970s', *Conference in Applied Economic Research,* Reserve Bank of Australia, Sydney.

Gregory R.G. (1982) 'Work and Welfare in the Years Ahead' (Joseph Fisher Lecture 1981, *Australian Economic Papers,* December.

Gregory R.G. (1990) 'Jobs and Gender: A Lego Approach to the Australian Labour Market', Discussion Paper No. 244, Centre for Economic Policy Research, Australian National University.

Higgins C.J. (1979) Comment on Gregory and Duncan 'The Labour Market in the 1970s', *Conference in Applied Economic Research,* Reserve Bank of Australia, Sydney.

INDECS (1981) *State of Play,* Allen & Unwin, Sydney.

Junankar P.N. (1986) *Costs of Unemployment: Main Report,* Commission of the European Communities, Luxembourg.

Junankar P.N. (1987) *Costs of Unemployment: Annex on Social Costs of Unemployment,* Commission of the European Communities, Luxembourg.

Junankar P.N. (1988) *Very Long Term Unemployment,* Commission of the European Communities, Luxembourg.

Junankar P.N. and C. Kapuscinski (1990) 'The Duration of Unemployment in Australia: Memory and Measurement', Discussion Paper No. 238, Centre for Economic Policy Research, Australian National University.

Junankar P.N. and C. Kapuscinski (1991) 'The Incidence of Long Term Unemployment in Australia', Discussion Paper No. 249, Centre for Economic Policy Research, Australan National University.

Jackman, R. and R. Layard (1988), 'Does Long-term Unemployment Reduce a Person's Chance of a Job?: A Time Series Test', Centre for Labour Economics Discussion Paper No. 309, London School of Economics.

Karmel T. (1989) 'The Dynamics of Unemployment Duration', Department of Employment, Education and Training, Economic and Policy Analysis Division, Discussion Paper No. 5, Canberra: AGPS.

Kenyon P. (1990) 'Insiders, Outsiders and Corporatism', paper presented to the 19th Conference of Economists, University of NSW, Sydney, September.

Keyfitz N. (1977) *Applied Mathematical Demography,* New York, Wiley.

Layard R. and Nickell S. (1986) 'Unemployment in Britain', *Economica,* 53, S121–S169.

Lewis P.E.T.and M.G. Kirby (1987) 'The Impact of Incomes Policy on Aggregate Wage Determination in Australia', *The Economic Record,* 63: 156–161.

Lewis P.E.T. and M.G. Kirby (1988) 'A New Approach to Modelling the Effects of Incomes Policies, *Economic Letters,* 28, 81–85.

Mitchell, W.F. (1987) 'The NAIRU, Structural Imbalance and the Macroequilibrium Unemployment Rate', *Australian Economic Papers,* 26(48): 101–118.

Moore D. (1989) 'Industrial Relations and the Failure of the Accord: What should be Done?', *Australian Bulletin of Labour,* 153–183.

Mortensen D.T. (1986) Job search and Labor Market Analysis, in O.C. Ashenfelter and R. Layard (eds), *Handbook of Labor Economics,* Amsterdam: North Holland.

Murphy C. (1989), 'The Model in Detail', *Mimeo,* Economics Department, Research School of Social Sciences, Australian National University.

Newell A. and J. Symons (1987) 'Corporatism, Laissez-faire and the Rise in Unemployment', *European Economic Review,* 31, 567–614.

OECD (1983) *Employment Outlook,* September, Paris: OECD.

Panitch L. (1980) 'Recent Theorisation of Corporatism: Reflections on a Growth Industry', *British Journal of Sociology,* 31 (2), 159–187.

Pissarides C. (1987) 'Real Wages and Unemployment in Australia', Centre for Labour Economics Discussion Paper No. 286, London School of Economics.

Reserve Bank of Australia (1979), *Conference on Applied Economic Research,* Sydney.

Schott K. (1985) 'Australian Wages Policy', *Mimeo,* Sydney.

Sheen R. (1990) 'Australian Industrial Bans, PhD thesis, Department of Political Science, Research School of Social Sciences, Australian National University.

Simes R. (1988) 'The Role of Wages in the Australian Macroeconomy', paper presented to the Australian Economic Congress, ANU, Canberra.

Simes R.M. and C.J. Richardson (1987) 'Wage Determination in Australia', *The Economic Record,* 63 (181): 144–155.

Stilwell F. (1986) *The Accord... and Beyond,* Sydney, Pluto Press.

Treasury (1977), *Budget Statements, 1977–78,* Budget Paper No. 2, Canberra, AGPS.

Treasury (1989), *Budget Statements, 1989–90,* Budget Paper No 1, Canberra: AGPS.

Trivedi, P.K. and W.T. Hui (1987), 'An Empirical Study of Long-term Unemployment in Australia', *Journal of Labor Economics,* 5: 20–42.

Watts M. and W.F. Mitchell (1990) 'Australian Wage Inflation: Real Wage Resistance, Hysteresis, and Incomes Policy 1968(3) –1987(3)', *Manchester School,* Vol LVIII (2), 142–164.

Appendix

Table 4.3.A1 Estimating the Trend Rate of Growth of Participation by Age and Gender

Years 19..	T	A	FW	MW	$\bar{R}^2$	s.e.	Het	Reset	DW
Group F15–19									
66–67	–1.5	–1.0	4.1	#	.66	1.3			2.7
	(–3.6)	(–1.4)	(2.2)						
77–89	–0.1	0.6	X						
	(–0.4)	(2.5)							
Group M15–19									
66–67	–1.3	–1.0	#	4.6	.64	1.4			2.1
	(–3.1)	(–1.4)	#	(1.9)					
77–89	–0.4	0.8	#	X					
	(–3.4)	(3.0)							
Group F20–24									
66–67	0.7	–1.0	#	–0.5	.97	0.9	* *		2.1
	(11.6)	(–2.4)		(–1.5)					
77–89	X	0.3	#	X					
		(6.3)							
Group M20–24									
66–67	–0.1	0.1	#	–0.7	.77	0.8			1.9
	(–0.5)	(1.1)		(–1.2)					
77–89	–0.03	X	#	X					
	(–1.0)								
Group F25–54									
66–78	1.2	0.6	0.5	#	.99	0.4	* *		1.6
	(23.8)	(7.1)	(2.8)						
79–89	X	X	X	–1.6					
				(2.3)					
Group M25–54*									
66–89	–0.2	#	#	0.1	.96	0.3		* *	2.1
	(–6.5)			(0.9)					
Group F55–59									
66–89	0.3	0.6	0.1	#	.67	1.1	* *		2.1
	(2.9)	(3.3)	(0.3)						
Group M55–59									
66–67	#	0.4	#	–2.0	.99	0.7			1.9
		(2.9)		(8.5)					
78–89	–1.0	X	#	0.7					
	(–12.9)			(0.6)					

(continued)

Table 4.3.A1 Continued

Years 19..	T	A	FW	MW	$\bar{R}^2$	s.e.	Het	Reset	DW
Group F60–64									
66–80	–0.1	0.9	#	#	.90	0.7			2.3
	(–2.9)	(4.0)							
81–89	0.3	–0.1	#	–4.5					
	(2.4)	(–0.6)		(–2.6)					
Group M60–64									
66–78	–1.5	3.2	#	#	.99	1.3			2.2
	(–14.8)	(6.6)							
79–89	–1.0	1.9							
	(–6.9)	(7.6)							

Notes:

Dependent variable: the participation rate (%) in August of each year 1966–89, for male (M) or female (F) of specified ages.

Explanatory variables:

T Time trend

A Aggregate employment as a percentage of the 15–64 year old population

MW and FW: Average real hourly earnings for males / females at 1980–81 prices, using junior or adult earnings as appropriate. OLS coefficients are reported with t-statistics in brackets (corrected for heteroscedasticity where appropriate).

\# Indicates that a variable has been omitted because it is not significant at the 20% level.

x Indicates that a coefficient is stable over the two periods.
Where sequential Chow tests have indicated a structural break, the coefficients which are significantly different at the 10% level are reported for both periods; otherwise, the coefficients are assumed to be stable.

* Because a Chow test reveled that there was no structural break between the two periods, the estimated parameters are taken to be constant over 1966–89.

** Indicates heteroscedasticity or functional form mis-specification significant at the 5% level.

4.4

Aboriginal Employment and Unemployment: An Overview

P.N. Junankar and Cezary A. Kapuscinski

Introduction

Aboriginal people face an exceedingly harsh climate[1] in the Australian labour market. They have lower employment rates, lower participation rates, and massively higher unemployment rates than non-Aboriginals. They have lower earnings, are employed in mainly unskilled manual occupations, in short-term dead-end jobs (except in the public service), often in seasonal work, and with no career structure. Life for Aboriginal people in Australia is, in Hobbes' eloquent phrase, "nasty, brutish, and short". Aboriginals have poorer health, higher mortality rates,[2] less education, less training, poor housing and living conditions.

A proper analysis of the labour market behaviour of Aboriginals should distinguish between Outstations, Aboriginal towns, non-Aboriginal towns, and the urban section (cities and large towns).[3] An important analytical distinction is that between Aboriginals who live in a traditional life-style and are not part of a formal labour market, and those who participate (or attempt to) in a formal labour market in urban or rural areas.[4] In a traditional society there is no formal employment (wage labour) or unemployment, although various tasks may be done in a particular structured and traditional manner with the produce beirig shared without the use of a market process. By contrast, there is a formal labour market in both the rural and urban sectors where there is the possibility of wage employment.

There is a direct analogy with the Lewis dual economy model[5] for less developed countries (LDCs) with a traditional non-capitalist sector and a modern (capitalist) sector. However, unlike LDCs, the Australian traditional sector does not provide food for the modern urban sector but only

Reprinted from 'Aboriginal Employment and Unemployment: An Overview' by P. N. Junankar and Cezary A. Kapuscinski in *Economic Papers*, 10 (4), 1991, 30–43. With kind permission from John Wiley & Sons, Inc.

provides some labour that may migrate on a seasonal or semi-permanent basis (although some Aboriginals return to their traditional areas as they get older.[6] The only flow from the modern urban sector to the traditional sector consists of government transfers (unemployment and other social security benefits). These typically provide the wherewithal for the purchase of (for example) motor vehicles, and alcohol. For purpose of analysis we shall consider the labour market to consist of a traditional sector, a rural capitalist sector, and an urban sector (sub-divided into secondary and primary segments).

As mentioned earlier, Aboriginal unemployment rates are very high and the recent downturn in the labour market will almost certainly lead to a more than proportionate rise in their unemployment rates. It will also lead to growth in long term unemployment which will tend to persist for a long time after the recession is over.

Employment, unemployment and participation rates

Introduction

One of the striking features of the Aboriginal labour market is that Aboriginal people have very low participation rates compared to the non-Aboriginal population. This is true in urban areas as well as in rural and remote areas. Similarly they have very low employment/population ratios. Finally they have massive unemployment rates and high long-term unemployment. After providing a conceptual framework, we discuss some of the limitations of the concepts of employment, participation rates, and unemployment rates and then highlight some of the major changes in the Aboriginal labour market with the limited data available. Finally we discuss some of the explanations for the lack of success of Aboriginal people in the labour market.

Conceptual framework

As mentioned earlier, it is possible to think of the interaction of Aboriginal and non-Aboriginal people in the economy in terms of a Lewis-type dual economy model (see Figure 4.4.1). The "traditional sector" consists of Outstations and Aboriginal towns, while the "Modern sector" consists of non-Aboriginal towns and cities and large towns. The distinction we are suggesting is in terms of traditional versus "Western" rather than between rural and urban sectors. The traditional sector provides flows of labour (usually young people of 15–24 years of age) to the modern sector, while the modern sector provides flows of government transfers (unemployment and other social security benefits). In addition, the traditional sector provides some traditional goods and artefacts to the modern sector while the modern sector provides some modern goods (motor vehicles and alcohol) to the traditional sector. There also appears to be a reverse migration from the modern sector to

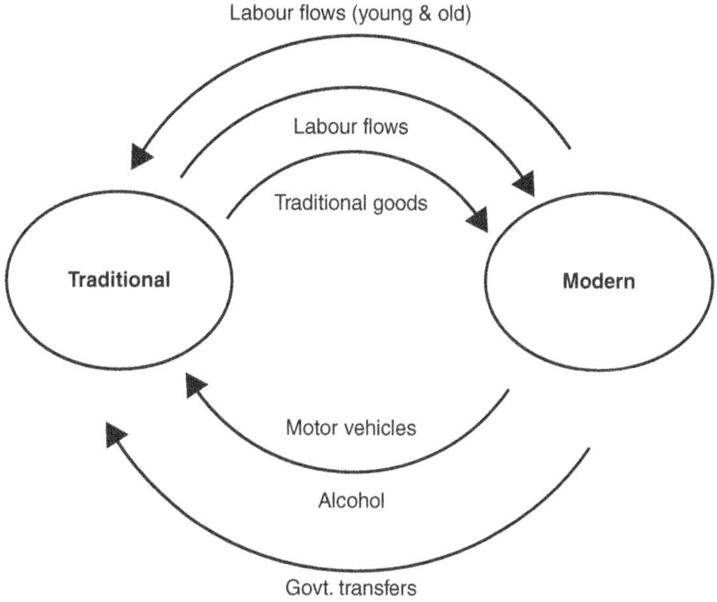

Figure 4.4.1 Lewis Model, traditional and modern sectors

the traditional sector of very young and older Aboriginal people, the former perhaps to obtain family and kinship support, while the latter due to the lack of success in the modern labour market as well as due to housing difficulties. This migration process can be thought of in terms of a Harris-Todaro (1970) model with people migrating from the traditional sector in response to the expected modern sector income (i.e., the wage times the probability of finding work).[8] The migrants to the modern sector would then search for work in a fairly hostile and unfamiliar labour market, without adequate housing or the social support systems they left behind. This would lead to an attempt to congregate in ghettoes. Thus to slow down migration flows we need to make the traditional sector more attractive, rather than increasing employment in the modern sector as it simply attracts more people from the traditional sector without alleviating the unemployment problem. To prevent the flows of the very young and older people from the modern to the traditional sector would require better housing and support systems for families with young children.

We consider the urban labour market as consisting of two main segments: a primary segment with highly paid educated employees with long term jobs and a career structure, and several favourable conditions of work; and a secondary segment consisting of unskilled, poorly educated workers in short term low paid jobs. We expect most of Aboriginal people in the urban sector would be working, or looking for work, in this secondary segment.

The concepts of employment, unemployment, participation rates are really applicable in an economy with a developed wage labour market. For Aboriginal people this is true in the urban sector and in the rural sector in pastoral areas, but it is not true in the traditional communities in remote areas and Outstations. This was emphasised in the Miller Report (1985), "... in these [remote] communities ... conventional labour force concepts such as employment, unemployment and income are often largely irrelevant" (p. 337). This suggests that we should be cautious in interpreting some of the survey data (census or otherwise) which show low employment and participation rates. Even in the modern sector, the concept of unemployment may be inappropriate if people have given up looking for work because they have become discouraged. For these discouraged workers the line between unemployed and not-in-the-labour force is very thin.

The evidence

As mentioned earlier we shall discuss the Aboriginal labour market in terms of modern and traditional sectors. In the modern sector, which includes urban and rural capitalist enterprises and state (Federal, State or local government) enterprises, Aboriginal people may be employed, unemployed, or not-in-the-labour force. Almost all the data we have on Aboriginal people come from the Censuses. Besides problems with self assessment of much information, there is a very high rate of non-response especially to labour force questions.

Although comprising a small proportion of the population (1.5%), the Aboriginals face some of the greatest problems of all disadvantaged groups in the labour market. Unfortunately data on Aboriginals is very limited. The main source of data on labour force status is contained in the five yearly censuses. In addition the Australian Longitudinal Survey provides limited information on unemployment and duration of unemployment for young Aboriginal people. There are various limitations on the data and most commentators believe the data are underestimates of unemployment rates.[9]

Before turning to the labour force aspects, let us look at a few demographic features of the Aboriginal population. Firstly, the Aboriginal population is highly concentrated in a few States. Of the 227,645 Aboriginals in 1986, 52.8% lived in New South Wales and Queensland, with another 31.9% in Western Australia and the Northern Territory. Secondly, 66.7% of them live in Major Urban or Other Urban areas.[10] Thirdly, the population is very young with 40.0% under the age of 15 years, and 52.5% under 20 years. The working age population is 57.6% of the total. This is a reflection of the high birth rate and the high mortality rates.

Many Aboriginals are not involved in the formal labour market, and many are "working" in the government's Community Employment Programme/ Community Development Employment Programme. For many of these people this is not really employment but simply a form of unemployment benefits. Employment in subsistence living is not included as employment. Some Aboriginals live in remote rural areas and may not remain in the same place for long. All this means that the data on employment, unemployment, and participation for Aboriginals should be treated as being subject to an undefined measurement error.

Not withstanding that, the official unemployment rates of Aboriginals are usually *at least* three times that of the non-Aboriginal population. Just as the overall unemployment rate has tended upwards over the 1970s and the early part of the 1980s, the Aboriginal unemployment rate increased dramatically (see Table 4.4.1). In 1971 the Aboriginal unemployment rate was 9.2% (9.7 for males and 8.1 for females) of the labour force increasing to 24.5% (25.9 for males and 22.3 for females) in 1981 and to a massive 35.4% (36.0 for males and 34.2 for females) in 1986. Another indication of the difficulties faced by Aboriginals is to look at the Employment/Population ratio. The Employment/Population ratio fell from 41.4% (60.4 for males and 21.7 for females) in 1971 to 31.3% (40.4 for males and 22.7 for females) in 1986. This is in contrast to the overall Employment/Population ratio which decreased from 79.1% to 66.9% for males and increased from 36.3% to 42.3% for females.

Another feature of the Aboriginal labour market is the very low labour force participation rates. In 1986 the participation rate for Aboriginal males was 63.1% and 34.5% for Aboriginal females. This contrasts with 73.5% for all males and 46.8% for all females.

The Census data for 1986 (Table 4.4.2) provide an interesting description of unemployment rates for Aboriginals and non-Aboriginals by State and Urban/Rural breakdown. This again shows clearly that the Aboriginals have higher unemployment rates in all States and in Major Urban, Other Urban, and in All Rural areas. This is true for males and females. If we ignore the ACT as being unrepresentative, the Aboriginals have unemployment rates of between three and /our times the non-Aboriginals. The highest Aboriginal unemployment rate is for the Rural sector of New South Wales while the lowest is for Rural Tasmania. The unemployment issue for Aboriginals is not only a rural problem but also a significant urban problem with unemployment rates of 43.4% in West Australia, 32.1% in Queensland, and 29.7% in NSW for males in the major urban areas.

The evidence from unemployment rates by age provide another worrying picture of unemployment among Aboriginals. Young Aboriginals (15–19 year olds) experience almost twice the unemployment rate of all Australians. Table 4.4.3 shows the unemployment rates and employment/population ratios by age for the 1986 census year. The unemployment rates decline more or less uniformly with age while the employment/population ratios follow an inverse U-shape. Again these figures show the serious nature of the problem, especially for young people, with unemployment rates of between

Table 4.4.1 Labour Force Status of Persons Aged 15 Years and Over: 1971–86

Year	Employment/ Population (%)	Unemployment rate (%)	Labour force/ pop. (%)
		Aboriginal population: males	
1971	60.4	9.7	66.9
1976	56.2	18.3	68.8
1981	47.0	25.9	63.4
1986	40.4	36.0	63.1
		Aboriginal population: females	
1971	21.7	8.1	23.6
1976	25.1	16.9	30.2
1981	24.8	22.3	31.9
1986	22.7	34.2	34.5
		Aboriginal population: total	
1971	41.4	9.2	45.6
1976	40.7	17.8	49.5
1981	35.7	24.5	47.3
1986	31.3	35.4	48.3
		Total population: males	
1971	79.1	1.5	80.3
1976	76.1	4.0	79.3
1981	73.1	5.4	77.3
1986	66.9	9.0	73.5
		Total population: females	
1971	36.3	2.2	37.1
1976	41.6	5.0	43.8
1981	42.5	6.8	45.6
1986	42.3	9.6	46.8
		Total population	
1971	57.7	1.7	58.7
1976	58.7	4.4	61.4
1981	57.6	6.0	61.3
1986	54.4	9.3	60.0

Note: The Not Stated in 1986 are included with those not in the labour force.
Source: Tesfaghiorgis and Altman (1990).

40% and 50%. The comparable data from the 1981 Census show that the situation has got worse rather than better, with unemployment rates consistently higher for each age group in 1986 compared to 1981.

Employed Aboriginal people are mainly wage and salary earners (95.7%) and a large proportion are employed in the public sector (43%, which is likely to be an under estimate as people employed in publicly-funded community organisations are treated as private sector employees). (Public sector

Table 4.4.2 Unemployment Rates (In Per cent) For Males And Females Aged 15 To 64: 1986

Area	Males		Females	
	Aboriginals	Non-Aboriginals	Aboriginals	Non-Aboriginals
		Australia		
Major Urban	31.2	8.3	27.3	8.8
Other Urban	39.9	9.9	37.2	11.5
All Rural	35.1	9.6	37.0	9.5
		New South Wales		
Major Urban	29.7	9.0	27.0	9.5
Other Urban	48.2	11.1	45.7	12.7
All Rural	52.1	12.1	47.7	11.4
		Victoria		
Major Urban	20.0	6.2	18.8	7.5
Other Urban	28.9	7.2	31.2	9.4
All Rural	27.7	6.5	25.8	7.4
		Queensland		
Major Urban	32.1	9.8	30.0	10.6
Other Urban	36.3	11.1	37.0	12.7
All Rural	29.3	10.9	39.0	11.3
		South Australia		
Major Urban	40.4	9.8	31.6	9.2
Other Urban	45.4	10.6	39.5	11.1
All Rural	24.7	8.2	18.7	7.3
		Western Australia		
Major Urban	43.4	9.2	35.1	9.1
Other Urban	44.0	8.6	40.8	11.1
All Rural	33.4	7.3	32.7	7.7
		Tasmania		
Major Urban	22.6	8.8	20.3	8.3
Other Urban	23.4	10.1	22.3	11.2
All Rural	17.7	10.6	17.4	10.3
		Northern Territory		
Other Urban	30.9	7.7	23.1	8.1
All Rural	39.3	7.4	40.0	6.8
		Australian Capital Territory		
Major Urban	10.9	4.1	9.5	5.4
All Rural	48.7	3.2	38.9	7.6

Notes: (1) Major Urban = Population in excess of 100,000.
(2) Other Urban = Population between 1,000 and 100,000.
(3) All Rural = rest of State or Territory.
(4) Source: ABS 1986 Census Microfiche.

Table 4.4.3 Aboriginal Labour Force Status, By Age, 1986

Age	Unemployment rate	Employment/ Population rate	Unemployment rate	Employment/ Population rate
	Males		Females	
15–19	51.3	24.0	51.7	18.3
20–24	41.5	43.6	38.5	27.3
25–29	34.2	50.4	31.1	25.6
30–34	32.2	51.8	24.0	27.6
35–39	28.3	53.0	22.8	29.8
40–44	25.5	51.4	21.1	28.2
45–49	24.8	49.5	22.4	23.9
50–54	26.2	41.0	20.5	18.3
55–59	24.4	35.1	18.1	14.4
60–64	27.1	20.0	27.9	5.8
15–64	36.0	41.9	34.0	23.8

Source: ABS 1986 Census.

employees are not, of course, in a secondary segment.) Figure 4.4.2 illustrates the levels of full-time employment in the Australian Public Service of Aboriginals and All Australians. Since 1980 there is an increase in absolute numbers in employment as well as in their employment relative to the total.

The main industries of employment were community services (30%), public administration (13%), wholesale and retail trades (10%), manufacturing (9%) and agriculture (7%). Almost three-quarters of the employed Aboriginal males were concentrated in three occupational groups, labourers and related workers (39%), tradespersons (19%) and plant and machine operators and drivers (15%). Aboriginal women were concentrated in clerical (33%), labourers and related workers (23%) and personal services and sales (16%). Not surprisingly, there were very few employed in managerial and professional occupations (9% compared to 24% for all Australians).

The extent of long-term unemployment for Aboriginals is significantly higher than non-Aboriginals and increased over the 1980s. Data on unemployment duration are scarce and in Table 4.4.4 below we present information based on the Commonwealth Employment Service data on Unemployed Awaiting Placement (UAP). This is based on the CES UAP register of a quarterly stock figure showing the number of records held for persons who indicated, when registering with the CES, that they were unemployed or worked for less than 15 hours per week (note that for the ABS definition of unemployed they cannot work for more than one hour a week) and were seeking full time work. Generally the UAP figures are much higher than the ABS figures and are not really a reliable indicator of unemployment." It is a very imperfect measure but may still provide some rough

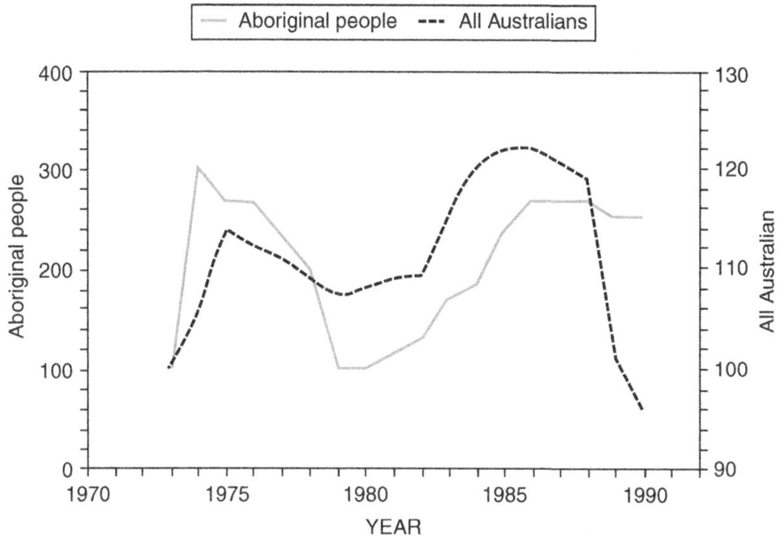

Figure 4.4.2 Full-Time Employment In The Australian Public Service (Index Numbers: 1973 = 100.0)

Table 4.4.4 Unemployment And Long Term Unemployment: CES Data

Period	**Aboriginals**			**Non-Aboriginals**		
	UAP(1)	*LTU*(2)	*PLTU*(3)	*UAP*	*LTU*	*PLTU*
Sept. 1983	20352	8260	40.6	755510	230555	30.5
Sept. 1984	21960	7645	34.8	730940	211409	28.9
Sept. 1985	23474	8387	35.7	687647	204443	29.7
Sept. 1986	29231	6972	23.9	739396	134853	18.2
Sept. 1987	33720	7873	23.3	769906	162819	21.1
Sept. 1988	35623	11630	32.6	706696	175970	24.9
Sept. 1989	29655	8931	30.1	562637	109095	19.4
Sept. 1990	35188	10684	30.4	740961	116294	15.7

Notes: (1) UAP = Unemployed Awaiting Placement.
(2) LTU = Long Term Unemployed defined as 9 months and over for the period 1983/1985 and 12 months and over for the period 1986/1990.
(3) PLTU = Percentage of unemployed who are LTU.
(4) The data for 1990 is for June—the latest data available.
(5) *Source*: Commonwealth Employment Service, unpublished tabulations.

indication of the problem of long-term unemployment (LTU) amongst the Aboriginals. Table 4.4.4 shows that the proportion of Aboriginals who were in LTU fell from 40.6% in September 1983 to 30.4% in June 1990. For non-Aboriginals the corresponding figures are 30.5% and 15.7% respectively. In other words, Aboriginals have a higher proportion of LTU and although there was a fall in Aboriginal LTU proportions, the fall was much greater for the non-Aboriginals. We suspect that the real figures may be worse because of the problem of recurrent unemployment faced by Aboriginal people who work in seasonal and other short-term jobs, so that many more may face long total spells of unemployment over some period.

Miller (1987) (presented as Table 4.4.5) shows that Aboriginals have a significantly higher proportion in long term unemployment (*defined* here as 39 weeks or more). In general, the higher the unemployment rate the greater the duration of unemployment and hence we would expect the duration of unemployment amongst Aboriginals to be greater than non-Aboriginals. Miller (1987) also shows that the expected duration of unemployment of Aboriginals is significantly higher than of non-Aboriginals controlling for various family and labour market characteristics.

As is well known, the level of schooling received by Aboriginal people is low, especially in the rural and remote areas.[12] Almost 65% of Aboriginal people over the age of 15 had left school before 16 years of age, 8% (of those not at school) had never been to school, and only 15% had any post-school qualifications (compared to 26% for all Australians). This low schooling may be one of the explanations for the high unemployment rates.

Labour market programmes[13]

Over the years there have been several labour market programmes aimed at the unemployed and the long term unemployed, and these are discussed in

Table 4.4.5 Percentage Distribution of Young Unemployed Across Duration Categories: June 1985

	Duration category					
	Less than 14 weeks	14–39 weeks	Over 39 weeks	Less than 14 weeks	14–19 weeks	Over 39 weeks
	Age group: 15–19			Age group: 20–24		
MALES						
Aboriginals	41.53	37.84	20.63	34.39	35.73	29.90
Non-Aboriginals	41.83	42.86	15.31	40.24	38.49	21.27
FEMALES						
Aboriginals	41.02	38.04	20.95	34.08	36.11	29.81
Non-Aboriginals	41.74	42.03	16.23	40.28	37.68	22.04
PERSONS						
Aboriginals	42.33	37.53	20.14	35.21	34.76	30.03
Non-Aboriginals	41.93	43.86	14.20	40.17	39.92	19.90

Source: Miller (1987).

Cass (1988). Labour market programmes are of different kinds: firstly, training programmes, general or specific; secondly, job creation programmes; thirdly, job subsidy programmes; fourthly, job placement and counselling programmes. Some of the programmes have been aimed at the LTU, e.g. JOBTRAIN, Community Employment Programme, or JOBSTART. Assistance for Aboriginals is provided by the government under the Aboriginal Employment Development Policy (AEDP). There are a series of programmes to help provide employment and training in the modern labour market as well as in rural and remote communities. Some of these come under the Training for Aboriginals Programme (TAP) and for 1990/91 the budget allocated $87,440 to cover an estimated 14,700 persons.

In Table 4.4.6 we provide some information on the numbers of (mainly) LTU people who were supported by government programmes. Support for Aboriginals is also given in the table under the Aboriginal Employment and Training programmes.

In the 1990/91 Budget a complete revision of the unemployment benefit system was announced. Unemployment benefits would be abolished and replaced by a Job Search Allowance for the first twelve months of unemployment and then followed by a NEWSTART allowance for the LTU. The

Table 4.4.6 Number of Approvals for Various Labour Market Programmes

Financial year	**Labour market programmes**		
	JOBSTART	**Community Employment Programme (CEP)**	**Aboriginal Employment and Training**
1981/82			4533[e]
1982/83			5594[e]
1983/84		30450[c]	9162[3]
1984/85		46670[c]	9998[e]
1985/86	36065[a]	37019[c]	10173[e]
1986/87	64589[a]	20934[c]	11426[f]
1987/88	46147[a]	9659[d]	12700[f]
1988/89	40385[a]		10720[g]
1989/90	34600[b]		12745[h]
1990/91	44000[b]		14700[h]

Note: Numbers in italics are estimates.

Sources: (a) JOBSTART Evaluation, prepared by the Programme Review and Income Support Branch for Training and Adjustment Assistance Branch, December 1989.

(b) DEET, 1990/91 Programmes, p. 72.

(c) SWRC Report and Proceedings, September 1989.

(d) Labour Market Policies for the 1990s, OECD, Paris, 1990.

(e) DEIR, Programmes 1986/87, August 1986, Appendix B.

(f) Skills for Australia, 1987.

(g) DEET, 1989/90 Programmes, August 1989, Appendix 2.

(h) DEET, 1990/91 Programmes, August 1990, p. 85.

important new change was to make the transition from the JOBSTART Allowance to NEWSTART non-automatic. The unemployed have to prove to the DSS that they are actively searching for work. Under the new Active Employment Strategy an integrated package of assistance comprising JOBTRAIN, JOBSTART, and various placement and counselling services are to be provided. These new provisions begin next year at a time when the labour market is going into a downturn. It is not clear how provision of more skills and active placement and counselling would help in a situation where the number of job vacancies are falling rapidly. Recent work suggests that in periods of high unemployment, these programmes are not effective, see Stretton and Chapman (1990).

Policies and policy recommendations

It is difficult to follow the recommendations of the excellent Miller Report (1987) with anything like the same depth and comprehensiveness. The policies can be roughly subsumed under two heads: (a) those policies that provide training and assistance for Aboriginal people to enter the modern sector urban labour market; and (b) those policies that encourage the improvement of the traditional sector (say) via assistance with traditional activities like artefacts for sale to the modern sector.

We would recommend that a major avenue to improve the condition of Aboriginal people requires the granting of land rights which would provide them with the economic base for a sustained improvement in their lifestyle. To quote the Miller Report (1987):

> We believe the ownership of land as an economic base is fundamental to Aboriginal prospects for providing for their livelihood, (p. 17)

Even though some land has been transferred (large amounts in the Northern Territory, but only small amounts in New South Wales), most of it is poor quality land and mineral rights are limited.[14]

The importance of land rights is not simply in terms of gaining an economic base but also in providing cultural identity and self-respect. Almost as importantly, in our Lewis/Harris-Todaro framework, land rights would decrease migration from the traditional sector to the modern sector where many of the Aboriginals are unemployed or have poorly-paid, short-term employment with inadequate housing and social support systems. This policy would decrease unemployment as well as increasing the welfare of the traditional Aboriginal society.

Another suggestion for improvement of the employment prospects of Aboriginal people would be to have positive discrimination. The aim of the Commonwealth to employ at least 1–2% of the Australian Public Service from the Aboriginal population is a start, although at present it is just over 1%.

Our last suggestion is to improve the quality of data on Aboriginal people. This would be ideally done by carrying out a longitudinal survey, but failing that at least annual surveys. If money is a major problem these surveys could be restricted to a couple of States, e.g. Queensland and New South Wales. Finally, we would recommend that data collected by the CES, DSS, and other government agencies on Aboriginal labour force status be published regularly.

Conclusions

In this paper we have argued that Aboriginal people have a low employment rate, high unemployment rates, and high long-term unemployment. Given that the Aboriginal population is expected to continue to grow, we need to create several thousand new jobs over the next ten years (approximately 56,000 jobs) to keep the unemployment rate at its 1986 level. However, if we want to decrease the Aboriginal unemployment rate by the year 2001 to a "modest" 10%, we would need to create an additional 78,000 jobs.[15] Based on the 1986 Census figures, this translates into 14,000 new positions in the industry sector (mining, manufacturing and construction) and 58,000 new positions in the services sector. This is a massive undertaking especially as the economy is now in a recession.

We have argued that a significant improvement cannot come about unless there is a major effort on the part of government to provide land and mineral rights. This would not only improve the conditions of those in the traditional areas but also slow down the flow of Aboriginal migrants to the urban areas to join the poor, unemployed, poorly housed, and down and out.

Notes

Public Policy Program, Australian National University. Paper presented to a Workshop organised by the Academy of Social Sciences in Australia and the Centre for Aboriginal Economic Policy Research on Aboriginal Employment Equity By The Year 2000, held at the Australian National University, Canberra, 20–21 March 1991. We are grateful to Steve Albin, Jon Altman and Habtemariam Tesfaghiorghis, Robert Castle, Don Clark, Bob Davidson, Russell Ross and Alan Stretton for helpful conversations and providing us with some of the data used in this paper. Margi Wood and Yong Ping Li provided excellent research assistance. They are not, of cour+se, responsible for sins of omission or commission.

1. Many of them live in an exceedingly harsh physical climate as well.
2. See Thomson (1991).
3. This is emphasised in the Miller Report (1987), see p. 33 ff. However, Census data only allows a distinction between Other Rural, Rural, Other Urban, and Urban areas.
4. Altman (1988) makes this distinction as well.
5. See Lewis (1954).
6. See Gray (1989).

7. See Miller (1987), Ch. 2.1, for a brief review.
8. This is consistent with the findings of Gray (1989).
9. See Castle (1987) for an interesting study of rural NSW. Also see Ross (1990).
10. The breakdown between urban and rural areas in the census is affected by the time at which it is carried out as some Aboriginals move from rural to urban areas at some times of the year. This suggests caution in using this data without qualification.
11. In addition to other problems data on duration for Aboriginals may be underestimates because of people moving away from one location to another. CBS Offices may also not be available in remote areas.
12. Table 6.21 of ABS (1991) provides details.
13. See Stretton and Chapman (1990) for a recent analysis. A useful summary of various labour market programmes is given in Kesteven (1987).
14. For an interesting paper on land rights, see Altman (1990).
15. This is based on some crude projections by the authors.

Bibliography

Altman, J. (1988), "Economic Status", in *Australian People: An Encyclopedia of the Nation, Its People and their Origins*, Sydney, Angus and Robertson.

Altman, J. (1990). "The Economic Impact of Australian Aboriginal Land Rights", paper presented to the New Zealand Association of Economists Sesquicentennial Conference, Auckland, New Zealand.

ABS (1991), *Australia's Aboriginal and Torres Strait Islander People*, Canberra, Commonwealth of Australia.

Cass, B. (1988), *Income Support for the Unemployed in Australia: Towards a More Active System*, Social Security Review Issues Paper No. 4, Canberra, AGPS.

Castle, R. (1989), *Employment Prospects /or Aboriginals in Rural Labour Markets*, Report to the Australian Council for Employment and Training, Canberra, AGPS.

Gray, A. (1989), "Aboriginal Migration to the Cities", *Journal of the Australian Population Association*, 6 (2), 122–144.

Harris, J.R. and M.P. Todaro (1970), "Migration, Unemployment and Development: A Two Sector Analysis", *American Economic Review*, 60 (1), 126–142.

Junankar, P.N. and C.A. Kapuscinski (1991), "The Incidence of Long Term Unemployment in Australia". Centre for Economic Policy Research, ANU, Canberra, Discussion Paper No. 249.

Kesteven, S. (1987), *Commonwealth Employment and Training Schemes Since 1973*, Current Issues Paper No. 1, 1987–88, Legislative Research Service, Department of the Parliamentary Library.

Kryger, T. (1990), *The Australian Longitudinal Survey: 1985 to 1988—Dynamics of the Youth Labour Market*, DEET, Monograph Series No. 4, Canberra, AGPS.

Lewis, W.A. (1954), "Economic Development with Unlimited Supplies of Labour", *Manchester School*, 22, 139–191.

Miller, P.W. (1987), *The Structure and Dynamics of Aboriginal and Non-Aboriginal Youth Unemployment*, Report to the Australian Council for Employment and Training, Canberra, AGPS.

Ross, R.T. (1988), "The Labour Market Position of Aboriginal People in Non-Metropolitan NSW", *Australian Bulletin of Labour*, 15, 29–56.

Ross, R.T. (1990), "A Probit Analysis of the Factors Influencing Labour Market Success of Aborigines in NSW", Paper presented to the Nineteenth Conference of Economists, University of NSW.

Saunders, P. and A. Jamrozik (eds) (1989), *Social Policy and Inequality in Australia and New Zealand,* Social Welfare Research Centre, University of New South Wales, Sydney.

Stretton, A. and B.J. Chapman (1990), "An Analysis of Australian Labour Market Programs", Paper presented to the NBEET Conference on "A Clever Country? Australian Education and Training in Perspective", 1–3 November 1990, Coffs Harbour, NSW.

Tesfaghiorghis, H. and J. Altman (1990), "Aboriginal Socio-Economic Status: Are There Any Evident Changes?", Paper presented to the Australian Consortium for Social and Political Research, Brisbane.

Thomson, N.J. (1991), "Recent Trends in Aboriginal Mortality", *The Medical Journal of Australia,* 154, February 18, 235–239.

4.5
Unemployment in Australia: Models, Myths and Mysteries

P.N. (Raja) Junankar

The aim of this paper is to discuss the problem of unemployment and long term unemployment in Australia. We shall discuss the causes of unemployment, the policies introduced by different governments to alleviate the problem, and the consequences of high unemployment. Some economists believe that unemployment is caused by a lack of aggregate demand, and the impact of structural and technological change on the labour market. The popular myths are that unemployment is caused by: high wages, inflexible labour markets, "generous" unemployment benefits, "unfair" competition from Asian low wage economies. However, unemployment rates in most OECD countries follow similar paths even though they have different institutional and policy frameworks. This suggests that unemployment is still a mystery to be explained. Finally, the paper discusses the serious consequences of unemployment for the unemployed, the families of the unemployed, and for the employed: mental and physical illness, increased crime and social problems, and loss of income. Given these high economic and social costs, why do governments allow unemployment to remain at such high levels?

A spectre hangs over the OECD: it is the spectre of mass (and continuing) long term unemployment.

1 Introduction

Full employment has ended. Even as a policy goal it is dead. Most political parties seem to think it is a mirage. The best we have is a target of a 5% unemployment rate by some unspecified date in the future[1]. In most western countries the labour market has changed irrevocably: there has been a shift from full time male employment in the manufacturing sector (with life-long jobs) to part time (mainly female) short term unemployment in the service sector. This has been accompanied by an increasing trend in unemployment

Reprinted from 'Unemployment in Australia: Models, Myths and Mysteries' by P. N. (Raja) Junankar in *Economic Papers*, 18 (1), 1999, 11–32. With kind permission from John Wiley & Sons, Inc.

(especially youth unemployment), long term unemployment, increasing wage inequality, and the growth of an underclass. The response of (many) governments has been to set up Commissions of Inquiry, publish White Papers, tighten up social security benefits, lower tax rates for the rich, and to emasculate the trade unions. However, unemployment remains a major economic, social, and political problem. What explains these trends? Why are governments unable to tackle this serious problem? What is to be done?

An especially worrying feature of the growth of unemployment is that it seems to go up rapidly but decrease very slowly, and on each successive occasion the trough of unemployment is higher. This process that the path of unemployment takes appears to be time dependent is called "hysteresis". The reasons for hysteresis are thought to be the lower probability of the long term unemployed finding work because of decreased job-search by them due to a loss of self esteem, because of skill atrophy, and employers rejecting them because they use unemployment as a signal of poor qualities. In addition, in the macroeconomics sphere the long term unemployed have no impact on wage bargaining and hence it increases the so-called non-accelerating inflation rate of unemployment (NAIRU). At the end of each recession there are more people who are unable to find work for longer and longer periods.

Many of the unemployed who are over 45 years old have reached their "use by" date as far as the labour market is concerned. They have been dispatched to the dust bin of history. Almost 50% of the unemployed in the European Union (EU) have been unemployed for more than one year, and almost half of these long term unemployed have been unemployed for more than two years. The numbers for Australia are a little better as about 35% long term unemployed and more than half of the long term unemployed have been unemployed for more than two years.

One of the obvious forces behind these trends in employment and unemployment is the growth of gross domestic product (GDP). However, there have been significant structural changes with a shift away from industrial production toward the service sector. Technological change has led to a shift in employment away from large scale production in "smoke stack industries" using full-time unskilled labour to small high tech firms in the "sunrise industries" using skilled part-time labour. Another reason often suggested for these trends in western developed countries is competition from the 'Asian tigers". However, the evidence for this is still to be produced. So-called rational economists argue that the high rates of unemployment and long term unemployment are due to the "generous" unemployment benefits that are paid for long periods of time. It is also argued that the interaction of the tax system with the social security benefit system decreases the incentive for low skilled workers accepting low paid jobs. However, the welfare state in Australia prevents the growth of an alternative labour market status: criminal activity. In the United States, measured unemployment rates are relatively low, with very poor social security payments, which means that the unemployed have to hustle on the streets to survive. There are increasingly large numbers of young people in Australia who have very high unemployment rates and are slowly falling into the so-called underclass.

The costs of unemployment are very high both for the unemployed and their families, and for society in terms of social problems like physical and mental illness, family breakdown, and increased crime. There are also significant economic costs for society in terms of loss of GDP in the present and in the future. Why, then, do governments not try to eliminate unemployment? Most EU governments (like the Australian government) have several active labour market policies: training for the unemployed, wage subsidy programs, etc. Unfortunately, the Coalition government has been abolishing many of these labour market programs and introduced work for the dole programs that do not provide adequate training. However, these active labour market programs usually work in association with macroeconomic policies to stimulate the economy. But most governments seem to be overly concerned about the impact these policies may have on the inflation rate even though inflation rates in most of the OECD countries are at historically low rates. We need to persuade governments that they should wage a "war on unemployment": encourage expansion of labour intensive industries (social services, health, education), provide training and assistance for the unemployed, provide subsidies to employers to hire the long term unemployed, and provide a stimulus to the economy. Governments should not sacrifice thousands of unemployed people to appease the "gods of inflation".

2 Definitions of Unemployment and Long Term Unemployment

The most common measure of unemployment is based on the ABS Labour Force Sample Surveys: every month the ABS sends out a survey to households and a "responsible adult" answers on behalf of the household. A person is considered to be unemployed if he/she is not working for more than one hour in the relevant week, is looking for work, and is available for work. However, the data are subject to recall errors and to respondent error. Long term unemployment is usually defined as a continuous spell of one year or more.

It is worth noting that the unemployment rate in the UK is measured as the number of people in receipt of unemployment benefits. As a result it is possible to reduce their unemployment rate at the stroke of a legislative pen. That is exactly what former Prime Minister Margaret Thatcher did. It appears, in the light of a recent discussion paper from Mr Reith's office[2], that the Australian government has taken a leaf from Thatcher's book, and all the long term unemployed will be required to work for the dole—which by definition removes them from unemployment.

Usual measures of unemployment are measures of the *stock* of unemployment at a point in time. Changes in this stock of unemployment come about by inflows into the stock and outflows from the stock. The inflows (those joining the unemployment stock) may have come from employment, not in the labour force (NILF), or new entrants (some from educational establishments). The outflows from unemployment may find work, leave the labour force (retire early, fall sick, or give up hope, i.e., join the NILF), or go into labour market programs, e.g., training schemes, see Figure 4.5.1D In simple form:

$$U_t = U_{t-1} + I_t - X_t \tag{1}$$

where the U's are unemployment stocks at the end of periods, and I denotes inflows into the unemployment stock and X denotes outflows (X for exits) from the unemployment stock (the flows are measured over the period).

$$\text{Inflows } (I_t) = \text{Quits} + \text{Fires} + \text{New Entrants}$$

Outflows (X_t)=New Hires+Retires, Deaths+New participants in Labour Market Program.

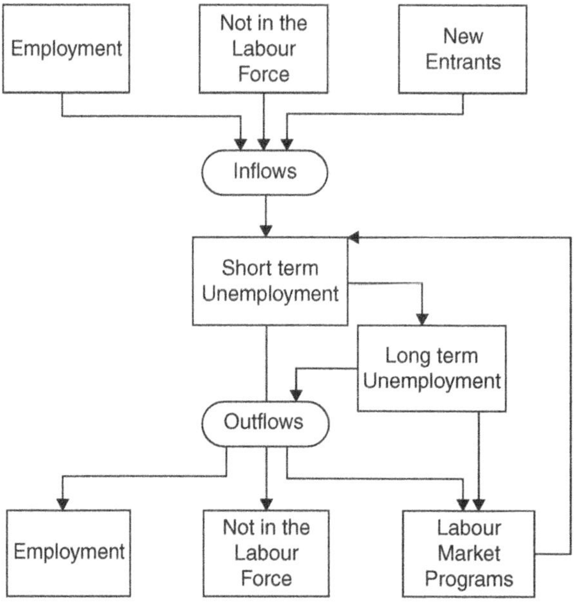

Figure 4.5.1D Unemployment: Stocks and Flows

What is interesting is that there are very large flows between these different labour market states: simply looking at the stocks may give a misleading picture (see later under Section 5).

3 Recent Trends in Employment and Unemployment

To provide a context to our discussion on unemployment we present some information on broad trends in employment and unemployment over the past few decades. A look at the aggregate time series data shows that female full time employment has grown faster than male full time employment; however, male part time employment has grown faster than female part time employment since the early nineties, see Figures 4.5.1 and 4.5.2[3]. This is contrary to popular mythology that female employment growth has been mainly part time and male employment growth has been mainly full time.

Unemployment rates for both males and females have been increasing over the past two decades, although in the earlier period female unemployment rates were higher than male unemployment rates. Since the early nineties male unemployment rates exceed female rates, see Figure 4.5.3. It appears that unemployment rates increase with each recession but never come down to their original levels during the subsequent recovery: there appears to be hysteresis in the process. Hysteresis, the time dependent nature of unemployment, it is argued, is due to either the unemployed workers losing skills (skill atrophy, or loss of human capital) which makes

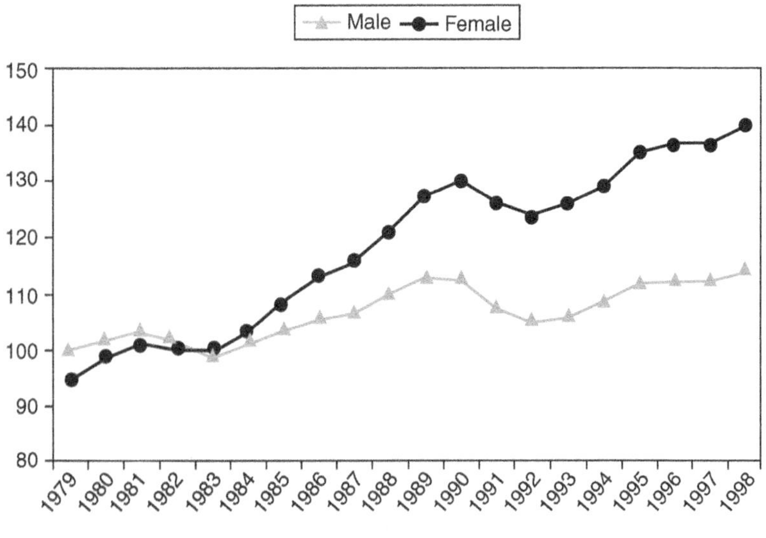

Figure 4.5.1 Male and Female Full Time Employment 1979–1998 (1983=100)
Source: ABS 6203.0.

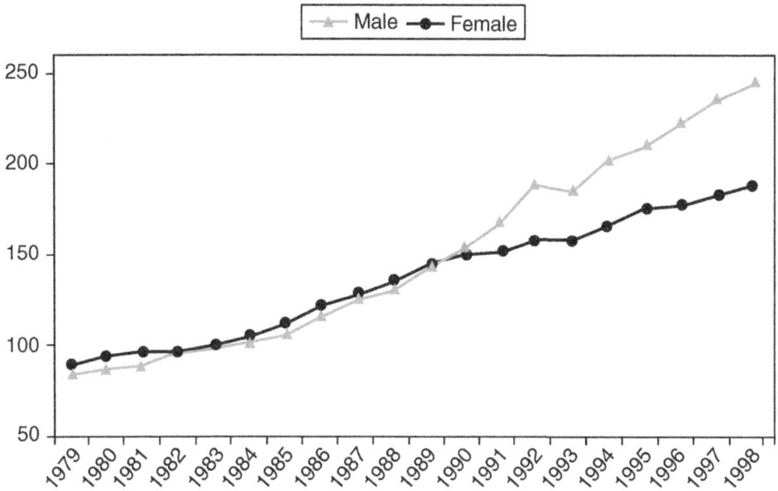

Figure 4.5.2 Male and Female Part Time Employment 1979–1998 (1983=100)
Source: ABS 6203.0.

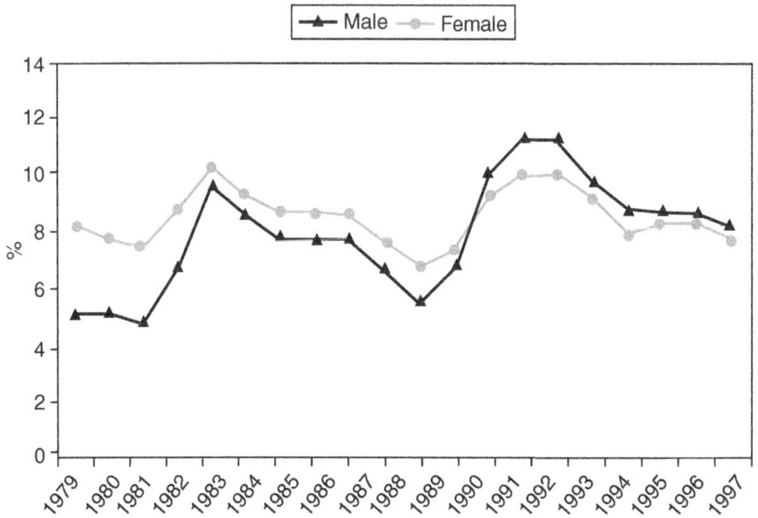

Figure 4.5.3 Male and Female Unemployment Rates 1979–1998
Source: ABS 6203.0.

them less employable, or due to employers using their unemployment status as a signal that they are "unemployable", or both. Hence an unemployed person has great difficulty in finding work and it becomes increasingly difficult with the duration of unemployment. This concept of hysteresis is used to explain the ratchetting up of unemployment over the past few decades.

When we look at unemployment rates by educational levels it is clear that the less educated have higher rates of unemployment. This is illustrated in Figures 4.5.4a and 4.5.4b. There is much evidence that the probability of finding work for the less educated is much lower than for the more highly educated, and hence they have longer spells of unemployment. However, when we look at the time paths of unemployment rates with and without post school education we note that they move very closely together. In fact, the *percentage increase* in unemployment rates from 1979 to 1997 is *higher* for those with degrees than those with post school qualifications, although it is true that the unemployment rate has increased substantially for those without post school qualifications (see Table 4.5.1). A simple regression of the unemployment rate of people with post-school qualifications on the unemployment rate without post school qualifications gives a positive relation with an adjusted R squared of 0.81, i.e., a fairly close correlation between the two series.

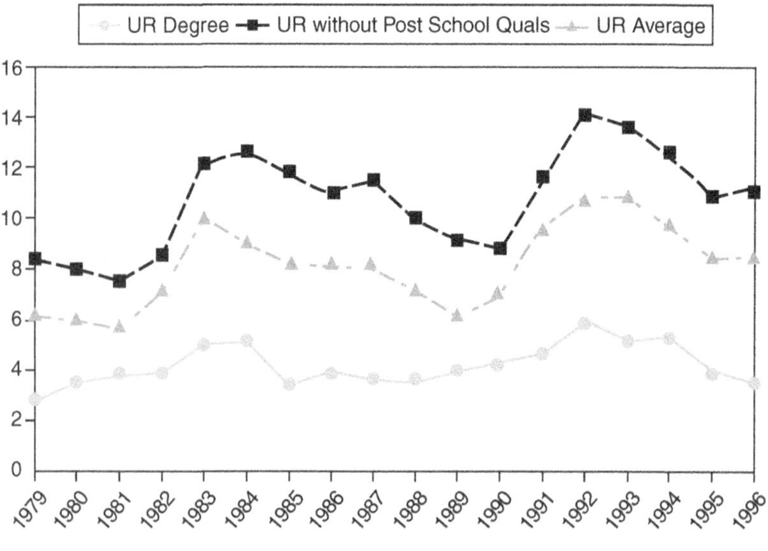

Figure 4.5.4a Unemployment Rates: With Degrees and Without Post School Qualifications
Source: ABS 6235.0 and 6203.0.

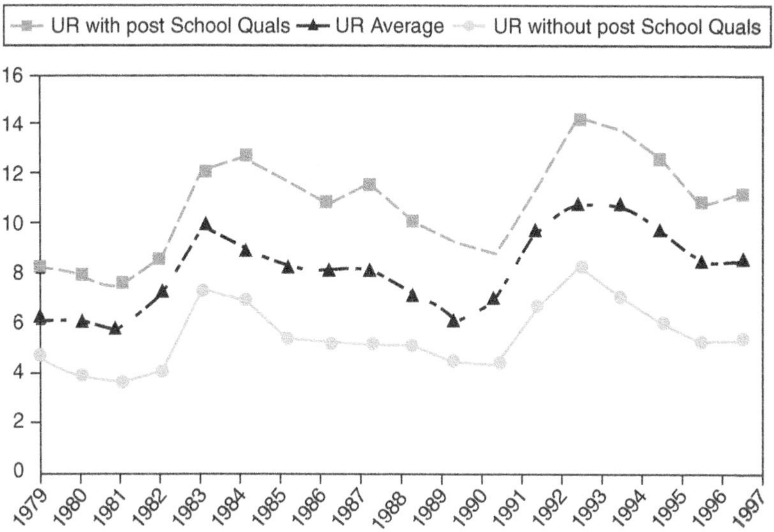

Figure 4.5.4b Unemployment Rates: With and Without Post School Qualifications
Source: ABS 6235.0 and 6203.0.

Table 4.5.1 Percentage Increase In Unemployment Rates By Educational Levels

	1979	1997	Percentage Increase
UR with post school qualifications	4.7	5.4	14.9
UR with degree	2.8	3.6	28.6
UR without post school qualifications	8.3	11.2	34.9

Source: ABS 6235.0 and 6203.0.

A short while ago the government announced that the unemployed would have to take a literacy test and those who refused to go back to school would be penalised by having their dole cut. What the time series evidence suggests is that, although it is true that the less well educated have higher rates of unemployment, it makes little difference if they simply increased their education levels; there is a fallacy of composition. One individual may increase her probability of finding a job, but if everyone gets more education it does not help unless we increase the number of jobs available. As Figure 4.5.4 shows the unemployment rate of graduates has increased even though the number of graduates has increased significantly.

This suggests that simply increasing the educational levels of the workforce does not necessarily solve the problem of unemployment. There is a problem of a "credentialism inflation": as the job market gets tighter employers demand higher qualifications for the same job.

There has been an increasing use of casual and part time workers, a growth of so-called "non-traditional" forms of employment, with increased job insecurity. With increasing unemployment there has been increased pressure on the unemployed to work harder and to increase efficiency: this has resulted in increased unpaid overtime, see Wooden (1997). There has also been a shift from blue collar to white collar employment in most OECD countries including Australia, see OECD (1992). These changes in the labour market have also led to increased wage inequality, see Borland (1996b), Gregory (1993b) and King, Rimmer and Rimmer (1992).

Another interesting feature of the labour market has been the growth of employment in the service sector and a decline in the manufacturing sector. This is illustrated in Figure 4.5.5 where we see that the share of employment in manufacturing has declined steadily over the last decade or so.

A comparison of Australian unemployment rates with the OECD shows clearly (see Figure 4.5.6) that they move together fairly closely although they

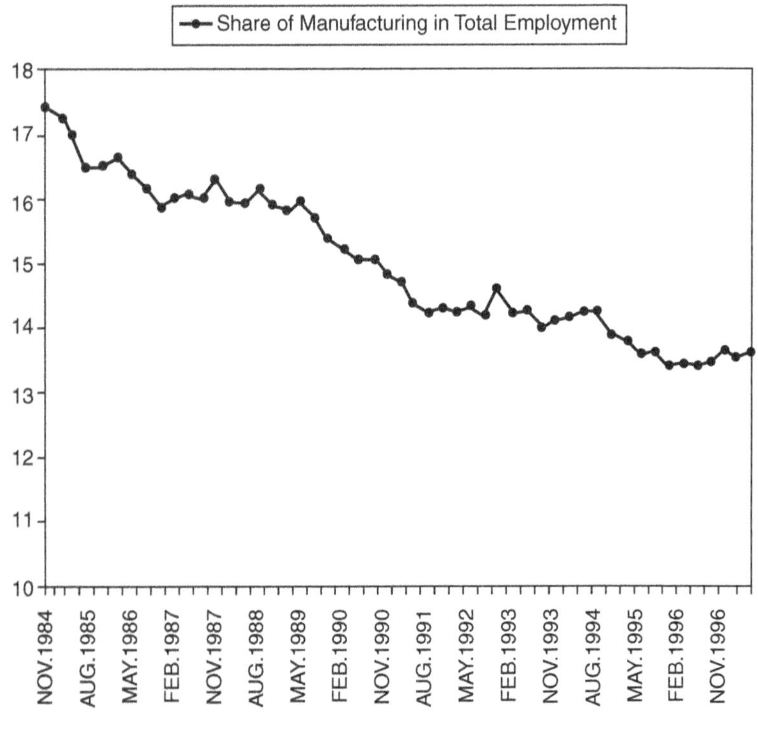

Figure 4.5.5 Share of Manufacturing Employment
Source: Ausstats, seasonally adjusted data.

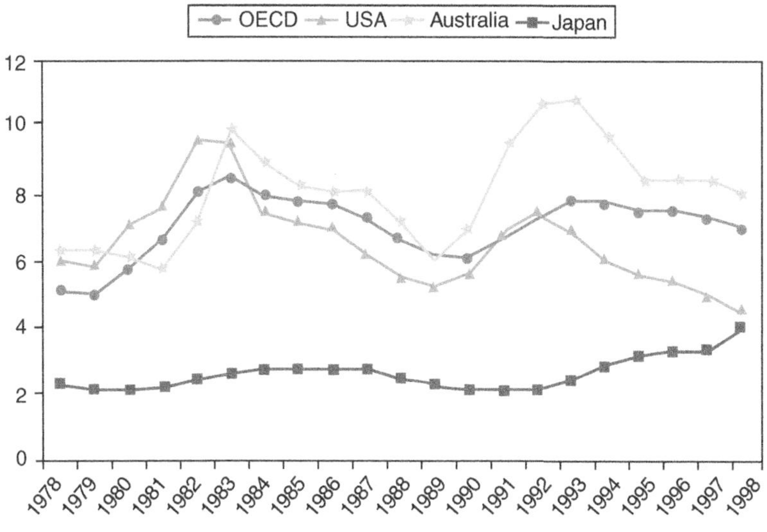

Figure 4.5.6 Unemployment Rates %

are at different levels. (Japan has had very low unemployment rates although this is changing.) This is seen more clearly if we graph the percentage rate of change of unemployment for OECD countries and compare it with the Australian performance, see Figure 4.5.7.

If we compare Australia over the period of the Accord with the UK after the advent of Thatcherism, it is clear that labour market flexibility does not necessarily provide ideal outcomes. Australia followed a quasi corporatist strategy with a tight incomes policy (the Accord) and maintained its award wage system, while the UK deregulated the labour market and decreased unemployment benefits. Australia performed better than the UK in terms of most macroeconomic variables including unemployment and long term unemployment. It is only since March 1996 that unemployment rates in the UK have fallen significantly below Australian unemployment rates, see Figure 4.5.8. Coincidentally, that is exactly the time that the Coalition government took office in Australia.

A comparison over time and across different countries leads to the conclusion that deregulated labour markets do not necessarily lead to full employment and regulated markets do not always lead to high unemployment. In the sixties unemployment rates in the USA (a deregulated labour market) were higher than in Japan (a regulated labour market). In the sixties and seventies West Germany (a regulated labour market) had very low unemployment rates, but it has very high unemployment in the nineties. The USA in the nineties has relatively low unemployment rates but had high unemployment rates in the sixties and seventies.

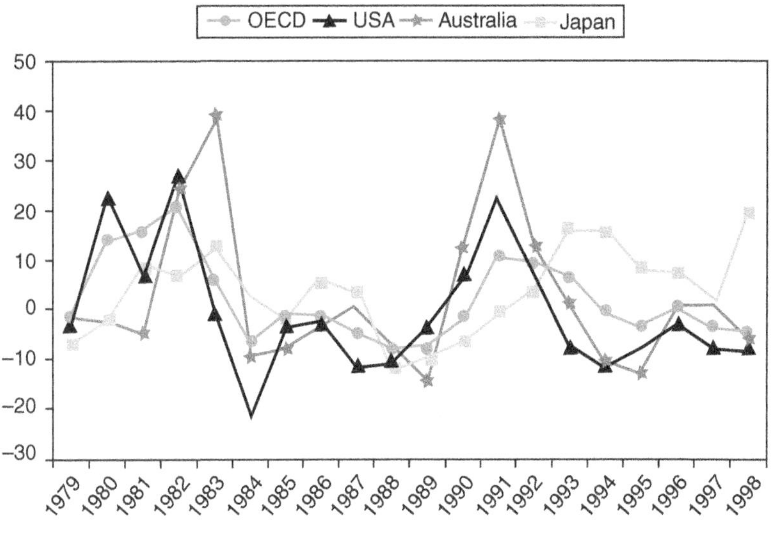

Figure 4.5.7 Unemployment Rates (% Change)

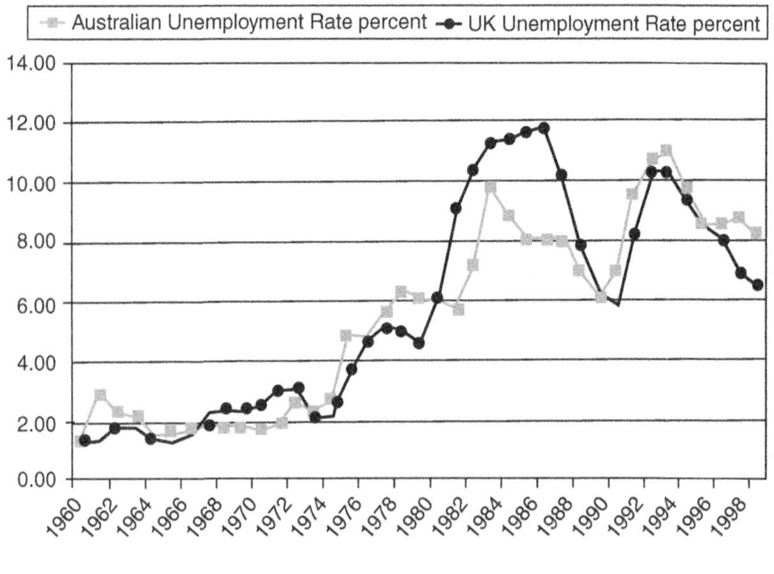

Figure 4.5.8 UK and Australian Unemployment Rates

4 Long Term Unemployment

An important issue that has not been dealt with so far in this paper is the problem of long term unemployment. As unemployment rises the numbers in long term unemployment rise quite rapidly. When unemployment falls the long term unemployment falls, but slowly (see Figure 4.5.9). After every recession we are left with a higher level of the long term unemployed. In some earlier work, see Chapman, Junankar and Kapuscinski (1992), we estimated a simple forecasting model which related the percentage of long term unemployment (PLTU) to unemployment rates lagged. Looking at Figure 4.5.9 it is easy to see a fairly close relationship between the two series with a time lag. Using the estimates from our model up to the time when Working Nation labour market programs were introduced in 1994 quarter 1, we project into the future what would happen to long term unemployment given the actual unemployment rates over the period. Figure 4.5.10 shows that during the course of the former Labor government's programs, our forecasts of the percentage of long term unemployment are consistently *more* than the actual values. This suggests that the introduction of Working Nation programs led to lower long term unemployment for any given level of unemployment. However, after the arrival of the Coalition government in 1996, we see that the forecasts are consistently *less* than the actual values, suggesting that the new policies were leading to higher levels of long term unemployment given the actual unemployment rates. In other words,

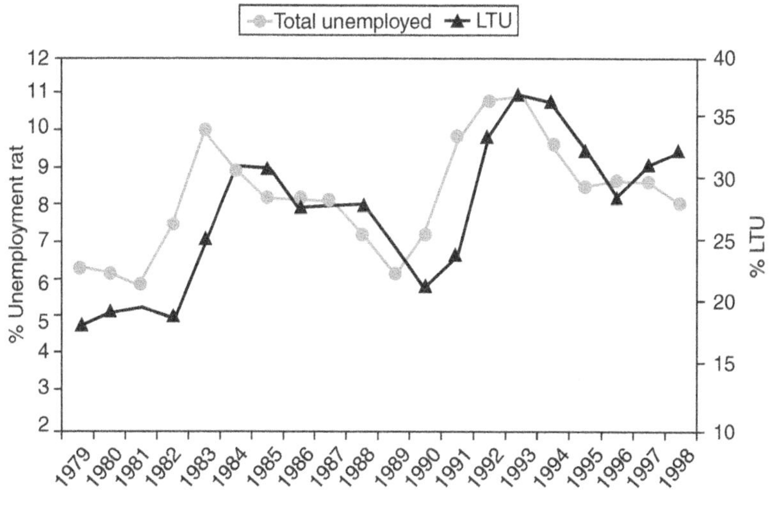

Figure 4.5.9 Unemployment Rates and Proportion of Long Term Unemployed 1979/1998

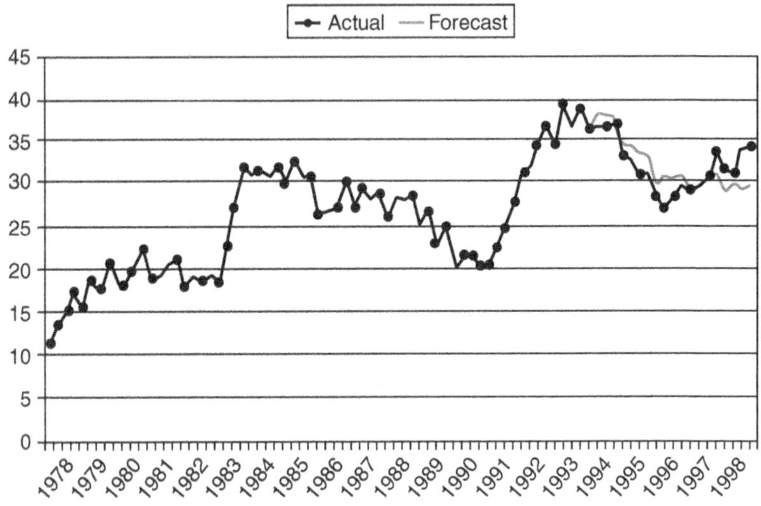

Figure 4.5.10 Proportion of Long Term Unemployment: Forecasts Compared to Actual Series PLTU: Persons

successful labour market programs introduced by the Keating government were abolished by the Coalition government.

5 Job Creation and Job Destruction

The economy is in a process of continual change with the setting up of new firms and new industries, the expansion of existing firms, the closing down of (unprofitable) firms, and the decline of existing firms. Schumpeter (1934) argued that technological change leads to what he called "creative destruction": old firms and industries close down but new ones are set up. During this process new employees will be hired by firms from the new entrants to the labour force, while some are hired from other firms or from the stock of unemployed or not in the labour force.[4] On the other side, some employees will leave existing firms (either voluntarily or involuntarily), some firms will shut down and make workers redundant, and some firms will "downsize" their labour force. The approach we follow is to study this process, which has been dubbed "job creation and job destruction" (see Davis, Haltiwanger, and Schuh, 1996), in the Australian economy.

What is striking is the large amount of labour mobility that takes place. In 1991 there were about 540,000 jobs being created and 603,000 jobs destroyed for males, with net job *destruction* taking place, in 1994, there were 610,000 jobs created and 528,000 jobs destroyed for males with net job *creation* taking place. Both in the recession year and the recovery year there were a large number of jobs created and destroyed: in the bad year there was net job creation and job destruction, while in the good year there was net job creation. What is important to note is that job creation and destruction takes place *simultaneously*. Figures 4.5.11 and 4.5.12 show the large amounts of job creation and job destruction taking place both in a recession year (1991) and in a recovery year (1994).

Approximately 268,000 males moved from non-employment (i.e., from unemployment or not in the labour force) into jobs and about 330,000 moved from jobs to non-employment in 1991.[5] The corresponding figures for 1994 were 365,000 and 280,000. In other words, for males in a recession year 1991 there was a net movement into non-employment, while in a recovery year 1994 there was a net movement into employment from non-employment. The cyclical effects are very clear.

The picture for females is very different. In both years there were *more* jobs created than destroyed. Again we see that for females in both the recession and the recovery years there was a net flow from non-employment into jobs.

When we compare males and females we see clearly that there has not been job destruction for male jobs and job creation for female jobs. For both males and females there have been large amounts of job creation and job destruction and the means for job creation *increased* from 1991 to 1994

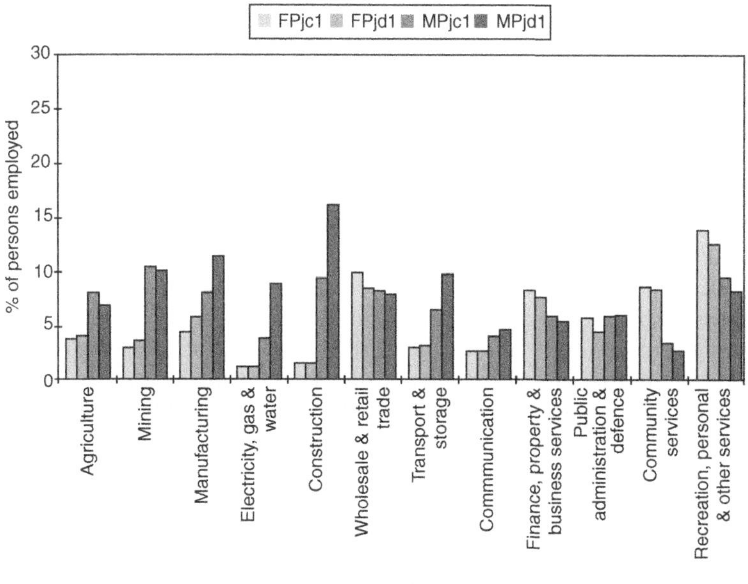

Figure 4.5.11 Job Creation and Job Destruction, 1991
Source: ABS Labour Mobility Australia 6209.0.

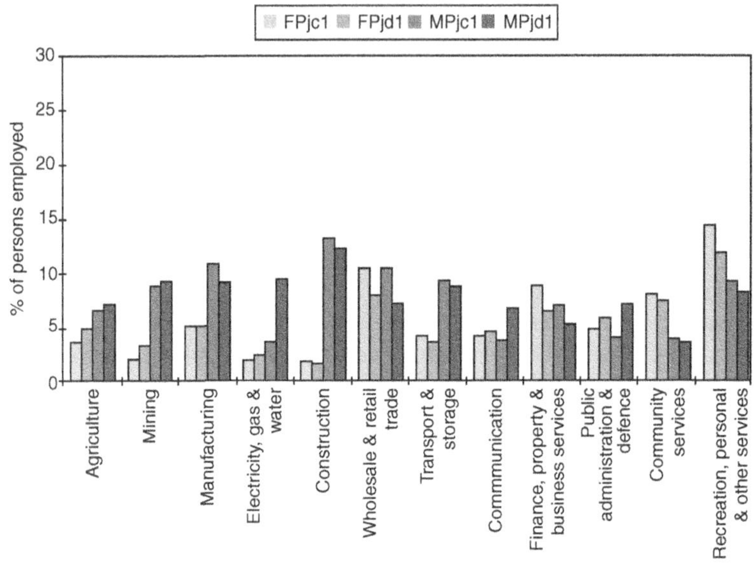

Figure 4.5.12 Job Creation and Job Destruction, 1994
Source: ABS Labour Mobility Australia. 6209.0.

while the means of job destruction fell. Similarly, the standard deviation for job creation increased while the standard deviation for job destruction fell over the years 1991 and 1994. The standard deviation of net job creation for both males and females increased. This suggests that there has been increased "turbulence" in the labour market between 1991 and 1994.

Technology, Trade, Labour Market Flexibility and Jobs

We argue that job creation and job destruction are the result of four major factors.[6] The first consists of the long-term (or permanent) shocks of technological innovation and progress which bring about relocation of firms, industries and occupations. A second factor is structural change in the economy due to microeconomic reform (deregulation and tariff reform) and corresponding changes in international trade. These changes lead to a shift of resources away from some industries (e.g., Textiles, Clothing and Footwear) and an expansion of others like tourism, banking and financial services etc. A third factor, the business cycle, affects job creation and job destruction. Some industries are more cyclically sensitive (e.g., construction) than others. A fourth factor is firm specific factors, personal and family reasons. As a result of the combined action of these factors we would expect to observe rates of job creation and job destruction. Some of the reasons for job creation and destruction are involuntary (e.g., if a worker is fired for any reason, including redundancy or voluntary (moving to find a better, or more highly paid, job), or for personal reasons (e.g., due to getting married or separated).

It has been argued that technological change increases job creation and job destruction. The impact of technological change on the labour market and on job creation and job destruction is significant but often has contradictory impacts. Technological change is usually defined as being either a change in the *product* (for example the facsimile machine) or a change in the *process* of production (for example, the use of robotics in the automotive industries). Technological change which leads to the introduction of new products would lead to either new firms setting up, or old firms expanding into new product lines which would lead to increased employment. However, as demand for the new products may be at the expense of some other competing products there would be some reduction in labour demand elsewhere in the economy.

Similarly, process technological change may lead to the substitution of capital for unskilled labour and hence lead to a decrease in labour demand. It may also lead to an increase in the demand for skilled labour as it is argued that technological change in recent years has involved a complementarity of capital with skilled labour, see OECD (1996). Process technological change has also affected the nature of production: "just in time technology" has revolutionised the nature and role of inventories. Employers now often use part time labour as a substitute for inventories of goods. Process technological change has led to a change in production methods such that physical strength is no longer necessary to work in factories so that females are no longer disadvantaged. These factors are likely to have led to an increase in female job creation and an increase in male job destruction.

However, process technological change that lowers costs of production may lead to an increase in the demand for the product, increased production and hence increased labour demand. Which of these effects dominates depends on several factors and is an empirical issue to be ascertained by looking at the data, see for example Van Reenen (1997).

Another issue not usually considered is that technological change may also affect the supply of labour, see Chapter 4, OECD (1994). For example, the product technological changes that introduced the contraceptive pill and household labour saving appliances may have led to increased female labour supply. The introduction of computer technology and mobile telephones may also have increased female labour supply by allowing more flexible working patterns, e.g., telecommuting.

The impact of trade on job creation and job destruction depends on several factors, including the interdependence of trade and technological change.[7] Standard Hecksher-Ohlin theory suggests that developed countries should be exporting capital intensive (and skilled labour intensive) products and importing labour intensive products. Technological change has important implications for trade. Product technological change should lead to an expansion of exports, while process technological change should lead to an increase in competitiveness and hence to increasing exports and decreasing imports. These should have a positive impact on job creation and negative impact on job destruction. With a lowering of tariff protection we should expect that there is likely to be an increase in job destruction and a decrease in job creation, unless the firms facing external competition become more productive, expand demand and hence help job creation and hinder job destruction. Wood (1994) suggests that labour saving technologies may be introduced in anticipation of increased competition from low wage developing economies and hence the loss of employment that is ascribed to technological change should really be ascribed to trade with low wage countries.

Our evidence suggests that there are more female jobs being created in high tech industries, but fewer male jobs being created in these industries. We find that there is a strong positive relationship between job creation and job destruction. We found some evidence to suggest that the higher the technological level of the industry, the greater the female jobs created, and fewer male jobs created. We found some evidence to suggest that, for the manufacturing sector, the greater the import penetration the fewer female jobs created.

6 Policies

"When the rich argue that tax cuts for the rich and wage or social benefit cuts for workers are the only way to cure unemployment about which the rich care deeply, every economist's eyebrows should rise" (Freeman, 1998, p. 15.)

Policies to lower the level of unemployment depend to some extent on what are believed to be the causes of unemployment by the government in power. Whether the government introduces policies to lower unemployment also depends on the priority given to unemployment over other economic variables in the economy. In particular, it is believed that there is a trade-off between inflation and unemployment: if the government introduced policies to lower unemployment it is believed that it would lead to an increase in inflation. Some governments believe it is more important to control inflation than to be concerned with unemployment, while some believe that the trade-off is too great. Given that inflation world-wide is at historically low levels, it seems that many governments are still stuck in a time warp when we had high inflation rates subsequent to what was clearly an unusual circumstance—the OPEC oil price rises of the seventies.

There are several myths about the causes of unemployment: these range from the view that selfish grasping unions have extracted rents from the employers and increased real wages and hence caused a fall in the demand for labour. A casual glance at the data shows that the strength of unions has been declining in the eighties in most OECD countries, notably in the UK.

However, unemployment rates in most OECD countries have gone up in the late eighties and early nineties. Another myth is that generous unemployment benefits have led to workers enjoying leisure at the expense of the tax paying public (the "dole-bludgers", in Australian English). Again, a glance at the data suggests that most OECD countries have lowered their unemployment benefits and tightened the conditions for receiving them, e.g., the UK. A popular view in the eighties was that the high rates of inflation, or unanticipated inflation, were the main culprits. However, we have now seen an era of world low inflation rates, with actual rates of inflation less than the expected rates. Other popular explanations are to do with oil price shocks (although oil prices have been falling in the past decade), technological change (although it is difficult to find any hard evidence to support this), and competition from Asian tigers, see Krugman and Lawrence (1994) for a rebuttal. Any attempt at using a mono-causal explanation of unemployment is unlikely to be successful in explaining such a complex economic phenomenon.

Keynesian economists believe that if we want to lower unemployment we should increase aggregate demand via monetary policy (lower interest rates) and fiscal policy (increased government expenditure and lower taxes). Curiously the champion of free trade and orthodoxy, the International Monetary Fund, is now attempting to persuade the Japanese government to do just that. In addition, most Keynesian economists would support the use of so-called active labour market policies, namely labour market training programs, subsidised employment, etc.

Neoclassical economists, or what Australians call economic rationalists, believe that unemployment is due to "interference" in the labour market by the unions and by the government. The unions, it is argued, raise wages above what the "market can bear" and governments introduce minimum wages and provide "generous" social security benefits to encourage dole bludgers. It is this view that has captured the imagination of the coalition government who are introducing measures to deregulate the labour market by making unionism (and industrial action by unionists) more difficult to organise. It is curious that it is necessary to introduce democracy in the workplace by having ballots for industrial action but no necessity to have ballots by shareholders when employers decide to close down plants.

A fairly common argument is that high real wages leads to unemployment: at present the Coalition government is trying to introduce policies to lower real wages for the long term unemployed and by deregulating the labour market. What is clearly important for employers is not simply the wage they pay but the productivity they receive per dollar of wage payment, or in other words the unit labour costs. Several economists have argued that firms deliberately pay higher wages in order to get higher productivity from workers. There are several variants of this argument: firstly, a higher wage prevents "shirking" since if the worker does not perform she may be fired and join the dole queue. The threat of unemployment persuades the worker to be productive. A second variant of this is that higher wages attract higher quality workers who have higher productivity. A third variant is that high wages lower worker turnover and hence keep down the costs of production. A fourth variant is based on "sociological" arguments that high wages lead to workers feeling well treated by the employer and hence provide greater productivity ("partial gift exchange relationship"). An important implication of this set of theories is that firms *choose* to pay higher wages to extract increased effort and higher productivity from workers. Hence they would not wish to cut the wages of their employees. Wage cuts are not even a rational response to the problem of unemployment.

In some recent work Bewley (1998) has produced evidence from the US that in a recession period employers were not willing to cut wages because of the likely impact on productivity via morale effects. It is true, that during the period of the Labor government's Accord, real wages were cut and employment increased. However, that was an agreement with the unions with increases in the "social wage" and with employers increasing investment due to the improved economic climate due to the Accord.

One of the ironies of present times is the current debate on minimum wages. Due to the introduction of laws banning discrimination on the basis of age, it would be illegal from the year 2000 to have junior wages that are a fraction of adult wages. The Coalition government, in general an ardent supporter of free markets, is insisting that minimum wages for youths must be entrenched in the workplace while the union movement is encouraging the move to abolishing minimum wages. However, the idiological arguments are carried out independently of evidence. Some work by my colleagues and I,[8] shows that employment of young people is not affected significantly by minimum wages; that is, if minimum wages were abolished and as a result youths earned higher wages, employment would not be affected.

The latest Reith discussion paper (or the parts leaked to the press to date) would have the compulsory work for the dole scheme for young people extended to adults. However, other than the satisfaction derived by the well off seeing the unemployed working in menial jobs in order to receive benefits, there is little hard evidence to show that this scheme increases the probability of the young finding "real" jobs. The idea of "reciprocal obligation" has an air of smug superiority: what about reciprocal obligations for the captains of industry who receive multi-million dollar payments? A newspaper account (*Australian* 19th February 1999) reported that Solomon Lew had received, tax free, something like $7 million. Should we expect the old and the sick pensioners to clean hospitals for free? The idea that we should force the unemployed to go back to school assumes that there are jobs out there just waiting to be filled. As discussed earlier we saw that the unemployment rates rose for all categories of workers, with and without post school qualifications. However, the evidence is clear: the unemployed are not refusing jobs as there are very few unfilled vacancies compared to the number of unemployed persons (approximately 10 unemployed persons to every vacancy).

7 Costs of Unemployment

The costs of unemployment can be grouped into economic, social and political costs. These costs are borne (to a differing extent) by individuals (both unemployed and employed persons), by their families, by social groups or classes, by political parties (including the government) and, of course, society in general. These costs of unemployment are both short run (static) and long run (dynamic). We find that the cost to the economy in terms of lost output is immense: of the order of 5–6% of GDP. Once this GDP is lost, it is lost forever. In fact we believe that high unemployment *now* leads to lower GDP in the *future* as well.

Unemployed individuals suffer in terms of lost income: single persons have the lowest replacement rate while married people with dependants have slightly higher rates. However, even married couples with two children only receive social security benefits amounting to about 65% of average weekly earnings. The long term unemployed who use up all their savings are in financial distress. Even employed persons suffer in terms of decreased job mobility. With high unemployment the government loses revenue in terms of taxes and has to spend on social security. The skill level of new immigrants is also affected adversely by high unemployment. High unemployment also leads to physical and mental illness, family breakdown, and increased crime (including homicide).

Why do societies allow such high unemployment to remain given these high costs of unemployment? Is it because they believe that the benefits in terms of lower inflation outweigh these costs of unemployment? Is lowering inflation really worth giving up at least 6% of GDP per annum? The government should not sacrifice thousands of unemployed people to appease the "gods of inflation".

8 Conclusions

This paper has covered a large number of important issues. The main theme has been that unemployment is a serious problem in most OECD countries and that we should attempt to tackle it by a concerted effort by the OECD as a whole. Simple remedies like deregulation do not provide a panacea. The worries about inflation should be left behind.

The world economy is still in a precarious position: the possibility of a stock market collapse in the US, the continuing problems of the Japanese economy and the possibility of the Chinese economy going through downturn. The best way of controlling the level of unemployment is to prevent a recession. Once unemployment goes up it comes down very slowly and remains at a high level. In these circumstances we should be wary that we do not suffer like some of our Asian neighbours.

There are many things that we do not understand. One mystery is why unemployment rates seem to follow similar paths in different countries with different social and institutional frameworks. The USA in the sixties had consistently higher rates of unemployment than Australia but now has suddenly emerged as a *wunderkind.* But then so did the West German economy in the post war period: it is now suffering high rates of unemployment not substantially different from its European neighbours.

Notes

Department of Economics and Finance, University of Western Sydney, Macarthur.
Text of Inaugural Lecture delivered at the University of Western Sydney, Macarthur, 23 February 1999.
I am grateful to Matthew Waite for excellent research assistance in writing this paper. This paper is based on my work done in collaboration with Dr Cezary Kapuscinski over the past 10 years and I am most grateful to him. Some of this work was done in collaboration with Professor Bruce Chapman, Dr Jakob Madsen and Dr Meng Xin. None of my collaborators is responsible for any errors or views expressed in this paper. However, I owe a debt of gratitude to all of them.

1. The Treasurer, Peter Costello, recently put up this target unemployment rate but did not specify when he hoped to achieve it by.
2. See Media Release from Martin Ferguson, Parliament of Australia, House of Representatives, 17th February 1999.
3. There are similar trends in other OECD countries. For a discussion see OECD 1996, pp. 158 ff.
4. Curiously, Davis, Haltiwanger and Schuh (1996), or earlier versions of their thesis, do not refer to Schumpeter. History of Economic Thought is clearly not a subject which is considered important these days.
5. The data are from the ABS Job Mobility Surveys and include people who had a job sometime in the previous 12 months, hence excluding the long term unemployed.
6. Davis and Haltiwanger (1996) discuss reasons for simultaneous job creation and destruction. They favour an explanation which depends on firms facing uncertainty and learning about cost conditions and some firms accumulate favourable information and expand while others who are not as efficient contract.
7. "Yet the impact of trade cannot be examined separately from that of technology. International trade is increasingly technology-driven, and the balance between the direct labour-displacing and the indirect price and income—'compensating'—effects of technology on jobs is now determined to a large extent in international markets," (OECD, 1996, p. 75.)
8. See Junankar, Waite and Belchamber (1998).

References

Australian Bureau of Statistics (1994), *Labour Mobility, Australia,* Cat. No. 6209.0, ABS, Canberra.

Bewley, T.F. (1998), "Why not cut pay", *European Economic Review,* 42, pp. 459–490.

Borland, J. (1996a), Job Creation and Destruction in Manufacturing Industry in Australia, *Economic Record,* 72 (216), pp. 46–62.

Borland, J. and R. Wilkins (1996b), Earnings Inequality in Australia, *Economic Record,* 72 (216), pp. 7–23.

Chapman, B.J., P.N. Junankar and C. Kapuscinski (1992), "Projections of Long Term Unemployment", *Australian Bulletin of Labour,* vol. 18, pp. 195–207.

Davis, S.J., J. Haltiwanger and S. Schuh (1996), *Job Creation and Destruction,* MIT Press, Cambridge, Mass.

Freeman, R.B. (1998), "War of the models: Which labour market institutions for the 21st century?", *Labour Economics,* 5, pp. 1–24.

Gregory, R.G. (1993), Aspects of Australian and U.S. Living Standards: The Disappointing Decades 1970–1990, *Economic-Record,* 69 (204), pp. 61–76.

Junankar, P.N., C.A. Kapuscinski and X. Meng (1997a), "Labour mobility in Australia in the nineties: a preliminary look at the effects of technological change", Centre for Economic Policy Research, ANU, Discussion Paper No. 373.

Junankar, P.N., C.A. Kapuscinski and X. Meng (1997b), "Have Women taken away jobs from Men? Job Creation and Job Destruction in the Australian economy", paper presented to the New Zealand Association of Economists Meetings, Christchurch 1997.

Junankar, P.N. and C.A. Kapuscinski (1992), *Costs of Unemployment in Australia,* EPAC Background Paper No. 24, Canberra, AGPS.

Junankar, RN., M. Waite and G. Belchamber (1998), "The Youth Labour Market: Anecdotes, Fables and Evidence", paper presented to a Joint Workshop on "Do Youth Wages Matter?", at the Centre for Economic Policy Research, ANU and the Productivity Commission, 23 November 1998.

King, J.E., R.J. Rimmer and S.M. Rimmer (1992), "The Law of the Shrinking Middle: Inequality of Earnings in Australia 1975–1989", *Scottish Journal of Political Economy,* 39 (4), pp. 391–412.

Krugman, P.R. and R.Z. Lawrence (1994), "Trade, Jobs and Wages", *Scientific American,* 270 (4), pp. 22–27.

Meng, X., P.N. Junankar and C.A. Kapuscinski (1997), "Technological Change and Job Mobility in Australia", Australian National University, mimeo.

OECD (1992), *Employment Outlook,* Paris: OECD.

OECD (1994), *The OECD Jobs Study,* Parts 1 and 2, Paris: OECD.

OECD (1996), *Job Creation and Loss: Analysis, Policy and Data Development,* Paris: OECD.

OECD (1996a), *Technology, Productivity and Job Creation,* vol. 2, Analytical Report, Paris: OECD.

OECD (1996b), *Job Creation and Loss: Analysis, Policy and Data Development,* Paris: OECD.

Schumpeter, J.A. (1934), *The Theory of Economic Development,* Cambridge, Mass., Harvard University Press.

Solow, R. (1990), *The Labour Market as a Social Institution,* Oxford: Blackwell.

Van Reenen, J. (1997), Employment and Technological Innovation: Evidence from UK Manufacturing Firms, *Journal of Labour Economics,* 15 (2), pp. 255–279.

Wood, A. (1994), *North-South Trade, Employment and Inequality,* Oxford, Oxford University Press.

Wooden, M. (1997), Unpaid Overtime, National Institute of Labour Studies, Discussion Paper.

4.6
Are Wage Cuts the Answer? Theory and Evidence

P.N. Junankar

This paper investigates the possibility of using wage cuts to lower unemployment. The paper first discusses the role of wages in various economic models (neoclassical, models with imperfect competition, efficiency wage models, insider-outsider models). It argues that in many of these models it is not rational for firms to cut wages as it would decrease their profits, while in some models wages are endogenous. It then considers how a government can cut wages in a market economy and argues that it is not feasible for the government to cut wages. The next section discusses the evidence on labour market flexibility and unemployment. The paper concludes with the argument that wage cuts do not lead to a decrease in unemployment.

"When the rich argue that tax cuts for the rich and wage or social benefit cuts for workers are the only way to cure unemployment about which the rich care deeply, every economist's eyebrows should rise." (Freeman, 1998, p. 15)

1 Introduction

The world economy appears to be on a precipice: there are gloomy predictions from the Governor of the Federal Reserve Bank, Alan Greenspan, that the world economy is likely to enter into a depression[1]. With most OECD economies already facing high levels of unemployment, the future looks bleak for the unemployed and those likely to become unemployed.

A comparison over time and across different countries leads to an inevitable conclusion: deregulated labour markets do not necessarily lead to full employment and regulated markets do not always lead to high unemployment. In the sixties unemployment rates in the USA (a deregulated labour market) were higher than in Japan (a regulated labour market). In the sixties

---

Reprinted from 'Are Wage Cuts the Answer? Theory and Evidence' by P. N. Junankar in *The Unemployment Crisis in Australia: Which Way Out?* edited by Stephen Bell, Cambridge University Press, Cambridge, 2000. With kind permission from Cambridge University Press.

and seventies West Germany (a regulated labour market) had very low unemployment rates, but it has very high unemployment in the nineties! The USA in the nineties has relatively low unemployment rates but had high unemployment rates in the sixties and seventies. The UK deregulated its labour market under Margaret Thatcher from 1979 onwards but its unemployment rate rose sharply and remained very high until the last couple of years. There are many economists, politicians and policy makers who believe that a simple remedy of wage cuts exists to cure unemployment. This is certainly the consensus in Canberra. This chapter argues that this argument is specious and false.

The chapter proceeds as follows. Sections 2 and 3 discuss orthodox accounts of unemployment. Section 4 discusses unemployment in models of imperfect competition, Section 5 discusses efficiency wage models and Section 6 discusses insider outsider models. Section 7 discusses a key issue: how can the government impose wage cuts? Section 8 discusses the evidence on labour market flexibility and unemployment. Section 9 concludes the paper.

2 Unemployment in a Neoclassical Model of a Competitive Economy

The orthodox (or neoclassical) view of the labour market is based on an idealised market: there are a large number of buyers and sellers of labour services who act independently of each other (i.e. there are no unions and there are no monopolies). The market behaves like an auction market: if there is excess demand the price is bid up, if there is excess supply the price is bid down and trade only takes place at an equilibrium price (wage rate).

In this abstract world, the demand for labour is determined by profit maximising firms facing a given production function (technology) and given prices of output and inputs (including labour). Firms can hire as many workers (or as many hours of work) as they please at a *given* wage rate. Since it is assumed that firms are maximising profits they would hire workers until the extra revenue they get by selling the extra output produced by an additional worker just equals the additional cost of hiring the worker, i.e. the wage rate[2]. Workers are assumed to be driven by maximising utility (doing as best as they can given the conditions they face) where they can work as many hours as they wish at the given wage rate. Labour supply and labour demand determine equilibrium employment and unemployment, independently of the goods market or the money market.

Unemployment in this model is voluntary: the unemployed are those people who are unwilling to work at the current market wage but would be willing to work only if they were paid higher wages. In this model monetary or fiscal policies that affect aggregate demand have no impact on unemployment as these policies (by assumption) do not affect the marginal productivity of labour. Only supply side policies that affect the production function (and hence the marginal product of labour) or changes in labour supply due to changes in tastes or due to tax or social security policies would influence unemployment. *Involuntary* unemployment is simply due to rigid wages.

In this model involuntary unemployment is possible if for some reason wages are fixed above equilibrium, either by governments imposing minimum wages or by non-competitive forces like unions. With wages fixed above market clearing rates unemployment would result. In this case a reduction in real wages would lead to an increase in employment and a reduction in unemployment. Hence the orthodox case for cutting wages relies on a labour market that operates like an auction market for (say) fresh fish: if there is an excess supply for the commodity price falls, if there is an excess demand price rises to clear the market. The only reason for the market to not clear is due to "interference" by the government or by unions.

Orthodox economists would argue that if we abandoned minimum wages we would solve the problem of unemployment. Their argument is essentially based on a simple competitive labour market as discussed above. In the discussion below of alternative models we show how this conclusion is invalid in a model where employers have monopsony power (i.e. an employer has to pay higher wages if they wish to hire more people) or where productivity of workers is linked to the wages paid, see under efficiency wages below.

This version of the labour market was criticised by Keynes (1936) when he argued that the labour market was different from an auction market: if nominal wages were cut for one group of workers it would affect the *relative* wages of that group, who would oppose the wage cuts. He also argued that a cut in everyone's wages would lead to a fall in aggregate demand (as wages were incomes for workers) and it would lead to a fall in consumption expenditures and hence a *rise* in unemployment.

Another set of the criticisms of this classical/neoclassical model came from Keynesian theorists, e.g. Barro and Grossman (1971). Essentially these criticisms were based on a view that there was a coordination failure: because the output market did not clear (prices were not perfectly flexible) this led to a constrained demand for labour which was less than that required to produce full employment. For example, during a recession automobiles pile up in yards until eventually the firms cut back production and decrease overtime, stop replacing staff who leave, start laying off workers, and eventually make workers redundant. In other words they do not cut prices to clear the inventories that are piling up in the yards. Hence the problem of unemployment was not due to rigidity of wages (either due to governments or unions) but due to a failure of the price system to operate in the real world without any problems.

If for some reason the output price did not adjust in the face of excess supply, then firms would be quantity constrained (minimum of the demand and supply curves) and hence would only demand labour to produce the non-equilibrium output level which was less than the equilibrium level.

This would lead to unemployment: *cutting wages in this case would not be a solution as the problem was in the output market, not in the labour market.*

The importance of this literature was to shift the focus: instead of blaming workers for unemployment, the blame lay in the output market. This led to much debate about the problems of coordination failure of the price system: the Walrasian auctioneer[3] was a clever fiction invented to solve an important theoretical problem by allowing trade to take place only at equilibrium prices.

3 Some Neoclassical Models of Unemployment

Another set of models that argue that unemployment is essentially a voluntary phenomenon is based on views of imperfect information in the labour market. An early version of this is due to Lucas and Rapping[4] (1969) where unemployment is a result of individuals "intertemporally substituting leisure". The distinctive feature of this model is that unemployment (leisure) in the current period is substituted for unemployment (leisure) in the future period. Unemployment is voluntary: it is the difference between normal or long run labour supply and short run or current labour supply. The reason there is unemployment is because the unemployed are "enjoying" leisure now while the wage they are being offered is low, and they would work in the future when they expect to have a higher wage offered. It is assumed that they can borrow from their friendly banker to cover their expenditures now based on their expected future earnings[5]. To put it graphically, the unemployed are choosing to be unemployed because they expect to work in the future at a million dollars a week!

The model assumes that we are always in short run equilibrium and fluctuations in unemployment are due to fluctuations in the current wage relative to expected future wages.

This intertemporal substitution of leisure argument would suggest that workers would quit their jobs in a recession voluntarily: unfortunately (for the authors) the data show clearly that quitting rates are acyclical. Quit rates are low in a recession period and high in a boom. This model was tested on time series data but the tests did not support the theory of intertemporal substitution of leisure!

A more sophisticated version of this model is based on search theories of unemployment, Phelps (1970), Mortensen (1970). In this case unemployment is a voluntary choice on the part of workers who believe that they would get a higher wage offer than they have received to date. They are simply maximising their utility (satisfaction) by waiting for a higher wage offer. It is assumed that everyone receives wage offers (there is a normal distribution of wage offers). Unemployed workers decide on a "reservation wage" based on their estimation of the wage distribution, their discount rate and any income they may receive in the absence of accepting a wage offer (e.g. income from assets, unemployment or other social security benefits). The higher the unemployment benefits the higher their reservation wage and hence the longer their duration of unemployment (they can afford to wait longer for this ideal wage offer which exceeds their reservation wage).

A critical assumption made in these models is that search is either not possible when the worker is employed or that search is more efficient when the person is unemployed. However, for most people search is in fact more efficient when employed: we have access to stationery, phones, and most importantly have a network of contacts. Even for blue collar workers it is easier to find a job when you already have a job. To be unemployed provides a negative signal to the prospective employer.

It is, however, strange that most of the unemployed people happen to come from poor families, with low levels of education and training, etc. The highly educated and the well off somehow seem to spend less time searching for a highly paid job!

To quote Phelps (1970):

> "It would be as senselessly puritanical to wipe out unemployment as it would be to raise taxes in a deep depression. Today's unemployment is an investment in a better allocation of any given quantity of employed persons tomorrow; its opportunity cost, like that of any other investment, is present consumption." (p. 17)

It is difficult to believe that 800,00 unemployed people are busily investing like crazy when firms are cutting back on investment in real capital goods.

In this model wage cuts would simply lead to searchers spending longer looking for work since they would have formed expectations about their reservation wage on the basis of the previous wage distribution. In other words, a cut in wages would not lead to a fall in unemployment for quite some time until the labour market participants changed their reservation wages in response to the wage cuts. Unless there was an accompanying cut in unemployment benefits this theory would suggest that wage cuts would *increase* unemployment! The theory has no predictions about how *quickly* reservation wages would respond to an altered wage distribution: the dynamics of this model need much further research.

4 Unemployment in Models of Imperfect Competition

These models are based (essentially) on a paper by Bob Rowthorn (1977) (a Marxist scholar from Cambridge University) although discovered independently by Layard, Nickell and Jackman (1991) where unemployment is the mechanism by which the claims of the workers and capitalists (employers) are made compatible, given the available national output. If the demands of the workers and employers exceed the national output a wage-price spiral ensues until a higher level of unemployment eliminates the wage price spiral. If unemployment is too low, wage setters would try to raise their relative wages, only higher unemployment would stop this leap frogging. In equilibrium what people expect is just realised.

The model consists of firms that use a mark up system of pricing where the markup is an increasing function of the level of activity in the economy, proxied by the employment rate (or negatively related to the unemployment rate). Firms set prices by putting a markup on **expected** wages.

Wage setting is done by unions who set wages on a markup on expected prices, with the markup as an increasing function of the employment rate and negative function of the unemployment rate. In other words firms are not maximising profits but simply use some rules to fix prices: given the average cost of production they add on a profit margin which is higher the employment rate and the lower the unemployment rate.

In this model the equilibrium unemployment is that level of unemployment where the interaction of the workers who are more aggressive in their wage demands at times of low unemployment and the employers who have a higher profit margin when unemployment is low.

Note that in this model real wages and unemployment are determined simultaneously, hence we cannot argue that the cause of unemployment is the high level of wages. Instead the interpretation is that workers expect too high wages consistent with the level of unemployment. Alternatively, employers expect too high a profit margin given the workers demands. Since wages are determined by this interaction of the workers demands and the employers bargaining, we cannot prescribe wage cuts as a solution to the problem of unemployment (see below for a further discussion of this issue).

5 Efficiency Wage Models[6]

If we find that there is unemployment, why do real wages not fall to clear the labour market? An interesting explanation is provided by the efficiency wage model. There are several variants of the efficiency wage hypothesis. One version of the theory can be traced back to Marx's *Capital*, while another one can be traced to Leibenstein's theory for less developed economies. The crucial assumption of this theory is that the productivity of a worker is some function of the wage paid to the worker. The different versions of this theory are:

(a) **Shirking Model**: This is best known from a paper by Shapiro and Stiglitz (1984) where they argued that employers would pay a higher wage (higher than market clearing) and if the workers did not perform adequately they would be fired. Given that unemployment exists this would provide an incentive for workers not to shirk. This is similar to Marx's argument that unemployment is necessary in a capitalist system to force workers to work hard so that they are not thrown on the scrapheap and do not demand higher wages which would erode the capitalists profits[7].

(b) **Costs of turnover Model:** Firms pay higher than market wages in order to lower the costs of turnover of employees. This would be especially important where the workers had job specific skills and losing an employee would involve the firm in spending on recruitment and training costs. Again firms choose to pay higher wages in order to get higher profits and they would not want to cut wages.

(c) **Adverse Selection Model:** The higher the wages paid the better quality of workers apply for the job and hence productivity and profits are higher. In other words, firms choose to pay higher wages in order to get higher productivity (what used to be called Fordism) and would not want to cut wages[8]. This is similar to the adage: "if you pay peanuts you get monkeys!"

(d) **Sociological Models:** Higher wages may improve worker morale and hence lead to higher productivity. This may be more important where team work is necessary in the workplace. One version of this kind of model comes from Akerlof (1982) which he calls a *"partial gift exchange relationship"*. Employers pay more than they have to (i.e. higher wages than the market clearing wage) as a gift and employees return this in part by being more productive than they have to be. This is based on studies by sociologists, psychologists and anthropologists who emphasise the cultural context of decision making and the importance of treating people well to get the maximum productivity from them.

The bottom line of all these theories is that we can calculate the wage which would maximise profits: obviously an employer would not be willing to pay an infinitely high wage because she gets a higher level of productivity with higher wages. There is a trade off: the higher the wage the greater the effort provided by workers and hence a higher productivity, however, the higher the wage the greater the costs of production and hence the lower the profits. Assuming that the productivity increases with wages but after a point the increases become smaller and smaller there is a profit maximising wage (called the "efficiency wage") where increasing wages any more would lead to a greater increase in costs than in revenues [9].

One important result from efficiency wages models is that wages do not clear the labour market, that is wages do not adjust to eliminate unemployment. Employers *deliberately* choose a wage above the market clearing rate in order to get increased effort from the workers (and hence increased productivity) and hence higher profits. As a result wages do not respond to changes in supply and demand: there is wage rigidity which is not due to unions or government "interference" in the labour market but due to the conscious maximising behaviour of the employers! Unemployment is a necessary feature of a capitalist economy with profit maximising behaviour.

A criticism of this theory is that employers would find an alternative method of getting workers to increase their effort and increase productivity. It is argued employers could require workers to post a bond (i.e. when the worker is employed he has to deposit, say $1,000 with the employer, and if they were inefficient they would forfeit the deposit). This is analogous to tenants in housing who have to provide a bond and if the property is not properly maintained they lose some or all of the deposit. If this were possible it is argued that firms would not have to pay efficiency wages. However, due to imperfect capital markets this is not likely: it is unlikely that workers would have sufficient savings to post such bonds and it is unlikely that a bank would loan the money for such purposes. Furthermore, if firms are likely to cheat then this is not an optimal solution. With housing it is relatively easy to get an independent judgement on damage to property, in labour markets it is impossible to get an independent judgement on an appropriate level of effort or productivity. Since it is very difficult to measure the effort put in by any worker or measure the productivity of a worker the employer could fire the worker just because she wants to have a smaller workforce. There would be several cases of legal disputes for wrongful dismissal as the employers would have an incentive to cheat. Hence, this is not a valid criticism of the efficiency wage models.

An important implication of this set of theories is that firms *choose* to pay higher wages to extract increased effort and higher productivity from workers. *Hence they would not wish to cut the wages of their employees*! Wage cuts are not even a rational response to the problem of unemployment.

6 Insider Outsider theory

In a series of articles and books Lindbeck (1993) has argued that unemployment is due to bargaining between employers and unions where the unions are concerned about the plight of their employed members (the insiders) and tend to ignore the plight of the unemployed (the outsiders). Wage bargaining then sets wages which are "too high" to clear the labour market and hence unemployment would persist. If for example productivity increases due to improved production methods, the workers would demand higher wages for the "insiders" and ignore the "outsiders", and hence unemployment persists. Gregory (1998) argues that the reason for the different time paths of US and Australian unemployment rates are partly explained by the insiders in Australia capturing the productivity gains (especially after the introduction of enterprise bargaining), unlike in the US.

7 How can government policy impose wage cuts?

Before we discuss how a government would be able to impose wage cuts it is necessary to distinguish between money wage cuts and real wage cuts. An employer may be able to cut the money wages of her employee but whether it leads to a cut in real wages depends on whether the price level remains constant or not. If all employers cut money wages then it is likely to lead to everyone being worse off and as a result workers cut their expenditures on consumption goods, see Malinvaud (1982). This then leads to a fall in consumer good prices and hence the fall in money wages may be alleviated to some extent or may even lead to a rise in real wages. Hence, the money wage cut may or may not lead to a real wage cut. What is necessary according to orthodox economists to increase employment (or decrease unemployment) is a cut in *real* wages. Malinvaud (1982) also argues that low wages may hinder capital accumulation and hence lead to lower productivity in the long run. Hence although wage cuts may be advantageous from the point of view of one firm/employer it may lead to negative consequences for the economy if all firms cut wages simultaneously. It should also be noted that what is important for firms is not the level of wages but the unit labour costs of production which depends on productivity. Hence, wage cuts may not be a solution if it leads to a fall in productivity and hence a rise in unit labour costs.

The simple solution, proposed by some politicians and some economists, to cut wages to lower unemployment is simply not feasible. If we had a competitive labour market wage rates are endogenous: they are determined by the demand for and supply of labour. The only way to affect wage rates is to influence the demand or supply of labour. In more realistic models with imperfect competition, wage rates are determined by the joint behaviour of firms who use a mark up pricing system and workers who are bargaining for higher wages. Again, government policy has to lead to a change in the behaviour of employers or workers: it is not obvious which policies would lead to employers or employees to change their behaviour such that they increase employment but at lower wage rates.

In efficiency wage models wage rates provide an incentive to workers to raise productivity. Hence government policy to encourage firms to cut wages would be counter productive.

Finally, wage cuts are feasible when minimum wages are legislated. In Australia we have a complex system of minimum wages which is slowly being eroded (first by Keating's enterprise bargaining, and now by the Coalition Government's Australian Workplace Agreements). The government could certainly introduce legislation to cut minimum wages for low paid workers (especially for youths). However, it would be difficult for the government to change the award wage system for the low paid workers without changing the industrial relations system even further, or by abolishing the Australian Industrial Relations Court. However, such drastic changes would require some form of agreement with the unions or another election victory with an election platform to remove award wages completely. The Hawke-Keating Accord on wages was a significant agreement that had been forged at a time of consensus politics and is unlikely to be repeated. The impact of the Accord on wages and employment is considered later when we discuss the evidence for the impact of wage cuts on employment and unemployment.

However, the simple theory that argues that a cut in minimum wages would lead to an increase in employment and a decrease in unemployment is based on a simple competitive labour market model. Recent work by Card and Krueger (1995) shows that if we relax the assumption of perfect competition a cut in minimum wages may lead to a decrease in employment. They show that if we allow for a monopsonist employer then the simple solution of wage cuts breaks down.

Similarly, if we use the efficiency wage arguments a cut in minimum wages may increase the turnover of low paid staff, and hence lower the average productivity of labour and hence lower the profits of the employer.

8 Evidence on Labour Market Flexibility and Unemployment

> "Unemployment is always and everywhere a real phenomenon," (with apologies to Milton Friedman, 1980).

For some time now the OECD has been arguing that labour market flexibility is likely to lead to higher rates of employment and lower rates of unemployment. What do they mean by labour market flexibility? Generally, it is taken to mean an absence of minimum wages, no restrictions on employers firing workers, an absence of unions, and limited social security benefits (low unemployment benefits relative to wage levels and restricted for short periods of time)[10]. In other words, labour market flexibility is usually taken to mean shifting the power balance in bargaining towards the employer and away from workers.

If we compare Australia over the period of the Accord with the UK after the advent of Thatcherism it is clear that labour market flexibility does not necessarily provide ideal outcomes. Australia followed a quasi corporatist strategy with a tight incomes policy (the Accord) and maintained its award wage system, while the UK deregulated the labour market. If we choose any of the usual criteria by which economic performance is judged, Australia outperforms Britain in all cases. If we look at GDP, industrial production, employment, unemployment, long term unemployment, inflation, net trade, we do significantly better, see Junankar (1997). The reason for the relative success of the Accord was not simply that real wages were kept under control but more importantly there was a climate of opinion that industrial peace had been declared which gave investment a boost which helped a rapid growth of employment, see Chapman, Dowrick and Junankar (1991).

(i) Minimum Wages

In a recent study of the impact of minimum wages on employment, the OECD *Employment Outlook 1998*, estimated cross country (pooled over time) regressions for a sample of OECD countries which had minimum wage legislation (curiously excluding Australia). They found that:

> Firstly, the results suggest that a rise in the minimum wage has a negative effect on teenage employment. Secondly, negative employment effects for young adults are generally close to or insignificantly different from zero. Thirdly, for prime-age adults, the most plausible specifications suggest that minimum wages have no impact on their employment outcomes. (OECD *Employment Outlook 1998*, pp. 47–48)

However, they are cautious in their conclusion and emphasise the "*fragility of the results in Table 2.5*", (OECD 1998, p. 47, emphasis added). They add:

> At the same time, it is important to note that these estimated effects are relatively insignificant in terms of explaining the large decline that has occurred in the teenage employment-population ratio in some countries. (OECD *Employment Outlook 1998*, p. 48)

The employment elasticities are significant for the 15–19 year old groups but are relatively small, of the order of about minus 0.4. These are relatively small and for a group of young people for whom there has been a large increase in education. In other words, they have not allowed for young people choosing to stay on in education and simply assumed that the differences in employment over time and country are due to the employers cost minimising demand functions. The OECD *Employment Outlook* (1998, p. 70) indicates that differences and changes in school retention rates are likely to affect the estimates and this is a matter for further research. In fact it is likely the result is due to estimating a hybrid demand and supply equation.

Most estimates of the responsiveness of employment to wage cuts suggest that it is relatively small. For example, Debelle and Vickery (1998), estimate that it would require a 10 per cent cut in *real* wage to increase employment by four percent. However, it is not clear how employers can cut real wages: they can cut money wages and the cut in real wages depends on the response of prices to the cut in money wages. If prices fall because of a fall in the demand for consumer goods then real wage may not decline at all or by a smaller amount than the money wage cut.

In a recent study of the youth labour market by the Productivity Commission Daly et al. (1998) assert:

> " ... even among teenagers, who are often most affected by minimum wages, the proportion being paid the minimum wage is relatively small. Minimum wage studies do not say anything about what would happen if the wages of the remaining teenagers were changed relative to employees in other demographic groups.

> "Studies that can examine this question look at substitution between particular types of labour. The estimated responsiveness of youth employment to youth wages in these studies is considerably higher than the estimates from the minimum wage studies. The weight of evidence suggests a relatively large (much more than proportionate) decline in youth employment in response to an increase in the youth wage." [pp. xii, xiii]

Junankar, Waite and Belchamber (1998) criticise the Daly et al. paper on several counts but especially because they use average wages rather than minimum wages and as a result use wage rates which are chosen by the firm to get increased efficiency. As it happens many of the workplaces in the Daly et al. study pay youths more than the minimum wage presumably because they believe that they would get higher productivity and hence higher profits as a result. In their research Junankar, Waite and Belchamber (1998) use minimum wages and employment of youths for every separate year of age but they are unable (in general) to find significant wage elasticities.

(ii) Centralisation

There has been a debate in the literature on whether deregulated labour markets provide better outcomes than regulated markets. In some seminal work Calmfors and Driffill (1988) showed that there appeared to be a hump-shaped relationship between centralisation and unemployment. Very low and very high levels of centralisation were good for unemployment, but intermediate levels were bad. This was based on studies of OECD economies using cross-section data. Freeman (1988, p. 79) found some supporting evidence although he emphasises the considerable diversity of performance and hence argues that there is no "particular set of labour market institutions as the simple key to success". In a more recent paper Freeman (1998) is circumspect about the hump-shaped relationship and discusses the problem that institutions themselves are influenced by economic history.

Similar results were obtained by Rowthorn (1992) where he showed that countries with high levels of wage dispersion (with unregulated labour markets) had worse labour market outcomes than those with low levels of wage dispersion.

However, in some recent work the OECD (1997, Chapter 3) found no statistically significant hump-shaped relationship between unemployment and centralisation. In fact it found that centralised/coordinated economies had a *lower* wage inequality and *lower* unemployment rates. In a recent paper Nickell (1997) argues that the popular view that the labour market in North America is flexible and hence there is low unemployment while in Europe the labour market is inflexible/rigid and hence there is high unemployment is wrong. If we look at a longer sweep of history we see that in the nineteen fifties and sixties unemployment rates in the USA were generally higher than most European countries while in the eighties and nineties the situation has reversed even though labour market institutions have remained more-or-less unchanged over the period (except for, especially, the UK).

Rowthorn (1992) using cross section data for the OECD finds a positive relationship between wage dispersion and decentralisation: where wage bargaining is decentralised overall wage dispersion is higher. Further he finds that there is very little empirical support for the view that wage flexibility (as proxied by wage dispersion) has a positive impact on employment. However, he finds some weak evidence for wage dispersion leads to lower unemployment rates.

In an interesting paper Gregory and Sheehan (1998) argue that employment growth in Australia has been more rapid in the bottom two deciles of the earnings distribution although wage inequalities have increased more in the US. In other words it is not necessary to reduce wages to increase employment. Or to quote them: "There is no evidence for the view that legislation to make the wage system more flexible will have any significant impact on unemployment." (Gregory and Sheehan,1998, p. 348).

A common theme that runs through many of these papers is that there is no simple answer to an ideal labour market institution that would solve all the problems of a society. Different types of organisation are appropriate for different economic and social circumstances.

(iii) Surveys of Employers (Bewley)

In some fascinating research conducted over several years Bewley (1998) has surveyed a large number of firms with in depth questioning about the role of wages and employment. He finds that in most cases firms laid off workers due to a decline in product demand or financial setbacks but not due to demands for wage increases. Firms were unwilling to cut wages in response to a fall in demand as it would affect productivity via morale effects a la Akerlof (1982). Workers would resent pay cuts and it would affect the reputation of the firm which would harm its chances of hiring good workers in good times. Lay offs only affected a minority of workers whereas pay cuts would affect the whole workforce and the laid off workers are no longer on the premises to affect the productivity of the remaining workforce. He also rejects the view that workers have unrealistic expectations about wages leading to their unemployment: "There were few indications that unemployed people had excessive wage expectations. On the contrary, many unemployed people were too flexible and found themselves rejected by firms as overqualified." (Freeman, 1998, p. 459.)

This is an important paper that debunks much of orthodox economic theories of the labour market.

(iv) Female employment and equal pay legislation

In Australia equal pay legislation in the sixties and seventies led to a significant increase in female wages, however, we saw a concomitant *increase* in their employment. This is clearly inconsistent with orthodox economic theory. Gregory et al in various papers have discussed this issue.

To summarise this section: there is no simple relationship between labour market institutions and unemployment or between wage flexibility and unemployment. More importantly, employers choose not to cut wages as they think it would affect them adversely. There is no way the government can force employers to cut wages if they do not wish to do so. In other words, *wage cuts are not desirable and they are not feasible.*

9 Conclusions

To summarise: money wage cuts may not lead to real wage cuts. Money wage cuts may lead to increased unit costs due to a fall in productivity. Even if money wage cuts led to a fall in unit labour costs the likely impact on employment and unemployment is very small. Finally, wage cuts are not a sensible policy because firms do not want to cut wages as it affects workplace morale and hence productivity. If firms do not want to cut wages then the government cannot impose wage cuts. The policy is neither economically rational nor is it feasible.

Wage cuts do not solve the unemployment problem. Cuts in welfare benefits do not solve the unemployment problem. Unless the government is willing to expand demand by direct government expenditures and by providing incentives to the private sector to expand investment and production we will continue to have high unemployment. Labour market programs in conjunction with appropriate macroeconomic policies would help the unemployed to find satisfying work. We cannot afford to continue to run an economy with high levels of unemployment. Besides the obvious waste of resources which could be producing large amounts of consumer goods we are also slowing down the future levels of GDP as investment is lower and human capital is being destroyed due to unemployment. What is needed is a concerted program by the OECD countries to expand aggregate demand in the economy. The old monetarist remedies which have been pushed by the IMF and many neoclassical economists have clearly not worked. It now seems that there is a change in thinking taking place: even the IMF is telling Japan it should expand government expenditure and cut taxes. That is a good Keynesian remedy. We should try it here as well!

Notes

1. See The Australian, October 9th, 1998 for a report about Alan Greenspan's comments.
2. In formal terms, they hire workers until the real wage rate equals the marginal product of labour.
3. In Walras' (1874) *Elements of Pure Economics* he suggested that an auctioneer would costlessly iterate on prices until an equilibrium price set was obtained, no trade would take place except at equilibrium prices. This meant that the equilibrium price was independent of the dynamic path of price adjustment.

4. In a curious twist of history, one of these authors (Rapping) whose name is so closely tied to this neoclassical model decided to change his paradigms and became a Marxist scholar. Lucas has remained a true blue neoclassical economist and went on to win the Nobel Prize in Economics for his contribution to the "rational expectations revolution".
5. Ask any of your unemployed friends of their experience of getting loans or over drafts from their bank!
6. See Akerlof and Yellen (1986)
7. Also see Kalecki (1943) for an elaboration of this argument.
8. Henry Ford who doubled workers' wages in 1914 said "Of course the higher wage drew a more productive worker. But that wasn't the real reason. The fact was, it was no good mass producing a cheap automobile if there weren't masses of workers and farmers who could afford to buy it." (quoted in Schmid, 1995, p. 433).
9. More formally, the efficiency wage is that wage where the elasticity of effort with respect to wages is unity.
10. See OECD Jobs Study and Gregg and Manning (1997)

References

Akerlof, G.A. (1982) "Labor Market Contracts as Partial Gift-Exchange", *Quarterly Journal of Economics*, 97, 543–69.

Akerlof, G.A. and J. L. Yellen (1986) Efficiency wage models of the labor market, Cambridge University Press, Cambridge.

Barro, R.J. and H.I. Grossman (1971) "A General Disequilibrium Model of Income and Employment" *American Economic Review*; 61(1), March 1971, 82–93.

Bewley, T.F. (1998) "Why not cut pay?", *European Economic Review*, 42, 459–490.

Calmfors, Lars and John Driffill (1988), "Bargaining Structure, Corporatism, and Macroeconomic Performance", *Economic Policy*, 6, 14–61.

Card, D. and A. B. Krueger (1995) *Myth and Measurement: The New Economics of the Minimum Wage*, Princeton University Press, New Jersey.

Chapman, B.J., S.J. Dowrick & P.N. Junankar (1991) "Perspectives on Australian Unemployment: The Impact of Wage-setting Institutions" (with), in *Australian Economic Policy: Conference Proceedings,* (Ed.) F.H. Gruen, Centre for Economic Policy Research, Australian National University, Canberra, (pp. 21–57).

Daly, A., N.H. Duc, D. Eldridge, O. Gabbitas and P. McCalman (1998) *Youth Wages and Employment*, Productivity Commission Staff Research Paper, Ausinfo, Canberra.

Debelle, G. and J. Vickery (1998) "The Macroeconomics of Unemployment", in *Unemployment and the Australian Labour Market* ed. by G. Debelle and J. Borland, Reserve Bank of Australia, Sydney.

Freeman, R.B. (1988), 'Labour Market institutions and economic performance', *Economic Policy*, 6, 63–132.

Freeman, R.B. (1998) "War of the models: Which labour market institutions for the 21st Century?", *Labour Economics*, 5, 1–24.

Friedman, M. (1980) 'Memorandum', Treasury and Civil Service Committee, House of Commons, UK, Session 1979–80, Memoranda on Monetary Policy, HMSO, London.

Gregg, P. and A. Manning (1997) "Labour market regulation and unemployment", in Unemployment Policy: Government Options for the Labour Market ed. by D.J. Snower and G. de la Dehesa, Centre for Economic Policy Research, Cambridge University Press, Cambridge.

Gregory, R.G. (1998) " Solutions to Australian Unemployment ", in *Unemployment and the Australian Labour Market* ed. by G. Debelle and J. Borland, Reserve Bank of Australia, Sydney

Gregory, R.G. and P. Sheehan (1998) " Unemployment trends in Australia and the US: The natural rate, wage flexibility and path dependence", in *Working for the Future*, ed. by P. Sheehan and G. Tegart, VUT Press, Melbourne.

Junankar, P.N. (1997) "Lessons from Britain's Thatcherite Experiment", *Economic Papers*, 16 (4), 65–70.

Junankar, P.N. and C.A. Kapuscinski (1992), *The Costs of Unemployment in Australia*. EPAC Background Paper No. 25, Australian Government Publishing Service, Canberra.

Junankar, P.N., M. Waite & G. Belchamber (1998) "The Youth Labour Market: Anecdotes, Fables and Evidence", Paper presented to the Joint Workshop on "Do youth wages matter?" at the Centre for Economic Policy Research, ANU and Productivity Commission, 23rd November 1998.

Kalecki, M. (1943) "Political Aspects of Full Employment", *Political Quarterly*, 14, 322–331.

Keynes. J.M (1936) The General Theory of Employment, Interest and Money, Cambridge University Press, Cambridge.

Layard, R., S. Nickell and R. Jackman (1991) *Unemployment: Macroeconomic Performance and the Labour Market*, Oxford: Oxford University Press.

Lindbeck, A.(1993) *Unemployment and Macroeconomics*, London: MIT Press.

Lucas, R.E., Jr and L.A. Rapping (1969) "Real Wages, Employment, and Inflation" *Journal of Political Economy*; 77(5), 721–54.

Malinvaud, E. (1982) "Wages and Unemployment", *Economic Journal*, 92, 1–12.

Mortensen, D.T. (1970) "Job Search, the Duration of Unemployment, and the Phillips Curve, *American Economic Review*; 60(5), 847–62.

Nickell, S. (1997) "Unemployment and Labor Market Rigidities: Europe versus North America", *Journal of Economic Perspectives*; 11(3), 55–74.

OECD (1997) *Employment Outlook*, OECD, Paris.

OECD (1998) *Employment Outlook*, OECD, Paris.

Phelps, E.S. (1970) *Microeconomic Foundations of Employment & Inflation Theory* (New York: N.W. Norton & Co. Inc.).

Rowthorn, R.E. (1977) "Conflict, Inflation and Money" *Cambridge Journal of Economics*; 1(3), 215–39.

Rowthorn, R.E. (1992) "Centralisation, Employment and Wage Dispersion", *Economic Journal*, 102, 506–523.

Schmid. G. (1995) " A New Approach to Labour Market Policy A contribution to the Current Policy Debate on Efficient Employment Policies", *Economic and Industrial Democracy*, SAGE, London, 16, 429–456.

Shapiro, C. and J.E. Stiglitz (1984) "Equilibrium Unemployment as a Worker Discipline Device" *American Economic Review*; 74(3), 433–44.

Solow, R. (1990) *The Labour Market as a Social Institution*, Oxford: Blackwell.

Walras, (1874, 1954) *Elements of Pure Economics*, translated by William Jaffe, Allen and Unwin, London.

4.7 A Political Economy of Unemployment: Causes and Consequences

P. N. Junankar

The British economy has been going through one of the deepest recessions in its history. The Government's restrictive policies are hitting the economy at the same time as an international recession. At the same time, there are long-term structural changes taking place in the economy: the so-called deindustralisation of Britain. Unemployment (including school leavers) in the UK has exceeded three million for some time: in January 1984 it was 3.1997 million (13.4 per cent.). Over 35 per cent, of the unemployed (in January 1984) have been unemployed for more than a year. Almost all forecasters (with the exception of maverick forecasts by Patrick Minford) agree that unemployment is unlikely to fall significantly in the next two years: it is expected to hover around three million. The post-war commitment to full employment has been abandoned (first by Callaghan in 1976[1] and then by the present Government) in its single-minded pursuit of "conquering" inflation. The present Government in fact, in espousing the New Classical/Monetarist ideas, claims that it cannot *control or affect the level of unemployment.*

The Scale of the Problem

Most capitalist economies go through phases of booms and recessions (see Figure 4.7.1 which compares the unemployment experience of OECD countries). The British economy has gone through a prolonged recession and although there are some signs of a weak recovery these are not expected to decrease unemployment significantly.

Unemployment data in the UK were collected until November 1982 by counting those people who *registered* as unemployed. Since then the Government has decided to collect and publish data on the basis of those persons claiming unemployment or supplementary benefits or national

---

Reprinted from 'A Political Economy of Unemployment: Causes and Consequences' by P. N. Junankar in *Political Quarterly* 56 (1), Jan–March 1985, 56–67. With kind permission from John Wiley & Sons, Inc.

Figure 4.7.1 Standardised unemployment rates for six industrialised countries (1966 to 1983)

insurance credits. For various reasons many people are excluded from this count: these include married women who are ineligible for unemployment or supplementary benefits, and many young people. In addition there are about three-quarters of a million people (in March 1984) on various Special Employment Measure Schemes (*e.g.* Youth Training Scheme) and if allowance is made for them, the unemployment total is estimated to rise by about 500,000. Early retirement schemes for older unemployed people similarly lowers the measured unemployment.

Total claimant unemployment in the UK (including school leavers) increased from 1,218,000 in May 1979 (election of the Thatcher Government) to 3,199,700 in January 1984. This represents an increase of 163 per cent, in just over four years—this is a remarkable achievement! Over the same period, youth unemployment (age less than 25 years) increased from 429,000 (old basis) to 1,259,700 (new basis), an increase of 194 per cent. The long-term unemployed (duration greater than six months) increased from 597,700 to 1,777,100, an increase of 197 per cent. The long-term unemployed (duration greater than one year) increased from 346,000 to 1,188,000, an increase of 243 per cent. In January 1984, 18.4. per cent, of the unemployed had been unemployed for 26–52 weeks and 37.1 per cent, for more than 52 weeks. This growth in unemployment had taken place at the same time as a *fall* in the working population even though the population of working age had increased. This is due to the non-registration of (especially) women and "discouraged workers". The unemployment rate in the United Kingdom for January 1984 for males was 16.0 per cent, while for females it was only 9.7 per cent. Another aspect worth noting is that unemployment is spread very unevenly across regions: in January 1984 the unemployment rate in Northern Ireland was 21.9 per cent., in the West Midlands 15.5 per cent., and in the South-East it was a mere(!) 9.8 per cent. Another feature of unemployment is that its incidence is concentrated amongst the unskilled, the ethnic minorities, and the young. These same groups also face *repeated* spells of unemployment.

Alternative Explanations of Unemployment[2]

(i) *Classical/Neo-Classical/Monetarist/New-Classical*
Although there are subtle differences between these alternative explanations this group of economists argues *either* that all unemployment is voluntary (assuming perfectly flexible prices) *or* that unemployment is caused by "institutional rigidities" (*e.g.* trade unions, minimum wage legislation, etc.) which prevent the labour market from clearing. The essence of the former explanation can be captured by the phrase "there has been a sudden attack of laziness amongst the population!" These attacks of laziness (like many other diseases) are obviously contagious since almost all the OECD countries face a similar problem (see Figure 4.7.1).

The theory underlying all these versions is of a perfectly functioning competitive system where wages and prices adjust rapidly (in some versions, instantly), where there are no externalities and where there is a complete set of markets (including state contingent markets). In such an Arrow-Debreu world the only unemployment that can exist is voluntary: workers *choose* to remain unemployed. Fluctuations in (voluntary) unemployment in this model can only arise due to changes in technology or tastes. This rarified micro-economic model is relied upon by this group of economists when they discuss/model macroeconomic variables.

Involuntary unemployment in Classical/Neoclassical models is simply due to institutional rigidities. If trade unions raise wages above the "equilibrium" rate this causes unemployment. Similarly, if the Government (so it is argued) imposes minimum wage legislation (above the "equilibrium") this leads to unemployment. Again the presumption is of a competitive model with a single "rigidity" introduced. (In non-competitive markets a minimum wage does not necessarily lead to unemployment.) Economists like Minford argue that the growth of unemployment in Britain is explained by union strength (growth of?), and high unemployment benefits (the latter increasing voluntary, "natural", unemployment).[3]

Neoclassical economists like Phelps (1970) and Mortensen (1970) explain unemployment as a voluntary search period while waiting for better wage offers. The higher the unemployment benefits, the lower the search costs and hence a greater time is "invested" in searching. Phelps (1970) in his introduction to this influential volume says, "It would be as senselessly puritanical to wipe out unemployment as it would be to raise taxes in a deep depression. Today's unemployment is an investment in a better allocation of any given quantity of employed persons tomorrow; its opportunity cost, like that of any other investment, is present consumption" (p. 17). It is rather strange that three (or really four) million unemployed workers are investing like crazy while capitalist employers have *reduced* investment significantly!

The Lucas–Rapping (1970) model is in the same paradigm. In their model workers mistakenly believe that today's real wage is "too low" relative to tomorrow's real wage, so that they substitute current unemployment for future employment. Even in a certain world, L–R would argue that intertemporal substitution would lead to unemployment[4]: if we all *correctly* believed that the wage rate *next* period would be a million pounds (dollars) a week we may all voluntarily *take* unemployment this period and work next week! Fluctuations in unemployment are caused, in these models, due to variations in the deviation of the actual and expected wage rates. *Misperception causes unemployment.*

The New Classical school led by R. E. Lucas and T. J. Sargent argue that people form rational expectations (RE) about relevant variables: individuals form expectations that are *correct on average*. In a perfectly competitive world with RE there can be no systematic deviations of relevant variables from that expected (e.g. real wages cannot deviate systematically from expected real wage rates) and hence there cannot be *systematic* fluctuations in employment (unemployment). Hence all fluctuations in unemployment are *purely random*. Unemployment is a random walk! The evidence for these theories is either negligible or non-existent.

(ii) *Keynesian*

This school treats unemployment as being involuntary and primarily due to inadequate aggregate demand. There is market failure: markets do not clear, wages are rigid, or at least not completely flexible. Keynesians argue that aggregate demand fluctuates (especially investment) and this leads to sympathetic movements in output and employment (and hence inverse fluctuations in unemployment). Keynes stressed the volatility of expectations which leads to volatile investment. Workers do not accept a money wage cut as this implies a cut in *relative* wages. A Keynesian interpretation of the recent recession is in terms of the OPEC oil price rises leading to a fall in the real incomes of OECD countries. This led to a decrease in demand for British exports by OECD countries. This fall in aggregate demand was the initial cause of the recession and unemployment. Tight monetary and fiscal policies by the Thatcher Government reinforced the fall in aggregate demand and hence deepened the recession. A variant of this is that a rise in oil prices led to a cost push inflation: the higher input prices led to higher output prices which led to workers demanding higher money wages to compensate for the loss of real income. The Thatcher Government in attempting to "conquer" inflation imposed tight monetary policy which caused the interest and exchange rates to adjust rapidly, there was an "overshooting" of the exchange rate. This decrease in competitiveness led to a fall in the rate of profit and hence a decline in production and inventories and ah increase in unemployment. A variant of this is the "Dutch Disease" explanation: the discovery of North Sea Oil and Gas led to a jump in the exchange rate. There is some empirical support for this explanation. This interpretation can be found in Buiter and Miller (1981, 1983) and Grubb, Jackman and Layard (1982).

(iii) *Marxist/Radical*

A Marxist explanation of unemployment begins with an analysis of the cyclical fluctuations of a capitalist economy. In a dialectical fashion capital attracts and discards labour in pursuit of profits. The *process* of capitalist development increases labour supply (via increased participation and increases in "efficiency units" of labour services) as well as increases in demand. Capital accumulation, which plays a central role in introducing technological change, takes place in a cyclical fashion leading to multiplier-accelerator cycles in production and employment (and hence unemployment). Technological change is presumed to be labour displacing and it is argued that this leads to unemployment. Like Keynesians, Marxists stress the volatility of accumulation (investment) but unlike traditional (bourgeois) economists they stress technological change as leading to unemployment. In one version as the economy is on the upswing unemployment falls, wage rates rise, the profit rate falls below some critical level, accumulation (investment) falls, output and employment fall and so the cycle continues. The increased unemployment (the industrial reserve army) keeps the "pretentions of the workers in check"—in other words puts a downward pressure on wage rates, and hence improving profit rates. There is clear evidence of falling rates of profit in the seventies and early eighties and a decline in investment. There is evidence, see, for example, Junankar and Price (1984) that aggregate demand is important in explaining fluctuations in unemployment. There is, however, no firm evidence that technological change, in aggregate, has led to increased unemployment (see, for example, *Scientific American,* 1982). However, the process of technological change displaces workers and if aggregate demand is held down by Government policy it results in unemployment.

Unlike Keynesians, Marxists argue that Government policies cannot eradicate unemployment[5]: unemployment is inherent in a capitalist system. The only way to remove unemployment, it is argued, is to remove capitalism.

The Costs and Benefits of Unemployment

After a brief review of alternative explanations I now turn to the social, political and economic consequences of unemployment. The aim of this section is to highlight the *costs and benefits* to individuals, classes, and to society of unemployment. It is important to remember that the stock of unemployment is continually changing due to inflows and outflows. Inflows into the unemployment stock consist of voluntary quits, fires (involuntary separations), and new entrants and re-entrants. The outflows from the unemployment stock consist of new hires, discouraged workers who leave the labour force, and workers retiring due to old age. There have been attempts in the United States (see Feldstein (1978) and Hall (1972)) to argue that completed unemployment spells are of very short duration (the so-called "new view") and hence unemployment is not a serious problem. Clark and Summers (1979) in an interesting paper argue that the mean of the completed spells of the *currently unemployed persons* is very high although the mean of all completed *spells* is low. Those with long duration spells account for a high proportion of all weeks of unemployment experience. In other words, most of the unemployment experienced is concentrated on a small group of people. Another feature worth mentioning is that many of the unemployed face *repeated* spells of unemployment. One's views on the appropriate measure of unemployment colours the costs and benefits of unemployment.

(i) *The Costs of Unemployment*

As mentioned earlier the costs of unemployment are borne, to varying extents, by individuals, by the working class, by elements of the capitalist class, and by society in general.

(a) *The Individual*

An unemployed individual faces a fall in his real income. If (s)he quit voluntarily (s)he would (presumably) have anticipated this fall in real income and weighed it up against the expected benefits. However, (s)he may not have correctly anticipated the length of time required to find another job. For this individual there is a loss of real income (as a voluntary quit the individual is not eligible for unemployment benefits (at least for a few weeks)) which may be substantial. For the person who was fired, or the contract came to an end, or was made redundant there is a sudden (unexpected?) fall in real income. Unemployed workers (if they have an adequate work history) are eligible for unemployment benefits to cushion the blow. A recent change in legislation by the Thatcher Government has abolished the "earnings related supplement" making the fall in real income rather dramatic for some people. People who are not eligible for unemployment benefits are eligible for means-tested supplementary benefits. However, a married woman who becomes unemployed is ineligible for supplementary benefits. If a married man becomes unemployed his wife's earnings are used to determine the level of supplementary benefits: there is an economic incentive for the married woman to give up her (usually poorly paid part-time) job.

These purely economic costs to the individual are greater the greater the length of unemployment. There is some evidence to suggest that there are permanent "scarring" effects of unemployment: the longer the duration of unemployment the more difficult it is to find another job. This may be either because the unemployed person gets disillusioned and decreases his search intensity and/or because employers treat long duration as a signal of unwanted characteristics. If you take the view that the mean of the completed spells of the *currently unemployed persons* is very high then this cost to the individual is fairly high.

High levels of unemployment also impose a cost on *employed* individuals. Firstly, unemployment may affect wage rates and/or earnings growth. Secondly, high unemployment leads to a decrease in job mobility and a decrease in voluntary quits. Because individuals perceive a decreased probability of employment they do not look for new posts and voluntary quitting declines. This increases dissatisfaction of the employed workers who are potentially mobile.

Besides the purely economic loss of losing a job (an income), unemployed individuals lose their social standing amongst their peer group. In a society where a person's worth is judged by his earning capacity an unemployed person is a social failure and misfit. Marsden and Duff (1975) mention the case of an individual who when made redundant still left his home at 9 a.m. with his sandwiches and "worked" in his garden shed until 5 p.m. when he returned home! The idea that having a job provides not only an income but also provides a person with psychological and social satisfaction is usually ignored by most economists.

Individuals who are unemployed seem to be more prone to illness (physical and mental) and some would argue are more likely to attempt to commit suicide, and to die through illness. There is much work to be done in this area but there are problems of disentangling cause and effect: are those individuals unemployed because they are prone to sickness or are they prone to sickness because they are unemployed? All these ailments lead to a poisoning of family relations and puts severe strain on marriages and family life.

(b) *Class*

Let us turn to the impact of unemployment on social classes: on the workers and the capitalists. Increased unemployment *apparently* hits both the workers and the capitalists.

Prolonged and high unemployment leads to a distinct shift in power (social, political and economic) away from the working class towards the capitalists. The prolonged and high unemployment that Britain is now experiencing (and has experienced only once before in the depression of the

1930s) has led to a profound change in Britain. It has led to a slowing down in the growth of real earnings and a fall in the share of wages in GDP. It has led to a weakening of trade unions: membership of unions has been falling quite significantly in recent years. Using strikes and strike days lost as an index of the power of unions we see that the present depression has led to a weakening of unions. Even Social Democratic Party economics Professors Buiter and Miller (1983) state "Since the Tories came to power in 1979 there has been a shift in the balance of industrial bargaining power away from the unions and toward management" (p. 358). Political activity which is centred around the work place and unions suffer. Governments can and do pass anti-union legislation in such periods of union weakness.

Prolonged unemployment (accompanying the depression) has, on the whole, a favourable impact on the capitalist class. A re-structuring of capital takes place: some of the smaller firms go into liquidation. According to the paradigm of a "good" capitalist economy it is the least efficient plants and firms that go to the wall. During a depression new investment and the introduction of new technology is likely to suffer and hence threaten future profits. To sum up, elements of the capitalist class suffer during a depression.

(c) *Society*

The biggest cost to society is the loss of output which could be produced. Estimates of these are enormous and it seems surprising that any society would *voluntarily* give up such large amounts of goods and services. During periods of high unemployment the Government has a fall in tax revenues and an increase in welfare expenditures (unemployment and other benefits) and an increased cost of ill health. It has been argued by Hargreaves-Heap (1980) that increased unemployment now leads to increased unemployment in the future: a process called hysteresis. Thus society will face even greater costs in the future.

A permanently high rate of unemployment imposes serious strains on the social fabric. These are likely to lead to increasing racial tension as people search for scape-goats. It has been argued that the riots in Brixton and Toxteth may be a side-effect of high unemployment in those areas. It is argued that society is likely to get increasingly polarised with political parties becoming more extreme. However, it is also argued (contradistinction to the above) that unemployment leads to a feeling of helplessness and alienation from the body politic. There is work which suggests a link between unemployment and crime, either because the unemployed have nothing to do and crime is a way of buying the good things of life, or like good neoclassical maximisers the opportunity cost of time had decreased. There is some evidence from preliminary work done by the author which finds evidence for a link between youth unemployment and crime by youths.

In the face of this the Thatcher Government has been at pains to give well-above average pay rises to the police force and the armed services.

If there is civil strife there are at least two groups who have been pampered and can be trusted. The recent armed confrontations between the police force and striking miners is only one such illustration of the changed industrial and social scene.

(ii) *The Benefits of Unemployment*

Although Monetarists and New Classical economists do not see any benefits from unemployment (except to the individual) I shall follow the earlier section and look at the benefits to individuals, to classes, and to society.

(a) *Individual*

An unemployed individual can benefit from leisure, at least for some time. S(he) can do various jobs around the house which were postponed: do the garden, paint the house, clean the shed/garage, etc. But to some extent these are done simply as time-filling occupations: a way of justifying to oneself that one is not useless and redundant. Outside leisure activities like sailing, swimming, watching sports all cost money: to enjoy these leisure activities you need a job! The unemployed person can search for a (better?) job and at least for some time this can provide some "excitement" to life. However, prolonged spells of unemployment are not "beneficial".

If the higher unemployment slows down the rate of price inflation (although Monetarists and New Classicals do not believe this) then the *employed* individual is better off. People on fixed incomes and creditors would also benefit (especially if it is an unanticipated fall in inflation). The Monetarists (and the Thatcher regime) believe that unemployment does not affect inflation (there is no Phillips curve trade-off, for the New Classicals not even in the short-run). (For Mrs. Thatcher it is inflation that causes unemployment.)

(b) *Class*

The class that benefits from unemployment is the capitalist class. High levels of unemployment increase the capitalist's control over workers. The sack is a powerful and credible threat if there is a large dole queue. One local Tory authority in Britain forced a reduction in money wage rates (of 25–30 per cent.) on the school "dinner ladies": a poorly-paid group who would otherwise have to face prolonged unemployment. British Leyland workers have accepted wage increases *below* the rate of inflation.

Periods of prolonged full employment increase the bargaining power of workers, and bosses lose their authoritarian position in the workplace.[6] With a large industrial reserve army the workers are reminded that their job is due to the bounty (beneficence) of the capitalist. The capitalist employer is in a position to extract more labour services from workers. Changes in work practices can be imposed more easily.[7] Absenteeism and strikes are likely to decline and productivity is likely to rise. The tories refer to a "new realism in industrial relations", what they mean is that they are (in Marx's words) keeping the "workers pretentions in check". All this helps to stimulate the rate of profit and hence future accumulation (investment).

A prolonged depression leads to an increase on *average* productivity via a closing down of the least efficient plants and firms. This helps to raise the rate of profit. Periods of recession lead to a re-structuring of capital with an increase in mergers and take-overs leading to increasing concentration. This helps larger (and perhaps more efficient) firms to benefit from the recession: they have greater resources to "ride the storm".

Unemployment is likely to put downward pressure on the inflation rate which benefits the rentier class. The evidence on Phillips curves for Britain is mixed: however the impact of prolonged unemployment on the inflation rate may be significant even if temporary increases to unemployment have insignificant effects.

(c) *Society*

It is important to note that even though millions of people suffer from poverty and hopelessness due to unemployment, *capitalist* society benefits. It helps to reinforce the power of capitalists over workers. It also provides for a reinvigoration of capitalism by weeding out the inefficient capitalists. A large reservoir of unemployed workers is necessary for a subsequent spurt in economic growth.

Thus a government which favours capitalism and capitalists must allow unemployment to persist. Hence the Tory Government chants "the Government cannot affect unemployment". Some capitalists and many workers may suffer but periodic bouts of unemployment are necessary to regenerate capitalist society. To quote Kalecki,

> "Lasting full employment is not to their (the 'business leaders') liking. The workers would 'get out of hand' and the 'captains of industry' would be anxious to 'teach them a lesson'."

Conclusions

The aim of this paper was to outline the scale of the problem of unemployment in Britain, to discuss alternative explanations of the causes of the growth of unemployment, and finally to discuss the costs and benefits of unemployment. It has been argued that the costs of unemployment are not simply the loss of an income but also the loss of an individual's social role. It was suggested that the working class and society in general suffered important economic and social consequences. However, it was argued that the benefits of unemployment accrued most importantly to *capitalist* society. Unemployment plays an important role in reinforcing the authoritarian position of the capitalist class and leads to a reinvigoration of capitalist firms.

The prolonged and high level of unemployment in Britain (and most OECD countries) should lead economists to question the rationality of an economic system which requires this to help maintain capitalist society. Economists should consider alternative forms of society where unemployment may one day be a thing of the past. Simply pointing to the horrors of a Stalinist Russia should not prevent us from questioning the underlying economic system. Perhaps people may prefer a capitalist society with perpetual bouts of unemployment to an alternative society without. But how do we know?

Notes

The author is Principal Research Fellow, Institute for Employment Research, University of Warwick, on leave from the Department of Economics, University of Essex. The research was completed while the author was a Visiting Fellow, Department of Economics, Research School of Social Sciences, Australian National University. He wishes to thank Simon Price for helpful comments.

1. Jim Callaghan as Prime Minister said to the Labour Party Conference in 1976: "We used to think that you could spend you way out of a recession, and increase employment by cutting taxes and boosting government spending. I tell you in all candour that that option no longer exists, and that in so far as it ever did exist, it only worked ... by injecting a bigger dose of inflation into the system."
2. A recent Special Issue of the *Review of Economic Studies* (1982) on Unemployment has Richard Layard introducing the volume thus: "Those models with sound theoretical foundations do not seem to fit the facts of unemployment either in the US or Europe, and those empirical models which claim to be a reasonable representation of the facts nave no convincing theoretical foundations."
3. Note however that the Thatcher Government has reduced real unemployment benefits in the past few years, especially since the abolition of the earnings related supplement.
4. A footnote expands this thesis: "the theory 'predicts' that the workers will concentrate their labour supply in years of peak earnings, consuming leisure in larger than average amounts in childhood and old age" (L-R (1970) p. 266, fn. 9). A non-neoclassical economist can only gasp in wonder at the power of neoclassical economic theorems!
5. Like the Monetarists and Neoclassical economists, Marxists believe that the Government cannot control the economy. Unlike them, however, Marxists believe that the capitalist economy is inherently unstable.
6. See Kalecki (1943).
7. See Oster (1980).

References

Bruno, M. and Sachs, J. (1982), "Input Price Shocks and the Slowdown in Economic Growth: The Case of UK Manufacturing", *Review of Economic Studies,* Vol. XLIX (5), No. 159, pp. 679–706.

Buiter, W. H. and Miller, M. H. (1981), "The Thatcher Experiment: The First Two Years", *Brookings Papers on Economic Activity,* 1981 (2), pp. 315–367.

—— (1983), "Changing the Rules: Economic Consequences of the Thatcher Regime", *Brookings Papers on Economic Activity,* 1983 (2), pp. 305–365.

Clark, K. B. and Summers, L. H. (1979), "Labour Market Dynamics and Unemployment: A Reconsideration", *Brookings Papers on Economic Activity,* 1979, (1), pp. 13–60.

Feldstein, M. (1978), "The Private and Social Costs of Unemployment", *American Economic Review,* Vol. 68, No. 2, pp. 155–158.

Grubb, D., Jackman R. and Layard, R. (1982), "Causes of the Current Stagflation", *Review of Economic Studies,* Vol. XLIX, pp. 707–730.

Hall, R. E. (1972), "Turnover in the Labor Force", *Brookings Papers on Economic Activity,* 1972 (3), pp. 709–756.

Hargreaves-Heap, S. P. (1980), "Choosing the Wrong 'Natural' Rate: Acclerating Inflation or Decelerating Employment and Growth", *Economic Journal,* Vol. 90, No. 359, pp. 611–620.

Junankar, P. N. and Price, S. (1984), "The Dynamics of Unemployment: Structural Change and Unemployment Flows", *Economic Journal,* Conference Papers Supplement, Vol. 94, pp. 158–165.

Kalecki, M. (1943), "Political Aspects of Full Employment", in *Political Quarterly,* Vol. 14, pp. 322–331. Reprinted in Hunt, E. K. & Schwarz, J. G., *A Critique of Economic Theory* (Harmondsworth: Penguin, 1972).

Layard, R. (1982), "Introduction to Special Issue on Unemployment", *Review of Economic Studies,* Vol. XLIX, pp. 675–677.

Lucas, R. E. and Rapping, L. A. (1970), "Real Wages, Employment and Inflation", in Phelps (1970), pp. 257–308.

Marsden, D. and Duff, E. (1975), *Workless* (Harmondsworth: Penguin). Mortensen, D. T. (1970), "A Theory of Wage and Employment Dynamics", in Phelps (1970), pp. 167–211.

Oster, G. (1980), "Labour Relations and Demand Relations: A Case Study of the 'Unemployment Effect' ", *Cambridge Journal of Economics,* Vol. 4, No. 4, pp. 337–348.

Phelps, E. S. (ed.) (1970), *Microeconomic Foundations of Employment and Inflation Theory* (New York: W. W. Norton & Co. Inc.).

—— (1970a), "Introduction: The New Microeconomics in Employment and Inflation Theory", in Phelps (1970), pp. 1–26.

5
Long-Term Unemployment

5.1
Projections of Long-term Unemployment

Bruce J. Chapman, P.N. Junankar and Cezary A. Kapuscinski

Australia now has a considerable unemployment problem. One of the most important and least visible consequences of a deep recession is a large and expanding pool of people who have been unemployed for a long period of time. This is a crucial issue which has in the past been accorded less weight in policy discussion than is warranted.

The phrase conventionally used to describe the phenomenon of being unemployed for twelve or more months continuously is 'long term unemployment' (LTU). There are two basic facts about LTU, now illustrated in Figure 5.1.1.

The first is that a short time after the onset of a recession, LTU numbers increase rapidly; from the diagram, for example, in the year following the considerable downturn in 1982–83, the expansion in LTU was almost threefold. Second, even with considerable job growth – such as that experienced in the 1984–90 period of an average of nearly 4 per cent per annum – LTU decreases at a very slow pace.

What emerges is that once a recession eventuates, LTU becomes a significant and continuing issue. It is the subject of what follows.

LTU is examined in theoretical and empirical terms. Explanation is offered for the facts noted above and the distributional and efficiency implications of LTU are explored. From time series models projections are offered of the likely future minimum and maximum levels of total as well as both male and female LTU over the next few years. The data imply strongly that the numbers involved exceed, and will continue to exceed by a large margin, the highest level of LTU in post-World War II Australian economic history,

---

Reprinted from 'Projections of Long-term Unemployment' by Bruce J. Chapman, P. N. Junankar and Cezary A. Kapuscinski in *Australian Bulletin of Labour,* 18 (3), September 1992, 195–207. With kind permission from National Institute of Labour Studies.

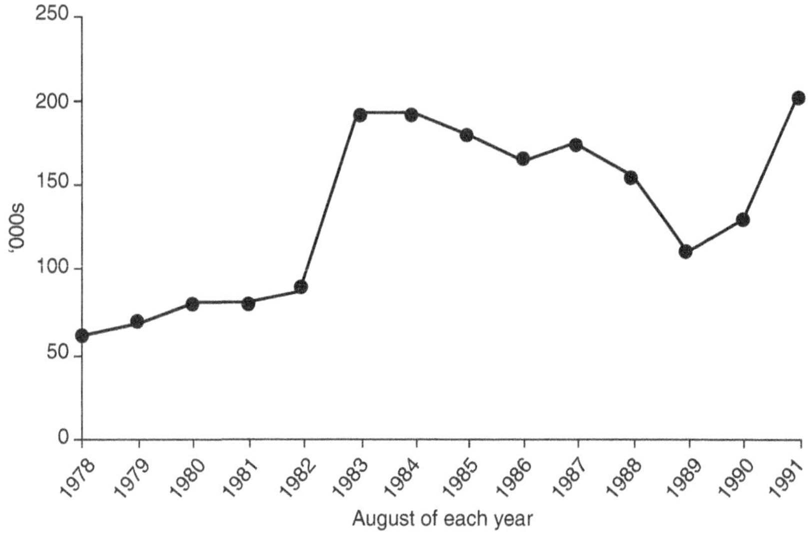

Figure 5.1.1 Long-term Unemployment (Persons)
Source: Australian Bureau of Statistics, Cat. No. 6203.

and that this will be true no matter what job growth ensues over the next few years.

The paper does not specifically examine recent Australian Government labour market program initiatives. The aim instead is to provide the theoretical and empirical bases important to understanding the issue.

Measurement and Theory

Measuring LTU

The current custom defines long term unemployment as a continuous spell of unemployment exceeding twelve months. This is arbitrary: in the earlier postwar periods LTU was defined as a continuous spell of six (and sometimes even three months).

There are several complexities associated with the measurement of LTU, the first of which relates to the notion of unemployment duration. In general an *uncompleted* spell of unemployment is measured at a point in time and constitutes the unemployment duration of people who are unemployed at that point of time.

However, during a recession many of the unemployed are very likely to remain unemployed for a further period. That is, most of those unemployed for 39 to 51 weeks are likely in the next quarter to be unemployed for over 52 weeks. Thus, in this situation, the uncompleted duration measure of LTU implies an underestimate of the true extent of the likely continuation of the LTU experience.[1]

Another complication is that the measure only includes people who have been *continuously* unemployed for 52 weeks or more. Those falling ill, or leaving the labour force because they are discouraged, are considered to have a zero duration of unemployment at the time of re-entering the unemployment pool. There is some evidence from the Australian Longitudinal Surveys that, for many people, recurrent spells of unemployment lead (over a certain period of time) to a cumulative duration exceeding 52 weeks,[2] but not as a continuous spell. This implies a systematic under-estimate of the extent of LTU.

In order to clarify some of the important conceptual issues associated with LTU, it is useful to think of the labour market as continually changing with inflows into and outflows from the unemployment stock. Thus,

$$U_t = U_{t-1} + I_t - O_t$$

where U_t is the end of period t unemployment level, I_t and O_t are inflows to, and outflows from, unemployment over the period t. The inflows consist of quits (voluntary separations), those who have been fired or made redundant (involuntary separations), and new entrants (or re-entrants) in the labour force. The outflows consist of people who find jobs, who get discouraged and leave the labour force, who fall ill, who retire or take early retirement, or who join labour market programs.

The stock of unemployed people consists of some people who have been unemployed for a short time, as well as those who have been unemployed for a long time. There is a distribution of people over different duration categories which is usually skewed with a large number in the shorter categories and a very long tail to the right of the longer term unemployed. By definition the inflows enter with a zero duration, while the outflows consist of those who are leaving from different parts of the duration distribution.

In general, the short term unemployed have a greater probability than the long-term unemployed of 'escaping' from unemployment into employment. The LTU have a lower escape probability into jobs because employers are less likely to prefer them, and therefore are more likely to discontinue job search, or take up early retirement.

The important point, as far as the relative probability of receiving job offers is concerned, is that as new people join the unemployment stock, the LTU seem to be pushed further and further back in the queue. A simplification is that the young and more highly skilled unemployed exit more easily from each new group of inflows, leaving behind the older and less skilled.

Explaining the LTU Experience

There are two main reasons for the LTU having low probabilities of securing employment. One is the apparent reduction in the intensity of job search, the other being a reluctance on the part of employers to hire those who have been unemployed for an extended period. These effects could be caused by demoralisation of the unemployed as their spell increases in length, and/or by employers regarding length of unemployment spell as an indicator of poor labour market qualities.

Within this second category there is a further distinction in the causes of increased unemployment duration, with the analogy of a flower shop introduced by Budd, Levine and Smith (1988a, 1988b) being useful in describing the processes at work. In the shop's stock of flowers there are blooms of varying age and brightness, with customers operating a double process of discrimination in selecting blooms. The newest flowers will be bought first and, if any are bought among the older flowers of any particular age, they will be the brightest. Thus for every passing day, remaining flowers both appear older and the cohort is losing the relatively bright blooms.

In the labour market context, similar processes may apply to the duration of current unemployment spell and a bundle of skills related to experience, education and so forth. First it is likely that employers compare someone unemployed for twelve months unfavourably with someone unemployed for less than three months, for any given common bundle of attributes, because of the belief that the former have lost skills or undergone adverse attitudinal changes from the LTU experience. This is known as the state – or duration – dependence effect.

The other effect is illustrated by noting that the cohort which has been unemployed for twelve months is different from a short-term unemployed cohort, since those with the better bundle of attributes will have already found jobs. This is analagous to the belief that the best flowers are purchased first, and is known as the heterogeneity effect. It works in the same direction as state dependence, with both effects implying that for those remaining the probability of leaving unemployment falls as the duration of the spell increases.

Related to this is the high probability that, as job opportunities improve, many of the 'new hires' seem to be from outside the labour force, that is, new participants and possibly previously discouraged workers. In other words, the competition for the limited number of vacancies that arises takes place not only between the different duration categories of the stock of unemployed, but also from the prospective new entrants without the characteristics observed in the LTU.

As noted, job search is also affected by the LTU experience. The longer a person has been unemployed the fewer contacts she or he is likely to have with a network of colleagues/workmates to provide information on job vacancies. Since the evidence suggests that these informal networks are very important for jobseekers, the LTU are in a disadvantaged position purely from a search perspective.

Clearly, then, there are several reasons for the LTU having poor current and future employment prospects. Moreover, there are significant costs associated with the phenomenon.

The Costs of LTU

The primary reason for a concern with unemployment duration is macroeconomic. Economic analysis in this area developed in important ways during the 1980s, most significantly with respect to the issue of 'hysteresis', in which the long-run positioning of the non-accelerating inflation rate of unemployment (NAIRU) is seen to depend on current and past rates of unemployment. In this literature LTU is considered to be an integral part of the hysteresis process.

Given both that employers are likely to view the LTU as poor employment prospects and that as a result the LTU will search less, it follows that at any given unemployment rate, job vacancies will be filled less quickly and with a poorer match when there is a higher proportion of LTU. From this perspective a reduction of LTU increases the likelihood of there being a more propitious matching of the pool of unemployed to job vacancies.

The adverse effect of increases in LTU on the operation of the aggregate labour market has been demonstrated empirically for the UK by Budd, Levine and Smith (1988a, 1988b). Similarly there is evidence that there have been effects from increases in LTU on the positioning of the Australian unemployment-vacancies relation (Hughes 1987, Hughes 1992, Williams 1989). Macro-economic modelling tends to support these latter findings with respect to estimations of changes in the NAIRU (Simes and Richardson 1987). Apparently, increases in both the proportion of unemployment which is long-term and the absolute number of LTU make the filling of vacancies more difficult and the rate of wage inflation higher at any given level of unemployment.

It follows from the above that there are likely to be compelling reasons from a long-term macroeconomic perspective for avoiding the creation of LTU. More obvious than this is that, *ceteris paribus*, a labour market characterised by increasingly high levels of LTU is one experiencing changes in income distribution (and life opportunities) towards the less equal.

Equity issues associated with LTU loom large for policy. There is little doubt that those with high unemployment duration are some of the most disadvantaged members of the labour force (Junankar 1988). Not only does this group have low contemporaneous incomes, it seems also to be the case that they have fewer skills and less education, and thus poorer employment prospects generally. This particular issue – the dynamic side of distribution – warrants some attention.

Over time, employed persons become increasingly different to unemployed persons in several senses. One is that the incomes of the former group typically increase, through real wage gains that average around 2 or 3 per cent a year, through individuals having more labour market experience and from the receipt of promotion. In other words, the differences between life-time job opportunities and acquired human capital levels of the employed and the unemployed become greater the longer the respective labour market states remain unchanged.

Empirical Estimates and Projections

In this section we set up simple forecasting models of female, male and total LTU. To minimise the data requirements, the concentration is only on the relationships between the proportion of the LTU in the unemployment stock (PLTU) and the unemployment rate (UR) for the respective groups.

The virtue of such an approach lies in the ability to generate forecasts conditional only on the past history of PLTU and lags of UR, with the profile of the future short-term behaviour of UR subjectively chosen against a low, medium and high level of expected unemployment in the period of the forecasts. The estimation period is from 1978(i) to 1991(iv) and the forecasts of PLTU are provided for the four years following (that is, until 1995(iv)).

The outer bounds of the forecasts of UR to the end of 1993 and constant thereafter were chosen to be 1.5 percentage points above and below the 1992(i) seasonally adjusted figures. Thus, for males, the three scenarios have values of 9.7, 11.2 and 12.7 per cent unemployment for the low, medium and high scenarios respectively. For females, these figures are 8.7, 10.2 and 11.7 per cent, and the forecasts for the total use the values of 9.2,10.7 and 12.2 per cent. Further, it is assumed that the transition to the terminal values at the end of 1993 takes place during the first eight quarters of the post sample period. The remaining period may then be regarded as a quasi-steady state.

Figures 5.1.2 and 5.1.3 provide an illustration of the recent history of both the PLTU and UR series for males and females. Consistent with earlier observations it is immediately apparent that while PLTU responds very quickly in the recessionary periods (as illustrated by the unemployment rates), it takes much longer to return to the pre-recession levels. The main conclusion from these graphs, however, is the clear link between UR and PLTU, a link which is empirically demonstrated in Chapman, Junankar and Kapuscinski (1992).

The models were tested with a range of fairly sophisticated empirical diagnostics, with the results being reported in Chapman *et al* (1992). As well, predictive tests both within-sample and post-sample (using Salkever's 1976 methodology) were performed to examine the usefulness of the models. In summary, it appears that there were no major problems in tracking the behaviour of PLTU within the estimation sample, with the models picking up most of the turning points.

As an illustrative example, Appendix Figure 5.1.1 demonstrates that the model for total LTU tracks the data quite accurately. This is true also for the models for males and females. Other predictive tests reported in Chapman *et al* (1992) also suggest that the models outperform the more simple techniques often used in the analysis of trends in macroeconomic time-series.

In short, the models employed for forecasting appear to be statistically healthy. They track the data well within the sample and outside the estimation period, and show no evidence of structural instability. Because of these

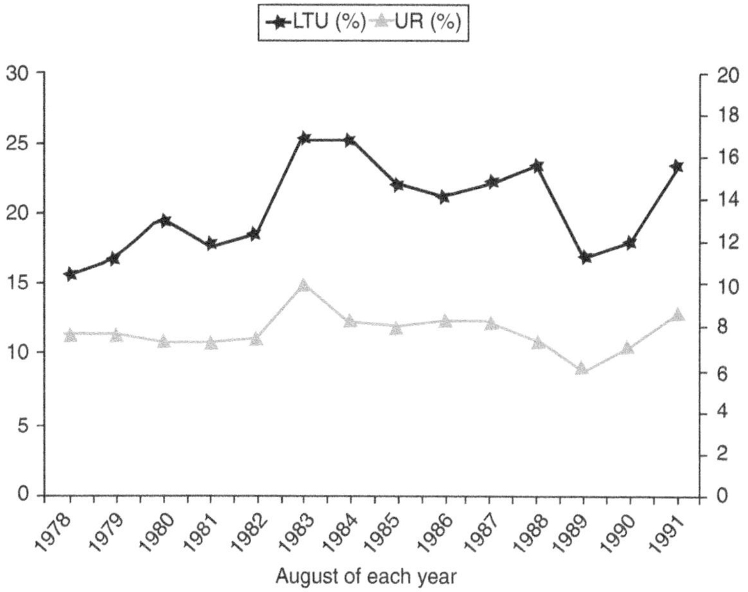

Figure 5.1.2 Proportion of Unemployment which is Long-term Unemployment and the Unemployment Rate (Females)

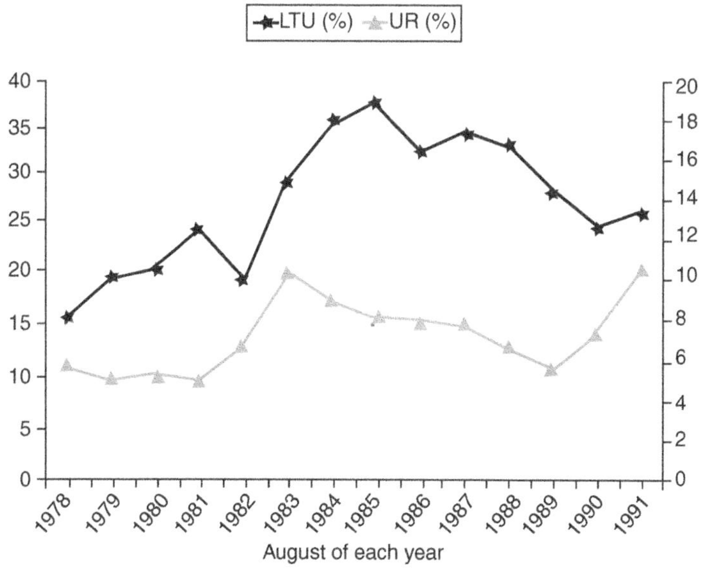

Figure 5.1.3 Proportion of Unemployment which is Long-term Unemployment and the Unemployment Rate (Males)

diagnostic characteristics, some confidence can be placed in the forecasts of LTU now reported.

Figures 5.1.4, 5.1.5 and 5.1.6 present projections of male, female and total LTU over the next four years. There is no presumption of what the actual unemployment rate (on which the forecasts are based) will be. But the minimum and maximum scenarios described previously seem to be reasonable boundaries for our purposes.

For males there is a relative stability in LTU projections in the next year or two, implying strongly that the short-term future course of LTU is pretty much determined by recent history. After this the 'low' scenario becomes much different to the 'high' outcome, with the most serious possible outcome being around 347,000 men in early 1995. But even the most optimistic forecast reveals no obvious decline from the historically high levels now being experienced.

There are two characteristics of the forecasts of the female LTU that differentiate them from the profile of the male LTU forecasts. First there is a higher proportionate difference between the 'low' and 'high' scenarios (more than double for females compared to less than 80 per cent for males). Second the female projections suggest some possibility of there being a decrease in this group's LTU given rapid job creation.

Figure 5.1.6 and Table 5.1.1 show the total forecasts with the projections suggesting the prospect of there being extremely high numbers of LTU over

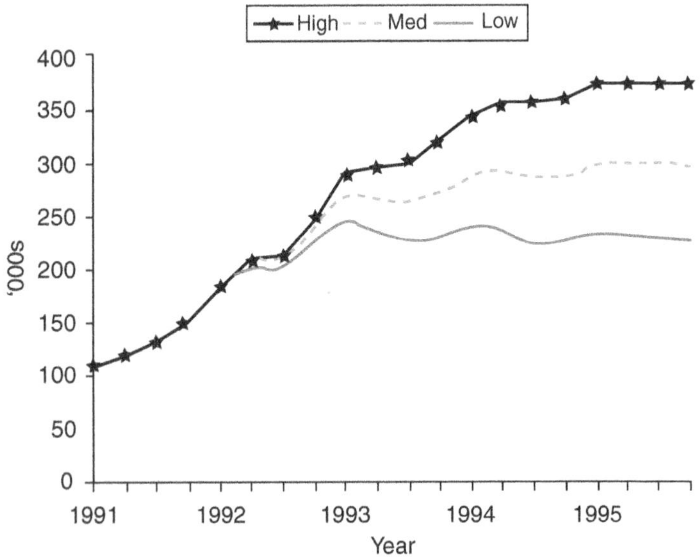

Figure 5.1.4 Post Sample Projections of Long-term Unemployment: Males

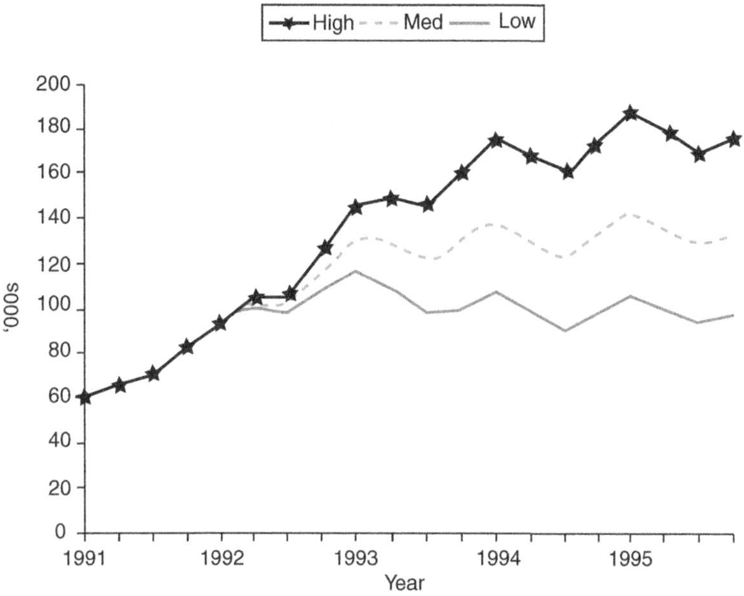

Figure 5.1.5 Post Sample Predictions of Long-term Unemployment: Females

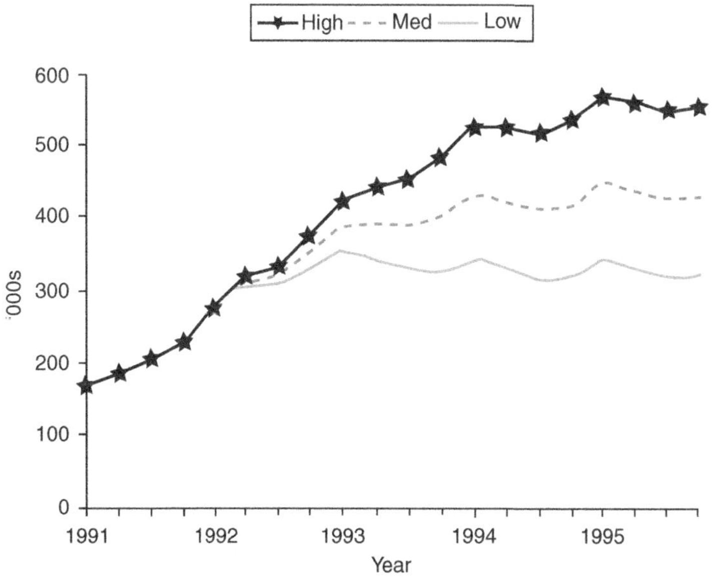

Figure 5.1.6 Post Sample Projections of Long-term Unemployment: Persons

Table 5.1.1 Long Term Unemployment Projections: Persons

Date	Low		Medium		High	
	UR(%)	LTU(000s)	UR(%)	LTU(000s)	UR(%)	LTU(000s)
1992 (I)	10.7	276	10.7	276	10.7	276
1992 (II)	10.4	304	10.7	309	10.9	315
1992 (III)	10.3	307	10.7	319	11.1	331
1992 (IV)	10.0	329	10.7	352	11.3	375
1993 (I)	9.8	356	10.7	390	11.6	425
1993 (II)	9.6	346	10.7	394	11.8	444
1993 (III)	9.4	328	10.7	388	12.0	453
1993 (IV)	9.2	324	10.7	400	12.2	482
1994 (IV)	9.2	319	10.7	418	12.2	531
1995 (IV)	9.2	323	10.7	431	12.2	554

the medium term. Even in the next two years it seems unlikely that there will be much – if any – fall in absolute LTU, with a reasonable suggestion (that is, the medium scenario) being that by early 1994 there will be about 400,000 people in the category, compared to about 190,000 in 1983. Much of this difference is attributable to growth in the labour force, but a part is a result of the effect of the ratchetting phenomenon: LTU tends to remain at high levels for a long time after a major recession, so that a further considerable downturn builds on this experience.

The important empirical point is that LTU over the next period will not be less significant than it currently is, and is likely to be of even greater magnitude. This assessment appears unlikely to be compromised by the state of the economy, which is consistent with the theory discussed earlier. A profound challenge relates to the implications these data have for policy.

Conclusion

In summary, the current state of the Australian labour market augurs poorly for those already disadvantaged in the labour force, of which there are, and will continue to be, very many. Our econometric estimates and projections imply strongly that the number of LTU will be at an unprecedented level and likely to be growing over the next two years. If past experience is a guide, it is now unlikely that this situation can be avoided.

A useful general policy point from the exercise is that an aggregate economic slowdown, even if planned to be of short duration, is associated with ongoing and long-term costs for the economy and individual members of LTU. Because members of the group tend to be placed at the back of the hiring queue, growing unemployment duration can persist for periods long after the bottom of a recession is reached. Unfortunately, rapid job creation has relatively little impact on the numbers of LTU.

However, it is clear also that there are considerable benefits associated with a pick up in economic growth in the next short period. That is, if the economy achieves an unemployment rate close to 9 per cent instead of increasing to around 12 per cent by the end of 1993, about 160,000 Australian workers will avoid the LTU experience, although it is unlikely that any of this group will be aware of this. As pointed out in the theoretical discussion, there are clear benefits to be had from the former result in terms of the efficiency of the operation of the macro-economy.

Notes

An earlier version of this paper was presented to the University of Wollongong Conference on Unemployment in February 1992. The authors are grateful for feedback from Conference participants and to Flora Gill for acting as discussant.

1. As against this so-called 'interruption bias', there is a counter-bias called a 'length bias'; the LTU are more likely to be sampled than the short term unemployed.
2. See Junankar and Wood (1992).

References

Budd, A., P. Levine and P. Smith (1988a), 'Real Wage Adjustment and Long Term Unemployment', in R. Cross (ed.) *Unemployment, Hysteresis and the Natural Rate Hypothesis*, Oxford: Blackwell.

Budd, A., P. Levine and P. Smith (1988b), 'Unemployment, Vacancies and the Long Term Unemployed', *Economic Journal* 98, 1071–91.

Chapman, B.J., Junankar, P.N. and Kapuscinski, C.A. (1992), 'Long-term Unemployment: Projections and Policy', Centre for Economic Policy Research Discussion Paper No. 274, Australian National University, Canberra.

Hughes, B. (1987), 'Immigration and the Australian Adult Beveridge Curves: Some Exploration of an Apparent Paradox'. Paper presented to the NBER Immigration, Trade and Labor Conference, Cambridge, Massachusetts, September 1987.

Hughes, B. (1992), 'Trends and Cycles in Unemployment Gross Flows: A Preliminary Investigation'. Paper delivered to the 21st Conference of Economists, University of Melbourne, July 1992.

Junankar, P.N. (1988), *Very Long Term Unemployment*, Commission of the European Communities, Luxembourg.

Junankar, P.N. and Wood, M. (1992), 'The Dynamics of Unemployment: An Analysis of Recurrent Unemployment', in R.G Gregory and T. Karmel (eds), *The Australian Longitudinal Survey*, Centre for Economic Policy Research, Australian National University.

Salkever, D.S. (1976), "The Use of Dummy Variables to Compute Predictions, Prediction Errors, and Confidence Intervals', *Journal of Econometrics* 4, (4); p. 393–97.

Simes, R.M. and Richardson, C.J. (1987), 'Wage Determination in Australia', *Economic Record 63*, 144–55.

Williams, J. (1989), The Single Girl's Guide to Steady State Relationships. Honours thesis, Department of Economics, The Faculties, Australian National University.

Appendix

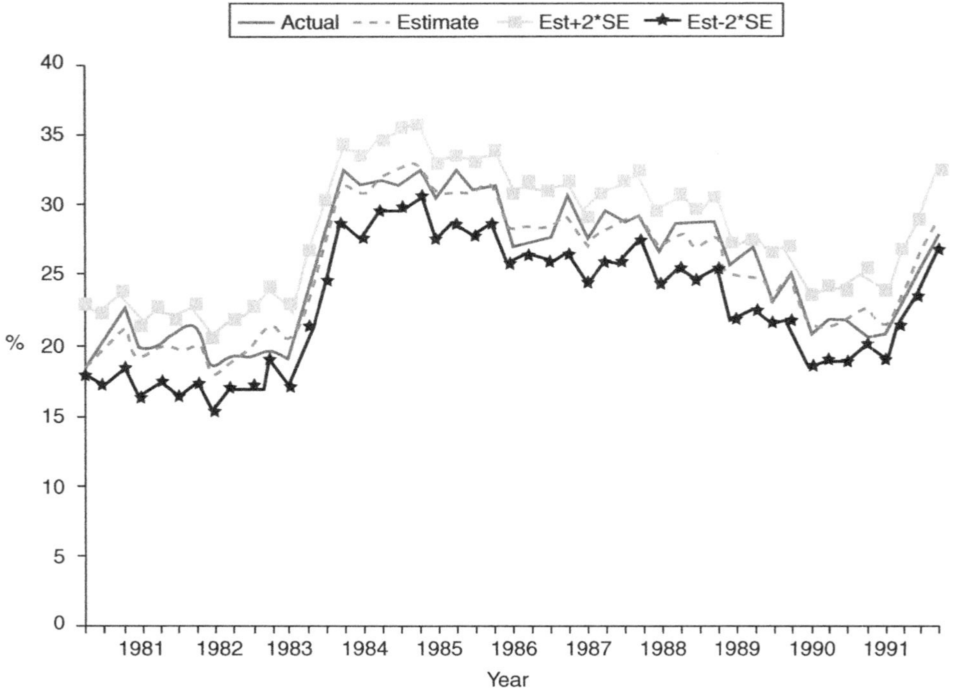

Figure 5.1.A1 Within Sample Predictions of PLTU: Persons

5.2
Was *Working Nation* Working?

P. N. Junankar and Cezary A. Kapuscinski

After several months of research and consultation, the Labor government introduced, in May 1994, with its publication of Working Nation, *a set of labour market programmes targeted at the long-term unemployed. With the new Coalition government taking office in March 1996, we saw the end of* Working Nation. *Did* Working Nation *labour market programmes lead to a reduction in general unemployment and a decline in long-term unemployment? This paper attempts to evaluate this particular aspect of its success by applying econometric method to macroeconomic data. Our results suggest that although* Working Nation *had a very short life, it succeeded in helping' the long-term unemployed: it was a valuable social and economic experiment.*

1 *Working Nation*: The policy package

The *Working Nation* policy package was introduced in May 1994. At that time unemployment and long-term unemployment had just begun falling, and as the business cycle continued with the recovery unemployment continued to fall rapidly. *Working Nation* included initiatives affecting both the demand for labour and the supply of labour, as well as policies designed to stimulate economic growth. The main features of *Working Nation* included a big expansion in labour market programmes, case management of the unemployed, a Youth Training Initiative, training wages for all trainees (including adults), New Work Opportunities (that is, direct job creation), a conditional guarantee of a job for long-term unemployed (the Job Compact), and changes to the social security system. The rationale behind these labour market initiatives included both equity reasons (to help the unemployed and, in particular,

Reprinted from 'Was *Working Nation* Working?' by P. N. Junankar and Cezary A. Kapuscinski in *Journal of Industrial Relations*, March 40 (1), 1998, 25–41. With kind permission from SAGE Publications.

the most disadvantaged group of the unemployed) and efficiency reasons (to decrease the loss of human capital through skill atrophy—see Piggot & Chapman, 1995).

The most tangible aspect of *Working Nation* that affected the long-term unemployed was the Job Compact. The Job Compact was designed to offer (usually) a full-time job (for at least twelve months), mainly in the private sector, to any person who had been on unemployment benefit for more than eighteen months after an agreement with an individual case management. Such an initiative involved subsidies to employers, 'encouragement and moral suasion' (to be supervised by NETTFORCE) and case management (to be supervised by the Employment Services Regulatory Agency) to make the unemployed 'job ready'. The Job Compact participant would have to 'accept any reasonable job offer', and would have a case management officer. It should be noted that women with employed partners were ineligible to qualify for the Job Compact programme. This was because they were not eligible for the receipt of unemployment benefit.

An important new feature of *Working Nation* (which Junankar (1988) had recommended to the European Community in the wake of the 1987 recession) was the targeting of labour market programmes at those who *are likely to become long-term unemployed* (the disadvantaged). As previous work has shown (see, among others, Chapman, Junankar & Kapuscinski (1992), Kenyon (1993) and Kenyon (1994), growth of the economy is *unlikely* to decrease long-term unemployment on its own. *Working Nation* acknowledged, therefore, that targeted labour market programmes are necessary to achieve such an aim.

Particularly notable features of the *Working Nation* policy were the reciprocal obligations of unemployed people with regard to job search and case management. Individual case management was designed to provide an assessment of the likelihood of unemployment continuing and tailor the assistance in the provision of Job Compact employment to the specific characteristic of each individual. A significant policy innovation was the use of non-government agencies to deliver case management—a process that was to be monitored by the Employment Services Regulatory Agency.

A substantial growth in employment and a decrease in unemployment led to a decrease in funding for *Working Nation* in the budget of 1995–96. The reduction in funding was also in response to pressures to lower the budget deficit (see Crean (1995) and a statement by Simon Crean, the then minister for employment, education and training, dated 19 October 1995). The 1995–96 budget cut expenditure on labour market programmes by $348 million in 1995–96 (Budget Statements 1995–96, Budget Paper no. 1, pp. 1–2). In addition, during the course of 1995–96 financial year there were also some revisions to the implementation of the *Working Nation* policy. As announced in the abovementioned statement by Crean, there had been some repackaging of subsidies, a greater emphasis on training rather than wage subsidies and some simplification of the programmes encompassing *Working Nation.*

With the election of the Coalition government in March 1996, *Working Nation* labour market programmes were terminated, and a significant overall decrease in expenditures on labour market programmes was announced in the 1996–97 budget. In particular, expenditure on labour market programmes was reduced by a further $575 million in 1996–97 and by $956 million in 1997–98 (see Budget Statements 1996–97, Budget Paper no. 1, table 4, pp. 1–18).

2 An evaluation of *Working Nation*

Various methodologies have been employed in the literature to assess the performance of labour market programmes in the light of their diverse objectives—that is, efficiency and equity. For example, effectiveness of labour market programmes is often evaluated by employment outcomes (at the aggregate and at the individual level), while efficiency outcomes have been assessed on the basis of changes of the duration structure of the unemployment pool and shifts in the Beveridge curve.

Most evaluations of labour market programmes, however, are fraught with difficulties. In the case of labour market programmes providing subsidies to employers, for example, the impact on employment and unemployment depends on several factors: (a) the *elasticity* of labour demand—the sensitivity of employment to changes in the wage; (b) the extent to which there is *deadweight*—the creation of jobs that would have been created irrespective of the labour market programmes; (c) *labour substitution*—the extent to which the target group is helped at the expense of the rest of the unemployed; (d) *job displacement*—the shift of employment to subsidised employers at the expense of non-subsidised employers; (e) labour force *participation* effects—the extent to which these programmes increase entry into the labour force; (f) *employers' attitudes* to the qualities of the target groups; and (g) subsidies as a *screening* device—the extent to which the employers can use the subsidies for hiring and training the unemployed at a lower cost. Major issues such as these are extensively discussed in Calmfors (1994), Dolton and O'Neill (1996), Organisation for Economic Co-operation and Development (1993) and Leeves (1997).

One of the first assessments of *Working Nation* was provided in Crean (1995). However, due to the impending federal election as well as the very short existence of the programme, Crean's report provided a rather generalised assessment of *Working Nation,* with a positive gloss on die labour market achievements.

An extensive evaluation of various aspects of *Working Nation* has been carried out by the Department of Employment, Education, Training and Youth Affairs (1996). Utilising a variety of administrative and survey data and a combination of both quantitative and qualitative methods, the report provides an assessment of the impact of *Working Nation* on issues ranging from aggregate trends in unemployment to the effectiveness of early screening of unemployed and the impact of case management on employment outcomes. However, while the department's evaluation of *Working Nation* on aggregate employment and unemployment discusses a number of factors affecting the programme's performance (such as employment and labour force growth), it does not go beyond this descriptive analysis.[1]

In this paper we apply econometric methods to assess the *macroeconomic* impact of *Working Nation* on unemployment and long-term unemployment. In particular, we estimate a model of long-term unemployment on a set of data up to the commencement of *Working Nation* and compare its forecasting performance after May 1994 with the actual data. Statistically significant positive differences between the forecasts and the actual data can then be used to infer that the labour market programmes of *Working Nation* were successful. Similar analysis is also undertaken with respect to the programmes' impact on aggregate employment by utilising simple employment functions. First, however, we compare the labour market outcomes of the 1983 recession with those after the recession of 1992 and discuss the underlying assumptions for such an analysis.

2.1 Comparison with previous recession

If we *assume* that the structure of the economy has remained unchanged, we would expect the labour market to behave in the same fashion during each business cycle. This is a strong assumption, which involves unchanged behaviour of the demand side of the economy (which affects employment), unchanged participation of labour (that is, the supply of labour) and unchanged policy response in each cycle. Figure 5.2.1 shows that the economy experienced more rapid growth after the 1983 recession than after the 1993 recession. Hence, we would expect, all else being equal, that employment increased more rapidly after the 1983 recession.

Turning our attention to the target group for the Job Compact, namely the unemployed of eighteen months or more (LTU-WN), we see that as a proportion of the total unemployment it has fallen very significantly since the introduction of *Working Nation*—see figures 5.2.2 and 5.2.3. It is interesting to note here, in view of our later results, that a comparison of this variable over the two cycles shows that men fared better in the 1992 cycle as compared to the 1983 cycle, while the profiles for women do not show substantial differences between the two cycles.

2.2 Forecasting long-term unemployment (duration eighteen months or more)

One method of studying the impact of *Working Nation* on long-term unemployment would be to use a structural model. In such a model a test of the impact of labour market programmes would involve an assessment of the extent to which the expenditure on labour market programmes affects long-term

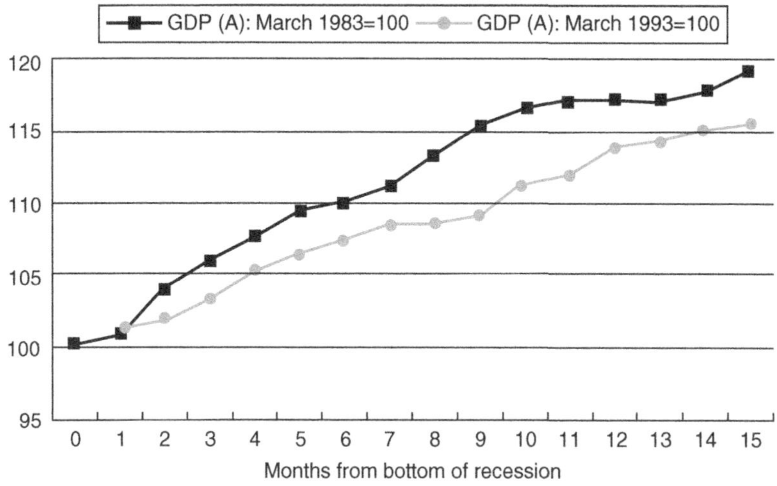

Figure 5.2.1 Gross domestic product (A) after two recessions: 1983 and 1993
Source: Australian Bureau of Statistics, Cat. No. 5206.0.

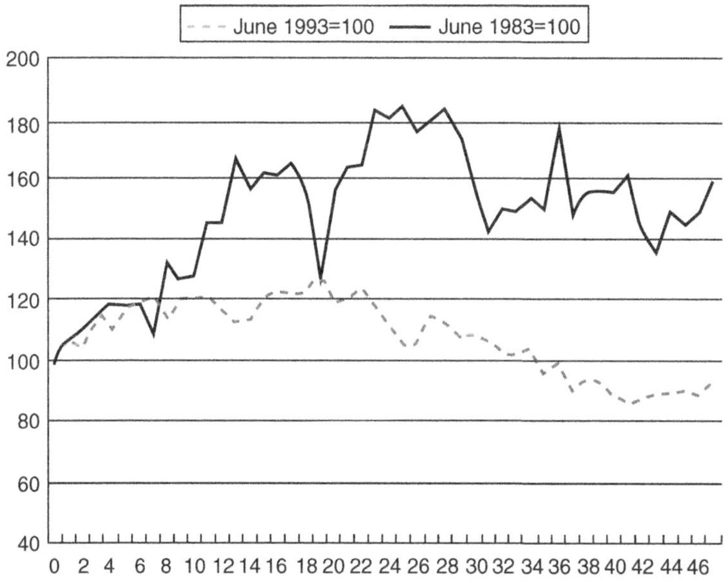

Figure 5.2.2 Proportion of LTU-WN: men
Source: Australian Bureau of Statistics, Labour Force Survey (unpublished).

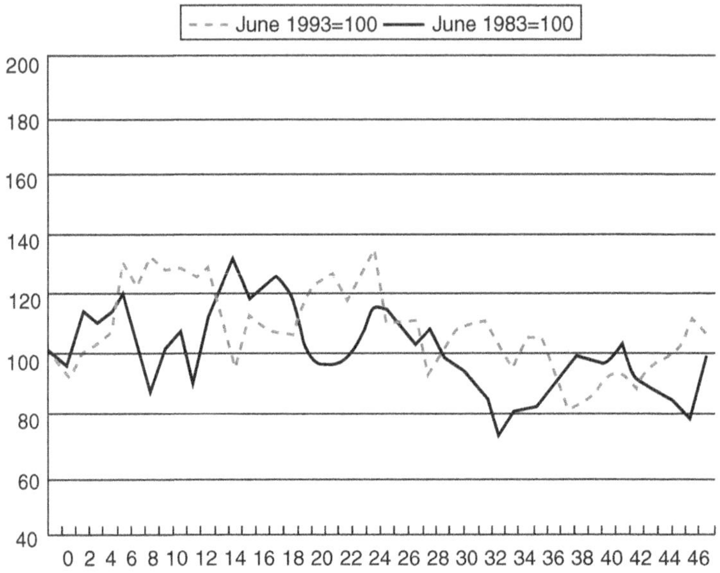

Figure 5.2.3 Proportion of LTU-WN: women
Source: Australian Bureau of Statistics, Labour Force Survey (unpublished).

unemployment. However, it is important to note that expenditure on labour market programmes (or the number of people on labour market programmes) is endogenous; when unemployment is high, expenditure on labour market programmes increases endogenously. Such models have been estimated for a cross-section of developed countries with mixed success—see Junankar and Pehkonen (1996)—but because of econometric problems (for example, no variation in the relevant explanatory variables such as duration of unemployment benefit eligibility) no estimation has been done for a single country.

As an alternative, we have employed reduced form models of long-term unemployment to forecast its behaviour after May 1994. This follows the approach from previous empirical work by Chapman, Junankar and Kapuscinski (1992), which utilised such reduced form time-series models to explain the proportion of long-term unemployment (PLTU) with the unemployment rate (UR) and the past history of long-term unemployment. Since the emphasis of *Working Nation* was on a slightly different target group of people (that is, those unemployed continuously for eighteen months and more) from the usual long-term unemployment (duration of fifty-two weeks or more) it seems appropriate to modify these forecasting models to fit this target population.

Given earlier work on adapting these models to the very long-term unemployed (people unemployed for two years or more—see Junankar and

Kapuscinski, 1992) the similarity of time-series behaviour of all three series dictated similar functional form and initial model specification for the LTU-WN. The final models estimated from May 1980 to February 1994 and chosen for the forecasting work are presented in table 5.2.1, with the basic diagnostic statistics presented in table 5.2.2. (The data for these models are from Australian Bureau of Statistics Cat. no. 6203.0 and Australian Bureau of Statistics, Labour Force Survey, unpublished.) In summary, these models fir the data accurately with no evidence of model misspecification (e.g. RESET test) or residual autocorrelation (e.g. LM(4) test for serial correlation up to the fourth order) and for each specification the standard error or the estimated regression is much smaller than the variability of the dependent variable. The data were consistent with standard prerequisite of cointegration (same order of stationarity of all the repressors).[2]

An interesting issue surrounding these models is their stability during the period when the *Working Nation* programmes were implemented. We have carried out two tests to evaluate the robustness of our models in the period 1994.2 to 1996.4. The Chow test is simply a test for a possible break in the structure at the official commencement of *Working Nation,* that is, in May 1994. As the results in table 5.2.3 reveal, there is no evidence of such instability. The Salkever test, on the other hand, tests the significance of prediction errors of our models in the post-1994.2 period. Again, the results suggest no evidence of structural problems at the 5 per cent significance

Table 5.2.1 Estimated models of the proportion of unemployment of eighteen months and more (LTU-WN)

	Men		Women		Persons	
Regressor	Coefficient	t-ratio	Coefficient	t-ratio	Coefficient	t-ratio
PLTU(-1)	0.625	3.97	0.706	8.47	0.533	3.90
PLTU(-2)	0.235	1.40			0.200	1.67
PLTU(-3)	–0.183	-1.38				
UR(-1)	–0.515	–0.88	0.676	1.87	–0.304	–0.81
UR(-2)	0.137	0.14	0.270	0.64	1.156	2.66
UR(-3)	1.583	1.63				
UR(-4)	–0.786	–0.79				
UR(-5)	–0.382	–0.33				
UR(-6)	0.814	1.22				
D4UE	–0.556	–0.67	–0.147	–0.21	–0.828	-1.51
Q1	0.163	0.09	-1.985	-2.64	-1.562	-2.63
Q2	3.733	2.41	0.081	0.07	1.555	1.96
Q3	2.221	1.24	0.056	0.08	–0.392	–0.65
Constant	–0.874	–0.64	-3.485	-2.50	-1.563	-1.94

Note: D4UE is a dummy variable equal to unity if one-quarter difference in UR lagged one year is positive. Ql, Q2, Q3 are quarterly dummies.

Table 5.2.2 Summary diagnostics of the estimated models of LTU-WN

	Men	Women	Persons
Adj. R-square	0.93	0.86	0.94
SEE	1.37	1.22	1.01
Std.dev.(y)	5.31	3.34	4.24
LM(1)	0.58	1.91	1.30
LM(4)	0.94	1.39	2.02
ACF: lag 1	-0.17	-1.55	-0.54
ACF: lag 2	0.59	0.92	0.51
ACF: lag 3	-0.55	1.17	-1.16
ACF: lag 4	-0.77	-1.21	-1.71
Reset (2)	3.42	7.67	0.97

Notes:
1. Adj. R-square is the adjusted regression coefficient of determination ($\bar{R}^2$). SEE is the standard error of the regression, while Std.dev.(y) is the standard deviation of the dependent variable.
2. LM(l) and LM(4) are the LM tests for serial correlation of order one and four, respectively. The critical value at the 1 per cent level is 2.57.
3. ACF is the residual autocorrelation function. The entries in the table are the *t*-ratios of the first four coefficients of the estimated ACF. The critical value at the 1 per cent level is 2.70.
4. Reset(2) is a test for regression misspecification. The critical value at the 1 per cent level is 7.31.

Table 5.2.3 Structural stability of the LTU-WN models

	Men	Women	Persons
Chow test	0.118	0.119	0.106
Salkever test	1.248	1.264	1.124

Note: The critical values for the Chow and Salkever tests at the 1 per cent level are 1.76 and 3.86 respectively.

level for all equations. Overall, therefore, these models can be described as capturing the essential elements of the behaviour of LTU-WN up to the end of the available data—that is 1996.4—and can be used as predicting models.

To evaluate the behaviour of LTU-WN under *Working Nation* we have utilised these models to forecast the expected outcomes of LTU-WN, given the actual levels of the unemployment rate in the 1994.2–1996.4 period. Such a procedure, under the assumption that the models capture the essential profile of LTU-WN series, can be used to provide indirect evidence about the success of programmes that remove unemployed from the stock of LTU-WN. We should stress, however, that since other policies can also result in the reduction of this portion of the stock of unemployment (such as short-term (re)training followed by a return to unemployment), this evaluation cannot be used as an unambiguous test of the effectiveness of the *Working Nation* labour market programmes.

The main results of our experiments are presented in figures 5.2.4, 5.2.5 and 5.2.6. These figures compare the dynamic projections of LTU-WN conditional on the actual unemployment rates with the actual profile of LTU-WN during the post-1994.2 period. For readability the series in these figures are smoothed. The figures also provide two standard error bounds on the forecasts of LTU-WN (which, statistically speaking, are equivalent to a 95 per cent confidence interval). In summary, *Working Nation* appeared to have a statistically significant impact in reducing male LTU-WN but was much weaker in affecting female LTU-WN.

While our forecasts of LTU-WN simulate the behaviour of LTU-WN on the basis of the pre-*Working Nation* structure of the labour market, the availability of data en commencements of laoour market programmes allows us also to assess these forecasts from the perspective of *Working Nation* outcomes. Thus, figure 5.2.7 presents the ratio of exits from long-term unemployment to total unemployment.[3] Again, the data unambiguously indicate that the *Working Nation* programme his had a more successful impact on men than on women (Corbett (1996) reported similar findings using gross flows data). In addition, the actual outcomes also indicate that during the life of *Working*

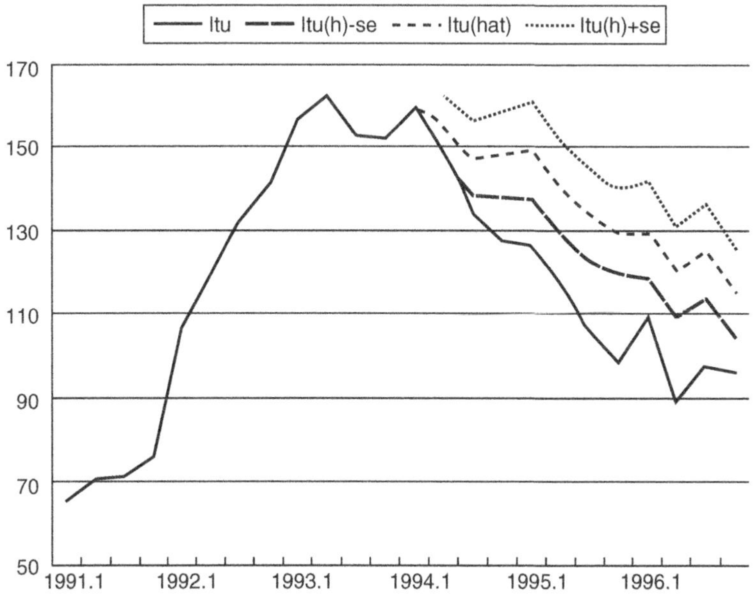

Figure 5.2.4 Actual and predicted LTU-WN: men

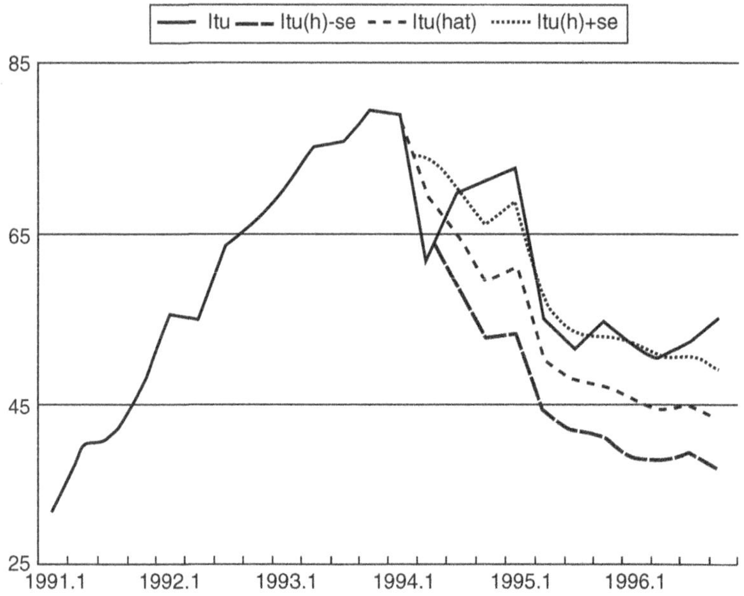

Figure 5.2.5 Actual and predicted LTU-WN: women

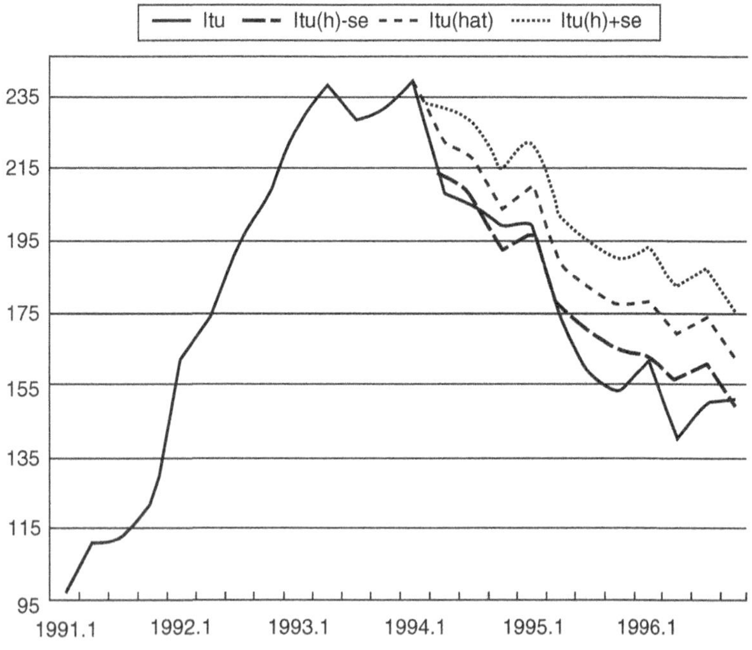

Figure 5.2.6 Actual and predicted LTU-WN: persons

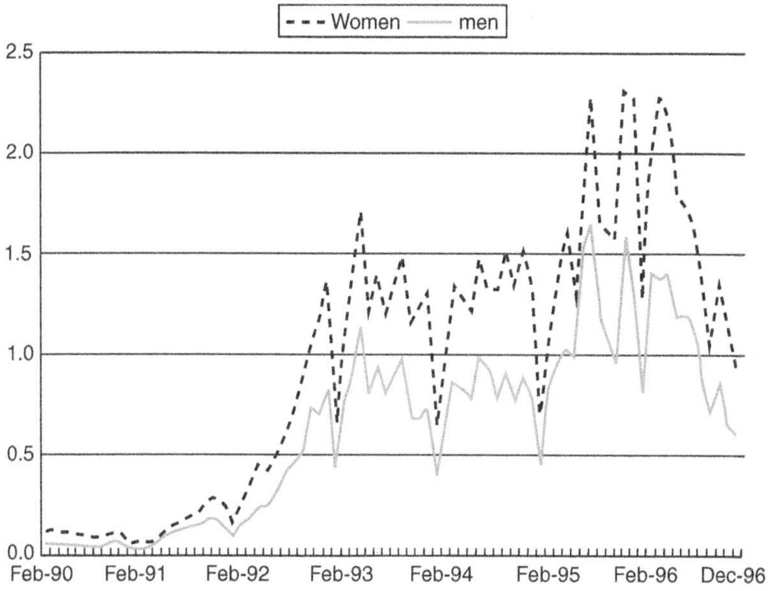

Figure 5.2.7 Exits from long-term unemployment to labour market programmes relative to total unemployment
Source: Department of Employment, Education, Training and Youth Affairs (unpublished).

Nation the gap between outcomes for men and women was consistently of the same order of magnitude.

To summarise, the major points from these experiments are as follows:

- There is a statistically significant effect from *Working Nation* on men and women.
- The effects, however are in opposite directions—men appear to be strongly benefiting from the programmes, while women appear to be adversely affected.
- As a result the net effect (i.e. for persons) is positive but weakly significant.
- These effects appear to be of constant magnitude almost to the end of the forecast period.

2.3 Forecasting employment

Another test of the effectiveness of labour market programmes is in relation to the change in *net* employment. Although it is that the general macro-economic stance of government policy is crucial to whether there would be an increase in net employment, the aim of labour market programmes is to facilitate an increase in employment, given the macroeconomic stance of the government. We would argue that the success of labour market programmes depends on the government pursuing monetary and fiscal policies that are expansionary at the same time that it is increasing expenditure on labour market programmes.

Given that the economic aim of wage subsidy programmes is to increase the quantity of labour demanded, such programmes would lead to an increase in employment.[4] Alternatively, labour market programmes can be viewed as increasing the supply of skilled labour, which, all else being equal, would increase the employment of such labour. As long as there is no substitution, deadweight or displacement, this would also lead to an increase in net employment.

In this context an assessment of the macroeconomic impact of *Working Nation* on the labour market can be carried out by estimating a simple employment function (see Russell & Tease (1991) and Organisation for Economic Cooperation and Development (1993)) and comparing its forecasting performance after May 1994 with the actual data. Our model uses the employment of wage and salary earners as the dependent variable (Australian Bureau of Statistics Cat. no. 6248.0). It should be noted that this variable was used rather than total employment because of the fact that employment of wage and salary earners would be most affected by the labour market programmes (with the exception of the NEIS programmes). Clearly, self-employed people would be less likely to be affected by labour market programmes. Explanatory variables in our model include lagged real unit labour costs, LULC, (constructed from total wage bill and employment, Australian Bureau of Statistics Cat. no. 6302.0 and 6203.0), lagged real gross domestic product, LGDP (Australian Bureau of Statistics Cat. no. 5206.0) and a lagged dependent variable. As the expenditure on labour market programmes is endogenous, we have not used this variable, unlike Organisation for Economic Co-operation and Development (1993). Clearly, when unemployment increases the government spends more on labour market programmes. Hence, we would expect that employment and the labour market programmes would be negatively correlated.

Our preliminary tests for cointegration indicated that all variables were I(1) (see tables 5.2.4 and 5.2.5), while the estimated employment function is presented in table 5.2.6.[5]

Given that there has been a substantial increase in labour productivity since the mid-eighties, we have also conducted tests of stability of the estimated functions (CUSUM-square tests). The results of these tests indicated that, past the initialisation of the recursive estimates, the estimated regressions do not suffer from structural breaks. This outcome can be taken as evidence that the gains in labour productivity have not been obtained significantly at the expense of employment levels. In summary, therefore, the

Table 5.2.4 Employment function: unit root tests

Variable	DF test	No. of lags
LWSEM	–3.44	4
LSWEF	–2.42	4
LGDP	–1.75	2
LULC	–1.76	4

Note: The critical value for the DF test at the 10 per cent level is –3.13.

Table 5.2.5 Employment function: cointegration tests

	DF test	No. of lags
Men	–2.83	4
Women	–1.77	4

Note: The critical value for the DF test at the 10 per cent level is –3.45.

Table 5.2.6 Employment function: men and women (dependent variables employed wage and salary earners)

Regressor	Men		Women	
	Coefficient	T-ratio	Coefficient	T-ratio
LWSEM(-1)	0.928	17.96		
LWSEF(-1)			0.887	8.98
LGDP(-1)	0.257	4.01	0.268	3.07
LULC(-1)	–0.165	–4.44	–0.116	–2.09
Q1	–0.014	–3.71	–0.028	–6.55
Q2	–0.005	–1.25	0.004	0.90
Q3	–0.031	–7.61	–0.028	–6.23
Constant	–1.739	2.70	–1.728	–2.58
	Diagnostics			
Adj. R-square	0.941		0.984	
LM(1)	1.35		1.52	
LM(4)	0.77		0.40	
ACF-lag 1	–1.39		–1.35	
ACF-lag 2	0.71		1.61	
ACF-lag 3	–0.88		–1.01	
ACF-lag 4	–0.70		–0.38	
Reset(2)	0.011		3.411	

Notes: See tables 5.2.1 and 5.2.2. The critical value for the Reset test at the 1 per cent level is 7.77.

employment functions fit the data well and there appear to be an statistical problems with the estimates.

Using our estimates of the employment functions on data up to the introduction of *Working Nation,* we then dynamically forecasted employment outside the sample period to assess whether *Working Nation* had made a significant difference to aggregate employment (see figures 5.2.8 and 5.2.9). The forecasts of wage and salary employment consistently overestimated the actual series, suggesting either that there was a structural break or that the model is not capturing some essential features of the employment relationship (sea also table 5.2.7 for two indicators of predictive accuracy). On face value, these forecasts would suggest that the labour market programmes were not successful in increasing net employment, even if they were successful in decreasing unemployment and long-term unemployment. It is possible that the tight fiscal grip that the government took in the 1995–96 budget has led to employers being more circumspect about employing new workers.

3 Conclusions

Our general conclusion is that labour market programmes under *Working Nation* appear to have had some effect on lowering unemployment and long-term unemployment for men (as well as an overall effect on persons), but

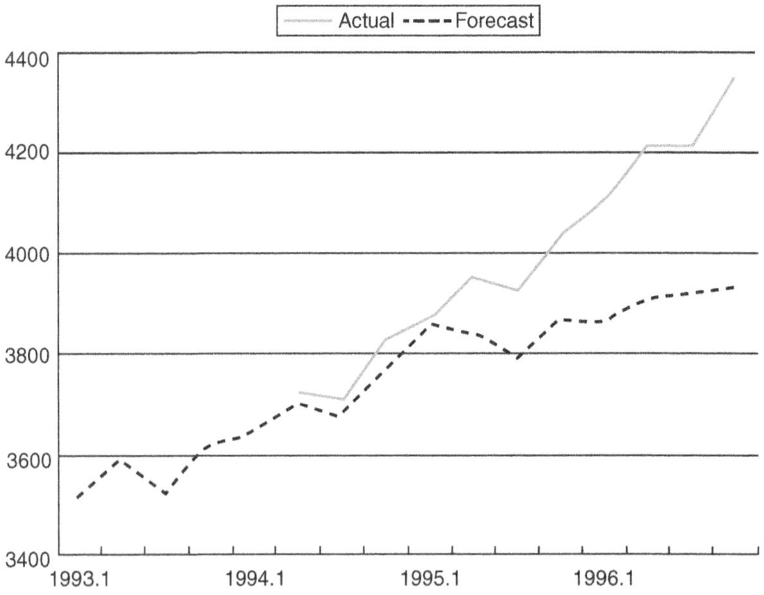

Figure 5.2.8 Actual and predicted employment of wage and salary earners: men

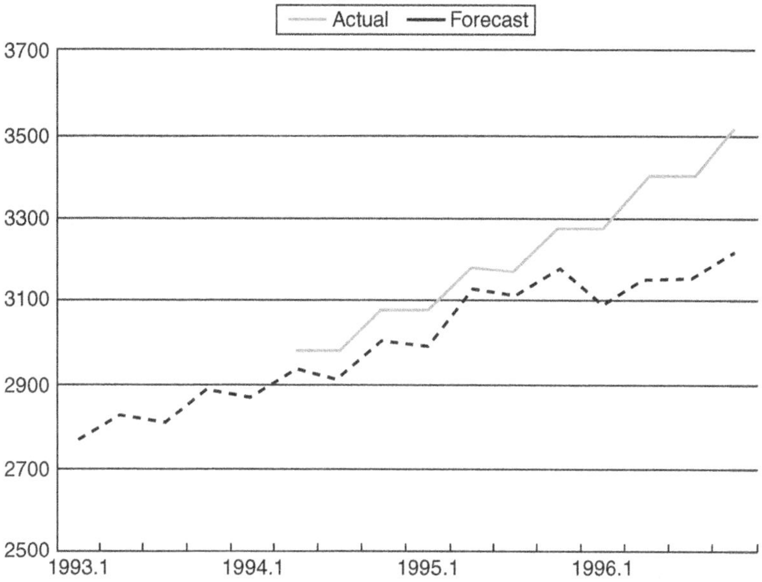

Figure 5.2.9 Actual and predicted employment of wage and salary earners: women

Table 5.2.7 Prediction evaluation

	Men	**Women**
RMSE	0.0506	0.0475
Theil's U	3.703	2.272

the results for women are ambiguous. Soon after the introduction of *Working Nation,* in the 1995–96 budget the government introduced tight fiscal policies to curtail the budget deficit and decrease expenditures on labour market programmes. However, with the new Coalition government the programmes were terminated. As a result, some of the labour market programmes had a very short life-span, and no final judgement can be made on the success or otherwise of *Working Nation.* We would argue that for the labour market programmes to be really successful, the government has to develop supportive macroeconomcc policies to increase the demand for labour.

Our analysis emphasises the importance of disaggregation by gender. Given that the programmes were aimed at the long-term unemployed, as explained above, *Working Nation* programmes were likely to be offered mainly, to men, rather than women. Any future labour mrrket programmes that target the long-term unemployed have to be designed to account for the ineligibility of sections of the target population under the usual indicators like the duration of receipt of unemployment benefits or attendance at Commonwealth Employment Service office.

Although our analysis has focused on macro effects, it is important to note that we cannot infer macroeconomic effects solely from macroeconomic studies because of the problems of substitution, displacement and deadweight. Further research is needed on microeconomic data, especially utilising the longitudinal study designed to provide information on the success of *Working Nation* (the Survey of Employed and Unemployed Persons).

To conclude, our results suggest that although *Working Nation* had a very short life, it succeeded in helping the long-term unemployed. It was a very valuable social and economic experiment, which was terminated prematurely.

Notes

P. N. Junankar, Chair of Economics, Department of Economics and Finance, University of Western Sydney, Macarthur PO Box 555, Campbelltown, NSW 2560, and Cesary A. Kapuscinski, Department of Economics, Research School of Pacific and Asian Studies, Australian National University, Canberra, ACT 0200. An earlier version of this paper was presented at the Public Policy Program seminar series at the Australian National University, and at the Macroeconomic Workshop at the University of New South Wales. The authors would like to acknowledge comments from participants at both meetings and, especially, comments from the discussant Nilss Olekalns. We would also like to thank Michael Keating for useful insights. The paper has also benefited from comments from anonymous referees.

1. A fuller discussion of these two evaluations of *Working Nation,* as well as the most recent Department of Employment, Education, Training and Youth Affairs assessment of labour market programmes, is provided in Junankar and Kapuscinski (1997).
2. In an earlier paper Chapman, Junankar and Kapuscinski (1992) found that the model supported a cointegrating relationship between the relevant variables. Also see Economic Planning and Advisory Commission (1996), Appendix 4.
3. Due to differences in the definitions of long-term unemployment used by Department of Employment, Education, Training and Youth Affairs (which is based on the Commonwealth Employment Service definition) and the Australian Bureau of statistics, we have used the gender-specific total number of unemployed as the deflator.
4. Michael Keating, the former secretary to the department of prime minister and cabinet, in a letter to us comments that the main purpose of wage subsidy programmes is not to increase labour demand but to increase the employability of the long-term unemployed. General macroeconomic policy, he argues, sets the scene for increasing employment.
5. See Appendix A for estimates using an error correction methodology.

References

Calmfors, L. (1994), 'Active Labour Market Policy and Unemployment—A Framework for the Analysis of Crucial Design Features', *OECD Economic Studies*, 22, Spring 1994, pp. 7–47.

Chapman, B. J., P. N. Junankar and C. A. Kapuscinski (1992), 'Projections of Long Term Unemployment', *Australian Bulletin of Labour,* 18, pp. 195–207.

Commonwealth of Australia (1994), *Working Nation: Policies and Programs,* Canberra: AGPS.

Corbett, L. (1996), 'Will *Working Nation* Work for Women?', Public Policy Project, Australian National University, Canberra.

Crean, S. (1995), *Working Nation: The First Year, 1994–95,* Department of Employment, Education and Training, Canberra.

Department of Employment, Education, Training and Youth Affairs (1996), *Working Nation: Evaluation of the Employment and Education and Training Elements,* Evaluation and Monitoring Branch, Economic and Policy Analysis Division, Department of Employment, Education, Training and Youth Affairs, Canberra.

Department of Employment, Education, Training and Youth Affairs (1997), *The Net Impact of Labour Market Programmes: Improvements in the Employment Prospects of Those Assisted,* Evaluation and Monitoring Branch, Economic and Policy Analysis Division, EMB Report 2/97, Department of Employment, Education, Training and Youth Affairs, Canberra.

Dolton, P. and D. O'Neill (1996), 'The Restart Effect and the Return to Full-Time Stable Employment', *Journal of the Royal Statistical Society,* Series A, 159, Part 2, pp. 275–88.

Economic Planning and Advisory Commission (1996), *Future Labour Market Issues for Australia,* Commission Paper no. 12 Canberra: AGPS.

Junankar, P. N. (1988), *Very Long Term Unemployment,* Commission of the European Communities, Luxembourg.

Junankar, P. N. and C. A. Kapuscinski (1993), 'Do the Long Term Unemployed Ever Find Work? A Preliminary Analysis of Long Term and Very Long Term Unemployment', paper presented at the 22nd Conference of Economists, Murdoch University, Perth, September 1993.

Junankar, P. N. and C. A. Kapuscinski (1997) 'Was *Working Nation* Working?', Discussion Paper No. 54, Public Policy Program, Australian National University, Canberra.

Junankar, P. N. and J. Pehkonen (1996) 'Long-Term Unemployment in OECD Countries: Do Institutions Matter?', School of Business and Economics, University of Jyvaskyla, Working Paper no. 162/96.

Kenyon, P. (1993), 'Policy Forum on Long-term Unemployment: Introduction', *Australian Economic Review,* 2, pp. 19–21.

Kenyon, P. (1994), 'The Job Compact: What does the International Evidence on Active Labour Market Policies Suggest About the Likelihood of its Success?', *Australian Bulletin of Labour,* 20 (4), pp. 272–97.

Leeves, G. (1997), 'Duration Specific Unemployment Outflows and Labour Market Training', Australian Labour Market Research Workshop, Fremantle, 13–14 February 1997.

Organisation for Economic Co-operation and Development (1993), 'Active Labour Market Policies: Assessing Macroeconomic and Microeconomic Effects', *Employment Outlook,* Organisation for Economic Co-operation and Development, Paris.

Piggott, J. and B. Chapman (1995), 'Costing the Job Compact', *Economic Record,* 71, pp. 313–28.

Russell W. and W. Tease (1991), 'Employment Output and Real Wages' *Economic Record,* 67 (196), pp. 34–45.

Appendix A: Estimates of error Correction models of the employment function

Based on the stationarity properties of the variables used in die analysis in Section 2.3, it is also possible to estimate an Error Correction Model linking the employment variable with the cost variable (ULC) and the aggregate demand variable (GDP). The following table presents an unrestricted specification of an Error Correction Model for men and women.

Given that not all the short-term dynamics terms in the Error Correction Model specifications are significant, we have also tested a simplifying restriction on our models with all the short-term dynamics variables excluded from the model. The results of these tests are given in table 5.2.A2. These results suggest the simpler form of the equation as given in section 2.2 as the preferable specification for both men (at the 10 per cent significance level) and women.

Table 5.2.A1 Employment function: Error Correction Models (dependent variable is change in employed wage and salary earners)

Regressor	Men		Women	
	Coefficient	T-ratio	Coefficient	T-ratio
Dlwsem1	–0.414	-2.15		
Dlwsef1			–0.362	-1.80
Dlgdp1	0.786	2.15	0.453	1.06
Dlulc1	0.154	1.20	0.086	0.61
Iwsem1	–0.032	–0.56	–0.023	–0.21
Igdp1	0.212	2.35	0.218	1.79
Lulc1	-0.142	-2.58	-0.154	-2.04
Q1	–0.004	–0.59	–0.019	-2.43
Q2	0.001	0.21	0.004	0.99
Q3	–0.021	-3.44	–0.017	-2.18
Constant	-1.639	-2.08	-1.731	-1.89
Adj. R-square		0.794		0.803
DW		2.185		1.958
ACF-lag1		–0.59		0.11
ACF-lag2		–0.96		0.33
ACF-lag3		–0.65		-1.09
ACF-lag4		–0.40		–0.61
RESET(2)		2.762		1.422

Table 5.2.A2 Tests of restrictions on the estimated Error Correction Models

	Men	Women
F-test	2.403	0.373
MSL	0.093	0.773

6
Costs of Unemployment

6.1
Unemployment in the European Community: Counting the Costs

P. N. Junankar

6.1.1 Introduction

In the past few years unemployment has grown rapidly and reached post-war record levels in the European Community (EC). The total registered unemployment in the EC in February 1988 was 16.6 million while the total in the 'big four' (France, Germany, Italy and the United Kingdom) was 11.5 million. An especially worrying feature has been the growth of youth unemployment as well as the increase in long-term unemployment. Table 6.1.1 gives a summary picture of these trends:

These high levels of unemployment have imposed significant costs on individuals (both unemployed and employed), on their families, on social classes, on the Government, and on society in general. The costs of unemployment are not only economic but also social and political. The aim of this paper is to discuss these costs of unemployment and to provide some estimates for the economic costs. The chapter is structured as follows: Section 6.1.2 discusses the problem of assessing the costs of unemployment, Section 6.1.3 provides some estimates for the output loss costs of unemployment, and Section 6.1.4 concludes the chapter.

6.1.2 Assessing the costs[1]

In this section we shall discuss some of the analytical problems involved in evaluating the costs of unemployment. The costs of unemployment are economic, social and political. These costs are borne (to differing extents) by individuals (both unemployed and employed), by their families, by social groups or classes, by the Government and, of course, society in general.

Reprinted from 'Unemployment in the European Community: Counting the Costs' by P. N. Junankar in *Unemployment in Europe*, edited by J. Muysken and C. de Neubourg, London: Macmillan, 1989, pp. 269–280. With kind permission from Palgrave Macmillan Ltd.

Table 6.1.1 Growth of unemployment in the EC

	Unemployment rate[1]	1979 Long-term unemployment[2]	Youth unemployment[3]	Unemployment rate[1]	1986 Long-term unemployment[2]	Youth unemployment[3]
Federal Republic of Germany	3.2	19.9	3.4	8.0	32.0	8.4
France	9.9	30.3	13.4	10.5	47.8	23.4
Italy	7.6	n.a.	25.6	10.9	n.a.	39.3
United Kingdom	5.6	24.5	10.6	11.8	41.1	20.7

Source: OECD, *Employment Outlook*, 1984, 1985, 1986.

Notes:

[1] Standardised unemployment rates.

[2] Percentage of unemployed with duration of 12 months and over.

[3] Percentage of total youth labour force (less than 25 years) unemployed.

n.a. = not available.

The economic costs faced by the individual depend on whether (s)he is employed or unemployed. If the individual is employed, the overall level of unemployment may affect the increases in (real) earnings as well as decreasing the probability of moving to better paid or more satisfying employment. For the unemployed person the economic costs are obviously the loss of income (less any social security benefits and the value of leisure). The economic costs to society are the loss of potential output both in the current period (static costs) and in the future (dynamic costs). The economic costs to the Government involve the extra social security payments plus the loss of tax revenue due to lower incomes and expenditure. However, except for the administrative costs, these are transfer payments and hence not a cost to society. The social (psychological) costs to the individual are the loss of status and esteem for the unemployed person while the social costs to society are due to increased social tension, civil strife, increased crime, morbidity and mortality. The social, and political costs to groups (classes) are in altering the balance of power (both in industrial relations and in the political process) away from workers towards the employers (capitalists). Governments may find that their political base is eroded by growing unemployment and may be forced to alter course. There are also signs of a growth of racism and an attack on ethnic minorities by the extreme right.

In evaluating the costs of unemployment, we need to aggregate the various costs and benefits of running an economy with a certain level of unemployment. In fact many of the costs and benefits are difficult (if not impossible) to quantify. However, even if we could obtain a numerical estimate for the different costs and benefits, it is not clear how these should be 'weighted' to obtain some aggregate measure of the costs of unemployment. Let us enumerate the different costs and benefits:

(a) current output loss (static costs);
(b) future output loss (dynamic costs);
(c) costs to the unemployed individual (loss of income minus social security benefits, loss of future income because of decreased probability of obtaining a future job);
(d) costs to the unemployed individual (increased morbidity, increased probability of mortality, psychological costs);
(e) costs to the employed individual (lower rate of increase of wages/earnings);
(f) costs to the employed individual (increased amount of labour services extracted because of the threat of losing one's job, decreased job mobility leading to dissatisfaction);
(g) costs to the family of unemployed individuals (both monetary and social – psychological stress, arguments, separation/divorce);
(h) costs to the Government Revenue Department (Exchequer) (higher social security payments, less taxes collected from lower incomes and lower expenditure);

(i) costs for society (greater social tension, strife, crime, etc.);
(j) costs (benefits?) to society in terms of changed balance of power between workers and capitalists (weakening of trade union power);
(k) benefits of lower rates of inflation;
(l) benefits of leisure to an unemployed individual[2];
(m) benefits of a revitalised capitalist economy by weeding out of inefficient firms and helping the concentration of economic power;
(n) macroeconomic effects on saving and investment of large Government expenditures on social security and declining tax revenues.

Clearly this is a wide range of costs and benefits to try to estimate and in many cases, they would be impossible to quantify. Even if we could quantify each of them we would have to avoid an element of double counting. For example, we cannot add together the output loss costs and the fiscal (Exchequer) costs. In an ideal world we would aggregate all these costs and benefits by attaching weights to the costs and benefits obtained by different individuals or groups (classes). However, this would require making a series of value judgements which would very likely be questioned. In this chapter we shall simply provide some estimates of the output loss costs of unemployment.

To be able to properly evaluate the costs and benefits of unemployment we need to specify:

(i) what caused unemployment to rise;
(ii) what lower level of unemployment we consider;
(iii) how is this lower level of unemployment to be achieved, i.e. what specific policies generate the lower unemployment level.

The implicit assumption in this chapter is that unemployment is avoidable, i.e. an alternative set of policies would lead to a lower unemployment rate. The view taken by this author is that the main reason for the growth in unemployment is a lack of effective demand. Some authors have argued that high real-wage rates, high social-security benefits, or increased power of trade unions, etc., have caused the growth of unemployment. Clearly one's view of the causes of unemployment affects the evaluation of the costs of unemployment. For example, if higher unemployment were caused by increased social security benefits, the unemployment is voluntary and therefore has no costs, if we ignore externalities in the search process (congestion costs).

6.1.3 The real costs of unemployment: output loss

The real economic cost to society of the high levels of unemployment lies in the loss of current and future potential output. If all (or perhaps, more accurately, many) of the unemployed found work today, they would be producing more goods and services and national income would be higher today. Clearly an interesting question is how much higher would national income have been if the unemployment levels in the EC were at a lower level (say that before the oil-price shock). If the answer to this question is that the order of magnitude is in excess of 10 per cent of national income, then society is paying a very high price for this unemployment. If the answer were less than 1 per cent, perhaps we would be justified in saying that it is not worth making such a fuss about unemployment. In addition, an interesting (but difficult) question is to what extent *future* output is affected by current high levels of unemployment. A slack economy lowers the rate of real investment in new capital goods and new technology. In addition, skills of unemployed workers deteriorate and they would be less productive in the future. However, quantitative estimates to this future loss are difficult to obtain. Implicit in our approach is that the unemployment levels of the past decade are not 'natural' or 'God-given' – society and governments can lower the unemployment level by alternative social and economic policies.

Having emphasised the importance of measuring the output loss costs of unemployment, we enter the problematic area of estimating this cost. Ideally, we would like to estimate the potential output (that level of output which would have been produced) if the unemployment level was at some lower level. Two problems appear immediately: first, which particular lower rate of unemployment do we assume? and second, how do we estimate the increased output from the increased employment (decreased unemployment)? One possibility is to use estimates of the so-called natural rate of unemployment. However, there are analytical problems in defining it, and there are several different estimates (or for some countries, none) of this rate and hence there is no obvious rate to choose. In our view, the concept of a natural rate is very unhelpful, especially when the natural rate seems to increase, *pari passu* with the actual rate of unemployment.[3] An alternative to using the natural rate concept is to use an *ad hoc* procedure: what would national income have been if unemployment levels were those experienced in (say) 1968–73 (prior to the first oil shock) or 1974–9 (prior to the recent international recession). In our discussion we shall use these alternative definitions.

As mentioned earlier, there are short-run (static) and long-run (dynamic) costs of unemployment. The static costs of unemployment are the opportunity costs of unemployment: what is the alternative level of national income (gross domestic product – GDP) is the unemployment level were lower? To answer this question completely correctly we need to know how this alternative level of unemployment would be achieved (i.e. what alternative policies or alternative values of exogenous variables would lead to this outcome) since this would provide us with information about which sectors' employment would increase (and with knowledge of the sectoral output response or elasticity) we could then evaluate and aggregate the increased national income. For example, if the current level of unemployment is 3 million and we want to know the loss of output due to this, we can ask how much extra output would be produced if unemployment were reduced to (say) 1 million. The extra output produced would depend on whether the policies were stimulating labour-intensive but low-valued products (say hand-crafted toys) or capital-intensive but high-valued products (say radio-telescopes). Again, if the unemployment were to be reduced by assuming alternative values of exogenous variables, we would get different estimates of lost output depending on the different assumptions, for example, a faster rate of growth of GDP (or higher rates of inflation) in America would stimulate exports and hence decrease unemployment. This sectoral information is particularly relevant since the recent growth of employment has been mainly in the services sector while the decline has been mainly in the industrial sector. However, this would require multisectoral econometric models of the economy with an amount of information and data which were not available to us. To reiterate, to get precise estimates, we need a well-specified multisectoral model and a well-specified alternative 'scenario': for each different scenario, we would get a different estimate.

In fact, what we have done (in line with previous investigators) is to assume that by some unspecified method, unemployment is lower and the previously unemployed are employed in different industries in the same proportions as the existing stock of employment. In some cases we have assumed that the unemployed would find work in the industries *from which they had lost their jobs*. We know that both these assumptions are approximations to reality and the longer the period over which we calculate these losses, the less precise the estimates become. This is because over the years the structure of the economy has changed enormously.

The dynamic costs of unemployment may be far greater than the static costs. However, they are difficult to estimate. As mentioned earlier, the dynamic costs of unemployment are the *future* output losses due to current high levels of unemployment. A high level of unemployment, a low level of capacity utilisation, depressed expectations of aggregate demand and profitability lead to lower levels of investment in real capital goods and slow down the introduction of new technology (via the new capital goods). This lower investment implies lower levels of future output and hence much greater economic losses. However, opposed to this view is the one put across by the UK government that the high unemployment is leading to a weeding-out of inefficient firms and industries and *increasing* productivity of workers due to a 'new realism in industrial relations'.

Perhaps an equally important dynamic (long-term) cost of unemployment is the *deterioration of human capital* due (especially) to long duration of unemployment. People who have been unemployed for long periods would lose their skills and, in some cases due to technological change, their previous skills would be obsolete. Of course, there is a high proportion of the unemployed who are unskilled workers without any formal training. But even so-called unskilled workers learn on the job and are more efficient than complete newcomers. The recent recession has seen a big increase in unemployment of older (presumably more skilled) workers and an increase in early retirement schemes. These schemes are equivalent to 'early-scrapping' schemes for physical capital goods. In addition, because of the growing problem of youth unemployment, investment in human capital has declined (at least in work-experience-related human capital). This means that future levels of production would be lower if and when the young of today find work.

There are several reasons why an estimate of the output loss costs is subject to measurement error.[4] Some of these factors might lead to an underestimate and some to an overestimate or, with some small probability, these two biases might just cancel out.

The factors that might lead to estimate of output loss being an underestimate are:

(a) Because the measured unemployment rates excludes certain categories of potential workers, for example, married women, young people who have never had jobs, early retirement of workers and, in Italy, those covered by the Cassa Integrazione Guadagni (CIG). In this paper we have relied on published statistics on unemployed so that, in general, we have made no allowance for these 'hidden unemployed'. Some of the methods of estimating output loss make no allowance for the fall in average hours worked, decreases in participation rate and lower rate of utilisation, which usually accompany the increase in unemployment.
(b) A particular problem, especially for West Germany, is that the unemployment figures do not take account of returned migrants.
(c) In general, the dynamic output loss costs are not quantified.

The factors that might lead to an *overestimate* of output loss are:

(a) The measured unemployment rate which includes the voluntarily unemployed (which for the New Classical school includes *all* the unemployed). In addition, a large proportion, so it is argued, of the unemployment rate is a 'natural rate' and hence should be deducted from the measured unemployment rate. The 'benefits' of leisure should be subtracted from the measured output loss costs.
(b) It is argued that a proportion (for some economists a very high one) of the unemployed is engaged in the 'informal sector' (or the 'underground economy') so that, if unemployment is reduced via growth in the formal sector, the informal sector would decline. Hence the net increase in real GDP (as opposed to measured GDP) would be small. Work done on the

informal sector by some sociologists, however, suggests that participants in the informal sector are more likely to have formal-sector employment as well. Employment in the formal sector provides the workers with a network of contacts as customers as well as intermediate producers. In addition, employees in the formal sector (for example, garage mechanics) have access to tools and equipment for use in the evenings or at weekends.

(c) Unemployed people are usually less skilled and often work in industries (occupations) with low productivity. To ascribe to the unemployed average productivity in the economy would lead to an upward bias. Some of the methods listed below attempt to make some correction for this bias.

(d) The high level of unemployment may lead to increased productivity of the employed labour force due to the threat of being fired (made redundant). Hence, if unemployment were decreased, productivity would then be biased upwards.

Thus we see that there are some conceptual problems as well as several measurement problems involved in estimating the output loss costs of unemployment. In other words, the numerical estimates we provide give a rough indication of the magnitudes of the costs. For purposes of comparability we have used annual OECD time-series data on employment, unemployment and GDP.

In this chapter we provide estimates for output loss using Okun's Law method which is a relationship between the percentage unemployment rate and the percentage output 'gap'. This output gap is defined as the deviation of actual output (GDP) from 'potential output' (GDP) expressed as a percentage of potential output (GDP). To obtain potential GDP we fitted simple exponential time-trends to GDP allowing for a break as a result of the oil shock in 1974. The time-trends were fitted up to 1980 and then extrapolated up to 1984. We then iterated around the estimated growth rate and constructed alternative series for 'Gap'. We then estimated (by ordinary least squares) an equation:

$$\mathrm{UR} = a_0 + a_1\,\mathrm{Gap}(i) + \varepsilon$$

where *UR* is the percentage rate of unemployment, Gap(i) is the ith series on which we iterated and ε is a random error. We then chose that equation which gave the best fit in terms of R^2s. If we find a_1 is 0.5 it means that each percentage point of unemployment implies an output loss of 2 per cent.

Table 6.1..2 provides estimates of the static output loss using this method. We estimated these costs assuming that unemployment is brought down (by unspecified policy measures) to the average levels of either 1968–73 or to that of 1974–9. The former period had lower levels of unemployment and hence implies a higher output loss, while the latter period had higher unemployment and, hence, lower output loss.

Table 6.1.2 Static output loss costs of unemployment (Okun's Law estimates)

	1980		1981		1982		1983	
	Low	High	Low	High	Low	High	Low	High
Federal Republic of Germany	—	6.69	3.00	10.25	8.74	15.98	13.38	20.63
France	6.14	13.27	9.59	16.72	12.00	19.14	14.06	21.20
Italy	3.43	6.77	7.06	10.40	9.48	12.82	13.51	16.85
United Kingdom	3.01	6.53	9.54	13.07	12.32	15.84	13.70	17.23

Notes: 'Low' estimates are when unemployment is brought down to the unemployment levels of 1974–9, while 'high' estimates are for 1968–73 levels.

Even ignoring the dynamic output loss costs, we find that the real costs of unemployment in terms of output loss have increased dramatically and, even allowing for measurement error, are massive.

To end this section, let me quote Okun: 'It is striking that a corrected estimate of social costs does not appear to be significantly smaller than output loss.... The loss of output is thus a good first approximation in assessing the social costs of recession and slack' (Okun, 1981, p. 272).

6.1.4 Summary and Conclusions

I began this chapter by outlining the problem of growing unemployment in the European Community and then discussed the problems of evaluating the costs and benefits of unemployment. I then provided some estimates for the (static) output loss due to unemployment: these estimates were all over 10 per cent of GDP which is a staggering cost to pay for a lower rate of inflation. Milton Friedman in evidence to the (British) House of Commons Treasury and Civil Service Committee (1980) argued:

> The best evidence is from the prior experience of the UK and other countries. As 1 read that experience ... I conclude that ... only a modest reduction in output and employment will be a side effect of reducing inflation to single figures by 1982 (House of Commons, 1980, p. 61).

In fact, what we see is that Friedman was clearly wrong – the output loss costs have been enormous and persistent. In our view the costs of unemployment are not only these output loss costs, but more long-term effects on individuals and society in terms of morbidity (physical and mental) and social tension. We do not really know what problems we are storing up for the future when we have millions of people who have experienced long-term unemployment. We are observing increasing social tensions in terms of civil riots as well as the growth of neo-Nazi movements in the EC. How long will it be before governments decide to engage in reflationary policies? To propitiate (appease) the gods of inflation do we have to sacrifice the lives of millions of unemployed people?

Notes

Acknowledgements: I should like to thank Sue Bowden and Mark Conaty for research assistance.

1. For a detailed discussion see Junankar (1985).
2. See Feldstein (1978).
3. See Solow (1985) and Hargreaves-Heap (1980).
4. Some of these issues are discussed in OECD (1982).

References

EUROPEAN TRADE UNION INSTITUTE (1984) *The Economic Costs of Unemployment in Western Europe* (Brussels: ETUI).

FELDSTEIN, M. (1978) 'The Private and Social Costs of Unemployment', *American Economic Review*, 68, no. 2, May, pp. 155–8.

HARRISON, R. (1976) 'The Demoralising Experience of Prolonged Unemployment', *Dept. of Employment Gazette*, pp. 339–48.

HARGREAVES-HEAP, S. (1980) 'Choosing the Wrong 'Natural' Rate: Accelerating Inflation or Decelerating Employment and Growth', *Economic Journal*, 90, September 1980, pp. 611–20.

HOUSE OF COMMONS (1980) 'Treasury and Civil Service Committee Session 1979–80, *Memoranda on Monetary Policy* (London: HMSO).

HOUSE OF LORDS (1982) *Report of Select Committee on Unemployment*, vol. 1, 10 May 1982 (London: HMSO).

JUNANKAR, P. N. (1985) 'The Political Economy of Unemployment: Causes and Consequences', *Political Quarterly*, 56, no. 1 January–March 1985, pp. 56–67.

JUNANKAR, P. N. (1986) *Costs of Unemployment, Main Report* (Luxembourg: Office for the Official Publications of the European Communities).

OECD (1982) *The Challenge of Unemployment: A Report to Labour Ministers* (Paris: OECD 1982).

OECD (1984) *High Unemployment: A Challenge for Income Support Policies* (Paris: OECD 1984).

OKUN, A. (1981) Prices *and Quantities* (Oxford: Blackwell).

SINFIELD, A. and FRASER, N. (1985) 'The Real Cost of Unemployment' March 1985, Dept. of Social Administration, University of Edinburgh.

SOLOW, R. M. (1986) 'Unemployment: Getting the Questions Right', *Economica*, 53, no. 2105, Supplement, pp. 523–34.

6.2
The Costs of Unemployment in Australia

P.N. Junankar and Cezary A. Kapuscinski

The authors wish to thank the participants of the seminar at the Office of Economic Planning Advisory Council for helpful comments and discussions on an earlier version of this paper. The paper has also benefited from comments provided by participants at the Annual Conference of Economists held at the University of Melbourne, and at the Economics seminar at the Research School of Social Sciences, ANU. We thank Bill Mudd for providing excellent research assistance. This research was supported by the Office of Economic Planning Advisory Council. The views expressed are those of the authors and not those of the Office of EPAC.

Unemployment now stands at a post-war peak of 11.4 percent and imposes a huge cost on society. The costs of unemployment can be grouped into economic, social and political costs. These costs are borne (to a differing extent) by individuals (both unemployed and employed persons), by their families, by social groups or classes, by political parties (including the government), and, of course, society in general. These costs of unemployment are both short run (static) and long run (dynamic). This study provides some quantitative estimates of some of these costs. We find that the cost to the economy in terms of lost output is immense: if unemployment in 1991–92 had been at 6.5 per cent our GDP would have been about six per cent higher. Once this GDP is lost it is lost for ever. In fact we believe that high unemployment now leads to lower GDP in the future as well. In other words our estimates provide a lower bound.

Unemployed individuals suffer in terms of lost income: single persons have the lowest replacement rate while married people with dependents have slightly higher rates. However, even married couples with two children only receive social security benefits amounting to about sixty five percent of average weekly earnings. The

---

Reprinted from 'The Costs of Unemployment in Australia' by P. N. Junankar and Cezary A. Kapuscinski in *Economic Planning Advisory Council*, Background Paper No. 24, Canberra, AGPS, 1992, p. 63. With kind permission from Economic Planning Advisory Council.

long term unemployed use up all their savings and are in financial distress. Even employed persons suffer in terms of decreased job mobility. With high unemployment the government loses revenue in terms of taxes and has to spend on social security. The skill level of new immigrants is also affected adversely by high unemployment. High unemployment also leads to physical and mental illness, family breakdown, and increased crime (including homicide).

Why do societies allow such high unemployment to remain given these high costs of unemployment? Is it because they believe that the benefits in terms of lower inflation outweigh these costs of unemployment? Is lowering inflation really worth giving up at least six per cent of GDP per annum?

In our view the government should not sacrifice thousands of unemployed people to appease the "gods of inflation"!

1 Introduction

The Australian economy in the late eighties and early nineties has been going through the worst recession in post-war history, which has led to a rapid rise in unemployment. With unemployment reaching a post-war peak of 11.4% (seasonally adjusted) in November 1992 almost every family has been affected directly, or indirectly, by the recession. Commensurate with this growth of unemployment there has been a rapid rise in the long term unemployment which is forecast to remain high for several years, even if the labour market recovers.[1] Many of us have a spouse, parent, sibling, child, or friend who is unemployed. What have been the costs of this unemployment? Who has borne the costs of unemployment? Is it possible to quantify them? This paper elaborates on these questions and attempts to quantify the costs imposed on the society, in general, and on the individual, in particular.

Unemployment is one of the most widely cited indicators of the state of the economy. From politicians to ordinary citizens, from professional economists to the popular press, everybody has a firm view about unemployment and its links with the economy. Few people, however, would dispute the proposition that unemployment implies some loss to society. For the unemployed the loss of employment and income is personal and immediate, for others it may involve less job security, lower business activity or increased concerns about the social fabric of the society.

According to a textbook model of an economy the endowment of the factors of production and the state of the production technology determine the capacity of the economy to produce output – the production possibility boundary. Any point inside the production possibility boundary indicates a situation where capacity is not fully utilised. Thus, the theory suggests that the total output can be increased without sacrificing the production of any commodities or services (*i.e.* there is zero opportunity cost of increasing output in terms of any individual outputs). However, there may be trade-offs:

inflation may rise, the balance of payments may worsen, productivity may be affected. These are important issues and we will return to them later in this paper. Given that the labour force is one of the factors of production, the substantial underutilisation of the available labour force implies that the economy is unnecessarily foregoing a proportion of its national income. These are the static (or short-run) costs of unemployment. In addition, there are dynamic costs of unemployment: high unemployment in the present may lower productive capacity (and, hence, future output) through a loss of human capital occurring as a result of skill atrophy experienced by the unemployed, as well as via lower capital accumulation due to weakened confidence in the economy. Why do societies willingly accept such a loss? Is it because they (or the government) think(s) that the benefits of such unemployment levels exceed the costs? We will discuss this issue later in this paper.

The Great Depression provided economists with a striking example of some of the most severe costs of unemployment. Since that time numerous researchers have attempted *ad hoc* evaluations of various aspects of the impact of unemployment on society. The post-war resurgence of Keynesian economics, however, has provided a scope for more formalised approaches. One of the conceptually simplest yet more enduring methods has been proposed by Okun (1962). It is based on the relationship between unemployment and economy's productive productive potential, (the static costs of unemployment). Other measures of the economic loss include simple accounting-type enumerations of the loss of output which rely on, *e.g.*, multiplying the average productivity of labour (or the average wage) by the number of unemployed people.

However, in addition to this economic dimension it is now widely acknowledged that unemployment has also other direct and indirect costs. These costs include the impact of unemployment on the psychological and physical health of people, the problems caused in society via increased crime, family violence, marital breakdown, *etc.* Unemployment also affects the political balance of forces, and may lead to governments losing support. This may reveal itself in the government changing policies in anticipation of an election – this is sometimes called the "political business cycle".[2] Although these costs are initially borne by various groups in the society it is, in the final analysis, society as a whole that loses from unemployment.

This paper is an attempt to quantify some of the costs of unemployment in Australia over the last decade or so. In order to set the scene we first review the analytical framework for assessing the costs of unemployment, and then review the concept of unemployment and its relationship to the measurement of the costs of unemployment. Next, we provide a description of the labour market in Australia over the recent past with particular emphasis on the unemployment record. The following sections concentrate on the three aspects of the costs of unemployment identified above with the final section containing some qualifications and general comments.

2 The concept of unemployment.

In order to identify and evaluate the costs of unemployment is is useful to review the concept of unemployment. There are two main methods of measuring unemployment: the labour force method, and the count of unemployment benefit recipients. The labour force method is based on a self-assessed response to a questionnaire. A person is considered to be unemployed if s/he was not employed, was actively looking for work at any time in the previous four weeks, and was available for work in the reference week.[3] Note that in this context a person is considered employed if s/he is in paid employment for one or more hours in the reference week. On the other hand, the Department of Social Security is concerned only with people in receipt of unemployment benefits (nowadays called Job Search Allowance for those unemployed less than 12 months and Newstart Allowance for those unemployed for over 12 months) from the Department of Social Security. However, this is not a very good indicator of unemployment since many unemployed people do not receive an allowance because their spouse may be working, and many persons receiving an allowance are not unemployed because they may be in part time employment (*e.g.* because their earnings from part-time employment are not sufficient to exclude them from an allowance).[4] Although these two measures are closely correlated, the differences between these series indicate one of the problems of estimating the costs of unemployment: focusing on a particular aspect of these costs (*e.g.*, loss of income of the unemployed) is unlikely to produce agreement because of the methodological differences behind the relevant data on unemployed.

In macroeconomic theory, unemployment is usually associated with an excess supply of labour at a given wage rate. Such a market outcome is further subdivided into an involuntary component which is due to demand-related factors and a voluntary component which is the labour supply response to, among others, the institutionally-set wages being higher than the market clearing wages. Our analysis, however, will proceed on the assumption that the current levels of unemployment represent an undesired economic outcome. Thus, the costs are not fully internalised by individuals as in normal (*i.e.* textbook) market transactions and outside assistance (in a form of, say, government labour market programs) may be used to reduce these costs.

At the microeconomic level, the theory of time-allocation (see Becker (1965)) suggests that an individual is able to adjust the supply of working hours in order to maximise utility subject to a budget constraint. Institutional rigidities, however, usually prevent fractional variations of the employment patterns for most people and result in suboptimal outcomes involving involuntary consumption of extra "leisure" (*i.e.* not-working). For instance, in one variant of neoclassical economics, individuals carry out an inter-temporal substitution of leisure. They are voluntarily unemployed because they are "taking" leisure now in anticipation of finding a highly paid job in the future. It is curious, though, that this voluntary unemployment is somehow taken by the less well-educated, the less skilled workers who are unlikely to have the access to powerful computers to solve lifetime utility maximisation problems!

In search theories of unemployment (see Mortensen (1986) for a survey) it is postulated that an unemployed person is looking for work in an uncertain environment and faces a probability distribution of wage offers. S/he sets up a reservation wage which depends on the costs of search (which include any unemployment benefits which arc available) and on the probability distribution of wage offers. If a wage offer exceeds the reservation wage then s/he accepts the offer and stops searching. Unemployment in this context is purely a voluntary choice. In a slightly more sophisticated version of this model the searcher faces a two-stage game with a probability of receiving an offer or not, and then conditional on receiving an offer a probability distribution of offers. In either case, the higher the unemployment benefits the higher the reservation wage and hence the higher the probability of remaining unemployed. This theory also *assumes* that search is more efficient when unemployed rather than when employed. This assumption, however, is unlikely to be supported by by evidence. However, given Australian industrial relations system individuals cannot accept wages below award rates, and of course employers may not offer such rates. Thus, individuals would be involuntarily unemployed.

Finally, we should also mention the efficiency wage theories and the natural rate school. The former explanation of unemployment is based on the efficiency wage arguments: employers pay a wage higher than market clearing rates because they get higher productivity from the workers (see Akerlof and Yellen (1986)). On the other hand, the natural rate school economists think in terms of a natural rate of unemployment, or a non-accelerating inflation rate of unemployment (NATRU) derived from Phillips curve estimates. However, recent work which stresses the problem of hysteresis (or dependence on the past situation in the labour market) suggests that the concept of a natural rate which increases with the actual rate is not a very useful analytical concept.[5] In fact, recent empirical work has produced estimates of such a natural unemployment rate which range from 5% to 8% making an arbitrarily selected value from this interval not a very useful tool in assessing the costs of unemployment.[6] However, for the purposes of considering alternative "scenarios" we have selected a particular value of this so-called natural rate, namely 6.5%. We shall return to this later in Section 5.

Essentially, therefore, the different theories of unemployment fall into two major categories: a Keynesian explanation which relies on inadequate aggregate demand (and sticky wages and prices) to explain (involuntary) unemployment, and neoclassical theories which use individual optimising behaviour and market clearing to explain (voluntary) unemployment.[7]

The importance of these philosophies to the evaluation of the cost of unemployment lies in their perception of unemployment. On the one hand, Keynesian economists assume that the unavoidable frictional unemployment represents only a small fraction of the currently observed levels of unemployment. The majority of unemployed are, therefore, involuntarily out of work and government policies can be used to reduce the size of the unemployment pool. The neoclassical view regards all (or most of) unemployment to be the result of some optimal market outcomes and, therefore, no government policies are necessary or desirable to influence the employment opportunities. Note, however, that even in a search model unemployment is not socially optimal if there are externalities in the search process, such as, "congestion costs".

Our work on estimation of the costs of unemployment is based on the assumption that a large proportion of unemployment is involuntary. Indirect evidence on this issue can be found by comparing the numbers of vacancies and unemployed. In May 1992 the total number of vacancies was only 2.6% of the total number of unemployed. For comparison, the average value of this ratio since February 1978 was 7.8% while in the late eighties it was above 10%.

Finally, we should note that there are different labour markets such as those characterised by geographic, locational, industrial and occupational specificity, gender, age structure, duration of previous unemployment distribution, *etc.* The estimation of the costs of unemployment, in fact, may vary depending on the disaggregation of labour force and the pool of the unemployed. For example, the costs of being out of work are likely to be different for a school-leaver living with the family and for a prime-age male in a single-income household.

3 The costs and benefits of unemployment: an analytical framework.

The costs of unemployment can be grouped into economic, social, and political costs.[8] These costs are borne (to a differing extent) by individuals (both unemployed and employed persons), by their families, by social groups or classes, by political parties (including the government), and, of course, by society in general. In addition the costs of unemployment can be divided into static (short-run) and dynamic (long-run) components.

Before we proceed further we should note that the costs of unemployment depend on what caused unemployed to occur (or to increase), what policies are used to lower the rate of unemployment, and what lower rate of unemployment the economy should achieve. To elaborate, if the unemployment is mainly voluntary then the costs of unemployment would be relatively small unless there were significant externalities. Different policies to stimulate the economy may stimulate different sectors of the economy which produce goods of different value (*e.g.* stimulation of low value added industries which are labour intensive as opposed to another policy which stimulates high value added industries), or have different impact on other objectives of the government or society. The lower level of unemployment to be achieved is important because the policies to lower the unemployment rate may lead to other economic problems, *e.g.* inflation may be a function of the level of unemployment.

Strictly speaking, to evaluate the costs of unemployment we need to identify all the costs and benefits to all individuals, groups, and to society in general. Having identified and evaluated them we need a method of aggregating them into a single measure. This would, however, require us to specify a "social welfare function" for the government or for society. This is beyond scope of this project: there are serious analytical and conceptual problems in proceeding in this direction. What we shall do is provide some macro measures of the costs of unemployment which implicitly weight individual utility measures. However, we should be careful not to double-count: the loss of output measure should not be added to any individual costs of unemployment discussed later.

Before we turn to discussing ways of measuring the costs them let us identify the different costs and benefits of unemployment.

3.1 Costs to individuals.

Costs to individuals can be classified according to the individuals' attachment to the labour force. In particular, the three main groups are the unemployed, the employed individuals and people not in the labour force.

1. *Unemployed individuals*:

The cost of unemployment to the unemployed person depends on whether the person is voluntarily or involuntarily unemployed. Even this distinction (which is not without problems) is too simple: we need to know whether the person became voluntarily unemployed and whether s/he remains voluntarily unemployed. For example, an employed person may *become* voluntarily unemployed by quitting from a job in the anticipation of finding another job quickly. However, that person may *remain* involuntarily unemployed because of the absence of job offers due to inadequate demand. For the truly voluntarily unemployed person, the benefits to him/her must be assumed (by revealed preference) to be at least as great as the costs. Unless there are externalities, or society somehow puts a different weight on the person's unemployment than the individual does, we can, however, ignore these costs of unemployment.

Involuntary unemployment in the present period may impose future costs on the individual in terms of lower future wages/earnings either due to loss of skills or due to the employer using a spell of unemployment as a signal of some unobservable inferior qualities of the worker and hence a lower employment probability. In addition, unemployed persons may suffer from a social stigma attached to being unemployed. This may lead to psychological or physical illness. (See also Section 7 below.)

Although unemployed persons are worse off in terms of losing an income they may gain in terms of increased leisure. In addition, those people who are eligible for social security benefits have some of the lost income replaced. Thus, increased leisure and social security benefits (partially) compensate the individual for loss of income.

Finally, an unemployed person imposes an externality on members of his/her family (or on others). This may mean simply that their consumption of goods and services declines (and they may be in poverty), or that they may be affected in terms of family violence, marital discord, *etc.* If unemployment also leads to an increase in crime, then the victims of crime are worse off. In purely economic terms the stolen goods are simply a transfer (admittedly, a non-voluntary one!) so there should be no net loss or gain to society. However, most crime involves some damage to property (which is a real economic loss) as well as psychological distress to the victims of crime. Another form of externality imposed by a voluntarily unemployed person is that the individual decreases the probability of employment of others in the labour market searching for work; these effects are referred to as "congestion costs".

2. *Employed individuals*:
Even employed individuals may be affected the by existence of (high) unemployment or increase in the incidence of unemployment Firstly, it may affect their income as a result of a fall in hours worked due to fewer overtime hours. Secondly, it may affect their future incomes. Thirdly, it may decrease job mobility and hence decrease their job satisfaction. Fourthly, they may be "persuaded" to work harder because the threat of unemployment (expressed or implied) looms on the horizon. This, from a social viewpoint, may be considered to be a benefit as it would increase the productivity of labour (as long as we ignore the increased disutility of harder work).

3. *Individuals who are not in the labour force*:
High unemployment may discourage workers from searching for work. Thus, some of the unemployed may leave the labour force and hence be worse off. Similarly, some people may not join the labour force because of the low probability of finding work. This category includes married women and students who stay on in education. Similarly, older workers may take early retirement because job prospects are bleak.

3.2 Costs to society.

A simple measure of the costs of unemployment for a society is to estimate the loss of output (GDP) by the under-utilisation of factors of production, especially labour. Society's welfare, however, does not simply depend on the goods and services produced (although we often use GDP per capita as an index of welfare in cross-country comparisons) but also on any benefits of leisure. It is difficult to obtain estimates of the value of leisure, and if people are involuntarily unemployed one can safely ignore this problem as we do in our paper. As mentioned earlier there are also dynamic costs of unemployment: future output may be less due to lower capital accumulation and skill atrophy leading to a lower level of human capital.

It is also argued that increased unemployment is the price society has to pay for controlling inflation and the current account deficit. In other words, the benefits of higher unemployment are expected to arise from lower rates of inflation and its impact on the overall functioning of the economy. These benefits are often asserted but rarely quantified.[9] However, increased employment *(via* increased aggregate demand) may lead to increased inflation and to worsening of the current account balance. If inflation imposes real costs on the economy (and there is much controversy about this issues, see EPAC (1991*a*)) we need to estimate these costs of inflation and subtract them from the output loss costs. Similarly, if the current account balance worsens some people may want to to argue that this imposes a real cost on society. Again, this would need to be estimated and subtracted from the output loss costs. The view we have taken in this paper is that we do not consider these costs to be significant. However, the reader may wish to subtract an appropriate value from the output loss costs of unemployment we have provided. We shall return to this issue later.

Another way of looking at the costs of unemployment to society is to sum the net private costs to unemployed individuals and the externalities imposed on others. In addition, there are some intangible costs like that of increased family violence, marital breakdowns, health status of the society, increased criminal activity *etc.* The private costs of unemployment are those faced by individuals (whether at an individual level or aggregated), while the social costs are those that allow for any externalities, that is, the impact one person's unemployment has on another person (or persons) through a non-market process. For example, the private costs of unemployment for an individual are based on lost income less any social security benefits less any benefits of additional leisure. The private costs to society are the sum of all the individual private costs, and the social costs of unemployment are the private costs of unemployment overall[10] plus (or minus) the value of any externalities, *e.g.* the value to society of the extra discomfort resulting from an increase in crime caused by the unemployment *etc.*

4 Recent trends in unemployment.

The decade of the eighties represents one of the most dramatic periods of the post-war economic history of Australia. The labour market, in particular, underwent a number of transitions the repercussions of which are affecting the position of the unemployed in the nineties. One of the more influential events was the recession of 1982. Figure 6.2.1 presents the movement of the gender-specific series of total unemployed as well as the gender-specific series of the unemployment benefit recipients. Thus, in the late seventies and early eighties the total number of unemployed oscillated around 211 thousand for males and 187 thousand for females. As a result of the recession these numbers nearly doubled in a period of less than a year. In fact, as Table 6.2.1 illustrates, the pre-recession means of the series are significantly different to the means in comparable periods after the recession. Although the numbers decreased over the decade, they did not return to the

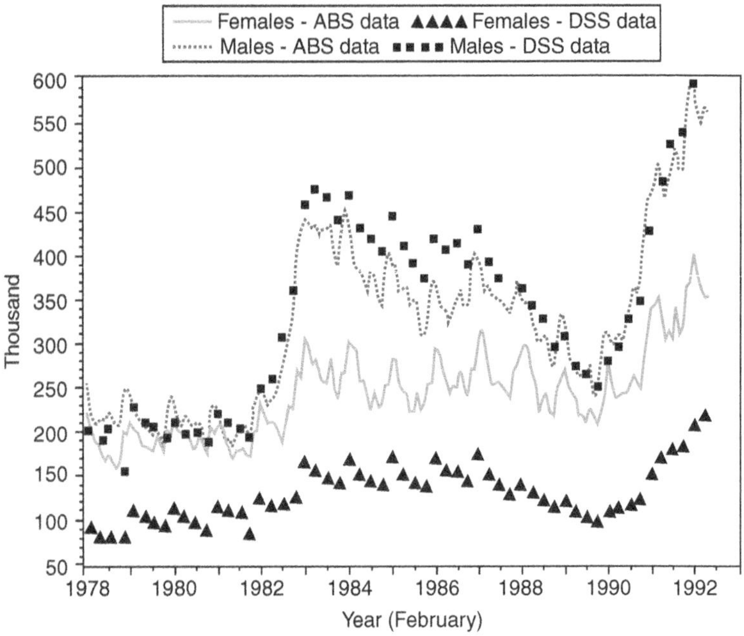

Figure 6.2.1 Unemployment series: by gender

pre-recession levels. In particular, the numbers of females unemployed in the second half of the eighties is no different to the period immediately following the recession of 1982.[11] In addition, the last sub-period identified in the Table (January 1989 – June 1992) includes the most recent recessionary period and clearly demonstrates the dramatic and very immediate impact of a recession on the level of unemployment.

Such an asymmetric response of the labour market to a recession has been increasingly emphasised in the literature as the *hysteresis hypothesis* – the influence of past history of actual unemployment on the future outcomes in the labour market (see the contributions in Cross (1988) for a fuller exposition and evaluation of this hypothesis). Thus, one can postulate that during a recession employers attempt to maximise profits by following a sequence of measures designed to minimise costs. On the labour demand side these measures might involve a decrease in overtime, a reduction in the number of shifts and no new hirings or replacements after which lay-offs and redundancies might begin. Finally, in the most drastic cases bankruptcies involve loss of employment for all employees of the given firm. Therefore, a major slowdown of economic growth and the associated loss of both current jobs as well as stagnation in employment creation, as in 1982 and in 1991–92, is usually associated with large increases in unemployment. During the

Table 6.2.1 Comparison of the levels of unemployment data.

	Gender category		
	Females	**Males**	**Persons**
ABS data:	**Total number of unemployed**		
Mean:			
Period I: 1978.7 – 1981.12	187.6	211.1	398.7
Period II: 1982.1 – 1985.6	249.6	363.9	613.5
Period III: 1985.7 – 1988.12	257.3	342.3	599.5
Period IV: 1989.1 – 1992.6	284.5	397.9	682.3
Tests across periods:			
$F_{Iv.II}$	143.54	196.04	195.73
$F_{Iv.III}$	248.66	686.06	544.43
$F_{Iv.IV}$	122.06	106.44	114.07
$F_{IIv.III}$	1.61	3.62	0.72
$F_{IIv.IV}$	12.65	2.65	5.23
$F_{IIIv.IV}$	8.47	9.13	9.22
DSS data:	**Number of unemployment benefit recipients**		
Mean:			
Period I: 1978.III – 1981.IV	96.2	200.7	297.0
Period II: 1982.I – 1985.II	142.0	399.6	541.6
Period III: 1985.III – 1988.IV	141.2	375.2	516.4
Period IV: 1989.I – 1992.II	141.1	394.7	535.8
Tests across periods:			
$F_{Iv.II}$	60.31	90.76	89.74
$F_{Iv.III}$	64.02	241.00	177.63
$F_{Iv.IV}$	15.41	29.99	26.22
$F_{IIv.III}$	0.01	1.14	0.76
$F_{IIv.IV}$	0.01	0.02	0.01
$F_{IIIv.IV}$	0.00	0.28	0.16

Notes:
1. The means are in thousands of persons.
2. The subscripts on the headings of the *F*-tests indicate the periods being compared.
3. The test statistics for the (monthly) number of unemployed are distributed as $F(1,82)$ with the critical values at 1, 5 and 10 % significance levels being approximately 6.956, 3.957 and 2.768.
4. The test statistics for the (quarterly) number of unemployment benefit recipients are distributed as $F(1,26)$ with the critical values at 1, 5 and 10 % significance levels being approximately 7.724, 4.225 and 2.909.
5. *Source*: ABS Cat. No. 6203.0, DSS *Quarterly Unemployment Benefits Recipients* (unpublished) and authors' calculations.

upswing, however, the growth of production tends to be sustained first by increased utilisation of the existing capacity rather than by expansion of capacity. On the labour supply side the effects of hysteresis include the progressive skill atrophy leading to a gradual deterioration of the quality of the economy's human capital as well as society's stigmatisation of the unemployed. We should also mention that the hysteresis hypothesis provides powerful theoretical arguments as well empirical evidence against the nomination of a specific level of unemployment as the "natural unemployment". In addition, in the face of record-breaking unemployment levels well above any reasonable value compatible with other targets, such as the non-accelerating inflation rate of unemployment (NAIRU), such discussions would seem to be misplaced.

A more complete picture of the transformations in the labour market emerges if we turn our attention to various measures of the incidence of unemployment. The most commonly quoted such indicator is the unemployment rate, which is a measure of under-utilisation of the available labour. Figure 6.2.2 illustrates a pronounced procyclical behaviour of unemployment rate irrespective of whether one looks at the unemployment rates of people looking for full-time jobs or all job-seekers. This is also confirmed by simple first-order autoregressive relationships of the unemployment rates

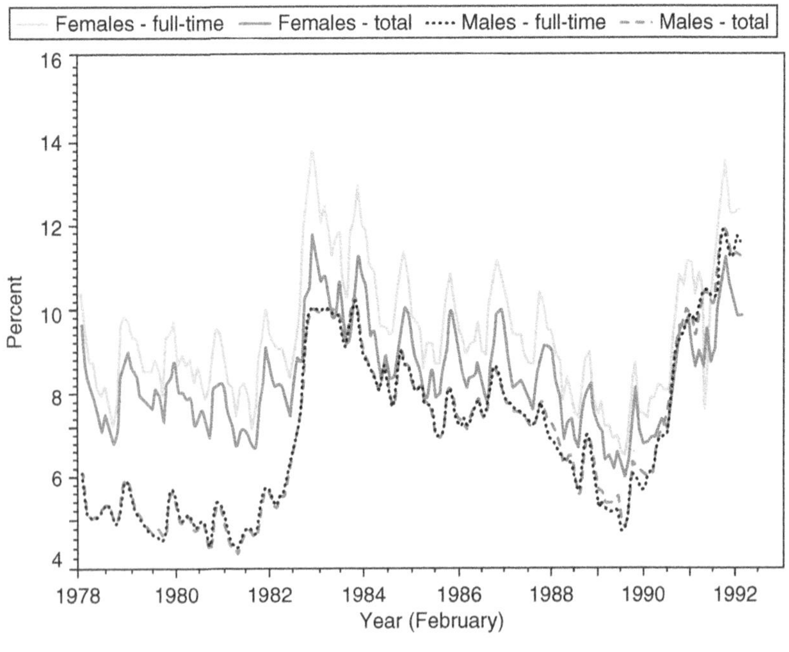

Figure 6.2.2 Full-time and total unemployment rates

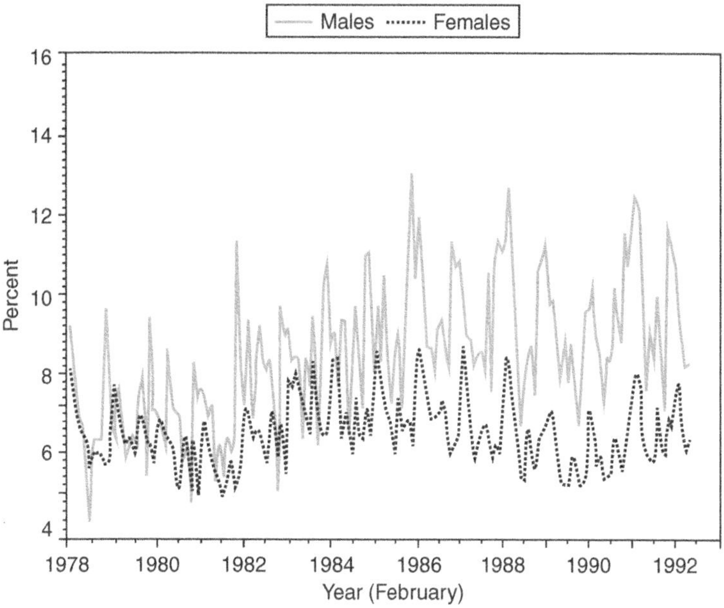

Figure 6.2.3 Part-time unemployment rates

which, for the full-time job seekers, yield coefficients of 0.96 for females, 0.99 for males and 0.99 for all persons while the equivalent coefficients for series involving total unemployment rates are 0.94, 0.99 and 0.98, respectively. It is interesting, however, that the unemployment rates among people looking for part-time work only seem to be much less cyclical (see Figure 6.2.3). The empirical coefficients in the autoregressions are 0.66 for females, 0.65 for males and 0.71 for all persons. Further evidence on this point can also be obtained from Table 6.2.2 which presents the results of comparisons of the full-time and part-time rates of unemployment across the periods identified in Table 6.2.1. In particular, whereas there is some statistical similarity between the unemployment rates for people looking for full-time employment, especially when the period encompassing the 1991–92 recession is compared with its immediate predecessor, all unemployment rates of part-time job-seekers displayed some degree of similarity. While we do not attempt to separate the costs of unemployment due to different job-seekers we should mention that the particularly active market for part-time work over the eighties may obscure the preferred labour market outcomes.[12] This may arise because, as has been pointed out in the literature (see, *e.g.*, INDECS ECONOMICS (1980)), the growth of part-time employment during a recession represents a sub-optimal choice on behalf of individuals who cannot find full-time jobs.[13] As can be observed from

Table 6.2.2 Comparison of the rates of unemployment data.

	Gender category		
	Females	Males	Persons
	Unemployed looing for full-time jobs		
Mean:			
Period I: 1978.7 – 1981.12	8.63	4.95	6.02
Period II: 1982.1 – 1985.6	10.72	8.27	8.99
Period III: 1985.7 – 1988.12	9.31	7.25	7.87
Period IV: 1989.1 – 1992.6	9.23	7.90	8.35
Tests across periods:			
$F_{Iv.II}$	74.85	169.38	154.54
$F_{Iv.III}$	14.61	373.02	210.04
$F_{Iv.IV}$	3.31	61.01	42.27
$F_{IIv.III}$	30.58	14.71	19.75
$F_{IIv.IV}$	15.89	0.66	2.34
$F_{IIIv.IV}$	0.06	2.90	1.71
	Unemployed looking for part-time jobs		
Mean:			
Period I: 1978.7 – 1981.12	6.08	6.95	6.26
Period II: 1982.1 – 1985.6	7.05	8.56	7.39
Period III: 1985.7 – 1988.I2	6.82	9.43	7.39
Period IV: 1989.1 – 1992.6	6.30	9.44	7.04
Tests across periods:			
$F_{Iv.II}$	37.21	31.48	59.04
$F_{Iv.III}$	19.72	61.65	44.73
$F_{Iv.IV}$	1.98	67.30	21.08
$F_{IIv.III}$	1.53	7.42	0.00
$F_{IIv.IV}$	18.44	8.18	3.88
$F_{IIIv.IV}$	8.22	0.00	3.13

Notes:
1. The means of the unemployment rates are in percent.
2. For further explanatory notes see Table 6.2.1.

Figure 6.2.3, however, the relatively small changes of the unemployment rates amongst the part-time job seekers across the business cycle support the negative impact of recessions even on the so-called secondary workforce.

An alternative measure of the extent of unemployment in the society is provided by the ratio of unemployed to population. Figure 6.2.4 provides a comparison of such rates for both males and females calculated with both the estimated unemployed looking for full-time jobs (the ABS data) and the enumeration of the unemployed receiving unemployment benefits (the DSS data). These two series are most closely related on administrative grounds and indirectly illustrate the impact of the recession on the behaviour of the unemployed.[14] This comparison reveals a number of issues concerning the

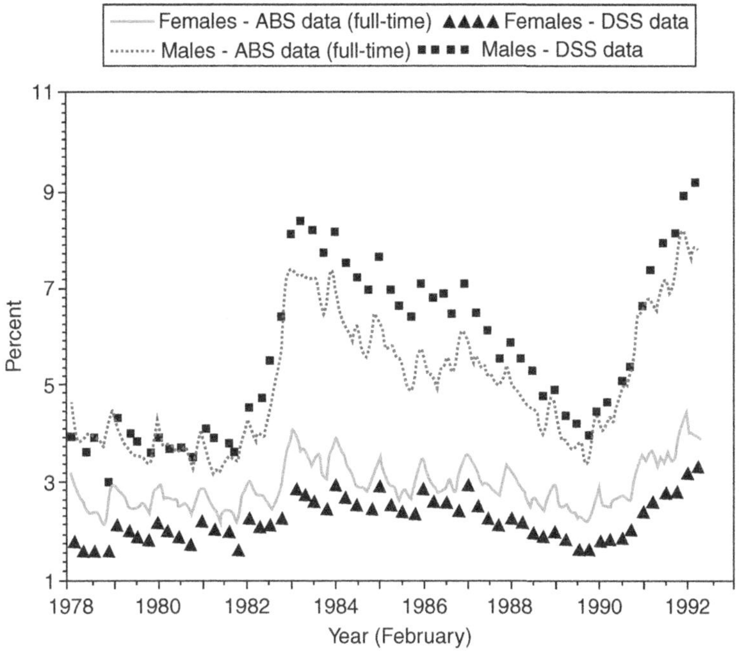

Figure 6.2.4 Incidence of unemployment

impact of unemployment on the population. Thus, while there are differences in the incidence of unemployment between the gender groups, the recessionary periods affect males much more severely than females. This is reflected not only in the differences based on the DSS series, which result from the administrative regulations concerning the eligibility for unemployment benefits, but also in the differences based on the ABS data. In addition, the much wider acceptance by males of unemployment benefits during a recession suggests that the workers perceive the cost of losing a job differently in times of recession than in boom times. Finally, it is worth re-emphasising that the incidence of unemployment measures the extent of unemployment in relation to the total population in contrast with, for example, the unemployment rate which relates unemployment to a particular sub-group of the population, namely the labour force. Therefore, observing one in twelve males and one in twenty five females out of work during recessions suggests that unemployment touches everybody in the society, either directly or indirectly through family or acquaintance links.

The last indicator that we will consider is the employment-population ratio or its mirror image – the jobless ratio, which is simply one minus the employment-population. A fall in the employment-population (or, equivalently, a rise in the jobless ratio) unambiguously indicates a deterioration in economic conditions irrespective of whether the unemployment rate rises or not. This is, in many respects, a more accurate description of the labour market than the unemployment rate, which may be biased downwards due to the "discouraged worker" effect.[15] Especially interesting is the comparison of the gender-specific and total rates (see Figure 6.2.5) in the context of the longer-term structural changes in the economy such as the increased early retirements and higher retention rates in schools. The male jobless rate increased substantially during the recession of 1982 and it did not return to the previous levels following the economic recovery later in that decade. In fact, the 1991–92 recession has all the indications of further aggravating the employment prospects for males. Given the dominance of male employment in the manufacturing sector it can only indicate continuing loss of high-value added output and, hence, continuing cost to the society of prolonged unemployment. On the other hand, the jobless rate for females shows a steady decline over the eighties which is a reflection of the continuing expansion of female part-time employment (especially in the low value-added service sector). The jobless rate for the whole of the population, however, clearly demonstrates the significant impact of recessions on the job market.

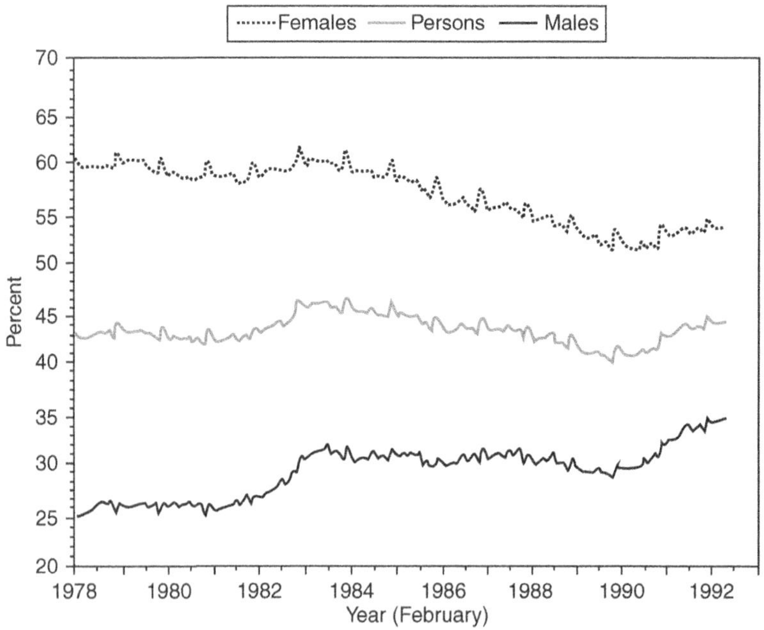

Figure 6.2.5 Jobless rates

It is also interesting to relate the concept of broader unemployment (or underemployment) in the context of the indicators of the unemployment incidence. One of the most often mentioned inadequacies of all the measures discussed above is their inability to capture the so-called "hidden unemployment". Hidden unemployment is said to occur when some unemployed move out of the labour force. Thus, even though they are not recorded in the official statistics on unemployment their potential inflow back into the labour force (mostly into the unemployment pool) will result in the unemployment rates showing smaller changes than would otherwise have resulted from economic recovery. The potential significance of the hidden unemployment lies, therefore, in its inverse relationship with economic growth and its nullification of the effects of job creation programmes on the overall unemployment situation. A simple method of calculating an approximate extent of the hidden unemployment has been suggested by Chapman, Dowrick and Junankar (1991) and it assumes a constant growth rate of the true labour force and adjusts the actual values of the labour force participation on the basis of the maximum observed over the business cycle. Following this methodology we have calculated the size of the hidden unemployment in Australia over the last decade and the relevant numbers are presented in Table 6.2.3. This Table also provides two sets of

Table 6.2.3 Estimated size of the hidden unemployment and its impact on unemployment rates: August values.

Year	Unemployment number ('000 persons)			Unemployment rate (%)	
	Hidden	Actual	Adjusted	Actual	Adjusted
1978	153.0	395.7	548.7	6.2	8.4
1979	271.3	373.8	645.1	5.8	9.6
1980	219.6	392.3	611.9	5.9	8.9
1981	292.0	377.1	669.1	5.6	9.5
1982	394.6	458.5	853.1	6.7	11.8
1983	476.9	684.1	1161.0	9.9	15.7
1984	500.9	604.6	1105.5	8.5	14.6
1985	494.5	571.1	1065.6	7.9	13.8
1986	396.6	595.6	992.2	8.0	12.5
1987	386.2	601.9	988.1	7.8	12.2
1988	357.8	538.8	896.6	6.8	10.9
1989	222.6	469.4	692.0	5.7	8.2
1990	176.7	587.5	764.2	7.0	8.9
1991	283.6	806.0	1089.6	9.5	12.4

Notes:
1. Columns headed *Hidden* refer to the estimated hidden unemployment. The adjusted figures are the sum of the actual unemployment and the hidden unemployment.
2. *Source*: ABS Cat. No. 6203.0 and authors' calculations.

unemployment rates – the official ABS series and our calculated series which include the hidden unemployment.

These estimates of the hidden unemployment indicate that a substantial proportion of the labour force withdraws from the official labour market during the recessionary periods. In particular, during the 1982 recession the size of the hidden unemployment pool amounted to about 40% of the adjusted unemployment while during the 1991 recession this proportion reached 30%. It is also worth mentioning that the recent discussions about the unemployment rate going into double digits would seem to have been misplaced by a decade if one accounts for the hidden unemployment.

This inadequacy of the official data has, however, been recognised by the ABS which now regularly collects information about the broader measures of unemployment and marginal attachment to the labour force through the annual supplementary labour force surveys. Thus, a person is defined to be underemployed if s/he would prefer to work more hours (if employed part-time) or did not work full-time hours for economic reasons, *e.g.* while being stood down or due to insufficient work (if employed full-time). A person is said to be marginally attached to the labour force if s/he is not in the labour force but wanted to work and, either, was actively looking for work but did not meet the criteria of unemployed or was not actively looking for work but was available to start work. One sub-category of the marginally attached consists of the discouraged jobseekers – people who did not actively look for work because of personal perceptions of unavailability of work.[16]

Table 6.2.4 presents the published data on these broader measures of unemployment with the first three columns providing a picture of the under-employment, the next three columns concentrating on the discouraged jobseekers and the last two columns contrasting our attempt to calculate a measure of broad unemployment with the actual standard unemployment rate. Thus, the underemployment rate is relatively stable although with the variations in the participation rate the number of underemployed varied from just over 200 thousand during the expansion of the mid-eighties to 450 thousand in 1991. Such numbers, therefore, have a significant impact on the rate of underutilization of the labour force (*i.e.*, the underemployment and the unemployment) which never fell below 10% percent since 1983 and approached 15% in 1991. The number of discouraged jobseekers, on the other hand, varies with the business cycle with more than 50% as many people in this category during 1991 than in mid-eighties. Although they account for about one to two percent of the labour force their pro-cyclicality significantly affects a broader measure of the unemployment rate. Finally, it is interesting to observe that an imperfect account of these two groups of people not in a preferred employment situation significantly pushes up the rate of broad unemployment.

We close this section with a brief look at the duration aspect of unemployment. In general, the unemployed have different experiences of

Table 6.2.4 Estimates of the underemployment of the labour force.

Year	Underemployment		Adjusted UER (%)	Discouraged jobseekers		Adjusted UER (%)	Broad UER (%)	Actual UER (%)
	Number ('000)	Rate (%)		Number ('000)	Rate (%)			
1983	285.5	4.1	14.4	118.2	1.6	11.6	15.8	10.3
1984	253.1	3.6	12.5	93.7	1.3	9.8	13.6	8.9
1985	226.9	3.1	11.5	83.0	1.1	9.0	12.5	8.4
1986	268.2	3.5	11.4	83.6	1.1	9.2	12.3	7.8
1987	306.9	4.0	12.2	94.4	1.2	10.0	13.2	8.2
1988	261.1	3.3	10.8	83.8	1.0	7.8	11.7	7.5
1989	313.8	3.8	10.1	76.1	0.9	6.8	10.9	6.3
1990	358.8	4.2	10.7	100.9	1.2	8.4	11.8	6.5
1991	457.4	5.3	14.8	138.2	1.6	11.5	16.2	9.5

Notes:
1. Columns headed *Adjusted UER* contain the rates of unemployment adjusted for the portion of the labour force described in the columns immediately to the left. Column headed *Broad UER* contains the unemployment rate broadly defined.
2. Values for underemployment are for May, while those for discouraged jobseekers are for September (except for 1987 when the survey was carried out in March).
3. *Source*: ABS Cat. No. 6265.0 and 6220.0 and authors' calculations.

unemployment and do not form a homogenous pool of unutilised productive resource. In fact, it is important to realize that the longer the duration of unemployment the higher the costs of unemployment are likely to be both for the individual and the society. Figure 6.2.6 demonstrates the trend over the past decade of increasing domination of the medium-term and, especially, the long-term, unemployed at the expense of the short-term unemployed.[17] In fact, the average duration of unemployment increased from 30.5 weeks in the pre-1982 recession period to 45.6 weeks in the period from 1988 to mid-1992. A more detailed picture of the distribution of the average duration by age and gender is presented in Table 6.2.5.

This table reveals that during the eighties the average duration of unemployment increased dramatically – more than doubling in some age groups. For a school leaver (*i.e.* an individual in the 15–19 year old group), who would be expected on average to have just over 100 weeks of labour force experience, the table indicates that a quarter of that experience is gained while unemployed. It is also worrying in the context of the 1991–92 recession that the average durations of unemployment (for most groups) are substantially higher than the durations in the corresponding period of the 1982 recession. Given the inherent lagging in the improvement of the unemployment position, and especially the long-term unemployment, behind an economic recovery such a situation in the initial stages of a recession suggests even longer durations can be expected once the recovery gets under way.[18]

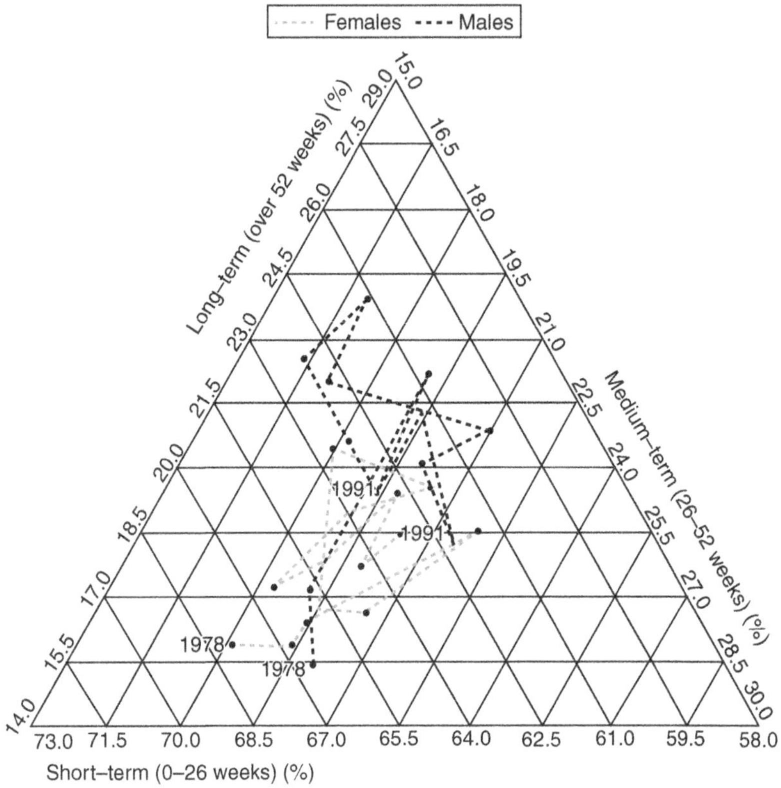

Figure 6.2.6 Decomposition of unemployment by duration: 1978–1991 (August values)

Table 6.2.5 Average durations of unemployment, in weeks: August values.

Period	Age group				
	15–19 year old	20–21 year old	25–34 year old	35–54 year old	Total
			Females		
1978–1981	27	34	25	19	29
1982–1984	29	42	32	46	37
1985–1988	30	41	34	46	38
1989–1992	26	35	37	50	38
			Males		
1978–1981	23	24	34	24	31
1982–1984	27	39	41	53	42
1985–1988	30	47	58	74	57
1989–1992	27	39	48	65	51

Notes:

1. The category "Total" includes the unemployed over 55 years old not identified separately.
2. *Source*: ABS Cat. No. 6203.0.

Such long average durations have very significant impact on the cost of unemployment and we will return to this point in Section 7.

[18]For empirical evidence from longitudinal data of this positive relationship between unemployment durations and unemployment rate see, for example, Dynarski and Sheffrin (1990).

6.2.5 Output costs of unemployment.

We begin our assessment of the costs of unemployment with measurement of the loss of output due to the underutilisation of the available labour input. Such calculations provide the most direct indication of the unemployment costs since they relate these costs to the economy's Gross Domestic Product (GDP). Thus, one can immediately gauge the importance of these costs both in real terms and as a proportion of actual output. In these calculations, as well as in those relating to the costs of unemployment for the government, the individual and the society, it is important, however, to distinguish between the marginal costs and the total costs. Thus, the marginal costs are defined as the incremental loss (or gain) in the output from, say, a one percentage point increase (decrease) in the unemployment rate. Such measures can usually be established in a regression framework and, in fact, Okun's coefficient is a popular example of the marginal cost of unemployment. The total costs, on the other hand, can be defined as the aggregate output that could be produced if the unemployment was reduced to a lower, predefined level. The choice of such lower level, however, remains one of the more controversial aspects of macro-economics. Given our earlier discussion about the inappropriateness of a yardstick such the NAIRU we have, instead, provided a range of estimates based on different scenarios of unemployment. For example, assuming zero unemployment yields the maximum output cost but it also assumes no adjustment costs in the economy from the substantial enlargement of the employment pool as well as the ability of the economy to cope with such a large structural change. An alternative to this rather unrealistic option is to assume a "low" and "high" levels of unemployment on the basis of historical evidence which would then correspond to a "high" and "low" cost of unemployment, respectively. In what follows we have defined the low unemployment level to be 4.5% to coincide with the average levels of unemployment in the latter part of the seventies after the first oil shock (*i.e.* from 1975 to 1977) while the period of high unemployment is taken to be 6.5% – the average value of the "equilibrium rate" of unemployment estimated for Australia in the 1980s (see EPAC (1992) for details). The choice of these rates will allow us not only a more accurate assessment of the cost of unemployment in terms of the lost output but also a historical perspective on the state of the unemployment in the eighties. We should stress, however, that these are hypothetical scenarios which do not imply or prescribe specific policy settings and abstract from transitional costs during the implementation of such policies.

Before we present our estimates of the output loss it is instructive to discuss a number of conceptual problems relating to the measurement of the loss. To start with we are concentrating on the static dimension of the output loss, which quantifies the opportunity cost of unemployment to the society based on some subjective measure of the normal (structural or frictional) unemployment. Such estimates are valid only within a short-run analysis since continuing high levels of unemployment lead to structural changes in the economy such as the reassessment of investment plans, changing capital-labour ratio, deterioration of the human capital of that portion of the labour force which is unemployed (and especially the long term unemployed), *etc.* Accounting for such factors would, however, involve the determination of the dynamic costs of unemployment. In other words, our estimates provide a *lower bound* to the real output costs if we were to take account of these dynamic losses.

Furthermore, the estimates of the output loss are subject to a number of qualifications due to possible measurement problems. In particular, there are a number of reasons which may lead to either underestimation of overestimation of these costs. Some of the problems leading to under-estimation are:

1. Discrepancy between the measured and the true unemployment, *e.g.* discouraged workers, early retirement of older workers, unemployed who fail the official test of unemployment. As discussed earlier this part of the labour force is often labelled as the "hidden unemployed".
2. Assumed constant participation rates and average working hours (both of which fall during a recession).
3. Constant utilisation rates for other factors of production as well as the normal replacement of the depreciating factors of production. (National Accounts indicate a cyclical nature of investment).
4. Omission of the dynamic costs of unemployment, namely the loss of future output due to lower human capital due to skill atrophy, and due to lower investment in physical capital stock (or long-term) costs of unemployment.

On the other hand, over-estimation may result from the following factors:

1. The inclusion of (unknown) voluntary unemployment in the measured unemployment.
2. The assumption of equal skill levels for the employed and the unemployed and the different categories of the unemployed (such as the short-term and the long-term unemployed or unemployed originating from different sectors of the economy).
3. The cyclically changing productivity of employees.
4. Differences between the productivity of different sectors of the economy.
5. The existence of the informal (or underground) economy, as argued by Cassel (1984), may be biasing crucial economic indicators (such as the

unemployment rate), while its generally counter-cyclical character (in relation to the official economy) may be undermining the effectiveness of traditional anti-cyclical measures. In particular, the number of people employed in the informal sector, may decrease during an upturn of the economy decreasing output of that sector as the output of the formal sector rises and replaces the output of the informal sector. However, most of the evidence suggests that people who are employed in the informal sector usually also have formal sector employment (see, *e.g.*, discussion in Fisher (1983*a*) and Fisher (1983*b*)).

5.1 Average wage method.

The average wage method of calculating the output loss focuses on the income side of the economy. It relies on the assumption that wages reflect the marginal product of labour. Thus, assuming that the marginal unemployed person, if employed, would receive the going wage rate we can calculate the total product potentially available through utilisation of the unemployed. This product (*i.e.* the output loss) is simply the total amount of earnings that the unemployed could obtain if employment was available. Our calculations use the average wage rates for the economy since we have no *a priori* knowledge about the sectoral specificity of the potential employment creation. In addition, the data requirements for such calculations are difficult to meet over our sample period. It is worth stressing at this point that as the economy absorbs more and more of the unemployed the average quality (or skill levels) of the unemployed declines. Therefore, the assumption of an identical wage rate to both the first and the last unemployed gaining employment may lead to a potential over-estimation of the output loss. This argument, however, can be counterbalanced with the observation that the actual levels of unemployment are well above the level at which such an employment selection process may be operating. In addition, we are ignoring the output that would result from the co-operating factors of production.

Given the availability of wage series for both the full-time and total employment and the corresponding data on both the total number of unemployed and the number of unemployed looking for full-time employment only, our initial calculations provide the orders of magnitude of the output loss based on disaggregation of the unemployed into gender and employment intensity. Thus, Table 6.2.6 presents the gender-specific estimates of the loss of GDP based on the potential employment of both the full-time job seekers and all the unemployed. As expected the values for males are much bigger than for females although there appears to be a much more pronounced cyclical variation in the male-specific losses. In fact, the output loss from male unemployment during a recession is more than double the value during the upswings of the business cycle. It is also interesting to observe that there is relatively little difference between the losses

Table 6.2.6 Calculated total output loss from gender-specific unemployment: average wage method

Fiscal Year	Females				Males			
	Based on $w_f^{F/T}$		Based on w_f^T		Based on $w_m^{F/T}$		Based on w_m^T	
	Value ($ m)	Proportion of GDP	Value ($ m)	Proportion of GDP	Value ($ m)	Proportion of GDP	Value ($ m)	Proportion of GDP
1981–82	3372.4	1.2	3759.4	1.3	5971.9	2.1	6454.6	2.2
1982–83	4444.7	1.6	4740.8	1.7	10303.3	3.7	10629.0	3.8
1983–84	4760.7	1.6	5082.1	1.7	11500.7	3.9	11966.2	4.1
1984–85	4458.1	1.4	4870.7	1.6	10551.6	3.4	11067.1	3.6
1985–86	4337.3	1.3	4836.7	1.5	9391.6	2.9	10030.2	3.1
1986–87	4537.0	1.4	4963.8	1.5	9819.2	3.0	10463.0	3.2
1987–88	4326.2	1.2	4882.5	1.4	8940.5	2.6	9645.0	2.8
1988–89	3958.6	1.1	4466.9	1.2	7632.5	2.1	8388.2	2.3
1989–90	3682.5	1.0	4296.3	1.1	7132.9	1.9	7924.3	2.1
1990–91	4954.7	1.3	5427.3	1.5	10958.6	2.9	11900.5	3.2
1991–92	6350.2	1.7	6568.7	1.8	14945.3	4.0	15511.8	4.2

Notes:
1. $w_j^{F/T}$ refers to the average ordinary time full-time gender-specific adult earnings. Calculations based on $w_j^{F/T}$ use the series of unemployed looking for full-time work.
2. w_j^T denotes average total adult earnings. Calculations using this wage series rely on the total unemployment series.
3. Values of output loss are in average 1989–90 prices.
4. *Source*: ABS Cat. No. 5206.0, ABS Cat. No. 5222.0, ABS Cat. No. 6203.0, ABS Cat. No. 6302.0 and authors' calculations.

calculated on the basis of full-time earnings and the average total earnings. This result can partly be attributed to the institutional link between the two wage rates which is reflected in a high correlation between the two sets of real wage series (simple correlation being 0.61 for females and 0.88 for males). In addition, as we have mentioned earlier, the cyclical differences between the series of unemployed looking for full-time employment only and the total unemployed tend to be proportionately less during the recessionary periods.

Tables 6.2.7 and 6.2.8 present the output loss from unemployment using both the average full-time earnings and the average total adult earnings. Both tables also present the estimates based on total unemployment as well as unemployment of less than two years duration which can be linked to a specific industry of last employment.[19] The combined output of such sectors averaged approximately 68 per cent of GDP between 1978 and 1992. The estimates indicate substantial output losses suffered by the economy as a result of unemployment. In particular, during recessions around 6 per cent of GDP is lost because of underutilisation of the available labour force. The picture is not much better during upswings either since the output loss does not decline by more than half of the recession value. Figure 6.2.7 also

Table 6.2.7 Calculated total output loss from unemployment: average wage method using average full-time earnings

Fiscal Year	Based on GDP*		Based on GDP	
	Value ($ m)	Proportion of output	Value ($ m)	Proportion of output
1981–82	6818.8	2.4	11386.4	3.9
1982–83	10961.7	3.9	17132.2	6.1
1983–84	10718.0	3.7	18735.6	6.4
1984–85	9325.4	3.0	17715.8	5.7
1985–86	8640.2	2.7	16729.5	5.2
1986–87	9243.7	2.8	17392.3	5.3
1987–88	8544.6	2.5	16463.4	4.8
1988–89	7368.7	2.0	14671.2	4.0
1989–90	7524.9	2.0	13952.0	3.7
1990–91	11645.6	3.1	19510.6	5.2
1991–92	14497.3	3.9	24945.1	6.7

Notes:
1. Calculations in the columns headed GDP* utilise the ABS estimates of total sector-specific unemployment which is based on unemployed with durations less than two years. The output of these sectors averaged 68% between 1978 and 1992.
2. Calculations in the columns headed GDP are based on the ABS estimates of total unemployment.
3. Values of output loss are in average 1989–90 prices.
4. *Source*: ABS Cat. No. 5206.0, ABS Cat. No. 5222.0, ABS Cat. No. 6203.0, ABS Cat. No. 6302.0 and authors' calculations.

Table 6.2.8 Calculated total output loss from unemployment: average wage method using average total adult earnings

Fiscal Year	Based on GDP*		Based on GDP	
	Value ($ m)	Proportion of output	Value ($ m)	Proportion of output
1981–82	6312.5	2.2	10541.1	3.6
1982–83	9865.0	3.5	15419.1	5.5
1983–84	9711.9	3.3	16981.2	5.8
1984–85	8393.6	2.7	15943.9	5.1
1985–86	7753.4	2.4	15012.9	4.6
1986–87	8222.7	2.5	15470.8	4.7
1987–88	7590.4	2.2	14625.5	4.2
1988–89	6518.3	1.8	12978.7	3.6
1989–90	6640.1	1.7	12312.6	3.2
1990–91	10204.2	2.7	17099.0	4.6
1991–92	12499.5	3.4	21506.1	5.8

Note: For explanatory notes see Table 6.2.7.

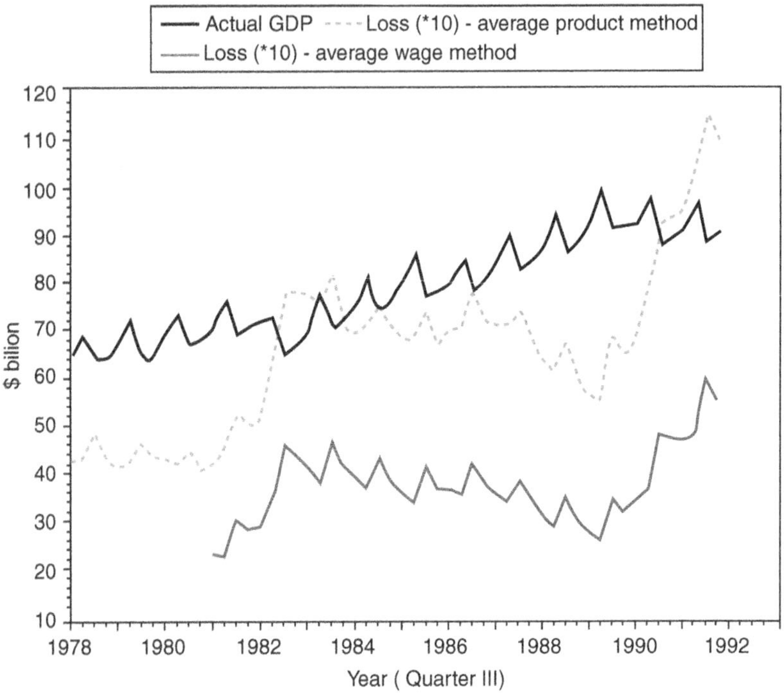

Figure 6.2.7 Calculated total output loss from unemployment

indicates that these output losses are very sensitive to the overall behaviour of GDP. In particular, a relatively small change in the GDP trend leads to a substantial change in the loss.

Table 6.2.9 presents the sector-specific losses from unemployment.[20] Although the traditional sectors of manufacturing and construction exhibit similar cyclical variations and the behaviour of the sector-specific losses reflects the behaviour of the total GDP losses, it is important to realise than the secondary sectors, like internal trade and recreation services, are inextricably linked to the fortunes of the rest of the economy. In fact, these sectors lose in recessions proportionally more than the traditional sectors.

Finally, Tables 6.2.10, 6.2.11 and 6.2.12 present the estimates of the total GDP loss as well as the sector-specific losses under alternative unemployment scenarios. As discussed earlier, our low unemployment scenario assumes the values during the post-oil shock period of 1975 to 1977 as representing the low unemployment period in recent history. The high unemployment scenario assumes that the unemployment rate is reduced to 6.5% which corresponds to the estimated "natural rate" during the eighties. For the sectoral

Table 6.2.9 Calculated total sector-specific output loss from unemployment: average wage method using average total adult earnings

Fiscal Year	Sector					
	Manufacturing	Construction	Wholesale & retail trade	Finance & business serv.	Community services	Recreation services
	Value ($ million)					
1981–82	1615.0	639.7	1506.5	328.6	579.3	607.5
1982–83	2728.8	312.1	2206.2	484.7	705.4	856.2
1983–84	2662.8	1236.0	2269.5	487.8	684.6	832.7
1984–85	1928.0	963.9	1925.3	419.9	709.2	844.9
1985–86	1715.0	746.6	1775.1	430.5	730.0	841.9
1986–87	1869.6	902.9	1923.9	487.0	704.0	818.9
1987–88	1676.5	764.6	1721.6	480.2	743.7	774.8
1988–89	1366.0	570.6	1477.4	445.0	699.1	699.6
1989–90	1448.6	737.3	1544.5	513.9	609.0	683.6
1990–91	2268.9	1353.3	2367.9	830.9	818.3	925.4
1991–92	2978.1	1838.3	2620.3	950.9	881.1	1101.5
	Proportion of actual sectoral output					
1981–82	2.9	2.6	3.1	1.2	1.9	5.2
1982–83	5.3	6.0	4.8	1.7	2.2	7.3
1983–84	5.1	5.6	4.8	1.7	2.0	6.9
1984–85	3.5	4.0	3.8	1.3	2.0	6.8
1985–86	3.1	3.0	3.5	1.3	1.9	6.5
1986–87	3.3	3.7	3.8	1.3	1.8	6.3
1987–88	2.8	3.0	3.2	1.2	1.8	5.7
1988–89	2.1	2.1	2.6	1.1	1.7	5.0
1989–90	2.2	2.6	2.6	1.1	1.4	4.7
1990–91	3.6	5.4	4.2	1.9	1.8	6.4
1991–92	4.9	7.8	4.5	2.3	1.9	7.5

Notes:
1. Values of output loss are in average 1989–90 prices.
2. SOURCE: ABS Cat. No. 5206.0, ABS Cat. No. 5222.0, ABS Cat. No. 6203.0, ABS Cat. No. 6302.0 and authors' calculations.

calculations the same benchmarks are assumed but are modified to account for the incomplete enumeration of sector-specific unemployment (available only for unemployed with durations of less than two years). The modification consists of weighting the benchmark figures with the shares of the sector-specific unemployment in the total unemployment. Before we look at the calculated output losses it is instructive to compare the unemployment situation during the alternative scenarios with the current outcomes. Thus, the average levels of manufacturing and total unemployment during our low unemployment period were 65 thousand and 273 thousand, respectively, (with the respective unemployment rates being 1.1% and 4.5%) while

Table 6.2.10 Calculated total output loss under alternative unemployment scenarios: average wage method using average total adult earnings

Fiscal Year	High unemployment				Low unemployment			
	Based on GDP*		Based on GDP		Based on GDP*		Based on GDP	
	Value ($ m)	Proportion of output	Value ($ m)	Proportion of output	Value ($ m)	Proportion of output	Value ($ m)	Proportion of output
1981–82	-63.6	0.0	-484.3	-0.2	1898.3	0.7	2908.2	1.0
1982–83	3496.4	1.3	4188.1	1.5	5456.0	2.0	7643.8	2.7
1983–84	3182.7	1.1	5385.4	1.8	5191.7	1.8	8953.4	3.1
1984–85	1564.0	0.5	3826.4	1.2	3665.4	1.2	7554.9	2.4
1985–86	860.0	0.3	2743.6	0.8	2981.1	0.9	6518.8	2.0
1986–87	1346.3	0.4	3281.4	1.0	3462.1	1.1	7031.9	2.1
1987–88	595.7	0.2	2280.1	0.7	2747.9	0.8	6078.7	1.8
1988–89	-765.4	-0.2	248.5	0.1	1475.7	0.4	4165.5	1.1
1989–90	-767.8	-0.2	-637.6	-0.2	1511.5	0.4	3347.1	0.9
1990–91	2623.1	0.7	3801.8	1.0	4955.8	1.3	7893.3	2.1
1991–92	4915.6	1.3	7986.8	2.1	7249.1	2.0	12146.6	3.3

Notes:

1. High unemployment is set at 6.5% – the average rate of the "natural rate" of unemployment. The adjusted rate for total sector-specific unemployment is 3.8%.
2. Low unemployment refers to the average level of unemployment between 1975 and 1977. This translates into unemployment rates of 4.5% for calculations using total unemployment and 2.6% for calculations using total sector-specific unemployment.
3. Calculations in the column headed GDP* utilise the ABS estimates of total sector-specific unemployment which is based on unemployed with durations less than two years.
4. Calculations in the column headed GDP are based on the ABS estimates of total unemployment.
5. Values of output loss are in average 1989–90 prices.
6. *SOURCE*: ABS Cat. No. 5206.0, ABS Cat. No. 5222.0, ABS Cat. No. 6203.0, ABS Cat. No. 6302.0 and authors' calculations.

the calculated figures corresponding to the high unemployment scenario (*i.e.* based on the 6.5% benchmark) were 82 thousand and 480 thousand, respectively. This compares with 121 thousand unemployed in manufacturing and total unemployment of 921 thousand in the second quarter of 1992 with the respective unemployment rates being 9.8% and 10.7%.

The output losses presented in these tables indicate a modest cost to the society of unemployment observed in the eighties. In particular, the low unemployment scenario leads to output losses very similar to the total output losses presented earlier and amount to about 3.3% of GDP during the 1991 recession. It is also interesting to note that the losses predicated on the high unemployment scenario result in negative quantities for some years indicating that the high unemployment benchmark may be set at a too high level.[21] The relatively smaller divergence for sector-specific unemployment series leads also to some industries occasionally registering a negative output loss under the high unemployment scenario. We should remember, however, that these industry-specific calculations are based on a subset of

Table 6.2.11 Calculated total sector-specific output loss from unemployment under the low unemployment scenario: average wage method using average total adult earnings.

Fiscal Year	Sector					
	Manufacturing	Construction	Wholesale & retail trade	Finance & business serv.	Community services	Recreation services
	Value ($ million)					
1981–82	437.6	123.5	518.2	97.8	221.7	216.6
1982–83	1587.8	807.7	1170.2	252.3	346.0	452.6
1983–84	1527.4	756.7	1290.2	238.2	301.2	413.4
1984–85	787.6	433.7	844.9	155.4	297.8	397.2
1985–86	619.4	220.7	670.7	145.4	306.2	387.1
1986–87	794.1	360.9	818.2	197.3	277.7	353.3
1987–88	590.5	230.6	591.5	174.6	316.4	279.2
1988–89	261.7	–15.8	298.3	115.9	245.6	188.3
1989–90	345.6	112.1	303.9	167.2	153.3	139.6
1990–91	1179.3	730.0	1120.8	471.0	348.5	369.5
1991–92	1899.2	1242.6	1365.5	594.9	391.3	500.5
	Proportion or actual sectoral output					
1981–82	0.8	0.5	1.1	0.3	0.7	1.9
1982–83	3.1	3.7	2.6	0.9	1.1	3.9
1983–84	2.9	3.4	2.7	0.8	0.9	3.4
1984–85	1.4	1.8	1.7	0.5	0.8	3.2
1985–86	1.1	0.9	1.3	0.4	0.8	3.0
1986–87	1.4	1.5	1.6	0.5	0.7	2.7
1987–88	1.0	0.9	1.1	0.4	0.8	2.0
1988–89	0.4	–0.1	0.5	0.3	0.6	1.3
1989–90	0.5	0.4	0.5	0.4	0.4	1.0
1990–91	1.9	2.9	2.0	1.1	0.8	2.6
1991–92	3.1	5.3	2.3	1.4	0.9	3.4

Notes:

1. Low unemployment refers to the modified low unemployment benchmark. The actual values for the tabulated sectors are: 3.6%, 4.1%, 3.0%, 1.6%, 1.4% and 3.7%.
2. Values of output loss are in average 1989–90 prices.
3. *Source*: ABS Cat. No. 5206.0, ABS Cat. No. 5222.0, ABS Cat. No. 6203.0, ABS Cat. No. 6302.0 and authors' calculations.

the unemployed, namely those with durations less than two years. As we have shown earlier, the continuing increase in unemployment durations is likely to lead to underestimation of these losses. The alternative losses of GDP are also presented graphically in Figure 6.2.8.

5.2 Average product method.

The average product method concentrates on the production side of the economy in calculating the loss of output due to unemployment. Thus, it

Table 6.2.12 Calculated total sector-specific output loss from unemployment under the high unemployment scenario: average wage method using average total adult earnings.

Fiscal Year	Sector					
	Manufacturing	Construction	Wholesale & retail trade	Finance & business serv.	Community services	Recreation services
			Value ($ million)			
1981–82	-85.7	-106.0	78.9	-4.8	62.9	43.0
1982–83	1080.7	583.5	709.7	149.0	186.3	273.2
1983–84	1022.8	543.7	854.9	127.2	130.8	227.0
1984–85	280.7	198.1	364.7	37.8	115.0	198.2
1985–86	132.5	-13.0	179.9	18.7	117.8	185.0
1986–87	316.1	120.0	326.8	68.5	88.2	146.3
1987–88	107.8	-6.7	89.3	38.8	126.5	58.9
1988–89	-229.1	-276.4	-225.8	-30.3	44.1	-38.9
1989–90	-144.6	-165.8	-247.5	13.2	-49.3	-102.1
1990–91	695.0	453.0	566.5	311.1	139.7	122.5
1991–92	1419.7	977.9	807.8	436.7	173.7	233.3
			Proportion of actual sectoral output			
1981–82	-0.2	-0.4	0.2	0.0	0.2	0.4
1982–83	2.1	2.7	1.6	0.5	0.6	2.3
1983–84	2.0	2.5	1.8	0.4	0.4	1.9
1984–85	0.5	0.8	0.7	0.1	0.3	1.6
1985–86	0.2	-0.1	0.4	0.1	0.3	1.4
1986–87	0.6	0.5	0.6	0.2	0.2	1.1
1987–88	0.2	0.0	0.2	0.1	0.3	0.4
1988–89	-0.4	-1.0	-0.4	-0.1	0.1	-0.3
1989–90	-0.2	-0.6	-0.4	0.0	-0.1	-0.7
1990–91	1.1	1.8	1.0	0.7	0.3	0.9
1991–92	2.3	4.2	1.4	1.1	0.4	1.6

Notes:

1. High unemployment refers to the modified benchmark of 6.5%. The actual values for the tabulated sectors are: 5.2%, 6.0%, 4.4%, 2.3%, 2.0% and 5.4%.
2. Values of output loss are in average 1989–90 prices.
3. SOURCE: ABS Cat. No. 5206.0, ABS Cat. No. 5222.0, ABS Cat. No. 6203.0, ABS Cat. No. 6302.0 and authors' calculations.

assumes that unemployed, if employed, would have contributed at the average level, *i.e.* their output would be the same as the average product of the employed labour force. As before, this method does not account for the differential skill levels of the unemployed and, therefore, neglects the issue of skill atrophy and non-homogeneity of the pool of the unemployed. It also does not acknowledge the cyclical variations in the average product of the employed labour force and, hence, tends to bias downwards the estimates of the loss of output. We should also mention that although the average product method is a conceptually equivalent way of assessing the loss to

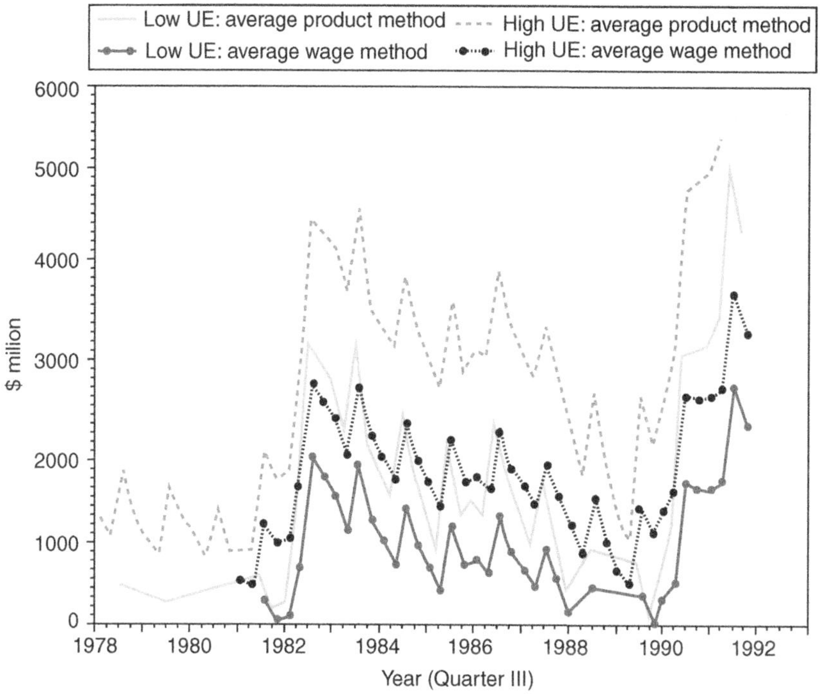

Figure 6.2.8 Output loss: low and high unemployment scenarios

the economy, the differences between the average wage and the average product methods could arise from the extreme simplifying assumptions behind these two methods. In particular, while various laws prescribe the wage rates that the unemployed could be potentially receiving there are no such regulations affecting their potential productivity. Hence the contribution to the national product of the last unemployed person is going to be higher when calculated with the average wage method than under the average product method.

Our estimates of the output loss for individual sectors and for the whole economy are presented in Tables 6.2.13 and 6.2.14. These estimates are comparable with the results obtained using the average wage method although, due to the accounting of the contribution of other factors of production, they are uniformly higher (see also Figure 6.2.7). In fact, a number of sectors as well as the economy as a whole register proportional output loss during recessions which is either close to or in double digits.

The estimates of the output loss under the alternative low and high scenarios are presented in Tables 6.2.15, 6.2.16 and 6.2.17. Figure 6.2.8 also compares the GDP losses under the two scenarios.

Table 6.2.13 Calculated total output loss from unemployment: average product method.

Fiscal Year	Based on GDP*		Based on GDP	
	Value ($ m)	Proportion of output	Value ($ m)	Proportion of output
1978–79	11089.0	4.2	17662.2	6.7
1979–80	10324.1	3.8	17295.8	6.4
1980–81	9777.8	3.5	17107.5	6.1
1981–82	11311.1	3.9	19062.6	6.6
1982–83	17467.9	6.3	27196.7	9.8
1983–84	17662.8	6.0	30762.6	10.5
1984–85	15256.4	4.9	28932.0	9.3
1985–86	14541.7	4.5	27959.3	8.6
1986–87	15727.0	4.8	29497.9	9.0
1987–88	14984.2	4.3	28862.5	8.3
1988–89	12855.5	3.5	25728.7	7.1
1989–90	13409.3	3.5	24913.4	6.6
1990–91	20126.0	5.4	33795.6	9.1
1991–92	24955.1	6.7	42724.5	11.5

Notes:
1. Calculations in the columns headed GDP* utilise the ABS estimates of total sector-specific unemployment which is based on unemployed with durations less than two years.
2. Calculations in the columns headed GDP are based on the ABS estimates of total unemployment.
3. Values of output loss are in average 1989–90 prices.
4. Source: ABS Cat. No. 5206.0, ABS Cat. No. 5222.0, ABS Cat. No. 6203.0, ABS Cat. No. 6302.0 and authors' calculations.

5.3 Okun's law method.

Both the average wage and the average product methods assumed that there is a one-to-one proportionate relationship between the output and unemployment. However, early work by Okun (1962) has demonstrated that due to various technological and economic reasons an increase in the utilisation of labour is likely to have more than proportionate impact on output. In fact, Okun's own estimates of such a relationship yielded a value of 3% points of extra growth in output from a 1% point drop in the unemployment rate – a relationship that has been named in the literature as "Okun's law".

Consequently, we have estimated the output loss from unemployment corresponding to the estimated values of the "Okun's law" coefficient. Our estimates of the law itself are based on two methods proposed by Okun and modified subsequently in the literature. Thus, we have employed the "First Differences" method as modified by Paldam (1987) and the "Trial Gaps" method as modified by Kalisch (1982). The former of these methods relies on estimating a relationship between the differences of the unemployment

Table 6.2.14 Calculated total sector-specific output loss from unemployment: average product method.

Fiscal Year	Sector					
	Manufacturing	Construction	Wholesale & retail trade	Finance & business serv.	Community services	Recreation services
			Value ($ million)			
1978–79	2563.7	1567.8	2167.8	587.9	641.7	697.5
1979–80	2647.1	1243.4	1943.4	544.1	649.0	654.7
1980–81	2549.8	1157.2	2032.0	530.6	547.9	599.2
1981–82	2887.4	1331.4	2317.3	655.0	703.3	706.6
1982–83	4776.4	2647.0	3132.0	975.5	889.9	999.2
1983–84	4805.8	2626.5	3639.3	933.5	862.2	960.1
1984–85	3542.7	1936.9	2857.1	807.9	863.4	937.6
1985–86	3333.3	1551.2	2615.7	835.6	904.7	953.6
1986–87	3780.2	1803.1	2809.8	1007.1	897.6	906.2
1987–88	3548.2	1608.3	2613.1	1018.8	979.6	839.9
1988–89	2979.4	1152.2	2273.0	930.3	893.7	753.0
1989–90	3252.6	1452.5	2295.0	1085.7	805.2	708.7
1990–91	5036.1	2473.6	3472.2	1661.5	1084.1	939.2
1991–92	6764.1	3420.3	3932.3	1844.3	1144.0	1064.4
			Proportion of actual sectoral output			
1978–79	5.0	7.3	5.0	2.5	2.2	6.5
1979–80	5.0	5.6	4.3	2.1	2.2	6.0
1980–81	4.7	4.9	4.4	2.0	1.8	5.3
1981–82	5.2	5.4	4.8	2.3	2.2	6.1
1982–83	9.3	12.1	6.9	3.4	2.7	8.5
1983–84	9.2	11.9	7.7	3.2	2.5	7.9
1984–85	6.5	8.1	5.7	2.6	2.4	7.5
1985–86	5.9	6.2	5.1	2.5	2.4	7.4
1986–87	6.7	7.4	5.6	2.8	2.3	7.0
1987–88	5.9	6.3	4.8	2.6	2.4	6.2
1988–89	4.7	4.2	3.9	2.2	2.1	5.4
1989–90	4.9	5.1	3.9	2.4	1.9	4.9
1990–91	8.1	9.9	6.1	3.8	2.4	6.5
1991–92	11.0	14.6	6.7	4.4	2.5	7.3

Notes:
1 Values of output loss are in average 1989–90 prices.
2 *Source*: ABS Cat. No. 5206.0, ABS Cat. No. 5222.0, ABS Cat. No. 6203.0, ABS Cat. No. 6302.0 and authors' calculations.

rate and the growth rate of the GDP. The inverse of the coefficient on the growth rate of output provides then an estimate of the trade-off between unemployment and output. The latter method is a two stage procedure which relies on fitting a trend growth line to the actual GDP and using the predicted output as a proxy for the potential output. The second stage then consists of estimating a relationship between the proportionate gap and the

Table 6.2.15 Calculated total output loss under alternative unemployment scenarios: average product method

Fiscal Year	High unemployment				Low unemployment			
	Based on GDP*		Based on GDP		Based on GDP*		Based on GDP	
	Value ($ m)	Proportion of output	Value ($ m)	Proportion of output	Value ($ m)	Proportion of output	Value ($ m)	Proportion of output
1978–79	609.3	0.2	-580.2	-0.2	3833.8	1.5	5032.9	1.9
1979–80	-367.9	-0.1	-1333.4	-0.5	2921.9	1.1	4398.7	1.6
1980–81	-1237.2	-0.4	-2093.9	-0.8	2152.0	0.8	3814.2	1.4
1981–82	-179.5	-0.1	-974.9	-0.3	3356.0	1.2	5190.5	1.8
1982–83	6141.8	2.2	7310.4	2.6	9626.8	3.5	13429.3	4.8
1983–84	5797.5	2.0	9740.4	3.3	9448.4	3.2	16208.8	5.5
1984–85	2821.6	0.9	6904.3	2.2	6647.7	2.1	13682.1	4.4
1985–86	1578.1	0.5	5049.5	1.6	5566.9	1.7	12098.6	3.7
1986–87	2562.9	0.8	6224.3	1.9	6613.4	2.0	13385.4	4.1
1987–88	1166.5	0.3	4470.9	1.3	5418.1	1.6	11976.0	3.5
1988–89	-1531.6	-0.4	434.4	0.1	2895.2	0.8	8217.2	2.3
1989–90	-1613.1	-0.4	-1371.9	-0.4	3009.1	0.8	6715.9	1.8
1990–91	5131.2	1.4	7416.4	2.0	9744.9	2.6	15533.1	4.2
1991–92	9795.3	2.6	15798.4	4.3	14459.8	3.9	24083.3	6.5

Note: For explanatory notes see Table 6.2.10.

unemployment rate. Our estimates of the Okun's law yielded values of 3.39 for the first method and 2.7 for the second method. These values compare with 2.7 obtained by Kalisch (1982) using the sample from the mid-sixties to 1980, 4.34 estimated by Paldam (1987) for the post-war period ending in 1985, 2.46 calculated from Murphy's contribution in EPAC (1991*a*) and 3.76 derived by Watts and Mitchell (1991) for the period 1968 to 1989.

As in the previous sections, we first present the loss of output due to total unemployment. Table 6.2.18 provides the financial year aggregates of the estimated potential output and the output gap based on the "First Differences" method.[22] In addition, the table also provides a relative indication of the magnitude of the output gap in relation to the actual GDP and the estimated potential product. These figures indicate that the loss is quite high, even during more prosperous times as in the mid-eighties during the extensive employment growth when the percentage proportion of output lost only managed to come to the levels experienced in the late seventies (which were characterised by much lower unemployment).

The estimates of the output loss under the low and high unemployment scenarios, as defined in section 5, are presented in Table 6.2.19 and are illustrated in Figure 6.2.9. These figures again paint a very depressing picture with even the estimates for the 1992 recessionary period under the high unemployment scenario yielding proportion of actual output lost in double digits and well above the losses during the 1982 recession. Overall, therefore,

Table 6.2.16 Calculated total sector-specific output loss from unemployment under the low unemployment scenario: average product method.

Fiscal Year	Sector					
	Manufacturing	Construction	Wholesale & retail trade	Finance & business serv.	Community services	Recreation services
	Value ($ million)					
1978–79	629.9	610.4	797.5	198.4	244.1	273.2
1979–80	630.9	278.9	529.3	132.1	242.5	226.1
1980–81	497.8	129.1	571.9	91.9	128.1	160.8
1981–82	774.6	253.3	795.7	193.4	267.2	248.6
1982–83	2760.9	1632.0	1654.0	508.9	435.3	528.5
1983–84	2761.3	1609.8	2091.8	458.0	377.1	476.4
1984–85	1447.9	870.5	1250.7	298.3	362.2	440.5
1985–86	1198.7	457.2	987.8	282.2	379.5	438.1
1986–87	1602.8	718.1	1192.0	408.5	354.3	390.6
1987–88	1250.4	485.9	897.5	370.5	417.0	302.6
1988–89	573.3	-32.0	456.8	242.5	312.8	203.7
1989–90	768.9	218.2	443.2	352.4	204.0	142.7
1990–91	2610.1	1335.2	1639.4	941.3	462.1	371.9
1991–92	4315.3	2311.8	2046.9	1154.1	507.3	483.1
	Proportion of actual sectoral output					
1978–79	1.2	2.8	1.9	0.8	0.9	2.5
1979–80	1.2	1.3	1.2	0.5	0.8	2.1
1980–81	0.9	0.5	1.2	0.3	0.4	1.4
1981–82	1.4	1.0	1.7	0.7	0.9	2.1
1982–83	5.4	7.4	3.6	1.8	1.3	4.5
1983–84	5.3	7.3	4.4	1.6	1.1	3.9
1984–85	2.6	3.6	2.5	1.0	1.0	3.5
1985–86	2.1	1.8	1.9	0.8	1.0	3.4
1986–87	2.8	2.9	2.4	1.1	0.9	3.0
1987–88	2.1	1.9	1.7	0.9	1.0	2.2
1988–89	0.9	–0.1	0.8	0.6	0.7	1.4
1989–90	1.2	0.8	0.8	0.8	0.5	1.0
1990–91	4.2	5.3	2.9	2.2	1.0	2.6
1991–92	7.0	9.9	3.5	2.8	1.1	3.3

Note: For explanatory notes see Table 6.2.11.

the Okun's law estimates confirm the earlier results obtained on the basis of accounting-type methods which demonstrated the significant magnitude of the output loss due to underutilisation of the available labour force.

5.4 Summary of the alternative estimates of the output loss.

We conclude this section on assessment of the output cost of unemployment by summarising the estimated losses under the three methods. As

Table 6.2.17 Calculated total sector-specific output loss from unemployment under the high unemployment scenario: average product method

Fiscal Year	Sector					
	Manufacturing	Construction	Wholesale & retail trade	Finance & business serv.	Community services	Recreation services
			Value ($ million)			
1978–79	-229.6	184.9	188.5	25.3	67.4	84.7
1979–80	-265.2	-149.7	-99.2	-51.1	61.8	35.6
1980–81	-414.2	-327.9	-77.0	-103.0	-58.4	-34.1
1981–82	-164.4	-225.9	119.5	-11.7	73.3	45.0
1982–83	1865.2	1180.9	997.1	301.5	233.3	319.3
1983–84	1852.6	1157.9	1404.0	246.7	161.6	261.4
1984–85	516.9	396.5	536.7	71.9	139.4	219.5
1985–86	250.0	-29.0	264.3	36.3	146.1	209.0
1986–87	635.0	235.8	473.0	142.4	112.9	161.5
1987–88	229.2	-13.0	135.0	82.4	166.9	63.8
1988–89	-496.1	-558.4	-350.4	-63.1	54.6	-40.4
1989–90	-335.0	-330.4	-379.8	26.5	-63.2	-108.9
1990–91	1531.9	829.2	824.8	621.2	185.6	119.8
1991–92	3226.9	1819.2	1209.0	847.3	224.4	224.8
			Proportion of actual sectoral output			
1978–79	-0.4	0.9	0.4	0.1	0.2	0.8
1979–80	-0.5	-0.7	-0.2	-0.2	0.2	0.3
1980–81	-0.8	-1.4	-0.2	-0.4	-0.2	-0.3
1981–82	-0.3	-0.9	0.2	0.0	0.2	0.4
1982–83	3.6	5.4	2.2	1.1	0.7	2.7
1983–84	3.6	5.3	3.0	0.9	0.5	2.2
1984–85	0.9	1.7	1.1	0.2	0.4	1.8
1985–86	0.4	-0.1	0.5	0.1	0.4	1.6
1986–87	1.1	1.0	0.9	0.4	0.3	1.2
1987–88	0.4	-0.1	0.2	0.2	0.4	0.5
1988–89	-0.8	-2.0	-0.6	-0.1	0.1	-0.3
1989–90	-0.5	-1.2	-0.6	0.1	-0.1	-0.7
1990–91	2.5	3.3	1.4	1.4	0.4	0.8
1991–92	5.3	7.8	2.1	2.0	0.5	1.5

Note: For explanatory notes see Table 6.2.12.

we discussed earlier all of these methods suffer from some deficiencies, for example in terms of under-estimation or over-estimation of the potential output. In order to provide some average of the losses Table 6.2.20 lists the losses from the three methods under both the high unemployment scenario (which corresponds with a lower output loss) and the low unemployment scenario (which translates into a higher output loss). In addition, the final two columns present averages of the output losses over these three methods. These mean values indicate that even if the current unemployment rate was

Table 6.2.18 Estimates of the foregone output: Okun's "First Differences" method

Fiscal Year	Potential Output ($ m)	Output gap ($ m)	Proportion of actual output (%)	Proportion of potential output (%)
1978–79	313448.8	50458.9	19.2	16.1
1979–80	320276.1	50968.0	18.9	15.9
1980–81	326428.2	48129.0	17.3	14.7
1981–82	343774.7	54568.5	18.9	15.9
1982–83	362229.8	83483.2	29.9	23.0
1983–84	378725.8	86070.7	29.4	22.7
1984–85	391357.5	81401.2	26.3	20.8
1985–86	405955.1	81455.1	25.1	20.1
1986–87	413735.7	85177.7	25.9	20.6
1987–88	428810.8	82416.6	23.8	19.2
1988–89	435153.3	71739.0	19.7	16.5
1989–90	452441.4	72964.8	19.2	16.1
1990–91	474768.0	102729.7	27.6	21.6
1991–92	495678.3	124154.7	33.4	25.0

Notes:
1. "Proportion of actual output" indicates that the gap is a percentage of the actual GDP.
2. "Proportion of potential output" indicates that the gap is a percentage of the estimated potential GDP.
3. Values of output loss are in average 1989–90 prices.
4. *Source*: ABS Cat No. 5206.0, ABS Cat. No. 5222.0, ABS Cat. No. 6203.0, ABS Cat. No. 6302.0 and authors' calculations.

to be lowered to 6.5% the output loss would be almost 6% of the GDP. Even if we assumed that there are significant costs of inflation[23] this would still constitute a significant net loss. The reader may wish to subtract an arbitrary percentage loss due to inflation. However, it would still leave a significant output loss due to unemployment.

6 Costs to the government.

In order to quantify the costs of unemployment to the government it is useful to treat the government as another economic agent. In such a framework the costs are easily seen as the expenditure of real economic resources associated with the provision of services to the unemployed. Such costs have to be distinguished from the fiscal costs to the government, such as increased unemployment benefits payments or reduced taxation revenue. These latter costs are, in fact, "transfer payments" and do not involve the use of economic inputs, and, therefore, cannot be classified in the same way as real economic costs. As an illustration, a recent study in the U.K. has found that the fiscal loss to the government due to the unemployment benefit payments and the foregone income tax revenue amounted to 5091 pounds

Table 6.2.19 Estimates of the foregone output under alternative unemployment scenarios: Okun's "First Differences" method

Fiscal Year	High unemployment				Low unemployment			
	Potential Output ($ m)	Output gap ($ m)	Share of actual output (%)	Share of potential output (%)	Potential Output ($ m)	Output gap ($ m)	Share of actual output (%)	Share of potential output (%)
1978–79	255419.1	-7570.7	-2.9	-3.0	273274.4	10284.6	3.9	3.8
1979–80	260852.4	-8455.7	-3.1	-3.2	279136.6	9828.5	3.6	3.5
1980–81	265020.6	-13278.7	-4.8	-5.0	283915.2	5616.0	2.0	2.0
1981–82	279960.3	-9245.9	-3.2	-3.3	299595.6	10389.3	3.6	3.5
1982–83	300723.4	21976.8	7.9	7.3	319648.5	40901.8	14.7	12.8
1983–84	314150.4	21495.4	7.3	6.8	334019.7	41364.7	14.1	12.4
1984–85	322964.5	13008.3	4.2	4.0	344008.5	34052.3	11.0	9.9
1985–86	334353.0	9853.1	3.0	2.9	356384.3	31884.5	9.8	8.9
1986–87	341238.3	12680.2	3.9	3.7	363545.2	34987.1	10.6	9.6
1987–88	352377.6	5983.5	1.7	1.7	375895.5	29501.3	8.5	7.8
1988–89	354964.7	-8449.6	-2.3	-2.4	379638.1	16223.8	4.5	4.3
1989–90	368708.5	-10768.0	-2.8	-2.9	394472.4	14995.9	4.0	3.8
1990–91	392676.5	20638.1	5.5	5.3	417935.4	45897.0	12.3	11.0
1991–92	413700.3	42176.7	11.4	10.2	438924.3	67400.7	18.1	15.4

Notes:
1. High unemployment is set at 6.5% – the average rate of the "natural rate" of unemployment.
2. Low unemployment is set at 4.5% – the average level of unemployment between 1975 and 1977.
3. "Share of actual output" denotes the ratio of the gap to the actual GDP.
4. "Share of potential output" denotes the ratio of the gap to the the estimated potential GDP.
5. Values of output loss are in average 1989–90 prices.
6. *Source*: ABS Cat. No. 5206.0, ABS Cat. No. 5222.0, ABS Cat. No. 6203.0, ABS Cat. No. 6302.0 and authors' calculations.

per unemployed person during the 1990-91 financial year.[24] Similarly, for Australia, Dixon (1992) calculated that the immediate fiscal loss to the government amounts to 50% of the private income lost as a result of unemployment. It is important, therefore, to realise that there may be secondary effects of these transfers (*e.g.*, changes in the consumption patterns in the society and the associated multiplier effects) which may have an impact on the allocation of real economic resources. Thus, government's fiscal policies affecting transfer payments (*i.e.*, taxation rates, eligibility for social security and the rates of benefits) should be taken into account in a full accounting of all costs of unemployment.

Our estimates of the costs of unemployment to the government concentrate on two aspects of government administrative expenditure which are directly dependent on the state of the labour market: the provision of the labour market programs (LMPs) and servicing the unemployment benefits. The first category groups together government expenditure designed to improve employment situation in the economy. Such an effect can be

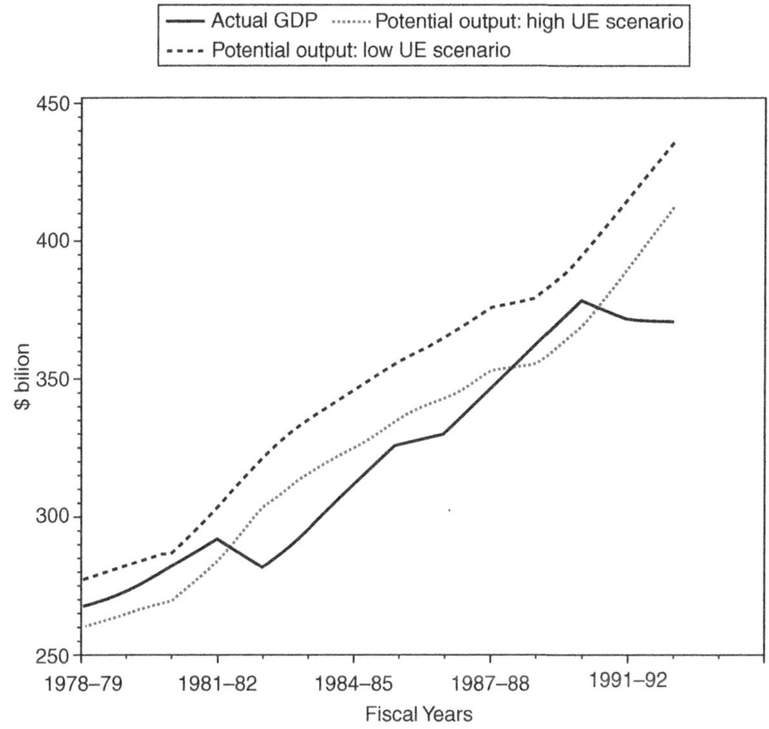

Figure 6.2.9 Actual GDP and potential output: Okun's method

Table 6.2.20 Summary of the estimates of the output loss under alternative methods. Proportion of the actual value of GDP

Fiscal Year	Average Wage Method		Average Product Method		OKun's Law Method		Average	
	High UE	Low UE	High UE	Low UE	High UE	Low UE	High UE	Low UE
1981–82	–0.2	1.0	–0.3	1.8	–3.2	3.6	–1.2	2.1
1982–83	1.5	2.7	2.6	4.8	7.9	14.7	4.0	7.4
1983–84	1.8	3.1	3.3	5.5	7.3	14.1	4.1	7.6
1984–85	1.2	2.4	2.2	4.4	4.2	11.0	2.5	5.9
1985–86	0.8	2.0	1.6	3.7	3.0	9.8	1.8	5.2
1986–87	1.0	2.1	1.9	4.1	3.9	10.6	2.3	5.6
1987–88	0.7	1.8	1.3	3.5	1.7	8.5	1.2	4.6
1988–89	0.1	1.1	0.1	2.3	–2.3	4.5	–0.7	2.6
1989–90	–0.2	0.9	–0.4	1.8	–2.8	4.0	–1.1	2.2
1990–91	1.0	2.1	2.0	4.2	5.5	12.3	2.8	6.2
1991–92	2.1	3.3	4.3	6.5	11.4	18.1	5.9	9.3

Notes:

1. "High UE" refers to the high unemployment scenario. High unemployment is set at 6.5% – the average rate of the "natural rate" of unemployment.
2. "Low UE" refers to the low unemployment scenario. Low unemployment is set at 4.5% – the average level of unemployment between 1975 and 1977.
3. *Source*: Tables 6.2.5, 6.2.15 and 6.2.19.

pursued through a number of initiatives ranging from increased training for the employed and the unemployed, direct job creation for the unemployed, and improvement in the workings of the labour market (*e.g.*, the efficiency of the Commonwealth Employment Service). Due to the possibility of "targetting" of such schemes, programs that affect the unemployed are of particular interest in evaluating the costs of unemployment and the provision of LMPs. We should point, however, that we do not attempt to evaluate the effectiveness of LMPs in attaining their objectives, in general, or their effectiveness in different phases of the business cycle, in particular. (For a policy-oriented evaluation of Australia's LMPs see Stretton and Chapman (1990).)

Table 6.2.21 provides a summary of the costs of all Labour Market Programs as well as those targetted on the unemployed. Overall, LMPs constitute a not insignificant proportion of the National expenditure and account for a large component of the Commonwealth expenditure. While the data suggest that at least part of the variations in the total expenditure may be a result of political convictions of the government of the day, it is important to note that a large measure of variation derives primarily from the government's assessment of the efficacy of various LMPs and its economic strategy in general. Thus, while the average amount spent per unemployed decreases in the early stages of a recession, the table suggests that it is not only as a result of an increase in the level of unemployment since the absolute amount spent on LMPs seems to decrease in the initial stages of a recession (both in absolute terms and as a proportion of government outlays). It is also interesting to observe that just before the onset of the current recession this average was comparable to the amount spent before the 1982 recession even though the unemployment levels in late eighties were significantly bigger than those before 1982 recession.

Additional insight into the cost of Labour Market Programs can also be obtained from the marginal effect of unemployment on the LMP expenditure. Thus, we have used simple models which relate these outlays to the state of the economy and the labour market situation. These models produced elasticities of the LMPs with respect to the unemployment rate of 2.90 for the LMPs targetted on unemployed and 2.03 for all LMPs. Thus, a one percentage point increase in unemployment is associated with a $170.2 million increase in spending on programs for the unemployed and $180.2 million overall increase in LMPs spending.

Turning to the assessment of the second aspect of government administration which directly uses real economic resources, Table 6.2.22 provides some data on the servicing of the unemployment benefits. Under the Social Security Act and related legislations the Department of Social Security administers income support predominantly for families with children, people with disabilities, retirees, the sick and the unemployed. In 1991–92 financial year the payment of unemployment benefits accounted for about 24% (the average over 1978/79 – 1991/92 being 18%) of the total payments under the

Table 6.2.21 Costs of Labour Market Programs

Fiscal Year	Programs for the Unemployed				All programs			
	Amount ($ m)	Proportion of Govt. Outlays (%)	Proportion of GDP (%)	Amount per unemployed ($)	Amount ($ m)	Proportion of Govt. Outlays (%)	Proportion of GDP (%)	Amount per unemployed ($)
1978–79	326.8	0.44	0.12	826.7	427.0	0.58	0.16	1080.2
1979–80	136.7	0.18	0.05	344.7	272.5	0.36	0.10	687.1
1980–81	175.5	0.22	0.06	424.3	355.2	0.45	0.13	858.8
1981–82	173.1	0.21	0.06	461.0	373.2	0.46	0.13	993.9
1982–83	359.5	0.42	0.13	799.2	559.9	0.65	0.20	1244.8
1983–84	946.5	1.01	0.32	1317.3	1172.0	1.25	0.40	1631.2
1984–85	935.2	0.94	0.30	1468.1	1192.6	1.20	0.38	1872.2
1985–86	680.1	0.68	0.21	1119.3	903.3	0.91	0.28	1486.7
1986–87	559.7	0.59	0.17	945.1	801.9	0.85	0.24	1354.1
1987–88	410.1	0.45	0.12	645.8	671.6	0.74	0.19	1057.6
1988–89	299.1	0.33	0.08	505.3	598.8	0.66	0.16	1011.7
1989–90	260.4	0.28	0.07	502.2	527.7	0.57	0.14	1017.7
1990–91	297.4	0.31	0.08	540.3	545.5	0.57	0.15	991.1
1991–92	555.3	0.61	0.15	683.7	830.3	0.91	0.22	1022.3

Notes:
1. "Govt. Outlays" denotes total government expenditure.
2. Values are in average 1989–90 prices.
3. *SOURCE*: Stretton and Chapman (1990), ABS Cat. No. 5222.0, Minister for Finance, *Press Release, Budget Statements. Budget Paper No. 1* and authors' calculations.

Table 6.2.22 Costs of administration of unemployment benefits

Fiscal Year	Amount ($ m)	Proportion of Benefits Payment (%)	Proportion of SS Act Payment (%)	Proportion of Govt. Outlays (%)	Proportion of GDP (%)	Amount per unemployed ($)
1978–79	382.5	42.03	5.67	0.52	0.15	1225.8
1979–80	402.4	43.49	5.49	0.53	0.15	1292.8
1980–81	423.6	42.55	5.21	0.54	0.15	1347.0
1981–82	482.6	39.42	5.10	0.59	0.17	1235.5
1982–83	532.3	23.67	4.62	0.62	0.19	838.2
1983–84	664.3	22.81	5.00	0.71	0.23	1136.5
1984–85	713.2	23.90	5.03	0.72	0.23	1270.4
1985–86	734.1	23.51	4.87	0.74	0.23	1288.5
1986–87	726.2	21.02	4.52	0.77	0.22	1318.2
1987–88	723.6	21.44	4.15	0.79	0.21	1523.0
1988–89	714.1	22.78	3.90	0.78	0.20	1831.1
1989–90	822.2	26.80	4.08	0.88	0.22	1921.3
1990–91	875.1	19.19	3.69	0.92	0.24	1293.2
1991–92	986.0	14.64	3.54	1.08	0.27	1157.6

Notes:
1. "Benefits Payment" refers to the total Unemployment Benefits payments.
2. "SS Act Payment" refers to the total expenditure under the Social Security Act.
3. "Govt. Outlays" refers to the total government expenditure.
4. Values are in average 1989–90 prices.
5. *Source*: DSS *Annual Report,* ABS Cat. No. 5222.0, Minister for Finance, *Press Release* and authors' calculations.

Social Security Act and, after the Age Pension payments, was the biggest single expenditure item amongst all the DSS programs. It is, however, the only program that is affected by the economic conditions rather than the demographic structure of the population. Thus, long-range demographic forecasts can be utilised to plan the administrative resources necessary for all programs except the income support for the unemployed. The short-term changes in the economic conditions and the corresponding number of potential unemployment beneficiaries implies that no such planning is feasible for the program of the unemployment benefits payment. DSS is also further constrained in the use of its resources by the Social Security Act which stipulates the delivery of "social security entitlements with fairness, courtesy and *efficiency"* (DSS *Annual Report,* 1989–90) (italics added). In addition, one also has to keep in mind the occasional policy changes affecting eligibility criteria of the unemployed (for example, longer waiting periods for school-leavers) and, therefore, the number of benefit recipients. Recent replacement of the unemployment benefits with Job Search Allowance and NEWSTART schemes which are differentiated by the duration of unemployment of the claimant also suggests that the government financial arrangement can be a factor in the budgetary allocation of income support.

The numbers in this table indicate that the total departmental administrative expenditure is of similar order of magnitude to the expenditure on the Labour Market Programs both in absolute terms and as a proportion of the National Product. The growth of the unemployment in the eighties, however, has resulted in a significant increase in the total outlays on unemployment benefits. Together with the tightening of overall government expenditure this has resulted in doubling of the proportion of unemployment benefits outlays to total government outlays over the decade of the eighties. It is also interesting to note that while the average LMPs expenditure at the end of the eighties has returned to the level at the beginning of the decade, the average amount (per unemployed) spend by the Department on administration has almost doubled over the same period. At the same time, administrative costs as a proportion of total unemployment benefits payment has declined as has the proportion with respect to the total Payments under the Social Security Act. Finally, our simple estimates of the marginal impact of one percentage point increase in the unemployment rate resulted yielded the elasticity of 0.58. This translates into $51.2 million increase in the administrative expenditure directly as a result of a 1 percentage point increase in unemployment.

7 Individual and social costs.

The costs of unemployment for an individual are more difficult to quantify than the pure output costs considered earlier. The main reason for this difficulty is the complexity and joint nature of pecuniary and non-pecuniary costs at the individual level. Thus, apart from the immediate financial losses as well as increased financial pressures from mortgage and consumer debt repayments, the unemployed suffer from the so-called "scarring" effect which affects their future employment and income prospects. This scarring translates itself into a lower probability of finding jobs due to employers (implicit?) preference for employed job-seekers over the unemployed applicants as well as for those with short-term unemployment history over the long-term unemployed. On the supply side, the scarring effect reveals itself with unemployed accepting lower-paid employment, usually at lower skill level. (See Bradbury, Ross and Doyle (1990) for estimates of the impact of scarring on wages and Junankar and Kapuscinski (1991) for a discussion of the effect of scarring and the resulting duration dependence and the composition of the long term unemployment.)

Given these qualifications, we will consider one of the most common indicators of the pecuniary costs of unemployment to the individual – the "replacement ratio" (RR). This measure is defined as the ratio of the person's net income in the state of unemployment to the net income when employed. As such, RR provides important information on the valuation of unemployment by both the society and the individual. The former aspect is conveyed when one considers RR as the ability of the nation's social security system to maintain the living standards of people moved from employment to the state of unemployment. The latter aspect is encapsulated by RR indicating the relative incentive for the unemployed to look for jobs and move out of the unemployment pool. It should be stressed, however, that the applicability of the concept of the replacement ratio is conditional on the eligibility of the unemployed for the unemployment benefits. For example, married women who satisfy the requirement concerning the attachment to the labour force usually fail the income test and are ineligible to receive the benefits.

In addition, the concept of the replacement ratio has several limitations. The most important of these is the non-uniqueness of RR. Thus, many components of benefits are subject to specific individual circumstances. For example, the conditional availability of family allowances means that unemployed people with identical personal characteristics except the family size will face different replacement ratios. A related issue arises also with individual differences in the usage of benefits that are available only to the unemployed. In particular, the assumption of a full take-up of such benefits is likely to bias upwards the RRs. Similarly, on the income side, the structure of the taxation system implies the existence of a number of RRs, one for each taxation level. An additional problem is also the distinction between a typical (or marginal) individual and an average individual. Thus, the average RR calculated from macro-data may differ from the marginal RR calculated from individual survey data. Finally, RRs can be defined as backward or forward looking RRs depending on whether the past (or actual) earnings and benefits or the discounted expected future earnings and benefits are used in the calculations. All these measurement problems provide a scope for a wide variation in the calculated RRs and, therefore, our estimates of RRs should be regarded as indicative of the likely range of RRs. We should, however, remember that with the present state of the economy when the unemployed form a substantial component of the population such conceptual differences between the various RRs are unlikely to affect the overall outcome of these calculations.

In order to present a broad picture of the range of replacement ratios as well as some indication of the severity of the pecuniary problems faced by the unemployed we provide a number of RRs. Thus, Table 6.2.23 contains unemployment benefit replacement ratios for hypothetical families with either a half or full average weekly earnings as the potential income in the state of employment and the appropriate level of unemployment benefits in me state of unemployment. In addition, the calculated incomes in both of these states are adjusted for various family and educational transfers and, where appropriate, taxation payments. The most striking fact about all of these RRs is their absolute size. For example, in 1989–90 a couple with two children could expect to be 40 per cent worse off in monetary terms when

Table 6.2.23 Unemployment benefit replacement rates for hypothetical families: 1978–79 to 1989–90.

Fiscal Year	Single adult		Couple with no children		Couple with 2 children		Couple with 4 children	
	0.5 AWE	AWE	0.5 AWE	AWE	0.5 AWE	AWE	0.5 AWE	AWE
1978–79	53.7	30.9	82.4	49.3	96.8	59.6	106.7	68.2
1979–80	50.0	28.4	82.7	49.1	96.1	58.7	103.9	65.8
1980–81	45.9	25.7	81.8	47.9	95.4	57.9	104.4	65.4
1981–82	43.8	24.3	79.7	46.6	92.8	55.5	101.5	63.0
1982–83	44.0	24.2	80.7	46.5	90.1	54.8	96.4	62.0
1983–84	47.2	25.8	83.3	47.6	84.4	56.2	85.4	64.1
1984–85	48.5	26.8	83.5	47.9	85.0	57.3	87.5	67.1
1985–86	50.5	28.2	83.7	48.5	85.3	58.6	87.8	68.9
1986–87	50.7	28.7	83.5	48.9	85.2	59.1	87.6	69.5
1987–88	52.6	29.7	87.1	50.7	88.4	62.7	90.5	71.6
1988–89	53.0	30.0	88.1	51.4	89.6	65.2	91.6	73.4
1989–90	52.8	29.6	87.3	50.7	89.2	65.0	91.2	72.0

Notes:
1. The numerator for these replacement rates is the total disposable income for the unemployed, the denominator corresponds to either half (0.5 AWE column) or full male average weekly earnings (AWE column).
2. *Source*: Bradbury *et al.* (1990), Table 3.1.

affected by unemployment. These figures improve slightly with the size of the family since non-unemployment benefit transfers generally increase with the number of children. These can, however, lead to some anomalies as in the late seventies and early eighties. In this period large families faced replacement ratios of over 100 per cent but these calculations arbitrarily assume that employment at half the average earnings would be expected by the unemployed. We should also stress that all of these replacement ratios exhibit similar fluctuations over time which reflects administrative changes to the base levels of unemployment benefits. Finally, it is interesting to observe that the state of the economy, as conveyed by the (lack of) growth of real average wages since the last recession, contributed to the slight increase of these replacement rates.

In addition to these detailed calculations of Bradbury *et al.*, we also present alternative replacement rates calculated from the macro-data. These estimates are given in Table 6.2.24 for both gender groups and in relation to both average earnings from full-time employment alternative and average earnings for all employed, which includes part-time employment. These figures show higher RRs for females than for males reflecting the lower average weekly earnings of females. In addition, due to the inclusion of part-time work in the calculations involving the average total earnings these RRs are

Table 6.2.24 Gender-specific unemployment benefit replacement rates: June quarter values

Year	Females		Males	
	Based on $w^{F/T}$	Based on w^{T}	Based on $w^{F/T}$	Based on w^{T}
1981	23.2	28.1	18.9	18.9
1982	22.6	27.6	18.2	18.0
1983	24.4	30.3	19.4	20.0
1984	24.8	30.6	20.3	20.5
1985	25.5	32.3	21.1	21.5
1986	26.8	34.3	22.1	22.4
1987	27.3	35.0	22.7	23.2
1988	27.4	35.4	22.8	23.3
1989	27.4	35.6	22.7	23.2
1990	27.6	35.9	22.9	23.4
1991	27.7	36.6	23.5	24.4
1992	27.1	35.5	22.6	23.6

Notes:
1. The numerator in these replacement rates is the single adult rate of the unemployment benefit.
2. The denominator is the gender specific adult earnings. $w^{F/T}$ denotes the average full-time adult earnings while w^{T} denotes the average total adult earnings.
3. Values are in average 1989–90 prices.
4. Values for 1981 are for the September quarter.
5. *Source*: DSS *Annual Report*, various issues; ABS Cat. No. 6203.0; ABS Cat. No. 6302.0 and authors' calculations.

larger than the corresponding figures based only on the average full-time earnings.

It is important, however, to put these RRs in the context of the family characteristics of the unemployed. Thus, in mid-1991, the ABS Labour Force Survey estimates revealed that 78.1% of all unemployed were classified as members of a family while 15.4% of all unemployed were single people. In addition, 25.5% of all unemployed people were married with dependents and 14.4% were married with no dependents.[25] On the other hand, 69.4% of all unemployment benefit recipients were single. Only 11.4% were married with no children and 18.3% were married with children.[26]

Summing up the discussion on the pecuniary costs of unemployment to the individual it is worth stressing that despite the low level of these replacement ratios they confirm that the unemployment benefits do provide some income support to the unemployed, especially the more disadvantaged. Thus, the proposals to reduce the unemployment benefit schemes should be regarded as adding to the costs of unemployment, especially for those least likely to bear these costs. In particular, such changes would dramatically alter the profile of replacement ratios with the long-term unemployed facing zero RR and only short to medium-term unemployed possibly being in a position to count on income support while out-of-work. Yet it is the long-term unemployed who are more likely to exhaust their savings and, therefore, be in financial distress. Given the unprecedented increase in the long-term unemployed in the current recession as well as the rising average duration of unemployment such changes would significantly increase the individual costs of unemployment.

Moving on to the non-pecuniary costs of unemployment for individuals and the society we should stress that this is an area subject to tentative claims, controversies due to different assumptions and relatively little of appropriate data (such as longitudinal surveys with both economic and social variables). Most authors agree, however, that employment is not only a source of income but also a provider of social inter-relationships, individual self-esteem and identity in the society and a set of goals outside the family. Thus, the loss of employment impacts on an individual on many levels with the loss of income being the most frequently mentioned aspect. Unemployment, however, also means loss of work-related social contacts, which may put increased strains on family structures and affect both mental and physical health. In the longer term, such degradation of life has also been linked with increased suicides and higher mortality through increased stress-related illnesses or inappropriate diet and life-style.[27] Although these links have been investigated by researchers from various disciplines ranging from demography to sociology the economic perspective is far from conclusive. The main problems for applied economists is the measurement and quantifying of the effects of unemployment on individual's behaviour. The use of proxies of these directly unobservable impacts in models which include well-defined variables, such as those describing individual's employment characteristics or the state of the labour market, often leads to statistically weak results and inconclusive tests. In the remainder of this section we briefly present some evidence on the cost of unemployment to the individual and the society.

Given the large and often controversial role of migration in Australia's economic and social development it is natural to postulate possible links between unemployment and migration. The focus of many studies, however, is on the reverse relationship, *i.e.* the impact of immigration on a given macroeconomic variable. For example, Junankar, Pope, Kapuscinski, Li and Mudd (1990) found no statistically significant influence of migration on wage or price inflation. There was, however, some evidence of unidirectional causal link between the price inflation, on the one hand, and the net rate of long-term immigration as well as the long-term arrival rate, on the other hand. Thus, it is reasonable to expect that the economic conditions in Australia (including the employment prospects) would be a factor contributing to the decisionmaking of potential migrants. Although our calculations of simple correlations between the net migration rate and the unemployment rate indicate a weak negative relationship (–0.48 over the period 1921 to 1989 and –0.23 for the post-World War II period) a more complete assessment of such impact requires a model accounting for lagged responses and the influence of other economic variables.

As an alternative we have attempted to model the impact of unemployment on the skill composition of migration to Australia. Withers (1989) constructed a migration skill index which measures a relative contribution of different occupation categories of migrants to the human capital formation. Given that the value of human capital directly influences the income per capita, such an index summarises the economic value of migration to Australia. Our single-equation model related the skill index to domestic demand variables (such as GDP) and the actual migration flows, among other variables. Since the skill index is essentially a weighted measure of earnings ability such a model can be viewed as a simple wage equation for immigrants. The movements in the skill index over time can then be regarded as a reflection of the relative attractiveness to migrants of various occupation categories in Australia as well as the immigration mix.

In order to account for the secular rise in the level of qualifications in the population in general we have estimated two alternative specifications with the time trend being a proxy for me exogenous progress in education levels. The fitted equations were quite satisfactory with R^2 of no less than 0.9 and high significance levels of the explanatory variables. The estimated elasticities of the skill index with respect to the unemployment rate were –0.036 for the model without the trend variable and –0.026 for the model with the trend variable. This translates into marginal effects of –0.72 and –0.51 at the means and –0.55 and –0.39 at the 1986 values of the variables.[28] While these numbers may seem low at first (the average value of the skill index was 99.6 over the full sample and 107.2 in the post-war period) it is instructive to consider the total impact of the unemployment on the immigration composition. Thus, completely eliminating unemployment would increase me skill index by 5.7 and 4.0 points (on the basis of these two models), *i.e.* by about 40 and 30 per cent, respectively, of its standard deviation. Recalculating these effects for a hypothetical reduction of unemployment to the average level over me entire sample (5.1 per cent over the period 1921 to 1986) resulted in increases of the skill index of 2.1 and 1.5 points (16 and 10 per cent of its standard deviation), respectively. Similar calculations using the post-war average of unemployment of 3.2 per cent yielded increases in the skill index of 3.4 and 2.4 points (33 and 23 per cent of the standard deviation of the post-war index). Finally, we have also utilised the low and high scenarios for the unemployment rate, as described in Section 5. The results from the two models suggest an improvement in the skill index of 2.5 and 1.8 points (approximately 34 and 24 per cent of the standard deviation of the index during the last decade of the sample) for the low unemployment scenario and 1.1 and 0.8 points (about 14 per cent and 11 per cent of the standard deviation) for the high unemployment scenario. These results imply that Australia's human capital formation is unnecessarily jeopardized by the adverse impact of high levels of unemployment on the immigration of advanced, highly skilled labour. In view of the continuing significance of immigration to Australia such costs of unemployment are affecting the whole of the society.

As we mentioned earlier unemployment is likely to affect not only the individual losing the job but also his/her immediate family. In particular, it has been argued that the state of unemployment with its large financial costs may lead to more stressed life-style resulting in increased domestic violence, break-up of marriages and a general loosening of family structures in the society as a whole. We have attempted to assess the link between unemployment and two indicators capturing the family structures – marriages and divorces. Simple correlations between unemployment and these variables provided an early indication of possible relationships – the unemployment rate and marriages are negatively correlated and there is a weak positive correlation between unemployment and divorces. In order to provide some structure to the models we have related both the marriage and divorce variables to regressors describing the age structure of the population, the urbanization rate and gender-specific wage rates. Although we cannot claim that such formulations account for all the demographic and economic causes they do provide a useful first approximation in assessing the impact of unemployment after controlling for major determinants of marriages and divorces. A summary of these results appears in Table 6.2.25.

As expected, the marginal effect of unemployment is negative for marriages and positive for divorces. Although the equations explaining divorces were not as good as those for marriages, the coefficients of interest were still at acceptable levels of significance (above 10 per cent). The interesting aspect of these estimates is their absolute size. Thus, while a 1 percentage point increase in the total unemployment rate leads to almost twelve hundred less marriages the effect on divorces is only about one-fifth. A possible explanation for this disparity may lie in the changing availability of and access to legal divorces over the seven decades of our sample. In fact, the ratio of divorces to marriages was 35 per cent in 1989 but averaged only 14 per cent over the full sample. Recalculation of the total impact of unemployment on the two indicators yields an even more disturbing picture of the costs of unemployment on the society. Thus, we have assumed no unemployment and calculated the hypothetical changes in the marriages and divorces both on average and in the last period of the data sample. These numbers also appear in Table 6.2.25. As an illustration, in 1989 unemployment could be attributed as the cause of about 3 per cent of all divorces as well as the main reason for reduction and/or postponement of over 5 per cent of marriages. It is also interesting to observe that the effects of male unemployment are very similar to the estimated effects of the total unemployment indicating that the periods of cyclical unemployment, which affect in the first instance

Table 6.2.25 Estimated impacts of the increase in the male and total unemployment rates on marriages and divorces

Measure	Change in unemployment rate	
	Males	Persons
	Effect on marriages	
Marginal effect	-1064.1	-1155.6
Elasticity (at means):	-0.068	-0.073
Total effect:		
- at mean values (number)	-5515.5	-5934.7
- at mean values (%)	-6.83	-7.35
- at 1989 values (number)	-5740.4	-6617.8
- at 1989 values (%)	-4.90	-5.65
	Effect on divorces	
Marginal effect:	199.8	220.5
Elasticity (at means):	0.075	0.082
Total effect:		
- at mean values (number)	1035.5	1132.4
- at mean values (%)	7.51	8.21
- at 1989 values (number)	1077.7	1262.8
- at 1989 values (%)	2.60	3.05

Notes:
1. Results obtained from estimation over the period from 1921 to 1989.
2. *Source*: Based on authors' estimates.

the primary work force (*i.e.* males between the ages of 25 and 55) are only marginally less costly to the society than the sustained chronic levels of high unemployment affecting all sections of the labour force. These numbers testify to the continuing severity of the costs of unemployment on the framework of the society.

So far in this section we have analysed the impact of unemployment on the individuals' financial position, the implications of high unemployment for the human capital formation and the cost of unemployment on the stability of family structures. We conclude this section with a brief look at more violent aspects of the costs of unemployment on the society. It has been argued that unemployment leads to higher mortality rates through changes in diet, stress and mental as well as physical health.[29] Junankar (1991), for example, using cross-sectional data from Great Britain found that unemployment is significantly associated with higher mortality rates after controlling for factors such as occupation and economic regions. There is also a long-standing controversy surrounding the link between unemployment and crime. The basic premise behind such links lies, according to Becker (1968), in relative opportunity costs of crime when the potential criminal is in employment as compared to the costs when in the state of unemployment. The supporting evidence behind these links is, however, steadily increasing. Thus, Junankar (1984) found positive impact of youth unemployment on crime as measured by the number of convictions and incarcerations in the U.K. In Australia, Dixon (1992) quotes South Australian statistics which point to a four-fold increase in unemployed offenders as compared with the total number of offenders in the seventies. Withers (1984) also used a measure of poverty (income shares), which is strongly associated with unemployment, and found it positively influencing both aggregated crime measure as well as selected crime categories. It is worth remembering, however, that such estimates of the impact of unemployment on crime provide only the immediate (or first-round) costs. There are, nevertheless, larger, long-run costs associated with increased criminal activity. They include, among others, increased private spending on insurance and larger share of government expenditure committed to law enforcement and correctional services.

Such studies are also invariably criticised from many quarters with the emphasis on inadequacies of the model specification, the deficiencies in the measurement of crime, or the type of data set used in estimations. In a recent study Kapuscinski, Chapman and Braithwaite (1991) have attempted to resolve some of these issues in relation to the impact of unemployment on crime and provided empirical support for the positive association in relation to a specific crime type – homicide. The authors argued that the disparities between the results from cross-sectional and time-series studies stem principally from a deficient and aggregated specifications of the impacts of unemployment. In particular, accounting for separate labour force attachment of males and females resulted in highly significant and positive impacts of unemployment on homicides. A summary of these results appears in Table 6.2.26. This table provides marginal effects of a 1 percentage point increase in the male and total unemployment rates on both the homicide rate and the total homicides. Thus, while the effects on rate of homicide appear to be quite small their translation into the actual murders provides figures unacceptably high by any measure. It is also sobering when one realizes that the current rates of unemployment are about twice the average over the past seven decades and, therefore, reduction of the unemployment to even long-term average would provide an invaluable impact on the homicide statistics.

We should close this section with a cautionary note. The analysis carried out on the individual and social costs of unemployment was primarily based on econometric regression methods. Such estimates indicate the impacts of the changes in the unemployment rate on a given indicator of the cost of unemployment. They should, however, be regarded as first approximations of associations between variables rather than as firm confirmations of causal relationships between unemployment and such indicators. Only

Table 6.2.26 Estimated impact of a 1 percentage point increase in the male and total unemployment rate on homicides.

Measure	Change in unemployment rate		Homicide indicator
	Males	Persons	
Elasticity:	0.090	0.102	
	Effect on homicide rate		
Marginal effect:			
– at mean values	0.27	0.31	15.68
– at 1989 values	0.32	0.34	18.95
	Effect on total homicides		
Marginal effect:			
– at mean values	2.62	3.01	155.47
– at 1989 values	5.35	5.71	319.0

Notes:
1. Homicide rate is the number of homicides per 1 million people.
2. The last column presents the sample values of the homicide rate and total homicides as indicated in the row headings.
3. Results obtained from estimation over the period from 1926 to 1989.
4. *Source*: Kapuscinski *et al.* (1991) and authors' calculations.

more complete models, both dynamically and structurally, could be used to assess the potential causal links between cost indicators and unemployment.

8 Conclusions.

We have attempted in this study to provide an evaluation of the costs of unemployment to the individual and the society, the government and the economy as a whole. We have argued that unless we have a well specified social welfare function we cannot aggregate the different costs of unemployment we have estimated. Readers may wish to adjust the output loss estimates by adding the costs of administration (*e.g.* of unemployment benefits) and then use their judgement on the costs of inflation to obtain a net cost of unemployment. This, of course, does not place a monetary value on social costs of unemployment (*e.g.* crime, disruption of social fabric *etc.*).

Moreover, we have concentrated on the first-round or impact costs and neglected the dynamic adjustments, the multiplier effects, the questions of micro-economic efficiency of the current levels of unemployment and the possible benefits of unemployment (*e.g.*, in terms of the Phillips' curve and the inflation-unemployment tradeoff or for the current account deficit). While this study is incomplete in these respects the results presented indicate that the unemployment at the current levels imposes significant costs on everybody in the society. In a broader context, therefore, one has to ask what are the appropriate unemployment-reducing policies and why the governments during the eighties have been reluctant to implement such policies.

To conclude, one of the main findings of this research is that the costs of unemployment, even if we take a low estimate, are very significant. Even making an adjustment for any benefits of unemployment society is losing about 5% of GDP in 1991–92. That is a very large number by all accounts.

Notes

1. See Chapman, Junankar, and Kapuscinski (1992).
2. For more detailed exposition of the theory behind the "political business cycles" see Kalecki (1943), Nordhaus (1989) and Alesina (1989), among others.
3. For a fuller discussion of the status of unemployment and other related concepts see ABS (1991).
4. Junankar and Kapuscinski (1990) provide a detailed investigation and evaluation of the theoretical and empirical problems of measuring unemployment using the two sources.
5. See, for example, Shulman (1989) for a critique of the concept of NAIRU.
6. More extensive information on these unemployment rates can be found in EPAC (1992).
7. For a recent paper discussing various explanations of the growth of unemployment in Australia from the perspective of the nineties see Chapman (1990).
8. See also Junankar (1986) and chapter 21 in McDonald (1992) for brief discussions of some aspects of this problem.
9. See EPAC Background Paper No. 11, April 1991 for an account of an interesting EPAC Seminar held on Australia's Inflation problem and the assessment of the benefits of lower inflation due to the increased unemployment.
10. There may, of course, be aggregation problem: the utility of individuals cannot be added together unless we assume identical and cardinal utility functions.
11. These trends were due partly to increased labour force participation rates (from an average of 60.6% between January 1982 and June 1985 to an average of 63.3% between January 1989 and June 1992). However, unemployment *rates* did come down during the eighties with increased employment growth. See also the discussion below on unemployment rates.
12. See Copland Oration by Gregory (1992).
13. It is also interesting to observe that the ABS publishes estimates of labour underutilisation which are based on individuals' responses to questions concerning preferred hours of employment. See *Labour Statistics, Australia*, ABS Cat. No. 6101.0.
14. See also Junankar and Kapuscinski (1990) for a more detailed empirical evaluation of the unemployment series from the two sources.
15. Strictly speaking, it is more accurate for the over 21 years old group.
16. These definitions are based on the concepts advocated by the International Labour Organization for measurement of informal employment and underemployment. See also ABS Cat. No. 6265.0.
17. Following convention, long-term unemployment is defined as unemployment with duration over 52 weeks. For expositional purposes we have defined the

short-term unemployed as having durations of less than 26 weeks with the balance of the unemployment pool being the medium term unemployed.
18. For empirical evidence from longitudinal data of this positive relationship between unemployment durations and unemployment rate see, for example, Dynarski and Sheffrin (1990).
19. These latter estimates are given under the heading GDP* in the tables.
20. Given the similarity of the output losses valued with the alternative wage series the calculations in this table and in the remainder of this section will be based only on the average total adult earnings.
21. Alternatively, one may think about the negative losses as the economy working at more than full capacity utilisation.
22. Due to the "Trial Gaps" method involving subjective choice in the determination of the potential output series and, therefore, an arbitrary nature of the output gap, our calculations of the total output loss and the loss under different unemployment scenarios are based only on the "First Differences" method.
23. Most estimates rarely exceed 1% of GDP. See also discussion in EPAC (1991*b*)
24. Unemployment Unit and Youthaid, *Working Brief*, October 1991.
25. These numbers are from ABS, *Labour Force Status and Other Characteristics of Families, Australia*, ABS Cat. No. 6224.0, June 1991.
26. DSS, *Quarterly Unemployment Benefit Recipients*, (unpublished), May 1991.
27. See Smith (1987).
28. The migration skill index is available only until 1986.
29. For a short outline of literature see Junankar (1986).

References

Akerlof, G.A. and J.L. Yellen (Eds.). *Efficiency wage models of the labor market.* Cambridge: Cambridge University Press, 1986.

Alesina, A. Politics and business cycles in industrial democracies. *Economic Policy*, April 1989, *8*, 55–98.

Australian Bureau of Statistics. *Measuring Employment and Unemployment.* Canberra: Australian Bureau of Statistics, 1991. ABS Catalogue No. 6279.0.

Becker, G.S. A Theory of the Allocation of Time. *Economic Journal*, September 1965, *75*,493–517.

Becker, G.S. Crime and Punishment: An Economic Approach. *Journal of Political Economy*, March/April 1968, 76(2), 169–217.

Bradbury, B., R. Ross and J. Doyle. Unemployment Benefit Replacement Rates. 1990. Paper prepared for the Department of Social Security Social Policy Research Centre.

Cassel, D. The Growing Shadow Economy: Implications for Stabilization Policy. *Intereconomics*, September – October 1984, 19(5), 219–225.

Chapman, B. The Labour Market. In S. Grenville (Ed.), *The Australian Macroeconomy in the 1980s*. Sydney: Research Department, Reserver Bank of Australia, 1990.

Chapman, B.J., Dowrick, S. and Junankar, P.N. Perspectives on Australian Unemployment: The Impact of Wage Setting Institutions in the 1980's. In F. Gruen (Ed.), *Australian Economic Policy.* Canberra: Centre for Economic Policy Research, ANU, 1991.

Chapman, B.J., P.N. Junankar and C.A. Kapuscinski. Projections of Long-term Unemployment. *Australian Bulletin of Labour*, September 1992,18(3), 195–207.

Cross, R.B. *Unemployment, Hysteresis and the Natural Rate Hypothesis.* Oxford: Oxford University Press, 1988.

Dixon, D. *Unemployment. The Economic and Social Costs*. Melbourne: Brotherhood of St Laurence, 1992 (2nd edition).

Dynarski, M. and S.M. Sheffrin. The behaviour of Unemployment Durations over the Cycle. *Review of Economics and Statistics*, May 1990, 72(2), 350–356.

Economic Planning Advisory Council. *Australia's Inflation Problem: Office of EPAC Seminar.* Canberra: Australian Government Publishing Service, 1991a. Background Paper No. 11.

Economic Planning Advisory Council. *Improving Australia's Inflation Performance.* Canberra: Australian Government Publishing Service, 1991*b*. Council Paper No. 48.

Economic Planning Advisory Council. *Unemployment in Australia*. Canberra: Australian Government Publishing Service, 1992. Council Paper No. 51.

Fisher, N.W.F. *An Expenditure Approach to Estimation of the Hidden Economy and Informal Labour Market*. (Working Paper No. 12). Canberra: Bureau of Labour Market Research, 1983*a*.

Fisher, N.W.F. *An Assessment of the Informal Labour Market in Australia*. (Working Paper No. 7). Canberra: Bureau of Labour Market Research, 1983*b*.

Gregory, R.G. Aspects of Australian Labour Force Living Standards: The Disappointing Decades 1970–1990. July 1992. Paper delivered as The Copland Oration at the 21st Conference of Economists held at the University of Melbourne.

INDECS Economics. *State of Play*. Sydney: George Allen and Unwin, 1980.

Junankar, P.N. *Youth Unemployment and Youth Crime: A Preliminary Analysis*. (Centre for Economic Policy Research Discussion Paper No. 106). Canberra: Australian National University, 1984.

Junankar, P.N. *Costs of Unemployment: Main Report*. Luxemburg: Commission of the European Communities, 1986.

Junankar, P.N. Unemployment and Mortality in England and Wales: A Preliminary Analysis. *Oxford Economic Papers*, 1991, *43*, 305–320.

Junankar, P.N. and Kapuscinski, C.A. *The Duration of Unemployment in Australia: Memory and Measurement*. (Centre for Economic Policy Research Discussion Paper No. 238). Canberra: Australian National University, 1990.

Junankar, P.N. and C.A. Kapuscinski. The Incidence of Long Term Unemployment in Australia. *Australian Bulletin of Labour*, December 1991, *17(4)*, 325–352.

Junankar, P.N., D. Pope, C.A. Kapuscinski, Y. Ping Li and W. Mudd. *Immigration, Wages and Price Stability*. Canberra: Australian Government Publishing Service, 1990. Bureau of Immigration Research Monograph.

Kalecki, M. Political aspects of full employment. *Political Quarterly*, 1943, *14*, 322–331.

Kalisch, D. *The Output Loss from Unemployment: Okun's Law Revisited*. (Working Paper No 10). Canberra: Bureau of Labour Market Research, August 1982.

Kapuscinski C.A., B. Chapman and J. Braithwaite. Unemployment and Crime: Resolving the Paradox. Paper prepared for the Criminology Research Council, June 1991.

McDonald, I.M. *Macroeconomics*. Brisbane: Jacaranda – Wiley, 1992.

Mortensen, D.T. Job Search and Labor Market Analysis. In O. Ashenfelter and R. Layard (Ed.), *Handbook of Labor Economics*. Amsterdam: North-Holland, 1986.

Nordhaus, W.D. Alternative Approaches to the Political Business Cycle. *Brookings Papers on Economic Activity*, Autumn 1989(2), pp. 1–49.

Okun, A.M. Potential GNP: Its Measurement and Significance. In *Proceedings of the Business and Economic Statistics Section of the American Statistical Association*. Washington, D.C.: American Statistical Association, 1962, 98–104. Reprinted in A.M. Okun (1970), *The Political Economy of Prosperity*, W.W. Norton and Company, New York.

Paldam, M. How much does one percent of growth change the unemployment rate? *European Economic Review*, 1987, 31, 306–313.

Shulman, S. The natural rate of unemployment: concept and critique. *Journal of Post Keynesian Economics*, Summer 1989, *11*(4), 509–521.

Smith, R. *Unemployment and Health*. Oxford: Oxford University Press, 1987.

Stretton, A. and B.J. Chapman. *An Analysis of Austalian Labour Market Programs*. (Centre for Economic Policy Research Discussion Paper No. 247). Canberra: Australian National University, 1990.

Watts, M. and W. Mitchell. Alleged instability of the Okun's law relationship in Australia: an empirical analysis. *Applied Economics*, December 1991, 23(12), 1829–1838.

Withers, G. Crime, Punishment and Deterrence in Australia: An Empirical Investigation. *Economic Record*, June 1984, *60*(169), 176–185.

Withers, G. The Immigration Contribution to Human Capital Formation. In *Australia's Greatest Asset. Human Resources in the Nineteenth and Twntieth Centuries*. Sydney: Federation Press, 1989.

6.3
Unemployment and Mortality in England and Wales: A Preliminary Analysis

P. N. Junankar

1 Introduction

In recent years a furious debate has raged in medical and health journals about the harmful effects of unemployment. Except for a few forays by economists, the debate has been between psychologists, epidemiologists, demographers and sociologists (see Smith (1985), Brenner (1979), Brenner and Mooney (1982), Stern (1983), Gravelle *et al* (1981), Moser *et al.* (1981, 1986, 1987), Warr (1983) and Platt (1982)). In this debate the general finding is that unemployment is a particularly stressful state which leads to physical and mental illness and, in extreme cases, to suicide, para-suicide or death. Economists, however, have taken issue on statistical grounds and dispute the findings: they argue that the verdict should be at best 'not-proven'. The aim of this paper is to provide a preliminary analysis of the relationship between unemployment and mortality using some limited data from the OPCS. The conclusions of this work are that there is a positive *association* between unemployment and mortality.

2 Background

Underlying this work is the view that employment provides an individual not only with an income, but also a set of social relationships which provide a structure and meaning to life. Unemployment, therefore, leads not only to a loss of income but also to a breakdown of social relationships. Not only do unemployed people suffer, but so do the immediate family, (Smith (1985)). Again, the family suffer not only because of a lower income, but also due to increased stress and anxiety. In addition, even employed people suffer

Reprinted from 'Unemployment and Mortality in England and Wales: A Preliminary Analysis' by P. N. Junankar in *Oxford Economic Papers*, 43, 1991, 305–320. With kind permission from Oxford University Press.

in periods (regions) of high unemployment. Job mobility is lowered during periods of high unemployment, the risk of losing a job causes anxiety, and the threat of unemployment may lead management to extract increased labour services from the employed. Thus an increase in the pace of work may increase stress and worsen health and lead to mortality. A recession may also lead employers to lower safety standards and, hence, increase the probability of work-place accidents. However, unemployment may be an escape from stresses related to work and from industrial accidents and pollutants at work.

An unemployed individual has a sudden fall in his/her income which (if unemployment is prolonged) could lead to poor diet, increasing susceptibility to illness, i.e. increasing morbidity and, in some cases, death. Besides the income loss, an individual suffers from anxiety and stress which may lead to cardiovascular diseases and hence to death. In addition, when an individual suffers from stress, there may be an increased consumption of tobacco and alcoholic drink which increases the probability of mortality.[1] Finally, unemployment may lead to stress which may lead to para-suicide and suicide.[2] For the family of the unemployed, the effects, it is argued, are very similar. (For the unemployed individual, there is a feedback from illness to unemployment: because he is ill, he does not find employment—the so-called 'selection' problem.) It is clear that there is a great diversity of individual responses to becoming unemployed. In addition, in a town, city, or region with high levels of unemployment, the state of unemployment may not cause the same degree of social stress or anxiety—there is little or no stigma attached to being unemployed. Similarly, for the same individual, the response to being unemployed in the booming sixties might have caused anguish while it may be a matter of indifference in the doleful eighties. Family and a social network of friends may, in certain cases, act as support groups to prevent the harmful consequences of unemployment. The impact of unemployment on an individual would depend on how he became unemployed: voluntarily or involuntarily. It would depend on the duration of unemployment, the number (and duration) of previous spells of unemployment as well as on the subjective and objective probability of finding work in the future. A person of fifty-five made redundant at the present time is unlikely to find a job again.

It is obvious that morbidity and mortality are affected by general ecological conditions (e.g. atmospheric pollution, environmental conditions, etc.) as well as by medical and health facilities available, general living standards, etc. In our work we shall assume that social class and regional dummies provide a reasonable proxy for all these other determinants. It is worth reiterating that unemployment may decrease the mortality rate because of the decreased probability of industrial accidents, exposure to dangerous pollutants and work related stress. On the other hand many fatal accidents happen at home.

There have been several studies[3] investigating this issue using time-series, cross-section, and longitudinal data. Pioneering work by Singer (1937), and

Morris and Titmuss (1944) using grouped cross-section data from England and Wales showed a positive link between mortality and unemployment.[4] In a series of papers Brenner (1979, 1983) using time-series data found a statistically significant link between mortality and unemployment. These studies have stirred up much controversy, see Stern (1983), Wagstaff (1985) for a sample of the critical evaluations. In a series of papers Moser *et al.*[5] have used, the OPCS Longitudinal Study find that the unemployed have higher standardised mortality ratios for various causes of death, even after controlling for social class and region.[6] In the next section we set up a simple econometric model to explain the link between unemployment and mortality.

3 Methods and results

In this paper we provide some preliminary results which suggest an association between mortality rates and unemployment rates. We postulate the following model:

$$SMR_{CR} = \alpha_0 + \alpha_1 UR_{CR} + \alpha_2 X_{CR} + \alpha_3 Z_{CR} + \varepsilon_{CR} \quad (1)$$

where

SMR_{CR} is the standardised mortality ratio for males in Class C in Region R. SMRs are defined as the 'percentage ratio of the number of deaths observed in the group studied to the number expected from the age-specific death rates for England and Wales' (OPCS (1978)).

UR_{CR} is the male unemployment rate for class C in Region R.

X_{CR} is a vector of variables like income, diet and nutrition, consumption of tobacco and alcohol, etc. for Class C in Region R.

Z_{CR} is a vector of variables like regional health facilities, environmental conditions, etc. for Class C in Region R.

ε_{CR} is a random error, assumed to be white noise.

The data for SMRs were obtained from OPCS (1978, 1986) and are annual averages of 1970–72 (henceforth called '1971') and of 1979–80 and 1982–83 (henceforth called '1981'). These data are based on the mortality of all males aged 15–64 for 1971 and 16–64 for 1981. The data are, therefore, both for the unemployed and employed males.

Since we did not have adequate data on the X and Z variables we proxied them by simple zero-one dummies. We assumed that Social Class would be a good proxy for X_{CR} i.e. for income, access to medical and health facilities, geographical location (in terms of housing and quality of housing) within the region, working conditions, and consumption of mortality increasing commodities like tobacco, animal fats, and diet generally. There is some evidence to suggest that this may be a reasonable proxy, but further work is necessary to find data on these variables separately.

We proxied Z_{CR} by regional dummies to take account of environmental conditions (pollution etc), regional health facilities, long-term unemployment, etc.

Unemployment Rates by Class and Region for April 1971 and April 1981 came from the OPCS longitudinal study.[7] They are defined such that UR lies between zero and one.

Since we have data for 1971 and 1981 we could have put a time subscript on the SMRs and URs. If the variables in the vectors X and Z are considered as 'fixed effects', i.e. unchanging over time we would not subscript them with time. However, it is possible that some of the X and Z variables are fixed effects while some are time varying.

The procedure we followed was to estimate the following equation (replacing X by Class Dummies and Z by Region Dummies):

$$SMR_{CR} = \beta_0 + \beta_1 UR_{CR} + \sum_{1}^{5} \beta_{2i} CD(i) + \sum_{1}^{8} \beta_{3j} R(j) + \varepsilon_{CR} \tag{2}$$

where CD(i) = 1 for Social Class i
= 0 otherwise
i = 1,2,3,4,5
and R(j) = 1 for Region j
= 0 otherwise
J = 1,2,3,4,5,6,7,8,9.

The OPCS social classes are

I	Professional etc. occupations	(Class Dummy 1)
II	Intermediate occupations	(Class Dummy 2)
III N	Skilled occupations: non-manual	(Class Dummy 3)
III M	Skilled occupations: manual	(Class Dummy 4)
IV	Partly skilled occupations	(Class Dummy 5)
V	Unskilled occupations	

(We did not use the data on the Armed Forces or the unoccupied.)

The Regions are the standard regions for England and Wales: North, Yorkshire and Humberside, North West, East Midlands, West Midlands, East Anglia, South East, South West and Wales. We used Dummies for all regions except the South East. In other words, the reference group is the Social Class V in the South East.

In this paper we use data only for males as there are problems involved in how to categorise the social class of women as well as difficulties with measuring unemployment rates.

The procedure we followed was to estimate equation (2) for the 1971 data set, repeat the estimations for 1981, and finally to pool the 1971 and 1981 data sets allowing for shift and slope dummies. It should be noted that unemployment rates increased enormously over the period 1971 to 1981 so that we may expect to see a change in the parameter vector from 1971 to 1981. In each case we estimated linear, log-linear, and semi-log forms and chose those equations that performed well in terms of the diagnostics on functional form, normality of errors, and heteroscedasticity.[8]

In this study we concentrated our attention on the SMR (All Causes) and SMR (Ischaemic Heart Diseases, International Classification of Diseases 410–414). The latter cause of death is often ascribed to stress factors and as such is particularly relevant for our study.[9]

Tables 6.3.1 and 6.3.2 provide the results of estimating equation 2 for 1971 and 1981 respectively for SMR (All Causes) and show a positive and significant relation (although quantitatively small) between the male

Table 6.3.1 Log SMR (All Causes), 1971 OLS Estimation

Constant	4.701	North	0.158
	(88.374)		(5.062)
Unemployment Rate	1.240	Yorkshire and Humberside	0.144
	(2.206)		(5.072)
Class I	–0.460	North West	0.215
	(–9.181)		(7.630)
Class II	–0.391	East Midlands	0.036
	(–8.048)		(1.321)
Class III N	–0.203	West Midlands	0.119
	(–4.469)		(4.395)
Class III M	–0.162	East Anglia	–0.083
	(–3.848)		(–2.960)
Class IV	–0.113	South West	0.027
	(–3.091)		(0.982)
		Wales	0.210
			(7.405)

$\bar{R}^2 = 0.954$ $F(14,39) = 79.678$

Diagnostic Tests	*L–M Version*	*F Version*
A. Functional Form	CHI-SQ (1) = 1.340	F(1,38) = 1.011
B. Normality	CHI-SQ (2) = 0.158	Not applicable
C. Heteroscedasticity	CHI-SQ (1) = 0.214	F(1,52) = 0.207
D. Predictive Failure	CHI-SQ (54) = 175.661	F(54.39) = 3.253
E. Chow Test	CHI-SQ (15) = 123.565	F(15,70) = 8.238

Notes:
A. Ramsey's RESET test using the square of the fitted values.
B. Based on test of skewness and kurtosis of residuals.
C. Based on the regression of squared residuals on squared fitted values.
D. The instruments were all the above regressors excluding the unemployment rate and with the unemployment rate for 1971 included.
E. t-statistics in parentheses.

Table 6.3.2 Log SMR (All Causes), 1981 Instrumental Variable Estimation

Constant	4.673	North	0.140
	(53.269)		(3.838)
Unemployment	1.393	Yorkshire and	0.102
Rate	(3.525)	Humberside	(3.141)
Class I	–0.548	North West	0.149
	(–6.227)		(4.332)
Class II	–0.441	East Midlands	0.041
	(–5.123)		(1.329)
Class III	–0.254	West Midlands	0.066
	(–3.268)		(2.035)
Class III M	–0.247	East Anglia	–0.120
	(–4.047)		(–4.093)
Class IV	–0.158	South West	–0.030
	(–2.870)		(–1.030)
		Wales	0.093
			(2.657)

$\bar{R}^2 = 0.980$	$F(14,39) = 133.633$
Diagnostic Tests	*L– M Version*
A. Functional Form	CHI-SQ (1) = 0.163
B. Normality	CHI-SQ (2) = 2.581
C. Heteroscedasticity	CHI-SQ (1) = 0.201

Notes:
See Table 6.3.1.

unemployment rate (by Class and Region) and the male SMRs (by Class and Region) even when we control for Class and Region. For Table 6.3.2, we used instrumental variable estimates to allow for mortality. Compared to Class V all other classes have lower mortality rates (controlling for unemployment rates and regional effects) and there is a positive gradient with Class I having the lowest mortality rate and increasing as we go down the social class ladder. All the Class Dummies are statistically significant at the 95% probability level. This finding is consistent with work by others, e.g. OPCS (1978), but in our case this positive gradient remains even after controlling for unemployment and regional effects. We also estimated this model with the response to unemployment being affected by Class, by using slope dummies (Class times unemployment). These were shown to be inferior when we carried out nested and non-nested tests. (We attempted to estimate equations with a proportion of long term unemployment added to these equations, but it led to a singular matrix. Unfortunately, we do not have data by Social Class and Region on long term unemployment.)

These results also show that regional differences are very important. There appears to be a North-South divide: the North (including Wales) doing badly compared to the South. Compared to the South East, all regions except East Anglia have higher SMRs when we control for Class and unemployment. The North West and Wales have significantly higher SMRs compared to the South East with the North, Yorkshire and Humberside, and the West Midlands coming in between. The East Midlands and the South West are not significantly different from the South East in terms of SMRs after controlling for Unemployment and Class. These cross-sectional results are consistent with the findings of Moser *et al.* (1986).

These results satisfy usual statistical criteria and tests of functional form suggest we cannot reject the semi-log model. The linear and log-linear models performed badly in terms of the functional form tests. Error terms satisfy the normality and homoscedascity assumptions. The fit (R^2) is good for a cross section study.

We repeated this analysis using data on SMRs for ischaemic heart diseases (ICD 410–14) (for 1971 and 1981 respectively) which are often linked to stress. This was in an attempt to focus upon those diseases which are likely to be caused by the stress faced by unemployed people. These results are presented in Tables 6.3.3, 6.3.4 and 6.3.5. (Table 6.3.5 provides estimates using an instrumental variables method and the results are very similar, except it *just* fails the heteroscedasticity test). We have, therefore, provided White corrected 't' statistics in parentheses.

These results provide some support for a relationship between the male unemployment rate and male SMRs from ischaemic heart diseases. When we control for Class and Region there is a statistically significant positive relation between male unemployment rate and male SMRs from ischaemic heart diseases. It is interesting to note that in 1971 Social Classes I, II, III M, and IV do *not* have significantly different SMR from Class V. Only Class III N has a significant and higher SMR. In 1981, there is a positive class gradient—SMRs (IHD) increase as we go down the social ladder. However, Classes III N and IV have relatively low t-values. These results are different from those presented in OPCS (1978) (pp. 54–5) but this may be because we have aggregated over all ages between 15 and 64. In OPCS (1978) the authors remark about the differences between different age groups, and for the 55–64 age group differences between Classes I and II disappearing. Thus our results may be different because we have aggregated over the adult age groups *or* because the positive gradient disappears when we control for unemployment and region. The negative gradient in Classes III N, III M and IV needs further investigation. (See OPCS (1978) p. 40 and pp 54–5).

The regional differences are again strong and (normally) statistically significant in both 1971 and in 1981. Again all the regions (except East Anglia) have higher SMRs from ischaemic heart disease. The Northern regions and Wales again appear to be doing badly, even after controlling for class and unemployment. The results suggest that if the reason for higher mortality rates is just inappropriate diet then this is true for *all* classes. However, even

Table 6.3.3 Log SMR (Ischaemic Heart Diseases), 1971 OLS Estimation

Constant	4.431	North	0.201
	(55.255)		(4.268)
Unemployment Rate	1.623	Yorkshire and Humberside	0.216
	(1.916)		(5.046)
Class I	–0.089	North West	0.272
	(–1.171)		(6.401)
Class II	–0.048	East Midlands	0.068
	(–0.649)		(1.660)
Class III N	0.183	West Midlands	0.104
	(2.672)		(2.546)
Class III M	0.082	East Anglia	–0.138
	(1.292)		(–3.287)
Class IV	0.072	South West	0.050
	(1.304)		(1.230)
		Wales	0.301
			(7.048)

$\bar{R}^2 = 0.855$	F(14,39) = 23.360	
Diagnostic Tests	*L–M Version*	*F Version*
A. Functional Form	CHI-SQ (1) = 2.831	F(1,38) = 2.102
B. Normality	CHI-SQ (2) = 0.751	Not applicable
C. Heteroscedasticity	CHI-SQ (1) = 4.314	F(1,52) = 4.515
D. Predictive Failure	CHI-SQ (54) = 133.139	F(54,39) = 2.466
E. Chow Test	CHI-SQ (15) = 132.179	F(15,78) = 8.812

Notes:
See Table 6.2.1.

if we control for regions unemployment is positively related to mortality rates. Again, the results do well in terms of usual statistical criteria.

We also estimated a linear equation and an equation linear in logarithms of SMR (Ischaemic Heart Disease) and unemployment rate. These results were inferior to those presented above.

As is obvious from the Chow tests in Tables 6.3.1 and 6.3.3, the model is not structurally stable when we pool the 1971 and 1981 data sets. Tables 6.3.6 and 6.3.7 provide results for this pooled data set for SMR (All Causes) allowing for a shift and/or slope differences between the 1971 and 1981 data sets. Table 6.3.6 allows for a shift dummy and regional slopes to vary between 1971 and 1981. The results, in terms of the diagnostic statistics, are good although several of the regional slope dummies are not significant. Table 6.3.7 allows for a slope difference in the Class effects (a shift dummy was not significant) and a non-nested test prefers this equation to Table 6.3.5. However, Table 6.3.7 suggests the existence of a mis-specified functional form. But in both cases the unemployment rate has a positive and significant coefficient, the Class Dummies and most of the region dummies are very

Table 6.3.4 Log SMR (Ischaemic Heart Diseases), 1981 OLS Estimation

Constant	4.550	North	0.233
	(58.876)		(6.106)
Unemployment Rate	1.082	Yorkshire and Humberside	0.210
	(3.081)		(5.967)
Class I	–0.413	NorthWest	0.249
	(–5.173)		(6.778)
Class II	–0.290	East Midlands	0.117
	(3.706)		(3.464)
Class III N	–0.075	West Midlands	0.111
	(–1.057)		(3.166)
Class III M	–0.122	East Anglia	–0.134
	(–2.153)		(–4.059)
Class IV	–0.089	South West	0.025
	(–1.732)		(0.755)
		Wales	0.199
			(5.382)

$\bar{R}^2 = 0.952$ F(14,39) = 75.824

Diagnostic Tests	*L–M Version*	*F Version*
A. Functional Form	CHI-SQ (1) = 2.758	F(1,38) = 2.046
B. Normality	CHI-SQ (2) = 3.524	Not applicable
C. Heteroscedasticity	CHI-SQ (1) = 2.796	F(1,52) = 2.840

Notes:
See Table 6.3.1.

Table 6.3.5 Log SMR (Ischaemic Heart Diseases), 1981 Instrumental Variable Estimation

Constant	4.491	North	0.218
	(48.237)		(6.226)
Unemployment Rate	1.358	Yorkshire and Humberside	0.120
	(2.719)		(6.750)
Class I	–0.354	North West	0.236
	(–3.895)		(6.038)
Class II	–0.232	East Midlands	0.110
	(–2.585)		(3.447)
Class III N	–0.024	West Midlands	0.101
	(–0.299)		(2.806)
Class III M	–0.083	East Anglia	0.137
	(–1.339)		(5.277)
Class IV	–0.055	South West	0.022
	(–1.032)		(0.864)
		Wales	0.185

$\bar{R}^2 = 0.951$ F(14,39) = 74.609

Diagnostic Tests	*L–M Version*
A. Functional Form	CHI-SQ (1) = 0.913
B. Normality	CHI-SQ (2) = 1.526
C. Heteroscedasticity	CHI-SQ (1) = 3.960

Notes:
See Table 6.3.1. However, t statistics are based on White corrected standard errors.

Table 6.3.6 Log SMR (All Causes) Pooled Data 1971 and 1981

Constant	4.682 (150.270)	West Midlands	0.119 (4.145)
Unemployment Rate	1.679 (10.252)	East Anglia	–0.088 (–3.059)
Class I	0.456 (–15.593)	South West	0.025 (0.880)
Class II	–0.369 (–12.866)	Wales	0.203 (7.089)
Class III N	–0.186 (–6.944)	North × D81	–0.022 (–0.534)
Class III M	–0.170 (–7.204)	Yorkshire and Humberside × D81	–0.046 (–1.130)
Class IV	–0.106 (–4.817)	North West × D81	–0.073 (–1.800)
North	0.146 (5.041)	East Midlands × D81	–0.001 (–0.015)
Yorkshire and Humberside	0.137 (4.785)	West Midlands × D81	–0.063 (–1.549)
North West	0.209 (7.296)	East Anglia × D81	–0.036 (–0.894)
East Midlands	0.034 (1.194)	South West × D81	–0.059 (–1.452)
		Wales × D81	–0.125 (–3.058)
		D81	–0.087 (–2.986)

$\bar{R}^2 = 0.965$	F(23,84) = 127.260	
Diagnostic Tests	*L–M Version*	*F Version*
A. Functional Form	CHI-SQ (1) = 0.324	F(1,83) = 0.250
B. Normality	CHI-SQ (2) = 0.048	Not applicable
C. Heteroscedasticity	CHI-SQ (1) = 0.425	F(1,106) = 0.419

Notes:
See Table 6.3.1.

significant. Table 6.3.8 provides similar results for SMRs (Ischaemic Heart Diseases). In all these pooled regressions, the unemployment rate is significant and positive, there is a positive class gradient, and Northern regions do worse than the Southern regions. In addition, the slope dummies suggest that the class gradient has become steeper and the regional divide is worse.

Taken together these results provide some support for the view that unemployment is associated with an increase in mortality rates independently of social class (and hence poverty, poor nutrition, etc.) and of regional differences. By using instrumental variables for 1981 we have attempted to overcome the problem of a possible endogeneity of the contemporaneous

Table 6.3.7 Log SMR (All Causes) Pooled Data 1971 and 1981

Constant	4.734	West Midlands	0.099
	(178.085)		(4.882)
Unemployment Rate	1.036	East Anglia	–0.098
	(7.771)		(–0.854)
Class I	–0.475	South West	0.001
	(16.518)		(0.036)
Class II	–0.405	Wales	0.161
	(–14.233)		(7.850)
Class III N	–0.216	Class I × D81	–0.151
	(–7.748)		(–6.464)
Class III M	–0.173	Class II × D81	–0.112
	(–6.359)		(4.791)
Class IV	–0.122	Class III N × D81	–0.127
	(–4.651)		(–5.066)
North	0.162	Class III M × D81	–0.127
	(7.758)		(–5.066)
Yorkshire and Humberside	0.131	Class IV × D81	–0.082
	(6.420)		(–3.240)
North West	0.192		
	(9.364)		
East Midlands	0.043		
	(2.131)		

$\bar{R}^2 = 0.965$	F(19,88) = 155.345	
Diagnostic Tests	*L–M Version*	*F Version*
A. Functional Form	CHI-SQ (1) = 12.765	F(1,87) – 11.661
B. Normality	CHI-SQ (2) = 1.666	Not application
C. Heteroscedasticity	CHI-SQ (1) = 0.865	F(1,106) = 0.856

Notes:
See Table 6.3.1.

unemployment rate, and hence the 'selection problem'. To reiterate, controlling for social class and region, we find a positive relation between the unemployment rates and mortality rates.

On the simple view that unemployment causes all the excess mortality, it is possible to provide a point estimate of the additional deaths caused by (say) an extra percentage point of unemployment using the estimated coefficient in Table 6.3.2.[10] The procedure followed was to calculate the increase in log SMR due to an increase of 0.01 of the unemployment rate (i.e. one percentage point), then find the increase in SMR (by taking exponentials), divide by 100 and multiply by the number of actual deaths,[11] i.e.

$$1/100\ [\exp((\beta)(0.01))]\ (\text{Actual Deaths})$$
$$1/100\ [\exp((1.3925)(0.01))]\ (84{,}275)$$
$$1/100\ [\exp(0.013925)]\ (84{,}275)] = 855$$

Table 6.3.8 Log SMR (Ischaemic Heart Diseases) Pooled Data 1971 and 1981

Constant	4.470 (127.379)	West Midlands	0.103 (3.830)
Unemployment Rate	1.373 (7.803)	East Anglia	–0.136 (–5.118)
Class I	–0.117 (–3.083)	South West	0.036 (1.368)
Class II	–0.075 (–2.004)	Wales	0.245 (9.009)
Class III N	0.157 (4.258)	Class I × D81	–0.225 (–7.324)
Class III M	0.057 (1.596)	Class II × D81	–0.145 (–4.715)
Class IV	0.050 (1.452)	Class III N × D81	0.169 (–5.413)
North	0.212 (7.699)	Class III M × D81	0.130 (–3.926)
Yorkshire and Humberside	0.209 (7.760)	Class IV × D81	–0.094 (2.827)
North West	0.255 (9.418)		
East Midlands	0.090 (3.355)		

$\bar{R}^2 = 0.916$	F(19,88) = 62.625	
Diagnostic Tests	*L–M Version*	*F Version*
A. Function Form	CHI-SQ (1) = 0.069	F(1,87) = 0.055
B. Normality	CHI-SQ (2) = 1.600	Not applicable
C. Heteroscedasticity	CHI-SQ (1) = 0.231	F(1,106) = 0.220

Notes:
See Table 6.3.1.

Thus the point estimate of additional deaths caused annually by one percentage point of unemployment is 855 (with a two standard error confidence interval of848to861).[12]

4 Discussion

We have found a positive association between the unemployment rate and the mortality rate after normalising for social class and region. This holds in the levels model as well as in the differenced model. We find a positive social class gradient for SMR(All Causes) but not for SMR (Ischaemic Heart Disease). We find a clear North–South divide: the North (and Wales) does significantly worse than the South.

The limitations of this work are, firstly, the high level of aggregation, namely class and region. Ideally, one should look at individual level data and estimate limited dependent variable models using, say, logit or probit. However, individual level data are not available from the OPCS. As a second best, we should disaggregate to (say) wards or travel-to-work areas, which we hope to do in subsequent work. A second limitation is the problem of disentangling the direction of causation. Our view is that the link is from unemployment to morbidity to mortality. However, we would expect a long lag between unemployment, and mortality (except for suicide). It can be argued (and has been) that ill health leads to unemployment (the 'selection problem'), ill health leads to morbidity, and hence mortality and unemployment are spuriously correlated. It has been argued that healthy people migrate to low unemployment regions, leaving the unhealthy in the high unemployment regions and hence an association between mortality and unemployment is observed. However, we have allowed for regional differences and even then there is a positive association between unemployment and mortality. A third limitation is that we have proxied a whole host of other causes of mortality by using class and regional dummies. Further work would include other explanatory variables like consumption of alcohol and tobacco, expenditure on health, etc. Finally, it needs emphasising that we have not used any data on the mortality of the unemployed themselves.

We are obviously aware of these limitations but nonetheless believe that our results provide additional support to the research done in this field by epidemiologists, demographers, etc. Much more work needs to be done to study the *causal* links between unemployment and mortality. Similarly, much work needs to be done to explain the social class and regional mortality differences. This would require longitudinal analysis of individuals from a richer data set which included information on several economic and other variables e.g. consumption expenditures on particular products (tobacco, alcohol, fats etc.), regional and environmental factors like pollution, quality of public health services, etc. Moser *et al.* (1984, 1986, 1987) have carried out some analyses of longitudinal data using information on class, a few broad regions, housing tenure, and employment status in one week in 1971 and 1981. However their analysis is limited to studying the impact of one variable at a time rather than in a multiple regression analysis context. We believe our results provide additional support to their analysis.

5 Conclusions

In this paper we have argued that there is a positive association between mortality rates and unemployment when we control for social class and geographical regions. We found that there was a positive gradient for SMR (All Causes): the lower the social class the higher the SMRs. This gradient was not noticeable for SMR (Ischaemic Heart Disease). Another major finding was the clear North-South divide, with the richer South East doing better than the poorer North, *even after controlling for social class.* We have argued that unemployment has an *independent* effect on mortality, in addition to the poverty associated with unemployment. We outlined further avenues of research which we hope to pursue later.

Notes

The analyses in this article are based on data from the OPCS Longitudinal Study. Crown Copyright is reserved. I should like to thank Mark Conaty and Abdul Latif for excellent research assistance. Nicky Hart was most helpful in guiding me around the literature. Comments from Joy Townsend, P. Goldblatt, and participants at seminars at Essex, Sheffield, Birkbeck College, Cambridge, and the AUTE Conference in Oxford in March 1988 helped to improve the paper. I bear sole responsibility for remaining errors as well as prejudices.

1. See Cook *et al.* (1982) where they found that the unemployed smoked more than the employed, correcting for age, social class and town of residence.
2. See Platt (1982).
3. A good review of the literature on unemployment and ill health (physical or mental), as well as unemployment and mortality, can be found in Smith (1987). A brief review is also available in Junankar (1986). For a critical review of some papers see Stern (1983).
4. See Stern (1983).
5. See for example Moser, Fox and Jones (1984), Moser, Fox, Jones and Goldblatt (1986) and Moser, Goldblatt, Fox and Jones (1987).
6. In 1981 the seeking work category was separated from those waiting to take up a job.
7. The data were kindly provided by Dr. P. O. Goldblatt. As mentioned earlier this data set does not include any labour market history.
8. See Stern (1983).
9. To avoid 'fixed-effects' bias we also estimated a differenced form of equation 2. The results supported the link between unemployment and SMRs.
10. See Scott-Samuel (1984).
11. According to Table 6.3.1, p. 19 of OPCS (1986) for the four year period actual deaths were 337,099 or 84,275 on an annual basis.
12. Just to give an idea of the magnitude of these deaths, in 1985, 3,379 men died in motor vehicle traffic accidents.

References

Brenner, H. (1979). 'Mortality & the National Economy: A Review and the Experience of England & Wales, 1936–76', *The Lancet* 15 September, pp. 568–73.

Brenner, H. and Mooney, A. (1983). 'Unemployment and Health in the Context of Economic Change', *Social Science and Medicine,* Vol. 17: 16, pp. 1125–8.

Cook, D. C., Cummins, R. O., Bartley, M. J. and Shaper, A. G. (1982). 'Health of Unemployed Middle-Aged Men in G.B.', *The Lancet,* 5 June, pp. 1290–4.

Fox, A. J., Goldblatt, O. and Jones, D. R. (1985). 'Social Class Mortality Differentials: Artefact, Selection or Life Circumstances?', *Journal of Epidemiology and Community Health,* pp. 1–8.

Godfrey, L. G., McAleer, M. and McKenzie, C. R. (1986). 'Variable Addition and Lagrange Multiplier Tests for Linear and Logarithmic Regression Models: Theory and Monte Carlo Evidence', Australian National University, Working Papers in Economics and Econometrics, No. 136, September.

GRAVELLE, H. S. E., HUTCHINSON, G. and STERN, J. (1981). 'Mortality and Unemployment: A Critique of Brenner's Time-Series Analysis', *The Lancet* 26 September, pp. 675–9.

JAHODA, M. (1982). *Employment & Unemployment: A Social Psychological Analysis,* Cambridge, Cambridge University Press.

JAHODA, M. and RUSH, H. (1980). 'Work, Employment and Unemployment', Science Policy Research Unit, Occasional Paper Series, No. 12.

JOHN, J., SCHWEFEL, D. and ZOLLNER, H. (eds) (1983). *Influence of Economic Instability on Health,* Vol. 21 in *Lecture Notes in Medical Informatics,* Ed. by D. A. B. Lindberg and P. L. Reichertz, Berlin, Springer Verlag.

KELVIN, P. and JARRETT, J. *(1984). Unemployment: Its Social Psychological Effects,* Cambridge, Cambridge University Press.

MADDALA, G. S. (1983). *Limited Dependent and Qualitative Variables in Econometrics,* Cambridge, Cambridge University Press.

MORRIS, J. N. and TITMUSS, R. M. (1944). 'Health and Social Change', *Medical Officer,* 26 August, 2 and 9 September, pp. 69–71, 77–9, 85–7.

MOSER, K. A., FOX, J. and JONES, D. R. (1984). 'Unemployment and Mortality in the OPCS Longitudinal Study', *The Lancet,* 8 December, pp. 1324–9.

MOSER, K. A., FOX, J., JONES, R. and GOLDBLATT, P. O. (1986). 'Unemployment and Mortality: Further Evidence from the OPCS Longitudinal Study, 1971–81', *The Lancet,* 15 February, pp. 365–6.

MOSER, K. A., GOLDBLATT, P. O., FOX, A. J. and JONES, D. R. (1987). 'Unemployment and Mortality: comparison of the 1971 and 1981 longitudinal study census samples', *British Medical Journal,* Vol. 294, 10 June, pp. 86–90.

NARENDRANATHAN, W., NICKELL, S. and METCALF, D. (1985). 'An Investigation into the Incidence and Dynamic Structure of Sickness and Unemployment in Britain, 1965–7 5', *J. R. Statist. Soc. A.,* 148, Part 3, pp. 254–67.

OPCS (1978). *Occupational Mortality.* The Registrar General's decennial supplement for England and Wales 1970–2. Series DS No. 1 (and data on microfiche) London: HMSO.

OPCS (1986). *Occupational Mortality.* The Registrar General's decennial supplement for Great Britain, 1979–80, 1982–83, Series DS No. 6 (and Part I Commentary data in Part II Micro for the Tables) London: HMSO.

PLATT, S. (1982). 'Unemployment and Suicidal behaviour: A Review of the Literature', *Social cience and Medicine,* Vol. 19, No. 2, pp. 93–115.

SCOTT-SAMUEL, A. (1984). 'Unemployment and Health', *The Lancet,* 22–29 December.

SINGER, H. W. (1937). 'Unemployment and Health' Pilgrim Trust Enquiry, Interim Paper No. 4.

SMITH, R. (1985). 'Occupationless Health'. (A Series of articles beginning 12 October 1985) *British Medical Journal,* 291, pp. 1024–7, 1107–11, 1191–5, 1263—6, 1338–41, 1409–11, 1492–5, 1563–6, 1626–9, 1707–10.

SMITH, R. (1987). *Unemployment and Health: A Disaster and Challenge,* Oxford, Oxford University Press.

STERN, J. (1983). 'The Relationship between Unemployment, Morbidity and Mortality in Britain', *Population Studies,* 37, pp. 61–74.

WAGSTAFF, A. (1985). 'Time Series Analysis of the Relationship Between Unemployment and Mortality. A Survey of Econometric Critiques and Replications of Brenner's Studies' *Social Science and Medicine,* Vol. 21, No. 9, pp. 985–96.

WARR, P. (1983). 'Work, Jobs and Unemployment', *Bulletin of the British Psychological Society,* Vol. 36, pp. 305–11.

Index

The manufacturer's authorised representative in the EU is Springer Nature Customer Service Centre GmbH, Europaplatz 3, 69115 Heidelberg, Germany. If you have any concerns regarding our products, please contact ProductSafety@springernature.com

Printed and bound by CPI Group (UK) Ltd, Croydon, CR0 4YY
10/10/2026
02231221-0019